Strategic Management
Creating Value in a Turbulent World

PETER FITZROY

Monash University

JAMES M. HULBERT

Columbia University

WILEY

JOHN WILEY & SONS, INC.

ASSOCIATE PUBLISHER   *Judith R. Joseph*
SENIOR ACQUISITIONS EDITORS   *Jayme Heffler/Steve Hardman*
DEVELOPMENT EDITOR   *Anna Rowe*
SENIOR EDITORIAL ASSISTANT   *Jessica Bartelt*
SENIOR PRODUCTION EDITOR   *Patricia McFadden*
MARKETING MANAGER   *David Woodbury*
PRODUCTION SERVICES   *Hermitage Publishing Services*
COVER CREDIT   *©Akira Inoue/Photonica*

This book was set in 10 point New Caledonia by Hermitage Publishing Services.
Printed and bound in Great Britain by Martins the Printers, Berwick upon Tweed, Northumberland.

This book is printed on acid free paper. ∞

ISBN 0-470-85731-5

10 9 8 7 6 5 4 3 2 1

With love and thanks to Margaret and Madge,
for their support, encouragement and assistance

Preface

In writing this book we have made every attempt to ensure that it reflects the competitive environment in which future strategic managers will work. The fact that we were starting anew, rather than re-writing an earlier text greatly facilitated this effort. We hope this has resulted in a book that is really current and reflects contemporary business reality.

The book is written for a capstone course in strategic management for MBA and advanced undergraduate students. We have consequently assumed that readers will have a sound foundation in marketing, economics, finance, accounting, information technology, and organizational behavior. Therefore the book serves as the basis for a course that integrates these subjects into an overall perspective on strategic management of the enterprise.

We have chosen to adopt a strategic management rather than a planning perspective. We view strategic management as the task of creating and maintaining organizations that generate value. Strategic management of a modern firm is a complex task; there are no easy solutions. The problems with which the modern firm is concerned are complex, unstructured and non-routine. The process of strategic management must involve a deep understanding of the environment in which the firm operates. Its essence is about making decisions that ensure not only the survival, but also the success of the firm. This task is becoming increasingly difficult for several reasons described below.

One characteristic of the world in which we live is that it is global and increasingly interconnected. This has implications whether one works for a multinational, a regional, a national, or even a local firm. There is no doubt in our minds that the ongoing process of globalization will profoundly affect the lives of senior managers in firms of any size. We have therefore drawn our examples not only from a wide range of industries, but also from a wide range of countries.

A second characteristic is the increasing rate of change and the increasing turbulence of that change. Change can be external to the firm or it may be change introduced to the firm by managers. It may be manifest in the blurring of industry and firm boundaries, driven by technology, deregulation, or, indeed, globalization itself. As a consequence, a vital task for the management of the firm is to create and respond to change. Change management will of necessity become increasingly important, and all managers will need to become accomplished in the management of change.

A third characteristic is the increased attention given to the performance of the firm. We take a value-based approach, emphasizing the firm as an economic entity. So we discuss how the performance on the firm can be assessed at both the corporate and business unit level. We also regard it as critical that strategic managers have an informed understanding of the impact of financial markets on strategy. Not only do financial markets put pressure on the firm for performance, they also facilitate and constrain the strategy adopted by the firm. However, while we are conscious of the importance of shareholders, we also understand that the modern firm has multiple stakeholders with interests in its performance. It is also true that environmental and social concerns have affected the operations of many companies. Yet in a competitive world—whether in product markets or capital markets—the importance of customers and shareholders should be self-evident.

Throughout the book we take a managerial perspective that the task of all managers is to create and manage the resources of the firm. Turbulence implies that managing change within the firm is critical and no strategy will last for long in today's and tomorrow's world. It is also the case that physical assets are becoming less important for the firm and are being replaced by intangible assets. It is through these assets that competitive advantage and value are created. The value of most firms is increasingly embedded in their people and processes. With the rise of the knowledge-based economy, the managing of intangible assets and the firm's knowledge base has moved inexorably to center stage, factors reflected in the coverage of our text.

Despite our concern that the firms generate value, the corporate scandals of the early 21st century have served to underline the importance of ethical behavior on the part of senior executives. The post-Enron environment is one where senior managers can expect higher levels of public expectation and more stringent scrutiny. The whole subject of corporate governance is critically important in an era where countless millions have become more and more dependent on private savings and pensions. We devote a separate chapter to the subject.

Perhaps one of the most important distinctions of our book is that we spend a great deal of time on the issues of corporate, rather than business, management. Too many strategic management books make the implicit assumption that the firm is a single-business entity, but this is clearly not the case for most firms of medium size or above. There is a whole set of issues that arise from the task of managing a multi-business entity that do not appear on the horizon of a single business firm. These we explore in detail.

We have organized our book to make it easy for you, the student, to follow, and for instructors to use the book in a variety of ways. We have adopted a more or less standard approach to the content of the book's chapters. Each begins with a definition of learning objectives—what you should get out of the chapter. We then introduce an opening vignette—a short business example that illustrates the relevance and importance of the chapter's subject matter. Each chapter then presents a theoretical framework typically illustrated with several charts and figures emphasizing key points. We have made every attempt to give you a straightforward structure to follow, with headings and subheadings clearly identified, and we hope you will find our text easy to read. Each chapter closes with a summary, a set of review questions, and extensive references to permit a more detailed follow up if you are interested.

☉ OVERVIEW

Chapter 1, Managing Strategically, introduces our model of strategic management and discusses the distinctions between strategic decisions, strategy, and strategic management. It focuses on the nature of the firm as an economic entity, measures of success of that entity, and the source of success, which we see as a synthesis between external market characteristics and the internal resources of the firm. We finally discuss some of the influences on the development of strategic management.

In Chapter 2, The Fundamentals of Strategic Management, we expand our discussion on the distinctions between strategic decisions, strategy, and strategic management. Strategic decisions are those hard-to-reverse major decisions taken by management. Strategy is the theme underlying a set of strategic decisions. Such strategies have several characteristics that are further developed. Strategic management is about creating organizations that generate value. A core concept here is change management. Following a discussion of business models, we address the question of value from the perspective of the firm's various stakeholders.

Strategic managers need a good understanding of the internal and external context in which they operate. This is the subject of Chapters 3, 4 and 5.

In Chapter 3, we cover the understanding of product markets—the broad environment in which the firm's products and services compete—as well as industry and business unit environments. It is here that many changes that affect the firm originate. These changes could be the development of a new product technology that threatens to make obsolete the firm's existing products. They also can be political or economic change in one of the major global markets of the firm, such as the introduction of the Euro in many European countries or the rise of China as a source of production and its entry in to the World Trade Organization. We address the importance of understanding the dynamics of the industry in which a particular business unit operates, including identifying when the boundaries are changing.

Global firms can be considered to operate in two fundamentally different markets: financial markets for debt and equity and product markets for customers. In Chapter 4 we review financial markets and their impact on strategy. Most firms raise some funds for growth and expansion in the global financial markets either by issuing debt or equity. The cost and availability of these funds have a significant impact on the firm's strategy. We review the characteristics of debt and equity markets and the pressure they place on firms for performance. Since financial markets are global, this pressure for performance is felt on a global basis. It is hard to hide behind national barriers. Finally, we review the nature and use of newer financial instruments such as derivatives.

While understanding the external world is critical, so is an understanding of the internal skills of the firm—what we call capabilities or what the firm is good at. Here we take a balanced view of the firm. Certainly the environment in which the firm operates can influence its performance, but so also do firm-specific resources. These resources may be tangible or intangible, and are combined to permit the firm to develop specific competences that may lead to competitive advantage and drive superior performance. We regard strategy as a synthesis of an "outside in" and an "inside out" approach. In a competitive world, there is an inexorable pressure for cost reductions, so we then address the major cost drivers such as economies of scale and experience curves. The chapter concludes with a discussion of the importance of knowledge and intellectual capital.

In Chapter 6, we turn our attention to the first step in generating strategy for the firm—creating a sense of the future of the firm, what it aspires to, and what it hopes to become. A firm, in our view, cannot be strategically managed unless senior management has a clear idea of where it wants to go. It is critical that senior management develop and communicate this vision throughout the firm, so that all staff is aware of and committed to the firm's aspirations. Management must also establish a set of values that can guide employee behavior in fulfilling these aspirations. A mission (a specification of the areas in which the firm will operate) and quantitative objectives for the firm and its components need to be established.

Chapters 7–9 are concerned with strategy. Chapter 7 addresses strategy for an individual strategic business unit, a unit of the firm that can be considered as relatively autonomous. Developing strategy at the business unit level requires an understanding of corporate objectives which will usually have a strong effect on the business. In addition, it requires an understanding of the business's own, specific environment. Strategy is then addressed, including the three major decision areas: where to compete, how to compete, and growth strategy. The concept of competitive advantage (how this can be developed and utilized) is of central concern in developing business unit strategy such as is the positioning of the business both vertically and horizontally. This determines what activities it undertakes and where it decides to compete.

Chapter 8 addresses strategy in the multi-divisional firm—the common situation for larger firms. Key decisions include which businesses should comprise the firm and how the combination of businesses create value. In multidivisional firms, a major task for corporate management is to allocate resources across the business units. Tools to identify which businesses should be supported are developed. This discussion is complemented with a discussion of the value of diversification. We then address a limited number of essentially financial decisions that are also the responsibility of senior management, such as establishing appropriate debt levels and dividends. The chapter concludes with a discussion of the risk profile of the firm.

In Chapter 9 we consider innovation within the firm. We cover opportunities for the firm to restructure its industry, innovate organizationally or change its mission. Successful firms must re-invent themselves and their mix of businesses, either through internal development or through mergers and acquisitions. Both means are discussed in some detail. We also address how firms can reduce their activities through divestments or spinouts.

Chapter 10 is concerned with managing change within the firm. In the text, we have placed considerable emphasis on the fact that change is an on-going feature of organizational life, and that change management must be a core competence for the firm. We develop a process model of change management and emphasize the role of leadership.

Chapter 11 continues the discussion of strategy implementation and is concerned with the design of some of the internal features of the firm, what we call organizational architecture. We look at several of the principles of designing organizational structure and some of the choices available to the global firm. With the increasing importance of process management, we review process improvement, information technology infrastructure and knowledge management systems. Finally we explore human resource concerns such as reward and appraisal systems and their alignment with the firm's strategy.

Chapter 12 is new for most strategy books. It looks at organizational performance from the perspective of the entire firm, as well as from the perspective of a component of the firm. While financial measures of performance, in particular economic profit, are highlighted, so are nonfinancial measures. This reflects the increasing importance of intangible assets. The chapter includes examples of performance measurement systems adopted by two firms.

Chapter 13 covers governance which includes the concerns of the board. The board has a number of legal and statutory responsibilities that must be met. While senior managers are responsible for developing strategy, the board is the group that is legally responsible for firm performance, and is accountable to shareholders. We examine the role, composition and structure of the board as well as board processes. We contrast governance procedures in different regions of the world, all with a view to ensuring that the firm acts to generate value in an ethical manner.

Chapter 14 is a short summary and review. It considers how strategic management may develop in the future. The chapter emphasizes the fact that both theory and practice are in constant evolution with new ideas, new theories, new practices, and new challenges constantly arising. As a would-be strategic manager, you, our readers, will face a lifetime of learning and change. You will certainly be living in interesting times!

⊙ SUPPORT MATERIAL

A comprehensive instructor's manual is available that details suggested teaching timetables, teaching notes and presentation slides. Suggested case studies for each chapter and guides on the end of chapter review questions are also available. These materials are available on the book's website: www.wiley.com/college/FitzRoy.

⊚ ACKNOWLEDGEMENTS

Many individuals and organizations have contributed to the publication of this text. Although anonymous, we are very grateful to the large numbers of MBA students in the United States, Australia, Europe, and Asia who have used some or all of the material as it was in preparation. We also owe a debt of gratitude to the anonymous reviewers who provided us with such useful feedback on our earlier drafts.

In addition, we would like to express our thanks formally to colleagues in several countries for their support and assistance. These include Neil Abromavage, Graeme Addison, Mohamed Ariff, Chris Ballenden, David Beim, Pierre Berthon, Walter Borghi, Wido Bosch, Noel Capon, Paul Coughlin, Andrew Dixon, Graham Edward, Wiveca Erlandsson, Jean Noel Ezingëard, Alexandre Fernandes, Peter Hawkins, Fred Hilmer, Graham Hubbard, Arnaud Humblot, Kevin Jagiello, Nell Kimberley, Mike Knowles, Roger Love, Wei Shan Lim, Rory Manchee, Vicky Mayer, Emma Meade, Nigel Morkel-Kingsbury, Mark Nicholson, John Papanidis, Chandana Perara, Eli Raskin, Janek Ratnatunga, James Sarros, Bill Schroder, Pelham Smithers, On Kit Tam, Bernard Taylor, Dianne Waddell, Gary West, Stuart Westmore, Greg Whitwell and David Wolf.

A number of colleagues have influenced our thinking and development over the years, and to these we owe a profound debt. They include Eric Abramson, Schon Beechler, Jeremy Davis, John Farley, Bradley Gale, Don Hambrick, Kathy Harrigan, the late John Howard, Madge Lyman, Gordon Mandry, Rita McGrath, Wayne Meinhart, the late William Newman, Atul Nerkar, Walter Nord, Dan Schendel, Kirby Warren and Bob Yavitz. To all these colleagues we express our deep thanks. We also wish to acknowledge the help we received from the secretarial and library staff at Monash and Columbia, as well as the constant encouragement of our partners, Margaret and Madge.

We also express our appreciation to several organizations for the use of material from their Web Pages, including BHPBilliton, Canon, Celemi, Ciba Specialty Chemicals, CitiGroup, Dealogic, Harley-Davidson, LEK Consulting, LG, News Corporation, Petrobras, Philips, Procter & Gamble, Siemens, Smithers and Co., Standard & Poors, and Unilever.

The staff at Wiley have been consistent and sympathetic advisors. We could not have hoped for a better publisher. Our thanks to Jessica Bartelt, Johanna Barto, Steve Hardman, Jeff Marshall, and Anna Rowe.

⊚ ABOUT THE AUTHORS

Peter FitzRoy is a Professor in the MBA Program at Monash University in Melbourne, Australia where he has taught Strategic Management for several years. He has held appointments at a number of institutions including Columbia University, the University of Illinois, the Manchester Business School, the Wharton school of the University of Pennsylvania, the University of Waterloo, and Purdue University. He also has extensive experience in lecturing on management development programs in Asia, Australia, the United Kingdom and the United States. He is actively involved in the Strategic Management Society, and has served for many years on the editorial board of the Strategic Management Journal.

James (Mac) Hulbert is the R. C. Kopf Professor Emeritus at the Graduate School of Business, Columbia University. He has taught or held visiting positions at the Fundacao Joao Pinheiro (Brazil), Henley Management College, the London Business School, Peking University, and UCLA among others. He has also taught on executive development programs in Europe, South America, North America, the Middle East, Africa, and

Asia. He has worked as a consultant with numerous global companies including Monsanto, 3M, IBM, General Electric, Chase Manhattan Bank, BASF, Ericsson, BHP Billiton, ICI, Unilever, and Visa International. His research interests are strategy and planning, which have resulted in several published books and numerous articles in the *Strategic Management Journal, Sloan Management Review, California Management Review, European Management Journal* among others.

Brief Contents

Contents

CHAPTER 1

Managing Strategically

Learning Objectives

Upon completing this chapter, you should be able to:

- Recognize the importance of strategic management to firm growth, innovation, and performance
- Distinguish among strategic decisions, strategy, and strategic management
- Realize that strategy involves a synthesis of external analysis coupled with an understanding of the internal resources and capabilities of the firm
- Accept that change is continual, with both incremental change and revolutionary change occurring
- Appreciate why firms exist as economic entities and be able to describe alternate forms of economic exchanges
- Understand the need for continual innovation and change: nothing is fixed; all attributes of the firm are variable
- Apply the model of strategic management developed in the chapter

To illustrate many of the principles of strategic management, consider a brief history of News Corporation,[1-3] a global news and entertainment firm.

1953	News Corporation owns a small newspaper in Adelaide, Australia, as well as two other small country newspapers; total assets are $AUM1.0 ($USM1.12)[4]
1950s	Acquires an unprofitable newspaper in Perth, a magazine publisher in Melbourne, newspapers in several regional centers in Australia, and a suburban newspaper publishing group in Sydney as well as a majority interest in the first Adelaide TV station
1960s	Acquires newspapers in Sydney and New Zealand
	Prevented from acquiring a Sydney TV license, so buys a regional TV station adjacent to Sydney
	Starts the first national newspaper in Australia
	Acquires an interest in a Hong Kong magazine company
	Acquires *News of the World* and *The Sun* in London, both of which are unprofitable
1970s	Acquires additional newspapers in Sydney as well as in San Antonio, Texas; acquires the *New York Post*, which is unprofitable
	Acquires an interest in a Sydney TV station
1980s	Acquires *The Times* and *The Sunday Times* in London, the *Boston Herald* and the *Chicago Sun-Times*, the *South China Post* in Hong Kong, *The Herald and Weekly*

1

Times in Australia; starts a new newspaper in Brisbane; moves all newspaper production in the United Kingdom to Wapping

Acquires 20th Century Fox and Metromedia (which owns seven TV stations) in the United States

Launches Fox as the fourth TV network in the United States; acquires an interest in satellite TV in the United Kingdom (SKY)

Acquires Harper & Row and Collins, book publishers in the United States, as well as a book publisher in Australia

Acquires Triangle Publications for $USB3.0

1990s   SKY and a competitor merge to form BskyB in the United Kingdom

MCI purchases an interest in the company, paying cash

Acquires New World Communications in the United States for $USB3.4

Purchases Star TV in Hong Kong

Expands into TV in Germany and Italy (Stream)

Expands into TV in Latin America

2000s   Acquires Telipiu, a competitor in Italian TV, from Vivendi, which is integrated with Stream; analysts anticipate losses over the first three years of € 700M–800M

Acquires a minority interest in DirecTV in the United States from General Motors

This short case illustrates many important principles of *strategic management*. First, a firm exists in a turbulent and rapidly changing *context*, which includes both the external world and the firm's internal skills. Strategy is about understanding and capitalizing on these changes. Context includes product market opportunities, which in the case of News Corp. included developments in satellite and cable TV. Context also includes the necessity for understanding the operations of financial markets. In early 1990 News Corp. had high debt and was almost brought down by a regional U.S. bank. The firm is proactive in its environment, actively soliciting support from a broad range of interest groups such as politicians, governments, regulators, financial markets, and allies in many countries.

The case also illustrates that News Corp.'s *strategy* displays both constancy and evolution over time. Its vision can be characterized as aggressive growth with global aspirations. At the same time, the firm has sometimes shown opportunistic behavior. Telipiu in Italy became an **acquisition** target due to cash flow problems experienced by its parent, Vivendi, and News Corp. was able to take advantage of this. In pursuit of its vision, it adopted both incremental and revolutionary strategies. Geographic expansion by purchasing several regional papers in Texas is incremental. Setting up a new TV network in the United States or a new national newspaper in Australia is revolutionary.

Strategy involves improving operating performance as well as the glamour of acquisitions. Acquisitions have been an important element in its strategy, but News Corp. has also improved the financial performance of many of its acquisitions, providing cash flow for further growth. It has also achieved ongoing improvement in existing operations, growing established markets as well as internally developing new businesses, such as the fourth U.S. TV network. These decisions have involved considerable risk, and the firm has been close to collapse several times, so good understanding of financial markets has been essential. The example also illustrates that *strategy is about making decisions* (not plans) even when the outcome is uncertain. These decisions may involve "betting" the company, as with News Corp.'s continued investment in SKY, which almost forced the firm into bankruptcy. Another high-risk decision was to move all U.K. newspaper production to Wapping, despite union opposition. In this, as in several other decisions, News Corp. achieved **first-mover advantages.** Within a few years, competitors had copied them.

Strategy is about change, both reacting to change (the emergence of satellite as a medium for TV broadcasting) and creating change (the launch of new newspapers). This has led News Corp. down a path of *continuous change,* with growth from geographic expansion, adoption of new technologies, and entry into new industries. Indeed, News Corp. was an important part of the forces driving these industry changes.

To support these initiatives, the **architecture** (characteristics of the News Corp.) has changed substantially. Its structure, processes, and people are different. The incentives are different, the values and culture are different, and of course not all staff have accepted some of these changes.

Finally, the **financial performance** of the firm has been remarkable. From its relatively humble beginnings, it has grown substantially. As of 2003, News Corp. was in filmed entertainment, pay and free-to-air TV, cable network programs, magazines, newspapers, and book publishing. In that year, the firm reported assets of approximately $AUB68 ($USB40) and revenue of $AUB30 ($USB20). As an indication of how far the firm has moved from its Australian and newspaper roots, 77% of revenue was generated in the United States and newspapers were responsible for just 16% of revenue.

The case study also illustrates the importance of strategic management. What makes News Corp. successful? Over this time period, many other news and entertainment firms have disappeared or been taken over. Why did News Corp. succeed where the management of *The Times* of London could not? We ascribe this difference to excellent strategic management, the ability to develop a strategy, to make decisions, to provide leadership, to create and get support for a vision, to develop the organization and its people, to build new skills and competences, to have the foresight and creativity to see what was happening in the world and the courage to take risks and to build the **organizational processes** to support development. Following the offer by News Corp. for Telipiu in 2002, its share price dropped 6.6%. Some investors felt that the firm should "slow down" and concentrate on profit, not growth, and develop strategies to reduce risk.[5] Instead, the firm aggressively pursued additional opportunities.

With its willingness to take risks and adopt a long time horizon, News Corp. has survived and prospered over the last 50 years. What the future will bring is hard to assess, but it is in a number of attractive industries and seems to have the skills in its staff to make the best of the opportunities it both creates and is presented with.

1.1 INTRODUCTION

As the example of News Corp. illustrates, this is an exciting and challenging time for all organizations. The high rate of change—reflected in rapid **globalization,** rapid shifts in technology, major political and social upheavals—is putting extreme pressure on governments, companies, and not-for-profits, affecting their ability to survive. In business, these changes pose both challenges and opportunities: some companies prosper while others atrophy, and significant new firms arise while others die.

The last few decades have seen the emergence of major new organizations. The United States witnessed the rise of Microsoft and Intel, Europe the success of Ikea and SAP. From Asia come Acer of Taiwan and LG of Korea, now well known around the world. At the same time, existing firms such as Nestle and Unilever have demonstrated continued success.

Cadbury Schweppes was formed in 1969 with a merger of Schweppes—created in Switzerland in 1783, and Cadbury—created in the U.K. in 1823. The firm has a history of innovation and growth, through both acquisition and internal development. It currently operates in over 200 countries, and in 2003 it had revenue of £B6.4 ($USB11.3) with operating profit of £B1.1 ($USB1.8).

Simultaneously, other firms founder or are at risk of failure. In 2002, Enron, Andersen, and Tyco formed a triumvirate that threatened the stability of U.S. capital markets. In Japan, companies with major problems include most of the banks and Mitsubishi (which is in an alliance with Daimler Chrysler). In the United Kingdom, Marconi has been in desperate straits, while in continental Europe, airlines such as Swiss Air and Sabena no longer exist in their original form. The Daimler-Benz merger with Chrysler is in trouble, as is Time-Warner AOL, while the one-time French corporate hero Jean-Marie Messier lost his job as Vivendi's stock price fell.

These examples illustrate the difficulty that firms experience in developing and executing value-creating strategies. While the rewards of success are greater than ever, so are the penalties of failure. In such a dynamic world, any strategy must be modified as the world changes. Successful firms have both constancy of vision and flexibility in execution. In a turbulent and unpredictable world, **innovation** in all aspects of the firm is the only route to sustained success. This constitutes the strategic management challenge: how to create value in the present while building a platform for future value creation. Strategic management is an ongoing, continual process, not a single event or decision.

Figure 1.1 shows a simplified model of the strategic management process. First, strategic managers must be aware of the changing **context** in which they compete. They need a deep understanding of environmental changes and their future impact. Coupled with this, they must understand what the firm is capable of, where it excels, what it is good at. In other words, what **resources** and competences do the firm and its members possess? These must also be seen dynamically: firms can develop new skills and competences, as forcibly demonstrated by News Corp.

Strategy will be driven by a combination of external changes and the skills of the people in the firm. Management needs to decide how to respond to both challenges and

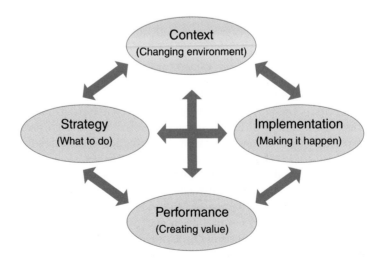

Figure 1.1 Simplified Strategic Management Process

opportunities. Since the world is changing rapidly, we can also expect the firm's strategy to do so. This may involve developing new bases of **competitive advantage** or completely new lines of business, either internally or via acquisition.

But strategic management is not just about what to do; it is also about how to do it, how the strategy will be *implemented*. New skills and competences will likely be required to take advantage of opportunities created by a changing environment. In addition, the future may call for new leadership skills, changing the structure and/or culture of the firm. The firm must to learn to operate in new environments with different competitors and possibly new technologies. Finally, the total strategic management process must result in organizations that *create value* over the long term.

As shown in Figure 1.1, these processes are interconnected. Strategic management and strategy development are not linear processes but are interactive and recursive.

Definition of Strategic Management Terms

This text focuses on strategic management, the managerial aspect of strategy. We begin by distinguishing several concepts that are often confused; namely, strategic decisions, strategy, and strategic management.

Strategic decisions are those that affect the long-term well-being of the organization. Such decisions involve major resource commitments and are difficult to reverse, implying a long-term commitment. Decisions that can be regarded as strategic can occur at all levels of the firm. What is strategic depends on the entity we are considering. In this text we will concentrate on two levels of decisions—corporate and business. **Corporate**-level decisions are those that affect the entire firm, whereas **business**-level decisions affect the particular business or division. Differences between these two will be clarified in Chapter 2. If there is only one business in the firm, then the corporate and business levels are identical. What is regarded as long term will also depend on the firm and the industry in which it competes. For a firm developing software, the long term may be as short as two or three years. For an oil company involved in all activities from exploration to retail, the long term may be 15 to 20 years.

> With News Corporation, we can easily identify a number of strategic decisions, such as the acquisition of *The Times*, the launch of the Fox network in the United States, or the acquisition of HarperCollins. These are all decisions that are risky; it takes time to see whether they were good decisions.
>
> Under the leadership of John Brown, BP has made significant investments in hydrogen technology. ExxonMobil, in contrast, has directed its R&D expenditures toward improving the emissions performance of existing fossil fuel technologies. In both instances, these are strategic decisions for the companies involved.[8]

Strategy is the common theme underlying a set of strategic decisions. In our view, an acquisition is a strategic decision, not a strategy. The strategy may be to change the scope of the firm or become global, and the decision to acquire a particular firm is part of that strategy. Such a strategy may involve other significant decisions, such as increasing the level of debt to fund the acquisition. Strategy is about the firm's relationship with the environment and developing the capabilities and competencies to enable it to prosper. It is our view that all firms have a strategy and that this strategy may be explicit or implicit, developed with extensive analysis or not, prespecified or allowed to develop in an evolutionary fashion. A firm's strategy can generally be expressed in relatively simple terms, although this may hide complexity within. When thinking about strategy, we must also recognize that in strategy nothing about the firm is fixed; it is all variable. The strategy may change a firm's scope, its culture, its structure, its vision, or all of the above. When developing strategy, we must therefore think creatively about a wide range of possible changes.

> The strategy of News Corporation is to become a global news, information, and entertainment company, not a newspaper company. The firm has been pursuing this for some time. Ikea has grown around the world with a strategy of organic expansion, exporting to many different countries a consistent store format and operating philosophy.

Strategic management involves creating organizations that generate value in a turbulent world over a sustained period of time. It is a management task that involves leadership, creativity, passion, and analysis—building an organization that both generates and responds to change, developing compensation systems to reward staff, devising appropriate structures and systems, competing for funds in global financial markets, and ensuring that necessary resources are developed and allocated to worthwhile opportunities. Strategic management means managing for the present as well as creating change so that the firm continues to prosper in a global, uncertain world.

> News Corporation has grown from a small regional Australian newspaper into a global business with interests in many areas of communications. This has involved leadership, developing new skills, and balancing growth with financial and other constraints. Growth has not been an accident; instead, the management of the firm has driven it.

The examples we have discussed underline the fact that *organizational innovation* is the key to strategy and wealth creation. The firm that finds an innovative approach is generally the one that shifts industry equilibrium in its favor. Further, our examples indicate that success is not predetermined by the industry in which the firm operates; successful and unsuccessful firms may coexist in the same industry. Indeed, two firms in the same industry can have different strategies, yet both can be successful: the so-called equifinality principle. Of course, success may be assessed in many ways, and different **stakeholder** groups, such as shareholders, customers, and employees, may use very different criteria. Of one thing we are confident, however: management makes a difference to organizational performance.

Only a few years ago, a great deal of effort was expended to improve forecasting models and forecast accuracy. Indeed, forecasts of revenues, costs, investments, and profit are central to much of the panoply of modern management. However, over time the business environment has become more turbulent, even chaotic, and too unpredictable for historical data to provide good guidance to the future, no matter how sophisticated the model. With turbulence, fixed investments and costs become more perilous, flexibility and variable costs more desirable. With these changes, it is becoming more and more important for firms to experiment and to learn quickly from their experiences. Yet we must not throw the baby out with the bathwater. Yes, forecasting has become more difficult, but at the same time the future is not completely unpredictable. Demand for many products and services, such as petroleum, electricity, steel, education, and banking, is remarkably stable. Further, predictions of environmental trends, such as population, have little error associated with them.

Developing strategy in today's environment is a challenging undertaking. When the world is turbulent and unpredictable, how should an organization respond? Should it respond purposefully or just drift? Some suggest that in such a world, strategy is obsolete before it can be developed. We reject this argument. We believe the firm must have a strategy for reacting and responding to developments. If it just drifts, it is unlikely to survive. A clear idea of where the firm is going is a necessary prerequisite to develop the resources, capabilities, and, ultimately, the products and services required by targeted markets. Managers need to understand the way the world is evolving and what responses are likely to enhance the firm's survival and prosperity. Without some sense of direction, albeit imperfect, the firm cannot operate.

This discussion leads us to consider, and to clarify, what we mean by firm success.

1.2 FIRM SUCCESS

We define an organization as a set of productive assets (including individuals) that voluntarily come together for a common purpose.[9] In this text, we focus primarily on **business organizations,** organizations whose common purpose is primarily economic. The primary purpose of many organizations, such as UNICEF or the Metropolitan Opera in New York, is noneconomic. Although such organizations must pay some attention to their economic performance, this is not their primary focus.

The definition of success of a business firm depends on whose eyes we are looking through. Shareholders have a different view from employees, who in turn look at things very differently from customers. The firm has many stakeholders or constituencies, but these three are undoubtedly among the most important. In Chapter 2, we discuss success from each of these perspectives in more detail. Here, we take the firm itself as the unit of analysis and explore three related questions:

What do we mean by the success of a firm?

What determines firm success?

What is the sustainability of that success?

What Do We Mean by Success?

At its simplest level, success may mean survival. If a firm survives only for a few years (or a few months, as was the case with many of the dot.coms), then we would not count that as a successful firm. By contrast, du Pont has been in business for more than 150 years, with significant changes to its scope and, of course, management. Success has not depended on a single individual. Rather, successful processes have been transferred to succeeding generations of managers. Continuity is certainly an element in defining success, but the challenge of strategic management is to create organizations capable of creating value over a sustained period.

We regard a firm as successful when it has the ability to create positive net **economic value** as an entity; that is, the value created by the firm is greater than the costs incurred in creating that value. The objective of strategic management is to develop strategies and to make strategic decisions so that this occurs. Let's look at what this implies in terms of value and costs.

The gross value created by the firm is the total revenue generated from the sale or lease of the goods and services it supplies to customers. This revenue must be larger than all the costs incurred in generating it. While there are many ways to classify costs, the most important ones are the costs of all inputs: material, labor, and capital. The value created by the firm as an entity is then simply:

Value created by the firm = revenue less all costs

TABLE 1.1   Economic Profit in the U.S. Computer Industry

	1993 ($M)	1994 ($M)	1995 ($M)
Data General	−219	−222	−187
Digital	−2,280	−2,546	−1,868
HP	−168	526	888
IBM	−10,188	−7,650	−252
Sun Micro	−181	−130	25
Tandem	−325	−180	−207

Source: D. Besanko, D. Dranove, and M. Stanley *Economics of Strategy*, (New York: Wiley) © 2000, John Wiley. This material is used by permission of John Wiley & Sons, Inc.

We will refer to this value as the **economic profit** of the firm. It is a different concept from the **accounting profit,** because in determining economic profit, we also consider the amount and cost of capital employed in the business. A firm may make an accounting profit but employ a huge capital base in order to do so. Since capital is not free, a capital charge must be included to measure economic profit. So we define economic profit as:

$$\text{Economic profit} = \text{revenue less all costs, including capital costs}$$

If a firm covers all other costs, but not capital costs, the firm is destroying value and hurting its shareholders. Since they may easily move their funds from one investment to another, failure to generate economic profit will motivate them to invest elsewhere rather than suffer opportunity losses.

Table 1.1 shows the economic profit earned by several U.S. computer firms, where economic profit is as defined above. We discuss the measurement of economic profit in greater depth in Chapter 12.

The table indicates that IBM generated an economic loss of $USM252 in 1995, destroying that much value for IBM shareholders. Note that this is the value of the firm as an ongoing entity; economic profit does not attempt to portray share prices, though they are undoubtedly influenced by economic profit. In that same year, HP created an additional $USM888 of wealth for its shareholders that they could not have received from other investments of equal risk. Firms that performed poorly in generating economic profit all suffered. Tandem, Data General, and Digital have disappeared or been merged out of existence, while IBM suffered a traumatic restructuring before reemerging as a strong and vibrant firm.

The purpose of strategic management is to ensure that the firm generates an economic profit that is available for distribution among its stakeholders or that the firm can use for innovation to create additional value. How this surplus is distributed, however, will be a source of debate within the firm, reflecting the values of managers, available growth opportunities, and the political power of various stakeholders.

What Determines Success?

Although many concepts such as **game theory** and **organization theory** have influenced the development of strategic management, the literature generally suggests that there are two main models of successful performance. These are referred to as the structure–conduct–performance (SCP) model and the resource-based view (RBV).

Structure–Conduct–Performance Model

The **structure–conduct–performance** model postulates that the dominant influence on firm performance is the external environment in which it competes. By contrast, the resource-based model postulates that the unique resources, skills, and competences of the firm that are the source of its success. We briefly discuss the contribution made by each model, subsequently developing our view that each is an incomplete framework for success.

With the SCP model, the **structural characteristics** of the industry are seen as determining conduct (or what we would regard as strategy), which in turn determines the performance of the business. Structural characteristics include, among others, such parameters as barriers to entry, customer concentration, existence of substitutes, and level of product differentiation between competitors. These characteristics determine the conduct of the business, including such elements as pricing, product strategy, R&D, advertising, and levels of investment. This conduct in turn is the primary influence on the performance of the business. This model has a long history in economics, with major contributions having been made by Caves[10] and Porter.[11]

The SCP model suggests that the industry in which the firm chooses to compete is more important than the choices managers make. Success occurs when the firm elects to compete in structurally attractive industries. Under this model, the emphasis in strategy is on optimal positioning: locate an attractive industry and attempt to become market leaders. The emphasis is on analyzing the firm's environment to assess the overall economic profit of the industry, since this is considered the major influence on firm profitability. We can see the importance of this approach in the airline industry, where average profitability is extremely low. This low profit arises from the structural characteristics of that industry—intense competition, high capital requirements, fluctuating demand, and so on.

However, even in the airline industry, some competitors do significantly better than others. This situation also arises in commodity markets such as those for oil or iron ore. Some firms may be more skilled at reducing costs, or possess unique knowledge in processing, or be in possession of a high-grade ore body—and thus be able to generate superior financial returns.

Under the SCP framework, strategy choices are seen as constrained by industry structure, with successful strategies being either producing at a lower cost than competitors or producing a differentiated product for which customers are prepared to pay a premium. Which is to be preferred is determined by industry structure. All firms are assumed to possess similar resources, although there is some discretion for the firm—it may be able to implement strategy better than competitors.

While we agree that these structural characteristics influence the nature of the strategy that leads to success, successful firms must also be able to develop the skills required to implement the strategy. In management consulting, the ability to offer a global client a consulting project at the lowest possible price may not be an advantage. Instead, the successful firms are those with credibility and the staff who can deliver on the proposal. Hence, while we regard industry structure as relevant, performance is linked to firm characteristics as well, which leads us to a consideration of the second approach—the resource-based view of strategy.

The Resource-Based View of the Firm

The **resource-based** perspective sees the firm as a collection of unique resources and competences that are the basis of its strategy and success. Resources are the more fundamental financial, physical, and intangible attributes of the firm. **Competences** refer to the firm's ability to combine and integrate these resources. In this view, differences in firm success are explained by differences in resources available to each firm, not industry characteristics. Such a view of strategy has a long history, with the early work having been on strengths and weaknesses[12] and distinctive competences.[13]

Such resources and competences can lead to superior returns only if they are specific to the firm, so they must be valuable to customers and difficult to imitate by competitors.[14] To be valuable, the resource must increase revenue or reduce costs compared with what they would have been without the resource. If it were easy to transfer resources from one firm to another, any advantage would be quickly competed away. These resources would then become the basis for competitive advantage, a necessary but not sufficient condition for success.

The resource-based view of the firm (RBV) focuses on the need to exploit differences between firms to establish unique positions of competitive advantage, a view aligned with the ideas of Porter, who notes that "competitive strategy is about being different ... choosing a different set of activities to deliver a unique mix of value".[15] Further, since the world changes, superior returns can be sustained only if new resources are generated.[16] In our consulting example, a successful firm develops the intellectual ability and knowledge of its staff to ensure that these are superior to competitors.

Synthesis

We consider both of these frameworks to be incomplete and now discuss some of their shortcomings.

The SCP model is concerned with the performance of a "firm" that is assumed to compete in a single industry. Yet most global firms compete in many industries; consequently, this model can be relevant only for a division, or what Chapter 2 describes as a business unit of the firm.

Most of the factors that the SCP model considers to affect performance are actually industry factors. Their impact must therefore be on a business unit, not the overall firm, which may compete in many industries. As we have seen, News Corp. competes in newspapers, film, and television, and the structures of these industries differ considerably. When we discuss "firm success," we need to be clear whether we are discussing the success of the parent or the success of a business unit within that parent. If it is the former, then considerations such as the firm's degree and nature of **diversification** or level of debt may be relevant. If it is the latter, industry factors have some relevance—but obviously they are not relevant for a diversified corporation; they can only be relevant for one of its businesses.

In addition, the focus on industry characteristics is also incomplete. If we consider a business unit, it exists in more than just an industry environment; it also exists in what in Chapter 3 we call the **remote environment.** This remote environment includes such things as antitrust legislation, an overall economy, average income levels of the members of the economy, and other factors that will influence the profitability of the business. Possibly as a consequence of this remote environment, we see successful firms in unattractive industries and unsuccessful firms in attractive industries.

The RBV is also incomplete. A specific resource or competence has no value independent of the environment in which the firm competes.[17] So a resource such as specialized knowledge may or may not be valuable. To return to our consulting example, the firm may have detailed and comprehensive knowledge of the auto industry. But if the firm has no clients in that industry, such knowledge has no value.

As shown in Figure 1.1, our model of strategic management is richer and more comprehensive than either of these two paradigms but uses both as partial inputs. First, the firm exists in a changing external world, and this world will have a bearing on its strategy. This external world has two elements, which we refer to as the **product/market** environment and the **financial market** environment. Both are relevant. The product/market environment includes such characteristics as the political context (say, antitrust law), which will influence many business units within the firm, and the industry environment. It includes the industry environment, which can affect only the performance of a business in that industry. Financial markets—the ability of the firm to raise debt and equity—will affect strategy and performance. We also need to distinguish what unit we are talking about: the entire firm or a unit within that firm. For example, if we are talking about the performance of a unit within a diversified firm, then we may expect characteristics of the parent to influence the performance of the unit.[18]

What the firm elects to do in the way of strategy will also be influenced by what the firm does well, what specialized resources and competences it possesses. However, strategic management is not only about a good idea; it is also about getting that idea to work. The strategy must be able to be implemented; if not, it must be changed. Finally, the firm estimates likely performance resulting from the chosen strategy. If this is not satisfactory, the strategy is likely to be revised. In addition, various performance measures can be adopted, which will be discussed in detail in Chapter 12.

Sustainability of Success

The challenge for strategic management is to build organizations capable of creating and delivering value over a sustained period. This has proved to be extremely difficult. Typically, firms seem to have their day in the sun and then decline, either absolutely or relatively, as new firms emerge in the growth sectors of the economy. Sustained success will occur only when strategic managers are able to both *manage for today* and *manage for tomorrow*.[19]

Managing for Today
Managing for today typically involves fine-tuning current operations, introducing incremental changes with strategy staying reasonably fixed. These changes are smaller, more evolutionary; the managerial focus is on managing complexity. Ideally, vision and values are in place, deeply embedded in the firm, well understood, and accepted by all. A key managerial concern is ensuring that the strategy is well understood and clear performance criteria are established and met. When managing for today, the firm's organizational structure is assumed to have been designed appropriately, as are the control system and performance management system.

Managing for Tomorrow
Managing for tomorrow requires different skills. To have the foresight and knowledge to imagine how the firm will look in the future requires creating a **vision** of what the firm and its environment is likely to look like, a topic to which we return in Chapter 6. To move toward realizing such a vision demands not only good leadership skills but also an understanding of what capabilities will be required and specific planning to acquire or develop them. This challenge will often require that we loosen up thinking in the firm. Managers and other employees must be open to change, willing to listen, keeping information systems open to external as well as internal inputs. Senior managers should not become overdependent on formal systems or their immediate staff. Useful insights may come from suppliers, customers, universities and technical bodies, and other such sources. Managers must seek leading indicators of change along all dimensions—technological, sociodemographic, political, and so on. The key is not so much to identify

trends but to spot turning points and points of inflection in growth curves. The company that is continually surprised by change is unlikely to deal with it well.[20]

> Consider Intel's dilemma. The cost of a computer chip factory for the new 300-mm silicon wafers is nearly $USB3, a significant sum even for Intel.[21] At the same time the future is unpredictable. What will be the impact of the Internet and network computing on the types of computers that will be purchased? What will be the future demand for computers? Has the market become saturated? What is the competition from contract chip manufacturers?
>
> It may take two to three years to build a new plant and perhaps three to five more years for the plant to pay off. Senior managers need to develop a view of the world to make the decision now as to whether or not to go ahead with the new plant, and this view of the world has a time horizon of at least four to seven years.

Given an uncertain future, a strategy cannot be set in concrete. It must evolve as the world evolves. At the same time, it needs to create a sense of common direction. Strategy making is an ongoing process, not something that is done periodically on a rigid planning cycle. The firm has to continually develop new ideas, a succession of initiatives over time. However, changes in strategy should be driven by changes in circumstances, not the passage of time.

We can link today and tomorrow by recognizing that long-term sustainability of success depends upon to two factors:

The sustainability of a competitive advantage in a given market or industry

The rate at which new industry sectors emerge and the ability of the firm to alter its scope and capabilities to compete in these new sectors

These two influences are depicted in Figure 1.2.

In a relatively free market, with no institutional barriers, any advantage will be competed away. Other firms will copy and/or enhance the initial competitive advantage. Unless the firm continues to enhance its advantage and develop new ones, its competitiveness inevitably deteriorates. Thus strategic management involves a process of ongoing change and improvement, adapting to a continuously changing world.

> IBM was at one time the most profitable company in the world. Fueled by its dominance of the mainframe computer business, it achieved the highest market value of any firm in the world. Yet, as the computer market changed, John Akers, the CEO, seemed unable to develop a strategy that "reinvented" the company; as a result, the firm sustained major losses, as we saw in Table 1.1. Lou Gerstner, a former executive of McKinsey then working at American Express, replaced Akers. Gerstner was able to turn IBM around, but only after he reinvented IBM's strategy.

Strategic management has to ensure the invention and development of offerings that will create value in an uncertain future, as well as creation of value through present offerings. If no value is created in the short term, the firm will lose the support of both customers and shareholders. However, if there is only a short-term focus, then the firm will have no future.

As we noted earlier, in strategy all characteristics of the firm are candidates for change. In the long term, nothing is fixed. Strategic management must create an organizational architecture that encourages continual reinvention alongside current operations. Strategic management therefore involves making either incremental and/or revolutionary changes to strategy to ensure sustained success for the firm.

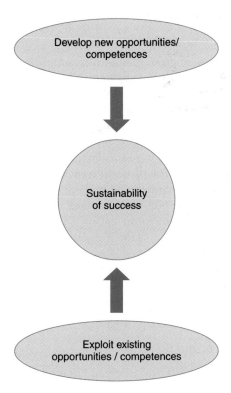

Figure 1.2 Sustainability of Success

Tesco, currently the leading U.K. supermarket chain, could continue to seek new supermarket sites for expansion in the United Kingdom, using existing methods of operating. Or it could change the layout within its existing stores. Both of these would be incremental changes to its existing strategy. However, by introducing online shopping, Tesco significantly changed its historic strategy, as it did when it chose to expand outside the United Kingdom. An even more radical change in strategy would be for them to become a global communications company such as AOL-Time Warner!

When a firm is in difficulty, it is often because its strategy and its underlying assumptions no longer fit reality. Assumptions about the nature and form of competition, what values customers are seeking, or the factors driving success become outdated. This is why the maintenance of an external perspective is a key element in strategic management. An early warning system is needed to see when the existing model is in danger of becoming inadequate. We explore these issues in more depth in Chapter 3.

Fundamental reinvention of strategy is much more difficult in practice than in theory. It requires innovation, creativity, and a deep understanding of the business, its customers, and how the environment is changing. Further, implementation of a new strategy may make existing capabilities out of date, requiring the firm to cannibalize existing products and even threaten existing jobs. Previously successful firms often demonstrate an inability to change; they perceive the world though increasingly obsolete eyes. Indeed, some believe that most innovation in an industry comes from firms outside the industry, which are not constrained by the incumbents' implicit assumptions and mind-sets.

Regardless, it is surely better that we cannibalize our business than allow others to do so. Yet many firms find this very difficult. They may reinvent themselves once, but then stop. For this reason, in many industries, relatively unknown companies that create and exploit new strategic positions have humbled once formidable companies with seemingly unassailable positions.[22] Nor are these innovative approaches limited to high-tech industries. Companies such as Aldi, the German discount retailer, Ryanair, the Irish low-cost airline, and Starbucks, the U.S. coffee chain, have brought major innovations to traditional industries and enjoyed strong commercial success. We have no doubt there will be many more examples in the future.

In summary, to ensure sustainability of success, a firm needs a *portfolio* of strategy initiatives—some focused on the short term and others on the longer term. The firm has to compete in product markets, and in these markets competitive advantage is a necessary but not sufficient condition for success. We can be successful relative to competitors but not create value as an entity. The challenge for strategic managers is to simultaneously create value in the present and set the stage for future value creation. This goal, in turn, poses a classic managerial dilemma: how much to invest in current businesses versus how much to invest in new businesses.[23] We believe that in a changing world, successful firms will be those that both create and adapt to change. They will be firms that have, in fact, helped to change the world.

◉ 1.3 THE CONCEPT OF THE FIRM

As was noted earlier, a business organization or firm is one whose primary purpose is economic. Since these firms are competing with other firms providing similar goods and services, they must organize themselves efficiently. An important determinant of firm efficiency is the selection of activities that it will undertake itself and those that will be acquired from others. Which activities are best grouped under common ownership and which are best handled by other arrangements? Should a firm employ its own accountants, or should this activity be outsourced? These decisions constitute a fundamental issue in strategic management: What should be the scope of the firm, and where should **firm boundaries** be defined?

> In the computer industry, firms such as Dell, IBM, and Compaq do not produce disc drives or memory devices, yet in the automobile industry Ford and GM still produce a substantial proportion of their subcomponents, despite having partially spun off their parts subsidiaries, Visteon and Delhi.

The question of which activities should be retained within the firm and which should be pursued by other means is the content of **organizational economics,** or the theory of the firm.[24] In this theory, it is generally considered that there are two archetypal forms of economic organization—the market and the hierarchy (or firm). With the former, the flow of goods and services occurs across separate legal entities. When transactions are handled within the firm, the economic activity is called a hierarchy and it is proposed that companies exist when these hierarchical relationships are more efficient than market transactions.

With a **market-based** system, exchanges occur between two separate and independent entities. When Dell purchases its computer chips from a company such as Intel, the transaction occurs in the market. In this arrangement, prices are used to coordinate flow of goods across separate legal entities, each of which has its own objectives.

These independent companies make their own decisions on what and how much to produce in response to price and demand signals. Incentives are relatively clear. Dell will continue to purchase from Intel provided Intel meets its requirements, and there is therefore pressure on Intel to understand Dell's needs.

With a **hierarchically based** system of exchange, goods are produced by and exchanged between different units of the same firm; that is, transactions occur between entities under common ownership. Such arrangements may be beneficial to the firm, since all individuals are employed by the same firm and should possess similar objectives. There is a bargain between the obedience of the subordinate and the responsibility of the superior, resting on the capacity to form relationships of trust to reduce conflicts of interest, where individuals act in their own interests rather than the firm's.

The question senior managers must resolve is: When are hierarchies better than markets? The answer is determined by three considerations: production costs, governance costs, and competences. Production costs can vary with each arrangement. Take the example of software. If it is produced within the firm, staff may be less skilled than outside specialists who have access to more sophisticated test and development equipment, making costs higher. On the other hand, software produced within the firm may have superior functionality, since it has been developed specifically for an internal application.

Governance costs are the costs associated with managing transactions.[25] With market-based transactions, these include the costs of negotiating, monitoring, and enforcing a contract with the external provider. Such governance costs also occur when transactions occur within the firm. These include coordination costs, costs of the bureaucracy, costs of complexity, and slow decision making. Under conditions of high external uncertainty, it is difficult to write a contract allowing for all future possibilities, thereby ensuring a fair return to both parties. Under these conditions, we would expect transactions to take place within the firm.

A final consideration affecting a firm's boundaries is its competences. Distinctive competences, based on tangible and intangible firm assets, can be used to extend the firm's scope. They are also key to developing a competitive advantage. The firm will want to ensure that current and future competences are kept within the firm, since they are the basis of future success. As firms become more knowledge intensive, they must develop, protect, and integrate this knowledge to enhance competitive position.

Managerial Implications

These two forms of economic exchange represent extremes, as shown in Figure 1.3. Economic exchanges may be at one of the two extremes or they may occur through one of a wide range of other relational forms, such as networks or alliances, long-term supplier agreements, licensing, contract staff, franchising, equity spinouts, and so on. Managers should consider a variety of alternatives, since they may permit a better balance between individual initiative and structured cooperation.[26]

Figure 1.3   Alternate Forms of Economic Exchanges

The issues described above have implications for a number of strategic decisions, including **mergers and acquisitions, networks, outsourcing, alliances, joint ventures, vertical integration,** and relationships.[27] At the same time, decisions on firm boundaries reflect mission, capabilities, and innovation. Since these drivers are themselves in flux, decisions regarding boundaries are a dynamic process. We now explore the likely impact of changes in some of these drivers. As firms become more knowledge intensive, we can expect to see an increasing use of outside specialist knowledge providers. Transactions involving high levels of non-firm-specific knowledge will tend to move outside the firm.

Various purchasing exchanges have been developed that allow the firm to reduce the costs of interacting with both customers and suppliers, permitting it to engage in more market-based transactions. The development of the **World Wide Web** has changed the economics of information, enabling a firm to effectively and cheaply utilize a network of other firms, drawing on the talents of many people to create products using e-mail, file transfers, Lotus Notes, and other means to achieve real-time coordination. These firms can be geographically remote, even in different countries. The net result of these developments is to encourage firms to concentrate on a small set of core competences, while making use of the core skills of other firms.

1.4 DYNAMICS OF CHANGE

Change is not a new social or technological phenomenon; it has always occurred. What characterizes the new century is the rapid pace and unpredictability of change, and its global nature.

Figure 1.4 indicates the changes in the rate of penetration of new technologies in the 20th-century U.S. market. Notice that technologies introduced in the early part of the century, such as automobiles and electricity, not only had much slower rates of overall growth than more recent introductions; they also had longer **latencies** before "take-

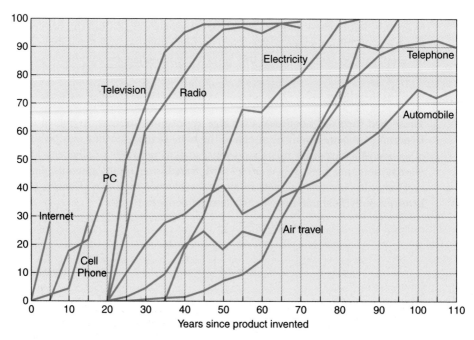

Figure 1.4   Rates of Penetration of New Technologies[28]

off" occurred. Mid-century technologies such as radio and television also had long latencies but then grew very quickly. But technologies introduced toward the end of the century had both minimal latencies and extremely rapid growth. Clearly, opportunities had to be realized quickly, or they might no longer be available. Developing strategy in these circumstances, which seem likely to prevail in the 21st century, cannot take place at the leisurely pace of earlier years.

Change is often thought of as existing along a continuum, from **incremental** or evolutionary to **revolutionary** or discontinuous. Looking at Figure 1.4, for example, the rate of growth of air travel looks like an incremental trend line. In contrast, the growth of Internet access comes much closer to a discontinuity. Other examples of incremental change would be the aging of the population, the addition of new product features to refrigerators, and the move to smaller families. Perhaps the most striking example of discontinuous change was OPEC's quadrupling of energy prices in the 1970s, which wrought enormous disruption to the world economy, since it made obsolete the capital stock that had been built predicated on relatively cheap energy. Another example would be the so-called Asian meltdown in 1997, which was not predicted by most economic analysts. In general, economic systems, macro or micro, tend to cope well with incremental change but experience shock when major discontinuities occur.

The pattern that characterizes many markets is periods of incremental change coupled with revolutionary change at various points. Such a pattern of change is referred to as **punctuated equilibrium.** Discontinuities are typically exogenous to the firm, in that it rarely creates them. The development of the Internet, for example, was not a result of activities by any of the automobile companies such as Ford, but the auto companies and their dealers have had to respond to this new technology to maintain their competitive position. Such radical changes are disruptive and are likely to fundamentally change competitive positions within the market as some firms adapt and others do not.

◉ 1.5 STRATEGIC MANAGEMENT PROCESS

Firms undertake the development of strategy in a variety of ways; the process can be formal or informal, intuitive or analytical. In this text we will emphasize more formal approaches. But we also have to remember that even when the firm has a formal strategy process, not all strategic decisions will flow from that process. A company may supplement the formal processes with a "project"-based process to decide on strategy. Acquisition strategies are often conducted on a project basis, although preemptive candidate screening is increasingly common.

Our model of the strategic management process is shown in Figure 1.5. As we have already noted, strategic management is about creating organizations that can continue to generate value in a turbulent world over a sustained period of time. Such a challenge requires a holistic process, from understanding the external and internal environment, to developing strategy, to getting that strategy implemented, to understanding likely future performance and whether or not this is acceptable. We now review the four main elements of our model—context, strategy, implementation, and performance.

Context

The firm exists within a changing environment, and managers have to understand these dynamics. This environment comprises two markets, the **product** markets within which the products of the firm compete for customers and the **financial** markets within which the firm competes for capital.[29] Managers must be able to identify prospective changes in these markets that are important for the firm. What is critical for one firm may not be

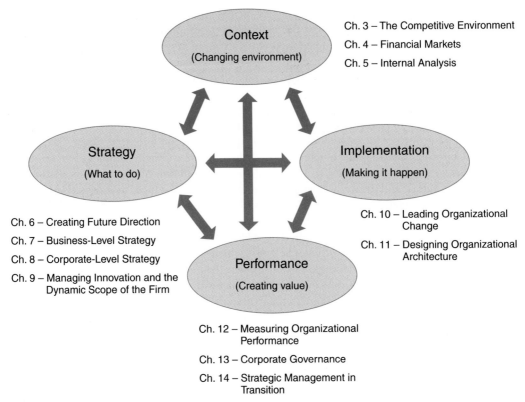

Figure 1.5 Strategic Management Model

for another. For banks, major changes have resulted from improvements in communications and information processing. These have resulted in the rise of nonbranch banking and a redefinition of banking. Which players will perform banking functions in the future? Will it be existing banks, new Internet-based entrants, or other retailers such as supermarkets? For aluminum producers such as Alcoa, the key environmental issues may be intermaterial substitution, recycling, and energy pricing. For electricity, the key change may be the rise of small local generators (CHP or co-gen), which could be installed by the power companies' customers, resulting in a move from large remote to small local generators. Managers have to ascertain the relative importance of changes that may occur, how significant they will be, when they may occur, and their likely impact, topics that will be further developed in Chapters 3 and 4.

At the same time, managers need to understand the firm's *skills* and *resources*. There is no point in developing a strategy that cannot be executed due to limited or non-existent resources. Chapter 5 explores the resource-based view of the firm. Here we take a holistic view. Strategy will be based on a combination of the skills and resources of the firm and the changes occurring in the external environment, recognizing that resources are not fixed. An important element of strategy, as we saw with News Corp., is the ability of the firm to generate new resources.

Strategy

Senior managers must decide on vision, strategy, and the firm's evolving business portfolio. Vision is a picture of an ideal future state. It should provide a purpose that will challenge and motivate staff and stretch the firm's capabilities. As will be discussed in Chapter 6, firms also need to establish a set of values to guide the behavior of the organization's members. These may be both implicit and explicit, and the former are typically more important because they are the de facto guides of behavior. Developing strategy also necessitates a mission, a statement that defines the scope of the firm, thereby delineating its boundaries.

Strategy describes the way in which the firm will accomplish the vision it has established and, as noted earlier, is the theme incorporated in a set of strategic decisions. These decisions affect the long-term well-being of the organization but are made in the present. As Drucker puts it:

One cannot make decisions for the future. Decisions are commitments to action. And actions are always in the present, and in the present only. But actions in the present are also the one and only way to make the future.[30]

Thus we must recognize that the future does not yet exist; it remains to be created by the actions of many, be they politicians, executives, consumers, or sports stars.

As noted, we will examine strategy at the corporate and the business unit levels. Corporate-level strategy is concerned with the present and future scope of the entire firm and the interrelationships among the firm's different activities and business units. Most global firms are comprised of a number of organizational entities that we will refer to as business units, and the composition of this mix of businesses changes over time. For a diversified global firm, this is possibly the most important strategic decision that the firm will make—what new business areas it should get involved in and how this will be accomplished. Business-level strategy focuses on how a unit of the firm competes in its industry, what will be its product/market scope, how it can obtain and sustain competitive advantage and related considerations.

We should recognize that some of the decisions we make today will shape the future of the firm. These decisions may be taken at different levels in the firm, sometimes unwittingly or without understanding of their longer-term impact.

> In his book on his experience in turning around the Chrysler Corporation, Lee Iacocca describes a decision to save $US2.50 on each of the Aspen/Volare series of automobiles by eliminating rustproofing of the undersides. He attributes a significant part of the company's fall from grace to this accounting-led decision, which ultimately alienated large numbers of consumers from Chrysler-produced cars.[31]

Implementation

Strategic management is not just about generating strategy; it is also about getting strategy implemented. For many firms, the challenge is implementation rather than generation. In a strategic context, all company characteristics are considered variable. Managers can change structure, culture, products and services, regions of the world in which the firm competes: all are under the control of management.

In Chapter 10 we explore the principles of how the firm can manage change. Most global firms are undertaking a number of strategic decisions simultaneously, so strategic management includes an element of project management—managing several change programs at the same time. Strategic managers need to decide who should be involved in these programs, what resources are available, what staff are used, and whether external consultants will be utilized. Implementation also involves the design of what we call the **organizational architecture**—the structure, systems, people, and incentives of the firm—a topic discussed in Chapter 11.

Performance

Strategic managers are responsible for the performance of the firm in both *financial* and *nonfinancial* terms. Financial markets expect a satisfactory return, as do other stakeholders such as customers. Thus part of the strategic management challenge is to ensure that the firm has a performance culture. Chapter 12 explores the issues involved in measuring the performance of the firm. We discuss a range of possible measures, financial and nonfinancial. The latter are often leading indicators of financial performance.

We must also appreciate that performance acts as a feedback element, reflecting the iterative nature of strategic management. The firm's performance will influence the vision that can be adopted as well as numerous other areas of operation. So strategic management is not a linear process; instead, it is an iterative, evolving, and learning process.

In Chapter 13 we explore **corporate governance,** which has become a critical issue in recent years. Corporate collapses, deceptive accounting, auditing failures, and unethical behavior by managers have all contributed to an intense public debate. Managerial salaries, perks, and share options have likewise caused concern. Strategic managers need a good understanding of governance, the role of the board, and how practices vary in different countries of the world.

✺ 1.6 WHO "DOES" STRATEGY?

There is no doubt that the primary responsibility for corporate strategy falls on the CEO, top management, and, ultimately, the board of directors. Nonetheless, in any successful firm, many others are also involved. Managers of major business units often have a role, and there may be a staff group supporting the strategic planning process. However, developing strategy is a line responsibility that cannot be delegated to a staff group.

CEOs must both manage today and be the architect of change for tomorrow, requiring that they be both inductive and deductive; intuitive and analytical; incremental and revolutionary. However, it is naive to believe that the fountain of all wisdom is the CEO, since new strategic ideas can come from anywhere within the firm Hence, good CEOs recognize they can neither do all the strategy work nor implement strategy without the support of others. They actively encourage strategic thinking throughout the firm, leveraging their personal time and effort by working through people, structure, and processes. Of course, the CEO carries primary responsibility for identifying where and how the company must change, but to transform a firm, the CEO needs committed and courageous entrepreneurs.

The CEO's task is extremely difficult. Strategy is more than an idea; it is also about making that idea work. CEOs must perform in many roles, requiring an almost holographic capability—as change agent, communicator, and public face of the company; as decider, facilitator, teacher, and mentor as well as learner. Garten suggests the major factors complicating CEO's jobs are:

- Conflicting demands from financial markets and the need for long-term investments in developing new capabilities and a talented workforce
- Inability to predict rapidly changing geopolitical and technological developments
- Emergence of new competition and markets that do not yet exist yet require huge investments if a sustainable position is to be attained
- The fact that the CEO increasingly has to play many roles[32]

We describe our own views on the major factors affecting strategy development in the next section.

⊚ 1.7 CHANGES AFFECTING STRATEGIC MANAGEMENT

Figure 1.6 summarizes major influences affecting strategic management. Although the diagram suggests that these influences are independent, they are all in fact interdependent. Many of the changes we briefly review in this section recur throughout the book and will be explored in more detail later.

Globalization

Globalization and increased competition in product, capital, and labor markets have been long-term trends since World War II. Most of us are personally familiar with product market competition as we select among domestically produced products and imports, between foreign and domestic brands. However, as businesses become more knowledge-intensive, it is also clear that competition for talent has erupted among countries as well as companies. Top talent managers and staff are now much more mobile, changing companies, industries, and countries.

Integration of world financial markets has dramatically increased the competitiveness of capital markets. There is more capital available, yet firms compete for it globally. New financial instruments for managing interest and exchange-rate risk (generally referred to as **derivatives**) have been developed, adding complexity to financial decisions. National financial markets are now linked, and trading occurs 24 hours a day.

There is also an international market for **corporate control,** with increasing numbers of cross-border mergers and acquisitions. Institutional investors own some 60% of

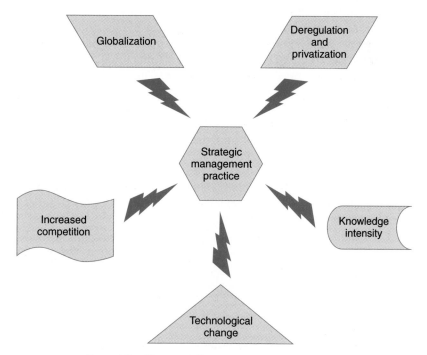

Figure 1.6   Changes Affecting Strategic Management

shares outstanding, with large pools of funds from insurance companies and pension funds. These investors have become more assertive in pressuring for performance, which in turn has driven the market for corporate control.

The last part of the 20th century also witnessed a coming of age for many emerging markets. The majority of the world's population, about 6 billion people, live in such markets. In the past, many multinationals sold products designed for the highly industrialized and developed Western economies in these markets. Today, however, there is much more widespread recognition that their needs are different, and they are increasingly seen as prospective customers despite relatively low income levels.

> Hindustan Lever developed a shampoo for the Indian market that was sold in single sachets at the rupee equivalent of 2 cents (a large proportion of the Indian population cannot afford to buy larger sizes). Despite the low selling price, the shampoo was a profitable success for the company.

Increased Competition

Most firms are facing increased competition in all markets—product, labor, and capital. Rapidly escalating competition based on price, quality, and innovation characterizes many markets, emphasizing the need for continual cost reductions to stay competitive. Squeezed net margins and shortened product life cycles underline the need to innovate new competitive advantages and build required competences. Firms also have to cope with increasingly unpredictable discontinuities, meaning greater emphasis on flexibility, as well as developing a vision that balances short-term performance and longer-term requirements. Increased competition also means that successful strategies will have shorter lives. New strategies must be invented, even if they destroy the validity of older strategies.

The blurring of traditional **industry boundaries** has also increased competition. As a result of deregulation and technological change, industries such as telecommunications, media, and computing are becoming hard to distinguish. Indicative of the change is talk of the TCM (**T**elecommunications/**C**omputing/**M**edia) industry. Other new words—such as *cosmeceuticals, edutainment,* and *nutraceuticals*—indicate that such changes are widespread, and not restricted to a few industries. Such changes make it increasingly difficult to identify competitors, suggesting that many firms will face a turbulent and less predictable future.

The net result of many of the above changes is that the very **structure** of industries has itself become variable. Increased outsourcing has locked many companies into cooperating networks, while the growth of contract manufacturing cuts across traditional industry boundaries. Information technology has both **disintermediated** some industries (reduced the need for intermediaries such as travel agents) and created new *intermediaries* such as AOL and Yahoo!

Further, companies themselves are engineering their own dissolution though spinoffs at the same time that others are merging and acquiring. The term **structural competition** has been coined to alert executives to the fact that if they are not playing an active role in creating structural change in their "industries," others are likely to do it for them!

> Typical of the many industries that have undergone enormous restructuring in recent years are banking, steel, pharmaceuticals, defense and aerospace, airlines and automobiles.

Technological Change

Technology has had the most important impact on the conduct of management of any change in the 20th century. Though by no means restricted to information technology, from the mid-20th century onward, the computer and associated telecommunications technologies began to have a profound impact. Companies implemented the automation of their accounts and then began linking with suppliers using electronic data interchange (EDI). In industries as diverse as airlines (American Airlines Saber reservations system), hospital supplies (American Hospital Supply/Baxter Healthcare's ASAP reorder terminals), drug distribution (McKesson Robbins Economost), and package shipping (FedEx's tracking system), applying information technology to solving customer problems led firms to strong, even dominant, positions in their industries.

Today, of course, we are all familiar with the Web, a worldwide information utility that is revolutionizing the relationship among firms, their customers, and their suppliers. The Internet permits customers to access company manufacturing operations to track order progress and enables a two-way dialogue with customers. It increasingly allows co-design of products, as part of a move to what is now called mass customization. The Internet allows a person to "work" in California while living elsewhere. With its 24-hour access, virtually infinite capacity, and open standards, the Internet has reduced the cost of search for buyers and sellers, with implications for firm boundaries. Transportation costs of such digital products as music and many financial products are dramatically reduced, creating the potential for a major new distribution channel. It also suggests that firms will need to work together to create networks of suppliers, distributors, and partners to create customer value, leading to more outsourcing.

Dramatic reductions in the cost of computing power and storage, increasing bandwidth, and lowered telecommunications costs combine to create enormously powerful forces for change. The scramble—undignified at times—of media companies to position themselves for the age of high-speed real-time downloading of audio and video products is indicative of the change that awaits all who conduct business in products and services that can be digitized.

All industries will be affected by the **information revolution** to a greater or lesser extent. There are likely to be severe shakeouts, with clearly defined winners and losers. The widespread availability of information technology will have dramatic effects on which activities are performed inside and outside the firm, for transaction costs will be changed. Similarly, the ease with which price information can be obtained will further increase the competitiveness of markets. Indeed, some commentators have already alleged that the low inflation experienced at the turn of the 21st century is a direct result of these changes.

Knowledge Intensity

Drucker and others describe advanced economies as "knowledge" economies because they are becoming less materials intensive and energy intensive all the time.[33] As *Business Week* put it, "The traditional factors of production—capital and skilled labor—are no longer the main determinants of the power of an economy. Now economic potential is increasingly linked to the ability to control and manipulate information."[34]

Knowledge intensity is increasing for most products. Direct labor is now a small proportion of total costs for manufactured products, and the market value of more and more firms is becoming independent of the tangible assets on the balance sheet.

With increasing knowledge intensity, there is a commensurate shift in recognizing the relative importance of **human capital** versus traditional fixed capital. The economics of knowledge products is different. Knowledge-based products generally show **increasing returns to scale:** The more widely they are used, the more valuable they become to a user. The value of Windows is enhanced by the fact that it has many users. Because of this, more people use it to write applications software programs, which again enhances its value. With such products there can be substantial benefits to early market entry, establishing the product as an industry standard. It may also be beneficial to share the product with others, forming alliances early on. We may not want to hoard the product but rather get wide application from others, including possible competitors. Note this is also a high-risk strategy, requiring major investment in R&D to develop and launch such innovations.

Deregulation and Privatization

Deregulation and **privatization** have occurred in many industries around the world, as governments have concluded that they do not do a particularly good job of running a business or that regulation has impeded consumer welfare.

Industries such as electricity, gas, water supply, banking and finance, telecommunications, airlines, railroads, and trucking have all witnessed significant change in many different countries. In virtually every case, there has been an increase in competition in these industries, together with increased rates of innovation not only in the core products and services but also in such areas as pricing and customer service.

These changes have dramatically affected the pecking order in many industries and have also introduced many new players who do not use the same "rules." They have required commensurate changes in supervision, for few governments are prepared to privatize monopolies without safeguards for consumer welfare. Dealing with these arrangements has often created a new arena of competition, with some firms notably more adept in coping with the regulatory framework than others.

◎ 1.8 SUMMARY

The foregoing discussion is replete with implications for the practice of strategic management. It is imperative that the firm add value to shareholders and other stakeholders, but a new managerial mind-set will also be required. Good strategic management will require much more flexibility and creativity. As firms become more knowledge intensive, the management of intellectual (human) capital becomes critical. Managers must be skilled at developing commitment—even passion—among their increasingly diverse workforce, for if human capital is the key to future success, then marshaling and managing these capabilities to their fullest potential will be essential.

New skills will be required to cope with the changing world. Creative strategic thinking and learning will be central to developing new business strategies in a world in which firm resources and capabilities are not fixed but must be continually developed.

Further, the very boundaries of firms and industries will be vague and changing. Questions such as how these boundaries should evolve, which activities should the firm engage in, which should be purchased from the market, what the core activities of the firm are, and what it does better than its competitors will be ongoing challenges to managers. New styles of organizations—emphasizing learning, anticipation, and quick response—will predominate. Processes, teamwork, and external networks will be constantly reviewed.

An uncertain environment makes forecasting more difficult, increasing the need for flexibility. The competitive landscape is complex and dynamic, and this, too, requires flexibility as well as speed and innovation. Managers need to manage both stability and change—to manage for the present and invest in the future at the same time.

Above all, we should recognize that strategic management is a process and that this process must incorporate ideas on motivation, structure, processes, incentives, and leadership. To neglect the human side of the enterprise and to focus solely on analytic tools is a crucial mistake given the prospective scenarios of the 21st century.

⊙ REVIEW QUESTIONS

1. Describe the strategic decisions taken by a global firm with which you are familiar over the last five years.

2. Analyze the differences between economic profit and accounting profit, and the implications of these differences for strategic management.

3. Provide examples of "strategies for today" and "strategies for tomorrow" for a global firm with which you are familiar.

4. What are the trends that could influence a firm to adopt a more market-based form of economic exchange?

5. Comment on the suggestion that management makes no difference to the economic performance of a firm.

6. Show how the strategic management concepts of context, strategy, and firm characteristics have led to superior economic performance for a global firm with which you are familiar.

⊙ ENDNOTES

[1] R. Belfield, C. Hird, and S. Kelly, *The Decline of an Empire* (London: Macdonald, 1991).

[2] W. Shawcross, *Murdoch: The Making of a Media Empire* (New York: Touchstone, 1997).

[3] News Corporation Annual Report, 2002: www.newscorp.com.

[4] Exchange rate of 1.12 US$ per AU$.

[5] J. Schulze, "News Hammered over Pay-TV," *The Australian,* June 12, 2002, p. 19.

[6] Exchange rate of 1.55 Swiss francs per U.S. dollar, "Federal Reserve Board Table G.5A," January 6 2003. www.federal reserve.gov.

[7] Cadbury Schweppes plc, *About Us,* www.cadburyschweppes.com

[8] M. Fagan, "Why They Hate Exxon," *Daily Telegraph,* May 19, 2002, p. B3.

[9] J. B. Barney, "Firm Resources and Sustained Competitive Advantage," *Journal of Management,* 17, no. 1 (1991), pp. 99–120.

[10] R. E. Caves, "Industrial Organization and New Findings on the Turnover and Mobility of Firms," *Journal of Economic Literature* 36(4) (1998), pp. 1947–1983.

[11] M. E. Porter, *Competitive Strategy* (New York: Free Press, 1980).

[12] E. P. Learned, C. R. Christensen, K. R. Andrews, and W. Guth, *Business Policy* (Homewood, IL: Irwin, 1969).

[13] P. Selznick, *Leadership in Administration* (New York: Harper & Row, 1957).

[14] A. M. Rugman and A. Verbeke, "Edith Penrose's Contribution to the Resource-Based View of Strategic Management," *Strategic Management Journal* 23, no. 8 (2002), pp. 769–780.

[15] M. E. Porter, "What Is Strategy?," *Harvard Business Review,* November–December 1996, pp. 61–78.

[16] C. Markides, "A Dynamic View of Strategy," *Sloan Management Review* 40, no. 3 (1999), pp. 55–63.

[17] R. L. Priem and J. E. Butler, "Is the Resource-Based 'View' a Useful Perspective for Strategic Management Research?" *Academy of Management Review* 26, no. 1 (2001), pp. 22–40.

[18] E. H. Bowman and C. E. Helfat, "Does Corporate Strategy Matter?," *Strategic Management Journal* 22, no. 1 (2001), pp. 1–23.

[19] These terms were first used by D. F. Abell, "Competing Today While Preparing for Tomorrow," *Sloan Management Review* 40, no. 3 (1999), pp. 73–82.

[20] N. Capon, J. U. Farley, and J. M. Hulbert, *Corporate Strategic Planning* (New York: Columbia University Press, 1988).

[21] M. Splinter, "Applied Chief Sees Brighter Times Ahead," *Financial Times,* July 15, 2003, p. 21.

[22] Markides, "A Dynamic View of Strategy."

[23] M. Baghai, S. Coley, and D. White, *The Alchemy of Growth* (London: Orion, 1999).

[24] O. E. Williamson, *Markets and Hierarchies: Analysis and Antitrust Implications* (New York: Free Press, 1975).

[25] For further reading, see R. H. Coase, "The Nature of the Firm," *Economica* 4 (1937), pp. 386–405; and O. E. Williamson, *Markets and Hierarchies: Analysis and Antitrust Implications* (New York: Free Press, 1975).

[26] J. D. Day and J. C. Wendler, "The New Economics of Organization," *McKinsey Quarterly* 1 (1998), pp. 4–18.

[27] D. J. Collis and C. A. Montgonery, *Corporate Strategy: A Resource-Based Approach* (Boston: Irwin/McGraw-Hill, 1998).

[28] M. Cox, "Rates of Penetration of New Technologies," *Federal Reserve Bank of Dallas* 2002.

[29] The firm also competes in other markets, such as the market for talented staff.

[30] P. F. Drucker, *Managing in a Time of Great Change,* (New York: Truman Talley Books/Dutton, 1995), p. x.

[31] L. Iacocca and W. Novak, *Iacocca: An Autobiography* (New York: Bantam, 1984).

[32] J. Garten, *The Mind of the CEO* (London: Allen Lane, 2001).

[33] P. F. Drucker, "The New Society of Organizations," *Harvard Business Review,* September–October 1992, pp. 95–104.

[34] "The Internet Economy: The World's Next Growth Engine," *Business Week,* October 4, 1999, p. 72.

CHAPTER 2

The Fundamentals of Strategic Management

Learning Objectives

Upon completing this chapter, you should be able to:

- Appreciate the complexity of strategic management in today's business environment
- Describe the critical characteristics of strategy
- Recognize the importance of innovation for the strategy of the firm and its implications for culture, systems, and structure
- Define the characteristics of a strategic business unit
- Design and/or modify a firm's business model
- Describe the managerial process involved in strategy development and implementation, including major impediments
- Articulate the concept of value for different stakeholders of the firm

During the 1980s, IBM was the most admired company in the United States, according to a *Fortune* survey, and its annual profits during this halcyon period were greater than the revenues of its nearest competitor.

During the early 1990s, there was rapid change in the industry and technology, particularly with the emergence of personal and networked computers, which replaced mainframes. These had much lower profit margins, and most industry profits went to Intel and Microsoft, not the computer manufacturers. By the end of 1994, the company had sustained losses of $USB15 over the previous three years and market capitalization had gone from $105bn to $USB32.

In response, a new CEO was appointed, the first from outside the firm. Other responses included laying off some 200,000 staff, trying to develop a new culture, removing the complacency that had crept in, and realigning the business portfolio toward information technology (IT) services and solutions. IBM developed IT into a major business, with revenue of some $USB30 in 2000, and was fast on its way to becoming the world's leading supplier of e-business solutions. In 2002, the company purchased the consulting business of PricewaterhouseCoopers (PWC) for $USB3.5.[1,2]

2.1 INTRODUCTION

As IBM's history illustrates, in today's fast-changing environment, firms cannot be complacent. Instead, strategy and many internal attributes must change to deal with the external changes the firm faces. Firm success is increasingly transient, as is its basis.

IBM's strategy was to exit some technology areas and concentrate on provision of services. Consequently, in 2002 IBM sold its hard-disk business to Hitachi for $USB2.05, at the same time purchasing the consulting arm of PWC. Such a purchase is likely to restructure the consulting industry, putting increased pressure on other firms such as McKinsey and the Boston Consulting Group (BCG). This episode also reflects what could be called the "opportunistic" nature of strategic management. In 2002, many accounting firms were under pressure from customers, governments, and regulators due to a perceived conflict of interest between their consulting and audit businesses. PWC was keen to sell, presenting IBM with an opportunity. Interestingly, a few years earlier Hewlett-Packard (HP) had attempted to purchase the same business for a rumored $USB18.[3]

As IBM's history demonstrates, the task of strategic management has become increasingly difficult, due to greater turbulence, complexity, and competitiveness of the business environment. To cope with this change, the firm must continually innovate and reinvent itself if it is to survive and prosper. Consequently, the firm will be in a state of continuous change. But the firm is always under pressure for performance in both financial and product markets. Here, then, is a fundamental challenge of strategic management. Throughout the ongoing change process, managers must ensure that the firm delivers *current value*, earning a return greater than its cost of capital, as well as establishing the strategies and organizational architecture required to *create future value*. To achieve these outcomes in a fast-changing environment, managers must increase the capability of an organization to deal with change, an agenda requiring formal planning and analysis as well as intuition and judgement.

Environmental turbulence represents both an opportunity and a threat. Changes are threatening since they will cause customers and competitors to behave differently. Firms must actively respond to the external changes over which they have no control. At the same time, firms can innovate, bringing change to the market in order to consolidate and/or improve their position. A significant amount of marketplace change results from the actions of firms in that market. When a firm invents new products or processes, adopts a new channel such as the Internet, or expands globally, the effects reverberate through its industry, affecting the behavior of both customers and competitors. Change in the firm will be both reactive and proactive, but only proactive change demonstrates managerial leadership.

In the preceding chapter we distinguished strategic decisions, strategy, and strategic management. We now explore these in more detail.

⊚ 2.2 CHARACTERISTICS OF STRATEGIC DECISIONS

Strategic decisions are those that affect the long-term well-being of the firm under consideration.

There will be a relatively small number of decisions that shape the firm's future development. What make these decisions and actions "strategic" is their likely future impact on the entire organization and its ability to create and capture value as well as the fact that these decisions are almost irrevocable: they are very difficult to reverse once implemented. Returning to our example of News Corp. from Chapter 1, we can identify several such decisions—the decision to move all the production of U.K. newspapers to Wapping, starting a fourth TV network in the United States, and purchasing 20th Century Fox, a major movie studio. With IBM, recent strategic decisions include terminating 20% of its staff and purchasing PWC's consulting business.

Figure 2.1 depicts four characteristics of strategic decisions, which we now review.

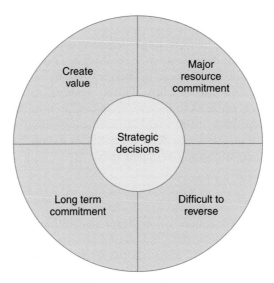

Figure 2.1 Characteristics of Strategic Decisions

Create Value

First, strategic decisions must be made with the goal of creating value for the firm. Of course, some decisions may not create value, while value in any case may not accrue until some time in the future. However, value creation involves more than the generation of sustainable competitive advantage. While creation of competitive advantage is a necessary condition for creating value, it is not a sufficient condition. A **competitive advantage** is an attribute possessed by the firm but not by its competitors, such as a low cost structure or a benefit for customers not offered by other firms. Nonetheless, firms could have an advantage that does not translate into superior financial performance. Industry structure may be such that suppliers or customers capture the benefits of the firm's competitive advantage. In personal computers, for example, almost all industry profit goes to Intel and Microsoft, with relatively little for the computer manufacturers. For this reason it is essential that strategic decisions are seen as those that create value for the firm.

Major Resource Commitment

The second characteristic of strategic decisions is that they involve major resource commitments by the firm, including acquisitions and divestments.

> In mid-2003, Manchester United announced the transfer of David Beckham to Real Madrid for a fee of £M30. The following day, Manchester United's stock price rose, reflecting investors' belief that the money was worth more to the future value of the club than David Beckham.

The point we are making is that strategy is about significant change to the composition of the firm in terms of the products and services it provides, the markets it serves, and/or the skills and competences required to accomplish the change. What is major obviously depends on the size of the firm: a strategic decision for American Airlines will usually involve more money than for a smaller carrier such as Ryanair. A decision is clearly strategic when it has the potential to put the future of the company at risk.

Difficult to Reverse

The third characteristic of strategic decisions is that they are difficult to reverse once made. The German firm Siemens is involved in a number of engineering businesses. It would be difficult for Siemens to drop its long-standing interests in engineering and reinvent itself as a fast-food firm. History matters! At the same time, while strategic decisions may be difficult to reverse, firms need to maintain a degree of *flexibility*, since future developments in the world are increasingly unpredictable. This requirement is often manifest in a desire to delay commitment to enter new businesses. Yet if delay is excessive, others will seize the opportunity.

Long-Term Commitment

Strategic decisions reflect a long-term commitment by the firm. A firm such as Exxon/Mobil has a long time horizon for its exploration processes, although firms in other industries may have much shorter horizons. But one of the essential features of strategic decisions is that they are concerned with the future and must have a long-term focus and commitment. Such decisions are not simply a continuation of the present, for with strategy nothing is fixed: everything is variable. A strategic decision may require changing the culture of a firm, recognizing that this is a multiyear commitment.

What is considered strategic and what time horizon is adopted will depend on the speed at which markets and technologies are evolving.

> In industries such as resources, airlines, steel, or plastics, strategic decisions about current and future capacity levels are necessary. In these industries a very long time horizon is required; for example, it may take 15 years to find, test, and develop a new oil field. The decision to commit current resources to exploration activities must be based on assumptions about the likely demand for and price of oil, its related products, and the nature of competition and costs over the next 15 years.

These long-term considerations are not just to do with the "old" economy.

> Amazon started in July 1995 with a clear focus on growth in revenue: to establish a strong Internet business by transforming book buying. After four years with a growth focus, Amazon changed to more balanced objectives of growth and cost reduction.[4] As of 2001, annual revenue was $3Bn, and in the fourth quarter of 2001 it reported its first pro-forma operating profit. To achieve this position, Amazon incurred cumulative losses of $USB2.8.[5] Whether or not the decision to start the firm in 1995 was a good one or not can still be debated. The company has indicated that it does not expect to pay a dividend, and the share price dropped from a high of $91.30 in the first quarter of 2000 to a low of $6.01 in the fourth quarter of 2001, reflecting investor concern at the firm's ability to sustain itself and the general disaffection with the Internet "bubble." By February 2004, the share price had recovered to approximately $45.

The firm may try to make a strategic decision *incremental*, where only a portion of the plant is built on the understanding that capacity can be expanded later. But there are limits to this approach: the new plant cannot be of such a scale that efficiencies are nonexistent. Indeed, the ultimate success or failure of B2B procurement portals or of many biotechnology firms will not be known for many years. Strategic decisions often exhibit the characteristics of a large bet.

These examples highlight a difficulty with strategic decisions, namely, getting this long-term commitment from management. High managerial turnover and the subjective nature of valuing outcomes of strategic decisions exacerbate obtaining such commitment. For strategic decisions are generally very difficult to evaluate on strictly quantitative grounds. Despite valiant efforts to forecast and develop *pro formas*, the future is often too uncertain for reliable forecasts. If there is a senior management change just after a strategic decision, the new managers may well try to reverse it, reflecting their need to make a perceived mark on the firm. Furthermore, strategic decisions usually generate net cash outflows before net cash inflows. Do managers have the courage to continue implementing decisions when cash flow is negative and the financial markets are demanding greater short term shareholder value?

⊚ 2.3 CHARACTERISTICS OF STRATEGY

Strategy is the common theme underlying a set of strategic decisions.

As we noted earlier, strategy can be both deceptively simple and extremely complex. For example, the success of Microsoft appears simple—it was able to get its operating system, MS DOS, installed on most IBM personal computers. However, this would not have guaranteed continued success since there were a number of other operating systems extant, including one developed by IBM itself. Microsoft strategy required a continual stream of decisions in a turbulent and dynamic environment. Of the many software firms contending for leadership in the so-called PC revolution, only Microsoft was successful in managing this stream of decisions; many others disappeared. Strategy requires both detailed understanding and the ability to develop a response that in retrospect is likely to be viewed as obvious.

As with a strategic decision, the purpose of strategy is to create value for the firm and its stakeholders, for which a competitive advantage is a necessary but not sufficient condition. Firm performance needs both a strategy and the means to put that strategy in place. In other words, the firm needs to excel at both strategy development and strategy execution. *Strategy is not just a good idea; it is making that idea happen.* So strategy also implies that the organization should possess the capabilities appropriate for implementing the chosen strategy as well as a strong performance culture, with clear accountability and incentives linked to performance.

Firms that are regarded as winners adopt strategies that are different from those of their competitors. Yet in many industries we see *strategy convergence*. All firms seem to adopt the same strategy, and differences between competitors are minuscule. Strategy differentiation is essential for success—but again, it is a necessary but not sufficient condition. However, when companies simply copy the leader, value is destroyed for all firms, including the leader. Lack of strategy differentiation in an industry leads to lower industry margins.[6] Thus strategy requires searching for new sources of advantage, inventing new rules and new games to become unique and create wealth.

We now review some characteristics of strategy, the common theme that links decisions together, as illustrated in Figure 2.2.

Incremental or Revolutionary Strategy

Two contrasting views of strategy are the incremental and the revolutionary. The difference is not merely a distinction between a short term and a long term. The two concepts involve fundamentally different ways to create value. **Incremental** strategies involve

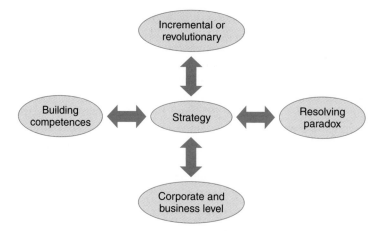

Figure 2.2 Characteristics of Strategy

managing current activities for high value. **Revolutionary** strategies are about success-fully creating major innovation in the marketplace.

Financial analysts often divide incremental strategies into two components. First is the estimated net present value of cash flows from **legacy assets** (assets that the firm currently controls and has accumulated over its entire history) on the basis of no change in strategy. Second is the estimated cash flow from **growth opportunities** realizable from these assets, such as market expansion.[7] We see both of these as incremental since they focus primarily on achieving competitive superiority through better management of current competences. *Revolutionary strategies* introduce major new products or serv-ices for which there was no preexisting market. They necessitate developing significant new competences, but, if successful, generate significant increases in firm value. The three-way distinction is shown in Figure 2.3.

Radical innovation is more likely to create significant new wealth than continuous improvement, albeit with higher levels of risk. This risk may, however, be reduced through processes that facilitate rapid learning and adoption of low-cost, low-risk exper-iments. Incremental strategy also has a risk—the risk that the firm will be made obso-

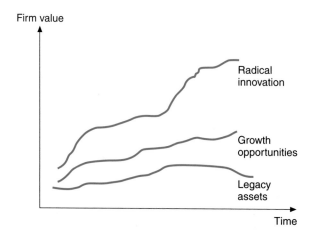

Figure 2.3 Value Components for a Firm[8]

lete by successful innovators. Incremental and revolutionary approaches are not mutually exclusive. Successful firms undertake both types of strategy at the same time.

We cannot discuss these strategy distinctions without also considering the firm's external context and, in particular, its markets. Markets are complex systems, comprising many dynamically interconnected parts. As Chapter 1 noted, their behavior can be described as punctuated equilibrium: periods of relatively slow change coupled with periods of dramatic change. The punctuated equilibrium model applies to both the environment faced by the firm and its response. Thus external changes can be incremental or revolutionary and strategy can be incremental or revolutionary. Markets also demonstrate **path dependencies,** where future developments are conditional on an earlier state.[9] For example, compact discs were designed with a specific diameter, and this has influenced the physical configuration of a range of devices using CDs.

This dichotomy between incremental and revolutionary change is illustrated in Figure 2.4. In Figure 2.4(a), firm change is aligned with the changing environment. Sometimes this change is fast, sometimes it is slow, but the firm keeps up with its changing environment throughout. In Figure 2.4(b), the firm is also changing, but the rate of change is insufficient to maintain its alignment; instead, the firm is drifting further and further away from where it should be, resulting in **strategic drift.**[10] At some point the firm will face a dilemma, either undertaking revolutionary renewal, with all the risks that involves (since it now has limited resources for change), or falling victim to a takeover or bankruptcy.

General Motors was a leader in the U.S. light truck market through GMC, but when the SUV revolution hit the United States, its long model development times meant it was initially left in the lurch by its competitors as they launched their SUVs first. GM had suffered strategic drift.

Incremental Strategy

Running a business today requires a strategy—defining the business through focusing its resources, capital, and people to meet the current needs of customers. This necessitates targeting customer segments, positioning the business relative to competitors, and deploying resources in line with these decisions. The firm searches the customer and competitive landscape for opportunities, attempting to leverage existing resources that afford best fit with the environment. Managers must also align functional and supply-

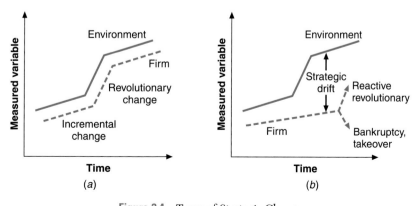

Figure 2.4 Types of Strategic Change

chain activities with the strategy and harmonize organizational structure, processes, culture, incentives, and people. Change occurs, but it is of a "tuning" type.

Incremental strategy usually focuses on *cost reduction* to create shareholder value by improving labor and capital productivity. Another common alternative is to increase revenues by targeting *growth segments* of the market, reducing customer defection and possibly making related acquisitions. Such a strategy can be successful, as is seen from the performance of Nestlé. It has been in business for more than 140 years, with revenue of CHFB88.0 ($USB67.0) in 2003. The firm has continued to innovate over this period, expanding into new geographic markets and launching new products, demonstrating a remarkable consistency.[11] Incremental strategy works reasonably well when environmental turbulence is low but may be less valuable as turbulence rises.[12]

Value from Legacy Assets

Any firm has a set of current activities. To support these the firm must focus on asset and employee productivity, operating efficiently in all respects. The rising level of competitive intensity and increasing pressure on margins necessitate an inexorable drive for improved productivity and cost reduction in existing operations. The importance of competitive costs is reflected in the downsizing undertaken by global firms over the last few years.

As Table 2.1 indicates, many firms have had major reductions in employment. Such reductions are obviously traumatic for the firm and reflect the fact that senior management sees no short-term alternatives. Clearly, managers must be cost-focused, and the firm may need to make major cost reductions. But improving year-to-year productivity in existing operations is unlikely to be enough to generate long-term wealth. Due to the dynamic nature of the environment, value created by legacy assets generally declines, so managers must consider alternatives.

Growth Opportunities

Firms can also create value through grasping growth opportunities in existing businesses. Line extensions, new product development, and market expansion—as well as related acquisitions—may all contribute. A common strategy for many firms has been *global expansion* with existing products. Indeed, the very label "multinational" reflects the historic strategy pursued by many large firms—namely, expansion into increasing numbers of national markets.

> The Anglo-Dutch firm Unilever has grown primarily through incremental means, staying close to its historic base of foods and detergents while expanding globally to the point where its turnover in 2002 was €B48.3 ($USB45.6) and it operated in more than 150 countries.

TABLE 2.1 Corporate Layoffs by Major U.S. Firms

Firm	Staff Layoffs (2001)
General Electric	75,000
DaimlerChrysler	26,000
Procter & Gamble	22,000
Lucent	16,000

Source: "Let the Bad Times Roll", *The Economist*, April 7, 2001, pp. 65–66.

Nonetheless, organic growth may fail to meet managers' and shareholders' growth objectives, in which case more radical growth alternatives must be considered.

Revolutionary Strategy

Major increases in wealth, for both firms and society, flow from innovation, not from optimizing present strategies. Some wealth is gained by perfecting the known, but venturing into and seizing the unknown, when successful, engenders large increases in wealth. This is the entrepreneurial challenge: to develop a deep understanding of our fast-changing world and to imagine the innovations that will create significant value. This requires managers to have *foresight* and *creativity*. It requires flexible thinking as well as the capacity to learn and adapt quickly, since the future is increasingly unpredictable. Innovation is about agility, experimentation, imagination, and diversity, while optimization is about scale, efficiency, and hierarchy. Radical innovation generally requires managers who are radicals, if not heretics, who go beyond the established orthodoxy of the firm or the industry.

In a rapidly changing world, the firm must innovate as well as improve productivity. Unfortunately, some managers may not be learning as fast as the world is changing. They fail to recognize that strategies become obsolete very quickly. Meeting the entrepreneurial challenge requires a future focus, by both the CEO (who could be called the chief change officer) and other employees. The firm must focus on what the future is likely to be, not only where it is today—a difficult task in a rapidly changing environment. To make decisions now that will pay off in the future requires managers who are both thinkers and doers, endowed with imagination, creativity, and passion.

Most firms find this combination of fundamentally different types of change— incremental and revolutionary—extremely challenging, partly because these processes require different skills and capabilities, a topic to which we return in Chapter 5. Further contributing to the difficulty of balancing short- and long-term considerations are financial market requirements that the firm continue to create value throughout this ongoing change process. Some, however, have excelled.

> Sony has been successful in developing and introducing a number of radical innovations, from the original Walkman to compact discs to an electronic camera to robotic pets, as well as continuing to improve their core products.

Revolutionary strategy can be thought of as a high-stakes game, starting when management develops a vision of the company's future, then makes major, hard-to-reverse decisions about where the company will focus its energies, capital, and people, hoping their vision is correct. Since the future is difficult to predict, the risks of this approach are correspondingly high.

Of course, not all strategy is revolutionary. Major changes are fraught with danger and may be traumatic for staff. We can categorize such dramatic change as either reactive or proactive. It is generally much better to take a large number of small, fast steps than one large one to try to catch up. However, firms and their management are often subject to inertia. Instead of a series of smaller changes, they wait until only a large dramatic change will ensure survival. This may require a substantial number of staff to be fired to quickly reduce costs. As we noted, IBM reduced staff by 200,000 in the mid-1990s. The company responded very tardily to a changing world and had to take radical steps to survive. Developing strategy requires the ability to ask strategic questions: What is changing, what is the rate of change, what is the likely impact, how should the firm respond? This should be done on an ongoing basis.

Revolutionary strategies may also be proactive, thereby becoming the force creating turbulence in the industry.

> Before the establishment of Amazon, Barnes and Noble itself created considerable turbulence in the book-retailing industry with the establishment of superstores, complete with armchairs, Starbucks coffee shops, and restrooms. Highly successful firms that either invented totally new industries or dramatically reinvented existing ones include Home Depot, Nike, Intel, Honda, SAP, and Sony.

In environments that are characterized by discontinuous change, the firm may have to respond in a revolutionary way, such as a radical redefinition of the firm or the industry, in order to survive. Such strategies are likely to challenge existing industry boundaries and norms and, if successful, reinvent the industry itself. In a discontinuous world, strategy reinvention is the key to wealth creation and survival. The Internet, for example, afforded many firms an opportunity to proactively reconfigure their supply chain, with consequences for power relationships, number of suppliers, prices, and so on. One may argue this is simply reacting to change, but the strategic innovation may well be novel in the originator's industry.

In other situations, the firm is beyond doubt creating change.

> Intel, with the invention of a standardized microprocessor, followed by continual development of faster and cheaper chips permitting new applications for personal computers, revolutionized its industry. It was prepared to cast aside its past in memory chips in order to accomplish this. Philips and Sony invented the CD and subsequently found many applications and developments that they had possibly never originally envisaged, including as a storage and recording medium for personal computers, digital video discs, and so on.

Such revolutionary strategies are about **leveraging** resources, about stretching the firm, as well as about the fit between the environment and current resources.[13] They often involve innovations that affect the entire business system—the value chain, the target customer focus, and the economic model may all be transformed.[14] They are more complex than product innovations and therefore more difficult to emulate. As a result, more sustainable competitive advantage is likely to accrue to the successful transformational strategy.

A radical innovation normally changes the rules of competition in the industry, leads to major changes in industry leadership, and strongly affects the previous incumbents. Federal Express's success had a major impact on UPS and the U.S. Postal Service, while Nucor's profitable mini-mill ultimately affected the strategies of many integrated steel manufacturers.

Sometimes called **breakout** strategies, these revolutionary strategies generally have delivery of a major improvement to customers as their core.[15] The improvement is large enough that it can be shared with customers to drive rapid growth, with some of the value retained to provide superior return to shareholders. In the commercial airline industry, the introduction of jet-powered aircraft provided such a major boost, lowering airfares in real terms and leading to a faster rate of growth in air travel. A similar boost took place when wide-bodied jets arrived.

Of course, these new models rarely emerge full-fledged. Learning and subsequent evolution occurs after the launch. However, when successful, these innovations produce major changes in industry structure, and the change in rules spawns imitators, forcing incumbents to respond.

Strategy at the Corporate and Business-Unit Levels

In a global firm, strategic decisions occur at several levels. We distinguish between strategy and strategic decisions at two levels of the firm—corporate and business unit, as shown in Figure 2.5.

Corporate strategic decisions affect the future well-being of the entire organization, while business-unit strategic decisions affect the future well-being of a unit of the total firm—a division, or what we will refer to as a strategic business unit. **Corporate strategy** includes developing a vision for the entire firm, making decisions about the scope of the firm, allocating resources among business units, developing objectives and performance measures for each business unit, managing the culture of the firm, managing the synergies among different business units, designing organizational structure, establishing relations with financial markets and product markets, and forming relationships with other firms.

Strategy at the **business-unit level** includes decisions on mission and objectives (normally negotiated with corporate staff), growth strategy (new products and new markets), outsourcing, and developing a competitive strategy, among others. In any firm, most value is created at the business-unit level; this is where most competition occurs.

Defining a Strategic Business Unit (SBU)

A **strategic business unit** is a unit of the firm that is relatively autonomous, an entity responsible for developing its own strategy. A business unit is responsible for its own products and markets, with its own competitors. Most assets required to run the business are under its control and it has its own managerial resources. At the same time, it is unlikely to be truly independent. There will be linkages with other units, either through markets served, technology, facilities and operations, or R&D. From the business-unit perspective, we have to ask what benefits the parent brings. If there were none, the business unit would be better off with another parent or as an independent entity.

Most value in a firm is realized in business units, through their ability to deliver goods and services at a profit. For the overall firm to create value, it must contribute to the competitive advantage of the business units comprising its portfolio. A key aspect of corporate strategy is therefore to decide whether business units are better or worse off because they are part of the firm. Managing the composition of the corporate portfolio (deciding which businesses should be part of the portfolio and how it should change over time) is the heart of corporate strategy. Consequently, a central question for corporate-level management is whether or not the firm creates value through its multiple-

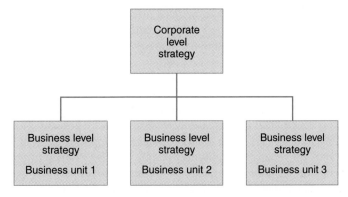

Figure 2.5 Corporate and Business Level Strategy

business activities. Ideally, the corporate center should create value greater than the costs of its overheads and greater than any other possible parent could create. In this way it can justify continued management of the firm's assets. The corporation would then indeed the natural owner (manager) of these assets.

Business-level strategy is concerned with how to manage and develop strategy of the relatively autonomous unit in the context of the firm's corporate strategy. For example, the mission of a business unit should be subsumed within the corporate mission, and its business objectives should be developed after discussion with corporate management. A key issue at this level is competitive strategy: How does the unit develop an advantage over its competitors? Note also that competition for customers occurs primarily at the business-unit level, not the corporate level. Competition is primarily a business-unit concept. Further, business-unit strategy includes decisions on growth strategy, what geographic focus to adopt, and what competences to develop.

Business-level strategy may also represent part of the implementation of corporate-level strategy. For example, a corporate strategy of international expansion is likely to have implications for all business units. A business also has to ensure that its strategies will deliver economic value, although this value may not be generated immediately. A growth business may sacrifice short-term profitability to create future shareholder value.

Decisions about a firm's business-unit structure should not be made lightly. The structure provides the basis for resource allocation decisions. If business units have been defined geographically, then resource allocation will occur on a geographic basis. If businesses have been defined on a product basis, then this will be the basis for resource allocation. In addition, decisions about the number of business units are corporate decisions and should be reviewed periodically. In large global firms, rather than a two-level structure of corporate and business strategy, three or more levels may exist.

Strategy as Building Competences

Regardless of how innovative a strategy is, it must be concerned with building firm competences. **Competences** are the skills and abilities of the firm, the things that a firm does better than its competitors. Competences are not static but must be built to support strategy. As Chapter 5 explains, a central element of strategy is building these competences faster and more effectively than competitors. The firm will have to forget old skills even as new ones are learned. For example, the U.S. retailer Wal-Mart has expanded into Central and South America, with 550 stores in Mexico alone. We would expect the company to use some of the skills, such as inventory management, that made it a superior retailer in the United States. But to succeed in its international expansion, Wal-Mart will need to build new skills, the most obvious one being language skills. In Mexico, Wal-Mart established a joint venture with CIFRA, Mexico's largest retailer, to overcome some of its competence deficiencies.

Strategy as Resolving Paradox

At the center of every strategy is tension between two apparently opposing thoughts: a paradox. The challenge was succinctly described by F. Scott Fitzgerald: "The test of a first rate intelligence is the ability to hold two opposed ideas in the mind at the same time and still retain the ability to function".[16] The essence of paradox is that the firm must operate at both ends of the spectrum simultaneously; it cannot operate solely at one end. The paradoxes include short term versus the long term, reflecting both creative and analytical approaches, demonstrating commitment to an idea and the flexibility to

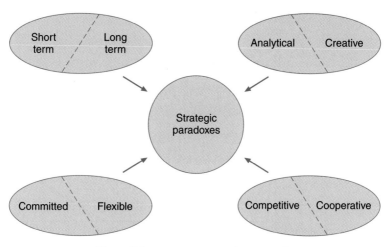

Figure 2.6   Strategy as Resolving Paradox

cope with unpredictable changes, being competitive as well as possibly cooperating with the same firms, showing some focus or centralization while permitting local autonomy, optimizing operations while allowing for innovation, and so on. Figure 2.6 indicates several of the relevant paradoxes to be addressed.

As we noted earlier, if the firm does not survive in the *short term,* then there will be no *long term.* British Airways reduced routes and staff to maintain short-term profitability in response to a major drop in international travel. If firms cease to meet the short-term requirements of financial success, they may become insolvent. Yet overemphasis on short-term results may put the long-term future of the company at risk. Short-term success can always be improved by starving the firm of long-term investment funds. The results of such actions may take several years (and a new generation of managers) to become apparent.

A new strategy often involves considerable investment in R&D, new facilities, and market and product development, with negative cash flows and economic profit, as illustrated in Figure 2.7. The firm must be able to fund this negative cash flow with funds from other parts of the firm, new debt, or new equity. Firms with less access to funding will find their innovation opportunities limited. Yet long-term success is dependent on innovation, implying investments that take time to come to fruition.

At the same time, the firm needs to decide when to call it quits, when to discontinue innovations that are unlikely to produce long-term success. This is not easy. There may be temptation to withdraw at the bottom of the cycle, just before things pick up. This is not helped by the tendency of managers to produce "hockey-stick" forecasts for their superiors.

Strategy must therefore reach an appropriate synthesis of the long term and the short term, addressing both the ongoing and innovation needs of the firm. If all management attention is directed at the ongoing business, innovation is stifled. Yet if too much attention is devoted to innovation, the core business may start to suffer.

Strategy also has to achieve a synthesis between the *analytical* and the *creative.* The former is characterized by detailed analysis of the environment, competitors, and so on, from which the firm constructs a reliable, rational, unbiased view of the world. However, too much analysis can lead to indecision, so-called paralysis by analysis, conflicting with the need to speed the pace of decision making. More data are always required, more

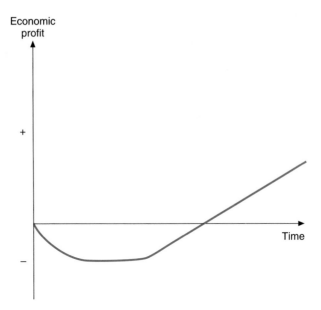

Figure 2.7 Economic Profit Profile of a New Strategy

studies have to be undertaken, and more risk needs to be removed from the decision. But, particularly for strategic decisions, we can never remove all risk. Strategic decisions always involve a significant element of intuition and judgment, which is risky if the decision maker lacks a valid mental model of the world and makes decisions based on prejudice and wishful thinking.

Another paradox is the tension between *competition* and *cooperation*. Strategy is not always a zero-sum game where if one firm wins, another loses. There may be benefits to be gained from cooperation, even with major competitors, as we see in numerous alliances. So while one purpose of strategy is to be creative, get an advantage, and outwit competitors, there are also times when a cooperative approach is called for. IBM and Sun Microsystems compete in some markets and cooperate in others.

Strategy also involves a synthesis between *commitment* and *flexibility*.[17] The firm needs to be committed to the pursuit of its vision and objectives. There will always be obstacles making this difficult. These may arise from changes in the environment (including competitors) or perhaps from employees unconvinced by the firm's strategy. Yet when the world has changed irrevocably, in ways that make the strategy untenable, or when performance is far below objectives and is unlikely to improve, the firm must change. Recognizing when commitment descends into outright stubbornness is an essential, but difficult, aspect of strategic management.

Other Characteristics of Strategy

Here we address other strategy characteristics more briefly. First, by its very nature, strategy is cross-functional, and different functional areas must be *aligned*. There is little value in attempting to become a global firm if the firm's human resources will not support this or if financial resources are inadequate. Different functional strategies must be aligned with the overall strategy. A corporate strategy focused on growth should lead to a discussion of how to fund this growth: Should the firm fund it through debt or equity and should the dividend policy be altered? If the firm decides to raise additional debt, what currency and maturity should be used? Similarly, a strategy to become more customer-focused may affect the human resources department's recruitment, training, development, and reward practices. Just as a particular strategy requires aligned resources, so may constrained resources limit strategic possibilities. Two key resources in this regard are skilled staff and financial resources. For example, if the firm is highly leveraged, then it may have to sell assets to ensure survival. On the other hand, if the firm is cash-rich or has access to cash in the form of debt or equity, it has a richer set of growth opportunities. There must also be alignment between strategy generation and implementation. There is little value in designing a strategy that cannot be implemented.

Strategy is also an *evolutionary* process. Strategy cannot involve an immutable timetable of what we will do in the future; the world is too turbulent and unpredictable for that to be successful. A strategy should incorporate a general direction and theme and, within that, sufficient flexibility to adapt as the world evolves. Strategy involves monitoring the changing environment, sensing changes, and making required adjustments to the strategy. *As a result, the actual realized strategy may not be the same as the intended strategy.*[18] In a world characterized by punctuated equilibrium, strategies need to be evolutionary,[19] and the learning issue will be addressed in more detail in Chapter 10.

Finally, given the size and complexity of global firms, most will be engaged in *multiple* strategic initiatives. A firm may be acquiring a European competitor, developing new products for an emerging market in China, exploring opportunities in telecommunications, attempting to change its culture to become more entrepreneurial, and designing and implementing new systems such as Customer Relationship Management (CRM) or Enterprise Resource Planning (ERP)—all at the same time. Sound strategic management may, and generally will, have a project management aspect, wherein senior managers are responsible for the design and successful execution of a number of initiatives. An important aspect of the CEO's job is to ensure that there are neither too few nor too many of these initiatives. Some firms suffer from "initiative overload," whereas the lack of required initiatives in a fast-changing environment will mean competitors soon leave the firm behind. Management must thus ensure that priorities are set appropriately.

At the same time, a firm may need to bet on a number of developments when it is unclear which will eventuate, and it may use a different strategy for each. A combination of alliances, internal development projects, and joint ventures can cover a number of possible developments. Here the firm is taking an options approach—placing small bets to see how a field develops, gaining information so as to act when appropriate. Because the future is unpredictable, experimentation is a good approach. At the same time, since resources are limited, trade-offs between these alternative futures will be necessary. No firm can cover all possibilities, particularly in capital-intensive businesses. The firm will need a mix of strategies in terms of time to fruition, risk, and degree of innovativeness.[20]

⊚ 2.4 CHARACTERISTICS OF STRATEGIC MANAGEMENT

Strategic management involves creating organizations that generate value in a turbulent world over a sustained period of time.

Strategic management is first and foremost about creating organizations, although those organizations have one important feature—they must create value. Such value creation requires continual innovation. In a world characterized by uncertainty, complex interactions, and ephemeral advantages, insight and foresight are essential managerial attributes. Certainly some industries are changing at slower rates than others, but disruptive change can arise from any number of sources, not just competitive or technological ones. So while foresight is always important, in some industries it will be essential.[21]

To repeat one of our themes, strategic management involves leadership skills and intuitive judgements as well as intellect, analysis, and planning. It is about organizations, the people who comprise them, their motivation and power, and the environment in which they compete. It is most definitely not a purely analytical activity.

We now review several of the features of strategic management, reflecting on both its importance and the challenge.

Creating the Organization

A fundamental role for strategic managers (including the CEO) is to create organizations that both respond to and introduce change. Change requires an entrepreneurial culture in the firm, one that encourages creativity and innovation, experimentation and learning. CEOs cannot do everything themselves; they need to work with and through other members of the firm. Thus strategic management also involves such tasks as designing organizational structure, systems, and decision-making processes; creating culture and values; developing compensation and incentive methods; and selecting and developing people—what we term the architecture of the organization.

Strategic management is deeply involved with such concepts as leadership, vision, integrity, empowerment, creativity, and risk taking. Despite the simplistic prescriptions of some gurus, there are rarely simple solutions to complex problems, and the strategic management agenda is therefore complex, requiring professional analytic skills.[22] Strategic managers need strong vision and a sense of direction about where the firm should go. They must be prepared to go into new areas, to create the future of their companies. They are often rule breakers, for to demonstrate industry leadership usually requires going outside traditional boundaries. They must also encourage such behavior in their people—hiring and developing staff who are skilled and entrepreneurial; who understand customers, competitors, and industry trends; and who bring both information and interpersonal skills to the organization.

Lack of an innovative and creative culture is often due to the frame of thinking that managers in the firm, and others in the industry, have acquired. Based on a combination of education, experience, consultants, and, often, the business press, this frame defines the company's understanding of itself and its industry. Managers have to continually challenge this **dominant logic,** which limits creative and lateral thinking. In some industries **strategy convergence** seems to occur, and all competitors follow a common industry recipe. Strategic management is about creativity, not following the herd. Winning companies have a strategy that is different from, and superior to, that of their competitors; a firm can never win if it has adopted a strategy identical to that of its competitors. Successful firms such as Nucor, Honda, SAP, Wal-Mart, and Dell have developed innovative strategies that have delivered significant improvements to customers, thereby generating substantial increases in shareholder value.

In a dynamic world, the organization must change and innovate if it is to be successful—although there is a risk with this, the risk of action is often lower than the risk of inaction.

Creating and Managing Change

To create value-generating organizations, strategic managers need an external perspective on the world and its developments. Given the turbulence and uncertainty we have discussed, it is becoming increasingly difficult for managers to develop strategies that sustain success. With a high rate of environmental change, *firms must change as fast or faster than their environment.* Strategies themselves have a shorter and shorter life: they rapidly become obsolete in a changing world, particularly when discontinuous change occurs. Unparalleled changes call for unparalleled responses. Part of the explanation for the short life of strategies is that intense competition quickly reduces any competitive advantage. Technology is creating frictionless capitalism, with lowered transaction costs, whereby any efficiency gains accruing to a firm are quickly competed away. So firms must force change in their businesses, becoming proactive and intellectual leaders of their industry.

Strategic management needs this external perspective. One key requirement is to recognize what Andrew Grove at Intel calls **inflection points**—points at which major changes occur due to new technology, regulatory changes, or changes in customer values and preferences.[23] These require the firm to make fundamental strategic changes, yet senior management, often far removed from the "coalface," is sometimes the last to notice the change. Rather than waiting until the performance of the firm has become degraded, strategic management must recognize when change is called for. It also needs the will to possibly cannibalize products and even businesses: to make a business obsolete before others do.

Strategic managers also need to recognize the possibility of new entrants, which often come from outside the industry but may not be new firms. These entrants could be established firms that are expanding their scope. In the United Kingdom, Tesco, a supermarket chain, is now a major gasoline retailer. We also see markets reaching saturation very quickly. Global firms operate globally, no longer launching in their home market and then following this up with a measured global expansion strategy. Instead, as with Microsoft's .Net, they launch globally on the same day.

Strategic managers should challenge the status quo, challenge the boundaries and positions within the firm, as well as consider how to invent new competitive spaces. They should challenge industry beliefs or norms, tap into the creative aspirations of all staff, and encourage ongoing questioning of traditional assumptions about the company and its businesses. Strategic managers must prevent cultural inertia, minimize resistance to change, encourage learning and experimentation, and develop new competences. This requires giving people the responsibility for engendering change, which involves both top-down and bottom-up processes. Management's job is to create an environment in which people can share knowledge, understand industry trends as well as their own business, understand strategy and competitors, and talk about the future and the need for change. With the increasing importance of intellectual capital and high-performance employees, monolithic, centrally managed firms are a thing of the past. One of Jeffrey Immelt's first actions after becoming CEO of GE in 2001 was to commission a group of younger managers to engage in a project aimed at defining the organization of the future. Interestingly, he did not give this assignment to very senior managers, but rather to those who would be managing that future organization.[24] A pattern of formal and informal groups, charged with the responsibility to innovate within some broad guidelines established by the parent, will characterize firms of the 21st century.

Creating Value

The organization created by senior managers, the activities with which it is involved, and the way in which it undertakes those activities must *create value.* A firm is primarily an economic entity. It may have social/political features, but the reason for its existence is economic—it promises to deliver products and services to its chosen customers in such a way that its revenue is larger than its costs, including capital costs. If the firm does not generate value, it has no reason to exist. It must meet the expectations of financial markets (a topic to which we return in Chapter 4). This is a considerable challenge. It is easier to create firms that destroy value rather than generate value. As Schumpeter noted, "creative destruction" is an ongoing process, and firms do not live forever.[25] *Firms do not have any intrinsic right to exist;* instead, this right must be continually earned in the marketplace against fierce competitors.[26]

Research indicates how difficult it is for firms to generate value over sustained periods of time. A major study[27] of U.S. firms over the period 1917–1987 found that only Kodak and GE outperformed the overall share market (such as the S&P 500), as measured by growth in market capitalization (although both have experienced difficulties in more recent times). Market capitalization is not the only measure of success, but it is at the very least a shareholder perspective, measuring the returns they get from holding the stock.

One explanation for this finding is that firms cannot innovate and change as quickly as the economy, and it is the economy that is reflected in any index of the overall share market. As industries grow and develop, the S&P, Nikkei, DAX, and similar indices are updated to reflect this, whereas firms such as USX are still basically in steel.

Ethics

Strategic management must also include a commitment to a set of **personal values,** including such things as integrity, trust, and fairness. There have been far too many examples of firms around the globe whose CEOs seem to have lost sight of this. Some CEOs seemed driven by a need for higher stock prices (possibly influenced by the options that they held), condoning loose accounting and ethical standards. CEO remuneration reached extreme heights and was too often unrelated to firm performance. A commitment to transparency is also necessary, with greater communication and sharing of information within the firm.

In summary, strategic management is about capturing the full potential of the firm today, meeting shareholder expectations, and choosing tomorrow's game in the light of turbulence and discontinuity. This requires imagining the future and what the firm will have to do to get there, a task that mandates considerable intelligence, learning, and feedback. By any measure, strategic management is not an easy task.

◎ 2.5 BUSINESS MODELS

Business models are a relatively new concept in strategic management, though Drucker used a very similar term *(business system)* in the early 1990s.[28] A **business model** is the method by which the firm generates revenue and profit; it addresses the fundamental question of how the business makes money.[29]

Management consulting provides an example of different business models. Firms such as McKinsey or BCG have traditionally charged a cash fee to clients, based either on a per-diem rate dependent on the number and seniority of the consultants involved or on a fee-for-project basis. Some consulting firms are changing this historical business model to one whereby the consulting firm offers an equity-for-service arrangement. The consultants takes an equity stake in the client, dependent on the success of their advice, allowing them to target clients that are cash-poor but have excellent growth prospects. This model has implications for the consulting firm in terms of cash flow and risk. The consulting firm may have a huge upside if the client is successful but is exposed to the downside risk of the client performing badly.[30]

A business model is a method of doing business by which a company generates revenue. Such a model spells out how a company makes money by specifying what activities it undertakes, where it is positioned in the value chain, and how it generates revenue. The business model idea is a very useful concept, but it is not the strategy of the firm, although some authors treat the two as synonymous.

In a given industry we may see two competing firms with fundamentally different business models. Dell and IBM employ different models in the PC industry—Dell with direct distribution, IBM with its value-added resellers. Thus there is competition between business models within an industry, and innovation can occur with the invention of a new business model that provides competitive advantage. In share trading, the traditional business model is the full-service broker. One wave of innovation followed the elimination of fixed fees, producing discount brokers such as Charles Schwab. A more recent invention involves another business model—online trading. Sometimes a new model renders the old obsolete (disruptive innovation); sometimes it just captures an increasing proportion of customer demand.

Innovation in business models is very important. Rather than being forced to reinvent business models by competitors, companies should be experimenting, on the alert for alternatives, whether precipitated by environmental change or by the firm itself.

Electronic commerce has given rise to new kinds of business models, and it is in this industry that the concept is widely used. eBay, for example, uses a traditional auction model, taking a commission on sales. Yahoo! provides content, usually free, and receives revenue from advertising banners and pop-ups associated with the site. Other firms adopt a utility model, with a customer fee based on usage, while still others raise revenue by selling data about consumers and their purchasing habits.[31]

A given business model has a life cycle—growth, maturity, and decline.[32] Strategic managers should continually challenge and test their firm's business model. Innovation in business models requires first that we understand the current model and then deconstruct it, understanding its underlying assumptions and analyzing what could cause it to lack consistency with the environment or technology. We should also explore business models of other industries (part of so-called best-of-class benchmarking) and consider constructing a new model. In some ways, the issues involved in business models parallel those in our discussion of strategy. The historical model for delivering shareholder returns was to reduce costs and explore revenue growth by targeting new growth segments—an incremental model. The new growth model instead places the emphasis on developing novel business models, which in turn requires a managerial model in which innovation, change, and uncertainty, rather than equilibrium, are the natural state—a revolutionary approach.

Components of a Business Model

A business model is the entire system for delivering value to customers and earning a profit on that activity.[33] It incorporates a set of assumptions about customers and economics, giving insight into how the firm expects to compete. The model must fit external reality and be internally consistent. It can be broken down into two components, value creation and value capture, as shown in Figure 2.8.

Value Creation
Value creation is how the firm creates value, which in turn depends on what activities in the value chain it is involved in. It includes customer selection and how the product or

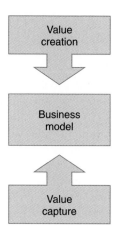

Figure 2.8   Components of a Business Model

service creates customer value (how it meets customers' needs). For some products, we should recall that customer value is determined by the total life-cycle cost of the product, not just the initial purchase price; this may provide opportunities for innovation. Since a business model also encompasses which activities the firm performs and which others perform, it may therefore involve a value network of suppliers and partners.

Value Capture
Value capture is how the firm gets rewarded for the value it creates, and this value capture is itself dependent on competitive differentiation. The normal way to capture value is through product and service fees, but, as we saw with electronic commerce, there can be other profit models. Gillette, for example, earns far more profit from the sale of razor blades than from the sale of razors. Automobile firms such as GM earn substantial profit not from the sale of cars but from the financing of car purchases. American Airlines earns money not only from flying passengers but also from fees received through its reservation system, which is used by travel agents and other airlines. Retailers of consumer appliances may make more money from the sales of add-on warranties than from the sale of the appliances themselves, while manufacturers of ink-jet printers often sell their printers at very low prices to ensure a stream of revenue from the sale of replacement ink cartridges.

Strategic managers need to think beyond new products to new business models that meet deep customer needs in unconventional ways. Sometimes a new model will destroy the old one; sometimes it captures an increasing proportion of the customers of the old model, reducing growth and profit for those companies that do not change. It introduces more strategic variety into a competitive domain, thus changing customer behavior. It is not a means of positioning against competitors but of going around them, and incumbents often find it difficult to emulate because they lack the required skills or are too slow to change. In many cases, incumbents are not prepared to cannibalize their existing model.

◉ 2.6 THE STRATEGY DEVELOPMENT PROCESS—A MANAGEMENT PERSPECTIVE

How do organizations, and managers within those organizations, actually develop strategy? In global organizations, senior line managers, often supported by a planning staff, typically develop strategy. Strategy is almost always the result of some type of collective decision-making process, with a number of managers involved. These processes are characterized by building diverse teams that challenge assumptions and increase the range of alternatives considered.[34] Firms also attempt to minimize internal political activity, although there is almost always a political aspect to the strategy process. Innovation may be required in this strategy-generation process to ensure that value-creating strategies result. This may require involving a wider group, crossing organizational and industry boundaries, and encouraging both new perspectives and experimentation.

Both managers and managerial researchers have debated the process of strategy development. The process appears to be a combination of the rational and the intuitive, of formal analysis and entrepreneurial activity. We know the future is uncertain and thus cannot be predicted with certainty, so strategic decisions have to be made without full information. The firm has a dilemma. Delay the decision until more and better information is available, or make a decision now without full information. If we delay, our competitors may decide to act and thus obtain a first-mover advantage. On the other hand, if a decision made with less information is incorrect, the firm suffers accordingly.

From one perspective, strategic thinking can be seen as a rational activity whereby managers gather facts, identify problems, develop alternatives, and choose the best alternative against a clear objective. This process requires substantial analytical skills to assess the importance of changes in the environment and the firm and the impact of these on the future.

Another view is that strategy is about intuition, judgment, and feel. Such a process is often claimed to generate more creative and entrepreneurial solutions. Creative solutions generally go beyond existing data; they represent an inferential leap into an uncertain future, requiring deep understanding that may not be fully supported by any formal analysis. Intuition is often more holistic, looking at problems in a more inclusive way based on the decision maker's prior experiences, knowledge, and values.[35]

In summary, some of the characteristics of the *strategy process* are the following:

- It requires analysis, but analysis will rarely remove the need for judgment.
- There is an increased need for speed in decision making, as the costs of delay are rising.
- Good decision processes should focus on the problem, not on politics within the firm.
- There is a need for creativity and developing original solutions.

Impediments to the Strategy Process

Strategic decision making may suffer from a variety of impediments, as illustrated in Figure 2.9, the elements of which we now examine.

Lack of Information

With fundamentally new products or major new business developments that take time to come to fruition, lack of sufficient information is common. Many firms attempt detailed financial analysis, but the quality of such analysis is often poor. Where risk can be assessed, risk analysis tools can be utilized.[36] In other situations, such analysis is virtually impossible since the future is too uncertain—and, in fact, unknowable. In these situations, strategic decisions rely mainly on judgment and intuition, supported with what analysis is possible, even if the latter has more of the characteristics of a ritual than of decision support.[37]

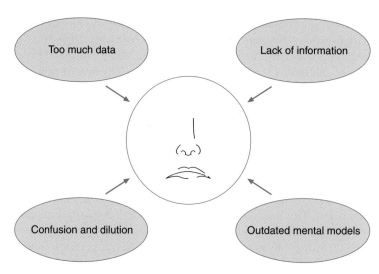

Figure 2.9 Impediments to Developing Strategy

Too Much Data

Sometimes strategic decision making can suffer from too much data but not enough information. We cannot determine what is important and what is not, and we cannot put the data into a context. In the information age, this will be an increasing problem.

Confusion and Dilution

We sometimes describe strategy and the process of developing strategy as the responsibility of the CEO, as if only the CEO is involved. This is far from the truth. Not only are there many individuals involved in collecting and analyzing data, there is normally a group of senior managers who actually make the final decision. This group has some interesting properties. Its composition is generally variable as some members join and other members leave (either the group or the firm). It is sometimes unclear who made a decision or even if a decision has been made. Decisions sometimes result from creeping commitment; they are not clear until some time after the event. Not only is responsibility for a decision thereby diffused, but sometimes the very solution chosen is the result of compromise, lacking clarity or direction.

Outdated Mental Models

We have noted that firms exist in a world of complex adaptive systems and that one characteristic of these systems is punctuated equilibrium, where periods of relatively slow change are interrupted by periods of radical and revolutionary change. As the world moves through these revolutionary periods, it becomes apparent that senior managers may be out of touch. Their experience and understanding was formed in a prior world; they have difficulty comprehending the new world. This discontinuity can be exacerbated by a tendency for senior executives to be insulated from reality, with staff not reporting bad news.

The difficulty here can be understood through the concept of a cognitive map or **mental model**—a set of assumptions about the industry environment and the nature of competition. For example, is competition local or global, who are possible entrants, what are the changing political/social trends that determine how we understand the world, and so on? A mental model is a process of organizing reality, of determining what is important and what is not.

In a study of General Motors in the 1980s, it was found that most senior executives of GM and other U.S. automobile firms had a set of assumptions for success that included the following:

- Cars are status symbols; styling is more important than quality.
- The U.S. market is isolated from the rest of the world.
- Workers do not have an important impact on productivity or quality.
- Managers only need a fragmented understanding of the business.[38]

In reality, these assumptions were wrong. They led GM down a very expensive path of underestimating the impact of overseas competitors, heavy spending on new plant, and declining quality. Table 2.2 shows significant market share losses in the critical North American market, dropping by almost 40% over a 20-year period, while GM incurred losses of some $USB9 from 1990 to 1992 and failed to generate shareholder returns for a significant period. While we would not claim that an incorrect mental model alone determined this performance, it reflects the fact that many GM managers were out of touch with the environment in which they competed.

A mental model is a set of ingrained assumptions and generalizations that influence how we understand the world and take action. They tell us what is important, what will be noticed. Mental models can be very dangerous to good decision making because they are typically tacit, not explicit. An auto executive may say, "People are only interested in styling," which really means, "I have a mental model which says that people are only interested in styling." These are actually very different statements. If the first, we believe it to be true. If the second, we could decide to test the model.

Mental models also develop over long periods of time and are therefore difficult to change. Further, a model becomes "objective" if it is widely shared within the firm. This is one reason why firms have difficulty putting new strategies into practice. New strategies

TABLE 2.2   Performance of General Motors

Year	Market Share (%) Units, U.S. Cars and Light Trucks	Share Price ($US) (December 31)
1980	45	22.5
1982	44	31.2
1984	42	39.2
1986	38	33.0
1988	35	41.8
1990	35	34.3
1992	34	32.2
1994	33	42.1
1996	32	55.8
1998	31	71.5
1999	28	72.7
2000	28	50.9
2001	28	48.6
2002	28	36.9

Sources: S. Zesiger, "GM's Big Decision: Status Quo", *Fortune*, February 21, 2000, pp. 71–74; "In The US in April 2003, General Motors' Car Sales Plunge; Honda's and Hyundai's Truck Sales Surge": *Auto on Info*, www.autooninfo.info/NAEd200305USSalesNews.htm, 2003.

fail to get implemented because they conflict with strongly held internal beliefs of how the world works. Managers and employees do not believe that the world has actually changed; if they see a change, they rationalize it as temporary: in the near future "sanity" (namely the past) will return. In this sense, management needs to undergo a paradigm shift, and this may require the injection of a completely new group of managers.

⟳ 2.7 STAKEHOLDERS AND ORGANIZATIONAL VALUE

A firm creates value when the revenue generated is greater than all the costs involved in generating that revenue, including capital costs. Indeed, the purpose of strategy is to ensure that the firm generates an economic profit that is available for distribution among its stakeholders or utilized for innovation to create additional value. However, a firm has numerous stakeholders, and it needs to create value for all. In this section, we will focus on three of the most critical stakeholders: shareholders, customers, and employees, as illustrated in Figure 2.10. How economic profit is distributed among these stakeholders will be a source of debate within the firm, reflecting the values of managers, available growth opportunities, and the political power of various stakeholders.

Shareholders

Shareholders have a financial investment from which they expect a return. Companies create **value for shareholders** when the return to equity is greater than the cost of that equity—or greater than what investors could earn from other investments with an appropriate adjustment for risk. Since shareholders have other investment choices, the firm must provide them with an acceptable return (generally financial). Shareholders can invest in government securities, which would generally be considered to have zero risk. So an investment in a higher-risk class such as a firm must generate a return greater than what could be earned from this risk-free investment.

Some shareholders may also have nonfinancial expectations, for example, that the firm will invest ethically. They may be concerned that the firm act responsibly on environmental issues, or that it trade only with acceptable countries (e.g., not invest in countries that exploit child labor), or that it pay staff in less developed countries at an acceptable level. While these issues may have to be considered, we will assume that the overwhelming reason for making and holding an investment is financial. Nonetheless, when assessing the magnitude of financial returns, an adjustment for risk must be made, and risk can be affected by the aforementioned ethical concerns.

Figure 2.10   Major Organizational Stakeholders

Creating value for shareholders is different from shareholder returns. **Returns to shareholders** are generated through share-price appreciation and dividend payments, and these returns are to some extent outside the control of management. Share prices are driven by factors apart from firm performance, as has been observed with the short-term volatility of share markets around the world. So while shareholder value, as defined above, is a useful criterion for decision making, return to shareholders—given its volatility—is less useful.

Should the firm not meet investors' expectations, shareholders may sell their shares, driving down the share price and increasing the possibility of a takeover by others who believe that they can manage the firm's assets better. This transferability of equity shares, and the rights associated with them, is referred to as the market for corporate control, a topic to which we will return in Chapter 4. The relevance of this market for the present discussion is that if managers do not produce acceptable returns for shareholders, it is likely that investors will cause management to be replaced.

Customers

Customers also make claims on the firm. At a minimum, they want products and services that meet their requirements in terms of functionality, quality, safety, delivery, and, of course, price. They also value innovation and the development of new products. In addition, they often have much broader expectations, related to the psychological and socio-psychological satisfactions from owning and/or using a product or service, as well as non-product-related expectations similar to those of shareholders.

Just as investors have a wide variety of investment alternatives, so customers have numerous choices. Markets are more competitive, and customers are more knowledgeable, more sophisticated, and harder to satisfy. They have strong sanctions they can exert over the firm: they may take their business elsewhere or, for many discretionary products and services, may choose not to purchase at all, instead saving or investing their money.

A firm cannot survive without revenue, so a *customer orientation* will be one of the foundations for the firm's success. Many firms find this competition for customers increasingly difficult and are wrestling with the challenge of acquiring a stronger customer focus.

Employees

The third vital stakeholder group is employees. Employees value both intrinsic and extrinsic rewards and are motivated by more than salary. If expectations about job satisfaction, growth opportunities, and the like are not met, they are likely to leave. Further, as competition becomes more knowledge-based, attracting and keeping high-caliber staff becomes critical. High-potential employees with valued skills have many choices in terms of where they work—for which firm and in which industry and, increasingly, in which country. Strategic managers need to ensure that these individuals remain committed to the firm. If their expectations are not met, they will leave the firm, substantially reducing its capabilities. The increasing knowledge intensity of business is reflected in a global labor market, changing the policies used to recruit and retain high-caliber staff.

Within a few weeks of the depths of Arthur Andersen's problems becoming evident, the firm began to dissolve as partners around the world initiated and secured arrangements that would protect their personal futures.

When we discuss the needs and requirements of these three groups of stakeholders, we have to ask: Can the firm deliver value to all three at the same time or does it have to make choices among them? If choices have to be made, how should these choices be made? On the first question, there is a wide difference of opinion. Commentators such as Copeland suggest that firms should adopt shareholder value as their only guiding principle. If they cannot deliver this, then they cannot deliver value to others.[39] Copeland suggests that companies that deliver to shareholders show better productivity and employment gains than low-performing companies. He sees a virtuous circle, with high shareholder value creating high value to customers and staff. The alternative view is that a firm could deliver superior value to shareholders and yet deliver low value to others. In other words, these three stakeholders are mutually exclusive: we can satisfy one only by not satisfying the others. If this view is adopted, one of the key tasks of the board is deciding what balance is to be achieved between these different stakeholders.

Other Stakeholders

While we have focused above on three key stakeholder groups, there are others. With the growth in outsourcing and networks, *suppliers* have often become extremely important, and supply-chain management is a major concern in many firms. We would like suppliers to provide a secure source, good products, competitive prices, and continual innovation. Suppliers typically have other customers, and they may be able to seek business elsewhere. Or they may not invest, thus reducing innovation, a situation that then has a cascading effect to us. Individuals and organizations that supply debt financing often receive special consideration, since debt is a major source of funds.

The firm must also attend to the needs of the social/political *community* in which it exists. Any firm is given some benefits from the legal system of the country in which it operates, such as limited liability or a defined tax rate. In return, it has to meet various social objectives and requirements. These include standards covering employment safety, occupational health, minimum wages, environmental protection, ethical behavior, and competitive behavior.

◉ 2.8 GETTING STRATEGY IMPLEMENTED

Strategy development, or generation, and implementation are normally distinguished, since they require different skills and are often done by different individuals and groups within the firm. *Strategy generation* is often the responsibility of senior management while *implementation* the responsibility of middle management. However, generation and implementation are obviously interrelated, since there is no benefit—and significant cost—to developing a strategy that cannot be implemented. There are good reasons to involve middle management in the development process, since this encourages commitment that assists implementation. In addition, the quality of the strategy that is developed may well be improved by the active participation of middle managers. They usually have good knowledge of the here and now, although in other cases—such as acquisitions—security requires that strategy be developed with little middle-management input.

A strategy needs to be broken down into smaller elements for implementation, necessitating a control system to ensure that the strategy is actually implemented. Strategy will be nested as it is implemented throughout the firm, and its numerous elements or components need to be aligned. CEOs cannot implement strategy on their own; others must do this. The role of the CEO and senior managers is to ensure that it is done, that resources for change are adequate, and that staff have the required skills. Senior managers must also recognize the difficulty of creating organizational change—there may be considerable resistance to change from other staff. The design of an incentive system that facilitates implementation is therefore another critical task for management.

Implementation of corporate strategy inevitably involves the use of *teams* that cross business functions. These teams require leadership at all levels of the firm. Since the firm will generally be implementing a number of strategies at the same time, there is also a requirement for project management skills. Given the complexity of the modern firm, it may have strategies to expand in Europe, to develop and launch new business in the United States, to change the culture to be more entrepreneurial and customer-focused, and to undertake a major cost reduction—all at the same time. Keeping these strategies aligned and implemented in an ongoing and timely manner is not easy. While large, centrally managed corporations are typically a thing of the past; so, too, are central strategy departments. Firms have decentralized. But at the corporate level, there will generally be a few groups of people who spend 60% to 80% of time on projects, such as planning and tracking, and the balance of their time on traditional strategic planning, such as industry analysis. High-potential individuals often rotate through these positions, not only getting useful knowledge from the business units but also ensuring that their mental models, at a minimum, reflect current marketplace realities.

◉ 2.9 SUMMARY

Managing global firms is difficult, for the world is changing rapidly and the future is very uncertain. Creating organizations that thrive and prosper in such an environment requires judgment and intuition as well as a deep understanding of the competences of the firm and its environment.

In a changing world, any strategy is likely to quickly become obsolete, so strategic management must be ongoing, continually developing new and different strategies. Value is typically created by innovation, not by mere replication of the present, but any change needs to be fully resourced, both financially and with human skills.

Strategy is not a single decision. It involves a stream of decisions, each significant in its own right. A strategy can be successful only when these decisions are aligned and integrated, and strategy therefore requires the commitment of the entire firm.

Strategic management is about managing the entire process, including implementation and generation of resources. A strategy for the future will generally involve competences not currently possessed by the firm, and only a holistic view will suffice.

◉ REVIEW QUESTIONS

1. Describe the differences between an incremental strategy and a revolutionary strategy and the circumstances when each may be used.

2. Specify what you would regard as the strategic time horizon for a national retail chain, a global resources firm, and a management consulting firm. What causes the differences?

3. Select a global firm with which you are a familiar. Provide examples of incremental and revolutionary strategies adopted by the firm. Comment on the result achieved with each.

4. Select a firm with which you are a familiar. Describe the strategic decisions made by the firm, its strategy, and the way that strategy has been managed over the last five years. Has the performance of the firm been satisfactory?

5. Select a firm with which you are familiar. Describe its business model. Can you develop an alternative business model for this firm?

6. What is a stakeholder? Can a firm satisfy all stakeholders simultaneously or does it have to be selective?

⊚ ENDNOTES

[1] Adapted from G. Hamel, "Strategy as Revolution," *Harvard Business Review,* July–August 1996, pp. 69–82.

[2] Adapted from D. Crowe, "IBM's $6.4Bn Consulting Shake-Up," *Australian Financial Review,* August 1, 2002, p. 1.

[3] Ibid.

[4] Amazon Annual Report, 2001, www.amazon.com.

[5] J. Davidson, "Whirls of Delight as Amazon's Profit Is Heaven Cent," *Australian Financial Review,* January 24, 2002, p. 3.

[6] P. M. Natterman, "Best Practice ≠ Best Strategy", *McKinsey Quarterly,* 2 (2000), pp. 22–31.

[7] R. Gupta, "A Case for Corporate Freedom," *McKinsey Quarterly,* 3 (1998), pp. 154–162.

[8] Note that the figure is illustrative and does not depict the actual value creation for any firm.

[9] E. D. Beinhocker, "On the Origin of Strategies," *McKinsey Quarterly* 4 (1999), pp. 47–57.

[10] G. Johnson and K. Scholes, *Exploring Corporate Strategy,* (6th Ed., Harlow, U.K.: Pearson Education, 2002).

[11] S. Wetlaufer, "The Business Case against Revolution," *Harvard Business Review,* February 2001, pp. 113–119.

[12] P. Berthon, J. M. Hulbert, and L. Pitt, "Innovation or Customer Orientation?," *European Journal of Marketing.* Summer 2004.

[13] G. Hamel and C. K. Prahalad, "Strategy as Stretch and Leverage," *Harvard Business Review,* March–April 1993, pp. 75–84.

[14] R. Buaron, "New-Game Strategies," *McKinsey Quarterly* 3 (2000), pp. 34–37.

[15] C. Lucier, L. Moeller, and J. Porsilieri, "Breaking Out: A Strategy Process That Works", Strategic Management Society Conference, Vancouver, September 2000.

[16] Quoted in C. Hampden-Turner, *Charting the Corporate Mind* (London: Blackwell, 1990).

[17] Quoted in P. Ghemawat, "Commitment versus Flexibility," *California Management Review* 40, no. 4 (1998), pp. 26–43.

[18] H. Mintzberg and J. A. Waters, "Of Strategies, Deliberate and Emergent," *Strategic Management Journal* 6 no. 3 (1985), pp. 257–272.

[19] E. D. Beinhocker, "On the Origin of Strategies," *McKinsey Quarterly* 4 (1999), pp. 47–57.

[20] H. Courtney, J. Kirkland, and P. Vigurie, "Strategy under Uncertainty," *Harvard Business Review,* November–December 1997, pp. 66–79.

[21] F. W. J. Barnett and T. B. Berland, "Strategic Thinking on the Front Lines," *McKinsey Quarterly* 2 (1999), pp. 118–123.

[22] F. Hilmer and L. Donaldson, *Management Redeemed,* (East Roseville, N.S.W.: Free Press Australia, 1996).

[23] S. M. Puffer, "Interview with Andrew Grove," *Academy of Management Executive* 13, no. 1 (1999), pp. 15–24.

[24] Personal communication with one of the authors.

[25] J. A. Schumpeter, *Capitalism, Socialism and Democracy* (New York: Harper & Row, 1976).

[26] R. N. Foster and S. Kaplan, *Creative Destruction* (New York: Doubleday, 2001), pp. 20.

[27] Ibid.

[28] P. F. Drucker, "The Theory of the Business," *Harvard Business Review,* September–October 1994, pp. 95–104.

[29] J. Magretta, "Why Business Models Matter," *Harvard Business Review,* May 2002, pp. 86–92.

[30] J. Henderson, B. Leleux, and I. White, "Untangling Service-for-Equity Arrangements", Strategic Management Society Conference, Vancouver, September 2000.

[31] A. Afuah and C. L. Tucci, *Internet Business Models and Strategies* (New York: McGraw-Hill Irwin, 2001).

[32] A. J. Slywotzky, *Value Migration* (Boston: Harvard Business School Press, 1996).

[33] A. J. Slywotzky and D. J. Morrison, *The Profit Zone* (St Leonards, NSW, Australia: Allen & Unwin, 1997).

[34] K. M. Eisenhardt, "Strategy as Strategic Decision Making," *Sloan Management Review* 40, no. 3 (1999), pp. 65–72.

[35] Intuition has been described as a cognitive conclusion reached on the decision maker's prior experiences and values. See L. A. Burke and M. K. Miller, "Taking the Mystery out of Intuitive Decision Making," *Academy of Management Executive* 13, no. 4 (1999), pp. 91–99.

[36] H. Courtney et al., "Strategy under Uncertainty."

[37] In many respects this type of decision parallels the situation faced by a startup business seeking funding. Great emphasis is placed on having a business plan, yet all venture capitalists and "angel" investors realize that these are hardly ever realistic and that their funding decisions are made largely on faith and assessment of the qualities of the individuals seeking the funds. Interestingly, Bower found that similar considerations apply when large firms are considering capital investment decisions. See J. L. Bower, *Managing the Resource Allocation Process* (Boston: Harvard Business School Press, 1970).

[38] I. Mitroff, *Break-Away Thinking* (New York: Wiley, 1988).

[39] T. E. Copeland, T. Koller, and J. Murrin, *Valuation: Measuring and Managing the Value of Companies* (New York: Wiley, 2000).

CHAPTER 3

The Competitive Environment

Learning Objectives

Upon completing this chapter, you should be able to:

- Identify the structural characteristics of the environment faced by the firm and how these drivers influence both competition and value creation

- Choose the appropriate level of specificity in environmental analysis, depending on the locus of the decision-making group

- Predict how changes occurring in the environment might influence future competition and value creation

- Incorporate understanding of environmental changes into the development of strategy

- Consider options for influencing changes in the firm's environment so as to improve future value creation

- Analyze customers and competitors to develop a competitive advantage and strategy

- Appreciate that strategy is realized in the future: decisions are made now but their realization occurs in the future

---

In late 2000, GE proposed to take over Honeywell. Both these firms are U.S.-based, and the value of the merger was $USB42. But a merger between two such large firms has global implications and ramifications. Although the U.S. Federal Trade Commission (FTC) had approved the merger, the European Union (EU) decided to oppose it on the grounds that it had the potential to reduce competition in Europe. Its concern was that GE's strong position in the manufacture of jet engines and its ability to offer finance, if added to Honeywell's aviation electronic business, would allow the merged entity to bundle their products together. This bundling would, in the view of the European Commission, amount to unfair competition.

At the center of the objection is the fact that GE owns a company, Gecas, which is an aircraft-leasing firm. In 2001, Gecas owned 790 aircraft, which it leased to airlines, and managed another 321 aircraft for other investors. The concern of the European Commission was that since GE owned this firm, there was the potential for Gecas customers to be forced to purchase GE engines and/or Honeywell electronics. GE's response to the rejection was to offer to put 19.9% of Gecas up for private placement, with this portion worth possibly $USB1.4. Since GE would still own 80.1%, it would maintain the ability to consolidate Gecas earnings.[1]

In the face of continued opposition from the EU, GE decided not to pursue the merger.

This example emphasizes that managers of global firms must recognize that they operate in multiple countries and that their strategy will be influenced by global as well as domestic considerations. Both GE and Honeywell are U.S. firms, and the U.S. Federal Trade Commission had approved the proposed merger. Nonetheless, the merger did not go ahead due to European Union opposition. Globalization adds a degree of complexity to decision making, and managers responsible for strategy development and implementation must understand this complexity. The example also illustrates how rapidly the business environment might change, shortening the life of a given strategy. Strategy must be reconfigured more frequently to reflect these changes.

The EU decision may also have been influenced by considerations independent of the proposed merger, such as decisions by U.S. antitrust authorities on mergers between European firms. However, both the firm and its competitors could influence external changes. GE and its European competitors were active participants in this process, lobbying their respective national governments in an attempt to influence the outcome. Finally, as a consequence of the EU decision, GE is likely to have to significantly change its strategy regarding aircraft engine and related businesses.

3.1 INTRODUCTION

The external environment faced by the firm and its business units affects the strategy of the firm, the value of the strategy, and thus the firm's performance. Environmental analysis is therefore not a passive exercise, but rather an active and essential input to strategy development, helping the firm and its business units identify attractive opportunities and make decisions on where and how to compete.

The drivers of change are for the most part external to the firm. As the global economy entered the new century, changes were taking place on multiple fronts at a very fast pace. Some of these changes made traditional business models and tools outdated, changing the rules for existing competitors and challenging the assumptions of others, both new and old. In this chapter we review some approaches that can guide us as we wrestle with the challenges of developing strategy in this fast-changing environment.

Strategy development requires the firm to understand what critical variables are changing, the pace at which these changes are occurring, and their likely impact on the firm, as illustrated in Figure 3.1.

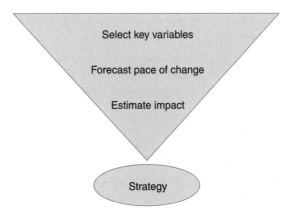

Figure 3.1   Process of Environmental Analysis

Select Key Variables

First, managers need to select the key variables that can affect their firm or business. What these are will depend on the firm and the judgment, knowledge, and intuition of the senior managers in identifying what is relevant. Consider, for example, forecasting the demand for automobiles. Knowledge of such variables as household income, interest rates, and consumer confidence would probably be very helpful. On the other hand, in forecasting the demand for baby food, the birth rate would be a key explanatory variable. So what is relevant and important depends on the business concerned.

Forecast Changes

Second, we need to estimate, or forecast, the nature and pace of these changes. If forecast changes are likely to occur in the distant future, we may just monitor. Continuing the baby food example, birth rates in much of the world are declining. This is a relatively slow process, occurring over many years, so while its impact in any year is relatively minor, its long-term impact is substantial. Other changes, such as those in data storage and communications, are occurring very rapidly, so the firm's response must be more immediate. In some industries the problem is to identify points of discontinuity, times when change is occurring very rapidly. Innovations such as the PC or electronic funds transfer, which generate entire new industries and place established firms under considerable pressure, are examples.[2] In addition, some of these changes, such as population growth, will be relatively easy to forecast while others, such as changes to the Russian legal system, are much less predictable.

Estimate the Impact of the Changes

Finally, we need to estimate the potential impact of these changes on the firm. Some changes will have a major impact, some a very minor one. The firm should allocate its environmental scanning resources toward those changes that have both a high probability of occurring within the relevant time horizon and a major impact on strategy. A variety of forecasting techniques may assist in this process. For example, in dealing with the trend changes of the type discussed in Chapter 1, times series and regression models can prove very helpful.[3]

The reason for trying to understand the changing world is that strategy and strategic decisions are realized in the future, not the present. Strategic decisions are made now, but their implications are not realized until the future.

The success or otherwise of a strategy depends not on the state of the world today but on the state of the world in the future.

In analyzing the external environment faced by a firm or a business unit, we distinguish three levels, designated as the *remote, industry,* and *competitive* environment, as shown in Figure 3.2. Successful strategy development requires an understanding of changes at all three levels.

> **Remote environment:** The broad social/technical/economic environment in which the firm competes. This environment is global in nature, exerts a powerful influence on strategy, and in many instances is slow-acting. Due to the breadth of these changes, they can be expected to affect a number of industries.

> **Industry environment:** Changes that impact on all competitors in a specific industry. Examples are changes in entry barriers from changing government regulations,

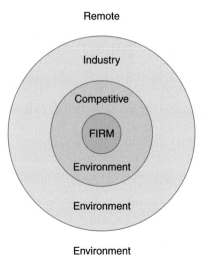

Figure 3.2 Environmental Analysis

technology, or the development of substitute products. Such changes influence all firms in the industry, possibly in different ways.

Competitive environment: Changes in customers and direct competitors that influence the competitive strategy of the business unit, such as the development of new products by competitors, the emergence of new channels of distribution, and the rise of new customer values.

Which level of analysis is required depends on the level of strategy that we are considering, corporate or business unit, as shown in Figure 3.3.

Strategy level	Analysis level	What analyzed	Strategic decisions
Corporate	Remote	Broad environmental trends affecting all business units	New opportunities, resource allocation among SBU's
	Industry	Structural changes in the industry	Resource allocation
Business unit	Remote	Environmental trends influencing the specific SBU	Competitive strategy
	Industry	Suppliers, entrants, substitutes	Competitive strategy
	Product/market	Customers, competitors	Competitive advantage

Figure 3.3 Levels of Environmental Analysis

When developing *corporate-level* strategy, key decisions are which businesses should the corporation be in, what should be its geographic scope, and how resources should be allocated among the business units. At the corporate level, analysis will generally be undertaken at two levels, the broad remote level and an analysis of developments in each industry in which the firm competes. Flowing from the remote analysis is a better understanding of major threats to the firm or opportunities that it may wish to pursue. For example, the firm may decide to move a substantial element of its manufacturing offshore to China. Since it is likely that such an investment may take several years to become profitable, the decision must incorporate a view on a number of broad economic variables, such as political stability in China and future exchange rates. Industry analysis is undertaken at the corporate level to ensure that the corporate level has a sound understanding of the attractiveness of the industries in which its various business units compete and thus can form a view on prospective profit levels of its businesses. Such decisions, whether to enter new businesses or to commit major resources to an existing industry, must be based on anticipated results for many years into the future, possibly as long as 5 to 10 years. The firm must have a view of the future before it can commit these resources, even if there is considerable uncertainty.

Business-unit managers need to undertake analysis at all three levels. Strategy for a given business unit will be influenced by certain developments in the remote environment, although which elements are critical will depend on the specific business unit. They must also understand changes specific to their industry. As we have noted, a business unit must create value, with revenue greater than its costs. But it is possible for the industry structure to be such that while the firm creates value, it cannot capture that value for itself. If the business is in an extremely competitive industry, buyers may capture all the value, with all productivity improvements and cost reductions passed on to customers. Alternatively, it may be that a firm in another industry has developed a substitute product with price/performance characteristics that will have a major impact on the revenue, and thus profitability, of the business. Thus an understanding of the nature of the industry, and how this is changing, is essential in developing strategy at the business-unit level.

Strategy at the business-unit level is interlinked with the concept of competitive advantage and should focus on developing such an advantage. This requires a detailed understanding of customer needs and how these differ across customer segments, how these needs are changing, and likely future strategies of competitors.

We begin this chapter with a review of the broader or remote environment and the various forces at work therein. We then focus on the more immediate industry environment, reviewing some of the analytic tools that can bring more insight to our understanding of that environment. Finally, we look at the firm's competitive environment, focusing on its relationships with its customers and direct competitors and the ways in which these are likely to change in the future. We conclude by summarizing the challenge to managers as they contemplate the likely changes that lie ahead.

In considering the subject matter in this chapter, there are two key ideas you should bear in mind. First, do not assume that the future will be a mere extrapolation of the past. Many alternative futures are possible, for the future does not yet exist. Where we are uncertain about the future, it may be very beneficial to consider alternative scenarios, opening our minds to the idea that change is inevitable and that we need to be flexible when changes cannot be accurately forecast.[4] Second, you should recognize that since the future does not yet exist, we might be able to influence it through our decisions. Do not assume that the remote or industry environments are not subject to influence. Some of the most successful competitive strategies have involved doing that very thing.

⟳ 3.2 THE REMOTE ENVIRONMENT

There are obviously many different aspects of the remote environment that can have significant impact on the operation of the firm, its competitors, and its customers. A simple acronym that can assist us in overviewing these aspects is the **PESTLE** model, so called because it covers the *political, economic, sociocultural, technological, legal,* and *environmental* aspects of the overall business environment, as shown in Figure 3.4

Figure 3.4 depicts the *firm as comprising a number of strategic business units* to reinforce our emphasis that the analysis of the remote environment will be undertaken at both the corporate and the business-unit level. Since the firm's strategic business units (SBUs) operate in different product markets, they each need to undertake their own analysis of the remote environment, analyzing the variables and changes appropriate to them. At the same time, corporate-level staff will also be analyzing the environment, possibly to identify merger and acquisition candidates or other growth opportunities. For example, both corporate and business-unit managers at DuPont may be monitoring economic developments in Malaysia. When this occurs, the firm needs to ensure that these two entities coordinate their activities. Firms often utilize corporate support staff to develop a view on relevant future variables, and all business units adopt that view. For example, corporate economic staff may forecast future exchange rates, and that view is adopted throughout the firm.

Political

Governments set the rules for business in areas such as competition policy, taxation policy, multinational agreements, and others, as shown in Table 3.1. Historically, governments intervened in national economies both to pursue political ends and to redress the perceived failure of market mechanisms to fulfill consumer welfare goals. In some countries, such as the United States, this intervention has involved government regulation while in others, such as the United Kingdom and France, state ownership of business corporations was vigorously pursued. In still other countries, such as India and Japan,

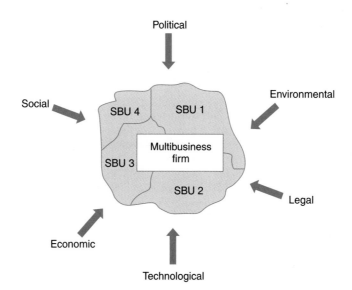

Figure 3.4   Framework for Analysis of the Remote Environment

TABLE 3.1 Selected Political Variables

Competition policy
Taxation policy
Privatization
Regulation of financial markets
Employment law
Government stability
Multinational agreements
Government spending

state-driven mercantilism to increase exports and reduce imports has been the pattern. In Japan, MITI was a key element in its drive for economic advancement.

For much of the 20th century, increased government involvement was the norm around the world. Since the early 1980s there has been a marked shift in *competition policy*, with an increasing reliance on free markets. Regulatory barriers around the world in such industries as airlines, banking, railroads, insurance, telecommunications, and trucking have been reduced. Governments seem to have realized that the regulations designed to protect consumers or competitors in an earlier era were no longer beneficial. Far too often regulation locked in inefficient competitive structures and restricted entry and innovation, denying consumers the benefits of competition. Such regulation also affected the liquidity of financial markets and the rights of shareholders.

> The EU is attempting to rewrite the takeover code to permit a larger number of hostile mergers, a move being strongly resisted by Germany. The EU proposals include that companies targeted by hostile bids consult shareholders before executing a defensive strategy, that the board maintain a neutral stance during a takeover bid, and that the board consult shareholders before taking "poison pill" steps to head off unwanted advances from another corporation.[5] If implemented, these measures may prevent the boards of European firms from rejecting takeovers that are in the interests of small minority shareholders.

On the other hand, as global competition has increased, some legislation has come to be viewed as limiting the ability of corporations to compete on a global scale. While this enforcement policy has changed somewhat, there may still be some way to go. Thus U.S. regulations have constrained overseas firms attempting to operate in the United States, and a similar pattern exists in the United Kingdom.

> RWE is a German utility, primarily in water. In the last few years it has been attempting to expand internationally, since it believes that there are limited investment opportunities in the domestic German market. In 2000 it bought Britain's Thames Water and in 2001 purchased American Water Works, the largest water company in the United States, for $USB4.6. In addition to becoming global, RWE is also attempting to become a multiutility company, but current U.S. law prevents the company from moving into gas or electricity.
>
> Interbrew, the Belgian brewer, was ordered by the U.K. government to sell Carling, Britain's most popular beer, as the price for the approval of the £B2.3 ($USB3.5) takeover of Bass Brewers. Carling was later bought by Adolph Coors, America's third-largest brewer for £B1.2.[6]

Another major area where government action affects firm strategy is the country's *taxation* regime. Corporate tax levels vary around the world; as a consequence, some firms have relocated their head office to such low-tax countries as Liechtenstein or Monaco. Another issue to consider is which income will be taxed in which country. U.S. firms are liable for U.S. tax on their worldwide income. The tax regime may also affect the repatriation of profits. Australia is attempting to renegotiate its joint tax arrangements with the United States, which currently applies a significant tax to profits earned in the United States by subsidiaries of Australian firms.

Germany has changed its tax system by removing any capital gains tax when companies sell their investments in other firms.[7] The impact of this has been small due to the decline in share markets, but it is expected to have greater impact in the future, when there could be a major reshaping of the German industrial landscape as shares in several of that nation's companies change hands.

In many countries, previously government-owned organizations such as airlines and utilities are being *privatized* and joining the private sector as governments adopt the view that private enterprise is more effective than government in promoting consumer welfare. This trend started in Europe in the 1980s and is now occurring even in such previously unlikely countries as the People's Republic of China (PRC). This trend has been aided by political change, such as the collapse of communism in the Soviet Union and Eastern Europe.[8]

Countries are increasingly entering into *multinational* agreements through bodies such as the World Trade Organization (WTO), the International Monetary Fund, and the United Nations. After many years, China has finally been admitted to the WTO despite the fact that this opens up many of its inefficient state-owned enterprises to global competition. In Europe, the European Union is taking on increasing importance as individual nation-state members are subject to its regulations, while many other countries have joined together to form economic and political unions, as shown in Table 3.2.

Looking forward in the political arena, we expect further attempts to increase economic cooperation as the world economy becomes ever more tightly integrated. There is a risk that the world may be moving toward a structure of regional trading blocs, as shown above, and that economic warfare might break out between the blocs. Most analysts consider this unlikely, but it is a scenario that prudent global managers should consider, particularly as they expand global sourcing. The ability of individual national governments to pursue independent economic policies has undoubtedly been limited by increased economic interdependency and emerging international institutions.

The *political stability* of a country is an important issue when considering investment decisions. In the recent past there has been considerable instability in such countries as Argentina (defaulted on its international debt), Yugoslavia (has split up into several independent countries), and the Middle East (affected by war and terrorism).

TABLE 3.2   Regional Trading Blocks

Asean	Brunei Darussalam, Indonesia, Laos, Malaysia, Myanmar, the Philippines, Singapore, Thailand, Vietnam
European Union	Austria,° Belgium,° Cyprus, Denmark, Estonia, Finland,° France,° Germany,° Greece,° Ireland,° Hungary, Latvia, Lithuania, Malta, Poland, Slovakia, Slovenia, Czech Republic, Italy,° Luxembourg,° Portugal,° Spain,° Sweden, the Netherlands,° United Kingdom
NAFTA	Canada, Chile, Mexico, United States
Mercosur	Argentina, Brazil, Paraguay, Uruguay

° = euro currency.

Economic

For most products, market attractiveness is strongly influenced by the size and growth of demand, which in turn is influenced by the country's economic well-being. There are a number of economic variables that may be relevant in determining opportunities, as shown in Table 3.3. Many related measures of economic well-being are available, but critical metrics include total *GDP* as well as per-capita measures such as *GDP per capita* and disposable income per capita. In addition, since we are interested in the future, we would also be concerned with the *growth rates* of these economic variables. China is an attractive market for many firms not because its GDP per capita is high but because its growth rate is high and it is expected to become a major market in the future.

With increasing globalization and interconnectedness among countries, the effects of an economic downturn in one country are no longer confined to that country alone. During the late 1990s, after having enjoyed strong economic growth for many years, such "Asian Tigers" as Indonesia, South Korea, and Thailand suffered recessions and unstable financial markets that reverberated around the world.

Of equal importance to strategists is not only the mean *per-capita* income but also its distribution across the population. In India, although average incomes are still quite low, there is a large middle class, estimated at over 200 million people, representing a significant market opportunity for quite sophisticated products. Major PRC conurbations such as Shanghai and Beijing provide similar opportunities.

The economic development of China has exerted significant pressure on the rest of the world, particularly since China has average manufacturing labor costs of $US0.6 per hour. Along with European and U.S. companies, Asian firms are also establishing production facilities in China. Half the information technology products of Taiwanese firms are currently made in China. This movement has resulted in many Asian firms attempting to change their position in the value chain. Manufacturing is outsourced to China, and Asian firms are attempting to concentrate on marketing, design and innovation, development of differentiation and brand image, and intangibles.[9]

For global firms, *exchange-rate* movements can have a major effect on profitability and costs. A resources company may find that its revenues are in U.S. dollars but its costs are in South African rand. Changes in the exchange rate can have a major impact on profitability unless the firm takes some hedging action. Firms use a range of derivatives, such as currency swaps, to attempt to reduce risk, as we discuss later in the book.

The European Union, the most advanced grouping of nations, introduced a single currency, the euro, in 12 member countries on January 1, 2001. For the first time, Euro-

TABLE 3.3 Selected Economic Variables

GDP, GDP per capita
Disposable income
Interest rates
Exchange rates
Inflation
Unemployment
Balance of payments
Savings rate
Capital productivity
Labor cost and productivity

pean consumers will be able to directly compare prices in different countries without having to worry about exchange rates. At the same time, firms will find it easier to assess the performance of subsidiaries operating in different countries, since they now all use the same currency. For example, a Dutch business such as Philips can more easily assess the financial performance of its Italian subsidiary, which now reports in euros. This common currency places restrictions on the member states, since if a member country faces economic difficulties, it is limited in the extent to which it can use exchange rates or interest rates in monetary policy.

These economic variables have to be treated holistically. For example, in 2002 there was concern about the sustainability of the U.S. economy and whether the United States was moving into recession at the same time that its trade deficit reached the unsustainable value of 5% of GDP, possibly plunging the world into a period of economic instability. Given the uncertainty about the future performance of the U.S. economy, together with the lack of transparency in audited accounting data of U.S. firms, it was feared that foreigners would no longer be prepared to support this trade deficit with inward investment.[10] Not only were foreigners investing less in U.S. shares; acquisitions of U.S. firms by foreign companies also slowed, reflecting concern about the future of the U.S. economy. As a result of these trends, there was significant fall in the value of the U.S. dollar.

Sociocultural

Strategy will also be influenced by changes in a number of sociocultural variables, as indicated in Table 3.4. *Culture* can be defined as "the distinctive customs, achievements, products, outlook, etc. of a society or group; the way of life of a society or group."[11] The society or group may be the inhabitants of a nation state, such as Chile; a geographic region within a nation state, such as the South or the Midwest in the United States; a geographic region encompassing multiple nation-states, such as the Hispanic countries; or a people without regard to geographic location, such as the Armenian, Jewish, and Chinese diasporas. Furthermore, a single individual may belong to multiple groups, each having different cultures, such as Turkish immigrants domiciled in Germany.

Cultures differ from one another on many bases, such as language, religion, values and attitudes, education, social organization, technical and material culture, politics, law, and aesthetics. They also change over time. Furthermore, within any individual cultural group, subcultures develop that may reflect both the broad group culture but also specific subcultural elements, such as baby-boomers and Generations X and Y.[12] The buying behaviors of these different cultural groups vary significantly. In Western families,

TABLE 3.4   Selected Sociocultural Variables

Culture
Population size and growth
Population age and ethnic mix
Lifestyle changes
Social mobility
Educational levels
Labor market participation rates
Religion
Attitudes toward technology

TABLE 3.5   Median Age by Country

Country	Median Age, 2000	Median Age, 2040
Australia	35.2	42.0
Japan	41.2	53.0
Niger	15.1	18.3
Spain	37.7	54.6
United States	35.5	41.0

Source: "UN Population Statistics": www.un.org.

for example, women traditionally did the shopping for many products and services, whereas in rural Bangladesh, men do the shopping.

Population size, growth, and *distribution* must also be analyzed. Significant strains may result from such demographic shifts. One of the best known is the impact on social security systems as birth rates drop, longevity increases, and the number of older beneficiaries rises relative to the number of contributors. Not only does this change raise possibly divisive strains; it has significant economic and political ramifications. As shown in Table 3.5, the median age in many countries is forecast to increase dramatically, raising the possibility of a crisis in social security systems. Indeed, some countries are considering raising their immigration rate to reduce the median age. In other countries, a growing proportion of the older population have private pension arrangements, which will ameliorate the state-funded pension problem. In turn, these demographic changes create new opportunities and relationships for insurance and mutual funds.

Other socioeconomic changes that may need to be analyzed are *lifestyle* changes, such as the increasing sophistication of customers, higher levels of education, better access to information, and a greater acceptance of and familiarity with technology. The advance of automation and information-based industries typically leads to (relatively) decreased demand for unskilled labor and increases in demand for highly skilled technical and professional labor. The net result is larger income differentials within societies, differentials that carry a number of social implications, such as permanent unemployment of those individuals who cannot cope with the modern knowledge-based society. Another component of these changes is the shifting attitude toward *globalization* and the tension between localism and globalism. On the one hand, individual groups both seek their own identities and act out their group membership in various ways. Important bases for group membership include religion and nationalism. Thus the growth of Muslim and Hindu fundamentalism is an important factor in the Middle East/North Africa and India. In such diverse areas as Turkey, Wales, the Basque country of Spain, and Brittany in France, these local and regional pressures are evident.

Concern has been raised about American influence—and Western influence in general—in many countries. The French government is fighting what some regard as a rearguard action against what it views as an American cultural invasion in general and an anglicizing of the French language in particular. However, concern is not limited to language. In late 1999, protests in many European countries against genetically modified foods led to rejections of and/or bans on Monsanto's Roundup Ready soybean seeds. In August 1999, several McDonald's franchises in Belgium and France were badly damaged or destroyed by protesters angry about the "globalization of food." Protesters angry at the impact of globalization have disrupted several WTO meetings. Malaysia and other Asian countries have also expressed concern at the "Westernization" of their societies and have issued calls for a return to Asian values.

To a large extent people don't notice culture on a day-by-day basis, but it becomes very evident when they encounter different cultures as firms move from domestic into foreign markets. Here, the issue is less one of cultural change than it is of attempting to understand a culture that is different. Companies acting in an ethnocentric manner may ruin an otherwise successful strategy implementation.

Technological

Virtually all observers of the business scene agree that not only is the pace of technological change extremely fast; it is accelerating. If we were to arbitrarily select the end of World War II as a start date, we would find that many of the products and services we take for granted today have been developed since that time. A partial list includes color television, dry copier machines, synthetic fibers and almost all plastics, cellular telephones, computers, integrated circuits, microwave ovens, passenger jet aircraft, communication satellites, virtually all antibiotics and numerous other life-saving drugs, ATMs, space travel, video and audio tape recorders, and CDs and DVDs. Many of these innovations represented disruptive technological change that fundamentally restructured industries. Some technological variables are shown in Table 3.6.

Information technology is having a pervasive impact on firms and their strategies, driven by the rapid and continuing reductions in price of these products. This rapid decline in costs is well expressed by **Moore's law**—that the number of transistors on a computer chip doubles every 18 to 24 months and thus that the speed of microprocessors, at constant cost, also doubles every 18 to 24 months. Although some observers anticipate that exponential gains in chip performance will eventually slow down, most experts agree that Moore's law will govern the industry for at least another 10 years. Intel has reportedly developed a chip with a speed of 10 gigahertz at room temperature, which is a major improvement over current (2002) speeds of 2.2 gigahertz. Other technological developments have resulted in faster processing speeds as well as and reduced heat and power consumption.[13]

Moore's law means that computing power will become ever faster and cheaper. Not only will increasing numbers of people around the world have access to powerful computing, but computer power will be built into devices other than computers themselves. Already, computers allow such diverse products as vehicles, aircraft, surgical equipment, and elevators to operate more efficiently, predictably, and safely. In the future we may even see computer chips in packaging as costs continue to decline.[14] These applications reflect the effects of the convergence of computing, communications, and

---

TABLE 3.6   Selected Technological Variables

Information technology
R&D spending
New products
New technology
Global technology transfer
Technological advantages of a country
The Internet
Incremental and disruptive technologies
Biotechnology

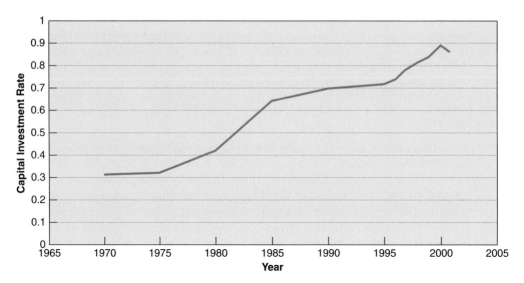

Figure 3.5 Ratio of IT Investment to All Other Investment by U.S. Firms

"Fixed Assets Tables, Table 2.7, Historical-Cost Investment in Private Fixed Assets," Bureau of Economic Analysis, 2002. www.bea.doc.gov.

media technologies as well as the growth of the knowledge economy, a topic to which we will return in Chapter 5.

The changes above are illustrative of the impact that information technology is having on business practices. This impact is also manifest in the changing mix of capital investment. As shown in Figure 3.5, U.S. firms have been allocating an increasing proportion of their capital expenditure to information technology, computer hardware and software, and communications equipment. This chart shows the proportion of investment in information-processing equipment and software to investment in all other fixed assets by U.S. businesses over the period 1970–2001. As can be seen, this ratio has increased dramatically, from 31.7% in 1970 to 85.4% in 2001, although there was a slight reduction in 2000 due to 1999 overspending in anticipation of Y2K. In dollar terms, IT investment has increased from $USB16 in 1970 to $B403 in 2001.

The Internet is a major new technology affecting the business landscape. The Internet is, or can be, many things. It is a distribution channel, a communications tool, a marketplace, and an information system. For example, it can alter the way in which the firm communicates with its customers and suppliers, the way in which it collects customer data, and the amount of information available to customers. We have already noted that firms are created because the costs of organizing and maintaining them are lower than transaction costs in the market. One of the implications of developments in computers, networks, communications, and data storage is that they have changed transactions costs and hence are opening up the possibility of significant industry restructuring. These developments may also create **disintermediation,** which means that the function of an intermediary can be dispensed with. When buyers and sellers of, say, insurance, can find each other easily over the Internet, who needs intermediaries such as brokers?

These changes are most likely to occur in industries where "products" can be digitized, among which are personal financial services. Table 3.7 shows the average cost per transaction in retail banking for five different modes. As the data indicate, there is a substantial incentive for retail banks to move to other channels of distribution, but they are

TABLE 3.7   Average Cost per Transaction in Retail Banking

Mode	Cost/Transaction ($AU)
In Branch Teller	5.40
Telephone; Customer Service Officer	5.20
ATM (Excluding Deposits)	0.60
Telephone; Voice Response	0.16
Internet	0.06

Source: Internal Costing Data; Major Australian Bank

constrained by their legacy assets of a branch network. A new entrant without this high-cost structure may find barriers to entry have been reduced, the new barrier being technology, customer acceptance of technology, and data security. Similar developments have occurred in industries such as hotels, car rentals, and share trading, where online trading now accounts for about 20% of all trades.

The Internet is an example of **Metcalfe's law,** namely that the value of a network to an individual user is proportional to the square of the number of users. Hence the interest in interconnection, open standards, and the development of new protocols such as XML, which carries information on what data are being transmitted as well as the format of that data. At the same time, the Internet has increased firms' concern with data security from external hackers or internal staff abusing the system. Data security is seen as a major obstacle to the widespread adoption of e-commerce, and developments in sophisticated encryption systems will be critical.

Major changes can also be expected in **electronic markets,** either business-to-business (B2B) or business-to-consumer (B2C), where firms interact with actual and potential customers and suppliers over the Internet. Such electronic markets are estimated to capture cost savings of 10% to 20%, but they also possess other benefits. Sellers can reach more customers, gather better data, and communicate more effectively. Buyers are able to compare products and prices from different suppliers, which may increase price competition between suppliers. Underlying all this is the capacity to reduce costs through better information and better systems. In the United States, the ratio of inventories to shipments across the economy has fallen from 2.0 in 1970 to about 1.2 in 2000, representing a huge increase in capital productivity.[15] Firms unable to achieve such improvements operate at a considerable disadvantage.

While future developments of these exchanges is uncertain, it is expected that they will grow in scope and importance, driven by developments in information technology and its cost-reducing potential. At the same time, we expect to see a range of structural forms of these exchanges. Some are likely to be vertical, with all members in a single industry. In the United States, Ford, GM, and DaimlerChrysler formed such an exchange with combined purchases of $USB240. The basic aim was to reduce costs in the supply chain, while forcing down supplier prices.[16] Others will be horizontal, based on products that span several industries. These exchanges will certainly be scrutinized by regulators to ensure that firms do not engage in anticompetitive behavior.

Many technological innovations are characterized by nonlinear growth patterns and often follow a logistics adoption curve. Managers who project initially low growth rates into the future may be surprised as inflection points are passed and rapid growth occurs.[17] As Christensen has noted, technological change can be categorized as sustaining or disruptive.[18] **Sustaining** technologies improve the performance of established products along the dimensions that mainstream customers in major markets have historically valued. This type of technological change rarely precipitates the failure of established firms—it represents a continuation of the present and is seen as more controllable by management.

Disruptive technologies are those that bring a new and very different value proposition to the customer. One such example is digital cameras; another is discount brokerage. Such products have features that are highly valued (initially) by a limited number of customers, often customers new to the market. These new products are often seen as inferior by existing customers, initially underperforming in comparison with established products, but they are often simpler, smaller, cheaper, and easier to use than existing products. In new applications, these attributes may have significant value. Such disruptive technology may precipitate the failure of leading firms since they pay too much attention to the issue of cannibalization of their existing products. The real problem often arises from their lack of awareness of the rate of technological change in, and consequent functional improvement of, the new technology. Since it is difficult to analyze such markets, established and bureaucratic firms are unlikely to give them the attention they require.

Business history is also replete with examples of major companies that turned down inventions that were ultimately extremely successful. Chester Carlson, inventor of xerography, was turned down by IBM, RCA, A. B. Dick, and many other companies before Joe Wilson, CEO of a relatively small Rochester company, Haloid Corporation, had the courage to bet the future of his company on Carlson's invention.[19]

All major appliance manufacturers turned down James Dyson, inventor of the bagless vacuum cleaner, when he approached them with his invention. He eventually started his own company, which by 2001 was the market leader in the United Kingdom and in 2002 entered the U.S. market.[20]

Legal

As we saw in the opening example, global firms must pay considerable attention to legal considerations and ensure that their strategies comply with legal requirements, as illustrated in Table 3.8.

The *legal framework* of a country influences firm strategy through its laws regarding such areas as mergers and acquisitions, capital movements, industry regulation, and employment conditions. Legal frameworks differ across countries. The United States and the United Kingdom have well-developed legal systems based on precedence and case law. In most of Europe the basis of the legal system is the Napoleonic Code. Other countries such as Russia are still trying to develop a strong and independent legal system. Similarly the Peoples Republic of China is struggling to develop a commercial code, and the laws governing business activities are still in evolution.

Different countries have different views on the *social responsibility* of the firm. The EU is strengthening the obligation of European firms to "inform and consult" workers'

TABLE 3.8   Selected Legal Variables

Legal framework
Status of the rule of law
Regulatory framework
Trade practices
Consumer protection

representatives about company strategy, and the EU employment commissioner has suggested that staff are the main stakeholders in a firm. This may affect the ability of a firm to close a plant or reduce staff in the EU, as experienced by Marks and Spencer when it attempted to close several stores in continental Europe. Some managers regard these requirements as an infringement on the right to manage, since it will make labor markets less flexible. Proposed regulations include consultation about layoffs in all companies with 50 or more staff after 2008.[21]

Many developed countries have an active and politically independent *regulatory framework*. In the United States, bodies such as the Environmental Protection Agency (EPA), Securities and Exchange Commission (SEC), and Federal Trade Commission (FTC) are powerful actors that have to be considered when establishing strategy. During the decade up to 2001, Microsoft was under investigation by the U.S. Justice Department, with the final resolution being made in the court. In the EU, there are several directorates-general responsible for defined areas of regulation. There is a D-G Competition, a D-G Environment, and a D-G Health and Consumer Protection. The latter body is responsible for food labeling in general and labeling of genetically modified foods in particular.[22]

The investment banking and accounting industries in the United States are under considerable pressure from the Department of Justice and the Securities and Exchange Commission to change their practices. There is concern about conflict of interest: can an audit firm provide an audit that is unbiased and independent when it also engages in consulting work for the same client? Can an investment bank provide unbiased investment reports on a firm when it is also soliciting for consulting work, mergers, and acquisitions or IPOs with that same firm? In late 2002, we saw most of the large accounting firms split off their consulting business, with PWC selling its consulting business to IBM for $USB3.5.[23]

Some professional bodies also have a major impact on firm behavior. International accounting bodies are attempting to get firms to record all financial assets and liabilities at their current market value rather than at their historical cost, since financial markets are now more volatile. This would have major implications for banks. The value of loans would fluctuate with changes in interest rates, and banks could be forced to write down loans if their credit quality was reduced. These changes would have to be incorporated into the bank's income statement, possibly producing a large accounting loss.

Looking at likely future trends, we believe that countries are likely to maintain policies that lead to competition in product markets. On the other hand, in such areas as health and safely, the environment, rights of various minorities, and so on, it seems likely that firms will face more stringent standards in the future. For example, the British government is considering mandatory paid paternity leave for fathers. Further, globalization is beginning to have significant repercussions on the legal environment. The U.S. FTC prevented the takeover of a British firm, BOC, by a combination of L'Air Liquide (French) and Air Products (U.S.).

Environmental

Senior managers can expect to have to deal with a variety of environmental issues that may have significant impact on their companies' future prospects, as shown in Table 3.9. Executives in the automobile industry, for example, have been subject to increased pressure from governments, environmental groups, various single-issue advocacy groups, and the public at large. Indeed, the European Union has proposed that car manufacturers bear the cost of taking back scrap cars from 2003 onward and be required to recycle or

TABLE 3.9   Selected Environmental Variables

Environmental legislation
Nongovernment organizations
Social responsibility
Triple bottom line

reuse 80% of a car's weight from 2005 onward. The industry and some governments—including those of Britain, Spain, and Germany—have resisted this proposal. Their counterproposal is that car manufacturers should bear such a cost, but only for new cars sold after the law is finally passed.

Some firms, such as BP, are committed to reducing their impact on the environment; in fact, their stated goal is to do no damage to the environment. In pursuit of this goal, BP claims their verified greenhouse gas emissions were 10% lower in 2001 than in 1990.[24]

Changes in the physical environment, roughly viewed as comprising the natural and man-made environment, affect our daily lives and the functioning of our organizations. Natural and man-made forces coexist in an uneasy equilibrium but whereas some natural forces seem independent of human action, other changes in the natural environment result from it. More fundamental changes may have a variety of consequences. For example, heightened awareness of the damage to the natural environment caused by pollution has given rise to new industries such as pollution control and renewable energy. In countries such as France and Germany, pollution has become an important political issue and legislators are elected as members of "green" parties. Indeed, in many countries, the strength of the environmental movement has led to strong legislation affecting firms' production systems, products, and packaging. In Germany, firms are responsible for the disposal of packaging in which their products are shipped. Perhaps as a consequence, German consumers used 11% less packaging in 1995 than in 1991, while disposable packaging use in the United States grew by 13% over the same period.[25]

In response to these pressures, some individuals have proposed that business firms should adopt the concept of the *triple bottom line,* suggesting that the firm must pursue social, environmental, and economic objectives.[26]

Although the PESTLE approach makes the elements of a remote environment scan easy to remember, there is a potential danger. Many of the changes we have discussed are in fact interrelated. Such technological innovations as the computer or the World Wide Web have enormous sociocultural and political implications. Legal-regulatory decisions may have vital economic, environmental, and political dimensions, and so on. There is therefore a danger of overcompartmentalizing, when in fact the important changes in our time typically have multiple and interrelated effects. When planning strategy, you should never allow debates over "which box?" to impede an understanding of the potential impacts of expected changes—after all, that's what's important!

Global firms, by their very nature, need to be aware of these changes in the remote environment in every region of the world. In addition, a diversified firm will need to undertake such an analysis at several levels. It will need to understand the changes occurring that are important for the firm as a total entity, such as the admission of China and Taiwan to the WTO. At the same time, we reiterate that each of the individual business units will need to undertake a thorough analysis of its own remote environment. We have used a general approach to analysis, but the specific dimensions and tools used to understand changes will depend on the specific firm and business unit for which strategy is being developed.

3.3 THE INDUSTRY ENVIRONMENT

While the remote environment will have a major impact on the firm's strategy, our next level of analysis goes deeper, exploring the structural characteristics of the industry in which a business competes and the effect of these on strategy. Since global firms are likely to operate in a number of different industries, this level of analysis is more appropriate at the business-unit level. Corporate-level staff would be expected to undertake this analysis when exploring mergers and acquisitions or when setting performance standards for a business unit.

Figure 3.6 depicts our model of **industry structure,** where industry structure includes suppliers, buyers, entrants, and substitutes as well as direct competitors. The depiction is based on the work of Michael Porter and is sometimes referred to as the five forces model.[27] The structural variables identified in the model affect all the firms in the industry, but not all firms will be affected equally. An industry analysis helps in understanding the power relationships among the players in the industry, which in turn influ-

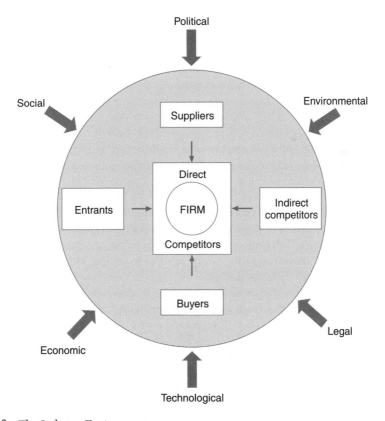

Figure 3.6 The Industry Environment

Adapted with permission of The Free Press, a Division of Simon & Schuster Adult Publishing Group, from *Competitive Strategy: Techniques for Analyzing Industries and Competitors* by Michael E. Porter, Copyright © 1980, 1998 by The Free Press. All rights reserved.

ence current and future levels of prices, investment in the industry, and firm profitability. Such an analysis may also assist the firm in choosing a basis for competitive advantage that capitalizes on opportunities or mitigates problems. As shown in Figure 3.6 the structural factors are generally grouped into five categories, and we now review each of these.

First is the pressure from *direct competitors,* or, to use another phrase, the competitive intensity of the industry. If intensity is high, profitability of firms in the industry is likely to be low. For example, a combination of slow growth and excess capacity is likely to produce lower margins, particularly if this is coupled with high exit barriers. The second factor influencing industry profitability is the ease of entry of new competitors. Industry profitability is likely to be low when *entry barriers* are low—when it is easy for competitors to enter and compete. Barriers to entry include the capital required to enter as well as nonfinancial barriers such as access to distribution channels, knowledge, and economies of scale, as we discuss in later chapters. Low industry profitability itself can also be considered as a barrier to entry. When industry profitability is high, this acts as a signal to other firms—including potential competitors who may be operating in the same industry in different locales (so-called parallel competitors)—to enter our market. The spread of the multinational, resulting in today's global marketplace, is a consequence of this behavior. An important strategic implication from the above is that good profits are often a leading indicator of increased competition. Too often, good results cause firms to be less competitive, complacency rendering them vulnerable to new sources of competition. Economic theory also suggests that under conditions of oligopolistic competition, we should devote considerable effort to attaining deeper understanding of our competitors (current and potential) and their likely future course of action.

Profitable markets, however, do not just attract potential direct competitors, those who do business in the same way we do; they also attract *substitutes,* or indirect competitors, the third factor influencing industry profitability. These are competitors capable of meeting the same customer needs as our own business but which do so in a very different manner. Thus plastic bottles compete with aluminum cans for beverages, while digital cameras compete with traditional film cameras.

Substitutes often feature new technology that has basic quality and high cost early in its life cycle. This may cause incumbent firms to dismiss the threat posed by the substitute. Too often, incumbents ignore the potential for rapid technological advancement with the substitute, as is illustrated in Table 3.10, which shows the price and performance characteristics of a nonprofessional single-lens reflex digital camera produced by Canon. The prices of these cameras have declined rapidly over time (Canon's competitors would have followed a similar pattern). At the same time the functionality of these cameras has improved significantly, so picture quality, measured by the number of pixels, has increased almost fivefold.

The challenge for incumbents making traditional film-based cameras is to comprehend the rate of this technological change. The rate of technological change for their product is likely to be very slow, since the product is technologically mature. In 1995 it would have been difficult for these firms to understand that in just seven years the prices of the competing product would decline from ¥M1.98 to ¥M0.358 while functionality improved. Physical size and weight have declined at the same time as picture resolution has increased, and prices have fallen dramatically. Since these are salient characteristics influencing purchase, the value of the product to customers increased significantly over the time period.

This is a classic example of the well-known **S-curve** of technological change: improvements occur slowly at first, accelerate, and then slow down as the technology reaches its limit.[28] It may be difficult for executives in firms using traditional technology

TABLE 3.10   Price/Performance Characteristics of Canon Digital Camera

Model	Date Introduced	Price (¥)	Picture Resolution (megapixels)	Weight (grams)
EOS DCS 3	July 1995	1,980,000	1.3	1800°
EOS D 2000	March 1998	1,980,000	2.0	1650
EOS D 30	October 2000	358,000	3.25	780
EOS D 60	March 2002	358,000	6.3	780

° = with battery.

Source: "Canon Camera Museum," 2003: www.canon.com. Reproduced by permission of Canon.

(e.g., film-based cameras), for which technological improvements are gradual, to recognize the threat posed by a disruptive technology.

Without doubt, technological advance and deregulation have combined to vastly increase the threats posed by indirect competition. The probability that new indirect entrants will be successful is typically viewed as lower than that for parallel competitors, but the effects of their infrequent successes may be devastating. They provide examples of the low-probability, high-impact event against which it it so difficult to defend.

The other forces bearing on the firm act vertically. The fourth is the pressure from *suppliers* which is very much dependent on their importance to the firm. Sometimes this can be assessed in terms of the importance of the input product as a percentage of the firm's total costs. In other cases, suppliers can be critical for different reasons. They may add appeal for the firm's subsequent customers, or their product or service may be critical to the continuity of the customer firm's production processes. Whenever dependency is high, however, the supplier's bargaining power is enhanced, and this tends to be reflected in their margins vis-à-vis those of their customer, as well as other dimensions such as delivery time and flexibility.

Of course, as the power of suppliers rises, so does the threat of their forward integration down the channel of distribution into competition with the firm. This may occur via direct entry or acquisition. In other cases, the supplier may engage in promoting its brand directly to the firm's customers, raising the firm's switching costs as their customers' preferences move toward products incorporating the promoting supplier's products. Intel provides one of the best-known examples. Many of their customers that manufacture PCs have co-branded *Intel inside* on their own products, recognizing that their customers' brand associations should be favorable and lead to improved sales of their products, compared with those using other manufacturers' chips. Intel's advertising budget at the time of writing was over more than $USB1.

Very similar forces operate with respect to the final set of factors, the firm's relationship with its *immediate customers*. If the firm becomes dependent on a few large customers, its bargaining power is significantly diminished. These large customers will pressure for discounts, and their margins will usually benefit at the expense of the seller's. In the early 21st century, these battles are being actively fought between the suppliers to the major automobile firms and their customers, the auto firms. Automobile firms are very powerful customers that, when faced with overcapacity, declining market shares in the critical U.S. market, and large losses, were able to pressure horrified suppliers for price reductions of up to 15%.

Structural characteristics may significantly affect firm and industry profitability. For some industries, structural characteristics are such that almost no firm in the industry is able to make an adequate return, yet firms refuse to exit. For example, profitability in the paper industry worldwide is poor—and has been for many years. The international airline industry has also been a poor profit performer, and the devastating consequence of September 11, 2001, is likely to be that other airlines beyond Swiss Air, Ansett, and Sabena will fall into insolvency or be merged out of existence.

Industry Value Chain

Industry analysis of the type discussed above is incomplete since it neglects the dynamics of what we will call the **industry value chain**—the linked set of firms and the activities undertaken by those firms. Interindustry competition is increasingly common in today's world. In such cases competition can be seen as occurring between two complete industry value chains. Consider the beverage-packaging market, with two competing packaging systems: aluminum cans and plastic bottles. Figure 3.7 compares the industry value chain for each type of container.

Changes at any level of the value chain for aluminum cans influence the competitiveness of cans versus bottles. For example, aluminum smelting is a very energy-intensive process, using huge amounts of electricity. Any increase in electricity costs will obviously increase the cost of cans. On the other hand, feedstock for the plastic bottles is dependent on petrochemical prices, which will undoubtedly be influenced by the actions of the OPEC cartel. Currently, bottles made from polyethylene terephthalate (PET) have high levels of permeability, making them unsuitable for beverages such as beer. Should technological developments overcome this characteristic, the impact on the aluminum can industry is likely to be severe. Whether a firm is in the aluminum, plastics, or packaging industry, its managers should be monitoring changes at every level of the chain, not only for their own industry but also for those with which it competes in end-use markets and applications.

Profitability may also vary dramatically at each stage in this chain, depending on power relationships. This, in turn, may influence decisions on where to compete. Consider the case of Microsoft and Intel, which were the main beneficiaries of IBM's decision to

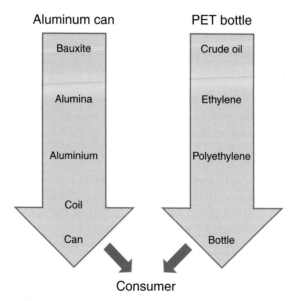

Figure 3.7   Industry Value Chain, Aluminum and Plastic Packaging

outsource the operating system and microprocessor in its personal computers. Their margins far exceeded the eventual meager leftovers that IBM received.

Industry value chains also allow us to examine disintermediation, where one level in the value chain is eliminated. The vast improvements in information technology and the advent of the Web have shifted the economics of direct marketing. As we have already noted, for information products such as airline tickets, disintermediation is quite widespread, as any ex–travel agent can attest.

Limitations of the Industry Model

Before moving on, we should note important limitations of the popular five forces model. First, it is predicated on the assumption that firms are *single-business single-industry* entities. Consequently, in a multibusiness firm the model is relevant only for an individual business unit. A firm such as du Pont has several business units, each of which competes in its own industry. But the corporation as an entity does not compete in an industry. The model of industry analysis can be applied only at the business-unit level, so its use is limited. Further, competition increasingly occurs among more or less formal alliances of firms or networks; again, the five forces model, with its concept of a clearly defined entity, is of little assistance in analyzing these cooperative/competitive conditions.

A second assumption is that we can define "an industry" with little difficulty. The mere fact that "substitutes" (indirect competitors) appear in the economic model suggests that the problem of defining "an industry" may be a little more difficult in reality. In the last part of the 20th century, some curious new words began to creep into the English language, terms such as *cosmeceuticals, edutainment,* and the like referred to in Chapter 1. Each of these words symbolizes the observation that the boundaries of an "industry" are indistinct, fuzzy, and often permeable. Where is the boundary between communications, entertainment, publishing, computing? Is Sony in competition with News Corporation? Anyone who has actually tried to define where one industry (or market) stops and another begins will testify that the problem is by no means as simple as it may at first sight appear. We are convinced that much innovation in fact occurs at the boundaries of what traditional players refer to as "the industry," with results that may be devastating for incumbents. Indeed, some specific innovations result from the juxtaposition and cross-fertilization of what were previously regarded as different industries.

Third, the model assumes that the *structure* of an industry has a major impact on the profitability of a business unit within that industry—in other words, that there are significant differences in profitability of business units across industries, resulting from structural differences between the industries. One study by Rumelt found that industry effects were actually quite small.[29] Other studies by Porter found more significant industry effects, although they did not use business-unit profitability as the dependent measure.[30] A more recent study found that firm-specific factors were more important than industry effects for industry leaders and laggards. For firms in the middle, neither dominant nor laggard, industry effects were important.[31] These researchers conclude that superior management works, irrespective of industry, while average management needs an attractive industry structure to be profitable. Perhaps we can conclude by saying that industry structure will have an impact—the presence of powerful customers, for example, normally depresses profitability, but it is not the only factor affecting business profitability.

Fourth, the model fails to convey the *dynamic* nature of most industries. Some industries are characterized by rapid changes in product innovation and rapidly escalating competition based on price-performance characteristics, with competitors attempting to establish first-mover advantages in both products and markets—a form of competition that has been referred to as hypercompetition.[32] Other industries, such as petroleum, steel, and cement, are characterized by relatively slow structural change. The automobile industry is going through a transition at the moment. Historically, firms such as Ford and General Motors built huge, vertically integrated systems that offered advantages through common ownership. Today, a different strategic pattern is developing. Both Ford and GM have announced that they plan to sell off their captive component suppliers—Delphi and Visteon, respectively. So the two firms are moving from hierarchy to market-based transactions—and expect to achieve cost and flexibility advantages.

It is vitally important that managers treat the structure of their industry as variable rather than fixed. The term *structural competition* was coined to capture the idea that today's senior manager must learn to think as much like an investment banker as an operating executive. Unless this game is played well, our firm may end up out in the cold, isolated by the structural moves of its competitors. Thus, to assist in developing strategy, we must concentrate on the dynamics: How will the industry look in the future? Will it remain attractive or should we consider exiting? As managers, it is essential to keep this future focus and not to regard the industry, its boundaries, or its structure as fixed.

Managers should also realize that industry structure is influenced by the firm's actions and that some strategic decisions are made to influence this structure. In the face of powerful buyers, suppliers may undertake horizontal mergers, increasing their power relative to buyers. Such mergers may also reduce competitive rivalry and move competition from a price to a nonprice basis, affecting average industry profitability. Faced with a powerful supplier possessing specialized assets, the firm may integrate backward to reduce the supplier's power.

Finally, the players that affect industry structure in the real world constitute a much more complex set than is portrayed in the simple five forces model. While some of these may be legitimately be viewed as among the external forces depicted in Figure 3.8, others belong inside the "magic circle." The issue of defining the scope of the players we should consider, and defining the boundaries of the industry, is the subject of the rest of this section.

Figure 3.8 portrays the complexity of the players involved in determining industry structure by showing examples of the entities that may influence that industry. We label as "allies" entities that may favorably influence structure. While these might be construed to include government agencies or regulators that could be viewed as influences in the remote environment, they also include those who benefit from our firm's activities even though they are not directly involved in its value chain. Inhabitants of local communities, businesses such as hotels and restaurants that benefit from their propinquity to the firm's facilities, and special-interest groups or non-governmental organizations (NGOs) might all conceivably constitute allied constituencies.

Just as some entities may support the firm's strategies, others oppose it. Union opposition is frequent when major changes of strategy threaten to disrupt the lives of union members, while those allied with the firm's competitors may have comparable influence. Further, trade bodies such as trade associations, professional associations, or technical groups may exert favorable or unfavorable influence. Finally, the growth of Internet access has made all firms vulnerable to the negative website phenomenon, where disgruntled employees, customers, and others may use "virtual organizations" to exert unfavorable influence.

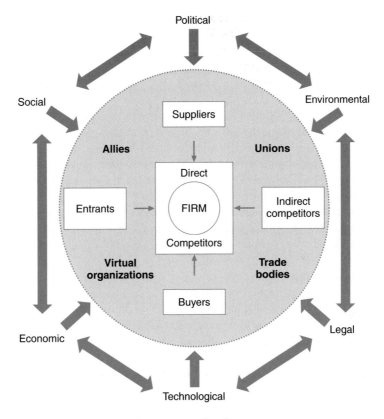

Figure 3.8 The Augmented Industry Environment

Figure 3.8 also indicates the importance of regarding "industry" boundaries as permeable by showing a dotted line rather than a solid line. Technology and deregulation are both powerful forces affecting the permeability of these boundaries. In many countries it was not so long ago that we had commercial banks, savings and loans (building societies), and insurance companies, but today the "financial services" nomenclature has become common as mutuals demutualize, building societies metamorphose into banks, and all scramble to develop an Internet presence.

Further, firms are moving away from a model of an independent entity with arm's-length transactional relationships with other firms. Instead, we now see the rise of network structures where firms work together to create a network of suppliers, distributors, other service providers, and customers. Value is created by the entire network, which also makes the concept of a rigid and well-defined industry somewhat questionable.

The moral that astute managers should draw from these examples is to keep their antennae tuned to the happenings at the periphery of what others regard as "the industry," for it is there that some of the most interesting and innovative competitive developments will occur.

3.4 THE BUSINESS-UNIT ENVIRONMENT

The final level of environmental analysis is undertaken to assess changes that could influence the position of the business unit relative to its competitors and the nature of its competitive advantage. The major focus is on identifying opportunities or problems resulting from changes in the competitive milieu and/or in customer requirements. This process should be seen as dynamic, creative, and opportunity-focused, based on sound analysis.

Customer Analysis

Customer analysis at the business-unit level involves developing a detailed understanding of customers, their needs and values, and how these needs may vary within a given market (market segmentation). In addition, emphasis must be on how these needs are changing and what the firm can do to introduce change to the marketplace. Growth comes not from doing the same thing as competitors; it comes from being creative, with the insight to understand the fundamental changes in the marketplace and how to respond to or create these. As with any analysis, the purpose is to understand—but more importantly, it is to identify the creative strategies that will generate value for the business.

Customer Value

Understanding the sources of customer value is a large and complex subject, better explored in a marketing course.[33] However, we should examine some of the basic issues involved in determining sources of value. One of the most important of these is understanding who the customer is. A broad perspective is vital, and we should therefore consider as a potential customer any person or organization involved in the channel of distribution or decision (other than competitors) whose actions can affect the purchase of the firm's products and services. This view recognizes that "customers" includes those who can influence the decision to purchase the firm's products and services, not just those who pay. We should also recognize that customers are always individuals, inasmuch as organizations do not make decisions; people in organizations make decisions. We also need to clearly understand the needs of customers as well as their dissatisfactions. Dissatisfactions may present opportunities to the business, an untapped market that it can exploit. Chapter 7 discusses measures of customer value.

Market Segmentation

Markets are characterized as comprising buyers, either individual or institutional, with different needs and requirements. Therefore meeting the needs of customers requires developing different types of offers, each focused on the needs of a defined segment. **Market segmentation** is the process of grouping together actual and potential customers whose needs are similar so that target segments can be selected and the appropriate marketing program designed. Particularly for industrial products, such segmentation requires a thorough understanding of customer economics, since such customers are likely to make purchases based primarily on economic criteria. One source of growth is identifying, and forcing if possible, the emergence of new segments. No method of segmentation will be perfect; there will always be some ambiguity. One possible test of successful segmentation is whether or not a competitor can have a profitable existence in the designated segment without being a competitor in a related segment. When this is possible, it suggests that there is little cost sharing between segments. Following segmentation, the firm should be able to do the following:

> Determine how to describe a market in terms of groups that demonstrate high within-group homogeneity and across-group heterogeneity
>
> Identify the needs and benefits required in each group

Determine which segments are attractive and how fast is the segment growing

Decide which segments to target and which competitive strategy to adopt for each targeted segment

Marketing theorists generally suggest that segments can be defined on the basis of one or more of the following characteristics:[34]

Geographic, such as country, region, or city size

Demographic, such as age, gender, firm size, firm profitability

Behavioral, such as use occasion, type of purchase situation

Social/psychological, such as personality, social class, organizational culture

Segmentation permits the firm to develop an offer that meets the needs of its chosen customers. It allows the firm to focus on those segments in which it has a competitive advantage and should permit greater differentiation of the offer and, consequently, better margins. Development of a competitive advantage can be achieved only with a detailed understanding of the market and its segments, since these characterize the variability in customer needs and values.

Since customer needs are constantly changing, the business unit will of necessity need to monitor and update its segmentation approach, both in terms of the basis for developing segments and the number and description of its chosen segments.

Segment growth also affects the ability of the firm to generate and sustain a competitive advantage. Rapidly growing segments typically exhibit increased turbulence, making share gain more feasible. Growing share in a very stable market is always going to be difficult. In a growing market there are new customers, new values, new needs and benefits required, and the possibility of designing products with different combinations of features—all of which may lead to rapid share gain if business-unit management has the foresight required to create the opportunity and build capabilities to exploit it.

When analyzing market segments, it may be useful to classify them as either a cost segment, a value segment, or a combination. In some market segments, there is relatively little variation in either the price charged or characteristics of the product or service. In these segments, customer choice will be based primarily on price considerations, with consequent implications for the competitive strategy of the business. Other segments may exhibit substantial variation in prices, with clear differences between the offerings of the various competitors, generally facilitated by strong differences in customer preferences between different offerings. In these market segments, price plays a lesser role, and the firm must develop a competitive strategy based on well-understood dimensions of customer value, In reality, most segments will be a combination of these two alternatives. The task of the business is to work out in which segments it can bring its capabilities to bear and to develop additional ones where worthwhile.

Customers often play different roles—such as gatekeeper, influencer, decision maker, buyer, and user—in a purchase process. Failure to understand these roles may preclude sufficient understanding of sources of value. Different customers will also have differing needs and wants, depending on sociocultural and situational factors, as well as differing roles in the purchasing process. There are clearly many ways to think about these needs and wants. However, considering three types of needs and wants—functional, psychological, and economic—provides a useful general framework for understanding the benefits delivered by a product or service. First, however, we must distinguish between features and benefits.

Features versus Benefits

In marketing a product or service, it is often critical to distinguish between features/attributes and benefits. Firms *produce and deliver* products and services but customers only *perceive* value in the benefits that these products and services provide. Some simple examples make this distinction clear. In its factories, Black and Decker manufactures electric drills whose features include color, drill speed, hardness of bit, drill bit gauge, drill weight, presence/absence of battery and battery life, ability to embrace other tools (e.g., sander), and so forth. For the most part, customers have little interest in these features per se; what concerns customers are the benefits offered by the drill, notably the holes it can make and the ease of making them. Similarly, retailers and wholesalers may care little for the specific products they sell; they are more interested in such benefits as net profit, sales per linear foot, and return on investment. Focus on benefits versus features has the important additional value of broadening the view of competition. To return to the Black and Decker example, when the focus of attention is on features, key competitors are other electric drill manufacturers. When the focus of attention is on benefits, the firm necessarily considers all other methods of making holes; for example, the substitutes or indirect competitors include nails, adhesives, water drills, and lasers, an important broadening of the competitive scope that prepares the firm for new forms of competition.

When considering the benefits offered by a product or service, it is useful to categorize these as functional, psychological, and economic.

Functional benefits serve a particular purpose, typically by allowing the individual, family, or organization to do something that needs to be done. They are generally concerned with such dimensions as performance level, performance reliability, time and place availability, accuracy, and ease of use. For example, food fulfils the function of satisfying hunger needs, disc brakes enable the car to stop, and a word-processing program eases the student's pain in writing an assignment.

Psychological benefits typically make people feel good in terms of such dimensions as status, affiliation, reassurance, reduced risk by not changing suppliers, security, and scarcity. These benefits may be associated with functional benefits but are different in kind. For example, in addition to the quality of the food, fine restaurants offer such benefits as perceived prestige and ambience; certain models and brands of automobiles offer status in addition to functional comfort and transportation benefits. Louis Vuitton products offer gift buyers a risk-reduction benefit and the near certainty that their gift will be appreciated.

With **economic benefits** the focus is on economic aspects of the purchase, such as price, cost savings, credit terms, and profits; some customers maintain that these are the only benefits that matter. Indeed, for many intermediaries such as wholesalers, distributors, and retailers, the core benefit from the purchase of goods for resale is the profit made on the spread between selling and buying prices.[35] For other types of customer, the economic aspect of the purchase is one of several benefits. In general, customers prefer to pay less rather than more for the functional and psychological benefits they receive because, as economists point out, this maximizes their utility. However, for some goods and services, customers may actually *prefer* higher prices because these bring psychological benefits such as status and prestige, as with designer brands and Rolex watches.

In many cases purchase decisions obviously involve a combination of motives, but failure to appreciate these, and the priorities placed upon them by different customers, may lead to inappropriate decisions with respect to value-chain modification. Chapter 7 presents frameworks for integrating consideration of value and cost in making business strategy decisions. In particular, we will discuss how these concepts can be integrated to develop the competitive strategy of the business unit.

Analyzing Competitors

Most competitor analysis is undertaken at the business-unit level. In undertaking to analyze specific competitors, we are making an implicit assumption that the unit in question is engaged in oligopolistic competition since under perfect competition there would be no purpose in the exercise. There is a defined process that we should follow in conducting a competitor analysis, the stages in which are shown in Figure 3.9.

Since the best competitive strategies are typically preemptive, identification is a very important stage that should encompass not only the competitors we must deal with today but also those that could represent a threat tomorrow. Further, we should define a competitor as any entity capable of meeting the same set of customer requirements as those that we intend to meet. Thus, in attempting to identify competitors, we should also consider substitutes, or indirect competitors. Whereas in day-to-day decision making actual direct competitors are likely to dominate in our thinking, the key to longer-term ownership of market positions is to anticipate potential competitors. Remember that microeconomics tells us that economic profits will inevitably attract competitors. Thus, we can argue that good profit performance is a leading indicator of increased competition. The old saying that an ounce of prevention is worth a ton of cure has much merit when developing competitive strategy!

Once competitors have been identified, we typically will have to target those that we believe represent the greatest challenge to us, that is, those that are most likely to prevent us from achieving our goals. Key to making this decision well is the ability to understand the world from the perspective of the competitor, for seen through the competitor's eyes, the world will look very different. If we are unable to do this, we are unlikely to be very successful in plotting competitive strategies.

Profiling competitors involves collecting a variety of information that will help us understand them better. As we noted, the prime focus of competitor analysis is typically at the business-unit level, but in Figure 3.10, we have illustrated the types of information about a competitor that might be collected at different levels.

Analyzing competitor information may employ a variety of techniques, such as analysis of resources and competences (see Chapter 5), assessment of financial capabilities (see Chapter 4), portfolio analysis (see Chapter 8), and close examination of the competitors' value chains (see Chapter 7). Yet without the ability to integrate the information and recognize underlying patterns, little that is useful will result.[36] Skill in pattern recognition is

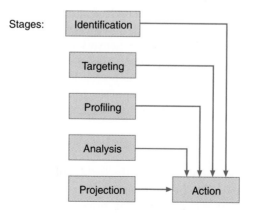

Figure 3.9 Process for Competitor Analysis.
Copyright: Christian and Hulbert, 1998.

Level of analysis	Financial performance	Portfolio	Functional strengths, weaknesses	Management capabilities, proclivities	Degree of vertical integration	Business system	Market performance	Positioning	Marketing mix
Corporate	✓	✓	✓	✓					
Business unit	✓	✓	✓	✓	✓	✓	✓		
Product-market	✓	✓	✓	✓	✓	✓	✓	✓	✓

Figure 3.10   Types of Competitive Information at Different Levels

one of the key requirements for good analysts, whether they work for the CIA or a global company. The difficulty was long ago acknowledged by Sun Tzu, the ancient Chinese strategist and author of *The Art of War* (ca. 500 B.C.), who explained it thus:

All men see the tactics whereby I conquer, but none see the strategy out of which victory evolved.

As the above discussion suggests, there can be no absolute certainty in competitor analysis. Nonetheless, the outcome of the work should be a number of likely projected scenarios, which are then fed into the planning of our strategy. Our strategy should be tested against these scenarios, seeking options that are likely to prove robust regardless of competitive actions. One of the most unimaginative, and often dangerous, competitive moves is simply to ape the actions (anticipated or otherwise) of a competitor. As global competition intensifies, attrition will ensure that, on average, the survivors are smarter and more adaptable than their failed predecessors. They will therefore be building strategies that capitalize upon their own distinctive competences. To imitate is tantamount to letting the competitor choose the weapons and the battlefield, a violation of a most basic principle of strategy.

3.5 MULTI-INDUSTRY COMPETITION

Much of our recent discussion has implicitly assumed that competition takes place among single-industry firms. Indeed, much of Chapter 7 will assume this context. Yet, as we noted earlier, in many industries, understanding competition and competitive strategy is a much more complex task than is implied by the industry model. We distinguish a minimum of four levels of competition: network-to-network, company-to-company, business-to-business, and product-to-product. The last is a market level of competition with which we will not concern ourselves in this book, while business-to-business competition will be dealt with in Chapter 7. In this chapter we conclude by briefly examining the issues raised by network-to-network and company-to-company levels of competition.

Network Competition

In response to rapid change and the increasing cost of business and product development, more and more firms are moving to organize themselves as **network competitors.** Other factors have assisted in precipitating this change. One, as noted earlier, appears to be a desire to variate fixed costs by more outsourcing. As markets become more competitive globally, retaining internally less-than-world-class activities obviously becomes less viable, and outsourcing typically results in networked relationships with suppliers. Firms find it increasingly difficult to be at world's best practice in all their activities, and competition forces them to outsource their poorly performing activities. The quality movement has contributed to a drop in the number of suppliers, as the buying firm becomes more demanding in seeking reliable quality and a relationship model prevails over the traditional bid-based transaction model. As firms globalize their activities, they also tend to seek global support, and suppliers that do not operate worldwide must enter into alliances and networks to maintain their business position. Finally, attempts to improve supply-chain efficiency and minimize working capital, again fostered by ever more competitive markets, result in closer, networked relationships among firms, which must cooperate in sharing information to derive benefit from the arrangement.

Rather than depict the firm's organization structure in the normal fashion, we might consider thinking about the network organization as member of a web of interrelationships, as depicted in Figure 3.11. Bluetooth is a development, led by Ericsson, to develop wireless technology with applications to computers and cell phones. Such wireless technology could potentially revolutionize personal connectivity, eliminating the need for wired connections. Bluetooth is a specification for low-cost radio links among cell phones, hand-held computers, and other communication devices, including the Internet, over short distances without the need for cable. It is designed for low-powered short-range operation between devices, and it costs some $20–$30 to install on a computer. This technology is beyond the capabilities of any single firm, and Ericsson has established a network of firms—including IBM, Intel, Microsoft, Motorola, Nokia, Toshiba, Agere, and 3Com—and more than 2000 associate firms to develop the required technology and applications.

This network of firms is itself in competition with another technology, and it is yet unclear which will be the winner. There are obviously large stakes involved, so first-mover advantages and standards will be critical. The second technology is currently denoted as Wi-Fi, a protocol permitting laptop computers within range of a base station to access the Internet at high speeds without the need for a cable. Microsoft has been reported as betting on both developments—it is part of Bluetooth and it is supporting Wi-Fi in its Windows XP operating system. It will be interesting to see how this competition develops. Bluetooth may have other market opportunities as a wireless payment system in shops and as an electronic travel pass, where its ability to transmit signals via

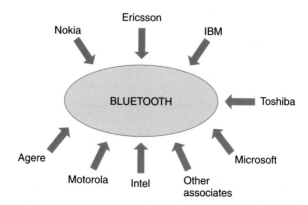

Figure 3.11   Network of Firms in Bluetooth
Source: "Bluetooth Membership," 2004: www.bluetooth.org.

short-range wireless would be an advantage.[37] There will certainly be competition between these two systems as each strives for dominance.

As Figure 3.11 indicates, the network model is by no means restricted to the firm and the suppliers with which it interacts in its now-deconstructed business system. Increasingly, erstwhile competitors are allying where they believe their joint interests are best served by such arrangements. Although Japan has long witnessed rivalry between major *keiretsu,* network-versus-network competition is fast growing elsewhere in the world. One of the most visible illustrations is provided by the airline industry. When the then CEO of British Airways (BA) first proposed an alliance with American Airlines, BA's major transatlantic competitor, he evidently failed to foresee the impact on American's major domestic competitor, United Airlines. United formed the Star Alliance, which has grown to be the biggest airline alliance in the world, subsuming a dozen airlines and more than 800 destinations. BA's One World alliance has also grown, but airlines not part of any such grouping are now desperately seeking partners, so successful has the Star Alliance become.

Corporate-Level Competition

Corporate-level competitors are perhaps best identified by assessing the overlap in their business portfolios. Shell and Exxon, GE and Siemens, Boeing and Airbus, GM and Ford are obviously corporate-level competitors because each pairing of companies competes in multiple businesses. Rolls Royce Aero Engines is an important business-level competitor for GE in its gas turbine business, but is not a key corporate-level competitor. The responsibility for competitor analysis and strategizing with respect to Rolls Royce would therefore lie at the business level within GE, although major strategic decisions with respect to its GE's aero engine business would rise to the corporate level.

Typically, targeting efforts in competitor analysis depend not only on the extent of the portfolio overlap but also on judgments about the intent of a particular competitor's management. This demands insight into both the competitor's capabilities and the intentions of its managers. Thus, while a typical corporate profile would involve gathering information about the competitor's financial performance, business portfolios, physical facilities, knowledge assets, functional strengths, and the like, it should also include gathering information and insight about the management of the targeted competitor.

◉ 3.6 SUMMARY

Sensing of the environment is key to strategic thinking. Broad environmental trends affect many industries and firms, including our own suppliers and our customers. Yet exposure to this external environment does not come of its own accord. Indeed, many of the admonitions to management, such as "sticking to the knitting" or "concentrating on core competences," create the danger of "cocooning," of insulating too many senior managers from the very forces that should be their preoccupation in strategy development.

We may overstate the case, but in most firms the pressures to focus internally far outweigh those that stress external focus. Of course, this is not an either–or problem; rather, it is essential to strike an appropriate balance. Most companies have at least some blinkers, whether operational or strategic. However the wise CEO will find ways to take off these blinkers, both individually and organizationally. We believe that such exposure is critical to creativity and innovation. To break the mold and come up with new paradigms requires an ability to separate one's thinking from the here and now. Activities such as encouraging people to go to external seminars (where they will meet people from other industries and firms), best-of-class benchmarking, and externally based measurement all help avoid the dreaded complacency that so quickly infests too many successful firms. The leader's task is to ensure that people don't get too comfortable, to maintain a state of organizational vigilance even when the firm appears to be successful.

We believe it is incumbent on managers to maintain an outward orientation toward the firm's environment, focusing on a realistic understanding of likely changes and their impact. Further, we must recognize that some change will be unpredictable and therefore balance focus and commitment with flexibility and responsiveness. The overarching need is to develop strategies that will be successful in the world of the future, not the world of the present.

REVIEW QUESTIONS

1. Why should a firm undertake a detailed analysis of its environment? Can the firm spend too many resources analyzing its environment?

2. "Since the world is changing rapidly and unpredictably, there is no value in attempting to undertake detailed analysis of the environment." How would you respond to this statement?

3. Select a firm with several business units. Which remote environmental variables, in your view, are important for the firm and for each business unit?

4. Give an example of a firm that appears to have failed to understand its changing environment. Can you provide reasons why this occurred?

5. Are any of the changes in the remote environment under the control of the management of the firm? If so, which?

6. Select an industry and review the factors that are affecting its profitability. Are the boundaries of this industry changing? If so, what is driving these changes? What is the likely structure of this industry in five years?

7. Does too much attention to direct competitors place the firm at risk? How?

8. Is the concept of an "industry" useful when so many firms are engaged in networks and outsourcing?

ENDNOTES

[1] D. Cameron and A. Hill, "Gecas at the Centre on Commission Concerns," *Financial Times*, June 29, 2001, p. 29.

[2] L. Downes and C. Mui, *Unleashing the Killer App: Digital Strategies for Market Dominance* (Boston: Harvard Business School Press, 1998).

[3] J. E. Hanke, D. W. Wichern, and A. G. Reitsch, *Business Forecasting* (Upper Saddle River, NJ: Prentice Hall, 2001).

[4] G. Ringland, *Scenario Planning: Managing for the Future* (New York: Wiley, 1998), pp. xi, 407.

[5] A. McCathie, "Berlin Breaks Ranks on EU Merger Law," *Australian Financial Review*, June 22, 2001, p. 28.

[6] "The World This Week," *The Economist*, January 5, 2002, p. 7.

[7] "Loosen Up or Lose Out," *The Economist*, December 7, 2002, p. 8.

[8] For a thoughtful discussion of the shift from government to market mechanisms, see D. Yergin and J. Stanislaw, *The Commanding Heights: The Battle between Government and the Marketplace That Is Remaking the Modern World* (New York: Simon & Schuster, 1998), p. 457.

[9] "Soaring Dragon, Busy Tigers," *The Economist,* April 27, 2002, pp. 63–64.

[10] G. Zucherman and C. Karmin, "Foreigners Disenchanted with US Stocks," *The Australian Financial Review,* May 21, 2002, p. 26.

[11] *The New Shorter Oxford English Dictionary* (Oxford, UK: Claredon, 1993).

[12] In the United States, Generation X comprises 17 million persons; Generation Y (echo boomers, the millennium generation) born between 1979 and 1994, comprises 60 million persons (versus 72 million baby boomers). E. Neuborne, "Generation Y: Today's Teens—The Biggest Bulge Since the Boomers—May Force Marketeers to Toss Their Old Tricks", *Business Week,* February 15, 1999, p. 80.

[13] J. Markoff, "The Increase in Chip Speeds Is Accelerating, Not Slowing," *New York Times,* February 4, 2002, p. C1.

[14] G. T. Ferguson, "Have Your Objects Call My Objects," *Harvard Business Review,* June 2002, pp. 138–144.

[15] "Let the Bad Times Roll," *The Economist,* April 7, 2001, pp. 65–66.

[16] "Seller Beware," *The Economist,* March 4, 2000, pp. 67–68.

[17] R. Foster, *Innovation: The Attacker's Advantage* (New York: Summit, 1986).

[18] C. M. Christensen, *The Innovator's Dilemma* (Boston: Harvard Business School Press, 1997).

[19] J. H. M. Dessauer, *My Years with Xerox: The Billions Nobody Wanted* (Garden City, NY: Doubleday, 1971).

[20] M. Rohrlich, "The Science of Suction Hits the Dirt," *New York Times,* August 29, 2002, p. F 1.

[21] "Inform, Consult, Impose," *The Economist,* June 16, 2001, p. 70.

[22] "Activities of the European Union", 2003, www.europa. eu.int/pol/index-en.htm.

[23] D. Crowe, "IBM's $6.4Bn Consulting Shake-Up," *Australian Financial Review,* August 1, 2002, p. 1.

[24] "BP Environmental and Social report", 2002, www. bp.com/envirsocial/index.asp.

[25] "Getting Green Dotted: The German Recycling Law Explained in Plain English," May 13, 2001. Raymond Communications, College Park, MD: www.raymond.com/library/news/227-1.html.

[26] J. Elkington, *Cannibals with Forks: The Triple Bottom of 21st Century Business* (Oxford, UK: Capstone, 1997).

[27] M. E. Porter, *Competitive Strategy* (New York: Free Press, 1980).

[28] Foster, *Innovation.*

[29] R. P. Rumelt, "How Much Does Industry Matter," *Strategic Management Journal* 12, no. 3 (1991), pp. 167–186.

[30] A. McGahan and M. E. Porter, "How Much Does Industry Matter, Really?," *Strategic Management Journal* 18 (*special issue*) (1997), pp. 15–30.

[31] G. Hawawini, V. Subramanian, and P. Verdin, *Is Profitability Driven by Industry- or Firm-Specific Factors? A New Look at the Evidence* (Fontainbleau, France: INSEAD, 2000).

[32] R. A. D'Aveni, *Hyper-Competition* (New York: Free Press, 1994).

[33] N. Capon and J. M. Hulbert, *Marketing Management in the 21st Century* (Upper Saddle River, NJ: Prentice Hall, 2001).

[34] Ibid.

[35] Of course, working capital–related issues such as inventory turns and time to pay are also important.

[36] J. A. Czepiel, *Competitive Marketing Strategy* (Englewood Cliffs, NJ: Prentice Hall, 1992).

[37] "Teething Trouble," *The Economist,* December 22, 2001, p. 78.

CHAPTER 4

Financial Markets

Learning Objectives

Upon completing this chapter, you should be able to:

- Understand the operations and actors involved in global financial markets
- Determine the value of a firm in the same manner as financial markets do
- Recognize the importance of senior management's responsibility in competing for investment funds in global financial markets
- Manage appropriate use of external funding to support firm strategy
- Supervise the use of derivatives to reduce risk

Table 4.1 shows the changes in the net debt levels of several global telecommunications companies during the late 1990s. The table shows that these telecommunication firms dramatically increased debt in the comparatively short time period of two years. They did this to obtain funds to purchase 3G (third-generation) licenses for cell phones in Europe. But this debt explosion had significant implications for their strategies, as financial markets subsequently pressured them to reduce debt levels. A rapid slowing of growth in existing markets exacerbated the problem, suggesting that the firms would have difficulty servicing their debt. Responses to these pressures varied among the companies. BT sold assets—in their case an interest in a Japanese joint venture (Yellow Pages Japan)—and subsequently floated their cellular operations, Cellnet, as MMO_2. AT&T witnessed a drop in its debt ratings, indicating the financial markets' concern with its ability to service its debt, and a consequent rise in the cost of debt. Partly to reduce debt, AT&T also tried to spin off a number of its constituent businesses. After a first half-year loss of $USB12 in 2002, the CEO of France Telecom was forced to retire. As of the time of writing, the board is attempting to raise $USB15 in new equity, which has put France Telecom's major shareholder, the French government, under pressure. They currently own 55% of the firm and thus would have to inject $USB8 in new capital, which could be seen as a state subsidy by the EU. On the other hand, selling down their investment would require a change in France's privatization laws and would be strongly resisted by unions.[1] At the time of writing, it is not clear how this impasse will be resolved.

4.1 INTRODUCTION

The example above underlines the importance of integrating all aspects of strategy and, in particular, ensuring that there is alignment between the financial position of the firm and its strategy. Financial markets, reflecting the interests of shareholders and debt

TABLE 4.1 Debt Levels of Selected Telecommunications Companies

Firm	Debt, End 1998 (€B)	Debt, End 2000 (€B)
AT&T	3	70
France Telecom	12	63
Deutsche Telecom	33	60
BT	2	50

Source: "The $250 Billion Gamble", p. 12 in "A Survey of Corporate Finance", *The Economist,* January 27, 2001.

holders, exert a strong influence on firm strategy. Decisions about the scope of the firm may be forced on the company by financial markets, without regard for the views of management. As happened with AT&T and the other firms described above, financial markets may require the firm to *divest* a business unit in order to reduce corporate debt levels, regardless of the apparent attractiveness of the unit. No firm is isolated from financial markets, and consequently it is critical that strategic managers have a deep understanding of these markets and of the relationship between financial markets and the strategic management of the firm.

To finance its operations, a firm can use either internally generated funds or external capital. Data on sources of funds indicate that global firms only generate 50% to 80% of the funds required for growth and innovation from internal sources (free cash flow from existing operations).[2] Most companies must therefore supplement their internally generated funds with external funds. In approaching financial markets for new debt or equity, managers must be aware of the demands and requirements of these markets. For example, if a company's debt has just been downgraded, new debt may be difficult to arrange. Or if there is turbulence in equity markets, new capital raising may be impossible, negating a variety of strategic options, including, for example, a proposed takeover.

Managers must also pay attention to the firm's **liquidity**—its ability to meet short-term financial responsibilities such as paying staff, suppliers, and debt holders. If the firm cannot meet such requirements, the directors must legally declare the firm insolvent and either they or the firm's creditors must then appoint an administrator. The administrator's responsibility is to run the business so that the needs of creditors are met first. Assets of the firm may be sold and the proceeds used to pay creditors, while other stakeholders such as customers, employees, and shareholders may receive little or nothing. In the United States, a special provision applies, namely Chapter 11, whereby the firm applies for insolvency but the existing managers retain control of the firm. A similar concept has been introduced in the United Kingdom.

The risk of insolvency is influenced by the firm's financial decisions, in particular the level of debt. If the firm is highly leveraged, interest payments as a proportion of cash flow will be high. Should product markets turn down and margins fall, cash flow and the ability to service debt deteriorate. Exchange-rate movements can similarly alter revenues and expenses quite dramatically, jeopardizing financial viability. These trends need to be understood and integrated with the firm's product market or business-level strategy.

At the same time, several factors are driving an increasingly competitive market for investment funds, which provides managers with additional alternatives. Financial markets have become global, and firms can raise funds in any market as the providers of funds see opportunities on a global basis. At the same time, these providers of funds assess investment opportunities globally, increasing the pressure on firms for performance.

Increasing deregulation of financial markets, as national governments remove restrictions on their operations, has further accelerated globalization. Due to technological developments, information about these markets is available in real time, while new financial products such as derivatives provide firms with many more choices for managing risk.

As is apparent from this discussion, financial markets determine the availability and cost of finance for the firm, and these in turn influence the firm's strategic options. The CEO and the board must be familiar with the operations of financial markets, the participants, and how they behave. In this chapter, we begin by clarifying the relationship between financial and product markets. We then explore financial markets in more depth, looking at both equity and debt markets. Next, we review cost of capital and methods of valuing the firm. Since CEOs are charged with maximizing shareholder value, these ideas are central to sound strategic management. Finally, we explain the role of derivatives in assisting in risk management.

⊚ 4.2 THE TWO MARKETS IN WHICH FIRMS COMPETE

Any large global firm can be considered as competing in two fundamentally different markets: *financial markets for debt and equity* and *product markets for customers*. Strategic management involves decisions about how to compete in both markets. This duality is represented in Figure 4.1. The ways of competing in these two markets are dramatically different, but in this chapter we focus on financial markets. Thus strategic management must address such questions as the following:

How will the strategy be financed?

What financial performance do these financial markets require?

How will financial risk be managed?

Competition in Financial Markets

Financial markets are where firms requiring funds for future investment come together with individuals and institutions with money to invest. At the corporate level, the firm competes for investment funds with other firms—and, indeed, with governments—in these global markets. If financial markets do not regard the firm as an attractive investment, it will be unable to raise the funds to secure its future. In this market, the interaction is solely with the corporate level of the firm, with the markets providing it with debt and equity funding.

Financial markets have grown in both complexity and importance over the last 25 years. In addition to debt, equity, and hybrid instruments such as convertible preference shares, a wide range of new financial products generally referred to as derivatives have emerged. These are investments whose value today, or at a future date, is derived from the value of an underlying asset. Managers now have many more choices regarding the nature, cost, and risk of an almost bewildering array of financial instruments. Strategic managers should be aware of the range and risks of these instruments.

Competition in Product Markets

The corporate level of the firm manages the collection of businesses that comprise its portfolio. Each business competes for customers in its respective **product market,** against other firms in the same or related industries. Through its parenting role, or through developing synergies and shared resources, the corporate level can influence results at the business level.

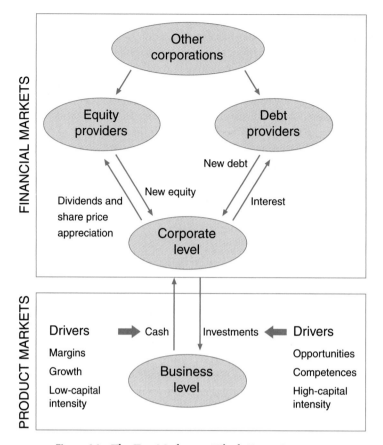

Figure 4.1 The Two Markets in Which Firms Compete

Relationship between the Two Markets

The funds raised at the corporate level are used to support the operations of the firm, which take place primarily at the business-unit level. Corporate management invests in a selection of business units depending broadly on the opportunities and costs of the business unit. The business units then may return net cash to the corporate level, with the magnitude of this cash flow being dependent on the margins, growth rate, investment intensity, and so on of the business unit. Corporate management uses these returns to pay external capital providers as well as to support innovation and growth.

Market for Corporate Control

Another form of competition at the corporate level is the market for **corporate control,** where different management groups vie for the right to manage the firm's assets.[3] The market for corporate control is the market for the buying and selling of companies or their components, as opposed to the market for products and services. This market is also referred to as the takeover market, both friendly and hostile—the latter being when the target firm's management resists the takeover.

Competition among management teams (and/or owners) for the right to manage a firm's resources limits divergence from shareholder wealth maximization by managers. Managers are assumed to act as agents for shareholders, but, as we discuss in Chapter 13, they do not always act in ways which maximize shareholder wealth.

The Managerial Challenge

Managing the relationship with financial markets is the responsibility of the CEO and the board, usually relying heavily on the advice of the CFO. As the opening example illustrates, financial markets put pressure on the firm for performance. Shareholders expect a return commensurate with the level of risk of their investment, while debt holders expect periodic interest payments.

We take it as a fundamental principle that a firm must create value, but what is meant by value depends on the perspective adopted. As we saw in Chapter 2, the firm has a variety of stakeholders and each defines value in different ways. Here, we extend that discussion and examine the concept of value from two perspectives, that of the firm and that of the shareholder.

Firm Value

We consider a firm to be primarily an economic entity. That entity creates value only when the revenue generated by the firm is greater than the costs incurred in producing it. In determining value, all costs must be considered, including the cost of the capital required to produce that revenue. Value defined in this manner is also called *economic profit* and is different from accounting profit. Economic profit includes explicit consideration of the cost of capital. We expect the firm to deliver a positive economic profit on an ongoing basis after all expenses, including tax and the cost of capital, have been included. When calculating accounting profit, a charge for depreciation is deducted, but this is not a capital charge per se; it is a period charge reflecting the decrease in the value of the fixed assets. We return to this topic, including how to measure economic profit, in Chapter 12.

Shareholder Value

From a shareholder perspective, the best measure of value is the **total return to shareholders:** share price appreciation plus dividends over a time period. However, since the current share price reflects expectations about the future, an individual shareholder may fail to get a return if market expectations change. Many shareholders would have lost heavily on Walt Disney if they bought shares at $42.50 on April 11, 2000, only to see the price collapse to $21.45 on January 2, 2002.[4]

Share prices are influenced by market sentiment about the future of the economy as a whole, as well as developments in the industry sector in which the firm is located, and therefore show substantial volatility. Consequently, while managers must be aware of and understand the importance of delivering value to shareholders, their ability to achieve this may, at least in the short term, be limited. First, other factors apart from firm performance drive share prices. Second, share prices exhibit considerable volatility and thus are difficult to use as an immediate criterion for management decision making. Nonetheless, it would be a brave manager who completely ignored market signals contained in share-price movements.

Risk Types

Risk is a central theme in strategic management. As we saw in Chapter 1, strategic decisions are made in the present but the consequences are realized in the future. This future is unknown and in some instances unknowable, and strategic management must therefore include an understanding of risk management—what risk is and what actions can be taken to control the level of risk. We classify risk into two broad categories, business risk and financial risk.[5]

Business Risk

Business risk is the year-to-year (or quarter-to-quarter) variability in the operating cash flow of the firm. Firm, industry, and competitive characteristics will influence the level of this risk. A firm with a high ratio of fixed costs to variable costs would have greater business risk since cash flow is extremely sensitive to relatively small changes in demand. Firms competing in markets in the early stage in the product life cycle would have high business risk due to the possibilities of competitor actions or substitutes. A high-technology startup would generally have a high business risk since the growth rate of the market, future market share, future competitive behavior, level of innovation, and the nature of innovation are all difficult to predict. On the other hand, a product in the mature stage of the life cycle would generally be considered to have lower levels of risk since such characteristics as market growth, competition, and innovation are generally easier to predict. Changes in commodity prices, as well as technology, competition, and changing customer requirements, all influence business risk. Note that debt holders, who receive a fixed interest payment, bear no business risk unless the firm goes into receivership, an example of insolvency risk for them.

Financial Risk

Financial risk is the ability of the firm to service its debt. Debt is a fixed charge that must be paid, regardless of the firm's financial performance. When a firm utilizes high debt levels, there will be a high fixed cost of repayments and consequently financial risk. If debt is not paid in full and on time, the firm becomes insolvent and new managers (administrators) are appointed to run it. These receivers are legally required to run the firm in the interests of debt holders, not equity holders. Common measures of financial risk are the firm's debt/equity ratio and its interest cover, the ratio of net income to interest expenses. The firm's capital structure therefore provides one means to assess financial risk, and this structure must be managed accordingly.

Total risk for the firm is the sum of these two components, business risk and financial risk. Financial risk is also described as leverage or gearing since financial risk magnifies business risk. We would expect firms with high levels of business risk to have low levels of financial leverage (low debt/equity ratios). Such firms are financed almost solely by equity, not by debt, as we see with startups financed by venture capital firms. In contrast, firms in mature industries with stable cash flows can sustain higher debt/equity ratios (higher levels of financial risk) due to the low level of business risk.

Should a firm become insolvent, there is generally a legally mandated order of payment, with secured creditors being paid first, unsecured creditors such as suppliers next, and, finally, shareholders. This is part of the reason shareholders are considered to have higher risk and expect a premium for assuming this risk. Consequently, the required return to debt holders will be lower than the required return to shareholders. Or to put it another way, the cost of equity to the firm will always be above the cost of debt.

⊚ 4.3 FINANCIAL MARKETS

Financial markets are comprised of debt markets and equity markets, with each market made up of a number of actors, as shown in Figure 4.2.[6] One group of participant in equity markets is individual shareholders, who buy and sell shares. Other important

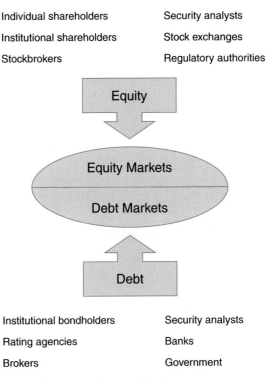

Individual shareholders   Security analysts

Institutional shareholders   Stock exchanges

Stockbrokers   Regulatory authorities

Equity

Equity Markets

Debt Markets

Debt

Institutional bondholders   Security analysts

Rating agencies   Banks

Brokers   Government

Figure 4.2   Financial Market Participants

participants are financial intermediaries: mutual funds, insurance companies, and pension funds, which typically collect the savings of individuals and corporations and channel them to firms to finance new investment. Other participants include banks, stockbrokers, financial advisers, security analysts, and exchanges such as the New York Stock Exchange (NYSE), together with various regulatory bodies, such as the U.S. Securities and Exchange Commission. Debt markets comprise some of the same actors as well as new ones: rating agencies and banks. Government also has a major role in both markets through legislation, taxation, the regulatory framework, and, sometimes, direct investment.

Financial markets have grown enormously over the last 20 years. In the 1970s, for example, a day on which 100 million shares changed hands on the NYSE would make headlines. Today, a billion and more shares trade daily without a murmur. Financial markets are becoming more efficient in many respects, including availability of information concerning a security's future prospects and its reflection in its price. *The Financial Times* and the *Wall Street Journal* are now available globally on the Web, as is *The Economist,* while services such as Bloomberg provide real-time data on financial markets. As a result, investors, institutions, and banks have become more sophisticated and more knowledgeable.

The world's major financial centers are New York and London, with others in Frankfurt, Hong Kong, Paris, Singapore, Sydney, and Tokyo. These financial centers differ in terms of liquidity and regulation. Liquidity is the ease with which financial assets may be traded. When there is a limited number of buyers or sellers, the market would be considered illiquid. Major markets such as New York and London are seen as having an advantage with their liquidity or depth.

U.S. financial markets, with their stringent rules on disclosure and insider trading, were generally thought to be among the most efficient, but the collapse of Enron and the difficulties experienced by Tyco and WorldCom raised doubts in 2002. The independence of auditors and security analysts has been questioned in the United States and elsewhere; as a consequence, several major accounting firms have separated their consulting and auditing practices. Tougher regulation is exemplified in the 2002 U.S. Sarbanes-Oxley Act, and more scrutiny of securities regulation is certain.

London is the leading center for international transactions in stocks, bonds, and foreign exchange.

> In 2001, Sony decided to move its currency and fund-raising activities from Tokyo to London. London was chosen for a number of reasons, including its access to market information, its infrastructure and people, and the lower trading costs. By comparison, Tokyo is less competitive and less innovative; has restrictive regulation, higher costs, and less liquidity; and lacks the high-powered human capital of London and New York. Sony expected to save ¥7B or $USM117 in commission payments per year through this move.[7]

All governments regulate the financial markets that fall under their jurisdiction, but the nature of the regulation varies widely, particularly with regard to the amount and accuracy of information available to investors. Regulations include rules on insider trading, capitalization ratios for financial institutions, and what activities institutions can engage in. Markets such as New York and London provide considerable information and are seen as more transparent. In Germany, banks can own equities, but this is not permitted in the United States. However, after many years during which it was prohibited, U.S. banks may now engage in both commercial and investment banking activities. In several European countries, shares and bonds may be issued as bearer instruments, where the ownership of the security is unknown,[8] while markets such as the eurobond market are essentially unregulated.

In Japan, banks are generally large holders of company shares, and during the past decade they have seen the value of these shares decline. Under new accounting rules, Japanese banks must now incorporate these book losses into their income statements, imperiling their capital adequacy ratios and threatening the entire Japanese banking system. To exacerbate the problem, Japanese banks are reported to have at least $USB355 of nonperforming loans on their balance sheet.[9] The Bank of Japan announced that it would purchase shares currently owned by commercial banks to give the banks some breathing space to strengthen their balance sheets. Not only may this put the Bank of Japan under some threat; it also introduces the problem of *moral hazard*. Can the bank pursue sound macroeconomic policy when it is a shareholder in specific firms?

Major Participants in Financial Markets

We now review some of the key actors and characteristics of global financial markets.

Shareholders

Shareholders are the firm's owners, and their holding of shares in the firm represents this ownership—the equity of the firm. A distinguishing characteristic of the modern firm is that the liability of shareholders is limited to the amount they paid for the shares. The firm is a separate legal entity, and the debts of the firm cannot normally be transferred to its shareholders. This may not be the case with other kinds of legal structures, such as partnerships. While shareholders are the owners, they do not exercise direct control as a result of ownership; instead, they have the right to attend the firm's annual general meeting, to appoint directors, and to vote on major changes to the firm, such as whether or not to accept an acquisition bid.

Shareholders get a financial return on their investment from two main sources—dividends and any appreciation in the price of the shares since the time of purchase (capital gain). In most countries, dividends are regarded as income to the shareholder and taxed accordingly. Share-price appreciation, however, is generally treated as a capital gain when shares are sold, which is usually taxed at lower rates.

Debt Holders

Lenders to the firm have a contract specifying their claims—generally fixed, periodic payments regardless of the firm's financial performance. They are also first to be paid in the event of bankruptcy, although in some countries there is ongoing political debate on whether secured creditors or employees should be paid first. Debt can be short term or long term, arranged through financial intermediaries such as banks or arranged directly by the firm. The cost of debt is affected by the financial strength of the firm, which in turn is influenced by ratings from agencies such as Standard and Poor's or Moody's. Interest payments on debt are generally tax deductible, reducing the true cost of debt to the firm.

Decisions regarding investment choices and the source of funds for new investments are central to strategic management. Strategies and associated new investments can be funded from three sources—retained earnings, new debt, or new equity. Firms generally demonstrate a clear preference order among these three sources of funds. Most firms prefer to fund investments from retained earnings and to maintain a steady dividend stream over time. If additional funds are required, the second preference is for more debt. Additional equity is issued only as a last resort. This is generally described as the **pecking order** theory in corporate finance. If there is excess cash, the firm is likely to pay off debt or exercise a share buyback scheme rather than increase dividends to shareholders.[10]

Since the cost of neither debt nor equity is the same for all firms, the cost of funds can be a source of competitive advantage, especially in capital-intensive industries.

Global Nature of Financial Markets

The global nature of financial markets is manifest in the choices that investors have about where to invest, a phenomenon illustrated in Figure 4.3. As seen in the Figure 4.3 potential investors can choose among many different regions of the world. Investors who decide to invest in the United States can choose among cash, equities, debt, or real assets such as property. Should they invest in equities, they can select any business sector, such as retailing, banking, or manufacturing. Within the broad manufacturing sector, they can invest in firms focusing on home appliances (such as Maytag), electronics, automobiles, and so on. If they invest in the automobile sector, they can choose among Ford, GM, or others. In addition, individual investors can invest either directly in a company or via a mutual fund such as Vanguard or Fidelity.

This wide choice is available to both individual and institutional investors, and both groups are becoming more sophisticated. Capital flows are now less *controlled,* with few restrictions in most countries for investing in other countries (although there are still some exceptions, such as India and Malaysia). Over the last decade, however, many countries, especially in the developing world, have engaged in strenuous efforts to

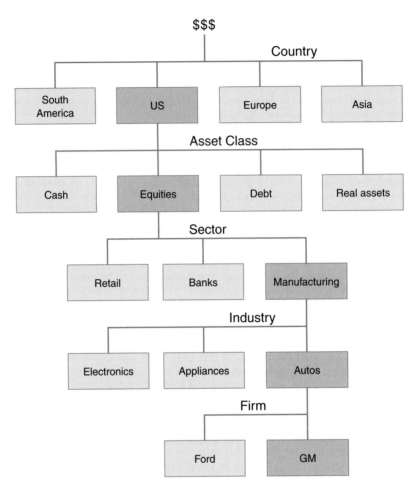

Figure 4.3   Global Choices for Investors
Source: Adapted from a chart prepared by G. Addison.

improve the liquidity and transparency of their financial markets. This reflects the increasing role of financial markets in economic development, a role likely to grow in the future. As a consequence of these changes, firms must be internationally competitive in terms of returns to shareholders. They cannot hide behind protective barriers but must generate appropriate shareholder returns or suffer the consequences of declining share prices.

There are some differences between capital markets in different countries. In the United States, for example, the role of banks in the provision of debt financing has decreased, an example of disintermediation. In contrast, Japanese banks are still the primary source of firms' debt and can own up to 5% of a company's stock. European and Japanese shareholders are generally seen as more passive than American investors. This may reflect the composition of the share register of companies where banks have significant equity holdings, as do other companies with whom the firm does business. Yet Europe is starting to see shareholder pressure for better returns, reflected in the increasing number of hostile takeover offers, such as Vodaphone's takeover of Mannesman. This trend is expected to continue despite the fact that Germany has successfully reduced opportunities for hostile takeovers. European and Japanese capital is often considered more **patient**, investors in these countries are more interested in long-term than short-term results. This observation should be treated with caution, however, since U.S. research suggests that up to 80% of the price of many shares is represented by expectations of future performance.[11]

In the United States, one feature of interest to non-U.S. firms is **American Depository Receipts** or ADRs.[12] With an ADR, a non-U.S. firm deposits some of its shares with a local (non-U.S.) custodian appointed by a U.S. depository bank. The U.S. bank then issues ADRs to the U.S. investor. So the ADR is a negotiable certificate backed by the underlying company shares. The holder of the ADR gets the dividend from the underlying non-U.S. firm—minus a fee to the bank. Through these ADRs, U.S. investors can purchase foreign shares as easily as shares in firms listed on the U.S. exchanges. Similar instruments exist in other financial markets outside the United States.

Another major trend has been a dramatic increase in the proportion of equity held by *institutional investors,* such as mutual funds and pension plans. Since they acquire stock on behalf of other investors, fund managers in these institutions pressure firms for superior financial performance, reflecting the pressure on them from their own senior management and investors. In these institutions, a small number of professionals make the buy/sell decisions on investments; although they are agents for their own investors, they represent a powerful set of shareholders with whose goals their incentives are not necessarily aligned. Indeed, the U.S. Magellan Fund has $USB60 under management, a considerable sum. Fund managers compare investment opportunities on a worldwide basis in the search for superior performance that can be passed onto their individual holders.

Large institutional investors are also becoming more active in corporate governance. Historically, institutions sold shares when firm performance was poor. Increasingly today, they pressure management for improvements, which may involve major changes to senior management. They also want more information on strategy as well as boards with strong, independent directors. This can produce a conflict for senior management and the board, since firms are prohibited from treating different shareholders differently. If they provide additional information to large institutional shareholders, there can be a problem with insider trading.[13]

Another major development in financial markets has been changes in *technology and communications.* This is manifest in the faster, smarter information systems—such as Bloomberg, Reuters, and Datastream—that provide real-time data on share prices and financial analysis globally. These developments have resulted in financial markets operating on a 24/7 basis, with online trading by individuals. It has become easy to monitor and execute orders from any country in many other countries; with the increasing number of institutional buyers, this trend is expected to continue. The information deluge also makes it difficult for managers to hide inferior performance.

Finally, during the 1980s and 1990s, the rate of *financial innovation* increased dramatically. Financial markets have witnessed the development of a range of innovative instruments, new products tailored to new sets of investors as well as products that take some of the risk out of interest-rate or currency fluctuations. Many of these new financial products are derivatives, such as interest-rate futures, which we discuss later. Such derivatives have been useful vehicles for managing risk despite such notable problems as Baring Bros. and Procter & Gamble.

Current Concerns with Financial Markets

During 2001 and 2002, considerable concern was expressed over the accuracy of financial reports prepared for investors, which we now discuss.

Accuracy of Financial Data

In the recent past there have been problems with the financial reports prepared by firms such as Enron, WorldCom, and Xerox, among others. U.S. regulatory and accounting procedures—once seen as a model for other countries—have been shown to be lacking, and a variety of remedial measures are being implemented.

Objectivity of Auditors

There has been deep concern about the objectivity of auditors. Auditors are appointed by and should report to the board. But auditors may get too close to management and lose their objectivity. Historically, the major accounting firms, which undertake audits, also had consulting arms. The audit part of their business was less profitable than consulting, so the accounting firm might use a "soft" audit as a way to get consulting business from the client. Recently, accounting firms such as Ernst & Young, KPMG, and PWC have all separated their accounting and consulting businesses or indicated that the accounting firms would no longer serve as consultant and external auditor for the same client. In making these changes, the accounting firms were probably acting just ahead of the regulators.[14]

Objectivity of Analysts

Concern has been expressed in the United States at the objectivity of financial analysts, particularly those employed within banks and brokerage houses. One study indicated that brokerage firms reward analysts who provide optimistic reports, including a "buy" recommendation, on stocks the brokerage firm is promoting.[15] Such reports can have a significant impact on a firm's share price, particularly in the short term. The market capitalization of Nokia, for example, fell over $USB60, or 26%, in one day due to downgrades by analysts after the firm indicated lower projected earnings.[16]

Senior executives should clearly be very careful about what information they report to the financial press. For example, speculation about possible future acquisitions must be handled carefully, not only to counter a major fall or rise in share prices but also to ensure that no insider trading occurs.

◉ 4.4 EQUITY MARKETS

To raise funds in equity markets, firms have numerous alternatives, some of which are discussed below.[17] The most common form of equity is ordinary shares, others being preferred and nonvoting shares. An ongoing firm may make a rights offer—an offer of new shares restricted to existing shareholders, generally at a discounted price. Such an offer has the feature of not affecting the distribution of shares—assuming all shareholders take them up. In contrast, a new offer may result in the addition of new shareholders and possibly the dilution of the power of existing shareholders.

An **initial public offering** (IPO) occurs when a firm issues a tranche of equity for the first time. It is generally difficult to set a price for these issues, as has been seen in the last few years with new technology stocks. Some dropped in price well below the listing price; others increased dramatically. An IPO can be expensive; the cost can be from 10% to 15% of the sum to be raised, depending on the sum.[18] Sometimes the price of the IPO is fixed; in other countries, such as Australia, the price can be flexible, having a price range dependent on demand for the issue or the type of investor.

Types of Investors

As noted, shareholders can be split into two broad groups: individual and institutional. Institutional investors include financial institutions such as pension funds, investment companies, and insurance companies as well as other nonfinancial companies investing surplus cash.

Over the last few decades, institutional investors have become more important. Recent data on individual and institutional investors in the United States are shown in Table 4.2. Part of this decline in the proportion of shares owned directly by the household sector in the United States has been offset by the increase in indirect equity ownership through mutual and pension funds. Growth in institutional investors also reflects the increase in equity held by investors from other countries as well as pension funds managed by local and state governments. A similar trend has occurred in other countries. The proportion of shares held by individuals fell from 55% in 1963 to 20% in 1994 in the United Kingdom and from 45% in 1960 to 20% in 1990 in Japan.[19]

This trend toward institutional investors has several implications. First, senior managers need to understand the needs of shareholders and how these vary among different types of shareholders. Some shareholders may prefer dividends; others may prefer capital gains due to a more favorable personal tax treatment. The preference between dividends and price appreciation will be influenced by the tax regime faced by the investor. If the shareholder is a tax-exempt investor, such as a pension fund in the United States, it pays no tax and therefore may prefer dividends.

In countries with a system of **imputation credits,** the company pays tax (at the corporate tax rate) on any dividend, and this payment is a tax credit for the shareholder.[20] The tax paid by the company can be offset against the tax due from the shareholder. The value of such a scheme depends on the tax rate of the investor. Investors who pay no or little tax would see no benefit, nor would foreign shareholders, since tax credits apply only in the country of origin of the dividend.

Shareholders may also differ in how they regard share ownership. Some institutional investors are more interested in the short term; they see the investment as just that—an investment. They are not interested in exercising ownership, and if the firm is not performing, they sell. Such investors seldom attempt to challenge management to achieve better performance. On the other hand, many believe small shareholders to be more patient investors; they are there for the long term.

TABLE 4.2 Percentage of Shares ($ Value) of U.S. Companies Held by Type of Investor

Year	Individual Investors (%)	Institutional Investors (%)
1950	84.3	15.7
1960	77.1	28.9
1970	57.5	42.5
1980	42.8	57.2
1990	36.7	63.3
1998	28.2	71.8

Source: "Survey 2000—Share Ownership Study," New York Stock Exchange, 2000. www.nyse.com/market information.

The contrasting needs and requirements of different investors suggest that there is an important role for investor relations. It may be necessary to apply marketing concepts such as segmentation to the share register to understand the needs of different investors and their possibly different risk profiles. These different requirements also highlight the need to communicate with investors, informing them about the firm and its strategy. Such investor relations are an important role for the CEO and the board.[21]

The Cost of Equity Capital

The fundamental assumption underlying shareholder value is that investors have numerous investment alternatives, as illustrated in Figure 4.3, and that the alternatives have different risk levels. Consequently, investors require a level of return on an investment commensurate with its level of risk. As the level of risk of an investment increases, so does the required return, as shown in Figure 4.4. The risk/return relationship may not be linear, as shown in the figure, but it is certainly monotonic. That is, investors require higher returns from risky investments to compensate for the possibility of losing their investment.

The lowest level of risk is a government security or, in the United States, a Treasury bill. These investments are assumed to be risk-free, since any national government is unlikely to default on the redemption or the payment of interest on any security issued in its name.[22] Since any investor can invest in these government securities, if the firm is to attract equity investment, it must promise the shareholder a return greater than this risk-free rate, the so-called risk premium.

We can express the rate of return required by an investor for a particular investment, as:

$$\text{Required return} = \text{risk-free rate} + \text{risk premium}$$

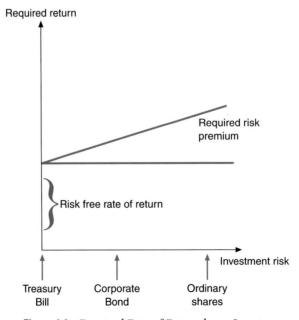

Figure 4.4 Required Rate of Return by an Investor

TABLE 4.3   Cost of Equity Capital for Global Firms

Firm	Cost of Equity (%)
Pacific Century CyberWorks	13
Xerox	12
Telecom Italia, Oracle, IBM	11
General Electric, Shell, HP	10
Unilever, Wal-Mart. Pfizer	9
Singapore Telecom	8
NTT	7
Nestlé, Toyota	6

"Marked by the Market," *The Economist,* December 1, 2001, pp. 59–60.

The risk premium is specific to the investment under consideration. To calculate this premium, modern financial theory suggests the use of the **capital asset pricing model** (CAPM),[23] whereby the rate of return required by the shareholder is given by:

$$\text{Required return} = \text{risk-free rate} + \text{beta} \times (\text{expected return on the market} - \text{risk-free rate})$$

In this formulation, the risk-free rate is the return on government securities, the expected return on the market is the average return from a portfolio of shares based on the share market as a total entity, and beta is a measure of risk for the security or firm in question. Values of beta are widely published.[24]

This required rate of return is the **cost of equity capital** for the firm. It is the return required by a shareholder to compensate for the level of risk of that investment. The cost of equity capital of several firms in 2001 is shown in Table 4.3.

Cost of equity depends on such factors as the nature of the industry (high-technology needs a high return) and stage of development (higher cost if the product or technology is in the early stages of the life cycle). Typically, young, entrepreneurial, high-technology firms have a very high cost of equity capital, reflecting the risk involved. Witness the high cost of capital of Pacific Century CyberWorks, a Hong Kong–based telecommunications firm. Nestlé and Toyota, in contrast, are well established firms operating globally, primarily in mature consumer markets. They are seen as having very low risk levels (reflected in a 6% cost of capital) and can undertake strategies forecast to generate lower cash flows than firms with high costs of equity such as Xerox or Oracle.

While the capital asset pricing model is commonly used to calculate the cost of equity capital, it does have some problems.[25] For example, the model is historical in nature. Values for the risk premiums are deduced from past data and may not be valid in the future. This poses a particular problem for new high-technology firms, which have no track record. The model also assumes that shareholders are interested only in risk and return, whereas noneconomic considerations such as religious or ethical criteria may influence investment choices.

Trends in Equity Markets

In recent years, many firms have engaged in extensive share **buyback** schemes, using their surplus funds to buy back shares on the open market. This increases share prices (thus possibly benefiting managers with share options) by reducing the number of shares outstanding, thereby increasing earnings per share, which is often used as a basis for valuing shares. Buyback schemes are also usually tax-efficient compared with increasing dividends, since capital gains taxes are generally lower than income taxes.

It is also increasingly common for firms to be listed on more than one exchange, with some of these cross-listings being quite complicated.

> Unilever has two parent companies, Unilever NV and Unilever PLC. Despite these two companies being separate legal entities, with separate stock exchange listings, the firm operates as a single entity. Unilever NV is listed on the Amsterdam, German, and Luxembourg exchanges, among others, while Unilever PLC is listed on the London exchange and as ADRs in New York.

◉ 4.5 DEBT MARKETS

Debt is a promise by the firm to pay a specified return for a specified time period. From the provider's perspective, debt has low risk and the holder will accept a lower return than an equity holder. From the firm's perspective, debt is cheaper than equity.

There is some risk to the debt provider, since the firm can default on paying debt due to insolvency. Consequently, firm debt carries higher interest rates than government securities. Yet holders of corporate debt are in a preferred position relative to shareholders, since they generally have some legal protection and are paid first in the event of insolvency. In addition, interest payments are a legal liability of the firm and are paid before any dividends. Creditors are often the trigger for instituting restructuring or formal bankruptcy proceedings, since if they have not been paid as required, they can establish a legal claim on the firm's assets.

> In Germany, Kirch Media filed for bankruptcy, an act that could have brought down the entire Kirch Gruppe. Some creditors formed a consortium to purchase the firm's 40% stake in Axel Springer, a publishing group. Other creditors such as Commerzbank agreed to a debt-for-equity swap and took over Kirch Media, even though it may have needed new capital of several billion euros.[26]

Many debt holders attach restrictive **covenants** to debt. These covenants provide more protection for the lenders since violations permit debt holders to call in their loans, which could cause insolvency and subsequent bankruptcy filing. Covenants might include limits on additional debt and capital expenditure or specify minimum levels of profit and maximum levels of leverage. Covenants inevitably reduce management's decision-making discretion.

Types of Debt

Firms employ a wide range of debt instruments in their search for funds. They typically utilize a mixture of short- and long-term debt, where "short term" is defined as debt that must be repaid within a year.[27] In debt markets, a bond is a generic name for tradable, long-term debt raised by a borrower who agrees to make specific payments, usually regular payments of interest and repayment of principle on maturity. Debt with a floating interest rate is generally priced with respect to a benchmark interest rate, such as the London inter-bank offered rate (LIBOR) or Treasury bills in the United States. A zero-coupon bond pays no interest but is issued at a discount below par or redemption value, so the holder gets capital appreciation through deferred interest, which normally means preferential tax treatment.

Debt also differs in terms of security. Senior debt that is paid first in the event of a default (before any subordinated debt is paid) has the lowest level of risk for the investor. The U.S. Federal Reserve Board publishes a more complete description of debt types and interest payment characteristics.[28]

A global firm will have a range of debt instruments, generally in different currencies and with different maturity dates. The cost will be influenced by several factors, including the general level of interest rates and the maturity of the debt, with the relationship between interest rates and maturity being expressed by a yield curve. As debt becomes due, the firm may roll it over, and here debt holders can exert substantial pressure on the firm to lower its risk profile and improve its ability to service the debt by divesting some of its current assets or businesses. So debt holders can exert a strong influence on the strategy of the firm.

As debt markets have become more volatile, some firms have replaced short-term debt with long-term debt, despite the higher interest rates.

> In 2002, AOL Time Warner replaced $USB6 of short-term debt with long-dated bonds although this added several million to their annual interest payments.

Firms also worry that short-term debt markets may lose liquidity and that market sentiment can change quickly, closing the bond market to the firm.

> In 2002, General Electric Capital Corporation issued a $USB11 bond to replace commercial paper borrowing,[29] indicating how strategic managers must keep abreast of changes in these critical financial markets.

Traditionally the banking sector was the major source of debt funds. Managers need to be aware that the ease and nature of lending by banks are often governed by regulations. For example, the Basel Committee on Banking Supervisions, under the auspices of the Bank for International Settlements, has proposed changing the capital reserve rules for banks.[30] The implications of these changes for nonfinancial organizations are likely to be greater differences in interest rates for loans of different quality or risk classes. So some firms will pay more for debt and others will pay less. These changes are still under discussion but are scheduled for 2004.

An increasing number of firms are issuing their own debt rather than using banks as an intermediary. These firms have the financial strength to issue high-grade debt without the use of a bank. In fact, some firms have a higher credit rating than banks! These firms often use a bank as an adviser, which has been reflected in the changing mix of business in banks, with fee income replacing interest income. The introduction of the euro has nullified national requirements for pension and insurance assets to be invested in the same currencies as their liabilities. So European stock and bond markets have become larger and more liquid, with debt being easier to raise from numerous providers. These financing options have lowered European firms' cost of capital and put competitive pressure on their banks.

There is potential for a conflict of interest between managers and debt holders. Managers may be tempted to undertake risky investments, since if these succeed the managers achieve large gains, as do the equity holders, who can get a return many times their investment. But debt holders get a fixed return, independent of the success of the firm. If the investment fails, debt holders may lose their investment. While the same is true for equity holders, the relation is not symmetrical. Equity holders can get huge returns; normally debt holders can never get more than the interest and/or the principal back.[31]

Ratings Agencies

Agencies such as Standard and Poor's (S&P) and Moody's, which rate the debt of companies and other organizations, play an important role in debt markets, since their ratings influence the cost of debt.

A credit rating represents the opinion of the agency—S&P or Moody's—on either the general creditworthiness of a firm, or the creditworthiness of a specific debt security. We will concentrate on the former. The credit rating for a firm is based on a number of factors such as financial measures of the firm together with a review of the industry, including its growth prospects, threat of technological change, and susceptibility to possible government regulatory actions. Such a rating is done independently of the firm, although the firm may be consulted prior to public release of such a rating.

Standard and Poor's rates industrial firms on a scale from AAA to D, where AAA is the strongest and D is used when the firm is in default. Ratings from AA to CCC may be modified by the addition of a plus or a minus. Definitions of the S&P ratings, in summary form, are given below:[32]

AAA: Capacity to meet its financial commitments is very strong.

AA: Differs from AA to a small degree; capacity to meet financial commitments is very strong.

A: Somewhat more susceptible to adverse changes in economic conditions, but capacity to meet financial commitments is still strong.

BBB: Has adequate capacity to meet commitments but adverse economic conditions could lead to a weakened capacity to meet financial commitments.

Firms rated as BB or lower are regarded a possessing significant speculative characteristics and are referred to as junk bonds:

BB: The firm faces major ongoing uncertainty or adverse conditions that could lead to inadequate capacity to meet financial commitments.

B: Adverse business or economic conditions are likely to impair the firm's capacity to meet financial commitments.

CCC: The firm is currently vulnerable to nonpayment and dependent on favorable economic conditions to meets its obligations.

So-called **junk** or **high-yield bonds** have a quality (rating by an agency) at less than investment grade. This is defined as a Moody's rating at or below Ba or a Standard and Poor's rating of BB or below. Such a rating is critical since the articles of some large institutions prohibit their holding junk bonds.[33] Nonetheless, there has been a significant expansion in this junk bond market. During the first six months of 1998, more than $USB110 in high-yield debt was issued by U.S. firms, suggesting that more firms, arguably of questionable credit quality, were raising debt funds, reflecting the environment of lower interest rates.[34]

While firms do pay attention to their credit rating and react negatively if it is downgraded, it is unclear just how important this is. In 2002, Bristol-Myers-Squibb had its credit rating by Moody's reduced to Aa2, an act which left just eight U.S. firms with a AAA rating. By contrast, in 1979, there were 58 U.S. firms with such a rating.[35] In the United States it appears that firms have increased debt levels to improve return on equity (ROE), leading to concern at the state of their balance sheets. Should there be any serious attempt to strengthen balance sheets by repaying debt, free cash flow will be reduced, ultimately hurting growth and innovation.

TABLE 4.4   Key Financial Ratios: Median Values for U.S. Industrial Firms, 1998–2000

	AAA	A	BB	CCC
EBIT interest cover (times)	21.4	6.1	2.1	0.1
ROC (%)	34.0	19.4	11.6	1.0
Operating income/sales (%)	27.0	18.6	15.9	11.9
Total debt/capital (%)	22.9	42.5	62.6	87.7

Source: Ratings and Ratios (2002). ©by Standard and Poor's, A Division of the McGraw-Hill Companies, Inc. Reproduced by permission of Standard and Poor's.

As Table 4.4 indicates, there are major variations in the financial performance of companies with these different ratings. Firms rated BB or lower have poor interest cover, low return on capital, and high debt—all as expected, due to their poor credit rating. The financial strength of a firm can be a significant competitive advantage: creditworthy firms are able to raise debt more cheaply than less creditworthy firms, as is evident in Table 4.5. Over the 17-year time period shown, AAA bonds averaged 2.99% (or 299 basis points) above Treasury bonds and BAA bonds averaged 3.98% above them. Creditworthy firms have therefore been able to raise debt considerably more cheaply, saving about 100 basis points on average, which may represent a considerable competitive advantage.

Rating agencies can put pressure on firms through their ability to downgrade their debt. Such a downgrade sends a negative signal to the market that the firm is now more of a credit risk, with a resultant rise in the cost of debt. For example, in 2001 Xerox had junk bond status, with a spread of 450 points over the LIBOR, up from a spread of 250 basis points previously.[36] The downgrading reflected the firm's need to improve net income and cash flow as well as future significant debt maturities.

Islamic Banking

What we have described above is the situation in a typical Western banking system. However, we need to be aware that there are other banking systems, the main one being the Islamic banking system—in wide use throughout the Middle East as well as in countries such as Pakistan and Indonesia.

The basic principle underlying Islamic banking is that interest is considered to be usury and is prohibited on religious grounds. Instead, under this system the investor or lender takes a share of any profits of the venture for which the money has been lent. Banks thus attempt to convert an interest payment to a capital gain. This generally involves some form of predetermination of profit and what percentage of this will be returned to the investor. Any losses are borne by the borrower. In addition, some Islamic

TABLE 4.5   Interest Rates for Treasury and Corporate Bonds

Bond Type	1985	1990	1995	2000	2001	2002
1-year U.S. Treasury bond	7.76%	7.36%	5.69%	5.85%	3.21%	1.67%
AAA Moody-rated corporate bond	11.37	9.32	7.59	7.62	7.08	6.49
BAA Moody-rated corporate bond	12.72	10.36	8.20	8.37	7.95	7.80

Source: Short-Term Rates (Washington, DC: Federal Reserve Board, 2003), Tables H-15 and G-13. www.federalreserve.gov.

investors are precluded from investing in some "undesirable" sectors, such as alcohol and gaming.[37]

🌀 4.6 COST OF CAPITAL AND FIRM VALUATION

The firm exists to create value, which it does when the revenues it generates are greater than all its costs, including the cost of capital. To determine whether or not value is created, we must understand how to calculate the firm's cost of capital. Indeed, comprehending how value is created and measured is critical to understanding the task facing strategic managers.

Cost of capital reflects the firm's capital structure, captured by the extent to which its operations are financed by debt and equity. These two sources of funds have different costs to the firm, reflecting their different risk levels. The firm's cost of capital is the weighted average cost of these two sources. So if we let D = level of debt of the firm and E = equity financing of the firm, then the total capital of the firm is $D + E$ and the weighted average cost of capital (WACC) is:[38]

$$\text{WACC} = (E/(D + E)) \times \text{cost of equity} + (D/(D + E)) \times \text{cost of debt} \times (1.0 - \text{tax rate})$$

This weighted average cost of capital is the value used to calculate economic profit and to discount future cash flows of the firm.

Firm Valuation

Investment analysts and shareholders use a number of measures to assess the value of the firm. These measures are not only critical for senior management in understanding the value of their own firm; they also play a major role in corporate strategy when the firm is manipulating its portfolio of businesses through mergers or restructuring activities of various kinds. We now discuss valuation models.

Market Capitalization
Market capitalization is the value of the firm as measured by the share market; it is calculated as the number of shares outstanding multiplied by the share price. Share prices are composed of two components: value from current operations (including incremental improvements) and value from expectations of future growth through innovation. Investors and analysts make explicit and/or implicit forecasts of the short- and long-term performance of the firm and its industry, and the expectations based on these forecasts are reflected in the share price. Share prices can thus be considered to represent the stock market's assessment of the net present value of all the firm's present and future strategies and capital investments at a given time.

One difficulty with using market capitalization as a basis for managerial decision making is that share prices demonstrate considerable volatility, as shown in Table 4.6, which indicates the volatility experienced by the NASDAQ and several individual shares as shareholder expectations changed over the period. In particular, the impact of the dot.com bubble of 2000 is apparent, with the share price of several firms reaching what proved to be unsustainable levels.

These data indicate that share price, and thus the market capitalization of a firm, is influenced by a number of transitory events outside of management control, such as government policy on interest rates, the performance of the economy, and the likely future performance of the sector in which the firm competes. All these influence expectations about the firm's future performance and the level of risk involved. Further, stock

TABLE 4.6   Performance of Selected U.S. Firms and the NASDAQ Index, January 1999–July 2003

Company	High		Low		Price July 31, 2003
	Price ($)	Date	Price ($)	Date	
Amazon	103.6	December 1999	6.2	September 2001	40.7
Cisco	77.8	March 2000	9.75	October 2002	19.3
eBay	111.8	March 2000	28.4	December 2000	108.2
Microsoft	58.8	December 1999	21.41	July 2002	26.2
Yahoo!	208.0	December 1999	9.1	September 2001	30.8
Nasdaq composite	5047	March 2000	1164	October 2002	1721

Source: "Share Prices," Thomson Financial, Datastream. www.thomson.com/corp/about.

markets often seem to display a herd mentality, chasing stock as prices are rising and selling stock as prices are falling.

Share prices are also influenced in the short term by the difference between actual performance and the *expectations* of investors and investment analysts. If these expectations are high and the company performs well but below these expectations, share prices will decline. Consequently, some firms seem to be on an expectations treadmill—the better they do, the better the stock markets expects them to do.[39] It is also not uncommon for a major shift in share price to occur with the departure of a current CEO or the announcement of a new CEO, suggesting that new expectations have been developed. Senior managers in global firms take an active interest in "managing" shareholder expectations through such actions as briefings to brokers and fund managers, ensuring that financial markets are aware of the strategy that the firm is pursuing.

Although it is difficult to use the share price as a basis for managerial decisions, senior managers favor high share prices for several reasons. First, share appreciation is often an important component in shareholder returns. Managers holding shares or options also benefit from such appreciation. In addition, high share prices discourage takeover attempts and put the firm in a strong position to take over other firms, particularly if shares finance the takeover.

> In the telecoms debacle of the early 21st century, Vodaphone, the world's largest mobile operator, escaped largely unscathed at the operating level because Sir Christopher Gent, architect of the firm's aggressive expansion by acquisition, had been scrupulous in using the firm's highly valued shares to make its purchases. While dilution inevitably resulted, Vodaphone became the leader in its industry.

Market Value Added

Market value added (MVA), developed by Stern Stewart, is the difference between the market capitalization of a firm and the accountants' account measure of all capital in the firm, both debt and equity.[40] It is expressed in monetary units and is a measure of how well the firm has created value over what has been invested in it.

From the balance sheet, capital employed is calculated as:

$$\text{Capital employed} = \text{total assets} - \text{current liabilities}$$
$$= \text{fixed assets} + \text{working capital}$$

which is equivalent to:

$$\text{Capital employed} = \text{long-term debt} + \text{equity}$$

TABLE 4.7   Market Value Added of Selected U.S. Firms as of October 31, 2001

Company	Market Value Added ($USB)
General Electric	312.1
Microsoft	298.8
Wal-Mart	198.4
IBM	142.6
Johnson & Johnson	137.4
Merck	135.6
Xerox	–6.7
General Motors	–34.5
Lucent Technologies	–42.0
AT&T	–94.3

Source: D. Stires, "America's Best and Worst Wealth Creators," *Fortune,* December 12, 2001, pp. 137–142.

Market value added is then calculated by:

$$\text{Market value added} = \text{market capitalization} - \text{capital employed}$$

MVA relates the current market-derived value of the firm to the amount of capital invested over the life of the firm.

Table 4.7 shows the market value added for a number of U.S. companies using market capitalization on October 31, 2001. Based on these data, it is easy to understand why GE is one of the most admired companies in the United States. As of 2001, it had a market capitalization of some $USB312 over and above the capital employed in the business. Contrast this with AT&T, which had destroyed some $USB94 of value over its life.

Market-to-Book Ratio (M/B)

Since MVA is in monetary terms, it is sensitive to firm size, complicating interfirm comparisons. This is overcome by using the dimensionless ratio:

$$\text{M/B} = \text{market capitalization} / \text{book value of capital employed}$$

Market capitalization is the share market's view of the total value of the future strategies of the firm. This can be expressed as the value that can be generated from the total asset base of the firm. As we will discuss in more detail in Chapter 5, the total assets of the firm can be categorized into two groups, tangible and intangible assets. Thus the market capitalization of the firm can be interpreted as the current value of both intangible and tangible assets, whereas book value of capital employed is the value of all tangible assets on the balance sheet. Consequently, the M/B ratio can be seen as a measure of the relative importance of intangible and tangible assets in the value of the firm. M/B ratios are high for firms whose capital is primarily intangible, representing the skills of staff, brand names, patents, and so on.

Across all firms in the *Fortune* 500, the average M/B was about 3.5 in 1998,[41] suggesting that accounting systems drastically undervalue the firm's assets when these are primarily intangible. Such undervaluation could lead to senior managers spending too little time managing the intangible assets and too much time managing the tangible assets, a topic to which we return in Chapter 5.

TABLE 4.8 Total Return to Shareholders for Selected European Firms, as of June 30, 2003

Company	Industry	Country	Average Annual TRS % over 5 Years
Nokia	Information technology	Finland	12.2%
Diageo	Beverages	United Kingdom	1.4%
ICI	Chemicals	United Kingdom	6.8%
Akzo Nobel	Chemicals	Netherlands	−12.2%
Nestlé	Food	Switzerland	−1.6%
Alcatel	Information technology	France	−26.1%

Source: L.E.K. Consulting, www.lek.com.

Total Return to Shareholders

Another market-based measure used to assess the performance of companies is the **total return to shareholders** (TRS), defined as the annualized total return to shareholders from maintaining their investment in a stock over a period. Looking at this measure simplistically, it is the total of dividends and price appreciation of the shares of the company over the time period. Table 4.8 shows the TRS measure for a number of European firms. The table shows the compounded average annual growth rate in the total return to shareholders for the different firms. As can be seen, Nokia has been an outstandingly successful company, generating an average annual return to shareholders of 12.2% over the five years from 1998 to 2003. Akzo Nobel has not performed well, in terms of shareholder returns, while ICI appears to be recovering from some earlier lackluster performance. These differences suggest that while industry affects performance, firm-specific factors also need to be understood.

Like market capitalization and MVA, managers may find it difficult to use TRS as their main decision-making tool. TRS focuses solely on the market value of a firm and its dividend stream. If the market is an efficient judge of business, then TRS will demonstrate the value added by management, although the impact of other factors on share prices must be recognized. Nonetheless, TRS overcomes difficulties that occur with accounting measures, such as book values bearing little relationship to current values or a high ratio of intangible to tangible assets.

Accounting Measures of Profitability

The firm's accounting system is the primary source of information for assessing a firm's financial performance. Accounting procedures and systems encapsulated in the Generally Accepted Accounting Principles (GAAP) were developed to indicate the state of the business as a going concern, and a number are used by financial markets in valuation. The most important are discussed below, although, as we will see, they are not always the most appropriate measures for assessing performance.

The measure most closely followed by analysts, stockbrokers, and investors is **net income** or earnings, both current and projected. This value is reported in the income statement and is broadly measured as revenue minus certain expenses. Both are reported on an accrual basis, meaning that net income is not a measure of cash flow. Net income is calculated after a combination of cash and noncash expenses, the most important noncash expense being depreciation. This presents some difficulties since depreciation is a partly subjective number, based as it is on historical costs and assumptions about the economic life of an asset. Net income may also be reported as pre- or post-tax, and before or after interest expenses. Given this lack of uniformity, other common measures are earnings before interest and tax (EBIT) and earnings before tax, interest, depreciation, and amortization (EBITDA). While the latter is more closely related to cash flow, it is not a true measure since changes in fixed and working capital are excluded. Such a measure favors firms with high capital expenditures since these do not appear on the income statement.

Although net income measures the firm's earnings, it doesn't include the capital necessary to generate that income. Consequently, there is a need for measures that explicitly consider the level of capital used to generate net income. In the ratios below, we use net income as the numerator, but it is also common to use EBIT, particularly at the SBU level. Efficiency measures include the following:

Return on equity (ROE): net income / shareholder's equity

Return on assets (ROA): net income / total assets

Return on capital employed (ROCE): net income / capital employed

Return on sales (ROS): net income / total operating revenue

Values for shareholder's equity, total assets, and capital employed are obtained from the balance sheet.

4.7 RISK MANAGEMENT AND DERIVATIVES

Strategic management involves making decisions now, knowing the consequences will occur in the future. Because how the world develops during this time is uncertain, uncertainty and risk are central themes of strategic management. As discussed earlier in the chapter, firms face risks from two primary sources. Business risk is related to the underlying nature of the business and industry in which it competes. Financial risk is related to interest rates, exchange rates, and changes in equity markets and commodity prices. For example, many firms have cash streams from different countries and currencies that expose the firm to exchange-rate risk. Alternatively, the firm may be considering raising additional debt in the future, and so it may face an interest-rate risk—the risk of a rise in interest rates. Should the firm need to raise additional equity in the future, changes in the levels of equity markets may present it with an equity market risk. Finally, some firms operate in commodity markets, purchasing or selling a commodity such as iron ore or oil, and these commodity markets are characterized by major price fluctuations, exposing firms to price risk.

Managers of nonfinancial firms generally accept and are responsible for the business risk of the firm. The question we pose here is whether the managers should accept the financial risk inherent in the firm. For example, if the firm is an exporter, does it bundle in an exchange-rate risk with the business risk of the firm? We believe the firm should quantify its risk exposures and select appropriate instruments to offset the risk. One important class of instruments is **derivatives**—a broad range of financial instruments whose value depends on the value of an underlying asset or index.[42] These can be used to limit risk for a firm, or allow it to seek higher profits at higher risk, and form a part of the risk management operations of the firm. When such instruments are used, risk is transferred, at a price, to another party prepared to assume it. Although risk management operations are the responsibility of specialist staff, it is important for the CEO to understand the role, uses, limitations, and the possible implications of risk management techniques. Such firms as Metallgesellschaft, Barings, Procter & Gamble,

Sumitomo, and Allied Irish Banks have all got into difficulties due to poor management of this activity.

With increasing globalization and turbulence in financial markets, firms are likely to be exposed to several of these risks and need to take action to limit their exposure. As an example, suppose that Alcatel, the French telecommunications firm, sells a component to Compal, the Taiwanese laptop computer manufacturer. We also assume this contract calls for the supply of the component from Alcatel over some time period at a fixed price. Since the component is globally traded, it is priced in U.S. dollars.

Alcatel faces a business risk with this component, which it is likely to sell to other manufacturers. What is the demand for the component? What are competitors doing? What is the likely future behavior of prices and margins? What substitutes exist? And so on. At the same time, its contract with Compal creates exchange-rate risk—it sells in U.S. dollars yet most of its costs are in euros. Should Alcatel decide to accept the risk of changes in the euro–dollar exchange rate, engaging in currency speculation? If it does, it is bundling exchange-rate risk with the product it is selling. Alternatively, should Alcatel hedge to reduce or eliminate exchange-rate risk arising from this contract?

Compal has even more difficult choices. Its value chain comprises a set of costs, some of which are in U.S. dollars (purchases), some in Taiwanese dollars (its R&D and possibly marketing expenses), and some costs in Chinese renmimbi, since the computer is made in its Chinese plant and sold to Compaq in U.S. dollars. Compal is exposed to three currencies and their exchange rates.

This simple example illustrates one impact of globalization: firms have the potential to be exposed to a high degree of currency risk, which has a major impact on profitability. Responsible strategic managers will attempt limit the exposure of the firm to such sources of risk by establishing a risk management program. The CEO does not manage all the details but should ensure that processes designed to adjust risk exposure are in place and that the appropriate risk management instruments are selected. Because much of this activity involves the use of derivatives, managers need some understanding of their features and use. Yet, since hedging has a cost, a firm cannot hedge all risks: managers have to decide which risks to hedge against. Given the devastating impact that poor decisions can have, many firms avoid leveraging positions that magnify risk and could be interpreted as speculation. Risk management processes will be discussed in more detail in Chapter 8.

The use of derivatives has increased so much that they are now the dominant activity in the world's financial system. Table 4.9 shows the size of the derivatives market for products traded over the counter (OTC). Instruments that are exchange-traded have been ignored. As can be seen, this a huge market with a total size in December 2002 of $USB141,737, with one form of derivatives—interest rate swaps—representing almost 56% of the market. Derivatives are generally classified into three main types, although there is a bewildering array of specialized instruments that are permutations of these basic types.[43] The three main types are forward contracts, options, and swaps, each of which is described briefly below.

Forward Contracts

A **forward contract** is an agreement between two parties, a buyer and a seller, to buy or sell something at a later date at a price agreed to when the contract is written. Each party agrees to do business with the other, so each party accepts a default risk that the other party can and will deliver. Futures are forward contracts operated through a

TABLE 4.9   Amount Outstanding, OTC Derivatives ($USB)

Instrument	December 1999	December 2000	December 2001	December 2002
Foreign-exchange contracts	14,344	15,666	16,748	18,469
Outright forwards and				
forex swaps	9,593	10,134	10,336	10,723
Currency swaps	2,444	3,194	3,942	4,509
Options	2,307	2,338	2,470	3,238
Interest-rate contracts	60,091	64,668	77,568	101,699
Interest-rate swaps	43,936	48,768	58,897	79,161
Options	9,380	9,476	10,933	13,746
Other	6,775	6,423	7,738	8,792
Other instruments	13,767	14,865	16,862	21,569
Total	88,202	95,199	111,178	141,737

Source: "International Financial Statistics," in *BIS Quarterly Review* (Basel: Bank for International Settlements, 2003), Table A99. www.bis.org.

futures exchange. They are a forward contract with standardized terms and can be traded at any time without contact with the original party. Futures are liquid, and default risk is borne by the exchange. They are very common with agricultural products and other commodities such as oil, coal, bauxite, aluminum, and gold. With these products, there are two markets—the physical spot market, where physical product is bought and sold, and the futures market, where promises to buy or sell in the future are bought and sold. Futures markets transfer risk from hedgers to speculators, from those willing to pay to avoid risk to those willing to assume the risk in the hope of gain.

In addition to these futures markets in commodities, there is also a wide range of financial futures such as currency, Treasury bonds, and stock market index–based futures. For example, a firm can use U.S. Treasury bonds to hedge against movements in interest rates. The trade in such contracts is generally done by direct negotiation or over the counter, since there is no central exchange. Table 4.9 indicates that foreign-exchange futures are a major market.

Options

An **option** is a contract in which the writer of the contract grants the buyer of the contract the right, but not the obligation, to purchase from or sell to the writer something at a specified price within a specified time.[44] For this right, the option writer charges the buyer a price called the option price. An option to sell is referred to as a **put option,** while the option to buy is referred to as a **call option.** Unlike futures, the option contract involves a choice for the purchaser. On the date the option expires, the purchaser can decide whether or not to exercise the option. If the purchaser decides not to exercise the option, the only thing that is lost is the cost of purchasing the option. Options may be issued over the counter or traded on several of the futures exchanges. With an option, risk is not symmetrical. The option buyer can lose no more than the option price if deciding not to take up the option, while the option writer assumes substantial risk.

In general, whether such an option is attractive to the buyer will depend on a number of factors, including the current price, the exercise price, the time to expiration, the volatility in the asset's price, interest rates, and the option price. Detailed formulas on how to value options, based on the models derived by Black and Scholes, is given in many texts on capital markets.[45]

Swaps

A **swap** is a contract in which two parties agree to exchange the cash flows from an asset or liability. As shown in Table 4.9, the most common form of derivative is an interest-rate swap, where one party swaps its liabilities on a fixed-interest loan with another firm that has borrowed at a floating interest rate. Swaps can have many conditions, such as setting a maximum interest rate or requiring that the interest be payable in one currency and the principal in another. A simple example of another common swap, a currency swap, follows.

Currency-Rate Swap

Consider an Australian wine and beer firm, called Aussie, that wants to expand its wine-processing plant in France. Since the firm is domiciled in Australia, Aussie has good bank contacts in Australia, but none in France. A French bank would view the Australian firm as risky, and Aussie would have to pay a high interest rate for any funds borrowed from a French bank. Suppose at the same time a French hotel chain, Eiffel, is considering building a new hotel in Melbourne. Eiffel faces a similar problem—it has excellent relationships with French banks but not with Australian banks. So the two firms trade.

Situation

Aussie wants to expand wine processing in France.

Eiffel wants to build a new hotel in Melbourne.

Resolution

Aussie borrows Australian dollars in Australia and gives the funds to Eiffel to build the hotel.

Eiffel borrows euros in Europe and gives the funds to Aussie to expand the processing plant.

Aussie receives euros from its plant in France and gives these to Eiffel to pay interest on the euro loan.

Eiffel receives Australian dollars from the new hotel and gives these to Aussie to pay interest on the Australian dollar loan.

Note that this arrangement is cheaper for both firms than if they had each borrowed in the foreign country. There is now a counterparty risk: either Aussie or Eiffel could default on its respective loan. To overcome this, there is generally an intermediary between the two parties, normally a commercial bank, that absorbs some of the risk for a fee. It is not necessary to have counterparties with equal and opposite needs. A bank may decide to commit to one side of the transaction and then look for parties for the other, perhaps aggregating a number of these. For readers seeking a more complex example, the chapter appendix contains an illustration of a cross-currency interest-rate swap.

In summary, derivatives markets provide a firm with opportunities to manage risk. They enable firms that wish to reduce their risk to transfer it to other firms for a fee.

They are an element in the overall risk management system of the firm and are generally utilized as a hedge—an action taken to reduce risk. Managers need to understand how they can be used and recognize that if leverage is involved, small price changes can lead to large profits or losses. Speculation is not one of the tasks of managers—they should be hedging, not speculating!

4.8 SUMMARY

This chapter has highlighted the importance of financial markets to strategic management. Financial markets impose their own performance measures on the firm. Managers must recognize that failure to meet these measures will result in significant changes in strategy.

Developing strategy requires that the firm be able to assess and incorporate the demands of financial markets as well as product markets. The firm competes for funds in increasingly global financial markets. Lack of success in obtaining these external funds severely limits the strategic choices available to the firm.

Risk is an essential component in strategic management since the future is uncertain. Risk can be categorized into business risk and financial risk, and managers must ensure that risk is managed, that the risk level of the firm is appropriate for its resources.

A firm has two primary sources of funds, debt and equity, and one of the tasks of strategic managers is to manage these two sources, with due regard for the cost, type, and availability of these funds. The cost of debt will be influenced by factors outside of the control of the firm, such as general economic conditions and the actions of rating agencies. Equity is not free for the firm; it has a cost that will always be above the cost of debt. This cost of equity is largely determined by the level of risk of the firm, and it is typically measured with the capital asset pricing model. The cost of capital for the firm is then simply the weighted average cost of capital, reflecting the firm's financial structure.

Strategic managers need to understand that financial markets have a set of performance measures, which influence their attitude toward the firm. These measures include market capitalization, market value added, and the market-to-book ratio. Such measures supplement the traditional managerial measures such as return on equity and return on capital employed. Failure to recognize the importance of these financial market measures may result in the firm experiencing difficulty raising the capital required to support its chosen strategy.

This chapter also highlighted current concerns with the accuracy of financial reports prepared by firms. There have been numerous examples of firms reporting financial results that are quite irregular. Since investors rely on these, as well as on the objectivity of auditors, for making investment decisions, such a lack of credibility is likely to lead to major regulatory changes to strengthen their objectivity.

Finally, the chapter looked at derivatives as a means for the firm to reduce risk. The firm does this by shifting risk, at a cost, from itself to other individuals and organizations that are prepared to accept that risk. This is a complex area of corporate finance, fraught with difficulties, but managers must understand when such instruments are useful, and what are the consequences of both using and not using these instruments.

⟳ REVIEW QUESTIONS

1. Why are most large firms not self-sufficient in cash flows?

2. Explain the linkages between competition in product markets and competition in financial markets.

3. Policymakers in some countries believe that the market for corporate control should be suppressed or eliminated. Do you agree with this perspective? Justify your argument.

4. How do leverage (gearing) and the contextual environment interact to affect prospects for bankruptcy?

5. Discuss the major reasons why investors have grown to distrust firms' accounting statements.

6. Institutional investors have become more active shareholders in recent years. Why is this occurring? Do you approve of this trend? Why or why not?

7. Why was it that only eight U.S. firms had a AAA rating from Standard and Poor's in early 2002?

8. The return on government securities is generally assumed to be risk-free. Do you agree with this assumption? What evidence can you present to support your point of view?

9. Explain the difference between economic profit and accounting profit. Why is this difference important to strategic managers?

10. Explain the role of derivatives in risk management.

⟳ APPENDIX: INTEREST-RATE SWAP

Let us now consider a more complex but more realistic example of an interest rate swap. This example is drawn from F. J. Fabozzi and F. Modigliani.[46]
The current situation is:

There are two entities, an AAA-rated U.S. bank and a BBB-rated U.S. industrial firm, each of which wants to borrow $USM100 for 10 years.

The bank wants to raise these funds at a floating rate, since it wants to protect itself from interest rate changes.

The firm wants to borrow at a fixed rate, since it wants to know what its future interest liabliliteis will be.

In the United States:

The bank can borrow at a floating rate of 6-month LIBOR + 30 b.p. (where b.p. = basis points, .01%).

The firm can borrow at a fixed rate of 12%.

However, in the eurobond market:

The bank can borrow at a fixed rate of 10.5%.

The firm can borrow at a floating rate of 6-month LIBOR + 80 b.p.

The decision faced by each firm is: Should it borrow in the U.S. or on the eurobond market, and should it borrow at a fixed or floating exchange rate? Also, do the differences between interest rates in these two financial markets provide either or both with an opportunity to get what they want at a lower cost? The structure of the interest rates in the two financial markets is:

Floating-rate securities:

The bank can borrow domestically in the United States at a cost of LIBOR + 30 b.p.

The firm can borrow eurodollars at a cost of LIBOR + 80 b.p.

So there is a spread of 50 b.p., since the bank is lower risk.

Fixed-rate securities:

The bank can borrow eurodollars at a cost of 10.5%.

The firm can borrow domestically in the United States at a cost of 12%.

In this market the bank is also seen as a lower risk, but the spread between the two entities in now 150 b.p.

The question is whether the difference in spreads of 100 b.p. between these two securities in these two financial markets presents the firms with an opportunity to raise funds more cheaply. We can assume that a financial intermediary will see this opportunity and enters into transactions with the bank and the firm. Under the circumstances described above, the intermediary is able to arrange a swap of interest payments between the bank and the firm, resulting in a lower interest for each, while at the same time getting a payment for its services. In essence, the difference in spreads of 100 b.p. is split between the three parties—the bank, the firm, and the intermediary—through a new transaction, the swap, making it attractive to all parties.

The intermediary sets itself up between the bank and the firm, accepting payment from each and making payments to each, while at the same time taking a margin on the business. The U.S. bank raises its $USM100 on the eurobond market at a fixed cost of 10.5% and pays the interest on this loan on a regular basis. The bank will also pay the intermediary a fee, a variable rate based on LIBOR, and in return get a fixed sum from the intermediary.

The payments made by the bank are as follows:

To the eurobond holders at a fixed rate of 10.5%

To the intermediary a floating rate of LIBOR + 70 b.p.

(*Note:* this 70 b.p. is negotiable; if it is too high or too low the transaction will not be attractive to one partner.)

The total sum paid out by the bank is thus:

10.5 + LIBOR + 70 b.p. = 11.2% + LIBOR

At the same time, the bank receives income from the intermediary:

Income from the intermediary at a fixed rate of 11.3%

(*Note:* Again, this is a negotiated figure; if it is too high or too low, one party will not find the transaction worthwhile.)

Consequently the bank's final position is:

Income received from the intermediary – 11.3%

Payments to bond holders and intermediary – 11.2 + LIBOR

Total cost (11.2 + LIBOR) – 11.3 = LIBOR – 10 b.p.

We see that the final position of the bank is a variable-interest-rate cost, as it had wanted, expressed relative to the LIBOR. In addition, this is less than if it had borrowed in the United States, where it would have paid a rate of LIBOR + 30 b.p. Thus the bank has saved 40 b.p. on its loan of $USM100, or $400,000 per year.

Let us now consider the situation from the perspective of the firm. The payments made by the firm are:

To the eurobond holders, a floating rate of LIBOR + 80 b.p.

A fixed payment of 11.3% to the intermediary

Total payments are thus LIBOR + 12.1%

(*Note:* Again, the fixed interest rate of 11.3% has to be chosen to make the deal attractive to both partners.)

The income received by the firm is:

A floating rate income from the intermediary, which we assume is 6-month LIBOR + 45 b.p.

(where the additional 45 basis points are chosen to make the deal attractive.)

Consequently, the firm's final position is:

Income received from the intermediary: LIBOR + 45 b.p.

Payments to bondholders and intermediary: LIBOR + 12.1%

Total cost: 11.65%

And the firm has now achieved its goal of a fixed-interest commitment, although this is made up of a combination of fixed and variable income and payments. In addition, this fixed interest rate is below what it would have been had the firm borrowed on the U.S. domestic market. In fact, the firm has saved 35 b.p. on its $USM100, or $350,000. From the perspective of the intermediary, the position is:

They paid the firm: LIBOR + 45 b.p.

They got from the bank: LIBOR + 70 b.p.

Net income 25 b.p. or on the sum of $USM100 a fee of $250,000

We should emphasize that whether this swap will be of value to all participants will depend on relative rates between the U.S. and the eurobond markets, the initial net spread of 100 b.p. As we noted earlier, the use of derivatives is partly dependent on the

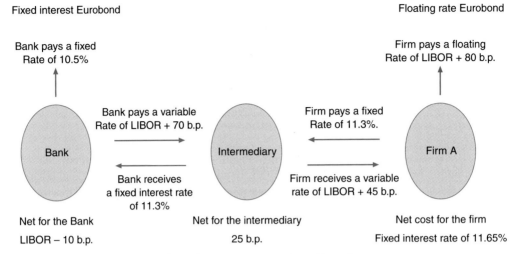

Figure 4.5   Interest-Rate Swap Example

relative value between different financial markets and the opportunities for arbitrage. In the example above, the net spread of 100 b.p. has been split:

25 points to the intermediary

35 points to the firm

40 points to the bank

The structure of this swap is illustrated in Figure 4.5, where it is clear that all three firms involved in the swap have been able to take advantage of the fact that financial markets in different regions of the world do not always move together.

ENDNOTES

[1] J. Tagliabue, "For France Telecom, Trouble at Every Turn," *International Herald Tribune,* September 14, 2002, p. 13.

[2] M. Grinblatt and S. Titman, *Financial Markets and Corporate Strategy* (Boston: Irwin/McGraw-Hill, 1998).

[3] M. Jensen, "The Market for Corporate Control," in *The Modern Theory of Corporate Finance,* C. W. Smith, ed. (New York: McGraw-Hill, 1990).

[4] "Disney Stock Quote History", 2002. www.disney.go.com/corporate/investors/stockhistory.html

[5] R. Pike and B. Neale, *Corporate Finance and Investment* (Hemel Hempstead, UK: Prentice Hall, 1996).

[6] Financial markets can also be classified as money markets (instruments with maturities of less than one year) and capital markets (instruments with maturities of more than one year).

[7] "London Calls as Sony Goes with the Money Flow," *Australian,* June 6, 2001, p. 39.

[8] J. M. Samuels, F. M. Wilkes, and R. E. Brayshaw, *Financial Management and Decision Making* (London: International Thomson Business Press, 1999).

[9] D. Pilling, "Hayami's Handout," *Financial Times,* September 19, 2002, p. 12.

[10] Grinblatt and Titman, *Financial Markets and Corporate Strategy.*

[11] K. Bruckner, S. Leithner, R. McLean, C. Taylor, and J. Welch, "What Is the Market Telling You about Your Strategy?", *McKinsey Quarterly,* no. 3, 2000, pp. 157–166.

[12] Grinblatt and Titman, *Financial Markets and Corporate Strategy.*

[13] Insider trading refers to a situation in which some investors are provided with information that is not provided to others.

[14] J. D. Glater, "Ernst & Young Latest Auditor Moving to Alter Some Practices," *New York Times,* February 5, 2002, p. C1.

[15] P. Taylor, "Bullish Analysts More Likely to Be Promoted," *Financial Times,* February 1, 2002, p. 27.

[16] "Star Turn," *The Economist,* August 5, 2000, p. 64.

[17] For a fuller treatment, see Grinblatt and Titman, *Financial Markets and Corporate Strategy.*

[18] E. F. Brigham and J. F. Houston, *Fundamentals of Financial Management* (Orlando, FL: Harcourt Brace, 2001).

[19] M. Useem, "Corporate Leadership in a Globalizing Equity Market," *Academy of Management Executive* 12, no. 4 (1998), pp. 43–59.

[20] Samuels et al., *Financial Management and Decision Making.*

[21] Note that large investors (institutional or otherwise) are often represented on the board.

[22] As we write, it appears likely that Argentina may default on its debt, while there is widespread speculation about Japan's increased indebtedness. The International Monetary Fund was reported to be considering ways to make it easier for countries to default on sovereign debt. These are yet further examples of how today's strategic manager must always question basic assumptions, for over time much of what was considered fixed has become variable, whether we consider interest rates, exchange rates, technology, or customer needs and wants.

[23] Grinblatt and Titman, *Financial Markets and Corporate Strategy.*

[24] R. A. Brealey and S. C. Myers, *Principles of Corporate Finance* (Boston: Irwin/McGraw-Hill, 2000), p. 227.

[25] Grinblatt and Titman, *Financial Markets and Corporate Strategy.*

[26] A. McCathie, "Creditors' Reprieve Gives Kirch Breathing Space," *Australian Financial Review,* February 18, 2002, p. 10.

[27] Samuels et al., *Financial Management and Decision Making.*

[28] *Trading and Capital-Markets Activities Manual* (Washington, DC: Federal Reserve Board, 2001).

[29] A. van Duyn, "Pay Now, Live Later Is New Borrowing Mantra," *Financial Times,* April 9, 2002, p. 19.

[30] "The New Basel Capital Accord: An Explanatory Note", Bank for International Settlements, January 2001. www.bis.org/publ.

[31] As result of financial innovation, this simple distinction is becoming fuzzier. As we noted, debt holders often impose a variety of conditions on borrowers, among which so-called equity kickers, whereby a debt holder may achieve an equity position under certain conditions, are becoming more common.

[32] S. R. Samson, *Corporate Rating Criteria* (New York: Standard and Poors, 2001). www.standardandpoors.com.

[33] Grinblatt and Titman, *Financial Markets and Corporate Strategy.*

[34] K. T. Liaw, *The Business of Investment Banking* (New York: Wiley, 1999), pp. ix, 337.

[35] J. Wiggins, "AAA-Rated Club Loses Yet Another Member", *Financial Times,* April 24, 2002, p. 20.

[36] "Bond Blues", p. 11 in "A Survey of Corporate Finance", *The Economist,* January 27, 2001.

[37] W. Edwardes, *Key Financial Instruments* (London: Pearson, 2000).

[38] Since interest costs are tax-deductible, the net cost of debt to the firm is lowered by its tax rate.

[39] R. F. C. Dobbs and T. M. Koller, "The Expectations Treadmill," *McKinsey Quarterly* 3 (1998), pp. 33–43.

[40] J. M. Stern, J. S. Shiely, and I. Ross, *The EVA Challenge* (New York: Wiley, 2001).

[41] R. K. Srivastava, T. A. Shervani, and L. Fahey, "Market-Based Assets and Shareholder Value: A Framework for Analysis," *Journal of Marketing* 62, no. 1 (1998), pp. 2–28.

[42] D. M. Chance, *An Introduction to Derivatives and Risk Management* (Fort Worth, TX: Dryden, 2001).

[43] F. J. Fabozzi and F. Modigliani, *Capital Markets: Institutions and Instruments* (Upper Saddle River, NJ: Prentice Hall, 1996).

[44] G. Crawford and B. Sen, *Derivatives for Decision Makers* (New York: Wiley, 1996).

[45] For example, Chance, *An Introduction to Derivatives and Risk Management.*

[46] F. J. Fabozzi and F. Modigliani, *Capital Markets: Institutions and Instruments,* pp. 642–645.

CHAPTER 5

Internal Analysis: Managing Competences, Costs, and Knowledge

---

Learning Objectives

Upon completing this chapter, you should be able to:

- Appreciate the role and nature of resources and competences in strategic management

- Be able to identify and appraise resources and competences

- Realize that an integral element in strategic management is building new resources and competences

- Use a value chain to analyze a business

- Determine the major drivers of costs and how these influence strategy

- Recognize the importance of managing intangible assets appropriately

- Understand the development of knowledge-based competition and its implications for management

---

Canon was founded in 1933 as the Precision Optical Research Laboratories with core technologies in precision grinding of lenses and the mechanics of camera operation, and these have been improved since that time. The company initially developed new competences in photocopiers through technology licensed from RCA but then developed a new process, based on its understanding of mechanics and optics as well as knowledge of chemicals. This alternative to Xerox's patented technology was further extended into a color copier. The technology was licensed to firms that subsequently became competitors. Canon entered the hand-held calculator business but was unsuccessful against Sharp, which was able to make much thinner calculators. The next development was a 35mm SLR fully automatic camera with a built-in microprocessor, using competences in precision optics, electronic circuitry, and manufacturing. The new camera had few parts and low production costs, based on the company's knowledge of calculators and mechanical cameras. Canon then developed a personal copier, drawing on its core knowledge of copiers. This copier incorporated a disposable cartridge, reducing the need for a service network, which had been a major barrier to entry. This was followed by a personal printer, which was a significant improvement on existing products, using a copier-like printer engine, with a disposable cartridge. Based on the company's manufacturing competences, this engine could be produced at low cost. It was used by other printer manufacturers such as Hewlett-Packard, and became the industry standard.[1]

⊙ 5.1 INTRODUCTION

Canon has successfully managed the transition from a small Japanese firm with limited skills and products into a global firm with a wide range of products in which it is a technological leader. In this transition, Canon utilized its existing skills and competences but also developed and built new ones. These have permitted the firm to launch an extensive range of new products capable of competing in high-growth markets, thereby expanding its scope and financial performance. Canon has adopted a number of approaches to generating the new skills required, ranging from the licensing of new technology to major investments in its own R&D. In some instances, these changes have been incremental, building on existing technology; in others, the developments have been revolutionary for the firm, permitting major new products to be developed. Nor is Canon's success due solely to its skills in R&D and technology; it has also developed world-class skills in manufacturing and marketing.

As we highlighted earlier, the fundamental question in strategic management is how firms achieve and sustain superior financial performance. Successful firms must achieve this superior performance in a world characterized by intense global competition, with strong rivalry in terms of the price/performance characteristics of competing products, where all firms are attempting to innovate with new products and business models. The Canon example demonstrates that success is strongly influenced by the unique skills and competences of the firm—what is referred to as the resource-based view (often abbreviated to RBV).[2] Strategy must be concerned with the development and deployment of firm-specific factors that will contribute to competitive advantage. This view contrasts with the structural view of success discussed in Chapter 1, which suggests that strategy involves the firm finding an attractive industry and taking actions to achieve a strong position within that industry. With this view, success depends on industry characteristics such as barriers to entry, weak customers, or the nonexistence of substitute products or services.

While structural characteristics of an industry are important, they are not the sole determinants of success.[3] This can be seen from data on the variability of firm profitability within an industry, as shown in Table 5.1 for the global chemical industry. No matter which measure is adopted, profitability varies widely within that industry. Ciba Geigy Specialty Chemicals shows a generally higher return than does du Pont.

We recognize that the firms shown in Table 5.1 operate in different segments of the chemical industry; Ciba Geigy competes in the printing ink market, while ICI competes in the decorative paints market. However, they all compete in certain other markets, such as construction, automotive, and engineering materials. Broader research confirms that industry factors account for only a small proportion of the observed variation in firm

TABLE 5.1   Variability of Firm Profitability within the Chemical Industry, 2002

Firm	Operating Profit/ Sales (%)	Operating Profit/ Total Assets (%)	Net income/Shareholders Funds (%)
BASF	8.2	7.5	8.9
Ciba Geigy Specialty Chemicals	11.1	6.7	9.3
du Pont	7.7	5.3	−12.2
ICI	8.7	10.0	35.9

Source: Annual Reports: basf.com; cibasc.com; dupont.com; ici.com.

performance.[4,5] Even in structurally unattractive industries (such as airline travel), some firms such as Ryanair and SouthWest are able to achieve superior financial performance. To explain success, we clearly must look at characteristics of individual firms, as well as those of the industry in which they compete, namely, the resource-based view of the firm. RBV emphasizes that the essence of firm profitability lies not in doing what other firms do but in exploiting the unique characteristics possessed by the firm.[6] We now address this topic.

The resource-based view suggests that firms succeed financially because they have unique and hard-to-imitate resources that permit them to develop a competitive advantage, thus generating superior financial performance. RBV conceptualizes firms as bundles of **resources**—stocks of important factors that a firm owns or controls in order to function. The approach assumes that these resources vary across firms (resource heterogeneity) and that they are difficult for competitors to imitate (resource immobility), so that differences may persist over time. Superior performance arises from the deployment of these resources, while sustainability requires the development of the new resources required to compete in a new and different world.

The resources developed by the firm must, of course, be aligned with the competitive circumstances it faces. The resources needed to be a successful clothing firm are different from those required to be a successful biotechnology firm. Resources may be deployed across all the businesses in the firm's portfolio, or they may be used only within one or a limited number of business units. A powerful corporate brand name such as Sony, for example, will typically add value to all products to which the name is applied, whereas GE's expertise in gas turbines does not help its NBC television network.

In a dynamic world, all sources of competitive advantage will have a limited life. Since competitors will eventually imitate the resources possessed by a successful firm, sustainability can be achieved only as a consequence of innovation. In addition, since the world is continually changing, what succeeds today may not succeed tomorrow. Because resources may depreciate in value as the environment changes, companies must manage their transition from dependence on one set of resources to another. In other words, continual renewal and/or extension of the resources of the firm is required for sustained success in a changing environment.

Nonetheless, resources in and of themselves do not lead to competitive advantage. For example, during the 1980s, General Motors possessed significant resources—substantial cash, large plants, good brand names, and an extensive distribution network—yet Japanese competitors gained significant market share from them in the critical U.S. market. Resources per se are a necessary but not sufficient condition for superior financial performance. It is the way in which the firm combines these resources that is critical to success.

These combinations of resources are what we will call **competences,** and it is the possession of competences that creates the value for an outside party that is crucial to financial success. Generally this outside party is the customer. However, competences could equally well create value for a supplier. We may have competence in supply-chain management that allows us to create value in the supply chain and share this with the supplier. This competence in supply-chain management may draw on resources such as information technology and human resources and may ultimately lead to additional customer value through lower prices. Thus a competence does not have to be restricted to something that directly adds value to customers; it could add value in other ways. In many parts of the world, the relationship with government is critical for success, and this could be one of our competences.

Summarizing, the resource-based view of the firm adopts the perspective that firm resources are central in formulating strategy. They are primary constructs on which firms build their strategies for profitably developing market opportunities. Competences are combinations of these resources, reflecting the ability of the firm to deploy resources. The key to the resource-based approach to strategy formulation lies in understanding the relationship among resources, competences, competitive advantage, and performance. This requires the development of strategies that exploit each firm's unique characteristics at the same time as ensuring that the resources and competences required for the future are being developed, so that sustained profitability can be achieved.

This resource-based view of the firm is illustrated in Figure 5.1. The basic elements are the resources of the firm. The linkages among these, the strategy of the firm (including its competitive advantage), and financial performance are illustrated in the figure. As the figure shows, the resource-based view emphasizes both **resource deployment** (how well we utilize current resources) and **resource generation** (how well we create new resources or new combinations of existing resources). It also distinguishes between superior performance and competitive advantage. A firm may possess a competitive advantage and yet not earn an economic profit. A competitive advantage is measured relative to competitors, while economic profit is measured relative to the capital employed in the firm.

We begin by examining the concept of resources, both *tangible* and *intangible,* and their contribution to strategic management. Next, we expand the discussion to introduce the idea of competences—combinations of resources that help us beat our competitors. The deployment of competences to obtain competitive advantage is the next topic, and from there we consider the dynamic or temporal dimension of competences, recognizing that old competences may no longer suffice and new ones must often be developed. We then examine the issues of value and cost, using the value chain or business system as a starting point. The understanding of costs and cost behavior is critical to the changes taking place in the world's economy, and it is therefore appropriate that we next cover the increasing role of intellectual capital in distinguishing successful firms from the crowd. We look at knowledge as a strategic resource and the management of knowledge

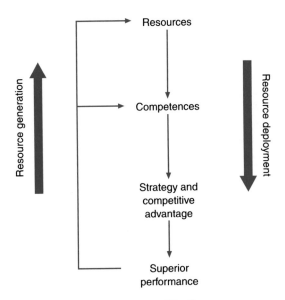

Figure 5.1   Resources and Performance

as a crucial competence in the years ahead, concluding with a brief discussion of the implications for managers.

⑤ 5.2 RESOURCES

Resources are firm-specific assets that enable the firm to perform activities in a manner superior to competitors. In the short term strategies are constrained by the firm's current resources and the speed with which it can acquire or develop new ones. Examples of resources are patents, trademarks, and knowledgeable staff. These are often difficult to transfer to other firms; that is, they are difficult to imitate. However, as we will see, resources may be more easily imitated than competences, since competences are integrated sets of resources.

Identifying resources is difficult, a good place to start is by examining the different types of each. The purpose of this analysis is not simply to describe the resource, although that is a necessary starting point. Instead, it is to try to understand whether the particular resource should be extended or modified, whether it can be used differently, or whether it can be used more efficiently. Such an analysis must also include an understanding of the changing environment, so that judgments can be made on what new resources are likely to be required and how these are to be developed.

To understand resources, we divide them into two broad categories—tangible resources, which appear on the balance sheet, and intangible resources, which do not.

Tangible Resources

The tangible resources of a firm can be broken down in to two main subgroups: financial and physical.

Financial Resources

Financial resources relate to the firm's capacity for future investment, whether this is in plant, people, processes, acquisitions, or innovation. If the firm has limited levels of financial resources, then its strategic flexibility is correspondingly reduced. Financial resources include the firm's borrowing capacity, its capacity to raise capital in the form of debt or equity, and its ability to generate funds internally as measured by free cash flow. These total resources determine the firm's capacity for investment expenditures in future products and facilities as well as its ability to innovate and handle fluctuations in demand and profits. In December 2003, Intel had some $USB8.0 in cash and cash equivalents and $USB5.6 in short-term investments, indicating substantial capacity to innovate.[7] These financial resources include the firm's credit rating, since this influences its ability to raise debt; the cost of that debt; and the ability to raise equity. But while financial resources are a necessary condition for innovation, they are not sufficient. Without financial resources, innovation is very difficult to achieve. If the firm has financial resources, these can be used wisely or they can be wasted.

Physical Resources

Physical resources include the firm's buildings and plant, the technical sophistication of its operations, the flexibility of its operations, and its reserves of raw materials. American Airlines, with its fleet of 978 owned and leased aircraft, has larger resources than Southwest Airlines, with its fleet of 355 aircraft.[8] Of course, in this industry the value of such a resource depends on other factors, such as age of the aircraft and the number of different types of aircraft in the fleet (SouthWest only has one type of aircraft, which contributes to its significant cost advantage). Other physical resources include the size of the firm, its geographic location, its information systems and databases, its distribution networks, and its customer information systems. For some firms, a major tangible resource is an automated warehouse system, which permits lower inventory costs.

Tangible resources may be standard across an industry and thus not a source of competitive advantage. For example, many firms in an industry might use very similar physical plant, resulting in little competitive advantage surrounding the plant itself. The Boeing 747 operated by Singapore Airlines is almost identical to the 747 operated by another airline.

Intangible Resources

Intangible resources are those that are not represented on the balance sheet and thus are more difficult to capture and to describe. They are less visible and consequently more difficult for competitors to understand, to purchase, and to imitate. As we will see later, these intangible resources are generally knowledge-based and may provide a relatively secure basis for competitive advantage.

Classically, the resources necessary for an industrial firm were considered to be the tangible resources of land, labor, and capital, where capital includes the financial and economic resources required. But in modern firms there is a new resource: the skills, knowledge, brainpower, and creativity of the firm and its members. These latter resources are what we call **intellectual assets** or capital, and these are increasingly important to many organizations. In management consulting or advertising, the factors critical for success are staff, not buildings or location. This trend is occurring in most industries where intellectual assets are displacing physical and financial capital as key factors of production. Intellectual assets and knowledge are demonstrating a defining role in determining competitive advantage, and the relative importance of intellectual capital continues to grow. Jobs are being redefined: the knowledge content of most jobs is increasing, whether we are talking of plumbers or doctors. The number of knowledge workers is increasing, and products themselves are becoming more knowledge-intensive.

It is not easy to quantify the increasing knowledge intensity of a firm due to the lack of accepted measures of intellectual assets; however, one surrogate for them is the M/B ratio of the firm. As was discussed in Chapter 4, this ratio is the market capitalization of the firm divided by the book value of the net tangible assets (or capital employed) of the firm, as shown in Figure 5.2.

Market capitalization reflects the views of financial markets on the prospects of the firm in terms of its ability to produce future cash flows. These cash flows can be interpreted as the expected return from all the assets of the firm, both tangible and intangible. Capital employed is based on historical accounting principles and reflects the value of the tangible assets of the business.

Thus the M/B ratio is a measure, possibly imperfect, of the *relative importance* of intangible and tangible assets in the valuation of the firm by financial markets. The intangible or intellectual assets include brand name or brand equity, the skills and knowledge of staff, customer loyalty, and patents as well as the knowledge base of the company in systems, technology, skills, and so on. Few if any of these assets appear on the balance sheet of the firm. The value of Merck or Coca-Cola is not based on bricks and mortar; the share market valuation is based on expectations of the value of the intellectual capital of the firms. In the case of Merck, this is the value of its patents and R&D, the ability to develop new drugs in the future. In the case of Coca-Cola, these intangible assets include the brand equity of Coca Cola, the value of which was estimated to be $USB70.5 in 2002.[9]

As a consequence of these developments, it is clear that the real value of companies, as expressed by share markets, is not given by traditional accounting measures as recorded

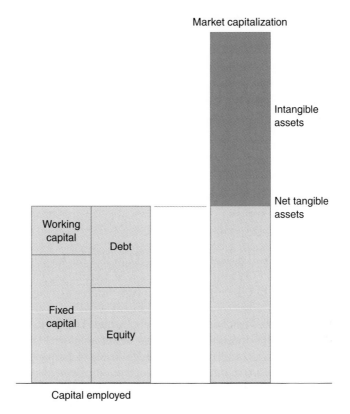

Figure 5.2   Tangible and Intangible Assets

on the balance sheet. When a firm invests in a tangible asset, the asset is booked on the balance sheet, with no cost on the income statement. The cost on the income statement occurs as the tangible asset is depreciated. Investment in an intangible asset such as R&D is shown on the income statement as a cost but not on the balance sheet. Yet the value of intangible assets is becoming more important, as reflected in the increase in the M/B ratios of firms over time. In fact it has been estimated that the median value of M/B values of U.S. firms doubled between 1973 and 1993.[10] In 1999, the average market-to-book ratio of the S&P 500 companies in the United States reached 6.25, where the denominator was the book value of equity, not the book value of capital employed.[11] However, these data do support the importance of intangible assets.

Table 5.2 shows the M/B ratios for a number of global firms. The table shows that Coca-Cola, Merck, and Nokia have high M/B, ratios reflecting the importance of intangible assets and future expectations. There are also significant differences between firms in the same industry, as illustrated by Wal-Mart and Sears. The high value for Wal-Mart reflects the growth expectations held for the firm because of its intellectual capital in the form of brand equity and its knowledge base in retailing and logistics. In contrast, Sears with a ratio of only 1.12 in December 2002, was seen as possessing little in the way of intellectual capital or future prospects.

Classifying Resources

Resources may also be classified in a manner which reflects their ownership. The categories which result are normally called human capital, structural capital, and customer capital.[12]

TABLE 5.2 Market-to-Book Ratios for Global Firms

Firm	Industry	December 2001	December 2002
Coca-Cola	Beverages	10.32	9.32
General Motors	Autos	1.38	3.03
Merck	Pharmaceuticals	8.33	7.00
Nokia	Electronics	15.33	6.47
Sears	Retail	2.46	1.12
Sony	Electronics	3.39 (3/02)	N/A
Toyota Motor	Autos	1.77 (3/02)	N/A
Wal-Mart Stores	Retail	7.62 (1/02)	5.36 (1/03)

Source: "Market-to-Book Ratios", Thomson Financial, Datastream Advance 3.5, 2003. www.thomson.com/corp/about

Human Capital

Human capital is in the minds of individuals; it is the knowledge, skills, ability, experience, intelligence, creativity, and motivation of individuals. The firm can use the human capital of its staff, but the firm does not own it. Staff with a high degree of human capital should be considered as volunteers, not employees—or, expressing this same idea a little differently, such staff can be rented but not owned. This human capital can be traded by the individual in the form of better salary, better employment conditions, or even a job with a new employer. Individuals with high levels of human capital are generally very mobile and can move to other firms if current employment conditions are not meeting their requirements. The firm itself cannot trade human capital unless it sells the entire group or division and the employees elect to stay with the divested entity.

The firm uses this human capital in its current operations. This knowledge may be about processes within the firm but could also be about relationships with customers, suppliers, and alliance partners. At the same time, the firm must facilitate the generation of new human capital, encouraging employees to develop new skills and more creativity. An issue for many firms is what knowledge is owned by the individual and what knowledge is owned by the firm, which brings us to a discussion of structural capital.

Structural Capital

Structural capital is capital that is owned by the firm, not by a specific individual. Structural capital is that which does not go home at night! It is contained in the firm's processes, hardware, software, databases, and structure, and it includes the company's values, culture, and philosophy. As an illustration, Tesco, the U.K. supermarket chain, has a customer clubcard, which permits the firm to maintain a complete record of customer purchases. This sophisticated database and data analysis system are valuable resources for the firm that are not currently possessed by its competitors.

If an individual leaves the firm, such capital stays with the firm. Its value and use are not confined to an individual; rather, it is a collective concept. Since the firm owns structural capital, it can be reproduced, shared, and traded. A patent owned by the firm can be sold; a process that has been developed by the firm can be licensed, as American Airlines has done with its reservations system or Amazon with its information system.[13] Unique market positions, technological knowledge, and accumulated experience may also create advantages difficult for competitors to copy.

Since one of the tasks of management is to build corporate assets, managers need to develop structural capital from the human capital of the firm's members. Whereas *the individual owns human capital, the firm owns the structural capital.*

So it is possible for a conflict to arise between the individual and the firm regarding what knowledge to share and what rewards will be offered to the individual to share this knowledge. What are the intellectual property rights of individual employees? What incentives will be offered to translate human knowledge into structural knowledge, which in turn is the basis for a competitive advantage for the firm? Human rights activists are increasingly concerned about these attempts. They argue that efforts to extract this knowledge from individuals and share it throughout the organization strike at the very heart of an individual's personal value in the labor market and see the whole area as the new frontier in a battle for individual freedom. Knowledge workers may also be more loyal to their profession than their employer. This is another reason for the increased popularity of gain-sharing rewards such as stock options, for there is a real need to improve the loyalty of knowledge workers as the role of intellectual capital expands. We are convinced that structural capital is likely to be a basis for competitive advantage for the firm, but it is difficult to manage and accumulate.

When structural capital can be legally protected, it is called **intellectual property** and is owned by the firm. Examples of intellectual property are trademarks, patents, and copyrights. The firm can extract the value of its intellectual property in a number of ways. For example, it could sell the intellectual capital to another firm, as when a firm sells a patent it owns. Or it could license it and obtain royalties, as Bell Labs did when it licensed the transistor to Sony. There is a growing market for trading intellectual assets, where the firm is both a buyer and a seller. Companies may buy knowledge to leverage their complementary assets; for example, many large companies are better at commercializing products than at developing them, and consequently they buy new ideas rather than developing them themselves. In 1997 pharmaceutical companies derived 34% of revenue from products licensed from other companies, a significant increase from 29% in 1992.[14] Such licensing allows the firm to access technological developments from a wide array of other firms—not just from its own R&D—although management must avoid overpaying for these licenses.

When the firm wants to trade this intellectual property, it needs to be aware of the level of legal protection afforded or the intellectual property regime that applies. A problem for many firms is the ease with which intellectual property can be copied in several countries. As a consequence, there is ongoing debate within the World Trade Organization (WTO) around the protection of the intellectual property rights of firms, whether these involve software, patents, or copyrights. In some Asian countries in particular, laws protecting intellectual property are relatively weak and it is easy to buy fake luxury goods such as watches as well as pirated CDs, or DVDs, and software. As a condition of its membership to the WTO, in 2003 China agreed to respect intellectual property rights in trademarks and copyright, reflecting a strengthening of the legal regime. As this regime gets established, we may expect to see increased trade in intellectual property, with firms taking a more aggressive stance toward its development. Other forms of knowledge have limited legal protection; consequently, some firms prefer not to patent new ideas, since they reveal what is being patented and hence make it easier for other firms to copy or enhance.

Customer Capital
Customer capital is the value of the firm's relationship with its customers, including understanding of customers' demands and preferences. Indicators of customer capital would be customer retention rates, satisfaction measures, profitability, and market share. Firms are increasingly interested in customer retention rates, since small increases in brand loyalty can have substantial impact on profit. It is generally more profitable to retain an existing customer than to acquire a new one. Indeed, there is a move-

ment to co-designing and even co-producing with customers, since these investments in joint innovation will usually build customer capital.[15] Not only do we want to be able to charge a premium to customers; we also want to enable them to charge a premium to their customers. A resource may be one that the firm has access to, even though it does not own it. For example, for many firms a major resource is its network of customers, but the firm does not "own" such a network.

For many firms a major intangible asset, and a major component of customer capital, is *brand equity*. The value of a brand name such as Samsung is owned by the entire firm and exists independently of the individuals who comprise the firm. A survey conducted in 2003 on the value of 100 global brands shows that Coca-Cola headed the list, with an estimated brand value of $USB70, as shown in Table 5.3. As the table indicates, industrial firms such as BP and Caterpillar possess significant levels of brand equity, implying that brand management is also relevant for them.

A number of leading fast-moving consumer goods companies have installed a system of brand health indicators to assess the direction of change, if any, in brand equity and to identify key issues that might otherwise pass unnoticed. These systems, further discussed in Chapter 12, also help remedy a major defect in the measurement of brand manager performance inasmuch as a focus solely on such results as profit, volume, or market share is rather like asking a corporation to show only an income statement. Brand equity can be seen as the balance sheet for the brand[16] and provides assurance that good short-term results have not been achieved at the expense of the brand's future.[17]

Intangible resources are a significant source of competitive advantage, since they are difficult for competitors to imitate and are often characterized by path dependency and causal ambiguity. For example, a competitor may be able to purchase modern equipment, but this does not imply that it can get that plant to operate efficiently and effectively. To do so requires an infrastructure, including other intangible resources such as a trained, knowledgeable, and committed staff. This leads us to a discussion of competences, the ability of the firm to integrate a number of resources—a process requiring time, money, leadership, and skill.

⊙ 5.3 RESOURCES AND COMPETENCES

An individual resource typically has no value in isolation; its value is realized when it is combined with other resources. These combinations of resources are what we designate

TABLE 5.3   Value of Selected Global Brands

Brand Name	Rank	Value $USB
Coca-Cola	1	70.4
Nokia	6	29.4
Mercedes	10	21.4
Sony	20	13.1
Samsung	25	10.8
Ikea	43	6.9
Louis Vuitton	45	6.7
BP	69	3.6
Caterpillar	75	3.4
Wall Street Journal	99	1.7

Source: G. Khermouch and D. Brady, "The Best Global Brands," *Business Week*, August 4, 2003, p. 69.

as the *competences* of the firm.[18] For example, strong finances are by themselves not a competitive advantage. They have value only when they are combined with other resources to constitute what we denote as a competence. This resource deployment and integration allows the firm to excel in the delivery of a process critical to an outside party. Such a process may be one that delivers quality to customers or a process that delivers benefits through the supply chain, but the essential point is that the competence ultimately contributes to the competitive advantage of the firm or its business units.

Competences are embedded in the firm's processes and organizational routines, such as new product development, order generation and fulfillment, brand management, or integrated logistics and supply-chain management. This is illustrated in Figure 5.3, where we have taken new product development and customer service as examples of competences possessed by the firm. Competence in new product development requires technical R&D skills, the ability to operate in teams, an excellent database system, and skills in understanding consumers. The firm will excel in this process—in other words, possess a competence in new product development—if it can integrate these disparate functional groups (among which there may well be interdepartment conflict) and their knowledge. The new product development process must be managed on an end-to-end basis, with all departments working together as a team toward a common objective. The new product development process has performance criteria—such as speed, time to launch, new product success rate, and resources consumed—that can be benchmarked relative to competitors to assess the magnitude of the competence possessed by the firm. Other examples of competences are:

Sony has a competence in miniaturization in consumer electronics, utilizing its resources in design, technology, marketing, and manufacturing.[19]

A bank might have a competence in front-line service, drawing on resources in its database systems, training, and human resources.

A textile firm might have competences in international transportation logistics, developing talented managers and linking operational goals to compensation plans and managing costs.[20]

Competences include discrete business-level organizational processes fundamental to running the business (e.g., order entry, customer service, quality control) as well as generalized organizational skills (e.g., miniaturization or tight tolerance engineering). So

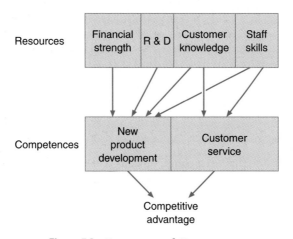

Figure 5.3   Resources and Competences

competences can exist at both the business and corporate level. Firms that are successful acquirers have developed competences in pre- and postmerger activities: they are able to assess the worth of a target firm and successfully integrate it into the existing firm. Because competences are hard to develop, any firm will possess only a limited number. By their nature, competences are global in character and, since they contribute to competitive success, should be assessed only relative to other firms.

Among the firm's relatively small number of competences, some will be more important than others. We will call these **core competences:** they are fundamental to performance and have the following properties:

> They have a disproportionate impact on ultimate customer satisfaction or the efficiency with which that value is delivered.
>
> They provide a basis for entering new markets.[21]

Obviously, the firm should excel at these core competences, while less critical competences may be considered as outsourcing candidates. If the firm possesses a core competence, it performs this activity in a manner superior to competitors. A core competence will generally focus on a user need (so that there is a source of revenue), be unique (so that prices can be set to some extent independent of competition), and be difficult to replicate (so profits will not be competed away). A core competence should not be very general, like marketing, but rather constitute "a combination of complementary skills and knowledge bases embedded in a group or team that results in the ability to execute one or more critical processes to a world-class standard."[22]

Hamel and Prahalad observe that Canon has four core competences—in precision mechanics, fine optics, microelectronics, and electronic imaging—and describe how these have been deployed across its product line.[23] In a study of a number of multinationals, core competences uncovered included superior technical know-how, reliable processes, and relationships with external parties.[24]

Core competences are seen as drivers of strategy, but they are difficult to identify and define and it is not always easy to separate core from noncore competences. As we will explore shortly, what is regarded as a core competence will change over time. For example, in the global automobile market, core competences have allegedly evolved from the possession of a global distribution network and quality production processes to niche marketing and flexibility.[25]

We now discuss the properties of competences that enhance their propensity to contribute to competitive advantage. Note that these would also be desirable properties of resources.

◉ 5.4 COMPETENCES AND COMPETITIVE ADVANTAGE

To evaluate the profit earning potential of a competence, we need to assess it in terms of a number of properties, as shown in Figure 5.4.

Valuable

The essential feature of a competence is that it makes a *significant contribution* to the fulfillment of customer needs. A competence is valuable to the extent that it allows the firm to reduce costs or increase revenue over what it would have been without the competence. Federal Express provides its customers with software, called Powership, free of charge, which allows them to schedule shipments, manage accounts, track packages, and order supplies electronically. To some extent using this system locks in

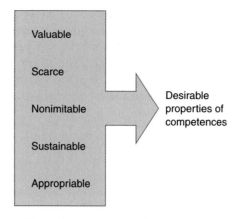

Figure 5.4 Properties of Competences

customers, but it also provides them with additional value. Sony has a competence in miniaturization of electronic products, which has been utilized in CD players, computers, and video cameras, since for such products smallness is a major consumer benefit. Wal-Mart, the company with the greatest sales volume in the world, possesses a set of resources and competences that include store location (reduced rental), brand reputation (reduced advertising), and supply-chain management (reduced logistics costs), which combine to provide a major cost reduction for Wal-Mart relative to the industry.[26]

Since customer needs change over time, the firm needs to continually reassess the extent to which its competences are contributing and whether or not new ones are required. IBM's competence in mainframe computers, for example, became less valuable when minicomputers were developed. In fact, in a changing world competences can sometimes become rigidities.

Scarce

A competence is valuable if it is not *widely shared* by other firms. If many firms develop the same competence, none will earn a substantial return on that investment. We can also distinguish competences required to maintain competitive parity from those that add to competitive advantage. In many markets firms need the competence to deliver high-quality products, but quality itself often fails to create competitive advantage: it has become a prerequisite for survival.

Nonimitable

Competences and resources differ in the extent to which competitors can *imitate* them. A resource such as location for a retail store is difficult to imitate. Similarly with a brand name. A competitor cannot easily duplicate the advantage that flows to Coca-Cola from its brand name. Competences that involve complex interactions are difficult to duplicate, partly because the competence demonstrates causal ambiguity; that is, it is not clear what it involves. The success of SouthWest Airlines, for example, is a complex mixture of culture, recruitment, schedule, routes, focus, planes, and so on.

A new factory provides little advantage when competitors can purchase the same plant from the supplier. However, if the resource is traded, the competitor may have to pay such a high price for it that all future benefits are capitalized in the price. The benefits a firm expects to accrue from possession of resources should not be dissipated in the competitive struggle to acquire them. The ease with which competitors can create a competence cannot easily be generalized. Sometimes the follower can create a competence at lower cost than the pioneer: the imitator learns from the pioneer's mistakes. In other cases, the pioneer has a significant advantage that is hard to dislodge.

Sustainable

Related to the above, it should be evident that the more difficult it is to imitate a competence, the longer it is likely to last. Other things being equal, the firm should obviously seek competences that are likely to prove *durable*. Since developing and sustaining competences are necessarily cost-incurring activities, we should always prefer one that promises a return over a longer period of time. As we see later in the chapter, such competences are more and more dependent on the possession of privileged knowledge not available to other firms. Sustainability of a competence will also be influenced by the rate of environmental change, which could result in the competence becoming obsolete, as well as the availability of substitutes.

Appropriable

Finally, there is the issue of whether or not the firm can *appropriate* the returns that the competence delivers. This is determined by property rights and the relative bargaining power of the actors. Ideally, the firm wants to capture the benefits of the competence, but profits may flow not to the firm that "owns" the resource but to employees, suppliers, or customers. In financial services, the competence may be the network of relationships with clients, but these often go with the staff member, not the firm. This may also be the case with an advertising agency.

> When the U.K. agency Saatchi and Saatchi broke up, the former partners of the firm took several major clients, such as British Airways, with them to their new firm, which has subsequently prospered. Cordiant, the renamed Saatchi and Saatchi, became insolvent in 2003.

The firm needs to exploit the full competitive potential of its resources by managing its structure, reporting system, and management processes, including incentives. As firms move toward more of a knowledge base, with a greater proportion of high-caliber professional staff, the need to capture the knowledge of individual staff members in systems and software increases.

◉ 5.5 DYNAMIC COMPETENCES

As we have emphasized throughout the book, organizations exist, and have to prosper, in a rapidly changing and unpredictable world. The competences and skills that lead to success today may not be those required for success in the future. Most competitive advantages are temporary due to imitation by competitors and substitution by other forms. There will also be changes in customers, competitors, and substitutes. Consequently, the firm must develop new competences, either by new combinations of pre-existing resources or by development of resources new to the firm. The processes involved must be an integral component of strategic management. The need to both deploy resources for current competitive success and generate the resources and competences required for future success is another of the dilemmas facing strategic management, yet another choice between stability and change.

We refer to these mechanisms for building and reconfiguring existing resources and competences as **dynamic competences.**[27] How good is the firm at changing its competences and resource base? How good is the firm at renewing itself, at creating and handling change? Long-term competitive advantage lies in the ability of the firm to develop the resources and competences required to address its changing environment faster, more astutely, and at lower cost than competitors.[28] This is like double-loop learning. The firm needs a set of competences to be successful today, but it also needs to be able to forget or terminate those that are no longer required, enhance some that have become more important, and build fundamentally new ones. Managing the transition from one set of competences to another is a considerable challenge and takes time to accomplish.

When we examine successful firms, it becomes apparent that they have developed a range of new competences, expanding out from their initial competences in a combination of incremental and revolutionary steps. Sony began as a firm repairing radios and making kits to convert AM radios into short-wave receivers. It then aggressively developed the competences that enabled them to develop miniature transistor radios, audio-tape decks, TV, color TV, VCRs, and many other products through a combination of internal development, alliances, and licensing of technology to such a degree that Sony is now the market leader in several global markets—a long way from the original radio repair business![29]

This need to create new competences is illustrated by the dilemma confronting firms that face the obsolescence of their core product. Do they focus their strategy on the changed needs of their current customers, or do they attempt to develop new markets for their current skills? Consider Kodak and the challenge it has faced, and continues to face, with electronic imaging for household photography. Does Kodak continue in the photographic image markets by improving traditional cameras and film or does it attempt to accomplish this using electronic technology, bringing it into competition with firms such as Canon, Sony, and others? Alternatively, does it try to utilize and develop its current competences in chemical imaging and attempt to launch into new markets?

We can visualize a firm as a *portfolio of competences* in which the composition and emphasis on each element will change over time in response to the changing environment, as shown in Figure 5.5. Some competences possessed by the firm in, say, 2003 will become less relevant in 2007. Others will become more important and will need to be developed through a combination of means. Some firms, such as Polaroid, have found it difficult to manage this transition,[30] while others have been remarkably successful.

These new competences may be generated internally through training, staff development, and selective recruitment, generally combined with multifunctional task teams. Alternatively, they may result from acquisitions, joint ventures, and alliances. Sony originally licensed the transistor from Bell Laboratories but was then able to improve the underlying technology, allowing it to develop major new markets, such as portable radios.

To identify a firm's competences, two approaches are generally used; a functional approach and a value-chain approach. Using the functional approach, competences are assessed relative to competition in each of the major functional areas of the business unit or firm. With the value-chain approach, the focus is on the specific activities undertaken by the firm and their competitive assessment.

We now go on to explore the concept of a value chain in more detail.

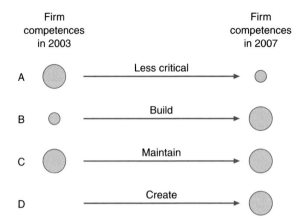

Figure 5.5 Dynamic Competences

⑤ 5.6 THE VALUE CHAIN

A useful tool for assessing competences and analyzing a business unit is the value chain, popularized by Michael Porter.[31] The **value chain** for a business describes that business in terms of the activities that the firm has chosen to undertake in order to be able to compete. These activities are the basis for examining the opportunities for reducing costs or adding value (improving differentiation) at each stage of this value chain.

We will organize our discussion of the value chain by first examining the drivers of cost, then looking at value added. However, ultimately cost and value must be integrated into an understanding of the complete chain. When they are not, we run the risk of attempting to reduce cost by eliminating or suboptimizing activities critical to adding value for customers.

Figure 5.6 shows the value chains for two directly competitive firms, one from Australia and the other from New Zealand. Each produces a timber product that is exported to Singapore. The data in the figure are the unit costs per tonne of the six major value-adding activities, from purchasing to service. Since this product is a commodity, they each sell it in Singapore for the same price: $600 per tonne.

As can be seen from the figure, the costs each firm incurs for each activity vary considerably. The value chain provides a better understanding of the magnitude of the cost variability and a framework for addressing the reasons why these costs differ. The New Zealand firm purchases the raw material, timber, at a lower unit price (of finished product) than the Australian firm. This challenges us to understand why this is so and question whether anything can be done to alter it. In this case, the reason has to do with climate and rainfall in New Zealand—trees grow faster and bigger there than in Australia. On the other hand, the forests in New Zealand are less accessible, so there is a higher cost involved in transporting the timber to the processing plant. The Australian firm also faces higher logistics costs in getting the finished product to Singapore—a combination of the location of the plant, less productive wharves, and high-cost shipping. The consequence of the different cost structures is that the New Zealand firm has a margin of $180 per tonne while the Australian firm has a margin of only $150 per tonne.

Such information is essential to fully understand a business's competitive position. When developing a value chain, we have to decide what level of detail to use. For example, in Figure 5.6 we used one activity—outbound logistics—but this could have been

	Australian competitor	New Zealand competitor
	Unit costs, AUD/tonne	
Purchasing	150	100
Inbound logistics	20	30
Operations	160	180
Outbound logistics	50	30
Marketing	50	60
Service	20	20
Margin	150	180
Price	600	600

Figure 5.6 Competitive Value Chains

broken down into more detailed elements, such as local freight, port handling, ocean freight, and Singapore distribution. Such a chain would be more complex but provide more complete information. We also have to decide which costs are relevant. Here costs were fixed and variable, including capital costs via depreciation, measured in terms of annual costs divided by annual volume in metric tonnes. Finally, two competitors in the same industry may use different value chains, depending, for example, on their out-sourcing decisions and their core competences.

Firms in other industries have their own value chains, different from the above. For example, in retail banking one critical activity is transaction processing. Transaction costs are generally considered a back-office function in the bank, with the total cost being a combination of processing and transmission costs, each of which has been influenced by technology. As transmission costs have fallen, banks and other financial institutions have been able to decouple the back office from the front office. Many call centers and trans-action-processing centers are in remote locations, such as India or Ghana. As with the forest products firms, the magnitude of the different cost elements varies from bank to bank. The management task is to understand their relative importance and what actions can be taken to reduce them—the concept of cost drivers.

◉ 5.7 COST DRIVERS

In a competitive environment, businesses have unrelenting pressures to reduce costs. The value chain provides a useful framework for understanding costs and their relative magni-tude. Here we will focus on the drivers of long-term cost behavior and how costs might be reduced. Ideally, we benchmark ourselves against competitors at each stage in the value chain. We first discuss two major drivers of cost: economies of scale and experience.

Economies of Scale

Economies of scale are a major driver of strategy. They are the rationale behind many mergers and acquisitions, based on the assumption that the merged entity will have lower costs through economies of scale. For example, when Chase and Chemical Bank decided to merge in the mid-1990s, they planned to combine their back-office functions of check clearing and loan processing. They hoped that this would reduce combined costs by some $USB1.5, a substantial sum.[32] Hewlitt-Packard and Compaq were aiming for even greater savings from their 2002 merger.

Figure 5.7 shows a typical relationship between long-run average costs per unit and a measure of firm size—the number of units produced per year. When **economies of scale** are present, unit costs decline as the size of plant increases. As shown in Figure 5.7, the plant producing 200 units per year has lower unit costs than the plant producing 100 units per year. This difference is not due to capacity utilization; it is inherent in the production technology used by the two firms. Consider the firm producing 100 units per year. At this production level, its costs are at a minimum. If it produces 95 units per year or 105 units per year, its costs will rise, since these costs are given by the firm's short-run cost curve, where technology is assumed to be fixed. Graphs of economies of scale assume that the firm is operating optimally, given the technology available for a particular size of plant. Economies of scale are determined by the industry long-run cost curve, which assumes different production technologies for different levels of output.

Relevant questions then become:

1. How significant are economies of scale? Economies of scale will be significant when the firm is capital-intensive. There are no economies of scale if all costs are variable. Consequently, there are major economies of scale in industries such as commodity chemicals, computer chips, and aircraft manufacture. In these industries, there are major benefits for being large—small competitors are cost uncompetitive.

2. In which activities do economies of scale occur? Scale economies are often thought to be confined to manufacturing operations, but they can also occur in other activities, such as R&D and marketing. It may cost $USM500 to develop a new drug—so the firm has to be large. On the other hand, capital requirements for production are often low, permitting the entry of relatively small generic manufacturers when the innovator's patents expire.

3. To what extent do scale effects act as a barrier to entry? If large-scale effects characterize the industry, entrants have a dilemma. Do they enter on a smaller scale, requir-

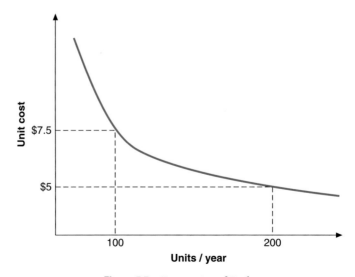

Figure 5.7 Economies of Scale

ing less capital investment and lower volumes to fill their facility, with the consequence that their costs will be uncompetitive? Or do they elect to construct a large plant so as to achieve economies of scale? This represents a significant investment, and the firm needs to gain a substantial market share to break even.

4. To what extent is optimal scale in the industry changing? Are there increasing benefits from scale or is the industry headed toward smaller scale, as shown in the two diagrams in Figure 5.8.

If there are *increasing benefits of scale* (Figure 5.8(a)), then the optimal size of plant is increasing and we would expect to see increasing industry consolidation, with mergers and acquisitions. Firms that recognize the change can proactively acquire other firms and have a better chance of surviving the consolidation while retaining their autonomy. In the auto industry, just such a process of consolidation built General Motors. More recently, Volkswagen A.G. has pursued just such a policy, grouping Audi, Seat, Skoda, Bentley, Bugatti, and Lamborghini under its corporate umbrella. Similar consolidation has occurred in the pharmaceutical, banking, chemical, supermarket, food, and insurance industries, as well as among such service companies as advertising agencies and law and accounting firms. When such consolidation occurs, firms not engaging in acquisition will likely become targets for others.

Alternatively, the graph of economies of scale could be moving to the left, with smaller plants or firms developing advantages over larger firms, as shown in Figure 5.8(b). This occurred in steel, where mini-mills had a significant cost advantage over large, integrated mills. A similar pattern may develop in power generation, historically an industry with substantial economies of scale. New technology permits the development of small-scale plants that can be located close to customers or even owned by them, thus eliminating the need for high-voltage distribution systems, massive chunks of investment, and even the utilities themselves.[33]

Scale economics rest on the ratio of fixed to variable cost; the volume sold and the impact of technology, on long-run average cost. Each of these assumptions needs to be examined carefully in the light of already existing knowledge as well as in the light of prospective future developments. Changes in economies of scale create substantial turbulence and change in an industry. Whether increasing scale leads to consolidation or decreasing scale produces new entrants and lower prices, changes in economies of scale are one of the drivers of industry restructuring. Firms that recognize that scale economics are changing, and act in a timely manner, will usually enjoy a competitive advantage. Com-

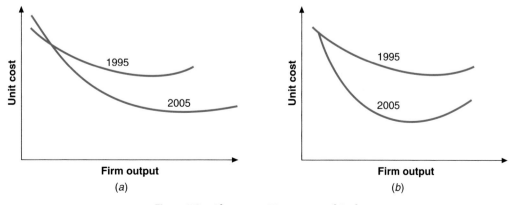

Figure 5.8 Changes in Economies of Scale

petitive advantage cannot be based on what was successful in yesterday's world; managers need to understand the economic characteristics of the world of the future.[34]

Learning

Another major driver of costs is experience or learning. As a firm performs a specific activity more often, it learns to do that activity better and more efficiently—in other words, its costs decrease.

As shown in Figure 5.9, the **experience curve** postulates that there is a relationship between unit cost and cumulative output, the total number of units of the product that the firm has ever produced, when the relationship is plotted on logarithmic scales. This cost decline has been observed in many industries but is particularly noticeable in electronics. There have been dramatic reductions in the price (and, of course, the cost) of disk drives in terms of price per megabyte of memory, measured in constant dollars, dropping from about $400 in 1977 to about $0.10 by the mid-1990s. This dramatic drop in price has created many new market opportunities for such devices. One cause of this cost reduction is learning, a concept different from scale. Learning means we do things better, faster, with less wastage. We modify the product to make it easier to manufacture, employ better inventory systems to reduce investment, adopt new technology and so on. These cost reductions do not occur automatically; they are made to happen by aggressive managerial action.

In a competitive market, a firm needs to reduce costs along the characteristic industry cost curve. If not, its costs become uncompetitive and it may not survive. If a firm can expand faster than its competitors, it may be able to slide down the experience curve faster than these competitors, reducing costs more rapidly. So growth may be the overriding objective for the business, particularly if the overall market itself is growing rapidly.

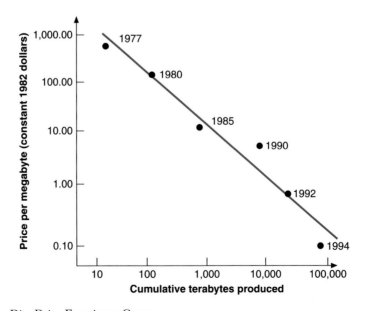

Figure 5.9 Disc Drive Experience Curve

Reprinted by permission of Harvard Business School Press. From *The Innovator's Dilemma*, Christensen, C. M. Boston MA 1997, pp. 8. Copyright © 1997 by the Harvard Business School Publishing Corporation: all rights reserved.

These ideas lead to a possible strategy imperative: find a growth market, have a strategy that focuses on growth, drive costs down with this growth, reduce prices to get faster growth, and end up with a dominant position in the market at maturity. At this time it may be impossible for the small-share producer to achieve the same cost structure as the market leader. So the strategy imperative is *dominate or divest,* epitomized by Jack Welch's admonition to GE's businesses to be number one or number two in every market in which they competed.

An important qualifier of this argument occurs when a major innovation takes place. New technology may change the design of the product or the production process, perhaps enabling a competitor with less cumulative experience to leapfrog the existing cost leader. In economists' terms, we have to distinguish between the long-run and short-term cost curves.

Value Drivers

As we noted earlier, any consideration of value chains that focuses exclusively on costs is potentially dangerous, for we should simultaneously consider how and where value is added for customers. Outsourcing or drastically reducing activities that are key to adding value for customers can create enormous problems.

> The British company Railtrack was responsible for maintaining the infrastructure of the British railroad system. However, it outsourced all maintenance (its supposed core competence) to independent engineering companies. When a major accident occurred, a crisis entailed and the company seemed incapable of managing its many separate outsourced contracts so as to ensure compliance and a sufficient level of safety. Very controversially, but nonetheless definitively, the company was forced into receivership.

◉ 5.8 KNOWLEDGE AND INTELLECTUAL CAPITAL

The national and international economy is being transformed by the increasing knowledge intensity of economic activity and by the growing importance of trade in knowledge products such as interest-rate swaps. As several commentators have noted, we are moving to a knowledge-based society, with firms becoming more knowledge-intensive. Indicative of this trend, the Organization for Economic Cooperation and Development (OECD) has developed a knowledge index for products, based on their R&D intensity. When this measure was used to assess the knowledge intensity of manufactured exports for the world economy as a whole, it was found that the index was stable during the 1970s at a level of about 0.70. However, by 1997 the index had risen to about 1.04, indicating the growth in knowledge intensity of products.[35]

Many of the successful companies of the last decade have been knowledge-intensive firms such as Oracle, SAP, and Merck. Other companies are using technology to develop products and services in which an increasing amount of knowledge is embedded. The economic value of a drug or a computer or a film is well beyond that of the materials of which it is composed. We can now purchase cars fitted with GPS systems, which provide a significant customer benefit in terms of locating lost or stolen cars. When digital city or regional maps supplement such systems, drivers can determine, in real time, better routes to their destinations that avoid heavy traffic or other impediments. Other knowledge-based innovations in autos include cars with features such as fuel management systems, active suspension systems, tires that detect punctures, and even diagnostics. Indeed, even our oft-maligned PCs have some such capability.[36] Massey-Ferguson has developed a satellite system to record agricultural yield per square meter, so that the company is now in the business of yield management as well as tractors.[37]

The increasing knowledge content of products and jobs arises from developments in information technology that have allowed "old" economy firms to develop smart systems containing substantial intellectual property rights. For example, Citibank developed sophisticated software to operate its retail banking system, including ATMs, but the value of this software is not on the balance sheet. Other companies have developed enhanced information systems to reduce inventory levels and the need for warehouses, reducing these firms' capital intensity and enhancing their financial performance.

In other sectors of the economy, there has been major growth in what are generally called **symbolic** goods, goods that can be compressed for transmission over telecommunication lines. There has been, and continues to be, growth in the ability to digitally store, locate, and transmit information.[38] Financial advice, X-rays, music, and movies can all be transmitted over an information network. The reach of these networks is not limited geographically, and innovation is further increasing the range of these goods. For example, in the finance sector there has been an increase in what can be traded, with currency and interest-rate swaps, index futures, and so on. Increasing electronic connectivity, arising from user-friendly interfaces, common standards and protocols, and the ability to digitize data, has facilitated these developments, which have been accompanied by explosive growth of the Internet and the World Wide Web. We are witnessing the emergence of a global knowledge economy, with the ability to deliver codified knowledge quickly and cheaply on a global basis.

These developments are being driven by the rapidly falling costs of information storage and transmission. CDs can now be produced and reproduced in the store or at home. Financial advisers distribute information electronically; consumers can buy and sell stock electronically; banks are allowing (or forcing) customers to perform their transactions electronically, via either ATMs or the Internet: the phenomenon is ubiquitous and pervasive.

An understanding of knowledge and its importance to strategy development is considered essential for strategic management. As Peter Drucker has noted, "knowledge has become the key economic resource and the dominant, perhaps the only, source of competitive advantage".[39] Before discussing knowledge and knowledge management, it is necessary to distinguish among data, information, and knowledge.[40]

Data consists of discrete objective facts about events, which are generally unstructured, without any meaning in themselves. Meaning comes from some analysis we perform on the data. For any firm there is generally a structured record of a transaction, which is the source of the data. For example, in buying groceries, we can describe the transaction in terms such as what products were purchased, at what price, who did the purchasing, what time of day, who was with the shopper, in which outlet the purchase took place. Other data would be historical share prices or the profit levels of an acquisition target. Nonfinancial data might include employees' qualifications or their attitudes as revealed on some scale. Such data are generally stored in a system, which can be evaluated in terms of cost, speed, and capacity as well as relevance and access.

Information is processed data that is intelligible to the recipient and is meant to change the way the recipient perceives something. Using the above example, information could be an analysis of the number of customers who bought, on the same shopping occasion, both products A and B. Information is data endowed with relevance and purpose, and it moves around a company in hard and soft networks. Hard networks include databases, reports, and e-mail, while soft networks would include presentations and conversations. Information gives us an analysis of the data; it can be formalized in databases, manuals, and documents and can be easily transmitted.

Knowledge is richer, broader, and deeper than information. It is a combination of information together with experiences, values, context, and insight. It reflects cognition and thinking. In the case of a potential acquisition, knowledge would be reflected in the answers to such questions as: Is the price acceptable? Can we integrate it with our current business? Knowledge is fluid, aware of what is not known, and contains judgment. Knowledge is thinking; it comes from experience tested against others and is informed by theory, facts, and understanding. It is fuzzy, hard to communicate, difficult to express in words, and depends on the owner. Knowledge is normally communicated by informal means and evolves with experience.

Knowledge can be considered to be a construction of reality rather than something that is true in an abstract or universal way. To the extent that knowledge represents "truth," it offers a reliable basis for making predictions and developing causal connection. In the context of an economic entity such as a firm, knowledge should be close to action and should be evaluated by the decisions and actions to which it leads. It is knowledge that makes data relevant and meaningful. Many firms have too much data and have difficulty turning this into knowledge that can be used for decision making. The firm is likely to get transaction data from such sources as an enterprise resource planning system, a customer relationship management system, a retail point-of-sale scanner, or e-commerce transactions, but it often has difficulty making use of this data. For example, in one study few firms indicated specific examples of decisions affected by ERP data.[41]

Following Sullivan,[42] we believe it is sensible to discuss knowledge from both an individual and a collective perspective. Certainly individuals possess knowledge, but we argue that organizations, as entities, also possess knowledge, such as values, group skills, and unwritten rules and procedures. Organizational knowledge may be concentrated in particular individuals, with problems for the firm if they leave. A firm can lose knowledge through downsizing, so managers need to understand the knowledge base of the company and how to develop it.

Types of Knowledge

Knowledge is difficult to come to grips with, but we need to be able to classify it to be able to discuss it in a meaningful manner and able to manage its generation, transmission, storage, and use. Possibly the most useful way to categorize knowledge is according to whether it is explicit or tacit. This relates to how easily knowledge can be codified in terms that enable it to be understood by a wider audience. If knowledge can be codified, it can be made explicit and easily transferred.

Explicit Knowledge

Explicit knowledge can be put on paper; it can be codified in sentences or articulated in books, scientific formulas, specifications, manuals, and reports. It can be transmitted using formal language.[43] Since explicit knowledge can be codified, it is readily and cheaply transferable. Explicit knowledge exists at both the organizational and personal level. Organizational explicit knowledge should be easily accessible by any member of the firm, have a life beyond the tenure of an individual staff member, and be continually updated and improved. It is typically codified in the firm's systems and databases. For example, the firm may have a formal process for the evaluation of acquisition candidates, with information on market characteristics, competitors, and so on. Under these conditions, an explicit document exists that can be examined, changed, improved, or modified. Documentation of processes enables them to be communicated, learned by new employees, and transferred from one set of staff members to another, providing opportunities for both individual and organizational learning. Management consulting firms, for example, try to document their experience on a given project, explicating what lessons were learned and what can be used on other assignments. Information technology, with its rapidly decreasing costs, has been a major enabler and facilitator in the transfer of explicit knowledge both within and between organizations. As we will see later, there are a number of technological platforms, such as data warehouses, which have been adopted to facilitate knowledge transfer.

Tacit Knowledge

Tacit knowledge is knowledge that is difficult to articulate in a meaningful and complete way; it is hard to see and to explain. It is tied to the senses, skills, and perceptions of individuals and is not easily transferred to others. Tacit knowledge is unarticulated and includes intuition, perspectives, beliefs, values, know-how, and skills. Tacit knowledge exists in people's heads and is augmented and shared through interpersonal interaction and social relationships. Often oral, it can be spread when people tell stories around the water cooler. However, it is deeply rooted in individuals' actions and experiences as well as in their values and emotions. It is therefore usually highly personal, hard to formalize, and difficult to communicate or share with others. Tacit knowledge is automatic; it is accessed and used with little thought. But it also can be wrong and is hard to change, which can pose formidable management difficulties.

Examples of tacit knowledge include the advertising executive who "knows" what a good advertisement looks like, an R&D scientist who "knows" that a particular technological solution will work, a CEO who "knows" that the organizational culture of a takeover target is compatible. In each case, the individual finds it impossible to clearly enunciate the basis for this knowledge.

We suggest that tacit knowledge also exists at the organizational level. Organizational tacit knowledge subsumes culture, values, and principles as well as ways of doing things. When we discuss knowledge transfer in Chapter 11, we will see that a major challenge for strategic managers is to find ways to transform individuals' tacit knowledge into organizationally explicit knowledge so that the firm as a whole may capitalize upon it. Some firms have developed expert systems and artificial intelligence systems to assist in this process.

Knowledge can also be categorized depending on whether it is firm-specific or not. The most general level of knowledge would be scientific knowledge that is widely known and understood by all professionals in a field. Examples would be knowledge of the statistical tools in market research or the scientific knowledge behind encryption for e-commerce security systems. Such knowledge is easily obtainable and equally valuable to many businesses.

Industry knowledge is widely known to all competitors within an industry, for example, how to operate a blast furnace or the principles behind electronic fuel management systems for cars. In some circumstances, firms can leverage such industry knowledge, as when a consultant or a lawyer specializes by industry and is used by many clients in the same industry.

These two levels of knowledge are essential to operating within an industry but generally do not provide any measure of a competitive advantage. They may provide a barrier to entry, since it may be more difficult for firms outside the auto industry, for example, to acquire detailed knowledge of technology currently used within that industry, whether it is satellite navigation systems or the fluid mechanics of automatic transmissions.[44]

In contrast, firm-specific knowledge is unique knowledge that exists in one firm but not in others. Since it is unique, such knowledge is difficult to duplicate by competitors.

To do so would take considerable time and resources. Knowledge of this latter type is the only real basis of a competitive advantage for a firm.

Characteristics of Knowledge Products

Knowledge is different from other resources such as labor and capital. Its unique properties influence how it can and should be managed as well as what kinds of strategies are appropriate. We now review some of its relevant characteristics.

Network Effects and Increasing Returns

Knowledge products often show **network externalities.**[45] Under these conditions, the value of the product or service to a given user increases with the number of users of the product or service. This phenomenon is referred to as Metcalfe's law. Examples of such network effects are the Windows operating systems or the Internet. Since Windows is widely used, other firms apart from Microsoft write compatible application programs, making it more valuable to users and thus even more widely used. In markets with strong network effects, when one brand gets a significant market share, the value to users rises, creating a strong incentive for people to use the product or service more.

In the production of physical goods, economists worked on the basis of diminishing returns, with the assumption that all industry participants were using the same production technology and that at some volume marginal costs increase, limiting the scale advantages of a firm (i.e., the long-run average cost curve eventually begins to rise because of so-called diseconomies of scale). Such is not the situation with many knowledge-based products. In knowledge-based industries with *increasing returns,* the firm that is ahead tends to stay there. No matter how a firm gets ahead in the early stages of a market, whether by luck or good strategy, increasing returns amplify the advantage. In technology markets, these increasing returns may also be driven by standards, particularly when these are "owned" by a single firm. The more a protocol gains acceptance, the greater the consumer benefits and the better chance the standard has of becoming dominant. A major goal for the firm in knowledge-intensive markets is therefore to ensure that the product or service that it has developed becomes the standard in the industry, actual or de facto. The innovating firm may even give away technology to help the product become the standard. Alternatively, it may enter in to alliances with competitors and customers to get the product adopted as a standard. As we saw in Chapter 3, Ericsson is trying to do this with its Bluetooth wireless applications, developing alliances with customers, suppliers, and competitors to ensure an industry standard that it has developed. Indeed, Linux has achieved great success in the server market based on giving away its operating system. Customers typically favor so-called open-systems approaches because of the freedom of choice they engender.

Since increasing returns tend to create winner-take-all markets, different corporate strategies emerge. In these markets, rewards go to the firms that excel at sensing and seizing opportunities. Seizing opportunities involves identifying and combining the relevant complementary assets needed to support the business. Winners are those with the cognitive and managerial skills to discern the shape of the play. Consequently, firms need to be highly entrepreneurial, with a flat hierarchy, powerful success incentives, high autonomy, and ability to navigate quick turns—in short, companies able to rapidly transform themselves. Once these leader firms are established, they become very difficult to dislodge. A classic example of the difficulty in replacing an incumbent is provided by the QWERTY keyboard, which was invented in the late 1880s for mechanical typewriters. The layout of the keyboard was established to minimize the possibility of the strikers hitting one another. Once this keyboard layout was established, it proved very difficult to replace, even though technology removed the original basis for its design.

High Leverage

The bulk of the costs of knowledge products lies in the fixed costs of their creation, not in their manufacture or distribution. Information technology has large up-front costs in research, development, and design engineering, so the first copy of a piece of software may cost millions of dollars. The second has a direct manufacturing cost of almost zero. Hence, winners in knowledge-intensive industries have to make huge bets early. Forming partnerships early is therefore not only helpful in establishing a standard but is also a method of risk reduction. Another alternative (if affordable) strategy is to operate with very low margins so as to build the business at the expense of short-term profit. This appears to be the strategy with Amazon, which has incurred substantial development costs.

Other Properties of Knowledge Products

Knowledge has some characteristics of a *public good,* in that it can be used without being consumed. One individual can use a piece of knowledge without diminishing another person's ability to also use it. Knowledge can be in more than one place at the same time, and we can sell knowledge to more than one person. This is not the case for tangible products. We cannot (or, at least, should not!) sell the same auto to more than one person. An airplane can be assigned to only one route, but an airline reservation system can be used simultaneously in multiple tasks with multiple customers. As is common with knowledge products, such a system is scalable. Systems can be designed to handle huge increases in use with little additional expense.

It is also difficult to judge the value of knowledge before you purchase. Knowledge has uncertain value; it is difficult to predict who will get the value from knowledge. The firm may bear the cost of development only to find that others reap the benefits, as would be the case with pirated software. These characteristics may result in the firm underinvesting in knowledge products. Further, the value of knowledge can depreciate very quickly. Knowledge of future share prices would have considerable value; knowledge of historical share prices has very limited value. So knowledge is often very time-sensitive. Finally, knowledge becomes increasingly fragmented over time; it gets deeper and more complex and has to be continually renewed and extended.

◉ 5.9 SUMMARY

In this chapter we have emphasized the importance of the resource-based view of the firm as a determinant of success. Firm performance is strongly influenced by the resources of the firm and how well these resources are integrated into competences. In addition, future success requires that the firm continue to develop and expand its resources and competences.

Strategy development also requires an understanding of where the firm creates value, the costs incurred in creating this value, and the drivers of these costs, such as economies of scale and learning. The value chain is a useful tool to use to disaggregate total costs into the relevant activities so that a better understanding of costs and their behavior can be developed. We would emphasize that such analyses should not be static. Managerial foresight in understanding how the firm's value chain is evolving can provide the basis for an innovative firm strategy. A firm that recognizes the increasing importance of economies of scale can develop strategies to exploit this understanding, such as a merger, to achieve a competitive advantage.

Managers are responsible for managing the assets under their control, both tangible and intangible, and for most modern firms the value of the intangible assets outweigh that of their tangible assets. Yet accounting systems focus almost entirely on tangible assets, which are represented on the balance sheet at cost less accumulated depreciation. These intangible assets complement the tangible assets of the firm, and managers need to reorient their attention toward them. When intangible assets are ignored in the financial statements of the firm, managers are likely to underinvest in these assets and overinvest in tangible assets, resulting in a misallocation of resources. At the same time, managers may not develop the skills required to develop and manage intellectual capital. Management of intellectual assets requires capturing and disseminating what the firm has learned over time, sharing ideas and experiences across functional and organizational boundaries. In a rapidly changing global world, these intangible assets, including knowledge, have become the key economic resource and the dominant—perhaps the only—source of competitive advantage.[46] This makes it imperative that the firm develop systems to measure, and manage, these intangible assets.[47]

Measures such as return on equity or return on assets will overstate performance, since intellectual capital is not included in the denominator. Leveraging intellectual capital means that managers should promote, not restrict, its use and ensure that it is disseminated and used throughout the organization. The firm must develop an infrastructure that facilitates the development, sharing, and use of knowledge. Connecting the relevant parties, capturing know-how in context, and delivering it when and where it is needed require the existence of a culture that values intellectual capital and provides incentives for knowledge generation, sharing, and use. This was a major motivation behind the concept of the boundaryless corporation articulated under Welch's leadership at GE.

Finally, developments in knowledge and information technology are affecting firm boundaries by altering the mix between those activities undertaken by the firm and those provided by outsiders. Knowledge-based theory suggests that activities with a high degree of non-firm-specific knowledge and that are also explicit will move to the market and be provided by outsiders. Already there is major growth in contracted staff and other forms of nonregular employment.[48] Only activities that involve high levels of tacit and firm-specific specialized knowledge will remain in the firm and become the core activities through which the firm generates a competitive advantage. Since information technology is likely to continue to reduce the uncertainty and complexity of market contracting, we expect to see more outsourcing, interfirm cooperation, franchising, disintermediation, and electronic markets.

Managing intellectual capital requires new organizational forms and new managerial skills. Firms will have to change the way they behave with respect to people, incentives, technology, and culture. The focus will be on attracting and retaining high-caliber staff, which requires a different culture and style in the firm—in particular, a move away from a command-and-control culture. In addition, the form of the firm's relationship with staff will change, with full-time employees increasingly being viewed as volunteers active in managing their own careers rather than employees per se. The firm does not own people, and individuals who possess valuable intellectual capital can walk out the door at any time if they think the firm is treating them poorly. If knowledge workers have loyalty to their profession rather than to the company, an autocratic style of management is unlikely to be successful. Firms of the future will have to pay considerable attention to attracting and retaining high-caliber staff and will need to develop rewards that align the personal interests of staff with those of the firm. For some staff, this may mean giving stock options and retention bonuses; for others, it may mean providing a sense of professional challenge and allowing the individual free time to create new knowledge.

But although managers may intuitively believe that strategic advantage comes from superior knowledge assets, they may still find it difficult to make the linkage explicit. Such an alignment is difficult when knowledge is primarily tacit and in the minds of individual staff members. The link between knowledge and culture is vital. Managers must facilitate a culture that values the creation, sharing, and use of knowledge, one that includes incentives for sharing.

◎ REVIEW QUESTIONS

1. Why is it important for a firm to understand its internal resources and competences? Is an understanding of the internal environment more important than an understanding of the external environment?

2. What are the differences between tangible and intangible resources? Are intangible resources a better basis than tangible resources for developing and sustaining a competitive advantage?

3. For a firm with which you are familiar, identify one or more competences and discuss these competences in terms of the five properties discussed in the chapter.

4. For the firm selected in question 3, can you identify any new competences developed by the firm over the last five years? How were these developed?

5. Select a retail firm such as a supermarket. Develop the value chain for this firm and discuss the changes occurring at each level of the chain. What new strategies could the firm adopt to take advantage of these changes?

6. Provide examples of firms who have restructured their value chain.

7. "Knowledge will become the dominant means of achieving competitive advantage in the future." Discuss this statement.

◎ ENDNOTES

[1] C. E. Helfat and R. S. Raubitschek, "Product Sequencing: Co-evolution of Knowledge, Capabilities and Products," *Strategic Management Journal* 21 Special Issue (2000), pp. 961–979.

[2] For a critique of the RBV, see R. L. Priem and J. E. Butler, "Is the Resource-Based 'View' a Useful Perspective for Strategic Management Research?" *Academy of Management Review* 26, no. 1 (2001), pp. 22–40.

[3] A. J. Mauri and M. P. Michaels, "Firm and Industry Effects with Strategic Management: An Empirical Examination," *Strategic Management Journal* 19, no. 3 (1998), pp. 211–219.

[4] R. P. Rumelt, "How Much Does Industry Matter?" *Strategic Management Journal* 12, no. 3 (1991), pp. 167–186.

[5] A. McGahan and M. E. Porter, "How Much Does Industry Matter, Really?" *Strategic Management Journal* 18 Special Issue (1997), pp. 15–30.

[6] G. Hawawini, V. Subramanian, and P. Verdin, "Is Performance Driven by Industry or Firm Specific Factors? A New Look at the Evidence," *Strategic Management Journal* 24, 1 (2003), pp. 1–16.

[7] Intel Annual Report, 2002, www.intel.com

[8] American Airlines Annual Report, 2002, www.amrcorp.com and SouthWest Airlines Annual Report 2002, www.southwestairlines.com

[9] G. Khermouch and D. Brady, "Cross-Culture Success: American Brands Still Lead the Way," *Australian Financial Review,* July 29, 2003, pp. 53.

[10] "M/B Ratio for US Firms," *The Economist,* June 12, 1999, p. 70.

[11] B. Lev, *Knowledge and Shareholder Value* (New York: Stern School, New York University, 2000).

[12] L. Edvinsson and M. S. Malone, *Intellectual Capital* (New York: HarperCollins, 1997).

[13] "Internet Pioneers," *The Economist,* February 3, 2001, pp. 73–75.

[14] A. Torres, "Unlocking the Value of Intellectual Assets," *McKinsey Quarterly* 4 (1999), pp. 28–37.

[15] P. Berthon, J. M. Hulbert, and L. F. Pitt "To Serve or to Create? Strategic Orientations Towards Customers and Innovation," *California Management Review* 42, no. 1 (1999), pp. 37–58.

[16] We are indebted to our colleague Tim Ambler of the London Business School for this insight.

[17] P. Berthon, J. M. Hulbert, and L. F. Pitt, "Brand Management Prognostications," *Sloan Management Review* 40, no. 2 (1999), pp. 53–66.

[18] Other authors use the term *capabilities,* e.g., G. Dosi, R. R. Nelson, and S. G. Winter, eds., *The Nature and Dynamics of Organizational Capabilities* (Oxford, UK: Oxford University Press, 2000).

[19] C. K. Prahalad and G. Hamel, "The Core Competence of the Corporation," *Harvard Business Review* May–June 1990, pp. 79–93.

[20] A. W. King, S. W. Fowler, and C. P. Zeithaml, "Managing Organizational Competencies for Competitive Advantage: The Middle Managment Edge," *Academy of Management Executive* 15, no. 2 (2001), pp. 95–106.

[21] Prahalad and Hamel, "The Core Competence of the Corporation."

[22] K. P. Coyne, "Is Your Core Competence a Mirage?." *McKinsey Quarterly,* no.1 (1997), pp. 40–54.

[23] G. Hamel and C. K. Prahalad, "Competing for the Future," *Harvard Business Review,* July–August 1994, pp. 122–128.

[24] B. Mascarenhas, A. Baveja, and M. Jamil, "Dynamics of Core Competencies in Leading Multinational Companies," *California Management Review* 40, no. 4 (1998), pp. 117–132.

[25] G. Johnson and K. Scholes, *Exploring Corporate Strategy,* (Harlow, Essex: Pearson Education, 6th ed., 2002).

[26] D. J. Collis and C. A. Montgomery, *Corporate Strategy: A Resource-Based Approach* (Boston: Irwin/McGraw-Hill, 1998).

[27] D. J. Teece, G. Pisano, and A. Shuen, "Dynamic Capabilities and Strategic Management," *Strategic Management Journal* 18, no. 7 (1997), pp. 509–533.

[28] K. M. Eisenhardt and M. Jeffrey, "Dynamic Capabilities: What Are They?," *Strategic Management Journal* 21 (Special Issue, 2000), pp. 1105–1121.

[29] C. E. Helfat and R. S. Raubitschek, "Product Sequencing: Co-evolution of Knowledge, Capabilities and Products."

[30] M. Tripsas and G. Gavetti, "Capabilities, Cognition and Inertia: Evidence from Digital Imaging," *Strategic Management Journal,* (Special Issue, 2000), pp. 1147–1161.

[31] M. E. Porter, *Competitive Advantage* (New York: Free Press, 1985).

[32] "When Bankers Marched in Two by Two," *The Economist,* April 6, 1996, pp. 75–76.

[33] K. Leslie, D. Kausman, and G. Bard, "European Power: Managing through Deregulation," *McKinsey Quarterly* 1 (1999), pp. 38–51.

[34] C. M. Christensen, "The Past and Future of Competitive Advantage," *Sloan Management Review* 42, no. 2 (2001), pp. 105–109.

[35] P. Sheehan and G. Tegart, eds., *Working for the Future* (Melbourne: Victoria University Press, 1998).

[36] G. Probst, S. Raub, and K. Romhardt, *Managing Knowledge* (Chichester, UK: Wiley, 2000).

[37] Ibid.

[38] R. Blumentritt and R. Johnston, "Towards a Strategy for Knowledge Management," *Technolgy Analysis and Strategic Management* 11, no. 3 (1999), pp. 287–300.

[39] P. F. Drucker, *Managing in a Time of Great Change* (New York: Truman Talley Books/Dutton, 1995).

[40] T. H. Davenport and L. Prusak, *Working Knowledge: How Organizations Manage What They Know* (Boston: Harvard Business School Press, 2000).

[41] T. H. Davenport et al., "Data to Knowledge to Results: Building an Analyical Capability," *California Management Review* 43, no. 2 (2001), pp. 117–138.

[42] P. H. Sullivan, *Value-Driven Intellectual Capital* (New York: Wiley, 2000), p. 276.

[43] This book is an example of explicit knowledge, but we would be the first to admit that successful strategic management requires tacit as well as explicit knowledge.

[44] Note that extensive use of outsourcing will change this knowledge barrier (see Chapter 7).

[45] D. J. Teece, "Capturing Value from Knowledge Assets: The New Economy, Markets for Know-How and Intangible Assets," *California Management Review* 40, no. 3 (1998), pp. 55–79.

[46] Drucker, *Managing in a Time of Great Change.*

[47] A system developed by Scandia to manage intangible assets is described in T. A. Stewart, *Intellectual Capital* (New York: Doubleday, 1999).

[48] A. Burton-Jones, *Knowledge Capitalism* (Oxford, UK: Oxford University Press, 1999).

CHAPTER 6

Creating Future Direction

Learning Objectives

Upon completing this chapter, you should be able to:

- Appreciate that an important task for management is creating a sense of the future of the firm
- Understand that developing a strategy requires an awareness of what that strategy is designed to achieve
- Apply the concepts of vision, values, mission, and objectives
- Apply these at both the corporate and business-unit level
- Recognize that these concepts must be linked in an integrated and consistent manner

The statements below describe how Canon saw its future direction in 2003:[1]

Canon's vision was "aiming to be a truly excellent global corporation," which it noted would have four elements:

Becoming number one in the world in all of Canon's core businesses

Building up the R&D capabilities to continually create new businesses

Achieving a strong financial position

Fostering employees that are enthusiastically committed to achieving their ideals and take pride in their work

To meet this vision, Canon stated a number of objectives; one of these was to "become the world No. 1 in semiconductor production equipment in 2005," an objective for one of its business units.

Other objectives were:

To eliminate the need for prototypes through simulation and 3D-CAD systems

Cost reduction through staff reduction and increasing commonality of product components

Expand production outside Japan, particularly in China

Decentralize R&D with the establishment of R&D in Europe and the Americas

As a result of these strategies, Canon expected to significantly improve its revenue and net profit, as shown in Figure 6.1.

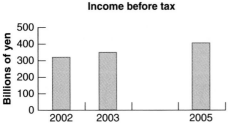
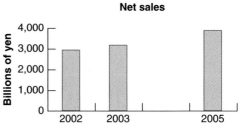

Figure 6.1   Canon Goals for 2005
Reproduced by permission of Canon.

As the figure shows, Canon expected to increase net sales from ¥B2940 in 2002 to ¥B3800 in 2005, primarily from the introduction of new products. At the same time, net income before taxes was expected to increase from ¥B330 in 2002 to over ¥B400 in 2005, indicating a small reduction in margins despite the cost reductions to be undertaken.

These statements attempt to convey the future direction for Canon as a corporate entity, as well as for its business units. They also describe specific objectives for the corporation as a whole as well as for one of its businesses (semiconductor production equipment). The strategy developed by the firm and its units will be designed to meet or exceed these expectations. As we will see in this chapter, a number of concepts can help strategic managers in establishing future direction, one of their most important functions.

⊚ 6.1 INTRODUCTION

The above example illustrates that Canon's senior managers see developing a sense of the future of the firm as an important component in the strategic management process. Managers and all employees in an organization have an interest in the future of the firm, and we believe that senior managers should be able to give reasonable answers to such questions as the following:

What do you think the firm will look like 10 years into the future?

What organizational values can we be committed to?

What changes can we expect in the next year or two?

What are we expected to achieve over the time period?

Answers to these questions mandate a sense of *purpose,* a sense of where the firm is going and what it aspires to be. This is a confusing area within strategic management, since firms use different terms to try to convey these ideas to employees and other stakeholders. Terms such as *mission, vision, purpose, intent, philosophy,* and *credo* all attempt to capture the need for the firm to be able to express, in some form, its aspirations for the future. The major reason for some kind of statement about future direction is the need to motivate and guide the efforts of employees. As we noted in Chapter 1, a firm is a voluntary collection of individuals with a common purpose, and this common purpose must, of necessity, give some guidance into the future.

Despite the evident importance of such a statement, Peter Drucker noted some time ago (and it is still true today) that business purpose and mission are major sources of business frustration and failure because they are seldom given adequate attention by senior managers.[2] We regard such a sense of the future as essential to generate employee passion and commitment. Employees seem to demonstrate commitment and enthusiasm when they have a strong personal attachment to the aspirations of the firm and what the firm stands for.[3] Over the last few decades, the need for such a sense of common purpose has increased rather than diminished. As organizations have decentralized and become flatter, decision making occurs deep down in the firm. To empower employees to make decisions without ensuring a shared organizational vision is downright dangerous for ensuring alignment. In addition, coordination across the firm becomes impossible. In our opinion, companies that continue to enjoy success have aspirations and values that stay constant while their strategies are continually adapting to a changing world.

Generating such a view of the firm requires creativity and imagination. Strategic management is not a purely analytical, left-brain activity but rather involves creativity, passion, and commitment. Contrary to the views that have permeated much of the literature on strategic planning, we must recognize that creativity and imagination are absolutely central to good strategic management. We would not be so foolish as to imply that these are the only qualities required in a CEO, nor would we wish to suggest that CEOs are the only persons in the organization in whom these qualities are desirable. Indeed, vision-setting is not simply a task for the CEO, for each unit or group within the firm can benefit from a shared vision that people in that unit can aspire to. However, the firm as a whole does need a sense of future direction, and developing this is one of the major responsibilities of the CEO.

We also believe that a manager who is incapable of imagining the future is incapable of creating it. Of course, creating is typically harder than imagining, but imagining is an essential first step. In this chapter, we begin with the concept of a vision statement, a critical and motivating feature. Next, we discuss values and their role in shaping behavior, before moving to the issues involved in mission definition. We conclude with the often-difficult but nonetheless vital task of setting objectives. Each of these concepts is applicable at both the corporate and business-unit levels of the firm. We discuss business strategy in the next chapter but defer to Chapters 8 and 9 the subject of corporate strategy per se.

In discussing the future direction of the firm, we will distinguish four concepts, as shown in Figure 6.2. Each of these will be briefly described, then examined in more detail later in the chapter. While we describe these concepts sequentially, it should be evident that they are very much interrelated, as indicated in the figure.

Vision

A **vision** for a firm is regarded as the ideal future state of the total entity. It is a mental image of a possible and desirable state of the firm. A vision needs to be realistic, credible, and attractive and should provide a bridge from the present to the future. Such a

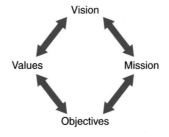

Figure 6.2   Elements of Aspirations

vision is essential for strategy formulation, since what the firm decides to do must be dependent on what it wants to achieve. The development of a vision is a major responsibility of senior management, since it is the logical antecedent to strategy development as well as a major motivator for employees. For this to occur, the vision must be communicated to and internalized by all employees.

Values

Values refer to the beliefs of staff members, which of necessity guide their behavior. Explicit values statements will usually include guidance on integrity and honesty, how employees will be treated, how customers and suppliers will be treated, and so on. Values may be quite general, but they should provide guidelines for employee behavior.

Mission

The **mission** specifies the domain of the firm: where and how it elects to compete. It specifies in fairly general terms the activities and operations of the firm. A mission statement should be specific to the firm and permit a person who reads it to understand what the firm is, what it does, and, just as important, what it does not do. Mission statements should clarify the firm's vision and provide a tangible direction that helps establish congruence among the actions of employees. Mission statements often reflect the firm's priorities among its key stakeholders and embrace a commitment to these stakeholders.

Objectives

Objectives are targets to be achieved by the firm and its units. These objectives typically specify in quantitative terms what the firm expects to achieve in both the short term and the longer term. Most firms have a hierarchy of such objectives, which cascade down from the corporate level to business units and beyond. They include both financial and nonfinancial objectives and represent the accomplishments that management believes must be attained in order to fulfill the mission and achieve the vision that has been established.

◉ 6.2 VISION

As our model of the strategic management process in Figure 1.5 indicates, strategic management is not a linear, step-by-step process. Rather, it is a recursive, interactive, circular process, with analysis leading to some ideas on strategy, leading to questions of how to implement them, leading to a forecast of potential results—all possibly leading back to a revised strategy. One element in this circular process is the generation of a vision for the firm. A firm is a voluntary collection of individuals brought together for a common purpose, and an important task for strategic managers is to generate a sense of the future for the entity that is widely shared within the firm. This is what we will refer to as the vision of the firm—a sense of what the firm is, where it is going, what it is trying to achieve. Such a vision can be expected to have a high degree of stability. But the world does change, and consequently the firm's view of its future may also change—in strategic management, nothing is fixed. We regard changing the vision to be one of the most challenging tasks for strategic managers.

A vision may be created at the corporate level, for the firm as a whole, or at a lower level, such as a business unit. Regardless, a vision should possess several characteristics. First, it must provide a general sense of direction, and thus it will focus strategy development and decision making. The other important property of a vision is that it must motivate employees. A well-designed vision statement provides the inspiration around which all members of the firm or unit can focus their energy and creativity.

The Vision Statement

Our definition of vision follows Bennis and Nanus, who described it as follows:

To choose a direction, a leader must first have developed a mental image of a possible and desirable future state of the organization. This image, which we call a vision, may be as vague as a dream or as precise as a goal or mission statement. The critical point is that a vision articulates a view of a realistic, credible, attractive future for the organization, a condition that is better in some important ways than what now exists.[4]

A corporate vision describes some ideal future state of the organization as a whole, but the concept is equally applicable at the business-unit or even functional level. Good vision statements should not be excessively restrictive, for employees must find in the vision something to inspire them personally.[5] Neither should visions be too specific or easily achievable, for their focus is the long run. A vision should be compelling, ambitious, and ask a lot of employees—although possibly its most important characteristic is the extent to which all employees are fully committed to it. A vision statement in which nobody believes is counterproductive, producing cynicism within the firm. Glaxo Smith Kline, the global pharmaceuticals firm, provides an example of such as vision statement.

> Our global quest is to improve the quality of human life by enabling people to do more, feel better and live longer.[6]

As we mentioned earlier, however, despite the desirability of some stability in a changing world, visions must also evolve—a good example of the paradoxes that often underlie strategic management.

> In 1999, Microsoft changed its vision from "A computer on every desk and in every home" to "Giving people the power to do what they want, where and when they want, on any device."[7] As a consequence of this change in vision, Microsoft has expanded its lines of business well beyond computers; it is now a major player in a number of new business areas such as PDAs, mobile phones, and video games.

Some firms use the term **strategic intent** to describe a concept similar to what we call vision, for successful firms often have bold ambitions, an obsession with winning, and the commitment to build the resources required for this success.[8] This obsession is referred to as strategic intent, which is not simply ambition. It is also an active management process, focusing on winning, on motivating people, and on communicating the value of the target while leaving room for individual contributions, sustaining enthusiasm, and using this intent to guide resource allocation. Starting resource positions are often poor predictors of future industry leadership; a firm can have lots of cash and talented people and yet lose its leadership position through complacency and poor decisions. Strategic intent is an animating dream that implies a significant stretch between existing resources and emerging opportunities rather than a focus on achieving fit between these two, an idea virtually identical with the vision concept we have articulated. The Finnish company Nokia describes its strategic intent as:[9]

> Nokia's business objective is to strengthen its position as a leading systems and product supplier in the rapidly evolving global communications industry. Nokia's strategic intent is to take a leading brand-recognized role in creating the Mobile Information Society by:
>
> Combining mobility and the Internet
> Stimulating the creation of new services

As we have noted, successful firms set ambitious aspirations that are audacious and not easy to achieve. Vision statements need to be grounded in reality, yet at the same time they must inspire employees, challenging them to do their best. We think that both terms, *vision* and *intent,* express a similar idea; an aspiration for the firm that is challenging, requires new competences, elicits strong commitment from all employees, and yet is seen as credible and realistic. Aspirations are based on current competences but also embrace evolving opportunities that will require the generation of new competences. As such, they reflect both an internal and an external focus.

A vision statement should be desirable to all stakeholders, should be feasible, should provide guidance in decision making, should be flexible enough to allow for individual initiative, and should be able to be communicated to all staff. It must be rooted in the reality of markets, competition, and technology. We would also suggest that strictly financial visions are unlikely to provide much in the way of motivation for employees. Instead, aspirations such as "to become the world leader in our industry in 10 years with the necessity for additional innovation to meet customer needs together with an increased global orientation" are likely to be seen as worthy of pursuit. Such aspirations are captured in the Glaxo Smith Kline vision described earlier. At the same time, the vision statement should not be so broad and grandiose that it loses all meaning.[10]

Having described what a vision statement is and its purpose, we now address the characteristics of vision statements and develop an understanding of the process used to create such a vision.

Characteristics of Vision Statements

The first and most important feature of a vision statement is its statement of the *desirable future* for the organization, which is an essential input to the strategy development process. In a turbulent world, we might question whether this is possible or even desirable. We believe, however, that all successful firms need a vision to provide a focus; otherwise, there will be distracting differences about what the firm is expected to achieve. However, since visions are generally fairly broad, this benefit should not be overstated.

At the same time, the vision statement must *motivate* and inspire all employees. The envisioned future should be ambitious, real, and visible but should also involve dreams, hopes, and a sense of passion.[11] Motivating people to implement plan-driven actions was never part of the lexicon of traditional strategic planning. Indeed, it was implicitly and blithely assumed that where the plan pointed, the people would follow. Not so! Hence the rationale for, and potential contribution of, the vision statement.

Effective vision statements result from activating the right side of the brain, which which deals with affect and emotion. As Peter Senge puts it:

A shared vision is not an idea. It is not even an important idea such as freedom. It is, rather, a force in people's hearts, a force of impressive power ... [It] is the answer to the question "What do we want to create?" Just as personal visions are pictures or images that people carry in their heads and hearts, so too are shared visions that people throughout an organization carry. They create a sense of commonality that permeates the organization and gives coherence to diverse activities.[12]

As Senge also emphasizes, many vision statements are imposed by senior management on organizations creating at best compliance rather than commitment. To evaluate the effectiveness of a vision statement, we must ask such questions as the following:

> Are we sure the vision is shared?
>
> Is the vision compelling and inspiring? Does it ask something of us?
>
> Does it create a sense of direction for the organization?
>
> Does it enthuse our people?
>
> Is it difficult to achieve, will it stretch the firm?
>
> Is it unique and differentiating?

One final point is perhaps the most critical of all. To be effective, a vision must be shared; it must be *owned* by all organizational personnel. If you ask most executives about visions, by far the majority will respond with a statement such as, "Well, the company has one…," implying that the executives have not internalized it. It is distressingly common for senior executives to agonize over developing such a statement, to pronounce it to various assemblies of subordinates, and to then be surprised that it isn't enthusiastically internalized and acted upon. A moment's reflection will reveal the naiveté embedded in such an approach. Visions that are not shared cannot be effective, and the only way we know of to ensure such sharing is to ensure the maximum possible participation in the visioning exercise. As with so many exercises involving the development of commitment, this may at first sight appear to be too lengthy and inefficient; yet, over the long haul, there is probably no greater inefficiency than having the current members of the firm acting without a sense of common purpose.

Creating a Vision Statement

In developing an effective vision statement, we must begin with the understanding that we are attempting to affect human emotions. You might ask yourself what are the phenomena that stir your emotions. Unless such stirring occurs, the vision will not achieve its intended ends.

Developing a vision statement is different from developing a cash flow statement— it requires intuition, creativity, and a sense of passion, together with an understanding of what drives human feelings. Creating the vision also requires foresight among senior managers, who are the organizational personnel primarily responsible for its creation.[13] **Industry foresight** is about becoming the intellectual leader in the industry—the firm which has a superior understanding of the industry and its structure, the customers and competitors, the current technology and that of substitutes as well as a deep knowledge of how these are changing and what the impact is likely to be. Managers should understand how the benefits current and potential customers seek are altering and what competences will be needed in the future to deliver these benefits, as well as the emergent technological possibilities that may create new needs and wants. Some managers have excellent backsight and poor foresight. They can easily identify the changes over the last 10 years but have considerable difficulty even contemplating likely changes in industry structure and the nature of competition over the next 10 years.

Creating good visions also requires some diversity of views to facilitate creativity. If all managers think alike, it will be difficult to envision new ideas, since new ideas are often on the boundary of the present. Again, a balance is needed. Too much diversity can be detrimental to progress; too much uniformity will inhibit creativity. There may also be diversity in process and subject matter, with a search for images and metaphors, with a focus on the future state of the firm, not how to get there.

Considerable time may need to be spent on this process. Developing a vision statement which is practical, which reflects the competitive situation and yet is also inspirational is a major challenge. At the same time, the vision statement for a firm should be relevant for some time—we do not expect a firm to alter its vision on an annual basis. However, as with any other firm attribute, there are times when the firm will have to alter its vision, and developing a new vision is one of the most challenging tasks for strategic managers. Vision and leadership have certain elements in common. As we will discuss in more detail in Chapter 10, one of the tasks of leaders is to create the vision for the future of the firm, and the ability to accomplish this is one of the distinguishing characteristics of a great leader.

Rather than asking current senior managers to develop a vision, some companies ask the people who will actually be managing the company in the future. A promising team of younger managers will also usually provide challenges to current thinking at the top of the company. This can also be the route to a fascinating and productive dialogue. Another projective technique that can be very effective is the organizational personality comparison, wherein executives are asked to describe an organization as a personality, comparing what they see now with what they believe they will have to be in the future. We also find that it is sometimes easier to ask executives to draw a picture of how the company will be rather than where it is today; again, this approach tends to activate the right side of the brain.

◉ 6.3 VALUES

The second element in creating a future direction is creating and reinforcing **organizational values**—a common set of beliefs that guide the behavior of organizational members. Values indicate how managers intend to conduct themselves, the principles that underlie how they go about their day-to-day activities. Values can be described as "the way we do business around here"; they are guidelines that govern the behavior of employees as they strive to achieve the vision of the firm. Such values may be implicit or explicit. Explicit values could address how colleagues will be treated (as trustworthy and respected?), concern for employee development, integrity and honesty in all dealings both inside and outside the firm, relationships with customers and the community, the risk of failure, organizational change, and so on.

Values include consideration of what is regarded as ethical behavior within the firm, a topic that has grown in importance since the difficulties with accounting audits and senior management behavior following the collapse of Enron and WorldCom in 2002.

> In early 1998, 57% of Britain's largest companies had or were preparing a code of business ethics versus 18% 11 years previously.[14]

As with vision, the task of infusing a set of values into the organization typically falls to the CEO and other organizational leaders. It is considered axiomatic that one feels a personal sense of mission, or finds meaning in work, when the organization's values match those of the individual. Such values can act as both a motivating factor and a control mechanism—one's behavior is consistent with one's values, and if these are in harmony with organizational values, a control system to ensure alignment is unnecessary.[15] Clear understanding of these organizational values is also important when recruiting new staff—we want individuals who are committed and who will act in accordance with the values of the organization.

We regard organizational values as integral to company success, but, with some notable exceptions, they have tended to be implicit rather than explicit. More recently, environmental pressures as well as pressure from shareholders have led executives to rethink corporate values and to make them explicit rather than implicit. Values can be thought of as **hard** (profitability and market share) and **soft** (integrity, respect for others, trust, and preeminence of customers).

As with vision, values statements are worthwhile only if they are embraced throughout the organization. Organizational members' "buy-in" is typically influenced by the extent of their participation in their development. Values can provide the "cultural glue" that enables some firms to thrive in times of rapid change whereas others struggle to survive.

Unfortunately, it is quite common to find that senior management behavior is inconsistent with the values statement of the firm. This was seen with Enron, which talked about integrity at the same time as senior managers were misleading shareholders and financial markets on revenue and debt levels. When such management hypocrisy is evident, there is likely to be a strong negative impact on the morale of employees, for employees pay more attention to action than they do to words.

As an example of a statement of corporate values, below we reprint the values for Procter & Gamble, a global consumer goods firm based in the U.S.[16]

P&G is its people and the core values by which they live.

P&G People　We attract and recruit the finest people in the world. We build our organization from within, promoting and rewarding people without regard to any difference unrelated to performance. We act on the conviction that the men and women of Procter & Gamble will always be our most important asset.

Leadership　We are all leaders in our area of responsibility, with a deep commitment to deliver leadership results. We have a clear visions of where we are going. We focus our resources to achieve leadership objectives and strategies. We develop the capability to deliver our strategies and eliminate organizational barriers.

Ownership　We accept personal accountability to meet the business needs, improve our systems and help others improve their effectiveness. We all act like owners, treating the Company's assets as our own and behaving with the Company's long-term success in mind.

Integrity　We always try to do the right thing. We are honest and straightforward with each other. We operate within the letter and spirit of the law. We uphold the values and principles of P&G in every action and decision. We are data-based and intellectually honest in advocating proposals, including recognizing risks.

Passion for winning　We are determined to be the best at doing what matters most. We have a healthy dissatisfaction with the status quo. We have a compelling desire to improve and win in the marketplace.

Trust　We respect our P&G colleagues, customers, consumers and treat them as we want to be treated. We have confidence in each other's capabilities and intentions. We believe that people work best when there is a foundation of trust.

Reproduced by permission of The Procter & Gamble Company.

Producing written statements of values may not be for everyone—British executives, for example, tend to be reluctant to develop such statements. But for many it provides another tool in the armory for creating and guiding organizational change.

For young entrepreneurial firms, organizational values are often strongly linked to the values of the founder, as is the case with Oracle or Microsoft. Sometimes, however, the values of the founder can persist for many generations of managers. The so-called "HP Way" at Hewlett-Packard is still considered a value and is attributed to Bill Packard, one of the founders.

Some of the most important organizational values are the (often implicit) values concerning risk, innovation, growth, and the future. In some firms, corporate values favor steady, incremental growth. In others, the values are at the other end of the spectrum. News Corp., as we have seen, has values that drive its growth and risk taking, values shared with firms such as Oracle, SAP, and Sony. Other firms, such as Exxon-Mobil and Nestlé, have values, perhaps implicit, that seem to espouse steady, long-term, and incremental growth, rather than explosive growth with the risks that entails.

Values as a Source of Problems

Values can also present problems. There may be significant variation in values across units within the same firm. Lawrence and Lorsch termed this phenomenon **differentiation,** and one of its most common manifestations is the difference in values across the various functional specialties within the company.[17] Such differentiation may also exist between the different business units of a multibusiness company, and the more diversified the firm, the greater this variation is likely to be. Both kinds of differentiation can result in difficulty in achieving coordinated strategies as well as implementation. Indeed, in many companies the values that actually guide behavior are implicit rather than explicit, and we must remember that when we talk of values in the context of strategic management, there is usually the assumption that these values are something that management is (or should be) actively managing. Clearly, it is easier to "manage" explicit values statements than to deal with implicit values. Further, the de facto values of the organization, while they may be implicit, are typically reflected in a variety of its systems and procedures ("standard operating procedures"), such that the very infrastructure of the organization serves as a major impediment to management attempts at change, a topic we explore in greater depth in Chapter 10.

Values can also impede the integration of acquisitions. The values of acquirer and the acquiree are often different, and, as we will see in Chapter 9, these value differences are a significant cause of postmerger difficulties.

Values also create difficulties in hiring. The values of individuals are often quite well formed by the time they take a job. Influenced by a prolonged process of acculturation, these values are therefore quite difficult to change. Further, as companies become global, these individual values are likely to become increasingly diverse and are less likely to reflect the values of the home country of the global firm and its cadre of senior managers.

> A successful Australian resources company moved rapidly into international trading of commodities. It found that a number of its new overseas recruits did not share the prevailing Australian values with respect to honesty and integrity and was forced to release a number of employees and rethink its hiring and training practices.

As most managements would undoubtedly prefer that their employees do "the right thing," it is instructive to consider where problems are likely to arise. Ignoring blatant

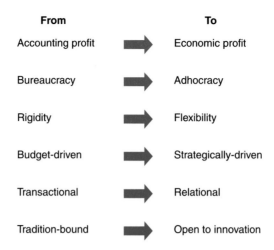

Desired Values Transformation

From		To
Accounting profit		Economic profit
Bureaucracy		Adhocracy
Rigidity		Flexibility
Budget-driven		Strategically-driven
Transactional		Relational
Tradition-bound		Open to innovation

Figure 6.3   Commonly Sought Values Transitions

dishonesty, which is outside the scope of this book, it is clear that, as the ethicists point out, the most difficult decisions are typically a result of a conflict between two "rights." A classic example arises when dealing with an unhappy customer, when the goal of profitability may to be appear in conflict with the goal of satisfying the customer. Systems that enable customer service representatives to adjudge the longer term as opposed to the immediate costs and benefits of alternative courses of action greatly assist employees in making appropriate economic decisions, for in these cases a conflict between the goals of firm profitability and customer satisfaction is a frequent and uncomfortable occurrence. Similar conflicts arise between the oft-avowed goal of developing a more entrepreneurial set of behaviors within the company and the strict budgetary limits that are imposed in order to ensure fiscal discipline. Systems may have to be significantly changed to facilitate changing the necessary behaviors.

Values also can create major impediments to organizational change. At times of significant change in the competitive environment, significant adjustment of firm values may be required. Imaginative use of the tools of human resource management—selection, development, appraisal, and reward—assist the change process. Without advance planning, however, wholesale employee turnover is likely to result if rapid change is required. This can create widespread dislocation of company operations, which can worsen what may already be a crisis situation. Figure 6.3 summarizes some of the values changes that companies are trying to accomplish at the time of writing.

◉ 6.4 MISSION

The third element in creating a future direction is creating a **mission** statement, an expression of the domain in which the firm and/or its businesses elect to compete. A mission statement describes the business the firm is in or the business in which it desires to be. Such a mission statement should be externally focused and contain a general description of the scope of the activities of the firm, often in terms of the products it intends to produce and the markets it will serve. Such a statement on the boundaries and scope of the firm and/or its businesses is ideally in line with the firm's vision and values and the expectations of major stakeholders.

A mission statement therefore defines the areas in which the company wishes to do business. It should simultaneously recognize areas of opportunity while capitalizing on the firm's competences. It should neither be so general as to admit too broad a variety of possibilities nor so narrow that it impedes all attempts at growth. Of course, multibusiness firms need to develop mission statements at the business-unit level as well as the corporate level. The missions of the individual business units should be subsumed by, and consistent with, the corporate mission. Mission statements not only codify opportunities where the firm does well or aspires to do well, however, for in doing so they typically demarcate the competitive set as well. Examples of mission statements for several firms are presented below.

The mission statement for IBM is as follows:[18]

> At IBM we strive to lead in the invention, development and manufacture of the industry's most advanced information technologies, including computer systems, software, storage systems and microelectronics.
>
> We translate these advanced technologies into value for our customers through our professional solutions, services and consulting businesses worldwide.

Unilever, the Anglo-Dutch consumer goods firm, has a much lengthier mission statement, which they call "Our Purpose":[19]

> At the heart of the corporate purpose, which guides us in our approach to doing business, is the drive to serve consumers in a unique and effective way. This purpose has been communicated to all employees worldwide.
>
> Our purpose in Unilever is to meet the everyday needs of people everywhere—to anticipate the aspirations of our consumers and customers and to respond creatively and competitively with branded products and services which raise the quality of life.
>
> Our deep roots in local cultures and markets around the world are our unparalleled inheritance and the foundation of our future growth. We will bring our wealth of knowledge and international expertise to the service of local consumers—a truly multi-local, multinational.
>
> Our long-term success requires a total commitment to exceptional standards of performance and productivity, to working together effectively and to a willingness to embrace new ideas and learn continuously.
>
> We believe that to succeed requires the highest standards of corporate behaviour towards our employees, consumers and the societies and world in which we live. This is Unilever's road to sustainable, profitable growth for our business and long-term value creation for our shareholders and employees.
>
> Reproduced by permission of Unilever

While lengthy, this statement reveals a great deal about the values that senior management believes should be guiding the behavior of company employees; it also, in referring to Unilever's "unparalleled inheritance," describes what senior management regards as the firm's distinctive competences.

Decisions about mission should be recognized as among the most important of strategic decisions and should not be taken lightly. Managing the evolution of mission statements is one of the most important responsibilities of senior management. The impetus to broaden the firm's mission statement may arise from a lack of sufficient growth opportunities in existing businesses. Alternatively, the firm may decide to narrow its mission, concentrating on core businesses, if resources are stretched too thinly or it is suffering poor financial performance. In addition, new leadership often sets new directions via a revised mission, and capital market pressure may play an important role, even for relatively focused firms, if financial analysts believe that company breakup will "release value." We have indicated that mission is associated with the domain of the firm, so decisions about changing mission are similar to decisions on the boundaries of the firm, as is illustrated below.

Underlying the concept of a mission is the idea of leveraging company capabilities by focusing on a limited number of opportunity areas rather than spreading resources, perhaps too thinly, over many different options. Academic research and general opinion suggest that, in general, companies succeed when they build on their core competencies,[20] focusing only on what the firm does well. However, this implies a strong internal focus, whereas the mission statements also need to include an informed view of market characteristics, including technology. Indeed, our research suggests that interrelationships among market opportunities (market relatedness) may be more important than technological competencies and synergies.[21]

Corporate versus Business-Unit Mission Statements

As we noted earlier, mission statements are useful strategic concepts for business units as well as for the firm as a whole. Consider the case of United Technologies, a diversified U.S. company that comprises a number of business units, such as Carrier (air conditioning), Otis (elevators), Pratt & Whitney (jet engines), and Sikorsky (helicopters). The corporate mission statement of United Technologies is necessarily broad in its scope:

> A Company that provides high technology products to the aerospace and building systems industries throughout the world.

Within the company, however, the Otis business unit has a much more focused description of its business:[22]

> Manufacturer, installer and maintainer of elevators, escalators, moving walkways and other people moving systems

Ideally, the business-unit missions for a corporation should be encompassed by the corporate mission but mutually exclusive such that the domain of each business unit is clearly specified and does not overlap with other business units. This ideal, however, may be shattered by innovation, which often seems to occur at the boundaries of what might have traditionally been considered as a "market" or an industry. Consider such new terms as *cosmeceuticals* (cosmetic products with functional "pharmaceutical" properties), *functional foods* (foods with demonstrable health benefits, such as cholesterol-lowering margarines), and *chilled foods* (neither preserved by freezing or canning nor "fresh" produce) or even the strategy of Mars in transforming its candy bars into ice-cream desserts. In every case, these innovations have wrought new patterns of competition and have caused strategic managers to rethink their strategies—and even their entire conceptualization of the business.

Characteristics of Mission Statements

Vision and values statements usually suggest ideals about how employees of the company will behave and what the company will become. In contrast, corporate and business mission statements have a more pragmatic and more immediate purpose. They exist to *guide* and to constrain the firm's future growth. They guide in the sense that they suggest where managers should be looking for future opportunity. They constrain by deterring selection of other kinds of opportunities.

As the examples above indicate, mission statements can be as short as a sentence or as long as a page. To be useful, as with vision and values, they must be communicated to and understood and embraced by all the members of the organization. Indeed, in our era of networked and outsourced organizations, this understanding can be usefully extended to other stakeholders, notably suppliers.

A mission statement should do the following:

- Encourage unanimity of purpose and specify what the organization does and, just as important, does not do
- Direct the search for new activities
- Highlight points of differentiation and the basis of competitive advantage
- Attract and deter potential staff
- Not change too frequently

Creating and Changing a Mission Statement

Although we do not believe that mission statements should change too frequently, obviously they cannot stay unaltered forever, and the faster the environment is changing, the more frequently they should be reviewed. New opportunities will arise even as older ones disappear, and a successful firm must inevitably outgrow its earlier missions. Most firms begin with a fairly simple and narrow mission statement, chosen from one of the types to be outlined below. As the successful firm grows, however, its mission statement will broaden, reflecting its growing competences and view of opportunities as well as possibly including several dimensions.

Bases for Mission Definition

Mission statements can be developed on several "pure-form" bases—three supply-side (natural resources, technology and product/service) and two demand-side (market/market segment and customer needs). We look at each in turn, illustrating how the mission definition can affect choices among opportunities.

Natural resources. These businesses maximize value from a natural resource. For example, the mission statement "We are a forest products company" should lead the firm to consider making any product, using any technology, and selling to any market, so long as the product is made from wood.

Technology. These businesses focus on a core technology, for example, "We are a glass company" or "We are an electronics company." An electronics firm's search for opportunity would be based solely on electronics: its products could be sold to any market and use any raw material, so long as they were based on electronics.

Product/service. These businesses focus on particular product(s)/service(s); for example, "We are an automobile firm." Although this mission implies a sole focus on automobiles, they may be powered by various fuels (gasoline, diesel, alcohol, LPG, natural gas), use various technologies (steam, internal combustion, electromechanical, gas turbine), and sold in many different markets around the globe.

Market/market segment. These businesses offer selected markets/market segments a variety of different products/services (made from various raw materials, using various technologies). For example, consumer packaged goods firms target families and offer various household and personal care products. Market-based definitions, often based on geographic or socioeconomic segments, are most common among retail and distribution businesses.

Customer needs. This mission focuses solely on customer needs. For example, a mission to serve transportation needs might lead a firm to offer bicycles, automobiles, trucks, helicopters, and airplanes.[23]

Individual pure-form missions may be used separately or combined with other bases to develop narrower mission statements. For example, Courtyard by Marriott's combines *product/service* and *market segment:*

> To provide economy and quality-minded frequent business travelers with a premier lodging facility, which is consistently perceived as clean, comfortable, well maintained and attractive, staffed by friendly, attentive and efficient people.

Mission not only influences choice of market opportunity but, via outsourcing, may lead firms to rid themselves of responsibility for activities that consume management talent and investment capital but do not provide significant competitive advantage. The most common everyday parlance for these kinds of changes involves managers talking about "refocusing on the core business." Unfortunately, these statements are often made in response to an earlier period of management excess. When firms are profitable, the principal–agent divergence often seems to provoke unwise diversification, usually via expensive acquisitions, that in later (often more difficult) times are remedied (often by different management) by refocusing on the core business.

Furthermore, our research suggests that rather than proactively managing mission statements and taking them seriously, most companies tend to forget about them when times are good and worry about them when they get into difficulty.[24] Even more common are those cases in which executives appear to ignore their businesses' missions. When decisions are made that are in obvious disregard of a mission statement, managers destroy their own credibility. We are convinced of the importance of mission statements but must reluctantly admit that when middle managers in an organization dismiss the whole exercise as mere "wordsmithing," they may well be giving an accurate description of what has occurred. This is an unfortunate commentary on the strategic management of their companies.

Some firms have been very successful in changing their mission statement when the environment changes or when analysis suggests that continuing with the current mission would not create desired levels of value. Others indicate that this is one of the most difficult strategic decisions to accomplish successfully.

> In 1995, Corning's revenues of $USB5.3 came from five major areas: health-care services (lab testing), 39%; telecoms (optical fiber) 22%; advanced materials (environmental and other), 16%; consumer (glassware), 13%; and information display (TV, computer screens), 10%. In 1996, a new CEO decided to transform the firm into a high-tech supplier; the firm

divested its health-care and consumer businesses and dramatically increased R&D from 3.5% of sales to 8.4%.[25] The Asian crisis of 1997, which saw fiber prices drop by as much as 50%, resulted in earnings problems in 1998. Despite this, the firm continued to build activities in telecommunications. Sales peaked in 2000 at $USB6.9, only to collapse to $USB3.1 by 2002. The firm reported losses of $USB5.5 in 2001 and $USB1.4 in 2002 due to restructuring charges and difficulties in the telecommunications businesses. In addition, some 19,000 jobs were eliminated over the period.[26]

One of the more successful examples is provided by the Finnish company Nokia, with its transformation to a telecommunications company. Nokia Corporation was formed in 1967 with the merger of three firms; a paper-making business, a rubber works, and a cable business. Over time it evolved into completely new areas of business, from radio telephones to TVs and computers. In 1992 a new CEO divested what were by then regarded as noncore businesses and focused on telecommunications and the digital age.[27]

◉ 6.5 OBJECTIVES

Organizations must specify what they hope to achieve in the future by formulating a set of **objectives**—measurable targets to be achieved. Objectives are clear, quantifiable, and measurable targets to be achieved by the firm, or a unit of the firm, within a defined time. All objectives should contain the following:

- An attribute that can measured, such as revenue growth
- A scale on which that attribute can be measured, such as dollars
- A level to be achieved, such as $USM100
- A time scale for the achievement of the target, such as the year 2007

Corporate and Business-Unit Objectives

Objectives are generally established in many areas of the firm, and there is typically a downward cascade—corporate objectives are established, then business-unit objectives, and then more detailed product/market objectives. The ideal, of course, is for all of these to be consistent and aligned. In practice, there is often a quite protracted negotiation process that involves consultation throughout the entire firm. The top-management team, in consultation with the board, will establish corporate objectives as well as review corporate strategies and corporate performance. Business-unit objectives will be established by business-unit managers in consultation with the top-management team, and there may be a secondary level of interaction with the board, depending on the importance of the business unit. Strategy development at the business-unit level involves primarily business-unit managers and corporate managers, although the board may be involved with major businesses. Business-unit performance, again, is primarily a matter between corporate managers and business-unit managers, with the board playing a secondary role in some circumstances. As is shown in Figure 6.4, objectives setting, strategy development, strategy implementation, and performance measurement are not linear processes but involve a series of iterations.

As would be expected, establishing objectives is generally a *political* process, characterized by bargaining and conflict coupled with rational analysis. Choosing appropriate objectives requires a deep understanding of the external environment and the opportunities it presents, together with an analysis of the competences of the firm, the vision and values of the firm, and the demands of financial markets.

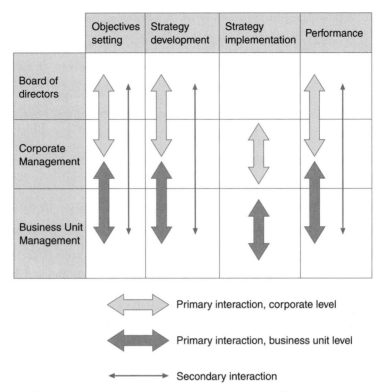

Figure 6.4 Iterative Loops in the Strategy Process (illustrative only)

Of course, the types of objectives that are set at the corporate level and the business unit level can differ quite significantly. At the corporate level, the CEO has to focus considerable attention on capital markets, whereas the concern of the business-unit manager is much more with product markets. However, the two perspectives cannot and should not be viewed as separate, for performance in the business units' product markets will affect growth in volumes and margins, which are the prime operating drivers of cash flow, and therefore of economic profit, and, ultimately, of return to shareholders of the corporation.

Table 6.1 contrasts the kinds of objectives that might be set at the corporate versus the business-unit level. Notice that in both instances there are financial and nonfinancial objectives, the subject that we explore next.

TABLE 6.1 Corporate and Business Objectives

Corporate Objectives	Business Objectives
Shareholder return	Growth
Economic profit	Economic profit
Growth	Quality
Net income	Market share
Income diversity	Employee development
Synergy	Productivity
Corporate citizenship	Knowledge generation

Although establishing objectives in a firm is normally a process that involves both a top-down and a bottom-up approach, sometimes senior management will issue an edict, such as: "Staff numbers have to be reduced by 5% in all business units within the next six months." Such an edict may follow from concern at the current and likely future profit levels of the firm, and senior managers may see no alternative but to adopt drastic and dramatic steps to improve profitability. Such objectives subsequently provide a basis for evaluating managers and units; they are an essential input to a control system, as we will discuss in more detail in Chapter 13. Thus, although ideally we would prefer that, as with other elements of this direction-setting process, we obtain acceptance and buy-in from all employees, there are times when objectives will be imposed from the top.

Financial and Nonfinancial Objectives

It is vitally important to recognize that business is not just about achieving good financial performance. The way in which financial performance is achieved is also important. Society recognizes this by imposing legal constraints on the way in which firms may choose to go about generating profit. These include regulations on such issues as competitive behavior (e.g., antitrust laws), pollution (e.g., U.S. EPA regulations), employment, minimum wages, child labor laws, and the like. Nor are concerns with means restricted to governmental regulations, for if company values statements are to be meaningful, then there must be some kind of mechanism for ensuring compliance, which may well be reflected in performance objectives (e.g., days lost to workplace injuries) and even reward systems.

As an illustration of the complexity involved in establishing objectives, consider the case of the petrochemical company BP. The chairman of BP, Lord Browne, announced that the target for 2002 was a $USB1.4 pre-tax contribution for BP. The contribution that each business was expected to make is shown in Table 6.2.[28]

In addition to these financial objectives, other objectives for BP in 2002 included:

- Increased returns in midcycle operating conditions
- Double-digit annual earnings growth
- Maintaining dividends at between 45% and 55% of earnings at midcycle conditions
- Gearing within the range 20% to 30% (net debt ratio)
- Organic capex in the range $USB12–13
- 5.5% reported production volume growth

TABLE 6.2   BP Objectives, 2002

Business	Contribution $USB
Upstream	0.6
Gas, power, renewables	0
Downstream	0.4
Chemicals	0.6
Overview	–0.2
Total	1.4

This example illustrates both the overall corporate objectives and the contributions expected from the various business units. There was a strong emphasis on financial results, supplemented by concerns for financial risk and for shareholder returns via dividends. (Here, capex refers to capital expenditure, excluding acquisitions.)

Setting Objectives

As we have seen, objectives may be stated in a variety of forms. 3M uses a "percent of revenue from new products" objective to stimulate innovation and product-line regeneration. More generally, however, a number of large firms break down their overall revenue growth objectives into three components: the organic growth component (sales growth expected from existing businesses), the new business (product) component (sales growth expected from the internally generated new ventures that will begin in the coming planning period), and growth from possible acquisitions and major new developments. The specific levels to be set here reflect a trade-off decision inasmuch as the stock price reflects a combination of investor expectations with respect to growth and margin. Clearly, higher margins can offset lower growth achievements and vice versa.

Categories of Objectives

The two major operating drivers for improving shareholder value are, as we saw in Chapter 2, revenue growth and operating margin. It follows, therefore, that if we accept the maxim that we should be increasing shareholder value, then growth and margin targets must be foremost in establishing the operational objectives of the corporation and its constituent businesses.

Revenue Growth

How revenue growth is attained is an important consideration. Sales increases resulting from existing operations (usually termed organic growth) are viewed differently from revenues received from new ventures. The latter are typically believed to be riskier, and investors seek higher returns from more risky investments. On the other hand, significant sales increases from such new ventures often have a disproportionately beneficial impact on the firm's share price, in anticipation of future profits resulting from the new venture. However, any management strategy aimed at increasing shareholder value should consider the risks, and perceptions of risk, associated with particular ventures together with the impact of these ventures on the firm's overall business portfolio, as will be discussed in more detail in Chapter 8.

As a consequence of these expectations, there may be times when management seeks to achieve more stable returns, possibly trading off profit quantity for profit quality, where high-quality profit is defined as a consistent stream of economic profit over time.

> A well-known ski resort was faced with the choice of developing ski trails on a neighboring hill or investing in facilities such as mountain slides and outdoor staging for the local symphony orchestra, which would make the resort more attractive to summer visitors. It elected to develop the summer facilities because of a desire to even out revenue and profit streams throughout the year.

Margin

The goal of improving margins has different implications at the corporate and business-unit levels. At the corporate level, the prevailing wisdom is that the group or corporate-level activities should ideally incur very low levels of overhead. Unless corporate activities are demanded by the operating businesses such that significant shared economies can be created by retaining them at the corporate level, they should instead be placed within the businesses, where allocation is no longer an issue and they can be prudently managed within a normal single-business framework. There is substantial justification for this philosophy in economic theory, for investors are capable of diversifying their own investment portfolio at very low cost.

Within a business unit, the value chain provides a very useful framework for understanding and generating opportunities for raising margins. In our experience, active management of the value chain is a fairly recent phenomenon, and there are still many companies in which managers restrict their actions to incremental changes and improvements in the existing business system but do not consider structural changes therein.

Strategic management implies that managers take an active stance toward margin improvement. The competitiveness of today's markets means that merely to maintain a position firms must improve their operations at the same rate as their competitors. To improve their position relative to competitors demands that managers reconsider many of their basic assumptions about the business, including considering the outsourcing any noncore activity that is performed at less than world-class levels of excellence. Margin improvement therefore demands ongoing benchmarking of performance versus best-of-class competitors and a willingness to innovate in seeking structural solutions that go significantly beyond traditional boundaries.

Level of Objectives

In addition to the pressures from the capital market perspective, however, there are very real pressures driven by the markets of individual business units. Decomposing corporate objectives to the business-unit level is in part a portfolio issue (discussed in Chapters 8 and 9), in part a competitive strategy issue within the firm's businesses, but also a behavioral issue. We address the setting of business-level objectives in Chapter 7, but suffice here to say that in general the level at which objectives are set demands finding an appropriate behavioral compromise. Objectives that are set at a level that lower levels of management regard as unfeasible motivate withdrawal behavior rather than higher levels of effort. On the other hand, some degree of "stretch" is necessary to motivate reconsideration of basic assumptions that might otherwise never be explored.

Too often, senior management neither ensures that their subordinates regard objectives as feasible nor pays sufficient attention to empowering lower-level managers to the point that they are willing to question and reconsider their basic, usually implicit, assumptions about how they run their businesses. Instead, the exercise too often deteriorates into a mind-numbing series of manipulations of budget numbers that bear little relationship to current or prospective reality. This is clearly detrimental to shareholders' interests, but unfortunately far too common.

In our view, an appropriate level of objectives can be established only by a participative exercise, with an open-minded attitude toward addressing the difficult trade-offs that must typically occur to resolve the tension between the top-down capital market pressures and the bottom-up pressures of competitive business markets. Time spent on these issues is usually time well spent from the shareholders' perspective.

Further, there are some important principles that should guide the setting of objectives. First, an overwhelming number of companies establish objectives and measure performance benchmarked against a previous period, often the previous year. When we see improvement over last year, this is often encouraging and motivating, but it can also be delusionary. We must never forget that business is a competitive game, and, wherever possible, more appropriate benchmarks are external. Company boards clearly neglected this principle in the bull market of the 1990s, when senior executives often received large rewards for company performance that lagged both their sector and the market. Whether we are looking at sales gains, ROEs, margins, or any other measure, we are well advised to compare these against competitors rather than the previous year.

A related problem is a tendency to look backward rather than forward. It is often said that "competition improves the breed," meaning that performance that may have sufficed previously is unlikely to do so in the future, an observation that is particularly likely to hold true in fast-moving high-tech industries. Companies that neglect the dynamics of competition in setting objectives are likewise headed for difficulties. Wherever possible, we should be looking forward and outward, offsetting what seems to be a frequently prevailing tendency to look backward and inward.

Problems in Setting Objectives

We now explore three major problems in setting objectives: determining priorities, excessive stretch, and unintended consequences.

Determining Priorities

Since the firm and its units must establish a nested set of objectives, cascading down the firm, we need to ensure that these are consistent with one another. For example, an objective of cost reduction may not be compatible with an objective of new product development. In other words, in setting objectives we must recognize that there are often trade-off decisions to be made, and it is essential that these decisions be made explicitly and clearly communicated. While, in an ideal world, we might wish to have everything at once, in the real world this will not occur. Consider as an example the potential problems posed by growth objectives.

As we saw in Chapter 4, the typical large company cannot fund its own growth solely from internally generated funds but must have recourse to financial markets. The reasons are quite straightforward: to grow requires investment funds, whether these go into new facilities, equipment, hiring and training new employees, or advertising. Whereas in some instances we may be able to generate sufficient funds internally, the faster we wish to grow (the more ambitious the growth targets), the less likely this is to occur, particularly for a single-business corporation that cannot internally cross-fund. In other words, there is a *trade-off* between *targeted growth rates* and *cash flow*. Unfortunately, there is a very human tendency to want to have everything at once, and unless the trade-off issue is addressed explicitly, disappointment is certain. Portfolio analysis techniques and the building of appropriate financial models can help avoid this problem, and we address these issues at more length in Chapters 8 and 9.

Excessive Stretch

In the last part of the twentieth century, some consultants were advocating the concept of BHAG—"big, hairy, aggressive goals"—to their clients.[29] In some companies this resulted in a meaningless numbers game. Allow us to explain.

The idea behind BHAG was that very ambitious goals could motivate people to achieve at much higher levels. We don't doubt that under appropriate conditions this may occur. Human beings have shown that they can sometimes achieve the extraordinary against considerable odds. However, to believe that the extraordinary can become routine is almost certainly a triumph of optimism over reality, while the constraints—implicit or otherwise—created by the organization too often guaranteed the impossibility of achieving the BHAGs. To achieve the exceptional may be possible but will usually require the availability of appropriate resources and/or the relaxation of constraints, such that the problem can be approached differently. Most companies advocating BHAGs had no such insights; they were not prepared to empower their midlevel managers by telling them to treat the organization as "boundaryless" or to relax rigid budget constraints that inhibited change, risk taking, and/or experimentation. As we will see in Chapter 9, this is why the changes that transform industries so often come from new players at the time, as was the case with Haloid (which became Xerox), FedEx (which deposed Emery Air Freight, previously the most profitable transportation company in the world), and Dell (which seized PC leadership from the mighty IBM).

Unintended Consequences

This problem is usually obvious in retrospect but is rarely seen at the time. Quite simply, human beings verge on genius when asked to perform against any particular standard. We find a way to do it! For many years, U.S. airlines competed, among other bases, by promoting the shortest scheduled times between airports. When, however, the U.S. Department of Transportation decided that passenger choice would be facilitated by publishing the airlines' arrival-time performance, the almost immediate response was to lengthen the scheduled times for their flights so that the on-time record immediately improved! When researching the management of multinational subsidiaries, we found that the response of subsidiary CEOs to what they regarded as unfair budget limitations from the head office (e.g., all expenditures over $50,000 must receive prior approval from HQ) was to ensure that invoices were paid with a series of smaller payments, none of which exceeded the budget limit.[30]

The only advice we can offer here is to avoid emphasis on any single measure by (1) achieving the balance of priorities we discussed earlier and (2) ensuring some measurement redundancy (i.e., measure the same construct by alternative means and methods wherever possible). In fact, deviant behavior is much less likely when objectives are negotiated and agreed upon, following the approaches we have advocated in this chapter. Where targets are externally imposed and perceived as unfair or arbitrary, and where reward and punishment are linked to performance against these objectives, problems become more likely.

Synthesizing the Concepts

So far we have talked about the concepts of vision, values, mission, and objectives but have spent little time talking about their interrelationships. We have discussed the idea that a vision cannot possibly become a reality if the values (and therefore the behavior) of the organization are not consistent with its realization. Similarly, along a chronological dimension, it would seem highly desirable that the evolution of a firm's business mission progresses over time toward the realization of its vision, even though we would expect a mission statement to be subject to much more frequent revision and to encompass considerably more detail. Similarly, we would hope that the corporate- and business-level objectives that are established will help the firm fulfill its mission.

⟳ 6.6 AN INTEGRATIVE EXAMPLE

We have covered a number of very important concepts in this chapter and have stressed how they should be integrated in a consistent manner. We will now illustrate this principle by using the example of Petrobras, the large Brazilian oil and energy company,[31] at both the corporate and business unit levels.[32]

CORPORATE LEVEL

Petrobras Corporate Vision for 2010

> Petrobras will be a leading energy company with a strong presence in the international market and leader in Latin America, focusing on shareholder value and social responsibility.

Values

- Creation of value for its main stakeholders: shareholders, customers, employees, society, the government, partners, suppliers, and local communities
- Entrepreneurship and ability to overcome challenges
- Focus on achieving top-tier results
- Continuous drive for business leadership
- Excellence and leadership in health, safety, and environment
- Competitiveness and innovation with a focus on differentiated services and technological competence

Petrobras Corporate Mission

> Operate in a safe and profitable manner in the oil, gas and energy industry, and in related segments, in Brazil and abroad, providing quality products and services, complying with environment issues, keeping in mind our shareholders' interests and contributing to the country's development.

2007 Corporate Objectives

Oil and Gas Production   (million bbl/day)

Brazil Oil and Gas	2.61
International Oil and Gas	0.50

Costs

Refining costs in Brazil (US$/bbl) 0.85

Investment

Invest $USB34.2 over the period, 2003–07, of which 57% will be from internal sources

Health, safety and environment (HSE)

Lost time injury frequency   0.7

Human resources

    Employee training index (hrs/employee/year)   80

Financial

    Leverage   38%
    Return on capital employed (Brent @ US$ 15/bbl)   12%

BUSINESS UNIT LEVEL STRATEGIES

Domestic Exploration and Production

    Increase production and reserves
    Strengthen expertise in deep and ultradeep waters

Gas and Energy

    Develop the natural gas market
    Participate in the development of alternative energy sources

International Mission

    Selective participation in Latin America, Gulf of Mexico and Western Africa
    Diversify the portfolio to reduce the cost of capital

Reproduced by permission of Petrobras.

The Petrobras website contains much more information on the details of company and business-unit strategies, but the excerpts above illustrate very well many of the concepts we have discussed in this chapter. A future sense of direction is clear from the 2010 vision statement, while both company and business-unit missions are described. The statement of corporate objectives contains both financial and non-financial objectives and emphasizes how important the latter are for a high-profile company such as Petrobras.

◉ 6.7 SUMMARY

In this chapter we covered some of the most important concepts in strategic management. They cover the gamut from the "soft" side of visioning and values to the "hard" side of missions and objectives—all of which play an important role in creating the future direction of the firm.

As Figure 6.5 illustrates, each concept plays a distinct yet related role in establishing the future direction of the enterprise.

The strategic management of an organization requires that you master both "sides", for one without the other will ensure that you fail in your managerial duties. As we have seen from the company examples examined, senior managers of virtually all large companies are very much aware that while achieving good financial results for shareholders

Vision, Values	Mission	Objectives
Tells us where we want to take the business...How we will manage it in the interim	Tells us what business we are in	Tells us the targets we wish to achieve
Revealing of culture	Revealing of scope	Measurable
Directional and aspirational	Directional	Level and time specified

Figure 6.5 Role of Different Concepts

is important, the firm has multiple stakeholders that can affect its future prospects. As the operations of large companies become more transparent, it is very clear that how results are achieved is as important as the results themselves, and good strategic managers will be aware that they cannot serve the longer-term interests of shareholders without regard for this important principle.

◉ REVIEW QUESTIONS

1. Choose a firm with which you are familiar. What is the vision statement for that firm? Do you think that this vision statement is correct?

2. Indicate, for the firm chosen in question 1, how the vision selected by the firm has influenced the strategies developed by the firm.

3. "All staff in a firm must have a good understanding of what the firm will look like in 10 years." Discuss this statement.

4. It has been suggested that too many vision statements are bland and do not generate staff commitment. Why does this occur?

5. What values do you think will become more important for global firms over the next 10 years?

◉ ENDNOTES

[1] F. Mitarai, "Corporate Strategy Conference," 2003: www.canon.com.

[2] P. Drucker, *Management: Tasks, Responsibilities, Practices* (New York: Harper & Row, 1973).

[3] A. Campbell, M. Devine, and D. Young, *A Sense of Mission* (London: Pitman, 1993).

[4] W. Bennis and B. Nanus, *Leaders: The Strategies for Taking Charge* (New York: Harper & Row, 1985), p. 89.

[5] J. C. Collins and J. I. Porras, "Building Your Company's Vision," *Harvard Business Review,* September–October 1996, pp. 65–78.

[6] Glaxo Smith Kline Annual Report, 2002: www.gsk.com.

[7] M. Moeller, S. Hamm, and T. J. Mullaney, "Remaking Microsoft: Why America's Most Successful Company Needed on Overhaul", *Business Week,* May 17, 1999, p. 106.

[8] G. Hamel and C. K. Prahalad, "Competing for the Future," *Harvard Business Review,* July–August 1994, pp. 122–128.

[9] Nokia Annual Report, 2002: www.nokia.com.

[10] G. H. Langeler, "The Vision Trap," *Harvard Business Review,* March–April 1992, pp. 46–55.

[11] Collins and Porras, "Building your Company's Vision."

[12] P. M. Senge, *The Fifth Discipline,* (New York: Doubleday, 1990), p. 206.

[13] Hamel and Prahalad, "Competing for the Future."

[14] "Ethics in UK Business," *Daily Telegraph,* March 2, 1998.

[15] T. E. Deal and A. A. Kennedy, *Corporate Cultures* (Reading, Ma: Addison-Wesley, 1982).

[16] P&G Annual Report, 2003: www.pg.com.

[17] P. Lawrence and J. W. Lorsch, *Organizations and Environment* (Cambridge, MA: Harvard University Press, 1967).

[18] IBM Annual Report, 2003: www.ibm.com.

[19] "Unilever Vision and Mission," 2002: www.unilever.com.

[20] C. K. Prahalad and G. Hamel, "The Core Competence of the Corporation," *Harvard Business Review* May–June 1990, pp. 79–93.

[21] N. Capon, J. U. Farley, J. M. Hulbert, and L. E. Martin, "Corporate Diversity and Economic Performance: The Impact of Market Specialization," *Strategic Management Journal* 9, no. 1 (1988), pp. 61–74.

[22] "Otis Mission," 2003: www.otis.com.

[23] T. Levitt, "Marketing Myopia," *Harvard Business Review* September–October 1975, pp. 26.

[24] N. Capon, J. U. Farley, and J. M. Hulbert, *Corporate Strategic Planning* (New York: Columbia University Press, 1988).

[25] "Has Corning Won Its High-Tech Bet?" *Business Week,* April 5, 1999, p. 64.

[26] Corning Annual Report, 2002: www.corning.com.

[27] Nokia Annual Report, 2002: www.nokia.com.

[28] BP Annual Report, 2002: www.bp.com.

[29] J. C. Collins and J. I. Porras, *Built to Last* (New York: HarperBusiness, 1994).

[30] J. M. Hulbert and W. K. Brandt, *Managing the Multinational Subsidiary* (New York: Holt, Rinehart & Winston, 1980).

[31] Readers should note that that we are not consultants to Petrobras and therefore have no views on whether or not the future directions the company has established are feasible or not. The information we have taken from the company's website provides an excellent example of how the concepts we have discussed in this chapter can be used and combined.

[32] "Petrobras Strategic Plan 2003–2007," October 2001 and April 25, 2003: www2.petrobras.com.br.

CHAPTER 7

Business-Level Strategy

Learning Objectives

Upon completing this chapter, you should be able to:

- Distinguish the differences between corporate-level and business-level strategy and their interrelationship
- Understand the importance of creating a future direction for the business
- Use the appropriate analysis tools in developing business strategy
- Define the major drivers of cost and value for a business
- Develop a strategy for a business that recognizes the three key decisions—where to compete, how to compete, and how to grow
- Define industry disintermediation and reintermediation and understand when outsourcing should be adopted
- Apply the concept of a competitive advantage and appreciate the need for ongoing enhancement of this advantage
- Describe the differences between a cost leadership, differentiation, and combination competitive strategy
- Select which growth strategy is suitable for a firm

Citigroup Inc. is a leading financial services company with operations in more than 100 countries, serving a wide range of business, consumer, and government markets. It has grown through both organic growth and acquisitions; as a result of this diversity, in 2003 the firm consisted of 17 business activities organized into five groups:

> Citigroup Global Consumer
>
> Global Corporate and Investment Bank
>
> Global Investment Management
>
> Citigroup International
>
> Smith Barney

Each of these five groups consists of a number of related business activities, which will be referred to as strategic business units (SBUs). The Global Corporate and Investment Bank Group includes the following six business activities:

> Global Equities
>
> Global Fixed Income
>
> Global Investment Banking

Global Relationship Banking

Global Securities Services

Citigroup Cash, Trade and Treasury Services

The corporate task is to manage the total mix of business groups and business units and how this portfolio will evolve over time, which is the topic of Chapters 8 and 9. In Chapter 7 we focus on strategic management at one of these business units, such as Global Equities.

The Global Equities business offers a range of equity financing arrangements, including initial public offerings, and in 2002 raised a total of $USB40.5 in capital. The Global Fixed Income business undertakes underwriting, structuring, sales, and trading across a range of debt instruments, including corporate and government bonds, as well as participating in syndicated loans. Since this is a global business, Citigroup operates in senior as well as subordinated debt and in a number of currencies, including the euro, yen, and dollar. The Global Investment Banking business provides strategic and financial advisory services to global firms and governments on mergers, acquisitions, and financial restructuring, among other areas. During 2002, as we will see in Chapter 9, the overall volume of mergers fell, but the business was able to increase its market share, particularly in Europe. Data for these three businesses are not reported separately in the annual report, but they are all significant global businesses—their combined net income in 2002 was $USB3.8.

Global Securities Services provides custody services to insurance companies and pension funds, while Citigroup Cash, Trade and Treasury Services offers cash management and trade finance to corporations and governments. This business has a Web-based cash management system that permits clients to integrate their supply chains and manage working capital more effectively.

All businesses in the Global Corporate and Investment Group are significantly affected by levels of activity in global capital markets, which are in turn influenced by macroeconomic and political policies and developments in the 100+ countries in which they operate. But the impact of this remote environment varies with the business. During 2002, some businesses reported decreased net income, due to lower business volumes, particularly in Latin America, as well as increased provisions for credit losses. By contrast, the net income of other businesses increased due partly to higher volumes and partly to reduced costs arising from prior investments in Internet initiatives.

Strategy at the business-unit level is concerned with the management of one of these business units, such as Global Equities. Each business unit faces different challenges, with possibly different industry structures, customers, competitors, and technologies. Consequently, each business will develop its own strategy, recognizing the opportunities and competitiveness in its environment, utilizing the resources and competences of Citigroup, and reflecting the strategy adopted by Citigroup as a corporate entity. A significant corporate resource (intangible asset) is the global franchise inherent in the names "Citigroup" and "Citibank," which is of value to all business units both with their customers and in raising debt. Other corporate resources could be information technology linking back-office systems in all the countries in which the firm operates.[1]

7.1 INTRODUCTION

Most large firms such as Citigroup are comprised of a number of business units. In this chapter, we focus the strategic management of such business units, while Chapters 8 and 9 address the issue of the strategic management of the overall firm. Of course, if the firm consists of a single business unit, then business-unit and corporate strategy are the same.

We begin by briefly considering the relationship between the firm and its business units before reviewing the issues involved in strategic management of a business unit. Business-unit strategy is significantly different from corporate strategy. The essence of **business-unit strategy** is how the business should compete in the industry in which it is located. A business unit has a specific focus and is therefore in competition with other firms producing similar products or close substitutes in essentially the same product/market. Thus business-level strategy is primarily concerned with product/market competition, with creating and maintaining a competitive advantage and generating and responding to changes in its industry.

Developing business-level strategy necessitates understanding the external context of the business, which we briefly review. We then outline useful analytic steps in developing a business strategy, paying particular attention to the value chain at the business level. We break the task of strategic management of the business down into a set of strategic decisions that we then examine in depth. We explore where the business should position itself, both vertically in the value chain and horizontally with respect to market segments. This is followed by a discussion of how the business should compete and a review of possible growth strategies for the business. We conclude with an example illustrating the need for alignment and integration not only with respect to the business strategy itself but also with respect to the supporting organizational architecture.

Corporate and Business-Unit Relationships

Different business units must develop their own individual strategy and be managed in ways that reflect their distinctive competitive context, while also drawing on resources provided by the corporate level of the firm. The challenges facing any particular business unit in the firm are likely to be different from the challenges facing the firm's other businesses, as illustrated by the two Citigroup businesses, Global Equities and Global Securities Services.

Nonetheless, while business units have a degree of autonomy and are managed relatively independently of other business units, they are all part of a larger enterprise, which can add value and/or create problems for the business unit. The existence of *synergy* among various business units, such as sharing of knowledge, skills, technology, and information, further compromises the independence of a specific business.

Business units may also share certain *corporate competences,* such as R&D, or certain corporate intangible assets, such as brand name. In addition, the mission and objectives of the business unit are negotiated with, if not dictated by, the corporate center. The strategy and performance of the corporate parent as well as the performance of other businesses also influence the strategy of a business. Sometimes, from a corporate perspective, a business unit is part of the implementation process for corporate-level strategies. To illustrate, a corporate strategy of "total quality management" has implications for all business units; it is not something that a given business unit can opt out of. In some instances, elements of business-level strategy follow directly from corporate level strategy, suggesting low levels of independence.

In truth, no business unit can be truly independent of either other business units or the corporate parent. Since one of the major tasks of a diversified firm is to enhance the synergy among business units to maximize corporate value, such cooperation should be viewed positively.

The corporate level is the *source of funds* and other resources for all businesses in its portfolio; no business unit would make an approach to financial markets for funds. The business unit is a recipient in the capital allocation process within the firm. It makes proposals for strategies and their associated funds, but the corporate level makes the final decision. In this allocation process, the corporate level must balance the competing demands for cash from the various business units. We also have to recognize that there are different styles of corporate centers.[2] In some firms the corporate center is deeply involved in strategy at the business-unit level so as to achieve synergy across the entire firm. In other firms, the corporate center acts essentially as an internal capital market, leaving strategy development to the unit. Which style is adopted by the corporate level will affect strategy at the business level, in particular the degree and nature of the interaction among a given business unit, other business units, and the corporate head office. Since a business unit is part of a larger whole, consideration needs to be given to strategy at the corporate level when we are developing business strategy.

Strategic Management of the Business

Strategic management at the business unit involves not only developing strategy but also the following:

Negotiating objectives, mission, and scope with the corporate level

Providing leadership and leading change within the business

Developing and implementing the organizational architecture to support the strategy, including structure, decision processes, human resources, and culture

Understanding technology requirements, including information technology

Accepting responsibility for the performance of the business.

Figure 7.1 reproduces the simplified model of strategic management (Figure 1.5 from Chapter 1), which can be applied at the business-unit level. In this chapter, we focus on analyzing the changing external and internal context of the business and on developing business-unit strategy. Discussion of implementation and performance will be deferred until Chapters 11 and 12.

A business unit faces a changing context, including changes in the industry, changes among customers and competitors, new technology, and so on. The changing internal context here has two dimensions: changes within the business unit, reflecting new resources and competences, and changes in the internal relationship with the corporate center, which may decide that the business is to be built up, run down, or even sold.

In response to these changes, the business may need to change its strategy (e.g., the segments it serves or the basis of its competitive advantage) and/or its architecture. Such

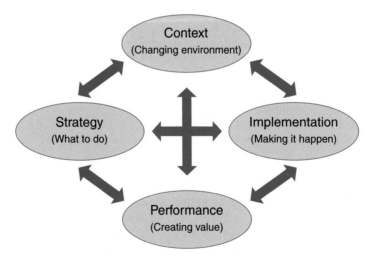

Figure 7.1 Simplified Strategic Management Model

changes might encompass structural change, implementation of a CRM system, modifying the culture to encourage employee empowerment, and so on.

Finally, the business unit must create value for the overall firm; its performance must provide a return greater than its capital costs. This value may not be created immediately or in the short term. The business may be one in which the firm is investing heavily with expectation of future returns. But the business must create value in either the short term or the long term or the corporation should exit the business.

Business Vision and Objectives

The concepts of vision, values, and mission discussed in Chapter 6 are, as we noted there, highly relevant for business units. So are objectives, and we now examine business-unit objectives in more depth.

Establishing a future direction for the business is a crucial task. However, a business unit's vision, values, and mission, while important to define, are qualitative and directional. The business unit must also have a set of quantitative targets, to be met by the strategy over some defined time period. These targets are the objectives for the unit. Objectives are a statement of what the unit expects to accomplish over a particular planning horizon. Strategy must be tested against these targets. If the strategy does not meet the objectives, then another strategy must be developed or the objectives revised. Of course, in a turbulent world, objectives may need to be revised as a result of unexpected developments. Nonetheless, successful businesses are characterized by a performance culture, part of which is the existence of defined quantitative targets, so that it is clear whether or not they have been reached.

As with vision, values, and mission, the corporate center plays a major role in establishing business-unit objectives. The center may unilaterally impose objectives for a given business or develop them more collaboratively, linking business-level and corporate-level strategy. If, for example, the corporate level were to dictate objectives to "become number one or number two in every industry" or "achieve 20% ROA," these would have major ramifications for all the firm's businesses.

Objectives are quantifiable, measurable, time-specific milestones of what the business wants to achieve. A business should have only a limited number of objectives, and they should be consistent with one another. Many firms set such objectives at levels that represent a "stretch" for the business, but they must be achievable if employees are to be held accountable for results.

Business objectives may be solely financial, but we recommend a broader approach. One framework for establishing a broader set of objectives, which we will discuss in more detail in Chapter 12, is the balanced scorecard.[3] This framework uses four major performance dimensions: financial (profit and growth), customer (satisfaction and retention), innovation (new products and processes), and internal measures (efficiency and costs). If we limit our focus for the moment to financial measures, however, common financial objectives are the following:

Growth: What growth in revenue, net profit, or assets is expected?

Net profit, measured as earnings before interest and tax (EBIT) or earnings before interest, tax, depreciation, and amortization (EBITDA): What dollar value of profit is expected, and is this to be measured before interest and depreciation or not?

Cash generation: Will the business be a net cash generator or user over the period?

Return on assets: What return on the assets is expected? This is a superior measure to margins, since it shows how well we are using the assets of the business whereas margins ignore any element of asset productivity.

Economic profit: What economic profit is the business expected to earn? We should not expect all businesses to earn a positive economic profit, for growth businesses in their early development typically will not.

A business cannot achieve maximum levels on all such objectives at the same time. It must make choices, and the strategy developed will depend on these choices. If objectives emphasize growth, immediate economic profit may be negative and the strategy to meet these objectives must be aggressive. If objectives focus on short-term profit, strategy might emphasize cost reduction or price improvement.

Objectives will be context-dependent, with choice influenced by such considerations as the product life-cycle stage, competition, the unit's market position, funds available, corporate needs for funds for other business units, and the unit's current profitability.

> During the 2000–2001 downturn, Cisco and Lucent drastically reduced employment in response to falls in revenue and profit. They had to reduce costs significantly, indicating the importance of these context-specific factors in short-term strategic decisions.

Objectives also need to achieve a synthesis between innovation and change on the one hand and efficiency on the other. Innovation is key to long-term performance, while efficiency may be vital for short-term survival. In competitive markets, pressures for cost reduction are always present and are exacerbated in a downturn.

⊚ 7.2 CONTEXT

Business-level strategy rests upon detailed understanding of the unit's external environment. Here we adopt the framework of Chapter 3, commenting on the need to understand changes external to the business, as well as the business itself and its economics.

Remote Environment

All business units face a changing remote environment, and the PESTLE model, introduced in Chapter 3, is a useful framework for understanding these changes. This model is an aid to thinking, not a rigid template to be applied mechanistically to all businesses. Strategic management is a combination of the analytical and the intuitive, and gaining insight into what external factors will be relevant for a specific business is at least partly intuitive. As highlighted previously, the principles of environmental assessment must be applied to individual businesses, since changes, their timing, and their impact will be different for different business units.

> Ford Motor Company owns Jaguar, a U.K. luxury car manufacturer. A number of external factors influence the demand for Jaguars, including, among others, exchange rates; disposable income; technological developments in car electronics such as GPS systems; developments in new materials and production processes. Another business unit of Ford, such as the truck division, will also be influenced by changes in its remote environment, but these influences will be different since the customers and competitors are different. Truck demand may be influenced by parameters such as business investment, legislation on road and rail use, and so on.

Industry

A business unit can be viewed as a member of a vertical network of firms that transforms inputs to deliver value to final customers. We have referred to this as the industry system or value chain. Such systems have both vertical and horizontal members. Vertical members are suppliers and customers, while horizontal members are entities providing inputs at the same level, such as accountants, market research firms, and law firms.

Industry analysis is most relevant at the business-unit level. The principles of competitive rivalry, substitutes, entrants, buyer power, and supplier power discussed in Chapter 3 are important to understand not just in the present but also dynamically, to reveal what changes are likely to occur. For example, are entry barriers for the industry falling, suggesting the likelihood of future entrants and lower margins? Changes influencing an industry affect some firms more than others; we need to understand possible impacts on specific business units.

Competition between Industry Systems

In many cases, competition is broader than that between two independent firms, instead occurring between two complete industry systems. There is competition between copper wire and optical fibers in telecommunications. Steel, aluminum, and composites compete in automobile manufacture, while in-store and electronic shopping compete for retail customers.

A vital initial step in developing business strategy is therefore to understand the extent, degree, and nature of competition between such industry systems. Whenever products from different technology platforms satisfy the same customer needs, each system must be thoroughly understood. Changes of costs or technology at any level in either chain will influence relative competitiveness and the strategy required to ameliorate or take advantage of such developments. For example, multinational environmental agreements (like Kyoto) will alter the basis of competition among coal, oil, natural gas, and renewable sources in electricity generation.

Value Creation and Capture in the Value Chain

We must also understand how much value is created in the complete system and which firms capture the value generated. Figure 7.2 shows the industry value chain for the Australian concrete and cement industry. This industry has four vertical stages of activity. Stage 1 consists of all firms making cement, which they sell to the concrete manufacturers. Similarly, a number of different firms make other input materials, such as crushed rock, also sold to the concrete manufacturers. Concrete manufacturers in turn sell the finished product to transport companies, who deliver the concrete to building and construction sites. If we analyze all the competitors in stage 1 we see that their price per ton of delivered concrete was $AU29, while their total costs, including capital costs, were $AU21 per ton. This first stage in the industry value chain generated $AU8 of economic profit over all competitors at this level. In total contrast, all firms in stage 3, concrete manufacture, generated zero economic profit; their revenue just covered total costs. While the industry generated a total of $AU22 per ton of economic profit, this was not distributed evenly across different levels. The final two stages, concrete manufacture and transport, generated zero economic profit. All economic profit generated in the chain was captured by the first two stages, manufacture of cement and other input materials. This distribution of value among firms involved in different stages of a chain will be influenced by such structural characteristics as relative power, the competitive intensity at different levels, entry barriers and costs, brand name, and product differentiation.

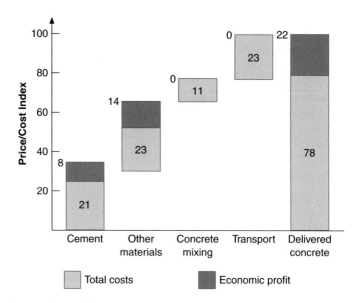

Figure 7.2 Industry Value Added, Australian Cement and Concrete Industry
Source: J. Stuckey and D. White, "When and When Not to Vertically Integrate," *Sloan Management Review* 34, no. 3 (1993), pp. 71–83. © 1993 by the Massachusetts Institute of Technology. All rights reserved.

All businesses in an industry system must decide where to position themselves, which activities they should perform, which activities should be done by other firms, and which organizational arrangements should exist among the firms. In the example above, concrete manufacturers might attempt to integrate backward to capture some of the economic profit generated at the previous stage. Further, while firms at the cement level regard the industry as very profitable, they should be concerned about the low returns at other levels. A business is less likely to invest if other players in the chain capture all the value created, and concrete manufacturers may decide to exit or reduce innovation. This in turn might encourage customers to switch to a different industry system, jeopardizing the prospects of the entire industry, including the profitable cement-manufacturing stage.

Within an industry system, value capture is often adversarial—a zero-sum game in which if I get it, you do not. But value creation can also be cooperative. Wal-Mart works cooperatively with suppliers to increase efficiency in the supply chain, by giving them access to Wal-Mart sales and inventory data. However, it also bargains very hard to extract for itself as much of the jointly created value as possible.

Industry System Changes and Disintermediation

Another consideration is whether or not the industry system is being reconfigured: Are stages being eliminated? Is the system undergoing a process of deconstruction and reconstruction? Such changes are disruptive and might allow new leaders to emerge.

Historically, the electricity industry was comprised of vertically integrated firms involved in all three stages of generation, transmission, and retail. More recently, this industry has begun to fragment, with the development of new businesses at these three levels as well as in the business of meter reading which is a new element of the value chain.[4] The value chain is being reconfigured in other industries, such as share trading, with Internet brokers such as E-TRADE or Charles Schwab and Internet providers such as Amazon.

Major drivers of disintermediation are developments in information technology and communications, enabling creation of new value chains. Managers must be aware of the nature of competition between different industry chains, the drivers of costs at each stage, and whether or not technology is causing stages to be eliminated or reconfigured. Value chains are a useful concept, but they should not be viewed statically, as they provide a framework for understanding the industry dynamics.

Competitor Analysis

A broad view of competition is essential to developing competitive strategy. We should be quite circumspect about any definition of competition that revolves around industry or products, for as we have just seen, intermaterial and interindustry competition is a very real phenomenon. Ultimately, the customer decides which alternatives compete to fulfill a particular need or application. Business-unit managers should therefore consider the following:

> Current direct competitors that want to improve their market position
>
> Possible new entrants that are expanding, perhaps because the segments are converging
>
> Firms with substitutes, that is, different products targeting the same customers or the same needs
>
> Suppliers and customers that could integrate forward or backward into the business

The end result of competitive analysis is to enable managers to construct better strategies. This requires projecting possible competitor moves and developing strategies that deal with this variety of projected scenarios. To accomplish this will typically require analyzing strategies competitors have employed in the past and how successful these strategies have been. We must also consider changes in competitors' circumstances (e.g., changes of ownership or management) before we can project what strategies they are likely to adopt and how we can address these. This analysis includes an understanding of what are they doing differently, how they compete in which segments, and their resources and competences. The results must influence our own business strategy, or we will have wasted our time constructing it.

⊚ 7.3 ANALYSIS FOR DEVELOPING STRATEGY

A tremendous variety of analyses can create insight for developing business strategy. We focus primarily on the use of the value chain or business system, an analysis that provides a very rich framework for analyzing a business unit, whether it is our own or that of a competitor,[5] and one that can generate useful and sometimes surprising options for strategic choices.

The Business Value Chain

A value chain for a business describes the activities that it has chosen to undertake in order to compete. These activities provide a basis for examining the opportunities for reducing costs or adding value (improving differentiation) at each stage. As Figure 7.3 indicates, to apply the value-chain concept we must first identify the activities involved

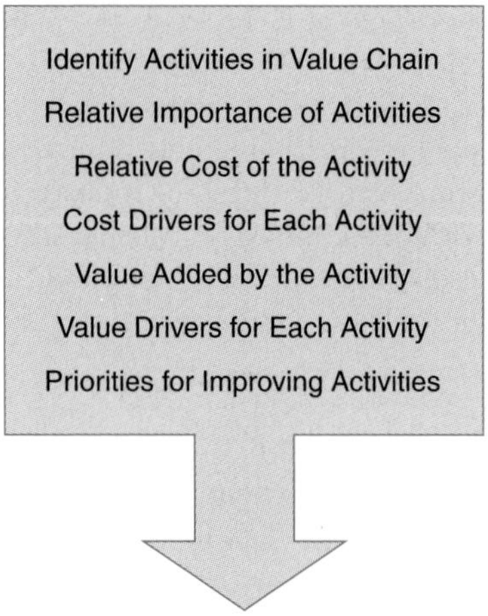

Figure 7.3   Using the Value Chain

in the value chain. To understand their relative importance, we must next identify their relative costs and value added for customers, as well as isolating the drivers of cost and the drivers of value added. However, to establish improvement priorities, we must integrate cost and value.

The first stage in this process is to describe the activities a firm has chosen to undertake in order to compete. Figure 7.4 describes typical value chains for the lending operation of a branch-based retail bank [Figure 7.4(a)] and a manufacturer [Figure 7.4(b)].

The activities of the *retail bank* have been collapsed into three broad stages; raising funds, processing transactions, and marketing of loans, together with a profit margin. This value chain provides a framework for ascertaining cost and investment drivers at each stage. The first stage is raising funds from depositors. The cost to the bank of these funds (the depositors' interest rate) depends on the general level of interest rates in the economy and the perceived risk of the individual bank. The former is dictated primarily by macroeconomic conditions and government policy, but management can influence the latter through its risk management policies.

Transaction costs are a back-office function, comprising a combination of processing and transmission costs. As data transmission costs have fallen, banks and other financial institutions have decoupled the back office from the front office. Many call centers and transaction-processing centers are in remote locations, even international ones, allowing the bank to capitalize on lower wage rates.

The costs of marketing loans depend on factors such as the bank's distribution channels, its branch network efficiency, and its use of technology to support these marketing activities. No company value chain is static, as businesses should constantly be seeking improvement opportunities.

The value chain can be employed to ascertain the nature and extent of our *competitive advantage* at any stage. This is illustrated in Figure 7.5, which describes a business unit with just two activities: manufacturing and logistics. The firm has analyzed its costs for these two activities, relative to industry best practice. Its manufacturing activity is operating at industry best practice with regard to cost. However, its logistics costs are well above best practice.

One interpretation of the situation in Figure 7.5 is that logistics is being subsidized by manufacturing. In highly competitive markets, such cross-subsidization is unsustain-

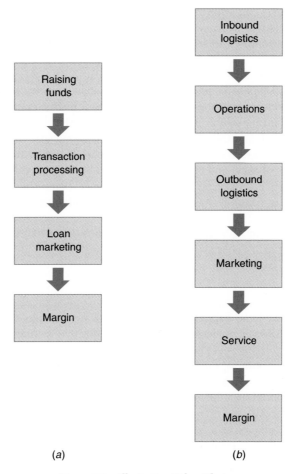

Figure 7.4   Illustrative Value Chains

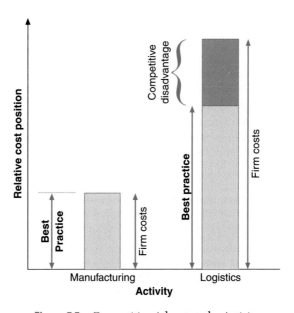

Figure 7.5   Competitive Advantage by Activity

able. No firm can afford to engage in activities in which it suffers a competitive disadvantage relative to competitors. The business must either improve its logistics performance or outsource it to achieve lower cost.

Cost Drivers

In highly competitive markets there is constant, unrelenting pressure for cost reductions, as well as innovation, if a business is to remain competitive. These pressures dictate that business-unit managers must understand the drivers of cost and value enhancement, and the value chain provides a framework for this understanding.

As discussed in detail in Chapter 5, two of the major drivers of long-term costs are economies of scale and learning. Both need be understood dynamically. As an illustration, economies of scale are a major rationale behind many horizontal mergers and acquisitions, where it is assumed that the merged entity will have lower costs.

> In the mid-1990s, Chase and Chemical Banks merged. The integration of their separate back-office functions of check clearing and loan processing was expected to reduce costs by some $USB1.5.[6]

Economies of scale are influenced by technological change and the relative importance of fixed and variable costs. If all costs are variable, then economies of scale are absent. However, management must be proactive in understanding the dynamics of scale, since changes create turbulence and consequent opportunities. If scale is becoming more important, the industry is likely to face restructuring through acquisitions as firms attempt to achieve lower costs. Firms unaware of this will end up as acquisition targets. Should scale become less important, the business can expect new entrants, with subsequent pressure on margins. Firms that act in a timely manner usually enjoy a competitive advantage as a result of such changes. Competitive advantage cannot be based on what was successful in yesterday's world; managers need to understand the economic characteristics of their world in the future.[7]

Learning

Learning effects can be particularly dramatic in high-growth markets, with significant cost reductions occurring as cumulative volume increases. This was illustrated in Figure 5.9, where the costs of disc drives declined from about $US400 per megabyte in 1977 to around $US0.10 per megabyte in 1994. Businesses unable to reduce costs in line with the average industry cost curve were forced to exit.

One possible strategy for a business, then, is to identify a growth market and develop a strategy focusing on high growth to ensure a long-term dominant position at the expense of short-term profit. One risk with this strategy is that a competitor, possibly with an inferior cost position, might introduce a major innovation, revolutionizing industry cost structures and thus nullifying the leader's advantage.

Customer Value

The value chain can also provide a framework for considering where and how to add value for customers.[8] These values are often in flux, but customers buy on the basis of the difference between price and the perceived value of the product or service, as illustrated in Figure 7.6. Buyers place a value of V on the product, which we assume to be greater than C, the cost to supply the product to the customer.

The value created by the business is then $V - C$. It creates value by converting inputs at a cost of C to generate a product on which customers place a value of V. The

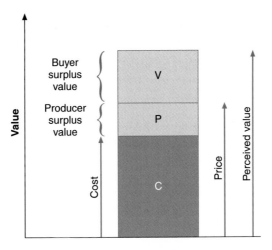

Figure 7.6 Price and Value Creation

business charges a price, P, which can be interpreted as splitting the surplus value, $V - C$, between producer and customer. The business may capture more value by either reducing costs while holding prices constant or by increasing value so that customers willingly pay higher prices (even though costs may rise). The level of P determines how the value the business has created is shared between producer and buyer.

Assessing Customer Value

Customer value is the difference between the perceived benefits received from the product or service and the perceived costs incurred in securing those benefits. For example, the customer is charged a price for the product but also incurs other "costs," such as time to search, effort in searching, and risk in the purchase. There are a number of ways to measure customer value, including perceived value, conjoint, and value-in-use analyses.[9] Here we describe one of these methods, perceived value analysis, which has the advantages of being easy to understand and apply.

Table 7.1 shows the perceived value of two brands of a particular product, an easy-chair. The analysis requires three steps: the identification of the benefits considered salient by the customer, the perceived relative importance of those benefits (estimated using a constant sum scale, where points summing to 100 are allocated across benefits to indicate their relative importance), and the perceived ability of the different competitive offerings to deliver these benefits, assessed with a 1–10 rating scale.[10]

TABLE 7.1 Perceived Value Analysis

Benefit	Relative Importance	Rating, Firm A	Total, Firm A	Rating, Firm B	Total, Firm B
Chair design	20	5	100	7	140
Comfort	30	6	180	8	240
Fabric quality	15	10	150	9	135
Fabric design	15	5	75	7	105
Ease of purchase	20	8	160	10	200
Total	100		665		820

Firm B's offering is clearly perceived as superior in the absence of price information. If firm A is priced at $500 and firm B at $450, then clearly firm B is offering the greatest value. B can take its reward in growth, using a combination of superior value and low price, or in margin by raising price. If there are multiple competitors in a market, results can be plotted on a two-dimensional chart, with relative price on one axis and relative value on the other.[11]

These data indicate where the firm could improve its offering, as well as useful dimensions of differentiation. Of course, it is always better to use data gathered from customers directly rather than substituting managerial judgment. Managers' judgments are sometimes quite far removed from those of the customer, which is why there is no substitute for good market research in trying to assess value.[12] Nonetheless, business-unit management needs to ascertain whether new bases of competitive advantage are being generated or are required, for in dynamic markets the basis of competition is always changing.

Business-Unit Analysis

As well as understanding the external context of business strategy development, we must also be intimately familiar with the business unit's strengths and weaknesses and those of the corporation of which it is a part. These are not part of the external context of strategic management, but the same disciplined and objective analysis is required. The resources and competences discussed in Chapter 5 must be subject to rigorous and objective analysis, benchmarked against competitors, and reviewed in the light of the requirements of customers not only in the current markets but also in those that the business unit expects to serve in the future. We may therefore want to develop a list of current sources of advantage and the unit's position on them, assessing them relative to the life cycles of the business's products and markets. We should also compare our financial and market performance with that of our competitors. We explore these analyses in more detail in Chapter 12.

The overall objective of the external and internal analysis we have just discussed is to get an understanding of who is winning and why, what the requirements of the market are (price or other forms of advantage), and whether or not we are using our competitive advantage well. This in turn requires an understanding of the economics of the business, its cost structure, and its value chain.

◉ 7.4 DEVELOPING BUSINESS-LEVEL STRATEGY

We have defined strategy as an integrated set of actions that require significant resources and commitment and that affect the future direction of the business unit. Its purpose is to generate value through creating competitive advantage in selected markets. Such strategy is based on the analysis undertaken by the unit. This analysis must facilitate rethinking the market, its segments, and emerging customer needs; rethinking the value chain or deconstructing the business; and, in general, helping managers find new approaches and opportunities. If the strategy process does not support these ends, it is not working properly.

Strategy is about doing different things or doing the same things differently from and better than competitors. This requires a balance between creativity and realism. Creativity is important in strategy development, since strategy is not formula-driven. Creative analysis can lead to major improvements in customer value, so-called value innovation.[13] Yet strategy must also be based on a sound understanding of the market, competitors, and our own competences. A strategy that cannot be implemented is unrealistic.

By its very nature, strategy has a future component. The business might not be creating value now but is expected to create value in the future. Managers must take risks, gambling that their insights into markets, customers, and competitors will turn out correctly. This exposes the unit to two different types of risk. One is that the future may turn out differently from what we expected. Consequently, a strategy will need a degree of flexibility to take advantage of external changes as they develop. The second risk is that we may not successfully implement the selected strategy. In our view, strategic management is about both a good idea and getting that idea to work.

Having developed a strategy, we need to estimate its expected returns and relate these to the returns from the current strategy. This involves posing numerous questions: What is the current strategy? Will the current strategy meet expectations? What risks are there with the current strategy? What is its cost structure, profitability, profitability by segment, channel of distribution, customer type or size, product line, geography? Where in the value chain are profits generated? When developing strategy, we should also try to test assumptions. For example, the assumption of no new entrants into a profitable high-growth market is unrealistic unless there are significant barriers to entry. If uncertainty is high, we should consider using scenario planning or performing a probability distribution of returns with a simulation exercise.[14] Alternatively, a real options approach, to be discussed in Chapter 8, may be adopted.

A Strategic Decision Framework

Developing business-unit strategy usually requires a number of strategic decisions, summarized in the framework in Figure 7.7. We can expand on the key questions of Figure 7.7 as follows:

Where to Compete

Vertical positioning of the business: Where in the vertical value chain should we position the business? What is the activity scope of the business? Which activities should be undertaken by the business and which should be outsourced?

Horizontal positioning of the business: In which segments should the business compete—how many segments, how many products? What is its width of market and product coverage? The vision and mission of the business, which should determine its scope, will obviously affect these decisions.

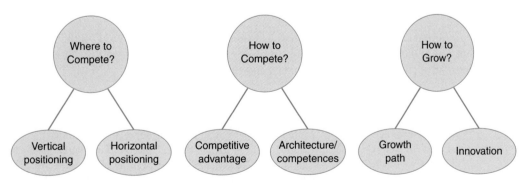

Figure 7.7   Critical Business Strategy Questions

How to Compete

Competitive advantage and strategy: Which combination of difficult-to-replicate factors does the business possess that will allow it to either produce at a lower cost or better meet customer needs than its competitors? How sustainable are these advantages, and how will the business develop new bases of advantage? How will these be deployed against competitors?

Architecture and competences: What competences are required to enable the business to implement its strategy and improve its competitive position? How competitive is its current knowledge base? Are its processes, systems, and structure supportive of the strategy? Does it possess the flexibility required to compete in a turbulent environment?

Business Growth Strategy

Growth and innovation strategy: What options does the business have for growth? Should it grow through new product development or by expanding into new market segments? Should these be executed by internal development, acquisition, or alliance? What are the alternatives and the risks associated with each?

We will discuss each of these decisions. Although we discuss them independently, they are nevertheless all interrelated.

◎ 7.5 WHERE TO COMPETE

Decisions about where to compete are obviously dependent on how the business's mission statement defines its scope, but managers must usually make more specific decisions about the vertical and horizontal positioning of the business. We now examine such decisions.

Vertical Positioning

Managers must decide which activities the business will undertake and which will be undertaken by others. They should question the traditional paradigm of owning the factors of production as the best way to achieve competitive advantage, instead deciding which activities are best done under *common ownership* and which are best done via *market-based* transactions. The value chain is a valuable framework for clarifying these issues.

> The CEO of a major textile and garment business once described his job to one of the authors as follows: "There are five stages of value added in our business. My job is to decide where in the world they will be performed."

Airline companies once believed that they had to own aircraft to be in the business, but today most lease their aircraft (and often other equipment), and many have outsourced such activities as maintenance and catering.

> The Australian airline Qantas uses mainly internal staff for maintenance. Qantas has never had a fatal accident in over 70 years of operation and sees its safety record as a major source of competitive advantage. (We could note that not all their customers may share this perception.) If we accept that this is indeed the situation, then a decision to outsource maintenance would be critical for Qantas, which has to balance possibly lower costs from external providers against the loss of direct control. If this activity is outsourced, will the

firm lose a core competence? Can the maintenance and safety record continue to be superior if it uses the same external providers as its competitors?

The emergence of the Internet has provided an opportunity for disintermediation and reintermediation in the airline industry. Historically, airlines used a network of independent agents to make reservations. Agents were able to make worldwide reservations on a common system. With the emergence of the Internet, consumers are now able to directly access airline websites and make reservations. The cost of such direct booking is low, but it places traditional airlines in direct competition with travel agents. In the pursuit of lower costs, newer airlines, such as Jet Blue in the U.S. or EasyJet in Europe, dictate that all bookings have to be made on the Internet (or by phone). In the airline industry, different firms have decided to undertake different sets of activities, and this choice has been a relevant component of their strategy.

When considering this vertical industry system, the firm must decide whether or not to expand its scope into immediately adjoining stages. This is normally referred to as vertical integration, and we now turn our attention to these decisions.

Vertical Integration

Vertical integration occurs when a firm acquires or develops a business that is the current concern of either its customers (forward) or its suppliers (backward), with the objective of getting higher profitability through the elimination of the customer/supplier, bringing their margins under the firm's control. Backward integration requires new operational skills; forward integration requires new marketing skills, while creating competition with existing customers.[15]

Vertical integration is motivated by the idea that the business can create additional value when more activities share common ownership. So where do these advantages come from? One source may be joint production economies—there are efficiency gains from linking two activities together.

A few years ago, Intel decided to integrate forward from chip production into motherboard production. Within a few months, half the motherboard manufacturers in Taiwan had gone out of the business.[16]

Integration may also provide protection against *asset specificity*, where the business can be held ransom by a monopoly supplier or customer. In these cases of market failure, the firm probably has no choice but to vertically integrate, as has occurred in some resource-based industries such as aluminum. In steel, however, the market for raw materials is more competitive, and few steel firms have vertically integrated backward into iron-ore mining.

There are several issues with vertical integration as a business strategy. Vertical integration inevitably results in an increasing proportion of a firm's or business's assets being in one industry, thus increasing dependency on it. In the automobile industry, for example, if we currently make cars and acquire a tire producer, we have not diversified in terms of industry; we have even more assets in the car industry, increasing exposure to changes in industry demand. Such actions may be taken defensively, to protect our original investment, although this may be dangerous, throwing good money after bad.

It may also be difficult to balance *scale* and *capacity*. We can see this by using a hypothetical but realistic example from the car industry. Suppose the efficient size of plant for cars is 400,000 units per year, requiring 2 million tires per year. Let us further assume that the automobile firm builds an efficient-sized tire plant that produces 3 million tires per year. The question, then, is what do we do with the extra 1 million tires per year? Do we attempt to sell them to our competitors—and will they purchase from a competitor? Or will we sell the extra product to the aftermarket for replacement tires? If so, we will need a strong retail marketing group. If neither of these alternatives seems feasible, the tire plant will only produce 2 million tires per year. If there are strong economies of scale, the plant will be a high-cost facility, making the cost of tires to the car company uncompetitive. An integration decision must be well thought out before choosing it as a course of action.

Vertical integration also opens up a *transfer-price* problem. If we are the upstream unit, selling to a sister business downstream, what should be our selling price? How are conflicts resolved? Is the downstream unit given the right to purchase the product on the open market? How do we ensure that the upstream unit is efficient? Is there a service agreement between the two units? There is often very vigorous debate over these matters, particularly if the intermediate product has no external market, making it impossible to determine a "fair" market price.

There are also quasi-integration strategies, such as long-term contracts, joint ventures, alliances, technology licenses, asset ownership (we own the asset but contract out manufacture), and franchising. These are various forms of cooperation between the firm and competitors, suppliers, and customers. These are looser forms of organization than normally implied by integration, which has an assumption of ownership.

There appears to be a movement toward less vertical integration.[17] The risk of market failure in many industries is reducing as deregulation permits new entrants. Faster and better communications have facilitated the emergence of global markets, increasing the number of potential suppliers and/or customers. In addition, low levels of vertical integration lead to greater flexibility, a source of competitive advantage in turbulent times. Finally, disintermediation has eliminated some players in industry value chains, while new intermediaries, often based around electronic markets, have arisen.[18] The market for corporate control is also pressuring integrated companies to restructure, which brings us naturally to the next strategic decision area: outsourcing.

Outsourcing

Outsourcing occurs when the firm transfers some of its recurring internal activities to outside providers, with the arrangement specified in a formal contract.[19] The resources for undertaking these activities are provided by the outside firm, which is also responsible for making decisions regarding those resources and meeting certain outcomes as specified by the contract.

> Dell outsources the design of most computer components, the production of many subassemblies, and some software. Its main tasks are assembling these components and, perhaps most important of all, managing the brand name "Dell" and the associated marketing and service activities.

In many industries, economies of scope are changing—firms and their suppliers are becoming increasingly specialized and outsourcing activities that are not regarded as core. The outsourcing movement is also driven by the increasing competitiveness of business. No firm can afford to undertake activities internally unless these activities are being performed at a world-class level, thereby contributing to competitive advantage. Yet for most businesses, a significant number of internal activities are likely to be being performed well below best practice. Increasing pressure for performance and the need to deliver economic value lead managers to search for new approaches, and outsourcing is one.

> Contract manufacturing is growing at 20% per year, "driven by two main developments: a growing concentration by original equipment manufacturers (OEMs) on core strengths—which are as likely to be in customer relations as in manufacturing—and technological changes that allow them to spin off part of the value chain without losing control of the product".[20]

These developments have been greatly assisted by improved communication systems. As search costs fall, firms seek outsourcing partners from a wider, often global, pool. Improvements in information technology permit outsourcing contracts to be better managed than before. The central reason behind outsourcing is that the business must focus its resources on activities essential to its survival and leverage peripheral activities.[21] In markets such as the United States and Europe, service firms have become large and sophisticated relative to the scale and expertise of service groups within integrated companies—so they may provide better and less costly services. These outsider suppliers can often develop better depth of knowledge, invest in software and training, be more efficient, and even offer staff better wages.[22]

If supplier markets were totally reliable and efficient, business managers might outsource everything except core competencies, although there are risks and some unique transaction costs for searching, contacting, and controlling these suppliers. In the longer term, the firm may become dependent on outside suppliers and may be held ransom, since outside firms now have specialized assets. With outsourcing, firms need more personnel involved in procurement and contract management. Lack of these skills is a major cause of outsourcing failure. However, there are often hidden costs of activities performed within the firm, since lack of innovation, delay, and internal bureaucracy too often go unrecognized. Possible reasons for outsourcing are summarized in Table 7.2.

TABLE 7.2   Reasons for Outsourcing

Strategic: The outside firm has a specific expertise, such as tax accounting, allowing the business to obtain specialized expertise in the area. Outsourcing may also provide increased flexibility in responding to changes in demand or technology.

Financial: Outsourcing normally reduces the need for capital employed by the business. The supplier may be able to obtain higher levels of capital productivity, and, since we do not provide the capital ourselves, our business is essentially variating its fixed costs and increasing its flexibility, which may help us respond to unanticipated changes in demand. In a turbulent world, this may be particularly advantageous.

Cost: A major reason for outsourcing is lower costs. For example, suppliers may achieve scale economies since they deal with multiple customers, and competition forces these cost savings to be passed on. But outsourcing involves transaction costs, which may make outsourcing cost more than performing the activities ourselves.

Organizational reasons: The business decides to focus on what it does best so as to increase customer value, outsourcing activities it performs relatively poorly. Here the business needs to take a long-term perspective. The U.S. electronics industry may have outsourced the foundations of future competences when it outsourced elements of its TV market, in particular screens. U.S. competitors lost the skills to develop and produce screens, which reduced their later participation in products with display screens, such as calculators and computer monitors.

Through outsourcing, business managers often expect to increase operating performance, obtain expertise, improve risk management, and acquire innovative ideas. Since suppliers have narrower scopes, they can perform better in what are for the business noncore areas, since these seldom get the resources to achieve world-class standards. Instead, we benefit from the supplier's superior resource package, sometimes even gaining additional market access through the provider's network. Staff who move to the external provider may have better career paths arising from the increased specialization of the outside suppliers' activities. On the other hand, many employees see outsourcing as a problem: their jobs are at risk.

Any activity in the firm's value chain can be done internally or externally and is a potential candidate for outsourcing. Activities such as IT, customer service, manufacturing, sales, and accounting are all possibilities, but of course such outsourcing can also be difficult to reverse—it is difficult and costly to terminate a 10-year contract in year 5! Since there is an increasing number of external providers for these activities, the relative advantage of internal versus external sourcing is constantly changing.

Insourcing

The core competences required by the business are not fixed; rather, they evolve over time, reflecting environmental and competitive changes as well as changes in customer needs. Activities related to future core competences are best kept in-house, where they can be nurtured to provide this future competitive advantage. This may even lead firms to bring previously outsourced activities in-house again.

> Optus, the number-two telecommunications company in Australia, has brought in-house some programming activities for SAP and its billing system, reducing its dependence on IBM and Hewlett-Packard, which formerly provided these as outsourced services. It may be the case that these skills exist in what is now the firm's new parent, Singtel.[23] Another possible reason is that because these skills are necessary to establish future competitive advantage, the firm decided to develop them internally.

The decision of what to insource and what to outsource must be periodically reviewed. Noncore activities probably should be outsourced, but the business is not likely to generate a competitive advantage from outsourced activities if the external supplier also serves competitors. This is one of several risks with outsourcing. Nonetheless, a business may be able to leverage its resources by focusing on a small number of core competences in which it can excel and which are important to customers. Managers should invest in exploiting and developing these competences as well as generating new ones. Activities in which the firm is not, or cannot be, best in class should be outsourced.

Horizontal Positioning

As we noted in Chapter 3, customers are rarely homogeneous in their needs: different customers have different needs. The business unit must group these disparate customers into **market segments,** groups of customers who have needs that are reasonably similar but whose needs across groups are different. We want to develop segments that show within-group homogeneity and between-group heterogeneity so that the unit can better accommodate the different needs of its marketplace.

Business-unit managers have to decide how many of these segments to target, how to provide the benefits sought, and at what cost. Most production systems or transaction systems have a cost of diversity; it is generally more costly to produce several kinds of bank loans, for example, than one kind of car. However, if customer requirements are such that a diversity of products is called for, the business must decide which, and how many of, these segments it will attempt to satisfy.

Here the business faces a dilemma: Should it produce a narrow range of products, at low cost, or produce a wide range of product variants, with possibly higher unit costs. This is never an easy decision, and it is made more difficult by the changing relationship between product diversity and unit costs. Advantages typically accrue to the firm that can innovate with a flexible production system that meets the diverse needs of the market.

> Vaillant is the biggest European maker of central-heating boilers. "Huge variation in customer tastes and building standards means … offer[ing] hundreds of different models … to reach across the continent." Boilers are manufactured to meet the specifications of many different countries, using as many common parts as possible so as to minimize the costs of customization "without narrowing the choice for the consumer."[24]

These principles hold for service as well as manufacturing firms. An insurance firm that can tailor products to specific customer groups, for example, will possess a competitive advantage as long as the incremental costs are reasonable.

The marketing group normally has the detailed knowledge of customer needs and wants as well as differences in these. The role for general management is to ensure that changes are identified so that a complete and realistic picture of the market is presented. The result of this market and customer analysis is a better understanding of:

- Changing customer needs
- Changing the basis of segmentation
- Changing relative importance of segments
- Changing ways of getting products to these customers—new channels

Business-unit management must monitor and update the basis of segmentation—tracking changing needs, ensuring that growth segments are identified, and making decisions on the number of segments in which the unit will compete. While the design of strategies for targeted segments is often delegated to marketing, business management must decide the unit's basis of competition, ensuring that the appropriate resources and architecture are developed.

In business-to-business marketing, the unit may treat each customer as a segment of one. This is also becoming an option in some consumer markets with the advent of mass customization. Here the Internet has helped, as has the development of computerized customer databases.

> The U.S. firm Lands End offered men's custom jeans for $54 in 2003. The customer provides a limited number of specifications of key measurements, which are the basis for making a pair of jeans specific to that customer, for delivery in three to four weeks. This customer information is saved by the firm, which not only makes reordering easy but also provides a valuable database for the company.[25]

Customer needs are critical because they define which type of competitive advantage can create the most value. Business-unit managers must therefore understand customer needs in each segment, how these are evolving, which needs are unmet or poorly met, and how potential customers might be enticed to purchase.

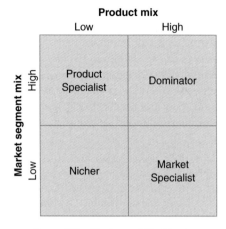

Figure 7.8   Horizontal Positioning

Horizontal positioning requires that the business unit decide in which segments to compete, as well as the range of products supplied to the chosen segments. It can be focused, operating in only one segment, or it can elect to be a broadly based competitor, competing in all segments; similarly, it can provide a limited or wide range of products. Figure 7.8 illustrates these options graphically. We now examine them individually.[26]

Market Specialist
Harley Davidson competes in a limited number of segments in the motorcycle market. Harley achieves a large number of product variations at reasonable cost by sharing very similar mechanicals, but all of its bikes are large-capacity road bikes. There are no small-capacity Harleys, nor does Harley compete in the motocross or off-road segments. More recently, the company has added the Buell brand to its lineup, but the Harley brand remains as a market specialist. Retail and distribution businesses are also good examples of market specialists, since their scope is usually defined around a socioeconomic or geographic segmentation.

Dominator
Honda is the dominator of the motorcycle business, competing in almost all market and product segments on a global basis. This was such a successful strategy that the motorcycle business funded Honda's development of its automobile business, the vision to which founder Soichiro Honda had always aspired.

As a broad competitor, a business has another decision to make: how to adjust its strategy across the different segments. Does it develop unique strategies for each segment (a higher-cost approach) or attempt to use similar strategies for each segment (a broad appeal that may completely satisfy no customers)? Modular design and production—or platform engineering, as it is known in the automobile business—is an important tool in achieving product variety at reasonable cost.

Nicher
Since we defined segments as groups with similar needs and wants and specified that the needs of customers in other segments are different, it follows that a business may be able to exist in one segment without having to participate or compete in other segments. If this is not the case, then our definition of segments is probably incorrect. Indeed, competitive advantage is generally defined with respect to a segment since a business

may have an advantage in one segment but not in another. Specialist car manufacturers such as Morgan and Ferrari are examples of niche-based competitors.

Product Specialist

Intel is an example of a product specialist because of its focus on standardized micro-processors, which it sells around the world for many applications. Of course, its product mix of chips broadened significantly as it grew. However, a specialist competitor such as Intel may be able to build significant expertise in a product, in a technology, or in relationships with the customers in a market segment. Nonetheless, there is considerable risk from more broadly based firms unless the specialist can erect barriers to minimize the threat of entry.

Part of business strategy is determining the proper segmentation, identifying seg-ments with good reward potential, ascertaining where the business is strong, and under-standing how boundaries may evolve and customer needs within the segment are likely to change. In addition, the choice of the number of segments in which to compete and the strategy to follow will be influenced by considerations such as segment size and growth, ease of serving the segment, and the capabilities of the unit.[27] In Chapter 8 we will examine the tools of portfolio analysis, which can be applied to make better choices among segment opportunities at the business level.

◉ 7.6 HOW TO COMPETE

Firm-specific factors are evidently important to business-unit success, for in Chapter 2 we observed wide variations in the performance achieved by different competitors within the same industry. These differences, if sustained over time, are attributable to the existence of a competitive advantage possessed by the business. A business has a **competitive advantage** when it is able to utilize its resources and competences to gen-erate a value-creating strategy that other firms find difficult to imitate. Such an advan-tage permits the business to outperform its competitors and is the only way to generate returns above the cost of capital on a sustainable basis.

Competitive advantage may come from a superior business definition, from unique capabilities, or from doing what other firms also do—but doing it better. Any such advan-tage must be assessed relative to competitors and must lead to one or all of: lower costs, higher sales volume, or higher prices. Otherwise, it is a phantom advantage.

The nature of the competitive advantage depends on the industry and marketplace in which the business unit competes. In management consulting, clients are unlikely to choose on the basis of price alone: having the lowest price is not necessarily an advantage in that industry. On the other hand, in commodity markets such as iron ore, sulphuric acid, or computer memory chips, many customers make decisions primarily on the basis of price.

Competitive advantage requires that the business is in a superior position on rele-vant sources of advantage and that competitors cannot easily replicate the drivers creat-ing these advantages. For example, for an advantage in product quality, drivers might include product innovation and customer understanding. If the advantage is customer access, drivers may be brand image and distributor relationships.

Competitive Business Strategies

Competitive business strategy defines the basis on which a business unit elects to compete for customers while withstanding competitive endeavors. It involves choosing activities that allow the business to deliver its products and services so as to produce superior economic results. We begin by looking at a simplified model of strategy and then elaborate.

Porter suggested there are two basic ways to achieve a competitive advantage:[28]

- Offer the lowest delivered price to the customer
- Provide a differentiated product

This is really just saying that to achieve success, we need to differentiate our offer from that of competitors and that the basis can be in price or nonprice features. Choice between these alternatives depends on segment response functions (demand elasticities), business competences, and the strategies of our competitors. If the segment is characterized by a cost/price game, the essential element of competitive strategy is reducing cost relative to prices. If the segment is primarily a value game, the essential element of competitive strategy is achieving superior price realization relative to costs. A market segment would be primarily a cost game when there is little price differentiation or difference in product offerings. On the other hand, a segment will be a value game when there is substantial variance in price realization, strong differences in customer preference between two offerings at the same price level, and a clear difference between product offerings. Note that these characterizations are not immutable. Innovation may shift a price/cost game to a value game, whereas lack thereof may do the reverse!

Low-Price Strategy

The essence of this strategy is that the price actually paid by the customer is the lowest among all available alternatives. While this is sometimes interpreted to imply that the business must charge the lowest price in the industry, we actually need to focus on the effective price paid by the customer, not the seller's realized price. Customers may incur costs outside the control of the business. For example, the customer may pay the costs of distribution, transport, taxes or tariffs—all costs that are outside the business's control but may be incurred by customers. When the business is pursuing a strategy of lowest delivered cost, it must achieve all sources of cost advantage. There is no point in having low-cost manufacturing, then selling through a high-cost distribution system.

Such a strategy can create value for the business's owners only if it is the industry's lowest-cost producer. Consequently, in these markets there is generally only one winner—the low-cost supplier. Other firms are unlikely to be creating shareholder value.

Low-price strategies are most appropriate when there are limited technological opportunities for product differentiation and few market opportunities for product variants. Sometimes the product's technical specification means all basic offerings will be the same. For example, the manufacture of sulphuric acid does not allow for much variation in product specifications, especially if all customers require the same quality. Such strategies are powerful when there is a high end-user concern with price, when buyer needs are primarily economic, and when the product represents a large proportion of the customer's total costs. Such conditions exist in coal-fired power stations, where coal represents 50% or more of the final cost of electricity produced.

A business pursuing a low-cost approach must make consistent decisions. Sustaining a cost advantage means understanding such cost drivers as scale economies and learning; avoiding marginal customers; and having a limited product range, low overheads, superior process effectiveness, and good management of working capital. Even low-price sellers need certain minimum levels of customer service, quality, delivery, and so on, but they should outsource any activity they cannot undertake at low cost, while maintaining constant vigilance over possible changes.

Compal, the Taiwanese computer firm, has moved a substantial proportion of its manufacturing to China to take advantage of the low labor costs there.[29]

With a competitive strategy based on lowest delivered price to the customer, cost-reduction initiatives often include downsizing, with major reductions in the number of employees. Such actions typically have a strong negative impact on staff morale,[30] and possibly reduced performance in the longer term.[31] Low-price strategies have other risks, the primary one being outsmarted by competitors who achieve technological breakthroughs that further reduce costs. Complacency can allow costs to rise, while technological change may result in new products or processes that the business does not adopt for fear of cannibalization.

Differentiation Strategy

A strategy of **differentiation** involves offering a product not at the lowest price but with features or characteristics that make it different from the competitive offerings and for which we can charge a price premium. Such a strategy is likely to be valuable when customer needs are diverse and when technology permits differentiated offerings to be produced. One measure of the extent of differentiation in a market is the difference in prices between essentially similar products. With a resource material such as coal, different coal mines price differentially, reflecting differences in impurities such as sulfur and heavy metals. Similarly, some oil fields such as Texas produce low-sulfur crude, earning a small price premium. Such products may reduce customer costs through reduced noxious emissions, and a price premium can be charged for this. Although the additional margin may be small, it can have a significant impact on economic profit. In other markets, however, we see very substantial differences in the prices of different offerings. Consider the automobile market: New cars can be purchased from as little as about $US6000 up to $US250,000 or more for Aston Martins and Ferraris.

There are many ways to differentiate offerings via quality, design, faster delivery time, more reliable delivery time, brand image, innovation, technological excellence, credit and or barter terms, and so on. Such strategies typically require an excellent understanding of what customers really value, good marketing capability, and strong interfunctional cooperation.

Some firms have been remarkably successful at differentiating through their brand name: they manage this intangible asset to create and extract additional value. U.S. brand names such as Wrigley's, Gillette, Coca-Cola, and Campbell have maintained a sense of uniqueness and strong market positions for many years.[32]

While the basic appeal to customers may be nonprice features, the actual price premium cannot be increased indefinitely—there are limits to the premium that customers are prepared to pay. This indicates some of the risks of a differentiation strategy. First, customers may cease to value the attribute that is the basis of differentiation, possibly because other competitors develop products with comparable attributes. Or the business may attempt to impose too great a price differential. In business-to-business markets, such a competitive strategy is likely to be more effective when the product represents only a small component of total costs for the end-user or when poor performance seriously affects the customer or the customer's customer.

Combination Strategy

The above two competitive strategies are sometimes viewed as mutually exclusive: the business must choose one or the other. Actually, the management challenge is to be both at the same time—to be both *low cost and highly differentiated.* In many industries it is indeed possible to be both. For example, higher product quality can actually reduce certain costs such as rework, returns, and recalls. Such a product may be both high in quality and low in cost. With a consumer product, the market leader may get economies of

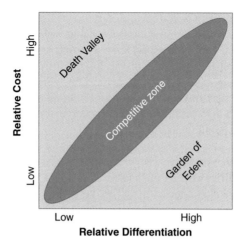

Figure 7.9 Competitive Business Strategies
Source: Adapted from a diagram developed by Geoff Lewis.

scale in manufacturing and advertising. The result is high brand image and thus high perceived quality coupled with low cost. This combination is obviously the most desirable competitive strategy in terms of the creation of shareholder value. Figure 7.9 juxtaposes the different options. Strategies in the diagonal zone can be described as competitive. However, the bottom right is the preferred zone and the top left definitely nonpreferred. Such a diagram can be used to follow competitive moves in an industry, where the historical and current position of the business and its competitors are plotted.

Dynamics of Competitive Advantage

The simple framework just discussed does not deal well with the dynamics of competition. Changes in customer demand and technology, the invasion of markets by new entrants, and blurring of industry boundaries can all lead to elimination of competitive advantage. In some financial markets, a business's competitive advantage from the time of launching a new product may last just days. In others markets, such as that for pharmaceuticals, patents may provide an advantage for a number of years.

Figure 7.10 illustrates this dynamic nature of a competitive advantage. As shown there, the importance of the "old" basis of competitive advantage diminishes as more competitors offer the attribute. So the attribute ceases to be a differentiator of competitive success, although it may still be critical for the customer. For the business to maintain its success, it must develop a new basis for advantage, based on detailed understanding of customer needs, competition, and its own competences.

During the 1980s and early 1990s, Japanese cars had a significant advantage in product quality. Over time, U.S. and European producers improved their quality levels, and now the difference between various models is much smaller. As a result, quality has ceased to be an effective differentiator. We need quality to be able to compete (it is a so-called qualifying attribute), but auto manufacturers must seek new sources of advantage. Many seem to have chosen image, as Toyota, Mercedes, Jaguar, Renault, and BMW are all now engaged in Formula One Grand Prix racing.

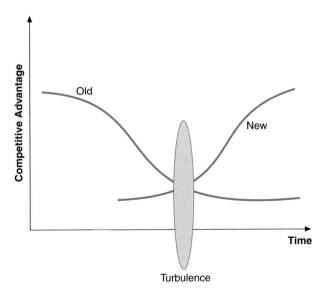

Figure 7.10 Evolution of New Bases of Competitive Advantage

The transition from one basis of advantage to another is a period of turbulence when market share can be gained or lost, when new competitors can gain share at the expense of incumbents. Eventually, some stability returns to the market, but success goes to the business that responds to the new environment and develops the required competitive advantage, enhancing its position while defeating competitors.

Figure 7.10 illustrates what has been called hypercompetition, an environment in which advantages are rapidly created and eroded,[33] replete with intense price/quality competition, rapid innovation, market invasion by global competitors, and redefinition of industry boundaries, among other characteristics. In such an environment, lack of innovation is likely to lead to gradual decline.

A firm that is late in responding to this turbulence has limited strategic options. Strategies for such businesses are likely to include retrenching to more attractive segments, reducing costs to improve profits, or developing new competitive advantages over the longer term.

Alternatively, when business units have a competitive advantage and generate returns above the cost of capital, strategies are likely to focus on such alternatives as investing in growth segments, extending competitive advantages in existing segments, and looking for opportunities in adjacent segments. For such businesses, operational improvements may be less important than growth. However, microeconomics tells us such superior returns are likely to attract competition. Management must therefore focus on ensuring future competitiveness, perhaps with nonincremental changes such as a shift of product form or new process technology.

Dynamics and Strategy

Different kinds of change create different implications for the organization. Businesses that are successful in commercializing new technologies or pioneering new markets need very different organizational configurations from those planning to address mature markets with low-priced entries. In this section we will illustrate these relationships by comparing resources required for entry at different stages of a product class or form life cycle. Notice that if a firm intends to compete throughout the life cycle required competences must change significantly.

Pioneer

Pioneer businesses attempt to create markets rather than enter existing markets. Their products and services often result from consistent and extensive R&D spending, with success built not on a single innovation but on a continuous stream of innovative products. These firms must develop in-house the R&D skills and organizational commitment to produce genuinely new products and services. Most importantly, pioneers must possess quite different, but equally critical, marketing skills that enable them to introduce new products into the uncharted waters of new markets.

Pioneer businesses require a risk-taking internal corporate culture, accepting of the inevitable failures that accompany innovation. The necessity to move quickly and enter early also mandates a degree of "organizational slack" so that they can speedily commit the required resources when fast-developing markets require them. They also need the financial resources to support heavy and consistent R&D expenditures (or the purchase of equity stakes or technologies) and the frequently high costs of market development.

Pioneering is a high-cost option, and governments typically recognize the unique contributions of such firms through patent law. Successful pioneers are able to secure limited monopolies for their discoveries, enjoying the resulting high margins. To secure this advantage, many pioneers employ armies of patent lawyers intent on protecting the firm's intellectual property. However, even in the absence of patent protection, significant advantage often accrues to the successful "first mover." Companies that frequently pioneer new products based on their own R&D include du Pont, 3M, Intel, Sony, and major pharmaceutical firms.

> 3M scientists spend most of their time on company-approved projects. However, they may also spend up to 15% of their time on individually designed projects, not subject to the corporate R&D bureaucracy. The most famous result of this process has been Art Fry's development of Post-It notes, a multimillion-dollar product for 3M.

Fast-Imitator Businesses

Rather than pioneer new markets, some firms await innovation by competitors, then follow the lead as quickly as possible. Companies using this approach avoid the high-risk financial outlays for projects that fail but risk allowing the pioneer to gain first-mover advantage or even patent protection. Fast imitation can be a viable option, but many that espouse this philosophy do so by default rather than design. Regardless, it implies a different organizational configuration.

While technology drives the pioneer, the major driver for fast-imitator firms is competition. Competitive intelligence is crucial: they may even identify pioneers' R&D projects before launch. Imitators focus on development rather than research. Either the development occurs in-house or the firm seeks to acquire products/entire businesses in developing markets. This is a "used-apple" policy. Let someone else take first bite of the apple—if it looks OK, go ahead; if not, stop![34] An ability to move fast when it becomes clear that the pioneer has developed a potentially successful product is crucial. Important capabilities include good development engineers and "can-do" lawyers to find weak spots in the pioneer's patent filings. Imitators often work very quickly. In the R&D-intensive pharmaceuticals industry, patents are typically circumvented within four years, at 65% of the innovator's cost.[35]

Examples of imitators include Matsushita, which successfully followed Sony into the home videotape market, and the Ethicon division of Johnson & Johnson, which consistently and successfully followed U.S. Surgical's (now Tyco) medical device innovations some 18 months later with lower-priced versions. A more contemporary example of a battle between a pioneer and a fast imitator was the struggle between Netscape and Microsoft in the Internet browser market, with Microsoft, the fast-imitator firm, eventually emerging victorious.

Segmenter Businesses

As markets develop, the number of competitors increases and power shifts from supplier to customer. Customers become more knowledgeable and accomplished in using the products and competitors more astute in listening to customers' emerging needs. As market growth slows and overcapacity becomes the norm, customer requirements typically become more specific, varying across the market and creating the segments that give this archetype its name.

Since the market has now grown significantly, segments can be very large. Segmenters offer products and services more nearly satisfying the needs of one or more segments than those of incumbents. Marketing research to understand customers and identify potential market segments and the ability to successfully address narrow market niches become more critical than technological expertise.

To address several segments simultaneously, a modular design philosophy and flexible yet cost-effective operating systems are required. Early entrants may be encumbered with inflexible and relatively costly operations systems, which are ill fitted to this stage of market development. Yet success for the segmenter demands close working relationships among marketing, product development, and operations—a considerable challenge to traditional functional organizations.

Examples from the automobile industry include Chrysler's highly successful introduction of the minivan into the mature U.S. automobile market (a segmenter innovation copied by all major automobile manufacturers) and Mazda's resuscitation of the long-dormant sports car segment with the much-imitated Miata (MX-5).

Me-Too Businesses

Entry is also common when the market is fully developed and is growing slowly, if at all. At this stage, price elasticity typically increases and the proportion of customers willing to choose among a set of competitors, all regarded as acceptable, usually increases.

Overcapacity and intense price competition often characterize these markets. To create shareholder value, me-too competitors with essentially similar offers must achieve a low-cost position. They need aggressive procurement operations and significant capability to reduce costs through value engineering. They must also be able to efficiently manage high-volume operations with low-overhead expenses. Me-too businesses typically have limited product lines and are often leaders in process innovation. Their strategies can wreak havoc in segmented markets where several competitors make value-added offers.

Companies that appear to have adopted a me-too approach are generic pharmaceuticals companies such as Novopharm and Patiopharm, which never invest in developing new drugs but rather focus on producing low-cost generic versions of existing drugs. Airlines such as JetBlue, Ryanair, and EasyJet provide other illustrations.

As noted earlier, the capabilities required by each of these four archetypes are in conflict. It is unlikely that a single business unit can embrace the entire range of archetypes at the same time, and even within a diverse corporation, the profound differences in required competences can pose real problems. A striking example of the difficulty in managing more than one of these archetypal entry strategies was Merck's much-publicized decision to build a separate facility in order to enter the generic pharmaceutical business and its subsequent pull-out before it even began operations.

In the short term, firms should select entry policies that optimize the relationship between their existing competences and marketplace demands. However, new opportunities will often require developing new competences. Given a choice between an attractive market opportunity plus little core competence, and a poor market opportunity plus significant core competence, most companies would be better off with the former, especially if they are committed to developing the requisite capabilities. Jeff Bezos, CEO of Amazon, had little in the way of core competence for running a dot.com retailer when he started Amazon.com, nor did eBay, the most consistently profitable B2C Internet business.

As markets develop over time, businesses choosing early-entry options must be concerned with potential competition from later entrants:

- Pioneers must be concerned with businesses adopting fast-imitator strategies.
- Pioneers and imitators must be concerned about segmenters.
- Pioneers, imitators, and segmenters must be concerned about me-too firms.

If the business intends to continue to participate in the market, it must therefore adjust its capabilities and competences over time. This is an important dynamic of strategic management for existing businesses, and failure to manage transitions associated with new market conditions has caused the demise of many businesses.

Competences and Architecture

The final step in determining how the business unit will compete is to design the architecture of the unit so that it reflects and supports the strategy, a topic covered in detail in Chapter 11. Strategic managers need to ensure that the firm's structure, processes, culture, and assets—human, organizational, and financial—enhance and support the selected strategy. The competences and architecture required by the business will be influenced by decisions on where and how to compete as well as decisions on the growth strategy for the business.

⊙ 7.7 BUSINESS GROWTH

Revenue growth is an important objective for many managers. The challenge is to ensure that the growth achieved creates a strong competitive position and increased economic value. Growth per se is insufficient to create value, since we can have growth that shows positive accounting but negative economic profit.

Growth requires funds to invest in market development, product development, R&D, new staff, and possibly new competences, underlining the need for coordination of business-unit and corporate objectives. If the business grows rapidly, with negative cash flow, the cash must come from the corporate level. The corporation must see this as the most desirable investment option, given the choices open to it.

Rapid market growth provides one of a limited number of opportunities for a change in relative competitive positions. Relative positions are more difficult to alter when the market is characterized by complete stability. Change of positions usually requires some disruption, perhaps from the emergence of new segments, a new technology, a regulatory change, or a shift in customer preferences.

Product/Market Growth Alternatives

A useful framework for discussing the growth options available to a business unit is the product/market matrix, originally developed by Ansoff and shown in modified form in Figure 7.11.[36]

As shown in the figure, a business unit can grow using one or a combination of nine alternatives. All except the upper-left-hand corner involve some degree of diversification, so that the matrix can be viewed as describing the degree of diversification involved in a particular growth alternative. Since risk is generally associated with degree of diversification, the matrix also serves as a qualitative means of assessing risk. Note that a particular alternative might be accomplished by internal development or acquisition, alternatives that are discussed in Chapter 9. We now briefly review several of the more important alternatives shown in Figure 7.11, chosen to reflect their significantly different approaches.

A *penetration* strategy is when the business grows by selling more of its current products to its existing customers. This can occur by increasing customer retention, increasing the amount customers buy and use in a given period of time, attracting customers from competitors, or attracting previous nonusers. In mature markets, when competitors' market shares are fairly stable, these options generally require a competitive advantage or some innovation. Yet penetration is often seen as a low-risk growth option, since we should understand our current market and products. On the other hand, there may be a strong competitive reaction and diminishing returns: after a certain point, the cost of gaining share will outweigh the benefits of growth.

Market *expansion* and *extension* occur when growth is achieved by taking existing products to new markets, where these new markets may be related to existing markets or completely new. These new markets may be geographic, as when the business expands its geographic scope, or via entry into a new industry sector. Such strategies

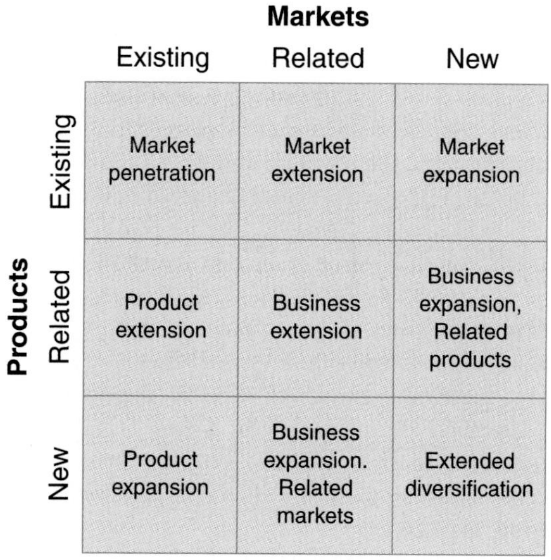

		Markets		
		Existing	**Related**	**New**
Products	**Existing**	Market penetration	Market extension	Market expansion
	Related	Product extension	Business extension	Business expansion, Related products
	New	Product expansion	Business expansion. Related markets	Extended diversification

Figure 7.11   Product/Market Growth Alternatives

involve higher risk than a penetration strategy, since the business must acquire understanding of customers in this new market and may meet new competitors.

Another growth option is to sell *new products* to existing markets. Again, these new products can be related to the existing product line, new to the business, or completely new to the market. When the product is new to the business but not the market, there will again be established competitors and the business will need to establish some competitive advantage.

Finally, the business may grow through extended *diversification,* developing new products for new markets. This strategy has the highest risk of the nine and should be required to earn the highest returns to offset this risk.

Business-unit managers must decide what combination of approaches will be adopted to achieve growth. Can the business do all at the same time, or is selectivity required? Generally it is difficult for the firm to do all at the same time since each requires different resources and competences. There is also a trade-off between market opportunity and organizational competence. If the business's strengths are in technology, then product development may be most attractive. If the strengths are in marketing, then the business unit is likely to attempt to enter new markets.

Innovation and Sources of Value

An alternative way of viewing growth options is according to the degree of innovation they encompass. The strategic management task at the business-unit level must include both operational and strategic innovation. Operational innovation involves reducing costs, increasing quality, and improving asset productivity, among other alternatives. But significant improvements in shareholder value will usually occur through strategic innovation. To get above-average returns, the business must go outside the current practice in the industry. Thus strategic management must concern itself with how the firm's markets and industry will be different in the future. Can the business set the rules for competition in its industry? Do managers understand the threat of new and unconventional competitors and substitutes?

Companies may focus too much on their core businesses, allowing their financial and other resources to deteriorate to such a level that they simply cannot grow. Should this happen, the firm will find it difficult to generate value. Profitable growth is not only important to shareholders; it also motivates staff, who find it exciting and rewarding, and suppliers, who like growing and profitable customers.

All business units need a stream of change initiatives, and these initiatives can be differentiated according to the nature and degree of innovativeness of the change. Business units should be engaging in a range of change initiatives—some relatively incremental in nature, others more radical. We will discuss the need for initiatives under three categories, depending on the degree of change, using the framework presented in Figure 2.3.

Ongoing Change

Ongoing changes are designed to improve efficiency without changing the basic mission or business model. Examples would be cost reductions or quality improvements. This is sometimes described as "managing for today"—shaping the business to meet current needs and managing current activities for excellence.[37] This is the traditional form of competition for many companies, which compete by enhancing the value of their product or lowering its price.

Ongoing strategies are those clarifying the segments in which we compete, the positioning within those segments, and resource deployment choices. They seek gaps in the competitive landscape and ensure that existing resources achieve the best fit with the environment. They also ensure that functional and supply-chain partner activities are aligned with company strategy and harmonized with organizational structure, processes, culture, incentives, and people. At the same time, the business must examine its cost structure to ensure that this is competitive, assess and expand competitive advantage, and improve quality and the value proposition delivered to customers. Such initiatives can also be described as focusing on operational effectiveness.[38]

An operationally effective business unit performs its chosen set of activities better than rivals. Many large firms have reduced headcount, downsized, reduced overheads, redesigned processes, and gone back to core businesses, which should lead to significant short-term improvements in performance. A business may need to undertake these measures if a crisis has developed but should aim to achieve excellence on an ongoing basis. Nonetheless, industry leadership over the longer term usually necessitates more ambitious changes.

Incremental Change

Incremental change results in modest changes to the unit's business model, encompassing expansion into new but related markets and products as well as process innovation. The term *business process reengineering* became somewhat faddish, but the fundamental importance of improving processes is undeniable. Nor should such improvements be limited to operations: the accounting, incentive, and performance management systems all provide examples of processes that might be improved.

Changes often mean performing different activities or performing similar ones in a different way. The **productivity frontier**—the trade-off between buyer value delivered and relative cost position of the firms in an industry—moves outward all the time as new technologies and management approaches are developed.[39] As a firm approaches a new frontier, competitors will imitate the means it used to get there.

Incremental innovation is often witnessed in low-growth markets. Examples would be breakfast cereal or cement, where there is little change in the sources of advantage and industry consolidation is often occurring. With more rapid but still evolutionary change, there may be more opportunities for innovation and segmentation, but such change does not pose the problems created by discontinuities.

Radical Change

Radical change is a proactive activity, initiated at the corporate or business level, that fundamentally redefines the business so as to compete more effectively in the future. Every business process and every dimension of competitive advantage has an associated improvement curve—the rate of improvement over time—generally an S-shaped curve.[40] After a business has been operating for some time, it and its competitors are likely to be on the top of the curve, so improvements are modest—reduce costs by 5%, cut product development times by 7%, improve customer retention by 4%, and so on. These improvements do not usually lead to breakthroughs in wealth creation, and radical change is sometimes required.

Radical change creates the future through such actions as changing the rules of engagement in a fundamental way, redrawing industry boundaries, and even creating new industries. It involves major changes in vision, mission, or the business model. Thus managers must address such questions as how customers are changing, how will the business address e-commerce, and what major new capabilities will be required. In an intensely competitive world, there is competition for industry leadership as well as market share.[41]

Some markets may be undergoing discontinuous change—driven by technology, regulation, or information technology—and these mandate radical change in the business. Markets are vulnerable to fundamental changes in technology or process that may devalue legacy assets. Data storage and popular music provide contemporary examples.

Under such conditions, significant changes in the sources of advantage, market share, and profitability of competitors can be expected,[42] often presaging the emergence of new firms with superior ways of meeting customer needs. Under these conditions, the competitive field is likely to be diverse and the unit may need to establish alliances to generate the required capabilities. Such major changes are also called "new games."[43]

Discontinuities are often the result of the development of a new technology, whose performance graph is generally initially below that of the current technology but whose development is faster and which rapidly overtakes the old technology on the S-curve. Management must recognize the limits of its existing technology and the threat posed by new, discontinuous technologies.[44] Some new technologies are disruptive, almost completely destroying their predecessors. Such disruptive technologies ultimately spawn products and services that yield substantial profits, but to cope with them requires radical change. Indeed, Christensen's research underlines the dangers of focusing too heavily on the needs of current customers. Businesses that do so are, to their detriment, likely to miss out on new technologies that, initially at least, may hold greater appeal for new customers than existing ones.[45]

Radical change requires management foresight, an understanding of future competition, insight into opportunities, and the ability to energize the company so as to get there ahead of competitors. It requires recognizing that there is competition for developing the required new competencies and the possible need for alliances. It mandates externally oriented managers who monitor breakpoints, times of dramatic change in market or technology.[46] When the occasion arises, managers must be willing to discard their current cognitive maps and models and adopt new ones.

Radical innovation is disruptive, and organizational transformation is required. There is a need to reskill people, to redesign processes, and to redirect resources. Ideally, this should not be reactive or done in crisis mode. For long-term success, the firm should build an innovation pipeline full of precedent-breaking ideas that have the power to transform industries and create new wealth.

Radical innovation does not mean that the business must throw away all of its past, but it may need to redeploy brands, assets, and competencies in new ways, and acquire new ones, to create new wealth. Radical innovation may appear to be high risk, but sometimes so is "steady as she goes." Radical innovation may take a business into areas where there is much to learn, but experiments and low-cost market incursions can limit risk.

Competition for the future involves creating and dominating emerging opportunities. We have to develop a view of tomorrow's opportunities and how to exploit them. The strategy here is stretch—not only to compete within existing boundaries but to shape future ones. These radical innovations have been referred to a "killer apps."[47] They take time to develop, need deep knowledge and the ability to work with other firms, and are typically not amenable to detailed financial analysis.

Foster and Kaplan[48] argue that only those firms which systematically destroy the parts of their firm that are yielding diminishing shareholder returns can expect to deliver high returns in the long term. Long-lived companies can prosper but will not deliver high returns to shareholders by working their patch and not venturing too far from it. Radical change may mean that we have to cannibalize our products before competitors do.

The management challenge is how to undertake a complete portfolio of changes at the same time. Business units that wish to ensure their future should be attempting to undertake all three types of changes—ongoing, incremental, and radical—simultaneously. This is not easy, since they each require different structures, incentives, and processes, the subject of Chapter 11.

🌀 7.8 ILLUSTRATIVE BUSINESS STRATEGY

Throughout the chapter we have argued for consistency and alignment in business strategy. Vision, values, mission, objectives, strategy, and supporting architecture should provide a mutually reinforcing network in a well-developed and articulated strategy for a business unit. If this is the case, problems of implementation should be much reduced. The remainder of this section is devoted to an example of such a strategy, recognizing that by the time this book is published, the circumstances that made this a good example may have changed. The ability of the chosen business to deal with these changes is at the present time unknowable.

Ryanair, the very successful Irish low-cost carrier, provides an excellent illustration of an aligned business strategy. Since Ryanair is a single-business company, there are no complications from attempting to differentiate corporate and business-unit strategy. The company flies only one aircraft type, the Boeing 737, which minimizes training and maintenance costs compared with airlines flying many different types. Much of the airline's cost advantage, however, comes from route selection. By flying between secondary airports, Ryanair keeps its airport and handling charges exceptionally low. Michael O'Leary, the CEO, claims that even more important is the fact that the lack of congestion enables 25-minute turnarounds. Ryanair's maintenance costs are also exceptionally low; the company carries out almost all routine maintenance itself, although the finance director explains that some of the maintenance cost shows up in staff costs because of its insourcing policy. The *Financial Times* summarized its cost advantages in six categories, as follows:

- Overhead: lower general administrative costs
- Distribution: direct sale only; no fees for third-party reservations systems; no commissions on ticket sales
- Passenger service: no catering; no in-flight amenities
- Crew costs: lower compensation; higher productivity; reduced crew complement
- Airport charges, ground handling: lower airport costs through use of secondary airports; lower taxes; lower ground-handling costs
- Seat density: 15% more seats per aircraft[49]

Each of these cost advantages is consistent, reinforcing the ability of Ryanair to offer low prices to customers yet still attain a margin (operating profit before tax to revenue) of 31.6% in its fiscal year ending in March 2003. At the same time, customer numbers in 2003 were 42% higher than in 2002.[50] This illustrates that when a company attains such complete alignment, it can have a dramatic impact even in a fairly mature market, and Ryanair's website boldly announces that it will be Europe's largest airline by 2011.

🌀 7.9 SUMMARY

In this chapter we examined the development of business-unit strategy. This task shares some elements with corporate strategy, the subject of the next chapter. Business management must create a future direction for the business, and the concepts of vision, values, and mission are as important at the business level as at the firm level. Business objectives and strategy, however, will differ, for whereas corporate strategy is typically concerned with a whole portfolio of businesses, a particular business has a much sharper scope, with a restricted range of products and markets.

We reviewed some of the analysis that is necessary to develop business strategy, looking at the context of the business and examining the use of the value chain in some depth. We emphasized the importance of understanding both the cost and value drivers of a business, as well as appreciating its strengths and weaknesses, before beginning strategy design.

Much of the chapter was devoted to the key strategic decisions that must be made in developing business strategy, namely, where to compete, how to compete, and how to grow. In each of these areas we explained a number of models that can assist in thinking through these decisions, emphasizing the importance of creativity and alignment in strategy design. We concluded the chapter with an example of a well-aligned business strategy, showing how the different elements of a strategy can be mutually reinforcing and underlining the need for a supportive architecture.

⑤ REVIEW QUESTIONS

1. Select a global firm with which you are familiar. Provide brief examples of strategies at the level of a business unit implemented by this firm over the last five years.

2. Which industries do you believe face the greatest threat of dis-intermediation by online Internet based competition.

3. Give some examples of industries in which economies of scale are changing. In these industries, are scale economies getting larger or smaller? What are the implications for firms in these industries?

4. Discuss the proposition that with increasing competition and knowledge intensity, outsourcing will become more common.

5. Give examples of business units within global firms that in your view are following a cost-leadership strategy

6. Do you believe that, in the future, combination strategies—a combination of cost leadership and differentiation—will become more important?

7. Discuss the proposition that with intense levels of competition, innovation is the only sustainable basis for competitive advantage.

⑤ ENDNOTES

[1] Citigroup Annual Report and Form 10-K, 2002: www.citi.com.

[2] M. Goold, A. Campbell, and M. Alexander, *Corporate Level Strategy* (New York: Wiley, 1994).

[3] R. S. Kaplan and D. P. Norton, *The Balanced Scorecard* (Boston: Harvard Business School Press, 1996).

[4] P. Crawford, K. Johnsen, J. Robb, and P. Sidebottom, "World Power and Light," *McKinsey Quarterly* 1 (1999), pp. 123–132.

[5] M. E. Porter, *Competitive Advantage* (New York: Free Press, 1985).

[6] "When Bankers Marched in Two by Two," *The Economist*, April 6, 1996, pp. 75–76.

[7] C. M. Christensen, "The Past and Future of Competitive Advantage," *Sloan Management Review* 42, no. 2 (2001), pp. 105–109.

[8] The sources of value were covered in Chapter 3; here we deal with customer value as a summary concept and how to measure it.

[9] N. Capon and J. M. Hulbert, *Marketing Management in the 21st Century* (Upper Saddle River, NJ: Prentice Hall, 2001).

[10] All perceptions are those of the customer, not the supplier.

[11] B. T. Gale, *Managing Customer Value* (New York: Free Press, 1994).

[12] Adapted from W. C. Kim and R. Mauborgne, "Charting Your Company's Future," *Harvard Business Review,* June 2002, pp. 77–83.

[13] W. C. Kim and R. Mauborgne, "Value Innovation: The Strategic Logic of High Growth," *Harvard Business Review,* January–February 1997, pp. 103–112.

[14] D. Vose, *Risk Analysis: A Quantitative Guide* (New York: Wiley, 2000).

[15] For a fuller discussion, see K. R. Harrigan, *Strategies for Vertical Integration* (Lexington, MA: Lexington Books, 1983).

[16] T. Jackson, *Inside Intel* (London: HarperCollins, 1997).

[17] J. Stuckey and D. White, "When and When Not to Vertically Integrate," *Sloan Management Review* 34, no. 3 (1993), pp. 71–83.

[18] P. Butler, T. W. Hall, A. M. Hanna, L. Mendonca, B. Auguste, J. Manyika, A. Sahay. "A Revolution in Interaction," *McKinsey Quarterly* 1 (1997), pp. 4–23.

[19] For a detailed discussion of outsourcing, see M. F. Greaver, *Strategic Outsourcing* (New York: American Management Association, 1999).

[20] K. Brown, "Sectors in Each Other's Pockets," *Financial Times,* October 20, 1998, p. 20.

[21] R. C. Insinga and M. J. Werle, "Linking Outsourcing to Business Strategy," *Academy of Management Executive* 14, no. 4 (2000), pp. 58–70.

[22] J. B. Quinn, "Strategic Outsourcing: Leveraging Knowledge Capabilities," *Sloan Management Review* 40, no. 4 (1999), pp. 9–21.

[23] M. Sainsbury, "Pain for Partners as Optus Cuts Back," *The Australian,* January 14, 2003, p. 25.

[24] P. Marsh, "Fired Up to Introduce New Ideas," *Financial Times,* December 10, 2002, p. 13.

[25] "Lands End catalog," 2003: www.landsend.com.

[26] J. M. Hulbert, *Marketing: A Strategic Perspective* (Katonah, NY: Impact Publishing, 1985).

[27] Capon and Hulbert, *Marketing Management in the 21st Century.*

[28] M. E. Porter, *Competitive Strategy* (New York: Free Press, 1980).

[29] Compal Annual Report, 2003: www.compal.com.

[30] K. E. Mishra, "Preserving Employee Morale during Downsizing," *Sloan Management Review* 39, no. 2 (1998), pp. 83–96.

[31] K. B. Lowe, "Downsizing and Firm Performance: Panacea or Paradise Lost?" *Academy of Management Executive* 12, no. 4 (1998), pp. 130–131.

[32] L. J. Bourgeois, I. M. Duhaime, and J. L. Stimpert, *Strategic Management* (Fort Worth: Dryden, 1999).

[33] R. A. D'Aveni, *Hyper-Competition* (New York: Free Press, 1994).

[34] T. Levitt, *Managing for Business Growth* (New York: McGraw-Hill, 1974).

[35] M. Christen, "Does It Pay to Be a Pioneer?" *Financial Times,* October 19, 1998, p. 1.

[36] H. I. Ansoff, *Corporate Strategy* (New York: McGraw-Hill, 1965).

[37] D. F. Abell, "Competing Today while Preparing for Tomorrow," *Sloan Management Review* 40, no. 3 (1999), pp. 73–82.

[38] M. E. Porter, "What Is Strategy?" *Harvard Business Review,* November–December 1996, pp. 61–78.

[39] Ibid.

[40] R. Foster, *Innovation: The Attacker's Advantage* (New York: Summit, 1986).

[41] G. Hamel and C. K. Prahalad, "Competing for the Future," *Harvard Business Review,* July–August 1994, pp. 122–128.

[42] D'Aveni, *Hyper-Competition.*

[43] R. Buaron, "New-Game Strategies," *McKinsey Quarterly* 3 (2000), pp. 34–37.

[44] R. N. Foster, "Attacking Through Innovation," *McKinsey Quarterly* 3 (2000), pp. 37–40.

[45] C. M. Christensen, *The Innovator's Dilemma* (Boston: Harvard Business School Press, 1997).

[46] Ibid.

[47] L. Downes and C. Mui, *Unleashing the Killer App: Digital Strategies for Market Dominance* (Boston, MA: Harvard Business School Press, 1998).

[48] R. N. Foster and S. Kaplan, *Creative Destruction* (New York: Doubleday, 2001).

[49] D. Dombey, "Low Cost Airlines," *Financial Times,* December 12, 2002, pp. 13.

[50] "Ryanair Annual Report," 2003: www.ryanair.com.

CHAPTER 8

Corporate-Level Strategy

Learning Objectives

Upon completing this chapter, you should be able to:

- Describe the differences between corporate and business-unit strategy
- Define the elements that comprise corporate strategy
- Apply the analytic tools of corporate strategy to resource allocation
- Describe the differences between related and unrelated diversification and how diversification affects firm performance
- Explain why it is a challenge for corporate management in a diversified firm to create value
- Understand the basis for corporate decisions on capital structure and dividend policy
- Discuss the nature of risk in strategy

In 1891, Gerard Philips established a company in Eindhoven in the Netherlands to manufacture incandescent lights, concentrating on making carbon-filament lamps, which had just been invented.

In 1914, the firm established a research laboratory to stimulate product innovation.

During this period, Philips started to diversify, initially into X-ray and radio equipment, introducing a medical X-ray tube in 1918, producing radios in 1927, and producing medical X-ray equipment in the United States.

In 1939, the company launched its first electric shaver. Philips's sales were 152 million guilders and worldwide employment was 45,000.

In 1940s and 1950s, the firm launched a rotary electric razor and did advanced work on transistors, integrated circuits, and TV camera tubes. It launched the compact audio-cassette in 1963 and integrated circuits in 1965.

The 1970s and 1980s saw developments in energy-saving lamps and key breakthroughs resulting in the launch, jointly with Sony, of the compact disc in 1983. The period also witnessed several acquisitions, including those of Polygram, Magnavox, GTE's U.S. TV business, and Westinghouse's lighting business.

In the late 1980s and early 1990s, the industries in which Philips participated became more competitive, and the company underwent considerable restructuring and a change of CEO. Sales subsequently grew steadily from 1994 to 2000, but the financial problems that had previously hurt the company were to recur. Despite a reduction in employment from a peak of 253,000 in 1995 to 189,000 in 2001 and further restructuring under two CEOs, 2001 losses were €B2.6, primarily due to writing down investments in Vivendi.

By 2003, sales in 60 countries generated turnover of €B29. The company remains active in lighting, consumer electronics, domestic appliances, semiconductors, and medical systems. Its stock is quoted on exchanges in New York, London, Amsterdam, Frankfurt, and elsewhere. Philips considers itself to be a leader in digital technologies for TV, wireless communications, and storage products as well as a world leader in lighting and shavers, with a strong position in medical imaging.[1]

⊙ 8.1 INTRODUCTION

The history of Philips illustrates some of the complexity involved in managing a large global corporation. Managers have had to deal with the firm's cycles of expansion and contraction, diversifying, then refocusing on core businesses (often accompanied by a new CEO). Geographic expansion led Philips into more than 60 countries, while product scope expanded from an early base of lighting into such new areas as integrated circuits and compact discs. These changes of scope were accomplished through a combination of internal development and acquisition, increasingly on a global basis, while both cooperative and competitive strategies were deployed at various times. Different technologies, products, countries with different cultures, governments with differing tax and legal systems—all these and more contribute to the complexity, while the rapid changes and turbulence of the contemporary business environment raise the bar still further.

Despite complexity and turbulence, however, we can state the overall objective of modern corporate management quite simply. The structure of the modern firm is that of a corporate center together with a number of semi-independent business units, which together comprise the business portfolio of the firm. The corporate center is responsible for developing and implementing corporate-level strategy, which includes such strategic decisions as allocating resources among different business units, making divestments and acquisitions, designing the structure of the firm, changing the culture, and overseeing relationships with financial markets, among others. The overall objective the center should achieve is to ensure that the market value of the firm as a whole is greater than that of its constituent parts. Algebraically, if the firm F consists of N business units, B_i, and V denotes the value of the firm or a business, then

$$V(F) \geq \Sigma \, V(B_i)$$

where the summation is over all the N businesses.

Consider a simple situation where a firm consists of just one unit, labeled A, and decides to diversify by adding a new unit, labeled B, to its portfolio. For this to add value, the following relationship must hold:

$$V(A + B) > V(A) + V(B)$$

Expressing it in words, the value of the combined entity $(A + B)$ must be greater than the sum of the values of the two businesses, assuming that they are independent. This simple relationship encapsulates perfectly the task of corporate management if we view the long-term objective to be maximization of shareholder wealth. Yet, while the objective seems straightforward enough, developing strategies to achieve the objective is much more demanding.

Due to the complexity of corporate-level strategy, we will address various aspects in two successive chapters. In this chapter we concentrate on managing the current scope of the firm and on allocating resources among the different businesses that comprise the portfolio. We begin with an overview of the components of corporate strategy and briefly review the issue of establishing direction. We next examine the different possible relationships between the corporate parent and its various businesses. We proceed to review a set of tools for managing the resource allocation process before examining the difficult and often controversial issue of diversification. We conclude with a discussion of financial policy and risk management.

In Chapter 9 we concentrate on managing the dynamic scope of the firm. In some sense this is inseparable from the issues of this chapter, but the importance of innovation, merger and acquisition policy, and participation in alliances, for example, is so great that they merit their own chapter.

Understanding Corporate Structures

Firms typically have their genesis as fairly simple organizations, often selling a single product or single line of products in one or a few markets. du Pont, for example, began as a manufacturer of black powder during the U.S. Civil War. Not only is it now a behemoth in comparison, but it no longer makes black powder! Over the longer term, virtually every aspect of the corporation must be regarded as a variable. Analogously, most of the early development of economic and business theory assumed a fairly simple structure, but this is increasingly at odds with the complexity of the modern corporation.

As firms developed in size and complexity, business and economic theorists begin to modify their work to reflect the new challenges, though it is often the case that practice runs ahead of theory building. Today's large global firms face unprecedented challenges for which management theory provides limited guidance. Nonetheless, path-breaking work by such authors as Chandler,[2] Rumelt,[3] Lawrence and Lorsch,[4] Williamson,[5] and others has generated significant insight into the problems posed by complexity. To illustrate the magnitude of the task, we will briefly examine the structure of Siemens, the German firm, which has worldwide assets of some €B90.

Figure 8.1 shows the Siemens organizational structure in abbreviated form. As with many large global firms, there is a third organizational level between the corporate level and the business units. Despite almost universal pressure to simplify structures and reduce the number of levels in the organization, many other firms are similarly organized. We will refer to this intervening level as the **group** level, where the group is a collection of interrelated business units. Accordingly, we may consider the group as possessing some of the characteristics of both a corporation and a business unit. However, the corporate level retains responsibility for relationships with financial markets, even though other functions may be devolved to the group level.

As Figure 8.1 indicates, Siemens has six groups, each with global responsibilities. A subunit within one of these groups comprises a business unit. Thus "automation and drives" is a business unit within the group "automation and control." In this chapter, the focus will be on strategy at the corporate level, and for ease of discussion the corporation will be assumed to comprise a number of business units; we will not discuss group-level strategy, since, as mentioned, it has characteristics of both corporate and business-unit strategy.

Siemens also has a number of corporate **departments** and **centers.** The departments include finance, personnel, technology, and corporate development. The five corporate centers are communications, information and operations, procurement and logistics, chief economist, and management consulting. It also has a financing and real estate group. Finally, there is also a Siemens Venture Capital Group, which identifies and funds investments in emerging and innovative technologies. As a global firm, Siemens has a regional organization, which is not shown in Figure 8.1, with regional companies, regional offices, agencies to support its operations in some 190 countries and its staff in 2002 of around 450,000.

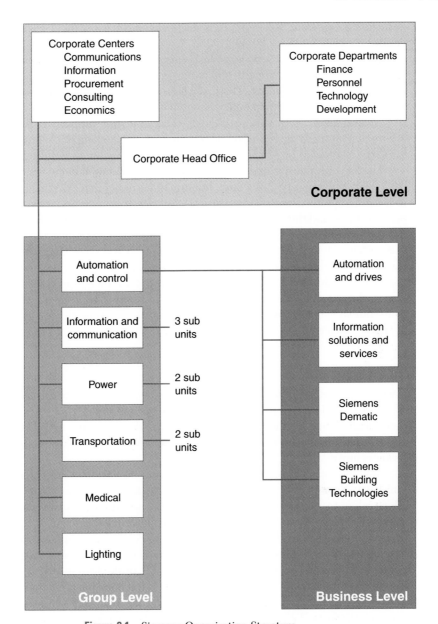

Figure 8.1 Siemens Organization Structure
Source: "Siemens Company Structure, 2003: www.siemens.com.

The essence of the corporate strategic management task is to manage a multiplicity of businesses, partners, geographic markets, technologies, and customers under the same corporate umbrella, such that the total entity delivers value to all stakeholders. As noted, the challenge is to ensure that the value delivered by the combined entity is greater than the value that might have been delivered under any other organizational arrangement, including where the business units act as independent entities.

This observation highlights the fact that strategy at the corporate level is fundamentally different from strategy at the business-unit level. At the corporate level, the strategic management task is not to manage any of the constituent business units or to develop strategy for these business units. Corporate staff, even though they are usually supported by centralized services such as corporate planning, finance, information technology, knowledge management, and so on, generally do not have detailed knowledge of a business or its environment. Their role is to manage the entire business portfolio, not an individual business. Corporate management delegates that task to senior business-level management, with various degrees of central staff support. It then attempts to ensure that mutually agreed-upon targets are met, recognizing that a business unit's performance is affected by its specific context, which varies across different businesses.

The key difference is one of breadth in terms of required decisions. A business unit has a degree of integrity; it is a more homogeneous entity that operates in a discrete and well-defined product/market. In contrast, the overall firm comprises a number of such business units, and these businesses may bear little apparent relationship to one another. Again, the challenge is to resolve a paradox. These business units can, and do, operate to a certain extent independently of one another. At the same time, they are part of a larger group and their performance should be enhanced by membership. So we need to combine the advantages of independence with the advantages of collective ownership. One of the corporate tasks is to influence relationships so as to create synergy, perhaps by encouraging one business to share its competence so as to improve the performance of another business.

Creating Value

If we accept that the objective of the corporate level should be to ensure that the value of the corporation's constituent businesses is greater under this particular corporate umbrella than under other any other ownership, then we must necessarily address the vexing question of how the corporate level adds value to the firm and its constituent business units.

In a diversified firm, most value is created in the business units, not at the corporate level. Nonetheless, a corporate center has specific decision areas in which it can affect value. Corporate is responsible for M&A activity, which can add to or destroy value. In addition, it is responsible for decisions regarding financing, dividends, and relations with financial markets, which again can affect value. Finally, corporate staff will have an impact in areas such as corporate culture and management values. So the corporate level can add to or subtract from the value of the firm in several ways, not only through its interaction with the business units. Yet, if each business in the firm's portfolio is independently maximizing its performance, *how can corporate staff add value to the total enterprise?* What is there for the parent to do? This question is fundamental to corporate strategy.

Since the parent corporation has no external customers (although it does have a relationship with certain external providers), it generates costs but no revenue. Ultimately, the parent must create value greater than the costs it incurs, despite the fact that its impact is indirect. However, the corporate center has an important intermediary role. It can influence business-unit decisions and strategies, and it stands between the businesses and financial markets. Thus, although primary value creation takes place at the business-unit level, parent and business unit should work together to enhance value creation.

Researchers have examined the effect of corporate ownership on the performance of firms' constituent businesses, and the results have been mixed. One researcher estimated that corporate effects account for as little as 0% and as much as 20% of the variation in SBU return on assets, with less corporate effect[6] as diversification increases. Other researchers have found even less corporate effect![7]

Part of the disagreement may arise from differences in methodology, including the use of different statistical tools, data sets, performance measures, and business-unit definitions. Nonetheless, overall, research suggests that the activities of corporate-level staff do make some difference to business-unit performance,[8] even though there may be uncertainty about the magnitude of the impact. Intuitively, it would seem quite anomalous to find that SBU performance was completely independent of the corporate-level staff! Nonetheless, it is often easier to see how the parent might destroy value than to see how it creates value, for poor acquisitions have historically been enormous destroyers of value.

> AT&T purchased NCR, a computer manufacturer, in 1991 for $USB7.8. After investing a further $USB2.8 in the acquisition, it sold NCR in 1996 for $USB3.4.[9]

In Table 8.1 we summarize how a corporate center might create or dissipate value in its relationship with its business units.

In an ideal world, the corporation would be described as the **natural owner** of its constituent businesses.[10] This term, introduced by McKinsey, means that the corporation's businesses perform better under this parent than they would under any other, including the situation of having no parent (being independent). If this is so, the firm should be relatively immune from unfriendly takeover, since it can earn more from the asset (the business) than any other owner, who cannot logically afford to pay more than its worth to the current owner.

Thus, for a corporation to exist on a sustainable basis, the corporate level must contribute to value creation, since otherwise the costs it imposes would render the firm vulnerable to takeover. The corporate center can create value through assembling a portfolio of business units, ideally with positive interdependencies and supported by a collection of competences. It can support business units in their decision making and add value to them through shared competences that create profitable opportunities for interdivisional cooperation. The corporation also acts as an internal capital market, possibly performing this role better than external financial markets due to better understanding of business-level opportunities (insider information!).

It is also evident that the corporate center must decide on the level and nature of its intervention in business-level strategy making. Given the turbulence in today's markets,

TABLE 8.1   Corporate Opportunities to Add or Destroy Value

Corporate can add value by...	**Corporate can destroy value by...**
Managing the dynamic scope of the firm, often through an active divestment and acquisition program	Making poor acquisitions, the majority of which add no value to the acquiring firm
Managing the linkages between businesses so that the performance of a given business is enhanced by the fact that it is part of the business portfolio of the firm	Imposing high overhead costs
Providing centralized services, where the quality/cost of these is superior to what the business could get from an outside supplier	Being slow and unresponsive, remaining remote from the business, and not assisting in strategy development despite the fact that it must approve strategy

firms have to be flexible, able to respond rapidly to unpredictable change. One common response has been greater decentralization, devolving more decision-making authority to the business units. Employees in these business units are closer to customers, competitors, and technologies and should be better able to make timely decisions that will create value for the business and hence the corporation.

The challenge for the diversified firm is for corporate managers to be able to demonstrate that they can improve the performance of business units when these units are part of a larger whole, that is, when they are no longer independent businesses. Corporate staff should only intrude in decision-making processes of the business when they are able to accomplish this.

◉ 8.2 ELEMENTS OF CORPORATE STRATEGY

Corporate strategy involves decision making in five interrelated dimensions, as shown in Figure 8.2. We now overview each of these elements and then develop each in more depth later in the chapter.

Creating Future Direction

As discussed in Chapter 6, developing a sense of direction for the entire firm is a critical role for the corporate center. In doing so, senior managers must cope with the often-competing demands of different stakeholder groups, whose claims on the firm will change in relative importance over time. If, for example, the firm faces a financial crisis, possibly brought about by a global recession, management may have to reduce employment or implement salary reductions to maintain the viability and profitability of the firm. Similarly, faced with a major quality problem, managers may have to reimburse customers at the short-term expense of shareholders' dividends.

Style of the Center

Corporate staff must also decide what kind of parent they will be and determine the principles that will guide their relations with the firm's various business units. This is often described as the parenting style of the firm,[11] which can vary between two extreme

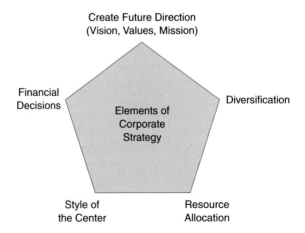

Figure 8.2 Elements of Corporate-Level Strategy

positions. On one hand, the corporate center may take a quite detached view of its business units. The traditional holding company model, for example, was one in which a very small center had a fairly passive attitude toward its holdings, as long as they performed satisfactorily. At the other extreme, corporate staff may be very involved in the development of strategy at the business-unit level, perhaps because all businesses utilize a common competence or technology or because of very restrictive financial guidelines, such as characterize some leveraged buyout (LBO) firms.

The style of the relationship between corporate centers and business units affects how intrusive corporate staff is, the level of business-unit autonomy, who establishes business objectives, and processes for establishing objectives. At the same time, corporate must decide whether or not to establish shared resource units such as finance and personnel to advise its business units. Style also affects policy decisions. For example, if the firm has a degree of vertical integration, does the downstream unit have to buy from the upstream unit?

> A paper manufacturing company also has a merchant division, which sells paper to printers. Does the merchant division have to buy paper from upstream in the company, or can it also source from outside the firm? If the merchant division is not given the option, then its viability can be threatened by poor performance of the manufacturing division.

A similar policy issue is whether or not a business must use certain corporate services. So, for example, if corporate has a legal group, do all businesses have to use this or can they go outside? Underlying these policy decisions are the kinds of paradoxes we discussed in Chapter 2: autonomy versus economies of scale, independent initiative versus the benefits of cooperation, local versus central control, and other similar dilemmas.

Resource Allocation

The corporate level is responsible for decisions on the *dynamic* scope of the firm: the portfolio of businesses that comprise the firm. For survival, a firm needs to continually renew itself, as products, markets, and technologies are replaced by substitutes or existing demands cease and new ones arise. The firm must be actively engaged in ensuring the emergence of new business opportunities, even as it abandons old ones. This may well encompass buying and selling business units, developing businesses internally, closing or exiting from existing businesses, forming alliances and networks with other firms, and redefining the businesses in the current portfolio.

Corporate management must manage the firm for both today and tomorrow, and it needs a relatively long planning horizon to do this. Corporate management must nurture self-renewal within the firm. Sustained growth will almost always require some diversification, as growth opportunities within the original line of activities diminish. Foster and Kaplan[12] argue that only those firms which systematically destroy the parts of the firm yielding diminishing shareholder returns can expect to deliver high returns in the long term.

Sometimes the firm completely reinvents itself, as with the earlier example of Nokia in Chapter 6. Some firms demonstrate that ultimately nothing about a firm is fixed; management can change all aspects over time:[13]

> In the late 1990s, Westinghouse Electric abandoned its technological roots, acquired CBS, changed its name, and focused exclusively in media. It later merged into the media giant Viacom.

In managing the dynamics of company scope, corporate managers must decide on the allocation of resources, financial and human, among the firm's various business units. They must also cope with myriad other issues, including acquisitions, mergers, takeovers, divestments, alliances, networks, spinoffs, and restructuring.

> In 2000, Sony decided to exit or downsize 28 of its 115 product categories in order to improve its economic profit.[14]

In addition, the corporate center is ultimately responsible for deciding the objectives to be met by each business unit. The firm should invest its free cash flow in businesses that provide the most benefit to shareholders. The corporate center is responsible for capital allocation across the business portfolio, judging which businesses should be supported with investment funds. In this capacity corporate acts as an internal financial market, supporting some businesses, providing less support to others, and perhaps withdrawing support entirely from still others. The firm may be better able to do this than financial markets because corporate managers may have better knowledge than would be available to financial markets. They may better understand the opportunities available to business units and consequently make judgments superior to those of financial markets. The resource allocation role implicitly assumes that the firm suffers from a capital shortage. A more appropriate view is that the purpose of the firm's center is to raise the capital required by all strategies that promise to deliver more than the cost of capital.

Diversification and Relatedness among Business Units

As noted earlier, successful firms inevitably outgrow their initial scope. To continue to grow, they must necessarily diversify. The extent, type, mode, and rate of *diversification* are all crucial questions for the corporate center. There is an ongoing debate in the research literature as to whether or not diversification creates value for the firm's shareholders. Economists like to point out that shareholders can diversify their holdings quite easily and cheaply. Their transaction costs are generally fairly small, particularly when compared with those incurred by a firm. Empirical research further suggests that not only does diversification destroy value, but that it often seems to be done for reasons of managerial hubris and ego.[15]

We expand on this topic later, but the general principle is that related diversification is generally more successful. Where businesses are related in some way and share a common set of competences, there is a better chance that synergy can be created. Multinational corporations provide an example of this principle in action. Although not all attempts at international expansion have been successful, the mere existence of the term illustrates the fact that many companies have been able to utilize their technological and product expertise across a wide variety of markets, and global expansion has become a major driver of diversification.

Financial Decisions

The most important financial responsibilities involve managing relationships with financial markets, including institutions and major shareholders; decisions on capital structure; and dividend policy. Related financial concerns include such matters as share buybacks, capital raising, sources of borrowings, risk management (including exchange-rate risk), and policies on stock options for staff, which are now closely scrutinized. Many of these decisions will have to be approved by the board, but the initiative is with corporate management.

In this section we have reviewed the major decisions comprising corporate strategy. Of course, there may be other important decisions to be made. Corporate managers will carry major responsibility for designing and evolving the architecture of the firm, which we discuss in Chapter 11. They must also respond to crises, such as a plant explosion or the bankruptcy of a major customer or supplier, and play a major role in managing relationships with governments and the broader community. In these respects, the CEO is the spokesperson for the company, and his or her behavior will be viewed as epitomizing the values and vision of the firm.

We now discuss each of the major elements of strategy in more detail.

8.3 CREATING FUTURE DIRECTION

Creating future direction is the most important task of corporate management. In describing vision and values in Chapter 6, we noted that a vision statement is aspirational. To serve its purpose, it should neither be easily attained nor frequently changed. Similarly, the firm's values should be sufficiently robust to provide enduring guidance in fulfilling the vision. These caveats do not, however, apply to the mission statement that defines the present and future scope of the firm. Missions should be regularly reviewed, in good times as well as in bad, for they must reflect and capitalize on both the effects of a dynamic environment and the firm's evolving competences.

Economic changes over the past few years have caused many firms to rethink their missions. As described in Chapter 3, corporate management must continuously monitor and analyze changes in the firm's external and internal environments. This is particularly challenging for global firms, since senior managers must be aware of developments in many countries, markets, and technologies. Such changes, like the Asian meltdown of the 1990s or the slowdown in the U.S. economy in the early 2000s, can have dramatic impact not only on firms but also on whole industries. They may mandate changing the mission, abandoning old businesses, entering new ones, implementing new organizational forms, creating alliances and networks, and so on.

A recession often brings much greater attention to issues of future direction. Growth hides a multitude of mistakes: a rising tide tends to help all firms. However, during a recession, managers have to focus on earnings and free cash flow, ensuring that costs are under control. A drop in demand, particularly when coupled with high fixed costs and break-even points, causes firms to contemplate major changes. Unprofitable businesses may need to be sold, balance sheets strengthened, debt levels and costs reduced. Firms may have to make decisions that are essential for the short run but may be at odds with any long-term view. Ideally, these decisions should not jeopardize future growth. Yet these same circumstances may present cash-rich firms with major opportunities, for they can pick up bargains. As noted in Chapter 6, however, companies tend to pay much greater attention to their mission statement in bad times, when they tend to talk of refocusing, on core businesses, and the like, than they do in good times, when the seeds of future problems are often sown.

8.4 STYLE OF THE CENTER

One key decision revolves around what we will call the style of the center—what decisions are made by the center and how intrusive the center will be in the strategies of the firm's businesses. In a study of the style of the center, Goold and Campbell examined a number of firms and characterized them on the basis of two dimensions:[16]

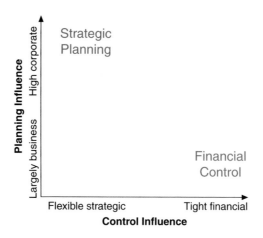

Figure 8.3 Styles of the Corporate Center

Planning influence: the degree to which the center influences strategy formulation at the business-unit level

Control influence: the type of control exerted by the center, what objectives are established, and how the center responds to business outcomes

On the basis of these two dimensions, corporations were classified into a number of **styles** of the center, as shown in Figure 8.3.

We will discuss two of the eight classifications: a strategic planning style and a financial control style. In firms where the center adopts a **strategic planning** style, the corporate center works closely with business units in developing their strategies. Corporate mangers of such firms believe they have an important role to play in developing business-level strategy and educating business units about the needs and skills of other businesses. These firms have extensive and explicit planning processes, with specified analytical frameworks and formats. Corporate personnel are involved in decisions on fundamental trade-offs (e.g., between growth and cash flow objectives) at the business-unit level.

With this style, the most important intervention by the center is managing interdependencies among business units. These firms typically exhibit considerable relatedness, such as shared resources, technology, or know-how, among business units. The center intervenes with the goal of maximizing overall organizational effectiveness. There is generally more senior-level input to the strategy process, and this is reflected in organizational structure, which is a combination of global product responsibility and substantial regional responsibility. Business-unit strategy needs to be coordinated with a geographic region strategy. The objectives established for business units are generally broader and more strategic—for example, to become the leading competitor. On the other hand, in this style of firm, there is less ownership of the strategy by the business unit, and failure to meet objectives may be attributed to the need to satisfy others in the firm, the regions, or the corporate level.

Firms characterized as possessing a **financial control** style differ considerably. There is limited corporate input into the business-level strategy process and much less attention paid to interdependencies among business units. Business-unit objectives are almost solely financial, and control is exercised more through the annual budgeting process than through the planning process. Once business-unit objectives have been established (almost entirely by the corporate center, with limited negotiation), business management is held accountable for meeting these objectives, with strong sanctions if they fail to do so.

The corporate center acts essentially as a financial market, funding proposals and strategies put forward by the businesses. Since objectives are clear and specific, the careers of senior business-unit managers may be in jeopardy if these are not met.

Goold and Campbell concluded that different styles of parenting could be successful, that there was no "ideal" style. Indeed, the style adopted was to some extent dependent on the management style of senior managers as well as the nature and type of the business units in the portfolio (which actually follows from the first). For example, if senior management elects to pursue growth via acquisitions, these are more likely to be unrelated, so that the firm adopts more of a financial control style. Another firm, with similar growth objectives, adopts a strategy of internal development, growing by transferring existing resources and competences into new areas for the firm. In these circumstances, the business units will likely demonstrate much greater relatedness, resulting in more of a strategic planning style for the center.

Synergy

An important concept in corporate strategy, related to the style of the corporate center, is **synergy,** the ability of two units to generate greater value when they are working together than when they work separately. So when both businesses are part of the same corporate parent, they may work cooperatively, permitting each to generate greater value.

Synergy could arise from a number of sources: sharing of know-how or skills; sharing common tangible resources, such as a manufacturing facility; or sharing an intangible asset, such as a brand name. While an attractive concept, however, synergy is not easy to create. Firms try to achieve synergy via cross-business teams, knowledge management and sharing of systems, and dissemination of best practices throughout the firm. But many managers seem to overestimate the benefits and ignore the costs and the difficulty of creating synergy.[17] This is probably one of the reasons why acquisitions are so often unsuccessful, as we discuss in the next chapter. Post-acquisition integration is difficult and synergies often fail to eventuate, so much so that one pundit commented that he now believed that synergy was a concept that only existed in a dictionary!

Despite these difficulties, some firms have developed effective mechanisms to achieve cooperation between business units in order to improve their competitive advantage, which is obviously easier when the various business units have a high degree of relatedness. With little relatedness, there are still possibilities for synergy with common processes, such as billing or customer service, but the opportunities are much greater when there are competences across business units that can be used by all.

> BP developed very effective mechanisms for sharing of knowledge and expertise among its exploration and production units spread around the world. This involved developing systems for the accumulation and retention of information, but also innovating with structural mechanisms for the dissemination of information among the business units. These included "peer assists" (temporary secondment), "peer groups" (quarterly meetings of peers from oilfields of similar maturity), "federal groups" (ad hoc groups on issues that cut across organizational lines) and, finally, personnel transfer. The company also fostered cooperative values and learning from outside the firm, with the whole effort supported by a new vision for the IT group.[18]

Sony, another global firm, intends to promote strategic collaboration across the entire Sony group, leveraging such resources as brand equity, knowledge, intellectual capital, and technologies across the firm's different businesses.

It should be clear from this discussion that there is an ongoing interplay between corporate and business-unit strategies. The strategic business unit (SBU) structure creates greater autonomy at the business level, and SBU general managers can be held accountable for results. The devolution of decision making should also permit quicker responses to changes in the market or in competition and allow the various businesses to develop systems and structures best suited to their own situations. At the same time, the parent corporation must find ways to add value to a business to justify its continued ownership thereof. Some commentators, such as Hamel and Prahalad,[19] have pointed out the dangers of treating business units as independent. Certainly there is a danger that a drive for autonomy by politically powerful business-unit managers can even jeopardize the future of the corporation as a whole.

Interfacing with Business Units

Corporations must decide which services to provide centrally and whether or not business units are required to use these services. Centrally provided services may achieve economies of scale in service provision, but offsetting this gain may be the dangers of lack of responsiveness to the differing needs of individual businesses. Most diversified firms share centralized legal and financial services. The corporate-level IT group is also increasingly important, as it establishes the information architecture for the firm as well as setting IT standards for each business unit. With R&D, there is a much more mixed picture. Some firms centralize research but decentralize development to their constituent businesses. Others have varied their approaches over time. The once-formidable central R&D operation of GE was almost completely decentralized, but CEO Jeffrey Immelt moved back to a more centralized model. In most cases, the debate revolves around the advantages of flexibility versus scale.

In virtually all cases, the corporate center has a role in establishing business objectives and monitoring business performance. As a result, it typically develops the planning system used within the firm, whether this is more budget- or strategy-driven. The planning procedures adopted by the parent also affect its influence on strategy development at the business unit. Thus, although competition in product markets occurs at the business-unit level and SBU managers usually have a better understanding of this than corporate managers, parents may be able to realize specific performance improvements in the businesses. For example, the corporation may excel at internal control (e.g., cost cutting), maintaining relationships with major customers that buy from a number of the firm's businesses, or squeezing suppliers. Finally, the business's strategy must generally receive corporate approval, and this process is likely to be more than a rubber stamp. In sum, business-unit managers are responsible for business-unit strategy, but corporate will intervene whenever it believes it necessary!

When deciding which businesses should be in the portfolio, we must also consider costs. In large corporations, people in the divisions often feel that the center does not add value; it is too remote, bureaucratic, and slow at decision making. Senior corporate executives may be out of touch with the realities of the competitive markets faced by businesses or lack understanding of cultural issues resulting from geographic diversity. If true, such characteristics limit the ability of the corporate level to add value to businesses. Corporate centers can destroy value by not agreeing to good investment proposals from businesses or through too much involvement in decisions at the business level.

⑤ 8.5 RESOURCE ALLOCATION

Given the complexity of the modern firm, some tools are required to assist in deciding which areas offer the most promise to the firm and how much to invest in them. Managing the firm's portfolio of businesses is a multidimensional task involving such important choices as the following:

Geographic market: In which countries will we compete? What balance should we seek between domestic markets and those in other countries? Which new countries should we enter?

Product: What products are we selling currently? Which are aging or are likely to become obsolete? What is our success at introducing new products?

Technology: Which technologies threaten our businesses? Are we entering new technologies? What competences would this require?

Market growth rate: Which of our businesses are mature? Do we have high growth businesses in our portfolio? Are we meeting corporate growth objectives?

Financial measures: How are our assets distributed over our businesses? Where are sales revenues generated? Where do earnings come from and how are these related to sales and asset distribution? What is the balance of the firm's cash flows?

The financial and market numbers lend themselves to a convenient tabular display that can be used for monitoring and tracking purposes, as is illustrated in Table 8.2. BHP Billiton is a global resources firm with revenue in 2003 of $USB17.5 and is listed on both the Australian and London Stock Exchange. As can be seen, the profitability of its different business segments varies significantly. Petroleum is one of the most profitable, with a return on assets of 35.8%. It earns 40% of the firm's total net income, yet utilizes only 16% of the firm's assets.

Similar tables could be constructed for geographic areas, product groups, or other breakdowns. Such data provide useful diagnostic information, and such a matrix could also summarize future objectives, again broken down by classifications of interest. The Korean firm LG published such a matrix showing how it planned to invest in R&D across different business sectors. The firm, which employs 130,000 people and gener-

TABLE 8.2   Segment Information for BHP Billiton, 2003

Business Segment	Turnover (%)	Assets (%)	Profit Before Tax (%)	EBIT/Net Operating Assets (%)	EBIT/ Turnover (%)
Petroleum Crude oil, natural gas	18.6	16.0	40.3	35.8	36.1
Aluminium Alumina, aluminium	19.3	24.8	19.9	11.4	17.2
Base Metal Copper, lead, gold	11.2	18.8	9.8	7.3	14.6
Carbon Steel Materials Iron ore, coking coal	21.1	12.5	35.7	40.1	28.3
Diamonds	8.4	7.4	10.2	19.7	20.3
Energy Coal	11.9	10.6	6.5	8.7	9.1
Stainless Steel Materials Nickel, ferrochrome	6.3	8.2	5.1	8.8	13.6
Total	100	100	100		

Source: BHP Billiton Plc Annual Report 2003, p. 94: www.bhpbilliton.com.
Reproduced with permission of BHP Billiton.

TABLE 8.3   Planned Allocation of R&D Expenditures, LG Corporation

R&D Investment Area	Amount (BKRW)°
Digital display	550 ($USM467)
Next generation mobile telephone	650 ($USM552)
Information and electronics components, life sciences	200 ($USM170)
Other	500 ($USM425)

° 1BKRW = $USM0.848 as of January 10, 2003.

Source: "Vision and Strategy," January 2, 2003: www.lg.co.kr.

ated revenues of $USB81 in 2001 across the globe, planned to spend $USB1.6 on R&D in 2003, distributed as shown in Table 8.3. These data indicate LG's R&D priorities across broad product groupings and give insight into its future direction.

Resource Allocation—Current and Future Portfolio

The distinguishing feature of a diversified firm is that it consists of a number of interdependent business units. The corporate center makes two crucial, interrelated decisions with respect to these units: what the *definition* of these business units should be (how they are delineated) and how *resources* are to be allocated among them.

The definition of what constitutes a business unit is important. As described in Chapter 2, we want the business units to possess a degree of integrity and to be able to be treated semiautonomously, with senior business-unit managers held responsible for their performance. But this structure also has an important impact on resource allocation, since corporate must decide on allocation of resources among these units. Thus a decision on the definition of business units is, of necessity, also a decision on the nature and type of resource allocation decisions to be made. If the units are defined geographically, then the first cut at resource allocation is among different geographic regions. If, however, the units are defined by product group, then resources will be first allocated among these groups. It is for this reason that some allege that "strategy is organization and organization is strategy." Nonetheless, managing this portfolio of businesses, rather than attempting to manage the individual businesses, is the major task of corporate management.

Corporate portfolios are, of course, dynamic, and corporate management must manage changes in the firm's portfolio over time. Figure 8.4 shows a firm consisting of three business units, called 1, 2, and 3. The question that corporate managers must address is what future portfolio they want. Will all business units be treated equally or not? Suppose that a corporate objective was to grow sales revenue at the rate of 10% per year for the next five years. Would we expect all business units to grow at this rate, or would we expect some to grow faster and some slower? Notice that this is a corporate-level decision. Senior corporate managers make this decision and business-unit managers are expected to follow.

Figure 8.4 suggests the corporation will have four businesses in the future, and thus its composition will have changed considerably. For business 1, the objective is to hold (maintain its current position in the market). This business is not seen as a growth opportunity, perhaps because its markets are mature, with limited growth opportunities. The firm believes it has better opportunities elsewhere, evidenced by business 2, which is given a growth objective, perhaps because it has international expansion opportunities. The question then arises of where the firm will get the funds to support the growth of this business. Remember that on average about 70% to 80% of funds for investment are gen-

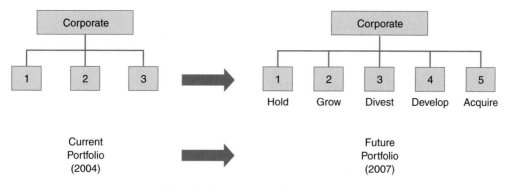

Figure 8.4   Current and Future Portfolio

erated internally within the firm. If business 2 is not generating the funds required to support its growth, they must come from elsewhere in the portfolio, perhaps business 1.

Business 3 is a business that the firm plans to divest; it is no longer considered relevant. This business may not fit a revised corporate mission or may be generating poor returns with little likelihood of improving. Divestment is clearly a corporate decision, but it may be executed in a variety of ways. The business might be sold to another firm, it could be spun out and listed as a separate firm (with or without an equity interest), the corporation could agree to a leveraged buyout by existing management, or it could simply be shut down. The pros and cons of these approaches will be discussed in Chapter 9.

Two new businesses appear in the 2007 portfolio. Business 4 is to be developed internally, while business 5 is an acquisition. Chapter 9 covers these options for changing scope.

Tools for Allocating Resources

Imbalance in a corporate portfolio can jeopardize shareholder interests. An overabundance of growth businesses can lead to liquidity problems, while too many mature businesses that generate excellent current results may have dismal future prospects. Since successful new businesses usually generate excellent operating margins, revitalization of the corporate portfolio is required for long-term shareholder value creation. In either case, a severe imbalance can lead to acquisition by firms seeking, respectively, growth opportunities or cash flow. In this section we examine a variety of tools that corporate management may use to manage the firm's portfolio.

Financial Analysis Methods

In Chapter 4 we discussed the importance of financial performance and some of the tools and techniques of financial analysis, issues to which we return in Chapter 12 when we address performance measurement. Our purpose in discussing financial methods at this point is twofold. First, since superior financial performance is a critical objective for management, analysis of potential investment returns is both important and proper. However, we also critique financial methods to illustrate why a corporate center should augment these methods with other approaches.

Whereas a few decades ago many companies made investment decisions based on historical accounting rates of return, today virtually all firms use financial methods that take into account the time value of money. Some firms, however, still use forecast rate of return on investment (ROI) calculated by projecting accounting data into the future. Because it considers the whole life of the investment, this method is often considered superior to payback (the period of time required to "pay back" the original investment). However, since neither method distinguishes between returns earned in different time periods, both are defective. The most commonly used methods that consider time are internal rate of return (IRR) and net present value (NPV).

- Internal rate of return (IRR) and net present value (NPV) both rely on discounted cash flow analyses, valuing returns (and expenditures) when they are earned (or paid out), discounting both future returns (cash inflows) and expenditures (cash outflows) to take into account when they are received/disbursed. For **IRR,** the value of an opportunity is measured as that rate (%) which equalizes the inflows and outflows. For **NPV,** the value is measured as an amount, typically secured by discounting the cash flows at a "hurdle" rate.

All financial analysis methods have several points in common. First, the result of the analysis is a single figure: months/years for payback, a rate (typically a percent) for ROI and IRR, and an amount for NPV. Second, the methods are conceptually simple; given the set of inputs—investments, sales revenues, and costs—the analysis is straightforward, even though complex calculations may be required. Third, the decision flowing from the analyses appears to be unambiguous: opportunities are ranked; those selected typically outrank and/or outperform the others on some criterion or exceed a hurdle rate that should be related to the firm's cost of capital. More complex techniques take into account the inherent riskiness of the project.

However, these methods suffer from two severe problems. First, each relies on estimates of future sales revenues (sales units and prices), costs, and investments. As any manager knows, judging the short-term investment required for a well-defined project is difficult enough; predicting sales revenues several years into the future is a daunting task. This task is also open to organizational game playing. As most managers have observed in their careers, opportunity-champions may be tempted to provide inflated revenue forecasts and low future cost estimates to turn marginal return projects into spectacular performers, particularly if they are moving to new positions shortly! By contrast, hard-nosed financial managers are just as likely to make "realistic adjustments" to these forecasts (sales revenues down, cost and investment estimates up), sending potential returns plummeting. As a result, investment decisions too often reflect the political clout of various functional managers rather than the intrinsic value of the opportunity. Resolving such conflicts also produces polarization between a proposal's proponents and those who judge it, too easily seen as opponents.

Second, financial analysis techniques are silent on strategic matters, since their logic dictates that opportunities be pursued in order of estimated financial performance, regardless of other considerations. A 22% return (assume IRR) opportunity will always be chosen over an 18% opportunity. However, the 18% opportunity may be central to the company's strategy, whereas the 22% opportunity may be peripheral. Strategically, the 18% opportunity should be chosen; financial analysis reaches the opposite conclusion. A related problem arises when companies allocate funds to individual businesses based on historic profitability. In this decision making mode, mature (no-growth) businesses tend to receive more investment than new businesses, which are starved of funds since current profits are low.

This danger of overinvesting in current businesses via incremental investments and simultaneously starving newer products is increased by the difficulty of forecasting several years into the future. Clearly, forecasting errors are much greater for newer versus more mature products. As a result of these risk perceptions, returns for new products are likely to be discounted to a greater extent than cost-reduction projects for existing products. Thus, management's quest for more conservative, less risky opportunities can easily lead to insufficient investment in potential new opportunities. As we will see in Chapter 9, these kinds of decision processes often create an advantage for the "attacker," an unencumbered new entrant that competes with newer technology.[20]

In order to deal with these problems, some financial managers treat risk explicitly via risk analysis techniques or even full-blown simulations. However, these procedures have found less favor than originally anticipated and managers continue to seek ways of dealing with the problem.[21] Rather than focus on refinement of the numbers, the major thrust has been closer and more explicit examination of the assumptions underlying the financial projections. For example, we might ask about the expected future growth rate of the market(s) in which the products will be sold and the targeted market share. Other questions arise: Against which companies will the firm be competing? What is the likely future market structure? How is technology expected to change? What is the role of government? And so forth. These questions cannot be answered precisely, but they indicate the need to take a much more strategic approach to major investment decisions. Asking and attempting to answer such questions requires that management explicitly address the validity of the assumptions underlying financial projections. In this process, companies have typically shifted from an internally oriented perspective on investment decisions to a more strategic, externally oriented focus. We now address several of these approaches, generically known as "portfolio analysis."

The Growth/Share Matrix

One of the earliest and one of the simplest portfolio approaches to resource allocation was developed by the Boston Consulting Group (BCG) and is referred to as the **growth/share matrix.** The approach was developed to assist managers in making decisions on business objectives, in particular, what objectives each business should have with respect to their cash position. Understanding the logic of the growth/share matrix, despite its problems, provides a good foundation for understanding why more elaborate schemes were later developed. We first explain the BCG approach and then critique its applicability, which is particularly questionable for information (digital) products with long-run average costs tending toward zero.

As we saw in Chapter 4, all real economic analysis deals with cash flows. Further, the survival of the firm depends on maintenance of liquidity. Therefore the corporate center must carefully manage the cash balance in its portfolio of businesses, planning how to manage any surplus or deficit. Most corporate portfolios will contain cash-generating (cash-positive), cash-neutral, and cash-consuming (cash-negative) businesses. Cash-negative businesses require support from elsewhere while, overall, the total firm must be in cash balance. The corporate center's task is to ensure that this balance is maintained from internal sources and the appropriate use of long and short term financing.

To assist in determining the cash position of businesses, the growth/share framework uses two independent dimensions:

The future rate of growth of the market in which the business competes

The relative market share of the business in the market in which it competes

Each of these dimensions is a surrogate for another underlying variable. The rate of growth of the market is assumed to be a surrogate of the need that a particular business has for cash. Rapidly growing markets create strong needs for cash if the business wants to maintain its position in that market, since expansion will require new facilities as well as probable increases in marketing and R&D expense. On the other hand, if the business is competing in a slow-growing market, its appetite for cash is very low, since its need for investment funds is limited.

Relative market share is assumed to be a measure of the ability of the business to generate cash. Here, relative market share is defined as:

Market share of the business/market share of the largest competitor

Hence the relative market share of a business can be anything from zero to infinity; it is not limited to a maximum of 1. A relative market share greater than 1 indicates that the business is the leader in its market. In the BCG framework, it is assumed that a business with a large relative market share is generating substantial levels of cash and one with a small relative market share is generating much lower levels of cash.

Note that the two dimensions of cash use and cash generation are independent of each other. For example, a business in a very rapidly growing market may need large amounts of cash for development. Amazon used cash for many years before it started to show an accounting profit, and at the time of writing was still cash-negative. During this period, the firm raised cash from financial markets in the form of equity. On the other hand, a business in a mature market may generate more cash than it can use. The surplus cash of such a business may be used by corporate to support cash-negative businesses.

> Microsoft Windows and Office businesses generate positive cash flows of approximately $USB12 per year. These funds can be used to support other businesses in Microsoft's portfolio.[22]

To use this tool, the businesses that comprise the firm's portfolio are plotted on a two-dimensional chart, with the two dimensions being future market growth and relative market share, as shown in Figure 8.5. To provide additional information, it is common to plot businesses as circles, with the size of the circle proportional to the size (say the turnover) of the business. The chart is split into four zones as shown. A relative market share of 1.0 separates high- from low-share businesses. Any business that is to the left of the cut point is **dominant** in its market; any business to the right of this cut point is nondominant. To separate high-growth from low-growth markets, a common cut point is GDP growth + 3%. Markets growing faster than this are considered to be high-growth; markets growing slower than this are considered to be slow-growth. Both cut points are somewhat arbitrary. For example, a business with a relative share of 1.01 may be the leader but is scarcely in a commanding position compared with the next-largest competitor.

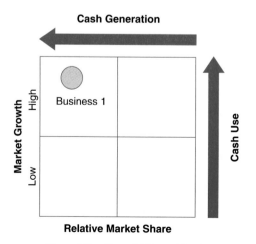

Figure 8.5   Growth/Share Matrix

To plot a particular business on this diagram requires two pieces of information: an estimate of the future rate of growth of the market in which it competes and the relative market share of the business. These, together with the size of the business, enable plotting its position, as we have done with business 1 in Figure 8.5. The figure also shows the likely cash position for each business type; for example, businesses in the bottom-left cell are likely to be cash-positive since they generate high levels of cash but use little of the cash they generate.

Any business that is above the cut point for market growth will ultimately fall below that cut point, since no business continues to compete in a high-growth market forever. All markets eventually mature, meaning that the market growth rate falls below the cut point. This downward vertical movement of the business over time is largely exogenous (outside the control of the management of the business). Sometimes a company with a high degree of dominance in a new technology can influence the growth rate of the overall market for such a technology, but, in general, Ford by itself cannot determine the long-term growth rate for automobile demand nor du Pont that for engineering plastics.

Management does have some control over the horizontal position of a business in the chart, since this depends on relative market share. A given business unit could gain, or lose, relative market share. If business management can increase its relative market share, the business moves to the left, as depicted in Figure 8.6.

Figure 8.6 illustrates the dilemma faced by business managers: When should they attempt to gain share with a business? It is generally considered easier to do this when market growth rate is fast, not only because competitive intensity may be lower but also because, if experience curve effects (Chapter 7) are important, firms may be able to generate a cost advantage. Further, during rapid growth periods, new customers are entering the market, new applications are being developed, and the technology is less settled—all of which may make share gain easier than in mature markets, where these features are absent.

As indicated in Figure 8.7, businesses in the bottom-left cell are expected to be cash-positive. They have a high relative market share, require lower rates of reinvestment, and thus are assumed to generate significant levels of cash. As we noted, Microsoft's Windows and Office products generated a net cash flow of about $USB1 per month in 2003. Cash from such businesses can drive SBU's in the upper right hand quadrant to a dominant

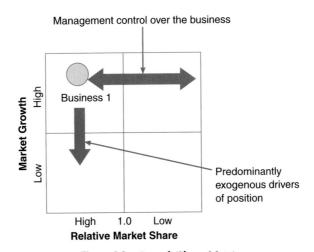

Figure 8.6 Growth/Share Matrix

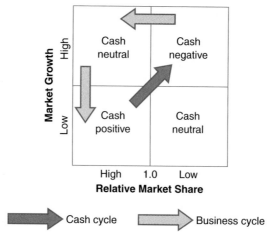

Figure 8.7 Cash Cycle of Businesses

position in their markets. As markets mature, such businesses will drop down into the bottom-left cell, thus providing funds for other top-right businesses. This can be viewed as a virtuous circle: grow share while the market is growing, then as growth slows, use the cash from the dominant businesses to support future cash generators.

As we have seen, the growth/share matrix emphasizes the relationship between entries in specific matrix cells and their financial characteristics. Products with high market shares are typically believed to be more profitable than those with low market shares; products whose volume is increasing quickly may require significant investment in fixed and/or working capital and market development, thereby reducing cash flow. In general, these correlations are supported by experience curve arguments and empirical research, as shown in Table 8.4, which shows the average profitability (in terms of ROI) of business units with different levels of market share. As Table 8.4 shows, business units with high levels of market share are clearly more profitable.

Typical recommendations from a growth/share analysis suggest that the strategy to be followed by a business depends on its position on the growth/share matrix.

Low Market Growth/High Market Share (Cash Cows) Businesses in this cell are typically highly profitable, both because of good cost position from economies of scale and experience curve effects and because market leaders are frequently able to command premium prices. Since the market is mature (low growth), required reinvestment should be low, with consequential benefits for cash flow. If they are well managed and major environmental change is absent, businesses in this cell may generate significant cash for many years, hence the term *cash cow,* although in some circumstances such businesses may not be net generators of cash that can be invested in more attractive businesses.

TABLE 8.4   **Market Share/Profitability Relationship**

Market share	< 10%	10–20%	20–30%	30–40%	> 40%
ROI	11%	18%	23%	27%	36%

Adapted with permission of the Free Press, A Division of Simon & Schuster Adult Publishing Group, from *The PIMS Principles: Linking Strategy to Performance* by Robert D. Buzzell and Bradley T. Gale. Copyright © 1987 by The Free Press. All rights reserved.

Cash cow businesses are generally given an objective of holding their market share since the cost of share growth is likely to outweigh the benefits. However, if significant environmental change such as a regulatory shift or the introduction of a radically new technology is forecast, a deliberate harvesting strategy aimed at increasing short-term cash flow, at the expense of market share, may be implemented. Specific actions may include increasing price, reducing/eliminating service, and/or cutting advertising and promotional support.

Overinvestment in mature products and businesses, driven by historical financial investment criteria, as discussed above, is also a serious issue; diminishing returns may set in as competitive spending levels are needlessly and unprofitably escalated.

In summary, low-growth/high-share products should represent the firm's primary internal cash source. The bulk of cash should be invested to support growth elsewhere—in newer markets, products, and businesses. The twin dangers of over- and under-investment demand a skillful balancing act from senior management.

Low Market Growth/Low Market Share (Dogs)   These businesses trail market leaders in low-growth markets. If the dominant firm's business is well managed (see above), low-market-share business should have inferior cost position, lower prices and consequently be less profitable than the leader. Yet, because follower firms may be better managed than the leader and have invested to force costs down, some low relative market share businesses can be quite profitable. However, if costs are bloated and/or relative market shares are quite small, low or zero profitability is likely.

The typical objective for better-placed low-share businesses is appropriate investment for long-run cash flow maximization, just as with high-share businesses. Poorly placed businesses should consider several different options: short-run cash maximization by liquidation, divestiture, new segmentation approaches that provide market niche dominance and a "kennel" strategy requiring acquisition of similarly placed businesses aimed at achieving viable scale.

High Market Growth/Low Market Share (Problem Children)   These businesses are typically viewed as the most risky both because of the inherent uncertainty in high-growth markets and their weak market share position, yet they may represent the future of the firm. They are often marginally profitable, but if they hold position and grow with the market, they consume substantial cash for investment in fixed assets and working capital. Unfortunately, such investment does not guarantee future profits since businesses managed in this manner may gravitate to the low-growth/low-share quadrant. As a result, the strategic investment decision for these businesses is often viewed as "double or quits." In other words, build market share and drive for dominance, ultimately seeking the low-growth/high-share cell via an intermediate high-growth/high-share position, or exit the business by gradual or more immediate means. Although the former strategy may be viable, largely depending on the actions of the market leader, very large investments are required for both market growth and market share gain. In many cases, a less risky approach is to seek dominance in a market segment.

High Market Growth /High Market Share (Stars)   These businesses are very desirable and yet are relatively rare. Typically, they are profitable, although not necessarily so at the very beginning of the life cycle, but investment in capacity expansion and increased working capital often means they may be cash-negative. Indeed, many new entrepreneurs with growing profitable operations find to their distress that profit and cash flow are not synonymous!

Growth markets are typified by considerable uncertainty with regard to ultimate market potential, evolution of customer needs, competitors, and technology. However, if relative market share is sustained, profitability and cash flows should improve as market growth slows. If dominance is maintained until maturity, "stars" cross the boundary to low market growth/high market share and should generate cash and support new growth businesses. The classic recommendation for these businesses is invest sufficiently to maintain and/or improve market position. The major danger is that management seeks profit too early, underinvests, and loses lead share position to a competitor, so that the business heads to the low-growth/low-share quadrant and poor performance. As with low-growth/high-share businesses, management must be concerned with overinvestment and overaggressive share-gaining behavior. Since market leaders can rarely drive all competitors from markets without incurring enormous costs, some optimal market share level should be set as an operational objective.

Difficulties with the Growth/Share Matrix

The growth/share matrix is a powerful tool for analyzing the business portfolio of a firm and for indicating possible strategic objectives for the businesses in that portfolio. However, we should be aware of several shortcomings and realize that the above recommendations cannot be applied without considering other issues. For example, the strategic recommendations neglect any idea of risk, the cost of gaining share, and the investment required. A business that is investment-intensive will require significantly more funds for growth than one that is less investment-intensive. Similarly, high-growth markets are typically viewed as attractive, yet, if many competitors rush to enter, installing too much capacity, prices may drop and all competitors may incur losses for considerable periods.

Good competitive strategy demands some element of contrarianism, particularly under the increasingly prevalent oligopolistic conditions of global markets. The major application of the growth/share matrix should be diagnostic—a means of raising, and discussing, "what-if" questions.

The growth/share matrix also has a number of technical problems. Any model for aiding decision making rests on a number of basic assumptions, and its value is only as good as these assumptions. The first assumption relates to the prior discussion: market growth rate alone may not signify an attractive market, even if it is associated with cash flow patterns. It is entirely possible to incur significant losses in growth markets, while if all competitors seek growth segments, they will be overoccupied, driving out the attractive returns that had originally led the market to be regarded as attractive.

A second core assumption is that strength of competitive position is captured by relative market share. In a static market, this proposition has some validity, but holding lead market position without having access to critical inputs is not a position of strength. Competitors may destroy strong market positions via securing scarce sources of supply or technological breakthroughs. Further, some generalizations underlying the growth/share matrix have been shown to be inaccurate. Using a large data sample from the PIMS project, Hambrick, MacMillan, and Day showed that the cash flow generalizations were not always accurate.[23]

The growth/share matrix makes two additional assumptions: the market share/profitability relationship and presence of downward-sloping cost experience curves. The results noted in Table 8.4 support the strong relationship between achieved market share and profitability, but this relationship may not hold universally, while gaining market share may be very costly. A related problem is that of market definition. Because of issues concerning level of segmentation and geographic boundaries, market definition is a vexing issue, yet it has a major impact on measures of both market growth and relative

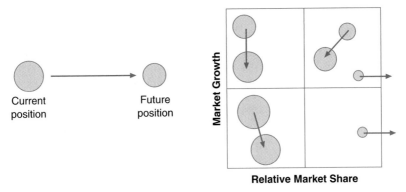

Figure 8.8   Current and Future Portfolio

market share—and hence on placement of entries in the matrix. If the served market of the business is defined too narrowly, the business will be assessed as dominant, which may be quite misleading. At the same time, market boundaries do change over time, suggesting that definitions of served markets should be reviewed periodically. Downward-sloping cost experience curves and comparable cost curves across competitors are supposed to drive the market share/profitability relationship. Once again, we do not expect this relationship to hold universally: well-managed small businesses frequently have better cost positions than major players, even though businesses with larger market shares might be relatively well managed.

> In intra-European service, Ryanair operated in 2001 with available-seat-kilometer costs of $US0.045, compared with $US0.12 for the three largest international European carriers, all of which have larger total volumes.[24]

Finally, the economics of many information products have very different cash flow implications than those suggested by the BCG model, since they are often characterized by very high development costs but marginal costs of almost zero, especially if distributed via the World Wide Web.

In summary, the growth/share matrix is a useful tool for analyzing the firm's business portfolio and can provide a good starting point for deliberations on setting appropriate objectives for different businesses. It can also be used to track historical evolution of the firm's business portfolio and to compare current and future portfolios, as shown in Figure 8.8. It becomes dangerous in naive hands, however, if treated as an automatic strategy generator.

Multifactor Portfolio Models

In part because of difficulties with the growth/share matrix, several other portfolio approaches have been developed and widely disseminated. Perhaps the most widely used is the **business screen** associated with GE. This approach redefines the two axes of the growth/share matrix—long-run market growth rate and relative market share—as market attractiveness and business strength, respectively, and then allows the user to identify a variety of factors to measure each dimension. In its original formulation, this approach was referred to as the stoplight matrix, a "colored" two-dimensional (market attractiveness/business strength) framework comprising three "green/go (invest/grow)" cells, three "red/stop (harvest/divest)" cells, and three "selectivity/earnings" cells (Figure 8.9).

Figure 8.9 Business Screen Matrix

This approach is conceptually more robust, since each of these dimensions comprises a number of elements or attributes. However, we now need to answer two questions:

What determines the attractiveness of an industry?

How can we assess business strength?

Industry attractiveness: Based on the theories of industrial organization economics; some of the structural factors that influence the attractiveness of an industry include:

Market growth rate

Customer concentration

Competitive intensity

Barriers to entry

Market size

Business strength: The competitive strength of a business unit is influenced by several factors, including:

Relative market share

Market share

Product differentiation

Relative costs

Competences

Of course, industrial organization economics is not the only source of ideas for the variables that will be used to construct such a screen. Results from empirical research such as the PIMS study may also provide insights, while some companies, as we noted in Chapter 5, have assembled and analyzed data reflecting their own experiences, which can also provide inputs.

For each dimension, the subfactors are combined in a weighting and rating scale, where the relevant dimensions are identified and then weighted in terms of their relative importance, using a constant-sum scale. The business unit is then rated 1–5 on each of these dimensions and a weighted total score calculated, as shown in Table 8.5 for the axis "business strength." A similar procedure is used to determine market attractiveness.

We can plot all businesses in the portfolio on the chart, as shown in Figure 8.10. As with growth/share matrices, it is usual to plot the business as circles, where the circle's

TABLE 8.5 Calculation of Business Strength

Factor	Weights (Σ = 1.00)	Business Rating(1–5)	Score
Market share	0.15	4.0	0.60
Relative market share	0.15	4.5	0.675
Differentiation	0.35	4.0	1.4
Cost	0.15	2.0	0.3
Margins	0.20	3.5	0.7
Total	1.00		3.675

size is proportional to the revenue of the business. Figure 8.10 is illustrative only and is not related to the calculations of Table 8.5, which is included only to show how the scores are computed.

The location of a given business has implications for investment, business objectives, managerial style, and incentives. Businesses in the upper-left cells, the green businesses, are those that the firm would find attractive investment candidates. Such businesses would have a growth objective and would likely require an entrepreneurial management style. Value is created by growth, and management incentives for these businesses would emphasize growth rather than current profitability.

Businesses in the lower-right cells are candidates for divestment—or at least limited investment. The objectives for these businesses would be cash flow, not growth, and would require cost-conscious managers who excel at cost reductions and squeezing assets for good returns. Here, value is created by cost reduction, not growth.

Thus business objectives, strategy, management style, and incentives may depend on the location of the business in such a portfolio chart. Indeed, some companies have gone so far as to classify their managers into three categories: overtakers, caretakers, and undertakers, based on a judgment of the preferred styles of these individuals. Many management theorists would disagree with such a procedure, arguing that managers should be able to adapt their styles to the requirements of the business.

Other Portfolio Methods

The need for competitive differentiation provides a strong argument for using company-specific multifactor analysis schemes. However, these may be constructed in many ways. McKinsey, for example, has developed a different kind of two-dimensional

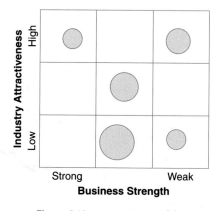

Figure 8.10 Business Portfolio

matrix, which attempts to directly integrate shareholder value considerations. The dimensions are:

> *The firm's ability to extract value from the business, relative to other potential own-ers:* Two categories are used here, "natural owner" and "one of the pack." The parent firm may have other businesses with which a particular business can share resources or competences. The firm as an entity may excel at financial controls, cutting costs, and squeezing suppliers or may have developed ways of sharing knowledge and resources among businesses, as in our BP example.
>
> *The ability of the business to create value as a stand-alone entity:* This can be expressed quantitatively or qualitatively. A qualitative measure might be based on a combination of industry attractiveness and business-unit position. A quantita-tive measure could be the NPV of the strategy of the business scaled by sales rev-enue to make it comparable with other businesses.

The resulting two-dimensional portfolio management is illustrated in Figure 8.11, where the size of the circle may be made proportional to the size of the business meas-ured in terms of sales, funds employed, or value added—always relative to other busi-ness units in the portfolio.

The decision as to whether or not a business unit should be kept in the firm's port-folio is dependent on both these considerations. The portfolio should consist of busi-nesses having the capacity to create value in their own right. This value in turn depends on the competitive position of the business and the attractiveness of the industry. In addition, the firm should keep in the portfolio only those businesses for which it has the ability to extract more of the value created than any other potential owner. The ideal portfolio would therefore be very crowded in the upper-left corner!

Comparison of Growth/Share and Multifactor Portfolio Methods
The value of various approaches to choosing among investment opportunities may be assessed by comparison across a set of criteria (Table 8.6). The basic trade-off is captured in the first three items: criteria, measures, and realism. The major advantage of the growth/share matrix is the limited number of criteria and their relatively unambiguous, more objective nature. Since the basis for investment decisions is reduced to market growth and relative market share, the ability of managers to manipulate individual entries is very limited. Although reasonable people may disagree about market growth forecasts, if agreement is formed on market definition, deriving relative market share is just a

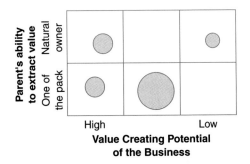

Figure 8.11   McKinsey Natural Parent Matrix

Source: K. McLeod and J. Stuckey, "MACS: The Market-Activated Corporate Strategy Framework," *McKin-sey Quarterly* 3 (2000), pp. 16–20.

TABLE 8.6   Comparison of Portfolio Approaches

Comparison Criteria	Growth/Share Matrix	Multifactor Matrix
Portfolio criteria	Limited but unambiguous	Unlimited but disputable
Measures	Basically objective	May be highly subjective
Realism	May lack	May have more
Manipulation of entries	Difficult	Easy
Implementability	Easy	More difficult
Communicability	Easy	More difficult
Accommodates new businesses	Not well	Yes
Explicit consideration of risk	No	Yes, if required
Underlying focus	Cash flow	ROI
Sensitivity to market definition	Yes	Yes

measurement issue. Conversely, the limited number of criteria is also a weakness since market growth and relative market share may be poor guides to resource allocation.

In comparison, the number of criteria in the multifactor matrix can range within reasonable limits. This approach may thus embrace many factors that the growth/share matrix omits and hence be more realistic. However, specific criteria are subject to dispute, and the weightings and ratings are typically subjective. As a result, political considerations and organizational power relationships may lead to manipulation of entries such that they enter the "required" cell. In our experience, in the multifactor matrix, investment opportunities tend to gravitate toward the high/high corner (high market attractiveness/high business strengths), possibly reflecting biased evaluations. By contrast, the majority of growth/share matrix entries by definition fall in the bottom right (low market growth/low relative market share).

The growth/share matrix has the advantage in ease of implementation and communicability. Senior management can view an entire complex, diversified organization arrayed on a single sheet of paper. Such a matrix can be used to analyze the trajectory of businesses over time, to evaluate customers and suppliers, and to test the likely results from pursuing different strategic options. Overall, it is easier to evaluate diverse businesses and market segments using the simple criteria from the growth/share matrix than to use the more complex multifactor matrix.

Conversely, whereas the multifactor matrix is useful both for assessing investment potential in current businesses and for evaluating totally new opportunities, the growth/share matrix is only really useful for assessing existing businesses. Indeed, since, by definition, all proposed new opportunities (other than acquisitions) have zero relative market shares, each such entry is a point on the right-hand side of the matrix. Whereas risk can be built into the multifactor matrix, it is not explicitly considered in the growth/share matrix. Furthermore, because of the market definition problem, the multifactor framework copes better with fragmented markets. Finally, neither matrix explicitly assesses the costs of changing market positions, meaning they are problematic in dealing with marketplace dynamics. However, at least the multifactor system clarifies the business strength improvements required to improve position.

Perhaps the bottom line for both approaches to portfolio analysis is that they are aids, not substitutes, for sound strategic thinking. Indeed, in our experience, the value of the approaches is less in the specific numbers and entries in either matrix than in the discussion that leads to their formation. Especially for the multifactor matrix, the discussion of which criteria to employ and arguments about weightings and ratings are frequently at a very high level, and managers gain significant insight about their choices.

Allocation of resources across the business units within the portfolio is a key corporate strategy decision. Business units are not identical. Each faces a particular competitive situation and consequently should be treated accordingly. In addition, they are each part of a larger portfolio, and corporate-level considerations may well outweigh business-level considerations.

⊘ 8.6 DIVERSIFICATION

As firms grow, they generally become more **diverse,** with an increasing range of businesses, technologies, and geographic regions. The degree, nature, and direction of diversification are some of the most important corporate strategy decisions. Managers may decide that growth has slowed in existing markets and there is consequently limited opportunity for creating future value. Or the firm may have surplus cash, over and above the amount that can be used profitably in existing businesses. While this cash could be returned to shareholders, either directly or via a share buyback, managers could diversify instead. However, if they invest in low-return initiatives, they destroy shareholder value.

The perspectives of shareholders and managers may differ on diversification. For managers, the reduction in cash flow volatility promised by diversification reduces business risk and may help the survival of the firm. For shareholders, some kinds of diversification can add value to the firm. For example, the diversifying firm may bring superior governance mechanisms or management skills to a new industry, perhaps transferring competences or economies of scope. **Economies of scope** occur when the unit product costs for a single firm producing two (or more) products are lower than the unit costs if each product was produced in separate firms. Nonetheless, we must always keep in mind that shareholders can diversify more easily than firms. Financial markets may place a conglomerate discount on the more diversified firm, indicating a belief that management will fail to extract all the value from its business portfolio and that the value of the component businesses is greater than the value of the total firm.

Diversification can take any of several forms, vertical or horizontal, related or unrelated with respect to industry, market, or geography. These options will be explored shortly.

> Many large retailers have attempted geographic expansion, often with mixed results. Marks and Spencer, one of the most successful retailers in the United Kingdom, diversified unsuccessfully into Europe, the United States, and Asia. Carrefour, the French firm that is world's second-largest retailer, had difficulty integrating its acquisition of Promodes. In contrast, Wal-Mart's acquisition of ASDA in the United Kingdom appears to be successful.[25]

There is considerable debate about the nature of diversity and its value to shareholders. Unfortunately, measurement of diversity is controversial.[26] Some measures concentrate on whether businesses compete in the same industry or market, whereas a resource-based view suggests measuring the extent to which different business units draw on common resources. Thus, another component of corporate strategy is the extent and nature of diversification: What is the relationship among the business units, are they related or not, and can resources and competences be shared between them?

> Canon is seen as having a competence in improving the effectiveness of a dealer network. This competence has been transferred from cameras to photocopiers, where the requirements are similar.[27]

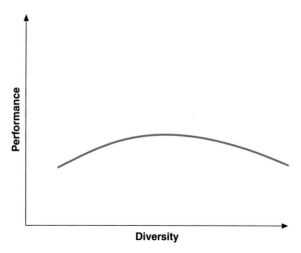

Figure 8.12 Relationship between Organizational Performance and Diversity

The degree of specialization of these resources also influences the nature of diversification. Collis and Montgomery concluded that firms with very specialized resources will compete in a relatively narrow range of businesses. For example:

> Sharp has specialized expertise in opto-electronic technologies such as liquid crystal displays. This technology may be used in many products, allowing the firm to continually expand its scope with a restricted range of related products.[28]

Managers must appreciate the difficulties of diversification. Due to bureaucratic costs, firms can easily destroy value through inappropriate diversification. It is not easy to manage a diversified company, and this could explain why many firms ultimately retrench to *core businesses*. The bulk of empirical evidence is that more focused firms outperform less focused ones. Firms seem to perform less well than the sum of their constituent businesses when there are no shared resources.[29] The general consensus is that some diversity is good but that there will be problems if the firm gets too diverse, as is shown in Figure 8.12, which suggests that firms with moderate levels of diversification outperform both highly focused and highly diversified firms. We should note that the management tools (such as communications and information technologies) needed to manage diversity improve over time, and managers should also become more adroit at managing diversity. The optimal degree of diversity may therefore increase over time.

Summarizing, some of the claimed advantages of diversification include the following:

Economies of scale and scope

The ability of the firm to act as an internal capital market

Market power or purchasing power

Financial and tax advantages.

There are some considerable disadvantages of diversification. A significant proportion of diversifications are driven by management ego—managers like to grow revenues and to run big businesses. As a result, they are tempted to invest in new ventures that may not deliver a return greater than the cost of capital, although they do bring revenue growth. This suggests an agency problem—managers are acting in their own interests, not those of the shareholders. In addition, it would be unrealistic to expect corporate managers to add value to a wide array of disconnected businesses. As a firm becomes increasingly complex, it is likely to also become unresponsive to the needs of its business units, slow in decision making, and high in overheads.

Related Diversification

To benefit shareholders, some kind of synergy should accompany diversification. This is most likely when some relatedness exists among the business units comprising the firm. Businesses in a portfolio are **related** when there is some sharing of or transfer of resources and capabilities among the different businesses, sometimes described as "fit." Relatedness may take any of several forms:

Tangible resources: The businesses achieve economies of scale/scope through sharing facilities, such as operations or R&D.

Intangible resources: The firm can transfer competences from one business to another. Competences might include a brand name, personnel, skills, and/or knowledge.

Market: The businesses share the same customers or distribution channels. Unilever or Altria, for example, would be expected to gain synergies in this way.

Management skills: These are often the most difficult to transfer from one area to another. Any relatedness would lie in the cognitive foundations on which the business operates, inculcating in managers the same business beliefs and assumptions.

> Senior management decided that GE should be a global leader in all its businesses. The firm reduced the number of organizational layers, delegated powers to decision makers, and cultivated entrepreneurship. These became the prevalent management philosophy, supplemented by a new incentive system to ensure implementation.

Finally, as described in Section 8.4, diversified firms can reallocate resources from one business to another in the corporate portfolio. Managers may be better at identifying opportunities than are external capital markets, with better information systems. This possibility may exist for money, technology, and personnel as well as capital.

Unrelated Diversification

Unrelated diversification occurs when there is little or no relationship among the businesses in the firm's portfolio, such as may occur in a holding company. The sole advantage of this type of company rests on the ability of a corporate center to make better capital allocation to businesses than can external financial markets. This could occur if corporate managers have superior information on opportunities available to a business, their costs, and likely future performance. This is not an unreasonable proposition, so long as the corporate center retains objectivity, since it typically has access to a large amount of information.

Unrelated diversification should reduce the variability of the firm's cash flow. The resulting lower risk should reduce the firm's cost of capital. Thus, although related diversification generally appears to produce superior returns to unrelated diversification, the latter can be successful under some conditions, such as:

Undervalued assets: The target firm has plants operating below capacity or real estate not being used to benefit shareholders.

Financial distress: The target is in financial distress, so its assets can be cheaply acquired.

Cash-short: The target is starved of capital but has good growth prospects.

Each of the above situations is basically a case of market inefficiency, suggesting that an astute buyout group may have an opportunity to make money by a policy of unrelated diversification. However, over time, if such buyout firms are seen to be making excess returns, these returns should be driven out by increasing numbers of buyout firms, making the market for corporate control much more efficient.

In summary, diversification is more popular among managers than among shareholders and analysts. Yet investment bankers and would-be sellers will continually solicit large public firms to make such deals. It takes a good understanding of strategic management principles to sort the wheat from the chaff in these situations, but there are some basic questions that we should always ask when considering such a move:

What can we do better than competitors?

What new strategic assets are needed?

Will we be a winner or just a player?

Will we learn from the diversification?

⊙ 8.7 FINANCIAL DECISIONS

Strategic management must include an understanding of certain financial decisions which influence the strategy that the firm adopts. The most critical of these are the capital structure and dividend policy of the firm, which we review below.

Capital Structure

Capital structure refers to the proportion of debt and equity used to finance the operations of the firm and is generally captured in the debt-to-equity (D/E) ratio, also called the financial leverage of the firm. We must be cautious when comparing the leverage of different firms, since some firms report leverage as D/E while others report leverage as D/D + E. These obviously have quite different arithmetic values. Organizational structures such as partnerships, alliances, joint ventures, and licensing also have differing capital structures.[30] Factors influencing capital structure are as follows:

Business risk of the firm: Volatility of demand and high fixed costs (heavy investment intensity) suggest the use of more equity rather than debt.

Tax position: Debt is tax-deductible, lowering the effective cost of debt. If a lot of the firm's income is already free of tax, then this is less of a benefit.

Financial flexibility: If the firm is already heavily indebted, then there is no flexibility for more debt. Indeed, if markets turn down or interest rates rise, the firm may have to roll over (renegotiate) existing debt.

Nature of assets, liquidity, and intangibility: The value of assets in liquidation is also important to lenders, who seek security. Tangible assets may be mortgaged, but if they are highly specialized, raising debt may still be difficult. For an advertising agency, assets are intangible, in the form of people and their creativity, not real estate or equipment. They are not a form of security for lenders.

Since debt is tax-deductible, there are advantages to high debt. In addition, high debt levels allow firms to leverage operating results, achieving higher returns on equity.

A safe, consistently profitable company with few intangible assets or growth opportunities should find a high debt level attractive. A retailer may have high leverage, while a new high-technology, high-growth company would be funded almost solely by equity. Table 8.7 shows the D/E ratios for a number of firms in 2002. As can be seen, Consolidated Edison, the New York–based energy supplier, which operates in a mature and still partially regulated industry, has a D/E ratio of almost 1, reflecting its low risk and a stable cash flow. By contrast, Intel, a high-technology computer firm, has a very low D/E ratio of just 0.03, reflecting the high business risk of the firm despite the fact that at this time it had substantial cash reserves of several billion dollars. Siemens, the German manufacturing firm, has a D/E ratio of 0.46, typical for a manufacturing firm. Intel must use retained earnings and/or new equity to fund any developments, while Consolidated Edison has a wider choice.

The balance of debt and equity and the nature of that debt and equity are important strategic management decisions and there is considerable debate as to whether or not there is an optimal level for a specific firm. The details of this discussion are to be found in a finance textbook.[31] Here we will briefly review some of the broader issues.

Financial theory suggests that the cost of debt should rise with increasing leverage such that, at some point, debt becomes too costly to employ. Another limit on the level of debt is the type of business. If the firm is characterized by stable cash flows, with substantial tangible assets, it can generally carry more debt. If the firm is cyclical, with most assets intangible, it will generally have less debt. Even in some mature businesses, technological change may mean that a firm is less likely to generate the stable cash flows needed to sustain high debt levels.

Since debt is cheaper, one could ask why firms are not funded solely by debt! With strong competition between banks and other financial intermediaries to provide debt funds, debt is normally easy to raise. However, as debt levels rise, debt providers increase their power over their customers through covenants on that debt that express their concern at the firm's ability to service its debt. The result is that financial markets monitor debt levels and may downgrade expectations of a firm if debt levels exceed prudent limits.

Firms that have difficulty servicing their debt may have to cut back research or advertising and sell assets if there is even a temporary cash flow problem. The reason for this is that debt must be paid, and if the firm cannot pay the required interest, or if the firm cannot raise more debt to pay the interest and principal, it is technically insolvent. This insolvency threat normally limits debt levels. Firms with high business risk compensate for this with low debt and thus low levels of financial risk.

An opposing view argues that firms should have high levels of debt because this may limit executives' tendency to invest free cash flow in core businesses with low returns (possibly below the cost of capital). It should also limit the tendency to diversify into unrelated businesses, since high debt levels must be serviced. So high debt and the replacement of equity with debt may stop uneconomic investment and encourage managers to return excess capital to shareholders.[32] However, as leverage increases, the cost

TABLE 8.7 Debt/Equity Ratios for Selected Firms

Company	Industry	Long-Term Debt	Equity	D/E Ratio
Consolidated Edison	U.S. energy	$USM6,168	$USM5,921	0.96
Intel	U.S. computer	$USM929	$USM35,468	0.03
Siemens	German manufacturing	€M10,243	€M23,521	0.46

Source: Company Annual Reports, 2002: www.conedison.com, www.intel.com, and www.siemens.com.

of both debt and equity will increase as the holders of these seek a higher return to compensate for increased risk.

Despite all the research, it appears there is no formula for the optimal capital structure; instead, it is a matter of judgment. This judgment of D/E ratios will be based on the tax rate, earnings variability or business risk levels of the firm, asset type (tangible or intangible), and the liquidity of these assets—as well as the general level of interest rates. In addition, current debt levels limit any increases—a highly leveraged firm will have problems further increasing leverage, regardless of circumstances.

Differences in Capital Structure

We observe a number of differences in capital structure based on factors other than those listed above. For example, German and Japanese firms typically operate with higher debt levels than, say, U.K. or U.S. firms, largely due to the different role of the banks versus other institutions and individuals in financing business operations.

In the United States, there has been a trend toward more use of debt.[33] Increased product/market competition has squeezed margins, reducing internally generated cash and increasing the need for external sources of funds. The desire to drive earnings per share via higher leverage, combined with low interest rates, has fueled increases in corporate debt, but at the expense of increasing firms' financial risk. The increase in debt and consequent levels of leverage of U.S. firms also reflect increasing merger activity, since this is generally financed by debt. The debt-to-equity ratios of U.S. nonfinancial firms rose from 70% in 1997 to 83% in late 2000.[34]

Dividend Policy

Dividends paid to shareholders restrict funds for future growth, and therefore some firms will be reluctant to pay them, particularly if they see good growth prospects.

> Microsoft's cash reserves grew to more than $USB40 before it finally announced that it would pay a dividend in 2003.[35]

Senior managers, in consultation with the board, are responsible for establishing dividend policy. Dividend payments are optional; there is no legal requirement that they be paid. However, dividends are important from two perspectives. From the firm's perspective, high dividend payouts reduce the funds available for future investment, meaning the firm can starve itself of funds for future growth and innovation if it adopts a high dividend regime. However, dividends are also a major factor driving shareholder value. We explore these perspectives below.

As noted, firms gain the majority of the funds required for new investment from their own cash flow. If too high a proportion of this cash flow is paid out in dividends, there will be insufficient funds for innovation and growth. At the time of writing, more U.S. firms are deciding not to pay a dividend, suggesting they are able to find good investment opportunities. On the other hand, managers who retain funds and invest them in alternatives that do not return the cost of capital are not serving shareholder interests. The real question is whether the firm has profitable uses for its cash—investment opportunities that are likely to return greater than the cost of capital. If not, then managers should return cash to shareholders, either by share buybacks or dividends.

Recall that investors obtain a return from both dividends and capital gains, and in the absence of dividends, shareholders can always sell stock. Some investors will prefer dividends, while others will prefer to take their return as a capital gain. This choice is strongly influenced by the tax regime in operation. Shareholders with high marginal tax rates may prefer to take their return as a capital gain and get the tax benefit. Shareholders such as pension funds may prefer dividends so that they can, in turn, pay their members.

The lack of dividends may also be another example of the principal/agent problem.

> There has been considerable debate as to whether or not Microsoft's cash hoard should be returned to its shareholders, permitting them to decide whether and where to invest. Microsoft instead invested in a range of securities, contributing to the net income of the firm but raising, to some extent, the question of whether Microsoft was an investment firm or a software firm.

Dividends, and changes in dividends, are also seen as having a "signaling" effect in financial markets. If the firm reduces its dividend rate, this could be interpreted as a signal that the firm is experiencing difficulties and the share price typically drops. If the firm introduces a dividend, or increases it, this could be seen as a signal that the firm has exhausted all good investment ideas and has limited future growth prospects.

In conclusion, there appears to be no real theory of optimal dividend policy, but managers need to be aware of the implications of their dividend decisions.

Share Repurchases

Share buybacks have become more common in recent years, when firms have engaged in purchasing their own shares on the open market. Share purchases can be seen as a complement to or substitute for dividends, since they should cause share price appreciation. U.S. firms, including such companies as GE and IBM, bought a net $2.7 trillion of their own shares in the five years leading up to 2001, and these stock repurchases have often been financed by debt.[36] GE has continued these purchases. During the first nine months of 2002, the firm returned $USB6.9 to shareholders, $USB5.4 in dividends, and $USB1.5 in share repurchases.[37]

Buybacks may be pursued for a variety of reasons. Managers may not see any desirable wealth-creating opportunities; hence they return money to shareholders. A firm may also repurchase its stock if it believes it is undervalued. Repurchase may also be a more tax-effective means to distribute cash to shareholders, since those who tender pay capital gains tax, not income tax.

Since any share buyback reduces the value of equity in the firm, it increases the firm's financial leverage, while earnings per share increase due to the reduced number of shares. This improvement may be positively regarded by financial markets, leading to a rise in the share price. This illustrates another potential *principal/agent* problem. Since buybacks increase share prices, managers with stock options or warrants (see below) may be acting in their own self-interest by engaging in buybacks. Whether share repurchases create value and for whom are legitimate issues to be debated. Nonetheless, it is a fundamental principle of shareholder value management that the firm should invest only in opportunities that return more than the cost of capital. When such opportunities are unavailable, cash should be returned to shareholders to decide how this will be invested. Buybacks are often a tax-efficient way to do this.

Management Incentive Options

In the last few years, many firms have modified their compensation systems to reward managers with **stock options** or warrants. These warrants are call options, giving the holder the right, but not the obligation, to buy a given number of shares in the firm at a given price up to a specified future date. This price is called the exercise price and is generally above the current share price. Such stock options are adopted to better align the interests of the firm with those of shareholders, since it is in the interests of the managers for the share price to rise to the exercise price. Options have frequently been offered to senior executives as part of their remuneration package, and in 2001 stock options represented some 58% of the compensation for CEOs of large U.S. firms.[38] However, over the years many companies have broadened participation in such schemes. Options have no value if the share price declines in the future, as has happened with many of the dot.com shares. Executives issued with such warrants are also generally restricted in when they can sell them. They may have to hold them for several years before they can be sold.

While options may indeed improve the alignment of interests between managers and shareholders, there are several concerns. First, how should options be reported on the income statement? Should they be treated as an expense, and if so how? Information on options is disclosed in the notes to the financial statements, but this information is not easy to follow. Options represent a future liability of the firm, and they are obviously an expense, since managers take them in lieu of salary. Yet few firms actually report them as an expense; if they are not included in the financial statements, the firm may be overstating its profit levels. Outright grants of stock also align interests of principals and agents, but because these must be expensed, they are used less frequently.[39] Both stock grants and options, however, can reward relatively poor performance in rising markets because very few firms insist on benchmarking performance against the market or their sector. Ironically, in the United States, options are considered expenses for tax purposes but not for the purpose of calculating net income or earnings. One study investigating the cost of employee stock options and their impact on reported profits found that the 1998 profits of large U.S. firms were overstated by between 18% and 27%.[40] Table 8.8 shows the reported net income, and the adjusted net income, where net income has been adjusted for the cost to the firm of management options offered to employees, for a number of U.S. firms. As can be seen, if Microsoft had expensed the cost of the issuance of options plus the change in the value of outstanding options, net income was estimated to drop from a profit of $USB4.5 to a loss of $USB17.8 The results shown in Table 8.8 are reflected in more recent data. If Sun Microsystems had been expensing options, its profits for the last three years leading up to 2003 would have been $USM700, not the reported $USB2.2.[41] It is easy to see why so many firms have actively resisted expensing stock options on their income statement. Certainly there are difficulties in evaluating the cost of these options, but this is conceptually no different from other accounting numbers such as depreciation, which has a subjective element. One valuation method proposed is that developed by Black and Scholes and discussed in any modern finance text.[42]

Following criticism from investors during the early 2000s, several firms changed their policies, with Citigroup, GM, GE, and Coca-Cola all announcing that they would

TABLE 8.8 Net Income and Adjusted Net Income for Selected U.S. Firms

Firm	Reported Net Income ($M)	Adjusted Net Income ($M)
The Gap	824	−1,686
GE	9,296	6,260
Intel	6,068	−1,814
Microsoft	4,490	−17,816

Source: D. Murray, *Employee Stock Options: The Fed Joins In* (London: Smithers & Co. Ltd., 2000)

now expense all stock options awarded to management, employees, and board members. Microsoft went further, announcing in July 2003 that it would cease offering stock options to employees and that it would now change its accounting practices to reflect the cost of such options.[43]

◉ 8.8 MANAGING STRATEGIC RISK

Strategic management involves making decisions now in anticipation of the future, when the chosen strategy affords the promise of an appropriate return. Since the future is unknown, and possibly unknowable, the actual return from a strategy is likely to be different from that anticipated when the decision was made. Strategic decisions are made in the face of risk and/or uncertainty. In a rapidly changing world, uncertainty can be very high, yet strategic decisions by their very nature take some time to eventuate. Who would be prepared to forecast U.S. GDP or political changes in China 10 years from now? Yet strategic decisions must be made in the present, even though their future returns are extremely difficult to predict.

All strategy involves risk. By **risk,** here we mean uncertainty in the return that is likely to ensue from the strategy. The realized consequences from the strategy may be different from the intended consequences, due to such factors as unanticipated changes in the environment or difficulties with strategy implementation. As we discuss below, one of the tasks of strategic managers is to choose strategies with "appropriate" levels of risk. A low-risk strategy could be to invest only in government bonds, but managers of such a firm add no value for shareholders, who can invest in these for themselves.

When evaluating strategy, we must consider a number of issues: the likely return, the level and profile of risk, and the time value of money. Here we focus on risk and return and the role of strategic managers in managing the trade-off between them. Of course, these are financial dimensions and represent only two of the many criteria that might be used to assess strategy. We look at a broader set of measures when we discuss performance measurement in Chapter 12.

While we need to be aware of the risk of action, we should not ignore the risk of inaction. Doing nothing can also be very risky if managers attempt to continue the status quo while the world evolves. This provides another classic paradox of strategic management. If we take no action, there is a chance of becoming obsolete, a probability that rises when change is rapid. Alternatively, we may adopt a particular strategy predicated upon a view of the future. This view is likely to be at best partly correct, indicating that there is a risk that the strategy may not deliver its intended results.

Nonetheless, we believe that managers must be proactive in introducing change, even though change will have an associated risk. Strategy takes time to design and implement, and without an element of creative foresight, the firm will almost certainly be overtaken by events.

Assessing Strategy

Any given strategy may be assessed on the basis of two characteristics:

The level of risk of that strategy

The expected return from that strategy over the planning horizon

If we ignore other characteristics of strategy for the moment and concentrate on risk and return, we may visualize possible relationships between risk and return, as illustrated in Figure 8.13. The horizontal axis is the return required by or anticipated for the strategy,

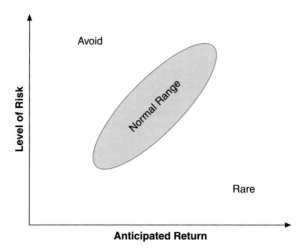

Figure 8.13   Risk/Return Trade-Off for Strategy

where this is calculated as the net present value of the strategy, discounted at the cost of capital of the firm (as discussed in Chapter 4). The vertical axis is the level of risk of the strategy. Here risk is measured as the variability in cash flow resulting from the strategy and reflects the strategy's inherent uncertainty. A strategy to buy government bonds would have very low risk, since there is little or no uncertainty in the future returns. A strategy to develop a new technology would have high risk. If the new technology is successful, the result is significant cash generation by the firm. If the new technology is not successful, the firm may lose a substantial sum. And, of course, we do not know whether the new technology will be successful.

As Figure 8.13 suggests, when a strategy is considered a high risk, the firm requires a higher return to compensate for the high risk. However, risk and return are independent characteristics of a strategy. Not all high-risk strategies offer the promise of a high return, hence our use of the term *anticipated return* for the horizontal axis. Ideally, we should seek strategies that have a low risk and yet promise a high return; the identification of such strategies encapsulates the challenge of strategic management. Yet these are rare, as indicated in Figure 8.13. Certainly, we should avoid strategies that are low-return and yet high-risk!

Managers have some degree of control over the risk level of their strategies, although they should also recognize that control is incomplete. Risk/return trade-offs depend on a number of factors. In theory, the choice should depend on the risk profile of shareholders; some will be more willing than others for the firm to pursue a risky strategy. However, there are likely to be differences in perspective between managers and shareholders. Managers may take larger risks since their money is not involved, while the personal values of senior managers and the firm's culture also have an influence. Clearly, different firms have different propensities for risk. Some are risk-averse, selecting strategies they believe have little risk, while other firms are more willing to adopt risky strategies.

Strategic Risk Profile

A firm will typically pursue a number of strategies that vary in their level of risk. Therefore we can develop the risk profile of a firm by assessing its range of strategies accord-

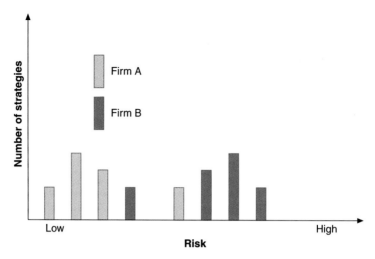

Figure 8.14   Risk Profile of Two Firms

ing to their associated risk levels, as illustrated in Figure 8.14, which plots the risk profiles of two firms, A and B. As can be seen, firm A avoids strategies with high levels of risk. It is risk-averse, limiting itself to relatively low-risk strategies. By contrast, firm B has a large number of high-risk strategies in place; it is much more entrepreneurial.

The choice of such a risk profile is yet another strategic decision by the managers of the firm, reflecting their trade-off between the overall level of risk for the firm and its anticipated return. Too many high-risk strategies may cause bankruptcy and destruction of shareholder value. Too many low-risk strategies may result in low growth and gradual decline, also resulting in the destruction of shareholder value.

Implicitly or explicitly, firms choose which risk profile to adopt and how much risk to accept in the pursuit of above-average returns. The risk level adopted by a firm is reflected in its beta used to calculate its cost of capital.[44] Firms such as Colgate Palmolive (beta = 0.63) and Nestlé (beta = 0.49) have low-risk profiles. Firms such as Amazon (beta = 2.17) and SAP (beta = 1.79) have higher-risk profiles.

Managing Risk

One of the most valuable ways to improve risk management is to open up the minds of managers to explicitly consider risk when developing strategy. When we address performance management in Chapter 12, we will urge that risk be explicitly incorporated into assessing performance by using sensitivity analysis. However, to consider risk a priori requires creativity and imagination. One of the most effective ways to do this is via the use of scenarios. These can be used to give management simulated experience in dealing with unpredictable events and to increase understanding of what may be the major drivers of return variability—and thus which things should be subject to more scrutiny.

Within a short while after its opening, it was clear that the long-awaited tunnel under the English Channel was not going to meet its financial objectives, and a complex refinancing followed. Among other factors, its owners had failed to anticipate the competitive response to their new services, for, within a fairly short time, the ferry operators had vastly improved their efficiency and rationalized their operations.

A firm can also opt to delay a strategy, which may mitigate risk. Faced with high uncertainty, we may purchase options. If we wait, some uncertainty may be abated, and that may be better than committing large amounts of capital prematurely. Many pharmaceutical companies chose this approach as the field of biotechnology appeared on their planning horizons.

Managing risk might well encompass a broad range of scenarios, subsuming decisions on how to keep key staff, the nature of service contracts with customers, environmental risk, occupational health and safety, security management (and, increasingly important, security related to the company's information technology), disaster and crisis contingency planning, and so on. Since, as we have seen, an increasing part of the firm's market value is dependent on intangible assets, shareholders are vulnerable to any incident that affects the company's reputation.

The following are estimates of the cumulative costs of reputation-damaging crises to the companies concerned:[45]

Exxon Valdez oil spill	$USB13
Occidental oil (Piper Alpha explosion)	$USB1.4
Barings Bank (collapse)	$USM900

The more recent Enron and WorldCom collapses dwarf the above examples, but their full costs are not yet known, and in any case these appear to have been due to quite blatant dishonesty on the part of a number of individuals.

Preemptive risk management is much the preferred approach, but managers must also realize that in today's society, perceived risk is as important as actual risk. Improved access to information, aggressiveness of global media concerns, and a resulting increased transparency of company operations combine to create a maelstrom of forces influencing public opinion. In addition, the "entrepreneurial" activities of various nongovernmental organizations (NGOs), often focused on a single issue such as the environment or animal rights, have found fertile ground in what has been termed the "risk society."

Societal change and uncertainty, fast technological change, and a lack of trust of authority have created a much more demanding environment for managing risk. Advocacy groups have become very sophisticated in their use of the Internet and media relations, to the point where large global companies that have in many cases made huge contributions to raising living standards in many parts of the globe are seen as villainous, if not downright evil.

No senior executive can afford to ignore these intersecting phenomena, for as the value of the firm becomes more and more dependent on the intangible assets we discussed in Chapter 5, the management of risk and the avoidance of crises becomes ever more important. Even a cursory examination of the ways in which the CEOs of major corporations have dealt with this type of problem indicates the enormous contribution that they can make at times of crisis.

A basic model for dealing with risk and uncertainty is shown in Figure 8.15. It suggests that managers should begin with an attempt to identify sources of risk and uncertainty and to examine their potential impact on the firm. Human beings are notoriously bad at intuitive risk assessment, and professional risk managers are increasingly employed to perform this task, often using actuarial data and models to assist them. Risk control involves considering ways to avoid, reduce, transfer, or neutralize risks and uncertainty. Activities of this type that many companies are committed to include health and safety practices at work, upgrading fire prevention systems, driver education and other kinds of training programs for employees, provision of first-aid kits on company

Figure 8.15 A Model for Risk Management

Source: Adapted from M. Regester and J. Larkin, *Risk Issues and Crisis Management* (London: Kogan Page, 2002).

facilities, wellness programs, health screening programs, installing firewalls and/or encryption protection for the firm's intranet, and so on. These activities, which might generally be described as loss-reduction programs, may well have a favorable impact on the cost of insurance for the firm. Of course, risk can be financed in a number of ways, regular insurance being only one method.

> When medical malpractice insurance rates first began their dramatic rise, one of our colleagues was CFO of Columbia–Presbyterian Hospital in New York, one of America's outstanding hospitals. Investigators found, as they expected, that the hospital's incidence of problems by medical procedure was extremely low. The hospital elected to self-insure for the first part of the risk and go directly to the reinsurance market for the remainder. The result was a disintermediation of the insurers—and a significant cost saving!

Of course, you can follow a similar strategy of increasing the deductible on your household or car insurance, but first be sure you assess the risk objectively! There are many options for hedging various kinds of financial risk. Some companies pass off credit risk to third parties by factoring their receivables or by requiring a letter of credit. As we mentioned in Chapter 4, it is quite common for large firms to hedge exchange-rate risk in similar manner, especially when large contracts in currencies other than the reporting currency are involved. All such programs require significant administrative management and controls, and the importance of these has been underlined by the collapse of Barings Bank through the actions of one rogue trader and the cases of company embezzlement and fraud that are uncovered all too frequently.

8.9 SUMMARY

With the expansion in the scale and scope of global firms, the complexity of strategy and strategic management has increased dramatically. The fundamental task for the management of a multibusiness firm is to ensure that the total entity creates greater value than would be possible if each of the constituent businesses were independent. Strategy at the corporate level has characteristics that make it different from strategy at the business-unit level.

Developing corporate strategy requires that managers make decisions in a number of areas, including the future direction of the firm, the style to be adopted by the corporate center, allocation of financial and other resources across the business portfolio, the extent and nature of diversification, and major financial decisions. These decisions need to be addressed in an integrative and holistic manner and cannot be made independently. A decision to follow an unrelated diversification strategy has implications for which style of corporate center is likely to be adopted by the firm. A number of analytical tools can be used to assist several of these decisions. In particular, the chapter emphasized the use of a number of portfolio management methods that are used to help decide what should be the objectives and strategy for different business units.

Finally, strategic management at the corporate level must concern itself with strategic risk and the risk profile of the firm. Addressing the trade-off between risk and potential return from alternative strategies is another key task for senior managers.

⊙ REVIEW QUESTIONS

1. Discuss the ways in which the corporate center in a multibusiness firm can add value.

2. Select a global firm and obtain a copy of its vision statement. Discuss how the firm's strategy has been influenced by the vision statement.

3. "The growth/share matrix is too naive to be useful in developing strategy." Discuss this statement.

4. Select a global firm (or a group within a global firm). Plot the business units of the firm on a matrix of your choice. What implications are there for the corporate strategy of the firm?

5. In the multifactor portfolio model, what factors contribute to an attractive environment for a business?

6. Explain the differences between related and unrelated diversification.

7. Many managers justify their diversification decisions on the basis of claimed "synergy." Is this claim always justified? Give examples of where you believe claimed synergy did not exist.

8. Discuss some of the ways in which financial markets impact on corporate strategy.

9. Provide an example of a firm with a high-risk profile and another with a low-risk profile. Illustrate by discussing the strategies adopted by each firm.

⊙ ENDNOTES

[1] Adapted from "Philips Profile," 2003: www.philips.com.

[2] A. D. Chandler, *Strategy and Structure: Chapters in the History of the American Industrial Enterprise* (Cambridge, MA: MIT Press, 1962).

[3] R. P. Rumelt, *Diversity and Profitability* (Los Angeles: Managerial Studies Center, Graduate School of Management, University of California, 1977).

[4] P. Lawrence and J. W. Lorsch, *Organizations and Environment* (Cambridge, MA: Harvard University Press, 1967).

[5] O. E. Williamson, *Markets and Hierarchies: Analysis and Antitrust Implications* (New York: Free Press, 1975).

[6] J. A. Roquebert, R. L. Phillips, and P. A. Westfall, "Markets vs. Management: What "Drives Profitability", *Strategic Management Journal* 17, no. 8 (1996), pp. 653–664.

[7] A. McGahan and M. E. Porter, "How Much Does Industry Matter, Really?" *Strategic Management Journal* 18 (1997), pp. 15–30.

[8] E. H. Bowman and C. E. Helfat, "Does Corporate Strategy Matter?" *Strategic Management Journal* 22, no. 1 (2001), pp. 1–23.

[9] "Fatal Attraction," *The Economist,* March 23, 1996, pp. 77–78.

[10] K. McLeod and J. Stuckey, "MACS: The Market-Activated Corporate Strategy Framework," *McKinsey Quarterly* 3 (2000), pp. 16–20.

[11] M. Goold, A. Campbell, and M. Alexander, *Corporate Level Strategy* (New York: Wiley, 1994).

[12] R. N. Foster and S. Kaplan, *Creative Destruction* (New York: Doubleday, 2001).

[13] "Westinghouse RIP," *The Economist,* November 29, 1997, pp. 63–66.

[14] Sony Annual Report, 2001: www.sony.co.jp.

[15] M. Hayward and D. Hambrick, "Explaining the Premiums Paid for Large Acquisitions: Evidence of CEO Hubris," *Administrative Science Quarterly* 42 (1997), pp. 103–127.

[16] M. Goold and A. Campbell, *Strategies and Styles* (Oxford: Blackwell, 1987).

[17] M. Goold and A. Campbell, "Desperately Seeking Synergy," *Harvard Business Review,* September–October 1998, pp. 130–143.

[18] "Case Study: British Petroleum (B): Focus on Learning" (Stanford: Stanford University, 1998).

[19] G. Hamel and C. K. Prahalad, "Competing for the Future," *Harvard Business Review,* July–August 1994, pp. 122–128.

[20] R. Foster, *Innovation: The Attacker's Advantage* (New York: Summit, 1986).

[21] H. Courtney, J. Kirkland, and P. Viguerie, "Strategy under Uncertainty," *Harvard Business Review,* November–December 1997, pp. 66–79.

[22] S. Ellis, "Squander Lust Over, Divas Flirt with Dividends," *Australian,* January 23, 2003, p. 22.

[23] D. C. Hambrick, I. C. MacMillan, and D. Day, L, "Strategic Attributes and Performance in the BCG Matrix—A PIMS-Based Analysis of Industrial Product Businesses," *Academy of Management Journal* 25 (September 1982), pp. 510–531.

[24] "As Regulators Launch an Inquiry into Suspected Illegal Subsidies, Is Cheap Air Travel in Europe Too Good to Last?" *Financial Times,* December 12, 2002, pp. 13.

[25] "When You Can't Sell the Goods, Sell the Shop," *The Economist,* January 18, 2003, pp. 53–54.

[26] J. A. Robins and M. F. Wiersema, "The Measurement of Corporate Portfolio Stategy: Analysis of the Content Validity of Related Diversification Indexes," *Strategic Management Journal* 24, no. 1 (2003), pp. 39–60.

[27] C. C. Markides and P. J. Williamson, "Related Diversification, Core Competencies and Corporate Performance," *Strategic Management Journal* 15 (Summer 1994), pp. 149–166.

[28] D. J. Collis and C. A. Montgomery, "Creating Corporate Advantage," *Harvard Business Review,* May–June 1998, pp. 70–83.

[29] B. Wernerfelt and C. Montgomery, "Tobin's q and the Importance of Focus in Firm Performance," *American Economic Review* 78, no. 1 (1988), pp. 246–250.

[30] D. R. Lessard, "Global Competition and Corporate Finance in the 1990's," in *Strategic Management in the Global Economy,* H. Vernon-Wortzel and L. H. Wortzel, eds. (New York: Wiley, 1997).

[31] M. Grinblatt and S. Titman, *Financial Markets and Corporate Strategy* (Boston: Irwin/McGraw-Hill, 1998).

[32] M. C. Jensen, "Eclipse of the Public Corporation," *Harvard Business Review,* September–October 1989, pp. 61–75.

[33] Grinblatt and Titman, *Financial Markets and Corporate Strategy.*

[34] "Corporate Finance," *The Economist,* January 27, 2001, special survey.

[35] "The Dividend Puzzle," *The Economist,* January 11, 2003, pp. 53–54.

[36] "Corporate Finance." *The Economist.*

[37] "GE Delivers 3rd Quarter Earnings of $Bn4.1 on 9% Revenue Growth," *Greenville Community News,* undated, 2002: www.greenville.com.

[38] "Coming Clean on Stock Options," *The Economist,* April 27, 2002, pp. 75–76.

[39] "System Failure," *Fortune,* June 24, 2002, p. 43.

[40] D. Murray, *Employee Stock Options: The Fed Joins In* (London: Smithers & Co Ltd, 2000).

[41] R. Waters and A. Michaels, "Sun Braced for Challenge over Stock Option Policy," *Financial Times,* July 14, 2003, p. 29.

[42] F. J. Fabozzi and F. Modigliani, *Capital Markets: Institutions and Instruments* (Upper Saddle River, NJ: Prentice Hall, 1996).

[43] R. Waters and S. Morrison, "Microsoft Ends Stock Options for Employees," *Financial Times,* July 9, 2003, p. 21.

[44] "Datastream Advance 3.5," Thomson Financial, 2003.

[45] M. Regester and J. Larkin, *Risk Issues and Crisis Management* (London: Kogan Page, 2002), p. 2.

CHAPTER 9

Managing Innovation and the Dynamic Scope of the Firm

Learning Objectives

Upon completing this chapter, you should be able to:

- Appreciate the importance of innovation for the firm and the necessity to manage the dynamic scope of the firm
- Describe the types of innovation that can be undertaken
- Articulate the differences between internal development and mergers and acquisitions as means of changing scope
- Define the issues involved in technological innovation
- Define the steps to be followed in mergers and acquisitions
- Apply the concept of synergy in mergers and acquisitions
- Utilize net present value to calculate the value of mergers
- Utilize the concepts of spinouts and restructuring as means of managing the changing scope

---

On January 9, 2003, William Morrison made a bid of £B2.6 ($USB4.2) for Safeway, the United Kingdom's fourth-largest supermarket chain, a bid which had the approval of Safeway management. Four days after this bid was announced, Sainsbury, the United Kingdom's third-largest retailer announced a tentative bid of £B3.0. One day later, Asda, which is owned by the U.S. retailer Wal-Mart, announced that it was also considering a cash bid for Safeway. Whether these bids would be proceeded with was dependent on the two firms undertaking due diligence on Safeway as well as receiving advice from the U.K. Competition Commission.

These bids reflect the fact that worldwide, retailers are finding it difficult to achieve required levels of profitability. Carrefour in France and Metro in Germany have both issued warnings that future profit levels are likely to drop. FAO Schwartz, the New York toy store, has declared bankruptcy. Kmart in the United States, operating under Chapter 11 protection from creditors, is closing stores, and has announced 37,000 job losses. Boots, the U.K. retail chain, has withdrawn from Japan, and Marks and Spencer, the U.K. retailer, seems to be withdrawing from global operations to concentrate on the United Kingdom. Retailers are seeking new strategies in a very difficult trading environment. Many firms in the industry have adopted a strategy of aggressive discounting—which has reduced margins, since operating cost increases have been greater than retail price increases. Other firms consider that a superior strategy is to reduce costs through mergers.

Depending on what transpires with Safeway, several retailers are likely to modify substantially their future strategy. If Wal-Mart were to be successful, this would consolidate its position in the United Kingdom and be a major contributor to its international success, particularly after the difficulties it experienced in Germany. If Wal-Mart were to be unsuccessful, it is likely to switch its attention to other countries in Europe, such as France or Spain. If Sainsbury were to be successful, Tesco (currently the major supermarket retailer in the United Kingdom) may be forced to switch to an international strategy based on acquisition rather than organic growth. This could be its only option despite the difficulties with international acquisitions in retailing due to variations in local tastes and the difficulties in achieving global synergies in purchasing.[1]

9.1 INTRODUCTION

As the above example illustrates, *mergers* and *acquisitions* are an integral element in corporate strategy. They are one of the means firms employ to grow, alter the scope of their operations, obtain new skills and competences, and reduce costs. Yet the process is fraught with difficulties. Major resource decisions must be made under considerable time pressure, with limited information. As illustrated above, the process is typically competitive and the outcome often dependent on external bodies such as regulators. Finally, future strategy will be influenced by the results of the bid—indicating that strategy has an element of path dependency.

In a rapidly changing and turbulent world, strategy innovation is essential to wealth creation—and even survival. The long-term health of any company is assured only if it possesses the capability for continual renewal via innovation and the development of new businesses. Putting this another way, *"the right of any corporation to exist is not perpetual but has to be continually earned."*[2] Whether developed internally, in combination with suppliers, by joint venture, acquisition, or some other means, the process will involve significant change and organizational innovation. In this chapter we begin by considering the nature of innovation in organizations. We do not regard innovation as being limited to research and development or to acquisitions. Rather, innovation includes the development of new market opportunities, the invention of new business models, the restructuring of an industry, the use of mergers to obtain new competences, and the deliberate refocusing of the scope of the firm.

We also explore how to organize for innovation and the characteristics that demarcate innovative organizations. We are firmly convinced that in the 21st century companies will find themselves having to create new markets rather than respond to existing markets, a change that mandates a much better understanding of how to organize for creativity and innovation than has traditionally been the case. Next we explore alternative approaches for developing new businesses. Today, most companies actively manage their business portfolio, adopting a number of approaches to ensure survival. These include development of new businesses internally, mergers and acquisitions, alliances, and partnerships as well as divestments and restructuring.

Firms need to focus on wealth creation rather than growth per se. Revenue growth can, of course, be a means of wealth destruction rather than wealth creation. However, substantial wealth creation occurs only with growth, not with cost reductions. Firms that exclusively "stick to their knitting" will, over the longer term, find themselves in real trouble. Changing customer preferences, technological development, the availability of substitutes, and, on occasion, government actions—all mitigate against what have been called vertically dominant corporate growth strategies. Yet as we saw in Chapter 8, firms can become too diverse, in geographic region, product, market, or technology. Too much diversity—too unrelated a diversification—is extremely difficult to manage. Many firms lack the management skills to do this well. Nonetheless, we must admit the possibility of organizational learning. Firms can learn to manage increasing diversity over time, and an optimal level of diversity 10 years ago may not optimal for today.

Despite the importance of innovation, many firms do not devote the time and effort required to develop a corporate perspective on the future.[3] Major intellectual effort is required to develop a view of the future, the competences required, the trajectories that could be used, relevant technological and political trends, all in a very uncertain world. Hamel and Prahalad call this foresight, an understanding of future technologies, competitors, core competences, and markets, among many others. They advocate a proactive rather than reactive approach to change. Downsizing and cost reduction are often inevitable consequences of late response to change. Leadership requires ongoing, continual innovation, both incremental and revolutionary. Long-term successful firms are able to transform industries, alter the boundaries between industries, and reinvent their industry before competitors do. Such firms have been described as industry revolutionaries. They break the rules of the industry, challenge industry norms and beliefs, and invent new competitive spaces, fostering a culture of creativity, risk taking, and experimentation.[4]

⑨ 9.2 INNOVATION IN THE FIRM

While the case for corporate innovation is easy to articulate, it has features that make it difficult for firms to manage, as illustrated in Figure 9.1.

1. *Degree*   Degree of innovation refers to the extent of the innovation, whether the innovation is *incremental* or *revolutionary*. Incremental innovation can ensure that a firm remains competitive within its chosen domain, but only revolutionary innovation will ensure long-term growth and value creation. Large firms seem to find incremental change easier, but rapid external change may require more revolutionary innovation. Revolutionary innovation may transform the relationship of the firm with its customers and destroy current products, generating new product categories and even industries. Revolutionary innovation is more difficult to undertake for established firms. As innovations become more revolutionary, they become riskier and more difficult to evaluate. Future returns are exceptionally unpredictable. Indeed, such revolutionary decisions often cannot be justified on purely financial, rational grounds. Revolutionary innovations generally evolve unpredictably and are sporadic, with many stops and starts and

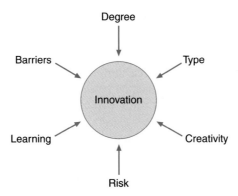

Figure 9.1   Features of Organizational Innovation

unanticipated outcomes. In addition, the benefits may not be what were initially expected, and flexibility and adaptability are needed.[5]

Tushman and O'Reilly argue persuasively that these different kinds of innovation demand very different organizational arrangements.[6] Their research indicates that while incremental innovation can be successfully managed within the existing organizational structure and system, revolutionary innovation cannot. If we add to their distinction Christensen's concept of a disruptive innovation, this argument seems to be even stronger. Perhaps the failure to heed this advice explains what Richard Foster described as the attacker's advantage,[7] for historically the advent of a discontinuous change in technology typically heralds a shift of industry leadership. Christensen has also shown that firms dominating one generation of technology often fail to maintain their leadership when a new technology emerges.[8]

2. *Type* We generally think of innovation in terms of the scope of the firm or in terms of a product/market, new businesses, and new products. But there are many other types of innovation, such as when the firm develops a new organizational structure, when the mental models of managers need to be updated, or when new management systems such as teams or a revised compensation system are introduced.

3. *Creativity* Creativity is fundamental to innovation. We regard creativity as a necessary but not sufficient condition for innovation. Creativity needs to be channeled to reflect the organizational vision. Innovators have a bias toward action, but this should not be at the expense of analysis. Innovators also have a focus on experimentation, on rapid learning and feedback, adaptive behavior, and flexibility. They have a degree of passion toward the innovation together with the ability to analyze and change when circumstances warrant. As can be expected, it is difficult to do both at the same time.

4. *Risk* Innovation reflects one of the most important dilemmas in strategic management, the tension between the old and the new. A changing world means that innovation and change are essential, but all change brings with it some level of risk, and the greater the degree of innovation, the greater the degree of risk. At the same time, there is a risk of inaction, which may never be given the attention it deserves.

5. *Learning* As with other organizational processes, firms can learn innovation skills; this can be accomplished in at least two ways. First, by doing something new, the firm develops a set of competences and skills in whatever comprises the new. Second, there may be double-loop learning as the firm learns how to manage innovation and change.

6. *Barriers to change* Any innovation needs to overcome barriers to change, often created by individuals within the firm. Some individuals seem to be inherently resistant to change; others may welcome change but only if they have been informed and consulted about the change and their role in it. Participation is often seen as a useful means to overcome this resistance, as illustrated by the experience of Honeywell in the United States. Up to 1993, the firm had been characterized by years of stagnation, with demoralized staff who felt that the firm was going backward. Barriers to innovation were seen in four areas:

A culture of risk aversion with little experimentation, where failure was punished

An internal environment in which innovation was discouraged

Few personal incentives for innovation and no corporate innovation goals

Inadequate processes for innovation.[9]

As a consequence of these characteristics, businesses within Honeywell were encouraged to manage themselves more efficiently, not to innovate. Following the appointment of a new CEO, the firm undertook a number of initiatives for innovation, primarily by identifying a large number of change programs of varying time horizons and encouraging staff to participate. It worked, but, as expected in a large firm, it took five years for the results to show up.

Organizing for Innovation

Some obstacles to innovation have been identified:

The inertia of success—why change when we are currently successful?

Uncertainty about what to change

Uncertainty about what to do—what new strategy is called for?

Uncertainty about how to do it—the challenges of implementation[10]

Our own empirical research suggests that innovation in an organization is not the result of any one factor but rather is a result of mutually reinforcing systemic factors. In Figure 9.2 we show the characteristics of more innovative companies, adapted from a survey of the *Fortune* 500 companies.[11] A cluster analysis revealed that only about a fifth of the sample could be considered to be innovative, and Figure 9.2 shows several of the characteristics they share.

The most striking aspect of Figure 9.2 is the holistic and systemic nature of innovative organizations. Too often, we believe, managers seek one easy answer to their

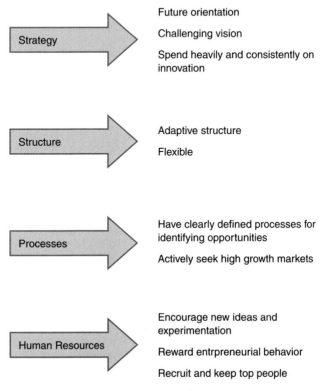

Figure 9.2 Characteristics of Innovative Firms

problems. As we have argued before, if strategic success were so simple, then it could be rapidly duplicated and any advantage competed away. In truth, the problem is more complex and usually involves creating an integrated, mutually supportive pattern that is self-reinforcing. Strategy needs to focus on the future, with changing rules of competition, with creating a competitive advantage, with developing industry leadership. But such a strategy is dependent on a culture of innovation within the firm, a willingness to take risks, an acceptance of failure. This in turn will be facilitated by the reward system in place: Is entrepreneurial behavior rewarded or not? What happens when failure occurs? Are people fired or does the firm learn from the experience? The firm also needs a structure that encourages innovation—not a highly formalized bureaucracy but rather a flexible and knowledge-based structure that can change rapidly to take advantage of opportunities.[12]

Types of Innovation

We think of innovation very broadly. Innovation can only be considered relative to the organization in which it occurs. Anything done for the first time by a particular firm is an innovation for that firm. Quite clearly then, what a firm considers to be innovative may not be considered so by its competitors, its customers, or its suppliers. Innovations that are new to a company, new to an industry, or new to the world are clearly very different in their implications, their risk, and their prospects of returns.

Much of the literature on innovation has focused on product innovation and creating new businesses. This is, of course, very important, and it tends to be somewhat easier to measure and track than other types of innovation. Nevertheless, other types of innovation are clearly important, and we have classified these into three categories: structural, organizational, and product/market scope, as shown in Figure 9.3, each of which we now explore.

Structural Innovation
Structural innovation refers to innovations that involve reshaping the structure of an industry, which may have vertical and/or horizontal dimensions. Reorganizing a supply chain into a novel constellation of partners would exemplify a structural innovation, and we are witnessing mammoth changes of this type as the information revolution unfolds. One driver of structural innovation is the interplay between the advantages of scale and specialization and the impact on these of developments in

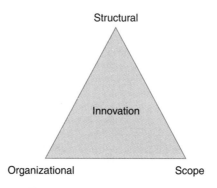

Figure 9.3 Types of Innovations

information technology.[13] Open architecture in computer systems can reduce transaction costs between firms, allowing firms to communicate more quickly and cheaply than before, with the possibility of outsourcing and disintermediation. Disintermediation is the partial or complete bypassing of a traditional channel member and has occurred or is presently occurring in industries as diverse as insurance, air travel, book-selling, and financial services. At the same time, new intermediaries have emerged, in a process referred to as **reintermediation.** The more successful dot.coms such as Yahoo! and eBay illustrate such changes. The growth of innovative outsourcing strategies represents further tangible evidence of the importance of structural innovation. In the auto industry, the Japanese producers have led the way toward using suppliers to deliver assembled modules (subassemblies) rather than discrete components, an innovation that has been an important contributor to the high levels of productivity that their plants have attained.

These supply-side innovations are increasingly mirrored by similar developments on the demand side. Much of Dell's success has been derived from its innovative system of working with customers to develop tailored offers. Co-development with lead airlines characterized Boeing's strategy for the 777, while retailer Wal-Mart engages in extensive data exchange with its suppliers, speeding supply and increasing the efficient management of working capital through faster inventory turns.

Yet another form of structural innovation is the development of new business models, with customers migrating from the old model to the new ones, which better satisfy the customer's important requirements.[14] Amazon could be seen as such an example, as were others discussed in Chapter 2.

The horizontal dimension of structural innovation refers to innovation at the same level in the supply chain. One of the most dramatic examples involves horizontal merger or acquisition, which changes the competitive structure of the industry. However, there are other horizontal maneuvers that must be classed as innovative yet fall short of such consolidation. The formation of an industry association, joint bargaining with unions, formation of R&D consortia, or the initiation of Japanese-style *keiretsu* or a Korean-style *chaebol* would all qualify on these terms.

Organizational Innovation

Examples of organizational innovation abound. Toyota's lean manufacturing system and the *kaizen* philosophy are Japanese contributions. Shewhart and Deming contributed seminally to the development of total quality management, General Electric invented "work-out," while the Boston Consulting Group contributed the experience curve and share/growth portfolios. It is difficult to ascribe credit for some of these innovations, but certainly CRM (customer relationship management), BPR (business process reengineering), and ERP (enterprise resource planning), aggressively marketed by various consultants, have had significant impact on the way organizations operate and assess themselves. Innovations in the organization of the firm also fall into this category. For example, Procter & Gamble's formation of customer-based business groups with their own bottom line was widely publicized, while many other companies have turned to forms of customer-based management, ranging from the basic adoption of key account teams all the way to full-fledged business groups of the P&G type. Other forms of organizational innovation include the formation of networks, process management, the use of cross-functional teams, new incentive systems possibly based on economic value, matrix, and other organizational structures. Each of these innovations is expected to deliver some value to the firm, but not all will lead to a sustained competitive advantage since they may be copied by competitors.

Business Scope Innovation

Our third classification is the one that most people think of when they consider innovation: Does the firm innovate by developing business units that cater to the needs of new markets or that represent completely new product groups? These new products may be either *new to the firm* or *new to the world*. When Sony and Philips created the compact disc, they created a new-to-the-world product. Innovations more removed from the current business typically incur significantly more risk. If successful, however, they may afford much greater returns. Indeed, major increases in firm value come only from innovations that are new to the world. In terms of the risk profile described in Figure 8.14, these innovations are very risky but have a possibility of creating enormous value and wealth for the firm. Conversely, relatively modest extensions to the existing product line would not be expected to generate remarkable returns but should incur very modest levels of risk. Indeed, Kuczmarski argues that different discount rates should be used in financial modeling of these different types of innovation options for exactly this reason.[15]

The categories we have discussed so far are by no means discrete even though they do create an organizing framework. New businesses necessarily imply organizational innovation, while structural innovation will almost certainly involve business scope innovation as well as organizational innovation.

> This linkage between the different forms of innovation is illustrated by the actions of Dow in the United States. The firm wanted to alter its business portfolio to get away from basic chemicals (cyclical, capital-intensive, and extremely competitive) and move its portfolio toward specialty chemicals (R&D-intensive, higher margin, knowledge-intensive). To support this innovation in business scope, Dow created a growth culture, aligned rewards with growth, and increased decision-making speed—all examples of organizational innovation. It also developed new business models, based on changes in the value chain, which we would see as illustrations of structural innovation.[16]

⊚ 9.3 A FRAMEWORK FOR MANAGING THE DYNAMIC SCOPE OF A FIRM

We have emphasized that the challenge for any firm is to ensure that it continuously renews and reinvents itself. Firms generally start with a single product line, which eventually becomes mature. Since growth and survival are two of the core objectives of the firm, mature and declining products or businesses must be replaced with new ones. As discussed in Chapter 2, the management challenge can be expressed as asking:

How does the firm manage its existing businesses efficiently?

How does the firm ensure growth with these businesses?

How does the firm develop new businesses?

All must be done at the same time, while creating value as an entity.

The typical multidivisional firm has a mix of business units, and the challenge for corporate management is to create the organizational arrangements and processes to encourage continual innovation. We regard this task—developing new business units—as critical for the prosperity and survival of the modern firm. Such innovation will both occur within the existing paradigm and expand the boundaries of the firm in response the change from within and outside the firm. In the longer term, strategic management recognizes that everything is variable: a firm can change any attribute—its technology, its culture, its product/market scope—to develop fundamentally different and new lines of business.

TABLE 9.1   Acquisitions and Divestments by European Firms, 1987–1993

Selected Firms Ranked by the Number of Acquisitions	Selected Firms Ranked by the Number of Divestments
Unilever (79)	Hanson (64)
Elf Aquitane (71)	BP (55)
Asea Brown Boveri (60)	ICI (52)
Grand Metropolitan (54)	Grand Metropolitan (44)
Siemens (51)	Unilever (35)
Fiat (46)	du Pont (35)

Source: G. Vitali, "Acquisition Strategy of the Top EU Leader Companies," Paper presented at the 25th E.A.R.I.E. Conference, Copenhagen, August 1998.

Some firms are very active in managing their business portfolio over time, as is clear from Table 9.1. Over the time period 1987–1993, Grand Metropolitan (now Diageo) sold 44 businesses and acquired 54. Unilever, often seen as primarily concerned with internal development, acquired 79 businesses and divested 35 others. As is clear, these leading EU firms have an active and aggressive portfolio management process, actively acquiring and divesting business units to ensure that their portfolio is appropriate to their resources and circumstances.

This need to manage the present and the future at the same time has been explored from a different perspective by Baghai, who recommends that a firm have a portfolio of businesses with different growth horizons, with the individual businesses classified in terms of their maturity.[17] The firm needs to maintain a continuous *pipeline* of business-building initiatives, since existing businesses will eventually fail. Businesses grow, mature, and decline; as they mature, we need a stream of others to take their place. Such a dynamic portfolio is illustrated in Figure 9.4.

Horizon 1 businesses are the current core businesses of the firm, which are generally mature. These businesses generate the cash and skills that provide the

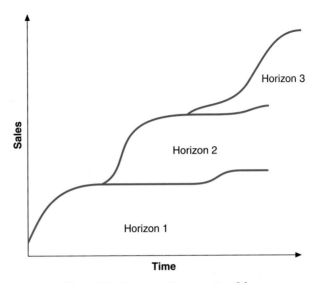

Figure 9.4   Dynamic Business Portfolio

resources for growth. In terms of Chapter 8's portfolio discussion, these are the cash cow businesses of the firm. The continuing ability of these businesses to generate cash is essential to the continued growth of the firm. Managers must ask: Are these businesses earning enough to allow us to invest in growth? What changes could affect our cost structure? Are we losing market share to competitors, direct or indirect? Are substitutes likely to be a major threat? Are the rules of competition changing due, for example, to government actions?

Horizon 2 businesses are emergent businesses—new ventures in which growth is accelerating. They can transform the firm but are likely to require considerable investment. Important questions for corporate managers are: Do we have new businesses capable of creating as much economic value as the current ones? Are they growing? Can we make the required investments? Do we have the entrepreneurial talent to manage these ventures?

Horizon 3 businesses are in the embryonic stage of the life cycle: they are real activities and investments, however small. They are the businesses that will secure the firm's longer-term future. These will be nonexistent unless senior management spends time reflecting about future growth opportunities. The pressure for short-term results is such that even senior managers may neglect the longer-term. Horizon 3 businesses require creativity as well as commitment. Generating the future requires foresight as well as resources!

The Baghai model suggests that firms need to commit to a series of business innovations and to build new competences to identify and exploit such opportunities. One relevant competence is the skills required to enable growth. For example, acquisition skills as well as postmerger and risk management abilities are likely to be crucial, since Horizon 3 businesses involve high risk. Throughout, noncritical competences can be outsourced, but the firm must develop and retain core competences since these determine how much of the future value is captured by the firm.

Management often needs to run Horizon 3 businesses with very different structures, incentives, and planning systems, indicating the interplay between the different types of innovation. Such growth can be stimulating for staff, providing new opportunities for them as well as shareholders. For example, spinouts may be used to encourage entrepreneurial behavior, though there may be consequent problems of autonomy and control. Many firms also encourage active adaptation: early development and launch, coupled with active feedback and learning, with flexibility to change as circumstances require.

> In the past, IBM has missed out on new technologies and new opportunities. The company has changed the way it identifies and pursues promising new ideas that may conflict with existing business units or fall between established organizational boundaries. They are managed as "Horizon Three" businesses separate from the rest of the organization. (Horizon One businesses are mature businesses like mainframe computers, and Horizon Two businesses are current growth businesses.) Horizon Three businesses are located in separate organizational units, with dedicated teams of managers. They are insulated from the company's established management methods and performance yardsticks, and they get personal sponsorship from a senior executive, to overcome resistance from middle management.[18]

A considerable number of new business initiatives will usually be required, since most will not grow to become successful businesses. The cost of development may be too high, or the environment may change in such a way that the development no longer makes sense.

Microsoft bets on several (competing) developments at the same time, whenever there is uncertainty about how the world will develop. Taking a stake, often through alliances, in several developments at the same time illustrates using real options as a hedge.

Developing the new clearly has associated risks. However, there is also a very real risk of inaction, namely, that the current business will either see substitutes develop or see its competitive position challenged so that it ceases to create and capture value. This creative destruction is a characteristic of competitive markets and can be seen in many product areas, such as when CDs replaced vinyl records, when full-service stock brokering was challenged by online brokering, or when letters were replaced by e-mail.

Of course, companies may focus too much on core businesses and lose the right to grow, or be under siege and therefore not have the resources to grow. Yet we must also recognize that profitable growth is exciting for staff and also creates shareholder value and employment.

The ability to create a continuous pipeline of new businesses representing new sources of profit distinguishes corporations that continue to grow. These exemplary performers can innovate in their core businesses and build new ones at the same time. Building and managing a continuous pipeline of business creation is the central challenge of sustained growth. Yet according to Baghai, companies boasting pipelines are the exception. Performance metrics rarely reflect the growth horizon of each business segment, yet if a firm relies on one management system across its entire organization, it tacitly assumes that all parts of the organization have similar management needs, which is patently ridiculous.[19]

This framework expresses the idea that the firm has a "staircase" of continuously expanding businesses, each of which requires new competences and skills. Since the future cannot be predicted, the firm needs to build new competences that create future options and opportunities. As new competences are generated, new opportunities open up for the firm. In an intensely competitive world, the firm must move quickly to exploit these opportunities before competitors enter or conditions change again.[20]

At the business-unit level, we need to recognize that each strategic business unit (SBU) must be managed differently. Each must develop strategy and processes appropriate to its unique characteristics. The corporate task is to ensure that its portfolio of businesses is being continually renewed. This is an ongoing task and has to be sequenced properly. Innovation costs money, time, and management resources, and the firm needs to decide to reallocate these from current businesses and apply them to developing the new. Shareholders interests are jeopardized if the parent waits until current businesses are almost gone before developing new ones.

By considering the dynamic aspects of business development, we can also begin to develop some insight into the capabilities that will be required to support different growth alternatives. Clearly, expansion into related and new markets places a premium on market research and the development of new marketing competences. If, as has been the case for global multinationals, the path of market extension and expansion involves new-country markets, then country expertise becomes a sine qua non. In contrast, adoption of product/technology extension and expansion mandates competences in development or, in the case of new-to-the-world products, perhaps in more basic research.

Means for Changing Scope

Firms have a number of choices about the strategy they pursue in terms of changing their scope over time. Two major alternatives are *internal development* and *mergers and acquisitions.* These two are seen as complementary; a firm is likely to adopt both simultaneously, although some firms have a predilection toward one more than the other. For many firms internal R&D will not create all the innovation required and other approaches are necessary. Since the future is unpredictable, many firms choose alliances, networks, and joint ventures to develop new lines of business. As the firm enters into new areas, each with a required set of competences, it generally also withdraws from existing areas through restructuring and spinouts. This dynamic approach to the business portfolio ensures that the firm continues to create value.

> The evolving strategy of Nestlé, the Swiss food company, illustrates this combined approach. Nestlé was founded in 1866 and by 2002 had revenue of $USB50 with pre-tax net profits of $USB5.5. Historically, substantial growth has been accomplished by internal development, by developing new products and businesses through extensive R&D. At the same time, over the period 1985 to 2000 it spent $USB26 on acquisitions, since organic growth in its established businesses had slowed. Its recent acquisitions have been in faster-growing markets such as pet foods and ice cream, with purchases of Haagen Dazs and Dreyers in the United States and Schoellers in Germany. In 2001 it spent $USB10.3 purchasing Ralston Purina in the United States.[21]

While we will shortly discuss these alternatives in more detail, the broad characteristics of each should be highlighted. Acquisitions are a fast means of changing scope; they can result in a new business being added to the portfolio in a matter of months. At the same time, the success rate of acquisitions is very low—only about 25% of them seem to add value to the acquirer. One reason for this low success rate is the premium firms pay for the target, meaning that it is difficult for the combined entity to achieve the required returns. The other reason is postacquisition problems, particularly the difficulty of merging corporate cultures. By contrast, internal development takes more time, requires the firm to develop a range of new skills and competences, yet is likely to overcome any cultural problems.

❺ 9.4 MANAGING THE CHANGING SCOPE—INTERNAL DEVELOPMENT

This method of achieving growth is widespread among major corporations. They recognize that technological innovation is central to improving productivity, developing new businesses, and generating sustained long-term value. High levels of R&D expenditure characterize these firms, leading to the development of new products and services. They also recognize that innovation requires commercialization. There is little value in inventing something that is never commercialized. Superior technology by itself is not sufficient for a successful business. Technology leaders are proficient at understanding changing customer needs, technological developments, and the strategies of both direct and indirect competitors to ensure that their leadership position is maintained. du Pont illustrates this approach to innovation, although its approach has evolved to give more attention to changing customer needs.

> du Pont spends about $USB2 per year to develop innovative products, unique technology, and new intellectual assets, with a research group of 1500 professionals. In 1998 the firm changed its approach toward R&D. Historically, R&D was meant to provide discoveries that du Pont could then commercialize. Since 1998, all research proposals are evaluated and selected on the basis of their technical and business case, a more market-based approach.[22]

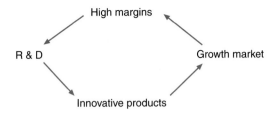

Figure 9.5 Virtuous Development Cycle

    Firms active in R&D attempt to create a virtuous circle, as shown in Figure 9.5. These firms use their high margins to invest in R&D to develop innovative products, which have high growth rates and margins, which in turn support a further cycle of R&D. Such leaders are close to markets, ensuring that technology is used to create new products that customers require, with a substantial advantage over current products. These firms attempt to maintain industry leadership through their development and use of technology. Indeed, the evidence suggests a strong positive relationship between R&D spending and corporate profitability.[23]

    Internal development has several advantages. First, and most important, everything is done in-house. As such, the firm has—in theory—total control over the entire growth process. Required resources are purchased/leased by the firm; it makes its own decisions on interorganizational relationships, such as those with suppliers and distributors; and shortfalls in human resources are dealt with by hiring to requirements and acculturating newcomers to the firm's way of doing business. Second, while alternative means of securing product/market access—for example, by acquisition—are available, internal development may be less expensive.

    The major disadvantages of internal development are timing and resource access. Internal development takes time. In an era in which market windows are shortening, in-house development may be a luxury the firm cannot always afford. Furthermore, at the limit, some required resources may just be unavailable to the firm or may be too expensive and/or too risky for the firm to develop on its own. These problems are leading firms to take a more holistic view of the growth process and to consider other mechanisms, such as acquisition and strategic alliances, to complement internal development growth strategies.

Technological Innovation

Figure 9.6 indicates the important issues to be considered in technological innovation.

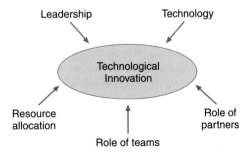

Figure 9.6 Issues in Technological Innovation

Source: Adapted from P. S. Cohan, *The Technology Leaders* (San Francisco: Jossey-Bass, 1997).

Technology Strategy

Technological innovation by the firm must be linked to the overall strategy adopted, and doing so involves a number of more specific considerations. First, the firm needs be able to define, develop, and utilize those technological competences that contribute to its competitive advantage. This will generally include decisions on which technology areas to explore and how these may change over time.

Technology leaders also have a deep understanding of the relationship between technological parameters and customer requirements, as discussed in Chapter 3. They understand the customer benefits that result from given improvements in technical product attributes.

From a managerial perspective, technology strategy also includes decisions on whether or not R&D will be *centralized,* in other words, which R&D projects will be done at the corporate level and which in the business units. This decision will reflect any economies of scale in R&D, since if these are strong, research is likely to be centralized.[24] The firm also must also decide on the R&D time span: Will it engage in primarily short-term development research, or will it engage in more basic long-term research, or what will be the mix between these?

Commercialization options must also be evaluated. Will the firm develop and sell the new products, license the technology to other firms, or sell the intellectual property represented by the innovation to other firms? We must also decide whether to patent the innovation. Patents give the firm some protection but reveal the innovation to competitors.

Commercialization must be the long-term goal of any R&D undertaken by the firm. For many firms, this last step has proved to be difficult, with many firms unable to commercialize their technological innovation so that the benefits accrue to the firm's competitors.

Technology Limits   Developing the firm's technology strategy also requires an understanding of the relationship between research effort and research output. As shown in Figure 9.7, this relationship generally follows an S-shaped curve. Initially, research effort results in small improvements in performance. Following this period, there are typically large increases in the performance measure for relatively small inputs in the research effort. Finally, the technology reaches a plateau where only small improvements are obtained even for large increases in research effort.[25] Recognizing these relationships is critical in developing R&D strategy, as they indicate when the research thrust needs to be altered. A product becomes a commodity within a market segment when all avenues for development are exhausted, when market requirements on each attribute of performance have been completely satisfied by more than one—often many—available products. As a given technology reaches its limit, the basis of competition typically changes and price competition becomes more intense.

Figure 9.7 indicates that when one technology, referred to in the figure as technology A, is reaching the limits of its performance, a different technology is often developing, one which has the potential to substantially improve the performance parameter. A well-known example of this would be when jet engines replaced piston-driven planes on commercial aircraft. No matter how much was spent to improve the speed of planes driven by propellers, there was a limit to the speed that could be attained. The only way to increase plane speed was to develop new technology—in this case, jet engines. As funds were invested in this new technology, plane speeds increased dramatically, again reaching a limit that called for another technology if speeds were to increase further.

Sustaining and Disruptive Technological Change   Christensen has extended our understanding of technical innovation with his distinction between sustaining technolo-

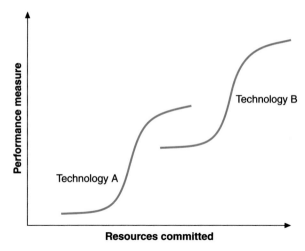

Figure 9.7   S-Curves for Two Technologies

gies and disruptive technological change.[26] **Sustaining** technological change improves the performance of established products along the dimensions of performance that mainstream customers in major markets have historically valued. **Disruptive** technological changes bring new and very different value propositions to the market place.

Christensen's research indicates that sustaining technological changes rarely result in the failure of established firms, since they find it easy to keep up. No modifications of managers' mental maps are required to appreciate the benefits of these changes. In contrast, disruptive changes often precipitate the failure of leading firms. Products based on these disruptive changes are often initially inferior, with features that appeal to new, not current, customers. They may be cheaper or even more expensive, but they frequently possess new kinds of functionality, for example, being smaller, faster, or easier to use. Because they are still under rapid development, however, their functionality improves rapidly until they challenge industry incumbents.

> Electronic share trading was not a major concern of many investors; they were happy with the concept of financial advisers. In addition, the margins on electronic trading were thin, and initially the market was quite small. So why would a stockbroker with a well-established business in providing advice on shares to its customers develop such a risky new technology, which few of its current customers would value?

As this example illustrates, it sometimes does not appear rational to invest in these disruptive technologies, for markets that do not exist cannot be analyzed. Further, these new technologies may reduce margins and are not desired by current lead customers. For this reason, firms external to an existing industry often develop such disruptive technologies.

The typical sequence is that a new technology, generally inferior to the established technology, finds limited application in some market segments that value the new benefit. The new technology then generally expands its market until it can successfully challenge, and possibly supplant, the existing technology.

Christensen also suggests that many of the incumbents' management practices make it difficult for them to develop these disruptive technologies. Firms currently seen as well managed have systems to ensure they listen to current customers, usually meaning they develop products with greater functionality using known technology. They find it difficult to allocate resources to R&D proposals that propose to develop products that current customers do not value, that offer lower margins, that have inferior performance parameters, and that can only be sold in small niche markets.

Leadership

A strategy of technological innovation requires leadership. Managers must understand those technologies important to the business. This understanding need not be in fine detail, but it is necessary at a broader level in order to decide which research projects to select. Managers need to understand customer requirements and how technological parameters relate to these. Thus leaders understand both technology and business: they recognize the importance of technology and at the same time realize that technological innovation must result in measurable business outcomes.

Leaders also realize that technological innovation is inherently difficult to manage; it is messy and rarely develops in a neat, logical manner. Instead, it is full of twists and turns, with many unpredictable events. Any major R&D program will have several sources of risk, such as the following:

Technological risk: How will this new technology develop?

Market risk: Is there a demand for the products and services that are expected to be developed?

Business risk: What investment in people and capital will be required?

Each of these risks must be understood and considered. Further, astute managers understand the need to employ good researchers, to keep the firm flexible, and to work at influencing or controlling industry standards in pursuit of their corporate goals.

Role of Partners

Firms on the forefront of technological innovation may not be able to develop all the required technology in-house. While they may be committed to internal development, with the high R&D expenditure that implies, they also realize that acquisitions and alliances may be required to stay ahead of competition.

This cooperative approach also arises from the *systemic* nature of many innovations, whereby an innovation must be embedded in a total system. For example, a computer is comprised of a central processing unit, an operating system, applications software, memory chips, power supplies, and communication devices. Innovation in any one of these elements must be consistent with, and integrated with, all the other elements. Modern technological innovation frequently requires that the firm collaborate and cooperate with others—hence the rise of networks. These require open communication with a number of firms, some of which may be direct competitors. As we saw in Chapter 3, the firm may be a member of various networks that allow the complementary competences of the different firms to be utilized.

It may also be the case that the firm will engage in a number of competing developments at the same time. As noted, Microsoft participates in many competing innovations when there is uncertainty as to which will ultimately win, an example of the firm taking out options on the various technologies.

Role of Teams

Technological innovation also requires that the firm eliminate boundaries between different groups within the firm. Innovation typically involves the use of *cross-functional* teams. Since many innovations also come from lead customers, innovation also requires close cooperation and input from such customers.

Since technological innovation is difficult, success requires specific human resource approaches. The best people need to be identified and recruited. The firm culture must encourage experimentation and risk taking, and incentives must support such a culture. In particular, the firm culture should not blindly resist cannibalization. This has been a major problem for numerous firms that have not supported new technologies because they promise to make existing products obsolete. In the longer term, it is usually better to make our own products obsolete than delay and let our competitors do this for us!

Resource Allocation

The CEO must play an active role in selecting the technologies that the firm is attempting to develop, ensuring that resources are allocated in accordance with the desired research portfolio. This requires scanning for new technologies and understanding which technologies are reaching their limits, which are likely to threaten existing technology, and which promise to deliver additional value to customers.

A specific tool that may be used to allocate resources is a matrix approach, similar to those discussed in Chapter 8, in which R&D projects are assessed on the basis of two dimensions:

The profit potential if the innovation is successful

The competitive position of the firm in this technology

Projects that score highly on each dimension are supported. Risk may be incorporated as a third dimension, or another portfolio of the risk and expected return from the research could be developed, recognizing the necessity to achieve a balance between these.

In summary, a firm active in R&D will have a range of projects that can be assessed on many dimensions. Some projects may involve basic research; others will be more developmental in nature. What it needs is a balance of projects, aligned with its corporate strategy and reflecting the culture of the firm.

9.5 MANAGING THE CHANGE OF SCOPE—MERGERS AND ACQUISITIONS

Mergers and acquisitions are a favored method of growth for many companies and an integral element in corporate strategy. Factors contributing to the increase in mergers and acquisitions are the ready availability of capital, globalization and the associated easing of regulatory regimes, and, finally, managerial motives—the desire of managers to grow their firms. We must emphasize that mergers and acquisitions are not solely financial issues—their success or otherwise is strongly influenced by behavioral issues, such as the merging of different corporate cultures and power conflicts between different managerial groups.

The terms *merger* and *acquisition* are often used interchangeably, and they do have some features in common. They are legal transactions, and appropriate legislation must be understood, whether in the country in which the planned merger is to take place or other countries. As we saw earlier, despite the fact that both GE and Honeywell are U.S. firms, regulators from the European Union blocked a merger between them.

An **acquisition** occurs when one firm, the acquirer, purchases a controlling interest in another firm, the target firm. An acquisition normally involves discussions with the management and board of the target, and when agreement is reached, the target's shareholders vote on the proposal. An acquisition can be friendly, when it is supported by the target firm's management, or hostile, when it is not supported. A takeover is normally an unsolicited acquisition bid, whereby the acquirer makes a direct appeal to the target's shareholders. Acquisitions can also be described as related or unrelated and as horizontal or vertical.

The acquisition may be of an entire corporate entity or of an individual business unit. The acquiring firm secures not only the target firm's product/market and technology portfolios but also its organizational structure, human resources, competences, and systems. It is the postacquisition integration of these that often causes difficulty.

A **merger** occurs when two firms agree to integrate operations on a friendly basis and agree to have virtually equal stakes in each other's businesses. Again, the bidder negotiates an agreement with management, which then submits the proposal to a vote by shareholders.

The majority of acquisitions do not produce a positive return to the shareholders of the acquiring firm, due either to the substantial premium over the current share price that is paid or to difficulties with postmerger integration. It has been estimated that some 75% of acquisitions fail essentially for one of these two reasons.[27]

> Discussing the resignation of the CEO of the British-Dutch steel firm Corus, analysts argued that the merger had been "beset with problems," producing four consecutive years of losses. They alleged that the merger had "simmering issues that just haven't gone away." British Steel, which had bought Royal Hoogovens, the other partner, "paid a premium and behaved as though they had paid a premium," said one analyst, suggesting that "post-merger integration was a sore point."[28]

When a firm acquires the assets and technologies of another firm, the acquirer generally has to pay a **premium** over the stand-alone market value of the target, reflected in the current share price of the target. Due to this premium, the acquiring firm finds it difficult to earn the margins required to make the purchase profitable for shareholders. Acquiring managers often make optimistic future earnings projections, overestimate cost reductions, and misjudge customers' attitudes toward the acquisition. Far too often, it proves impossible to marry the cultures of the two entities, leading to internecine warfare and/or future divorce. Further, it is not uncommon for senior managers in the acquired firm to leave, leading to a substantial loss of knowledge.

When considering a possible merger or acquisition, we need to address how the *competitive position* of the acquiring firm, or the target, will be affected by the acquisition. Since competition occurs primarily at the business-unit level, the competitive position of one of the entities should be improved, either through cost reductions or the transfer of competences from one to the other. The acquiring firm should manage the target better, bring some added benefits to the target, or bring benefits from the target to the acquiring firm. The acquiring firm must also be wary of unsustainable levels of leverage if debt financed the acquisition.

It is frequently alleged that big acquisitions are more difficult to implement than smaller ones. A strategy of many small acquisitions may provide higher returns than fewer large acquisitions. Growth strategies involving many small acquisitions may not make headlines but may be quite effective. For example, Microsoft, an organization with significant commitment to internal development, is nonetheless a very active acquirer.

One reason for the apparent success of many small acquisitions may be that the firm gains considerable expertise over time, lowering acquisition costs and improving effectiveness from identification all the way through to integrating into the acquired firm. Furthermore, market imperfections are more likely in the market for small acquisitions. Large acquisitions are usually highly publicized, and the acquiring firm is more likely to pay a proportionately higher price.

Mergers and acquisitions are corporate resource decisions that can quickly change the value of a firm, positively or negatively. All too often, shareholders of acquiring firms lose while those of targets win. Acquisitions are an unpredictable high-stakes game, a mixture of planning and opportunistic behavior on the part of the acquirer. They are often conducted under considerable time pressure as a candidate comes into play and other firms get interested. As we saw at the beginning of this chapter, after William Morrison made a play for Safeway in the United Kingdom, a

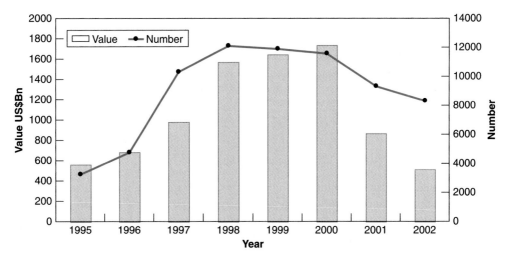

Figure 9.8 Number and Value of North American M&A Activity
Source: Reproduced by permission of Dealogic, London (2003)

number of other firms entered with competitive bids within a few weeks. Managers can easily get caught up in the excitement of the bidding process, losing sight of their original objectives. With such rapid change, detailed analysis may not be possible, particularly an analysis of how the two entities will be integrated and the human problems with the planned merger.

Size and Frequency of Mergers and Acquisitions

Aggregate merger and acquisition behavior shows considerable variation, with some periods of sustained activity followed by more benign periods, as shown in Figure 9.8.

As can be seen, the late 1990s and early 2000s were periods of intense activity, with the total value of U.S. mergers and acquisitions reaching $USB1,740 in 2000. By 2002, it had fallen away to just $USB515. Such a pattern is also true for Europe, as is shown in Figure 9.9.

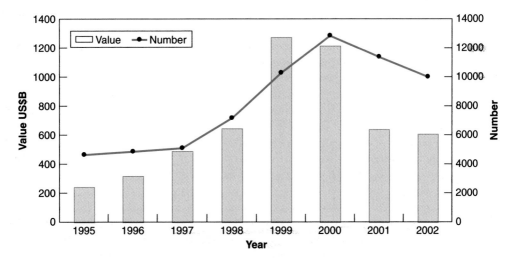

Figure 9.9 European Mergers and Acquisitions
Source: Reproduced by permission of Dealogic, London (2003)

Drivers of Mergers and Acquisitions

Mergers and acquisitions are a very common method adopted by firms to increase growth rates. They seem to be driven by a number of factors, not all of which are to the benefit of the shareholders of the acquiring firm.

Scale

A major rationale for mergers and acquisitions is the need to achieve scale economies. Thus when Hewlett-Packard and Compaq were considering their merger, they expected to achieve cost benefits of $USB2.5 by combining their previously separate operations. This driver is particularly important in mature markets, where firms achieve growth through acquisitions, thereby gaining market share and the ability to leverage their individual operations. Acquisitions are a commonly used method to become global, with a firm acquiring a small firm in the same industry in a new geographic area. Acquisitions may overcome entry barriers, although the premium can be considered such a barrier.

Competences

Through acquisitions, a firm can buy particular competences to augment its own. These may include an infusion of talent as well as new products, access to new and better distribution channels, and access to a new customer base.

Diversification

Acquisitions are a potentially useful way to diversify. They are quick, overcome entry barriers, and are generally lower-risk than internal development. While, as noted above, horizontal acquisitions are a common means of increasing the firm's growth rate, related acquisitions are a useful means of diversifying. When there are barriers to organic growth due to market saturation, diversification into new areas via acquisition is common, assisted by the ease with which finance can be obtained.

Management Ego

The other significant reason for acquisitions is management ego, reflecting the desire of managers to manage larger firms and the ego boost they get from making a major acquisition.[29]

Success of Mergers and Acquisitions

Despite the great popularity of mergers and acquisitions with managers, the evidence of their success is mixed. Acquisitions generally fail to yield returns to the shareholders of the acquirer.[30] All the benefits appear to flow to one of two parties: the shareholders of the acquired firm (from the premium that is paid) and the managers of the acquiring firm (they get a larger firm to manage). In 2001 a KPMG survey reported that 70% of the combinations studied failed to add value.[31]

Business leaders, as well as scholars, have spoken out against acquisitions. For example, George Bull (former CEO of Grand Metropolitan, now Diageo) asserted that organic growth (internal development) creates value for shareholders but that acquisition destroys value.

In mid-1997, drug company Eli Lilly reduced the accounting (book) value of its drug distribution arm, McKesson, by $USB2.4, over half the $USB4.1 acquisition price, a stark admission that it had overpaid.[32]

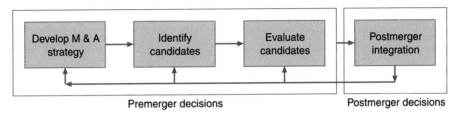

Figure 9.10   The Merger and Acquisition Process.

According to McKinsey, mergers often fail because revenue stalls. Only 12% of firms they studied accelerated sales growth in the three years after merging. Mergers create uncertainty, salespeople are targeted by competitors, redundancies damage morale, and managers become concerned with infighting, not running the business. Prior to the HP–Compaq merger, observers forecast sales declines of 15%, or $USB13![33]

Process Model of Mergers and Acquisitions

Need for a Process
Managers often see acquisitions and their integration as isolated events, not a process that can be improved. But for many firms, acquisitions are a normal part of their business. As seen in Table 9.1, for many European firms, mergers and acquisitions are a normal element in their corporate strategy. Similarly, GE Capital Services made more than 100 acquisitions between 1953 and 1998. Firms for which acquisitions are a key element of corporate strategy attempt to make acquisition selection and integration a core competence, a process that they can continually improve. Our recommended process is shown in Figure 9.10, which we now discuss in more detail. The process is split into two broad decision areas, pre- and postmerger. The process is shown as linear, but in reality it is an iterative, not linear, set of decisions.

Developing the Merger and Acquisition Strategy
Acquisitions based on an underlying strategy are more likely to succeed than those resulting from opportunistic reactions to the emergence of candidates. In far too many companies, these decisions are sporadic and different from normal experience. They are done with limited access to information and staff participation due to the need for secrecy.

The first step is to establish the strategy behind the merger or acquisition and determine responsibility for the process. There should be a good understanding of what the acquisition is expected to accomplish and the rationale behind the strategy. The acquiring management should provide a compelling reason for the acquisition and an explanation of how the acquisition will support their firm's strategy. Such an acquisition strategy should also state a vision for the combined entity. Such a vision helps to get employees of the target firm on board. Acquisitions can both reinforce and change a firm's direction, and the acquirer needs to be clear on what is expected.

Acquisitions create value when they enhance the capabilities of the combined firms. Managers must balance the need for autonomy of the acquired firm with the need to transfer capabilities between the two.

Developing an acquisition strategy also requires recognizing that different types of acquisitions can make very different contributions to the firm's renewal, as described below:[34]

- Deepen the firm's presence in its existing domain. This may result from the recognition of the need to strengthen its position in the industry, the possible need to deal with overcapacity in the industry, and the need to consolidate. The acquiring firm uses the acquisition to become more efficient, reducing costs through economies of scale. Alternatively, the acquirer may take the initiative in combining firms in a fragmented industry, again searching for economies of scale. These are often one-time opportunities and are difficult to do successfully since the firm has little experience.

- Broaden the firm's domain in terms of products, markets, or capabilities. This is often the basis for cross-border acquisitions, taking the firm into new geographic markets. Such acquisitions generally involve major cultural differences between the two firms, and here a history of successful acquisitions will help. Such acquisitions may also be a substitute for internal R&D.

- Bring the firm into new domains. Through the acquisition, the firm moves into new businesses that require new capabilities. Such an acquisition may substitute for internal R&D. Alternatively, it may reflect the belief of managers that industry convergence is occurring, and the acquirer puts together a combination of firms from those existing industries whose boundaries are eroding. Such a move may also reflect concern with the long-term situation in the firm's current domain and the need to find a new domain.

Acquisitions within the same industry offer the greatest scope for reducing costs, generating synergy between related products, achieving superior distribution by adding new products to established channels, and providing access to superior technology. When the acquisition involves an element of diversification, such synergies are more difficult to obtain. In these cases, we need to transfer competences between the firms. The less related the two businesses, the more difficult it may be to find competences that can be usefully transferred and shared.

Developing an acquisition strategy also involves establishing *responsibilities,* who is responsible for the entire decision-making process—the number of people involved, the speed, and the consideration given to strategic and organizational as well as financial issues. Any such process must involve senior management, but the team will involve many other staff members as well as external staff from consulting firms and advisers. Senior managers bring considerable experience and judgment to the process. Other staff bring a set of analytical skills, since considerable information on the target, its markets, and its performance must be analyzed. So we will need an acquisition team, and the responsibility of this team should be clear. This decision process should also give some consideration to the problems of integration—value is not created until after the acquisition, when capabilities are transferred and people collaborate to create the expected benefits.

Such a strategy statement should establish acquisition *criteria,* for example, what industry, what cost structure, what competences, what customers, and so on the target would ideally possess. Our view is that acquisitions, as with any decision of the firm, must create value for the firm as an economic entity. Mergers should be based on this as a principle, not on growth for its own sake. Acquisitions should be seen as a superior strategy to internal development in terms of cost, time, and ultimate performance. They should not be the means by which some managers preserve their jobs and get the opportunity to manage larger firms.

Identifying Candidates
The second step is to identify possible candidates, to make contact, and to undertake due diligence. The firm has already developed criteria for possible acquisitions that are

used to narrow the search for qualified candidates, including such characteristics as industry, size, geographic location, competitive strengths, management strengths, and price range. Possible candidates are then identified from trade lists and industry experts as well as banks and specialist merger advisers. Ranking these possible candidates is facilitated by a formal screening system, a weighting and rating scale.

Evaluating Candidates

Third, the firm must evaluate the candidate and negotiate the acquisition with the incumbent management as well as possibly with major shareholders in the target firm. At this stage it is also necessary to develop a price and guidelines for how the acquisition will be financed as well as what will be offered to the shareholders of the target firm, for example, cash, shares, or a combination of the two.

There is generally a courtship period during which the acquirer needs to build a compelling business case and create a constructive business relationship with the target as well as obtain support from major shareholders and other stakeholders—all under time pressure and in secrecy. This business case should be compelling and exciting, for otherwise little things can kill a merger. For example, European partners in a law firm are generally paid on the basis of seniority while partners in U.S. firms are paid on the basis of how much business they personally win for the firm. Any cross-border merger between law firms is likely to produce major tension within the combined firm. The location of the combined firm's head office or the choice of CEO of the combined entity could equally well cause difficulty. Regardless, it is important to contact the target firm and start the negotiation process.

Due Diligence   **Due diligence** includes an analysis of the financial strength, people, intellectual assets, environment, and operations of the seller. This provides the basis for making future forecasts as well as identifying any unknown legal or financial liabilities, or undervalued and overvalued assets. Such due diligence should also explore integration risks: How will this be done, what are the cultural risks, what are the differences? We know that postmerger integration is difficult, causing many mergers to fail, so there is a need to consider these issues early in the process. This indicates that the total acquisition process is iterative rather than linear.

Part of due diligence involves preliminary discussions with regulatory authorities and legal firms to identify potential obstacles. Any merger or acquisition must satisfy a number of legal constraints, and these get more complicated with the increasing size and global reach of the merger. There are also many accounting and tax issues to be resolved.[35]

Management must also decide how the acquisition will be structured and funded. Shareholders of the target firm may be offered cash or stock. With the latter, the acquiring firm buys the stock of the target with its own stock, which is especially advantageous if the acquirer has a high share price. Apart from the chance of some dilution in the value of these shares, however, the composition of the shareholder base then changes. Further, shareholders of the acquiring firm typically shy away from such dilution. Of course, an acquisition may be based on the understanding that the acquirer will sell some of the target's assets. If done well, these sales may finance a significant proportion of the acquisition cost.

A strong balance sheet aids the acquiring firm. In 1997, Apple had little cash and was under severe profit pressure. By 2000, the firm had $USB4 in cash, which gave it the option of pursuing acquisitions. Other firms divest part of their operations to provide the funds required for future acquisitions—reflecting a dynamic portfolio approach. On the other hand, if the firm is highly leveraged, additional debt to finance acquisitions will be difficult to arrange.

Synergy   The evaluation stage should also give consideration to the synergy in the proposed acquisition. **Synergy** is the increase in cash flows when the two firms are combined over what they would be expected to accomplish individually. Synergy results when the combination of various physical, financial, and intellectual assets is such that their value is greater than the sum of their individual worths. Assets might include brands, reputation, processes, and core competences as well as individuals with unique skills. However, no value is created without managerial actions and interactions between the firms. Synergy, if it is to occur, results from the transfer of capabilities between the firms and the improvement in the competitive position, and thus the performance, of the resulting combination.

Eccles suggests that there are five types of synergies:[36]

- *Cost savings:* These arise from eliminating jobs, facilities, and related expenses as well as economies of scale in purchasing. They are likely to be higher when the target is in the same industry in the same country.

- *Revenue enhancement:* Acquirer and target may achieve higher growth levels than if they stayed independent. Growth may arise from a larger customer base, but will they now buy from the combined firm?

- *Process improvement:* Managers can transfer best practices and core competences from one to the other, resulting in both revenue enhancement and cost reduction.

- *Financial engineering:* Management may refinance the debt of the target at the lower cost of the acquirer.

- *Tax benefits:* Management may be able to spread tax payments, pushing debt into high tax subsidiaries. This creates no improvement in competitive position.

In the majority of cases, acquiring firms pay a premium with respect to the share price of the target firm prior to any announcement of a takeover. The magnitude of this premium varies, but usually ranges from 30% to 50%, and it is paid up front, in expectation of future but uncertain cash flows. If we accept the efficient market hypothesis for a moment, then we have to conclude that the current share price of the target firm incorporates all the information available to financial markets about the value of the strategy of the firm, which leaves open an important question: How will the acquiring firm create value?

It is possible that financial markets are inefficient and undervalue the target firm. Thus the acquiring firm may see opportunities that financial markets do not. For example, the acquiring firm may see opportunities to generate additional value through the combination of the two firms, greater than either could generate individually, as discussed above.

The fact remains that managers who pay a premium commit themselves to delivering more than the market already expects from the strategy of the two firms. They must add value to the target in some way, making it more efficient with improved competitiveness. The magnitude of this additional value will depend on the characteristics of the acquirer and the target as well as management capabilities. Thus the same target will have different values for different acquiring firms.

In summary, we should remember that the onus—which is considerable—is on management to make an acquisition successful for the acquirer's shareholders. Shareholders can diversify their holdings at low cost, without paying the premium. Acquiring managers must see what the financial markets do not or the venture will join the estimated 70% to 80% that destroy shareholder value.

Valuing Acquisition Candidates

Valuing a potential acquisition requires calculating the net present value of future cash flows, discounted at the cost of capital, minus the investments made over time.

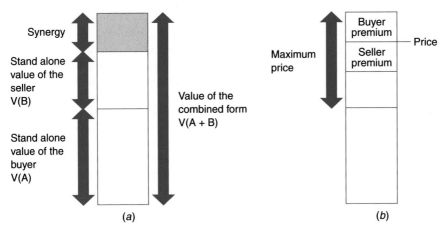

Figure 9.11 Valuing Acquisitions

Since any acquisition should involve some synergy, we need to estimate three terms:

V(A + B)—the net present value of the combined entity

V(A)—the net present value of firm A, the acquiring firm, without the acquisition

V(B)—the net present value of the acquired firm, without the acquisition

This gives us the situation shown in Figure 9.11.
With this formulation:

$$\text{Synergy} = V(A + B) - (V(A) + V(B))$$
(Synergy is the value of the combined firm
minus the value of the two firms independently.)

And the price should be between two limits:

$$\text{Lower limit for price} = V(A + B) - (V(A) + V(B))$$
(This is the lowest price at which the seller will sell, and at this price
the buyer captures all the synergy created by the acquisition.)

$$\text{Upper limit for price} = (V(A + B) - V(B))$$
(This is the highest price that the buyer will offer, and at this price the
seller captures all the synergy created by the acquisition.)

The price paid for the acquisition will reflect the relative negotiating power of the seller and the buyer and will vary with the nature of the buyer. Some firms will find greater value in a given target than others. Price will also depend on the position in the economic cycle, buyer and seller needs, and the state of financial markets.

> When the Air Touch share price was $US68, Bell Atlantic offered $US73, a 7% premium. Vodafone, a week later, offered $US89 and then a week after that got it for $US97 a share. For its shareholders to break even, Vodafone would have to find revenue generators and cost reductions of $USB20. But Air Touch offered greater synergies to Vodafone, in purchases and its European operations.[37]

How does the acquirer measure value? The recommended method of valuing a target firm is the present value of net cash flow over some horizon, where here cash flow is the free cash flow, net cash after all investments required to maintain the business being acquired. This analysis considers only operating cash flow; cash flow from nonoperating assets should be considered separately. Doing this calculation requires detailed estimates of future prospects for products and markets, cost structures, capital requirements, customers and competitors, and how they will respond to the acquisition as well as understanding of historical results.

The calculations involved in valuing an acquisition are illustrated with the example shown in Table 9.2. These calculations are for the value of the combined entity and thus contain certain synergies generated by the acquisition. They are also based on several assumptions regarding the performance of the combined firm, as detailed below. First, value is assumed to be given by the net present value of the entity over a defined time horizon plus the residual value of the entity after this time period.

The following has also been assumed:

In the base year of 2003, the combined revenue of the two firms would have been $10,000 and the net margin—defined as the ratio of earnings before interest, tax depreciation, and amortization—would have been 20%.

Due to postacquisition difficulties with the sales force and distributors, sales growth is assumed to be zero in year 1, then increase to 15% in years 2 and 3 as the benefits from the acquisition are felt, before falling away to zero as the firm reaches steady state. Similarly, the initial margin of 20% is assumed to reduce to 10% in year 1, reflecting restructuring costs, before increasing to 25% in year 3 as cost economies are achieved, and then reducing to the historical level of 20%.

It has also been assumed that the ratio of D/D + E is maintained at 50% and that new debt is issued by the combined firm to achieve an unchanged financial structure. The corporate tax rate is assumed to be 40%, while the WACC is 10%.

Given these assumptions and the use of the following formulas, the free cash flow of the combined firm can be calculated, over the five-year horizon, and each of these discounted back to the present. To this is added the terminal value of the combined firm.

TABLE 9.2   Calculation of the Value of a Combined Firm

Year	2003 Base	2004 1	2005 2	2006 3	2007 4	2008 5	2009 Terminal
Revenue ($)	10,000	10,000	11,500	13,225	14,548	15,275	15,275
EBITDA ($)	2,000	1,000	1,725	3,306	3,637	3,055	3,055
Capital ($)	5,000	5,300	5,670	6,103	6,693	7,423	8,081
Depreciation ($)	500	5330	567	610	669	742	808
Debt ($)	2,500	2,560	2,835	3,052	3,346	3,712	4,041
Interest ($)	225	239	255	275	301	334	363
EBT ($)	1,275	232	902	2421	2666	1,979	1,883
Net income ($)	765	139	542	1,453	1,600	1,187	1,130
Operating cash flow ($)	1,400	812	1,262	2,228	2,450	2,130	2,156
Free cash flow ($)	600	−138	62	778	750	430	986
Discount factor	1.0	0.909	0.826	0.683	0.467	0.218	0.047
PV of cash ($)	600	−125	51	531	350	94	

EBITDA = revenue × margin

EBITDA = earnings before interest, tax, depreciation, and amortization

Earning before tax = EBITDA − interest − depreciation

Net income = EBT (1.0 − tax rate)

Operating cash flow = NI + interest (1.0 − tax rate) + depreciation

Free cash flow = operating cash flow − increase in fixed and working capital

Terminal value = free cash flow at maturity/WACC

As can be seen from Table 9.2, the sum of the discounted free cash flows of the combined firm for the first five years is $US900. If we add to this the terminal value of the business, $US9,860 (986/0.1), we get a total value of the combined firm of $US10,760.

To provide estimates of the maximum and minimum price for the acquisition, as expressed in the above formulas, we then need to calculate the stand-alone values of each business.

The calculations above are not easy to undertake in practice since they require estimates of an uncertain future. Buyers may be too optimistic about revenues, profits, and cash flows, or expected cost savings may never eventuate. Competitive reaction may be misestimated, and so on. As a consequence, prudent buyers will use sensitivity analysis to look at alternative scenarios. A range of estimates of the impact of changes in firm growth, margins, expenses, capital expenditures, and discount rates can then be examined. The following example illustrates the difficulty in developing the precise value of an acquisition candidate.

> As has already been mentioned, IBM is moving out of technology into services. An element of this strategy was the purchase of PricewaterhouseCoopers Consulting in 2002 for $USB3.5. A few years previously, Hewlett-Packard had sought to buy the same consulting unit for $USB18.[38]

Other Methods of Evaluation The net book value (NBV) of the target's assets may be a consideration but is usually unhelpful. NBV is what was paid for assets, after deductions for depreciation, and is unlikely to reflect current value. NBV also ignores the value of intangible assets such as intellectual capital.

A more market-based method would be to offer a sum calculated by:

Price = P/E (for this type of firm) × E (of the target firm)

However, it is by no means clear that the P/E ratio chosen will be relevant to any specific firm. Further, not only are the earnings for just one year with no adjustment for risk (although this arguably may be reflected in P/E ratio used) but, as we have seen in recent years, accounting earnings are subject to considerable manipulation. Nonetheless, despite its weaknesses, a P/E value calculation is often used as a quick cross-check. These and other methods of valuing acquisition candidates are described in more specialized texts.[39]

Postmerger Integration

The acquiring firm needs to consider integration early in the process. What structure and reporting relationships will be adopted? How will the different firm cultures be integrated? How will the new arrangements be communicated to employees? What cross-business teams will be formed to work on business problems to assist in integration?[40]

Experience in mergers and acquisitions helps to facilitate postmerger integration, yet many managers have limited experience of this process. An acquisition can represent a huge change process, and there are many elements to consider, such as the following:

Redundancy: Will managers of the acquired firm be retained?

Job transfers: Will managers of the acquiring firm be transferred?

Restructuring: Should the organizational structure be altered?

Divestment: Should parts of the acquired firm be divested?

Cultural integration: How will this be accomplished?

Process integration: For example, how will the two accounting systems be integrated?

Postacquisition, there must be integration of what we refer to in Chapter 11 as organizational architecture as well as differing corporate cultures. Cultures involve a set of shared attitudes, values, beliefs, and customs—a set of basic assumptions (usually largely implicit)—that affect behavior. "The way things get done here" influences how managers behave as well as structure, systems, process, and style—that is, how the firm conducts business.

Acquiring management is often overconfident about the speed and ease with which they can achieve integration. Most firms find this an extremely difficult task, and it is the source of many failures. Although a compelling vision, fast transition, and effective planning assist integration, woe betide the acquiring management that assumes these problems away!

⊙ 9.6 MANAGING THE CHANGING SCOPE—HYBRID APPROACHES

Today there are many other alternatives to merger and acquisition as a method for altering the scope of a firm. These include strategic alliances, leveraged buyouts, joint ventures, licensing, technology purchase, and equity investment—alternatives that are not mutually exclusive but are part of a panoply of approaches that companies use to establish new businesses. Whereas some firms use several of these methods, others focus mainly on one or more implementation modes. We define various options, then explore their advantages and disadvantages.

Strategic Alliances

Sometimes a firm may be dissuaded from pursuing an opportunity because its managers conclude that they do not have the capabilities necessary to pursue the option. One way to secure these resources is via a **strategic alliance**, a partnership in which two firms combine capabilities to pursue mutual business interests. This partnership can be equity or non-equity (the latter is contractual). In general, the selection process for a strategic alliance partner involves matching strengths and weaknesses to provide the combined entity with a competitive advantage in the new business area. Partners should complement each other's strengths (or compensate for liabilities), not merely duplicate resources or capabilities.

Usually, however, alliances, unlike mergers, do not lead to cost reductions but instead offer revenue gains. Prototypical strategic alliances are between small, innovative firms with new technology and large firms with strong marketing capability, good reputations with customers, and financial resources. In some fields, the anticipated investment in potential new technology is so large and the risks so great that cooperation may be the only feasible way to pursue an opportunity. Strategic alliances also offer a way to dip your toe in the water with low risk, a valuable strategy in times of rapidly developing technology. They complement an outsourcing strategy, for if we retreat to our core business, we need many partners to fill noncore roles. They may also provide a way to extend geographically by forming an alliance with a local partner. Sometimes they can both complement resources and support geographic extension.

> Carlos Ghosn has been very successful at Nissan since Renault took a 36.8% stake. Losses of ¥B684 (or $USB6.1) for the year ended March 2000 were turned into a profit of ¥B331 in 2001, with operating margins improving to 4.75%, closer to the target of 8% by 2005. Ghosn formed cross-functional teams to break down barriers and get creativity, encouraging employees to take responsibility for outcomes. Nissan still has significant debts but at the time of writing appears to be much more successful than the DaimlerChrysler combination.[41]

Further, alliances have become much easier to run. Information technology, most notably the Internet, supports collaboration between companies at all levels, across time zones and geographies. Individuals can work remotely on joint teams and store information on common websites. Nonetheless, alliances still need trust, a clear set of goals, and good leadership.

In an increasingly turbulent environment, where knowledge of both specialized technologies and markets is essential for success, firms of widely different sizes and backgrounds should consider strategic alliances as one alternative method of implementing a growth strategy. However, although strategic alliances provide an attractive means of securing access to resources and reducing both risk and required investment, they are no panacea for firms implementing growth strategies. Many strategic alliances fail for reasons ranging from incompatible organizational cultures to a shift in focus by one of the partners, leading to a lessened interest in the strategic alliance.[42] A specific form of alliance is a joint venture in which two or more firms combine parts of their assets to form a jointly owned independent entity.

Licensing and Technology Purchase

Licensing and technology purchase are alternative methods of securing access to technology developed by other organizations. They differ both in terms of payment and in the extent of rights to use the technology. Typically, a **licensing agreement** specifies both a minimum royalty payment (fixed payment regardless of degree of use) and an earned royalty rate based on some measure of volume, for example, units, dollars, or profits. **Technology purchases** are typically arranged for a fixed sum. In both types of agreement, the firm secures access to the technology, but licensing agreements may constrain use by the buyer. For example, the licenser may restrict the licensee to certain markets, thus prohibiting access to other markets.

The main advantage of these two methods is that the acquiring firm avoids the risks and expense of the R&D effort that developed the technology. The disadvantage is that it may have to pay a high price for a successful technology. Firms adopting these practices need rigorous search processes to identify technologies that justify commercialization.

Equity Investment

Many major corporations have augmented their own R&D efforts by corporate venturing, taking ownership positions in startup companies. Here, again, the firm avoids direct R&D costs but has an equity position that it may be able to increase if the startup is successful.

Successful ventures are generally those that have a strong strategic rationale—where, for example, the technologies being investigated relate to the firm's own technology portfolio.

Consortia

Firms in Japan have historically engaged in joint development efforts, often supported by MITI. In the 1970s and early 1980s, when American and European firms were struggling to come to terms with the Japanese incursion, these consortia-based R&D efforts were viewed as key to Japanese success. In retrospect, other factors—such as emphasis on quality, customer focus, and efficient design and manufacture—were probably more important; today, MITI's attempts at industrial policy are viewed with much greater skepticism.

In Europe, such consortia were also accepted. Because of the huge cost of developing new commercial and military aircraft, collaboration among erstwhile competitors has become commonplace in the European aircraft industry. However, it was directly as a result of the Japanese onslaught that a concerted lobbying effort led to a relaxation of antitrust constraints on firm collaboration in the United States. The electronics industry was one of the first to engage in such a consortium-based effort, but in defense and aerospace such work is common; firms are now collaborating internationally when an innovation involves setting an industry standard.

Interestingly, the problems involved in standard setting provide excellent insight into the problems posed by consortia, for the seemingly interminable squabbling among participants often considerably delays the launch of an innovation. The arguments over DVD standards were protracted, as were those involving digital television, while—to the general detriment of consumers—in some cases no global standard was established. To state the problem simply, if you think it is difficult working in an alliance with one other firm, consider the potential problems in a consortium of many! Yet, despite these difficulties, some consortia succeed. Though controversial in American eyes, Airbus Industries, now to be separately constituted as a business, has a provided a series of competitive aircraft that none of the cooperating companies could have produced on their own.

Another form of consortia, discussed in Chapter 3, is the use of networks, where firms enter into collaborative arrangements with a number of other firms, including customers and possibly competitors, partly to supplement their limited competences and partly as a response to the high cost of new developments.

Option Buying

You may find it interesting to speculate on why, after decades of predominantly internally generated growth, the latter part of the 20th century witnessed such a proliferation of venture alternatives and a much broader perspective on admissible approaches within large companies. In our view, this is primarily due to much higher levels of uncertainty and risk. The structure of demand for innovative products has become more volatile. The much-heralded WAP phones collapsed, and at the time of writing, telecoms stocks were in a slump because of deepening concern over the slow pace of third-generation mobile deployment and an increasing fear that consumers won't be leaping joyfully into the new world of telecoms that was recently envisaged. Important technological flops of the last decade include CD-I (CD-interactive), DCC (digital compact cassette), DAT (digital audio tape), videophones, and many others. A second factor is the huge amounts of money required to deploy some of these technologies, for companies are understandably reluctant to put the company as a whole at risk to establish a new business.

One response to this change has been a very different philosophy with respect to the development of new business opportunities. The plethora of approaches now considered may be viewed as a way of buying options. If a given venture is risky and expensive, then perhaps we should be participating in a number of them, sharing the risk with others faced with a similar predicament, but thereby obtaining options to subsequently launch the successful few out of a portfolio of these risky and expensive ventures. The philosophy now needed is much closer to that of the venture capitalist, a factor that has had a major impact on the way large firms have approached the new business problem.

⦿ 9.7 MANAGING THE CHANGING SCOPE—DIVESTMENTS, SPINOFFS, AND RESTRUCTURING

As we saw earlier, firms actively manage their business portfolio, both acquiring and divesting businesses to reflect changing circumstances. Sometimes these changes, (particularly divestments) are forced on the firm by financial markets. In other cases, the firm takes the lead in altering its portfolio, usually reducing diversity and refocusing on a core business.

> Several Japanese electronics conglomerates are trying to reduce their scope. Currently they are vertically integrated, doing everything from making the chips to designing, building, and marketing the computers, cell phones, and so on that use them. Now Mitsubishi has announced it will stop making dynamic random-access memory chips, while Fujitsu is expanding its alliance with Siemens to share costs in the computer business. More specialized competitors such as Sony and Panasonic are doing better.[43]

Divestments and Spinoffs

A **divestment** occurs when a firm sells part of its ongoing business to another party. The firm may offer an **equity carve-out,** whereby it offers a minority position in a subsidiary through an initial public offering (IPO).

> du Pont raised $USB4.2 when it offered investors a 30% stake in its Conoco subsidiary.

When this is done, assets are transferred to the new firm, which has its own board, shareholders, and management. Depending on the number of shares offered, the original firm may or may not be a major shareholder. One advantage for the parent firm is that it receives cash from the sale of its equity in the subsidiary.

In contrast, with a **spinoff,** the entire ownership of a subsidiary is divested as a dividend to existing shareholders. Again, assets are transferred to the new entity and the management of this new entity reports to its own board. A spinoff might be considered when the original firm no longer seems a natural parent for the division or subsidiary that is being separated or even when there is a conflict or friction between the subsidiary's management and the head office.[44] The change is often accompanied by better financial performance of the spinoff as it escapes corporate shackles.[45]

A leveraged buyout is the purchase of shareholder's equity in part of the company by an external group which finances the purchase with debt. When led by incumbent management this is called a management buyout (MBO). Although firms appear to spend more time on acquisitions than on divestments, as we saw in Table 9.1, firms are actively engaged in both. Indeed, holding onto business for too long can have costs for the firm. It can encourage comfort and stagnation, stifle innovation and creativity, and thereby make it difficult to attract entrepreneurial talent. Troubled businesses can also absorb more corporate resources than they merit, in both dollars and time, detracting efforts from attractive opportunities.

Restructuring

As we have seen, corporate management involves the active management of the business portfolio, including acquisitions, divestments, spinoffs, and so on. Some of these are done to raise capital for the firm; with others, such as spinoffs, the firm does not receive any new cash. We have also discussed financial restructuring, whereby the financial structure of the firm is altered through a debt-for-equity swap or a leveraged buyout.

There is another form of restructuring, which we refer to as **organizational restructure.** This involves organizational redesign and downsizing. Organizational redesign will be discussed in more detail in Chapter 11; here we address some of the issues with downsizing. We consider downsizing to be a proactive reduction in the number of employees. Downsizing may reduce labor costs at the expense of loss of human capital.

Many U.S. firms downsized between September 11, 2001, and February 1, 2002, with almost a million layoffs. In challenging times, firms may see no other option for reducing costs. Layoffs are essentially short-term in their financial impact but may be much more negative in the longer term. Short-term cost reduction may result in low morale, loss of high-caliber staff, and atrophy of valuable intellectual assets. Indeed, some research indicates that downsizing does not help firm performance as measured by return on assets.[46] Certainly, downsizing will not fix a flawed strategy!

In a dynamic and changing world, the only path to continued success and wealth creation for a firm is innovation, continued renewal of the firm in all its aspects. Innovation is by its very nature risky, but so, too, is inaction where the firm is likely to become less and less competitive.

9.8 SUMMARY

Innovation is not easy, requiring creativity, risk taking, and leadership as well as financial and managerial resources. Innovation may occur in any aspect of the firm: its scope of operations, its organizational arrangements, or the structure of the industry in which it competes. While all firms have to react to external changes, real success comes when the firm is proactive in terms of innovation.

Key decisions in corporate-level strategy involve managing the dynamic scope of the firm—which new businesses it will develop and the means adopted to develop these. At the same time, decisions must be made on which businesses to exit, and how.

Two main means for increasing the scope of the firm are internal development, and mergers and acquisitions, and most global firms pursue both simultaneously. These two alternatives differ in terms of speed, resources, and competences required as well as the likelihood of success.

Firms pursuing internal development need to understand the importance of technological innovation, the need for R&D to be coupled with an understanding of customer needs. Senior managers must have a good understanding of those technologies critical for the firm, how they can be developed and commercialized, and whether firm competences need to be complemented by partners.

Mergers and acquisitions are an integral component of corporate strategy for most global firms, as is demonstrated by the rapid increase in the number of these over time. Such mergers may be undertaken to achieve growth, to acquire competences, and to diversify. However, many mergers and acquisitions fail to deliver value to the acquiring firm due to the high premium that must be paid and the difficulties in postacquisition integration. Many mergers are justified, at least in part, on the idea of synergy, which again is not always easy to capture. Mergers and acquisitons are major resource decisions of the firm, and it is recommended that formal means of evaluation, such as net present value, be adopted.

Finally, while firms are actively involved in expanding their scope, strategic managers also need to consider various options, such as divestments and spinoffs, as means of reducing their scope.

REVIEW QUESTIONS

1. Do you agree that it is important for a firm to innovate? If so, why?

2. Are the three types of innovation described in the chapter equally important? When would each be adopted, and what resources are required for each?

3. Discuss the relative merits of entering new markets by internal development versus a merger or acquisition.

4. For a firm with which you are familiar, obtain data on its changing scope over the last five years. Can you identify the strategy behind these changes?

5. Using the Internet, explore a current acquisition. Develop the strategic reasoning behind the acquisition, and discuss whether or not you think it will be successful.

6. How do firms create synergy through mergers? Do you think that this can ever be used to justify a merger?

7. Can a formal merger and acquisition process become a core competence for a firm? Discuss.

8. Why is net present value used to calculate the value of a merger? What difficulties are there with the use of this tool?

9. Are restructuring strategies likely to create wealth for shareholders? Discuss.

ENDNOTES

1 "When You Can't Sell the Goods, Sell the Shop," *The Economist,* January 18, 2003, pp. 53–54.

2 Robert Simon, quoted in R. N. Foster and S. Kaplan, *Creative Destruction* (New York: Doubleday, 2001), p. 20.

3 G. Hamel and C. K. Prahalad, "Competing for the Future," *Harvard Business Review,* July–August 1994, pp. 122–128.

4 Ibid.

5 By revolutionary innovation, we mean an innovation that improves known performance by 5 to 10 times, or involves a significant cost reduction, or that entails an entirely new set of performance features.

6 M. L. Tushman and C. A. O'Reilly, "Ambidextrous Organizations: Managing Evolutionary and Revolutionary Change," *California Management Review* 38, no. 4 (1996), pp. 8–30.

7 R. Foster, *Innovation: The Attacker's Advantage* (New York: Summit, 1986).

8 C. M. Christensen, *The Innovator's Dilemma* (Boston: Harvard Business School Press, 1997).

9 R. Peterson, *Creating Business Growth* (Vancouver: Strategic Management Society, 2000).

10 C. Markides, "Strategic Innovation in Established Companies," *Sloan Management Review* 39, no. 3 (1998), pp. 31–42.

11 N. Capon, J. U. Farley, D. R. Lehmann, and J. M. Hulbert, "Profiles of Product Innovators among Large U.S. Manufacturers," *Management Science* 30, no. 2 (1992), pp. 157–166.

[12] H. Mintzberg and J. B. Quinn, *The Strategy Process* (Upper Saddle River, NJ: Prentice Hall, 1996).

[13] J. I. Hagel and M. Singer, "Unbundling the Corporation," *McKinsey Quarterly* 3 (2000), pp. 148–161.

[14] A. J. Slywotzky, *Value Migration* (Boston: Harvard Business School Press, 1996).

[15] T. D. Kuczmarski, *Managing New Products: Competing through Excellence* (Englewood Cliffs, NJ: Prentice Hall, 1988).

[16] D. Ford, *The Corporate Role in Nurturing Growth* (Vancouver: Strategic Management Society, 2000).

[17] M. Baghai, S. Coley, and D. White, *The Alchemy of Growth* (London: Orion, 1999).

[18] R. Waters, "Never Forget to Nurture the Next Big Idea," *Financial Times*, May 15, 2001.

[19] Baghai, Coley, and White, *The Alchemy of Growth*.

[20] M. Baghai, S. C. Coley, D. White, C. Conn, and R. J. McLean, "Staircases to Growth," *McKinsey Quarterly* 4 (1996), pp. 38–61.

[21] "Nestlé: A Dedicated Enemy of Fashion," *The Economist*, August 31, 2002, pp. 43–44.

[22] "du Pont Overview," 2002: www.dupont.com.

[23] N. Capon, J. U. Farley, and S. Hoenig, *Toward an Integrative Explanation of Corporate Financial Performance* (Boston: Kluwer Academic Publishers, 1996).

[24] M. Dodgson, *The Management of Technological Innovation* (Oxford: Oxford University Press, 2000).

[25] Foster, *Innovation.*

[26] Christensen, *The Innovator's Dilemma.*

[27] M. L. Marks and P. H. Mirvis, "Making Mergers and Acquisitions Work: Strategic and Psychological Preparation," *Academy of Management Executive* 15, no. 2 (2001), pp. 80–94.

[28] C. Whitehouse, "Corus, British-Dutch Steel Maker Names a Chief," *New York Times*, April 24, 2003, p. W1.

[29] M. Hayward and D. Hambrick, "Explaining the Premiums Paid for Large Acquisitions: Evidence of CEO Hubris," *Administrative Science Quarterly* 42 (1997), pp. 103–127.

[30] M. Sirower, *The Synergy Trap: How Companies Lose the Acquisition Game* (New York: Free Press, 1999), p. 289.

[31] M. Devine, *Successful Mergers* (London: Profile Books, 2002).

[32] M. Freudenheim, "Lilly Cuts Distribution Unit's Book Value by $Bn2.4," *New York Times*, June 24, 1997, p. D. 7.

[33] S. London, "Secrets of a Successful Partnership," *Financial Times*, February 6, 2002, p. 9.

[34] For an alternative taxonomy, see J. L. Bower, "Not All M & A's Are Alike—And That Matters," *Harvard Business Review*, March 2001, pp. 93–101.

[35] J. F. Weston, K. S. Chung, and J. A. Siu, *Takeovers, Restructuring, and Corporate Governance* (Upper Saddle River, NJ: Prentice Hall, 1998).

[36] R. G. Eccles, K. L. Lanes, and T. C. Wilson, "Are You Paying Too Much for That Acquisition?" *Harvard Business Review*, July–August 1999, pp. 136–146.

[37] Ibid.

[38] D. Crowe, "IBM's $6.4Bn Consulting Shake-up," *Australian Financial Review*, August 1, 2002, p. 1.

[39] P. A. Gaughan, *Mergers, Acquisitions, and Corporate Restructurings* (New York: Wiley, 2002).

[40] R. N. Ashkenas, L. J. DeMonaco, and S. C. Francis, "Making the Deal Real: How GE Capital Integrates Acquisitions," *Harvard Business Review*, January–February 1998, pp. 165–178.

[41] "Halfway Down a Long Road," *The Economist*, August 18, 2001, p. 51.

[42] W. H. Berquist, *Building Strategic Relationships: How to Extend Your Organization's Reach through Partnerships, Alliances and Joint Ventures* (San Francisco: Jossey-Bass, 1995).

[43] "Welcome to the 1990s," *The Economist*, October 12, 2002, p. 66.

[44] L. Dranikoff, T. Koller, and A. Schneider, "Divestiture: Strategy's Missing Link," *Harvard Business Review*, May 2002, pp. 74–83.

[45] P. L. Anslinger, S. J. Klepper, and S. Subramaniam, "Breaking Up Is Good to Do," *McKinsey Quarterly* 1 (1999), pp. 16–27.

[46] W. F. Cascio, "Strategies for Responsible Restructuring," *Academy of Management Executive* 16, no. 3 (2002), pp. 80–91.

CHAPTER 10

Leading Organizational Change

Learning Objectives

Upon completing this chapter, you should be able to:

- Appreciate that organizational change and renewal are central strategic management activities
- Distinguish between the different types of organizational change, in particular incremental and revolutionary change
- Articulate how circumstances dictate the scale of organizational change
- Apply the defined process of change management
- Define leadership
- Describe the role of role of leadership in strategic management

---

British Airways (BA) is a major international airline, with operations in many countries. It was formed in 1971 through the merger of two British airlines, British European Airways (BEA) and British Overseas Airways Corporation (BOAC), both state-owned. For several years after this merger, both entities operated relatively autonomously. Both airlines had grown up in the post–World War II environment, with a substantial number of former armed forces pilots in management positions. There was little emphasis on profits—the airlines saw it as their role to arrive on time, show the flag, and extend routes, and there was a civil service mentality among the staff. There was little integration between the two original entities, no economies of scale, no common themes or culture. Further, productivity was low, costs were high, and service levels were poor. The situation got so bad that in 1981 a special bulletin was issued to all staff warning that the airline was likely to go out of business. In February 1981, John King, a successful business executive with little previous airline experience, was appointed chairman.

In September 1981 BA launched a survival plan, reducing staff from 52,000 to 43,000, discontinuing routes, and combining engineering bases. Six months later, another 7000 staff went. These staff reductions were accomplished with generous severance pay—indeed, there were more volunteers than places, and so employees were voting with their feet. In 1982, BA announced a loss of £M545 after taxes and extraordinaries, and took the opportunity to write off redundancy costs and reductions in its fleet value in an attempt to clear the decks. In February 1983, Colin Marshall, an executive with experience in car rentals, not airlines, was appointed CEO. BA launched a two-day training program called Putting People First. Some 40,000 staff went through this program, 150 at a time. The emphasis of the program was on positive relationships, at work and with customers, and mixed staff from different areas and levels. The major theme was customer service.

After this program had been completed, another 1500 managers went through a five-day program, Managing People First, which stressed the importance of trust, vision, and leadership. BA also launched new aircraft livery and uniforms, with much fanfare. It also took an interest in Galileo, a reservation system, and acquired an interest in USAir and Sabena, reflecting its global strategy. European regulators prohibited a merger with American Airlines, but eventually these two, plus other airlines, launched a global alliance, One World.

During the 1990s, the environment became more competitive following airline deregulation, particularly in the United States. Marshall became chairman, and the composition of the board was changed to bring in more nonexecutive directors. In 1996 a lawyer named Robert Ayling became the new CEO. In 1997 the company tried to refocus on customer service and new routes, and some £B6 were devoted to a major change program that included new aircraft, new routes, and extensive market research. BA also adopted more extensive outsourcing, introduced a pay freeze and new work rules, cut jobs, and reduced commissions to some travel agents. A new strategy of targeting intercontinental business, particularly business-class and first-class travel to improve passenger yields, was implemented. At this time, they were under increasing competitive pressure from new low-cost European airlines such as Ryanair. Despite these changes, the firm had a quarterly loss in 1999, and there was again a perception that ground staff were arrogant and uncaring.

In 2000, Ayling was fired and Rod Eddington became the new CEO. An experienced airline executive from Australia, he set out to repair the damage to the airline in what was becoming an increasingly hostile environment following the terrorism of September 11, 2001, the second Gulf War, and the outbreak of SARS.

As the British Airways example illustrates, organizational change is ongoing, driven by both external and internal events. Increasing competition arising from deregulation and new entrants fundamentally changed the airline industry, while events such as the Asian economic crisis and terrorism had substantial effects on passenger traffic. To respond to these changes, BA had to alter a number of its characteristics, including culture, work practices, levels of employment, route structure, and strategy. Some changes were relatively easy and predictable; others were major, with results very difficult to predict. Reaction to these changes by staff varied from enthusiasm to acceptance to rejection, with "sick-outs" causing major customer inconvenience. We cannot yet tell whether BA's recent changes will return it to consistently profitable status.

In a turbulent world, organizational change is the only certainty. Thus managing change is one of the major challenges facing firms, yet few do it successfully because managers lack the necessary knowledge and skills. However, executives must learn to manage and sustain change to achieve long-term health for their firms. As Michael Dell of Dell Computers has noted, "The only constant in our business is that everything in changing. We have to take advantage of change and not let it take advantage of us".[1] Dell operates in an extremely dynamic market place, with rapidly changing customer needs, technology, and competition, but Dell's challenge holds for any modern firm.

We distinguish external from internal change. Change in the remote or competitive environment is external. Sometimes the firm can influence this change—for example, by lobbying for changes in antitrust legislation—but more often it is outside its control. However, a firm may cause external change through its own activities. Intel may develop new and faster chips, which in turn drives change in the whole telecommunications industry. As Chapter 2 discussed, change in these external dimensions can be incremental or revolutionary.

The focus of this chapter is on internal change within the firm. Here we can distinguish both levels and types of change. A firm change can be incremental or revolutionary, with the latter involving a complete paradigm shift. Firm change can also be proactive or reactive. Anticipating external change may lead a firm to take action prior to a crisis. In other cases, the firm waits until the external change has become quite apparent before it responds, in which case it is behaving reactively. As the British Airways example demonstrates, a firm will often have a portfolio of change initiatives underway at the same time—some incremental, some more revolutionary. Strategic managers need to adopt appropriate tools while recognizing that there is a limit to the number of initiatives they can pursue simultaneously and that it is difficult to generate revolutionary change within an existing firm. Finally, change management requires leadership, and while the CEO must demonstrate this, leadership needs to occur at all levels of the firm since change is not purely a CEO issue.

⊚ 10.1 INTRODUCTION

Drivers of Change

The forces *driving change* within firms include new customer demands, rising consumer expectations, technological innovation, developments in communications and transport, and political changes resulting from increased global economic integration.[2] These changes create a need for continual improvement in organizational performance in order to maintain competitive position and create shareholder value. Competitive advantage is harder to sustain: the firm must simultaneously innovate, reduce costs, and cope with increasing uncertainty. At the same time, there are increased opportunities, with reduced barriers to operating globally. Yet, no matter how effectively managers plan, increased turbulence and uncertainty mean the unexpected will occur. Managers must develop organizations that respond quickly and effectively to environmental change, what Haeckel terms **sense-and-respond organizations**.[3] Hence, change management must become a core competence of the firm if it is to survive and deliver value to stakeholders.

In a dynamic world, a firm cannot afford to be stable and static. Further, the increased speed of external change means that managers must speed up change within the firm. Indeed, one of the tasks of strategic management is to introduce as much change as the firm can stand—take the firm outside its comfort zone—and even this may not be enough. At the same time, firms can suffer from change overload and fatigue, as well as cynicism. Too many change initiatives seem to peter out, only to be replaced by the next fad, leaving even the most loyal employees weary and confused.

Managing strategically implies that the firm must both respond to change and create change. For example, developments in communications and computers have produced changes that have influenced all firms. No firm is isolated from such forces. But these developments have also created opportunities for firms to innovate. Wal-Mart has created new supply-chain arrangements that have improved its competitive position. Similarly, the globalization of capital markets has put pressure on firms for performance but also created opportunities for new approaches to funding.

Changes in the Firm

Firms have responded to these external changes with a plethora of change initiatives, such as reduced centralization, new organizational forms such as alliances and networks, globalization of the firm, telecommuting by staff, a concentration on core businesses, and the extensive use of outsourcing. Other firms are attempting cultural change, the generation and adoption of new technology, organizational spinoffs, and downsizing. All these strategies are adopted in the expectation that the firm will create additional value. Most large firms will engage in several significant change programs at the same time. In its continuing search for competitive advantage, a firm may be simultaneously trying to do all of the following:

Reduce costs

Become more global

Become more customer-responsive

Develop new lines of business

Handle problems with postacquisition integration

Build e-commerce capabilities

The multiplicity of these change initiatives can cause change fatigue among staff as well as the problem of ensuring that these several initiatives are aligned and that they each produce results.

> To survive, IBM had to replace its chain-of-command management style, with its drawn-out product development times. The company has been turned around, reducing costs, accelerating technological innovation, reducing time-to-market, and refocusing on customers. It has moved from a make-and-sell approach to a sense-and-respond style.[4]

This example supports our view that change must be seen in a holistic manner, since change in one area may affect others. At the same time, from a strategic management perspective, change management can be about any aspect of the firm. While there is an ongoing need to innovate and change core operations, management must also think more broadly, addressing a range of possible changes from reinventing the industry to extending the domain of the firm to creating networks—all done to ensure continued value creation in the face of a turbulent and changing world.

Timing of Change

Managing change in the firm can mean many different things. At one level it means adapting to an external change, such as a new product launch by a competitor, a defensive but necessary move. It can also mean anticipating change, developing what we have referred to as foresight—insight into and understanding of likely future occurrences—and developing strategies to neutralize, or take advantage of, the expected change. Strategic managers cannot wait for the future to unfold. If the future is clear and unambiguous, leadership opportunities are lost. Change involves risk, but so does lack of change. The magnitude of the risks and the scale and frequency of changes will depend, among other factors, on the industries in which the firm operates. In fast-changing industries like electronics or communications, change is so rapid that any strategy is likely to have a short life. Continual change within the firm is the norm, and change management becomes a core competence. In such industries as oil and steel, change is usually slower and strategies may be longer-lasting.[5]

Change management is not only about responding; it is also about leading change, creating the changes to which other firms must react. Successfully launching new products, creating a new business model, changing the rules of competition, restructuring the industry, or changing industry boundaries—all might enable an innovator's advantage for the initiator, while other firms follow.

Change Management as a Core Competence

In a changing world, what is successful in the present is not likely to be successful in the future. Operational excellence is certainly required for current success, but it is limited as a source of sustainable competitive advantage, since competitors are continually destroying it. **Change management**—the ability to lead the firm into new ways—must become a core competence of the firm, so that it engages in continuous renewal and regeneration. Senior managers must show leadership and the ability to engage and empower staff to undertake continuous change. Even so, this is insufficient. The content of change, as exemplified by the corporate and business strategies adopted, is also extremely important. Westinghouse made many changes over a lengthy period, sub-suming several CEOs, with very little change in performance.[6]

Change Is Managed, but Not Neat

Change can be introduced to a firm in a number of ways, and some approaches are bet-ter than others. Nonetheless, managing change is not clean and neat; instead, it is messy and complicated. Change does not always turn out as expected, so it must be adaptive and evolutionary. Change programs often have to be altered while in progress. Substan-tial change takes time to implement. Meanwhile the world is changing, resulting in mod-ifications to change programs.

Any change will disrupt established patterns of behavior, values, and political power within the firm. Consequently, change managers must be aware of the consequences of change, its impact on employees, and any resistance to it. To tap into the skills and knowledge of staff, and overcome the obstacles of resistance, any change program should involve participation and be communicated to staff. Managers will usually need to conduct training sessions and put in place incentive systems that reward desired behavior.[7] Unfortunately, successful firms too often become complacent, developing a rigid, internal focus. They may become risk-averse, with reduced innovation and high levels of resistance to change.

Managing change may also require reshaping people's view of the world (their men-tal models), introducing new paradigms and new ways of thinking about the firm and its interaction with the world, which may be threatening to some employees. Transforma-tions normally require changes in people, structure, tasks, rewards, information, and decision processes, among many other factors.[8]

There is also a possible dark side of change: staff reductions, loss of skills, and declining morale. Some change programs, such as downsizing, can result in the loss of competences as people are forced to leave. Their skills may be hard to replace.

Change and Leadership

We take it as given that no change is likely to occur without leadership, whether this leadership is shown by the CEO or by other staff. We believe that the CEO should take a lead role in design and implementation of all major change initiatives—indeed, we regard the CEO as the chief change officer. No major change program is likely to suc-ceed without the active support and encouragement of the CEO.

Defining the precise leadership role of the CEO is not easy. With some change programs, the CEO may virtually dictate and manage the program. With others, the role of the CEO is to facilitate the change process. We discuss these alternatives in more detail shortly, but clearly change is never easy—it involves vision, leadership, and just plain hard work by many people. Whether the CEO is playing the lead role or not, change managers must adopt supporting behavior and use symbols appropri-ately. Successful change managers need to create dissatisfaction with the present, develop a clear vision of the future, build participation in the planning and imple-mentation of change, and reward behavior that supports the change—altogether a for-midable undertaking.[9]

Finally, astute leaders recognize that organizations are political systems, and power shifts among individuals, functions, and businesses are inevitable during any major change. They will recognize and seek the active support of key power groups within the firm. This may involve reshaping the executive team and removing senior staff who oppose, or only passively support, the change. Change may also require putting new people from inside or outside the firm in various management positions, as well as the use of external consultants who bring requisite skills and an external perspective to the process.

◐ 10.2 CHARACTERISTICS OF ORGANIZATIONAL CHANGE

As we saw in Figure 7.10, in the absence of action, the competitive advantage of a business unit and the firm overall will decline over time due to such factors as competitor initiatives, changes in customers and technology, political changes, and so on. Change is therefore mandatory for survival; the only questions are whether the changes will be large or small, proactive or reactive.

Change and the Environment

As discussed in Chapters 2 and 3, environmental change ranges from incremental to revolutionary. The firm should continually analyze its environment to identify these changes and their likely impact. We have reproduced Figure 2.4 as Figure 10.1, since it is useful in indicating the change possibilities and options required by the firm as it responds to and reacts to external changes.

Some firms are very successful at managing change, whether small (incremental) or large (revolutionary), as shown in Figure 10.1(a). These firms have demonstrated the managerial commitment to successfully handle change in all their activities and should be successful over the long term.

By contrast, Figure 10.1(b) demonstrates an inability to handle change. Such firms respond too late. Possibly they do not perceive the external changes, their mental models are outdated, or they regard change as too hard. They will inevitably arrive at a point where gut-wrenching decisions must be made, since their very survival is at risk. Unfortunately, at this late stage firm resources are often depleted, making renewal more difficult. The only options may be bankruptcy, takeover, or dramatic downsizing.

Figure 10.1 indicates that firms have options in change management, but if decisions are postponed, options are severely reduced.

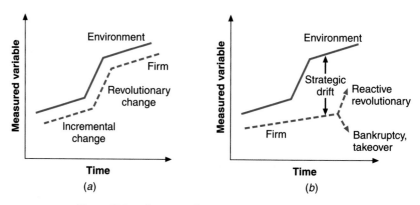

Figure 10.1   Change in the Environment and the Firm

Figure 10.2 Characteristics of Organizational Change

Change and the Firm

Figure 10.2 highlights some of the key change management decisions facing strategic managers. We will examine each in turn.

When to Change

Management must determine the urgency of the need for change. Is the firm in crisis? Is there sufficient time to implement change? Signals are weak to begin with, becoming stronger as the gap between performance and expectations increases.

So we can imagine a graph such as Figure 10.3, illustrating the need for change. The figure suggests the firm is initially doing well; the need for change is low. As performance declines, the need for change increases. The firm is not yet in crisis, since the deterioration is slow, but the signs are there.

If nothing is done, performance declines at an increasing rate, and the need to change increases. Unfortunately, since performance has declined, resources for change have been reduced, limiting available options. Obviously, change should be undertaken when adequate resources are available, but early on the apparent need for change is limited and it is difficult to get organizational support because there is little sense of urgency. Such a graph can be used to stimulate discussion. Where is the firm on this curve? Are assessments widely shared among senior managers?

Initiating a change program is a delicate balancing act. Initiate major change too early and employee resistance is likely. Wait too long and firm survival will be threat-

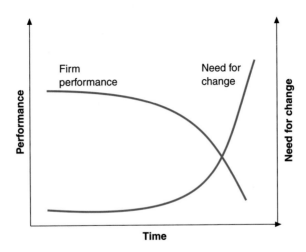

Figure 10.3 Need for Change

ened. In all change programs, some managers (probably the ones who believe they will benefit most from the change) will be enthusiastic. Others will be less enthusiastic, since they see no need for change or feel their careers are threatened. Key decisions revolve around timing and how much change to introduce.[10]

Anticipatory and Reactive Change

The ability to anticipate increases the time available for making changes, increasing the chances of avoiding a crisis. Unfortunately, because the precise nature of external changes and their impact on the firm are difficult to divine, the required organizational change is subject to uncertainty.[11] If the performance of the firm is good, the perception of managers is often that this will continue. Even under these circumstances, which are possibly unusual, some managers with excellent foresight believe that they have evidence that the future will be less munificent and that performance will decline in the future. The important point here is that there is time to implement the change program.

Anticipation normally permits a more measured response. Yet the need for change in these situations is often better understood by middle managers, who are closer to the "action," than by senior managers, who may be shielded from reality. Without anticipation, however, the firm can only react. Now, performance has deteriorated, growth rates or market share have started to decline, and margins are beginning to suffer. So change is required, although senior managers may disagree about the seriousness of the situation, with some calling for revolutionary change and others suggesting an incremental approach.

Finally, if change is left until very late, the firm may be in crisis. Performance is poor, financial markets critical, rating agencies have probably downgraded debt, and shareholders are unhappy. At his time, all staff should see the need for change. There is no problem with creating a sense of crisis—it is reported in the daily business press! Resources available for the change program are likely to be limited and change options reduced. Quick action may be necessary to ensure the firm's survival, but hopefully not at the expense of its long-term future. Labor market effects are likely severe. More mobile, highly qualified staff may leave the firm, and it is unlikely to be an employer of preference for new staff.

As a final word of advice on anticipation versus reaction, we must caution against "bottom-line" management. As we discuss in Chapter 12, the bottom line is a lagging indicator of changes in the business. The best strategic managers will lead anticipatory change, and to do this they will be tracking the leading indicators of change, recognizing that these provide the best guidance for securing longer-term shareholder value creation.

Change as a Sequential Search Process

Organizational change can also be characterized as a widening sequential search process. The firm initially tries a simple response; if this does not work, it tries a more comprehensive approach. We can even argue that this should be a continuous process. As Professor John Whitney, founder of the Turnaround Management Society, once remarked, "If you manage as though you are in a turnaround every day, you will never have to do a turnaround!"[12]

The central idea here is that organizational change is driven by a difference between performance and expectations. If current performance exceeds expectations, there is little incentive for major changes. As we saw in Chapter 4, managing expectations is an important role. Indeed, changing CEOs usually means establishing new expectations which may not be met by the existing strategy. We depict the process in Figure 10.4.

The sequential search model suggests that if performance is exceeding expectations, there is little impetus for change. If this is not the case, there is a widening search for

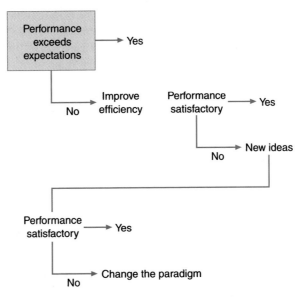

Figure 10.4 Change as a Sequential Search Process

options, starting with those close to the existing business and then getting further and further out. Of course, it is possible to leap straight to a radical option at the beginning of the change process, but a widening search for alternatives is more rational. Change is difficult and few firms succeed with the kind of radical change represented by the new paradigm—so why do it if it is not necessary?

The first step by many firms is to improve efficiency, generally through cost reductions.

> In 2003 the airline industry, faced with significant reduction in demand, discontinued routes and reduced flight frequency, while laying off staff and renegotiating union agreements.

Although cost reduction is a first choice for many firms, turnaround experts often suggest alternatives, including new marketing approaches.[13] If efficiency improvements do not produce desired results, the firm generally tries new ideas within the current business paradigm, which may include expanding product lines, expanding geographic market scope, or altering how work is performed.

Only if these options fail will the firm look at the most radical change—that is, a new paradigm for the firm. Such a change could be a divestment or, resources permitting, an acquisition.

> BHP Billiton, the Australian resources firm, is in the process of exiting the steel industry, which for many years has constituted one of its core businesses.

Such a model of widening search may have problems of predictability and even complacency, since at any time the firm may need to pursue a full range of change programs, some minor and others major.[14] Hamel argues that incremental and radical innovations are not mutually exclusive and must be pursued simultaneously. Incremental improvements, such as reducing costs by 10%, improving customer retention rates, or launching product line extensions, are all very well and good but are unlikely to produce large increases in wealth. Indeed, there may also be occasions when radical change is less risky than incremental change. When a firm only undergoes incremental change, another firm may introduce a radical change that destroys, or severely limits the potential, of the original firm. In addition, a firm can sometimes reduce risk through experimentation on a smaller scale, learning from the experience and subsequently expanding success models. Ideally, the firm will possess an innovation pipeline that is full of ideas, some of which will be precedent-breaking, with the power to transform industries and create new wealth.[15] Thus Starbucks, with its very different coffee consumption model, has 4% of Nestlé's revenues but 10% of its market value!

Scale of the Change

Change programs within the firm can be classified in terms of the magnitude of the change, whether the change is incremental or revolutionary, reflecting the punctuated model of change.[16] *Incremental* changes are those done on a regular basis and requiring no major changes in the architecture of the firm. Incremental change occurs when the company moves to a known future state over a controlled time period. The process is relatively slow and the transition path generally well understood, and it will typically involve a number of aligned changes. Implementing a new compensation system in a large firm would generally be viewed as incremental change, since levels of uncertainty would appear to be reasonably low. In some cases, however, such system changes have been extremely problematic, despite management confidence that this would not be the case.

Revolutionary changes, by contrast, will have an impact on all aspects of the firm, involving major changes to strategy, architecture, or culture; by their very nature, they are extremely difficult to accomplish successfully. With transformational change, the end state is generally unknown, as is the time period required for the change. Such changes involve a leap of faith and are often initiated when other options have failed. The difficulty of managing revolutionary change is exacerbated by organizational complexity, which in turn is influenced by organizational size and diversity in products, markets, and technologies. Today's global firms are characterized by this complexity, so introducing revolutionary changes within these firms is one of the most challenging managerial tasks. Revolutionary change is often driven by a major, external destabilizing event and may occur when the firm is in crisis, which provides the incentive for the change.

The differences between incremental and revolutionary change can be summarized as follows:[17]

Incremental change is done on a regular basis, with no fundamental changes to structure or processes.

Revolutionary change always requires a new strategy and vision.

Revolutionary change involves a large number of simultaneous changes.

Revolutionary change has no clear end, leads to an unclear future state, and takes more time.

Revolutionary change requires top-management support and leadership.

Locus of Change

Whereas there is a generally held belief that change must be led from the top of the organization, others hold to a different view. The basic question here is what kind of change is required. Discontinuous changes in the environment are likely to need center-led change in the firm. Any delay in response will probably mean it will be imposed coercively. Despite clear evidence of problems for the firm, however, change imposed from the top disempowers staff and may well result in strong resistance.

An ever-present danger of change programs imposed from the top is that they are typically standardized and may be focused on solutions, not problems. There is often an implicit assumption that TQM, 360-degree feedback, outsourcing, or benchmarking—whatever is the current management fad—will solve all our problems. Cynicism is too often the response of staff worn down by such initiatives. In contrast to a top-down approach, Beer suggests that the most effective way to change behavior is to put people into a new organizational context that imposes new roles, responsibilities, and relationships on them.[18] Such an approach is problem-focused, faces the competitive challenge, and encourages forming cross-functional teams around problems. Senior management's role is to facilitate the change, providing resources, training, and support needed by staff at the front line. With this model, change starts at the periphery of the firm, not at the center.

The above discussion clearly illustrates an interrelationship between change management and leadership style, which we will explore later in the chapter. One aspect of leadership style is be the degree of consultation that is used. Change driven by the center is more likely to be more coercive, less consultative.

Resources for Change

The requisite resources must be available for change to be successfully accomplished. This is not just a matter of resource availability, for the resources must also be commensurate with the scale and scope of proposed changes. For example, does the organization possess the required skills, or can they be acquired? Change is not cheap in either staff time or money. Adequate resources must be available; otherwise management may have to reshape the change initiative.

Two further questions must be considered before embarking on corporate change initiatives. First, how does the new initiative fit? There are two aspects to fit. The first is how the initiative meshes with existing organizational arrangements—in particular, with firm values. Initiatives closely aligned with existing values will be much easier to implement. As we earlier noted, radical departures will be much more difficult. One of the major difficulties with business process reengineering (BPR) which frequently leads to failure is the fact that the processes to be reengineered often cut right across the organization, requiring change on the part of all the business's constituent functions, thus raising enormous political opposition. Supply-chain reorganization raises some of the very same problems and requires great tenacity and insight for successful implementation. These types of initiatives clearly require good homework on change management, for they involve very significant departures from normal operations and may well conflict with the devolved values that characterize so many multibusiness companies. GE's embracing of the concept of a "boundaryless" organization was, in our view, one of the crucial elements enabling their BPR initiative "Work Out" to be so successful.

The second aspect of fit involves the relationship between a particular initiative and others that are either under way or occurred in the recent past. The trials and tribulations of British Airways provide a classic example of how a CEO can irretrievably destroy himself in such a way.

> Under Colin Marshall, British Airways changed itself from a moribund, government-owned underperforming monolith into a superior provider of customer service in an extremely competitive industry. Marshall's handpicked successor, Robert Ayling, correctly reasoned that the commercial airline business was becoming intensely competitive and that it was essential to reduce cost. However, the contrast between the initiatives of the two CEOs was enormous. As a consultant to BA put it, "Every time Marshall opened his mouth, he talked about customer service and the importance of the workforce. Every time Ayling opened his mouth, he talked about downsizing and outsourcing."

The consequences of this transition were that BA suffered from a series of employee "sick-outs" that stranded and/or inconvenienced thousands of passengers. As a result of this and other debacles, Ayling "succeeded" in halving the membership of BA's Executive Club (these were the premium passengers they were supposed to target!) and eventually—after a delay that some regard as inordinate—was fired by the board. The disastrous implementation of a strategy that was and still is essential to the future of the company cost him his job.

The second key question we must ask is how many initiatives can we sustain at the same time. There is clearly a limit on how much change people can accommodate. This is undoubtedly related to the history of the company. Adapting to change in an organization that has been stable for a long time is much more difficult. Organizations that have experienced a lot of change tend to be staffed by people who can handle it better, at least when the direction of movement is positive. High-tech companies have traditionally fallen into this category, although when their businesses ran into trouble in early 2001, it became very clear that the changes that accompanied declining performance were much harder for them to deal with. The other problem with multiple initiatives, however, is that they tend to make it very difficult for employees (and, indeed, other constituencies) to clearly understand the organization's priorities. Firms sometimes get themselves into terrible muddles as a result of these kinds of conflicts, as the following example illustrates.

> A European company's pharmaceutical division announced that it was forming global business teams around disease categories. These cross-functional business teams would work together from inception and discovery of a new chemical entity through the entire process to commercialization and marketing and would do so on an ongoing basis henceforth. This involved a major restructuring of the whole company and a very expensive training initiative. After the program had begun and been under way for only a few weeks, the very same corporate management banned all international travel because of a budget problem! The same division, a few years later, was put up for sale by the parent.

While we cannot give an absolute number of corporate-level initiatives to which a firm should restrict itself, we can recommend that no more than a few be considered at any one time. These should in any case be carefully cross-checked against any initiatives that are under way in the businesses that comprise the firm.

One useful tool that corporate management should consider using for dealing with multiple initiatives can be borrowed from project and product planning literature.[19] Wheelwright and Clark focus on the total resource requirements for a set of development projects and the balance of those projects, ranging from minor modifications to advanced development projects. Analogously, the CEO should be concerned about (1) the total resource requirements of corporate-level initiatives (which are typically imposed on top of business unit initiatives) and (2) the balance of these initiatives between the evolutionary and the revolutionary, or, if you will, between those aimed at ensuring short-term results and those aimed at securing the future cash flows of the firm. A portfolio overview of change initiatives, as suggested by Figure 10.5, may prove helpful in managing the strategy implementation process.

Simple summation of the resource requirements entailed by currently planned corporate change initiatives should lead to containment of corporate excess. In addition, however, consistent with our integral theme of planning for both today and tomorrow, CEOs should assure themselves that they have an appropriate balance of initiatives underway. Of course, Wheelwright and Clark developed their schema specifically for

Resource Implications

Implementation Programs	Tangible		Intangible		
	Financial	Physical	Human	Structural	Customer
Incremental					
Revolutionary					
Total					

Figure 10.5 Portfolio of Change Initiatives

product development projects, in which case it should be relatively easy to classify such projects along a continuum according to whether they represent R&D that is very basic, aimed at a fundamental breakthrough, all the way to relatively simple projects aimed at derivative developments ("flankers" in marketing parlance). However, throughout this book we have been at pains to underline the fact that innovation is not just about new products; it is a much broader concept, involving such ideas as new business models, new competitive strategies, new supply-chain arrangements, reconceptualization of business missions, and so on. To ensure the continued success of the business, it is essential that we not construe innovation narrowly, limiting its domain to that of new products.

10.3 THE CHANGE PROCESS

In the past decade, many companies have tried to remake themselves into better competitors to improve the level of corporate performance. These high-profile change programs have gone under many banners: total quality management, reengineering, rightsizing, restructuring, cultural change, and turnarounds. In almost every case, the goal has been the same: to cope with a new, more challenging market by changing how business is conducted. A few of those efforts have been successful. A few have been utter failures. Most fall somewhere in between, but with a distinct tilt toward the lower end of the scale.

As the business environment becomes increasingly competitive, the pace of change is likely to quicken, not slowdown. It is therefore imperative that strategic managers learn as much as possible about managing the change process and critical that they learn from the experience of others. The most common mistake is to underestimate the difficulty of change and to be too optimistic about the pace. Change involves numerous phases that, together, usually take a long time. Skipping steps creates only an illusion of speed and never produces a satisfying result. Critical mistakes in any of the phases can have a devastating impact, slowing momentum and negating previous gains.[20]

As we have noted, change initiatives often meet with a mixed response from employees. Some will be keen to act, recognizing the necessity for the change. Others—possibly the majority—will be less enthusiastic. Perhaps they do not see the need for change, for too often senior management assumes that others see the world as they do. They may also by cynically disillusioned by past corporate initiatives, believe that the change is simply a passing CEO fad, or perhaps feel personally threatened by the change.

The change process, consisting of three interrelated steps, is depicted in Figure 10.6. The process is not linear but—as we will see—interactive. First we describe each step, and then we examine them in detail:

- *Initiating change*—diagnosing and creating a perceived need for change and generating the new vision
- *Managing change*—planning and communicating, creating commitment, and empowering employees
- *Sustaining change*—institutionalizing a change philosophy

Initiating Change

Diagnosing the Need for Change

Diagnosing the need for change is a critical first step. This is often thought about as observing a gap between expectations and performance—but which performance measures matters enormously! As we noted earlier, accomplishing change in large organizations takes time, and if managers wait until a crisis is obvious, they may have left insufficient time to permit changes before a catastrophe occurs. Strategic managers must concentrate on *leading indicators* of performance and change, which means looking far beyond the bottom line. Achieving good profits may be a laudable goal, but the bottom line is a very poor choice to watch if we want to make anticipatory changes. Complacency about the need for change does not necessarily mean that managers are inept. Too often managers see no evidence that a change is needed because they are looking at the wrong indicators.

So where should we be looking? Chapter 9 emphasized the importance of turning points: shifts in the game or disruptive changes. Strategic managers must be attuned to identifying such turning points. As one consultant put it to us, "Change is always occurring. If you can't see it, you aren't looking hard enough." This is an important, almost Confucian, point. Change is the natural course of events; it is lack of change that is unusual. The locus of by far the majority of events necessitating change lies outside the firm, and it is therefore crucial for strategic managers to maintain a very strong external focus. Activities such as analyzing competitors, best-of-class benchmarking, attending professional meetings, and the like all have beneficial impacts with respect to spotting

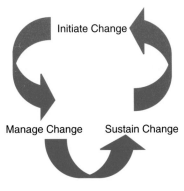

Figure 10.6   The Change Process

changes in leading indicators. Some CEOs insist that their senior managers become actively involved in various outside activities for exactly these reasons. Whether the need to change is precipitated by a competitive development, government action, a change in technology or a business model, or a change of supplier strategy, managers with strong external orientations are likely to be aware of the need earlier than their counterparts.

At the point where a need to change is recognized, the nature and magnitude of the required changes are likely to be unclear. In a large firm, no doubt other change initiatives are already under way, and divining the best course of future action is likely to be difficult.

Creating a Perceived Need for Change

The fact that a few perceptive individuals may recognize a need to change does not mean that the rest of the firm agrees. Establishing a felt need for change within the firm is therefore a critical prerequisite to any successful change effort. The difficulty arises from the fact that it is much easier for a workforce to believe things have to change when the firm is in evident crisis, but if senior management awaits this turn of events, there may be insufficient time to implement the change and save the firm. As a result, a key leadership task is to inculcate a state of dissatisfaction with the status quo. This generally requires establishing a *sense of urgency* or a sense of crisis before a crisis occurs! This can be problematic when all appearances are of success. This may be the case because performance measures are too historical, rather than leading, and there is little external information available and thus little understanding of a decline in competitive position. A sense of complacency may pervade the firm, especially when there are low performance standards with narrow functional goals. Strategic managers must then push up the urgency level, creating a sense of impending crisis while raising performance standards, widely distributing data on customer dissatisfaction, and opening dialogues with unhappy customers, suppliers, employees, and shareholders. Without recognition of a sense of crisis within the firm—the perception that the future of the firm is in doubt unless some action is undertaken—the outlook will be grim indeed.

At this stage, it becomes essential to create a *coalition* of individuals supportive of the planned change. No one person within the firm, CEO or otherwise, has all the information and knowledge needed. Political support within the firm is essential, for change normally requires a team with power, expertise, credibility, leadership, and resources to be successful.[21] As the change process begins, political considerations become crucial because major changes result in power shifts between groups and between individuals in the firm. Change agents need to gain the support of key power groups in the firm, which may involve reshaping the executive team or even replacing senior staff that opposes the change.[22] We return to these political considerations in the section below on managing change.

Generating a Vision

You should have recognized by now that creating change in large companies is a daunting task and not one that can be accomplished by just sending around a memo. It takes sustained hard work by many champions of the change. Change absorbs a significant amount of managerial resources and requires energy and commitment to keep it going. However, without some idea of what the change is intended to produce, the efforts will not be successful. Facile talk about change management is meaningless without some clarity about why the present state of affairs is undesirable and without creating a vision of the future of the firm that is both desirable and achievable. Clearly that vision cannot be a detailed blueprint. That is not the purpose of a vision. Equally clearly, change cannot be content-free.

As we saw in Chapter 6, such a vision should have several characteristics. It should be desirable, achievable, and as clear as is feasible under the circumstances. As with any vision statement, it should be inspirational and aspirational, going beyond the present and beyond strictly financial goals. A preliminary vision statement is often generated by senior managers in a team setting, based on a detailed understanding of the world and its developments,[23] but its refinement will ideally involve a much broader group, for they are essential to its realization.[24] To energize people in this way, the vision should have a limited number of themes, making it easier to communicate throughout the firm.[25]

Ideally, the vision of the firm's future will reflect how the world is changing and incorporate compelling reasons for why this vision is essential. Such a vision should be seen as attainable (possibly with some stretch) and be easy to communicate to all stakeholders, particularly employees. It should be brief and concise, but neither too vague nor involving "motherhood" statements. Such a statement may well mention how the vision will affect stakeholders, particularly customers, employees, and shareholders.

In some cases, the scale of required change will be almost all-encompassing. Changing the whole firm—its structure, processes, culture, and competences—is incredibly complex and cries out for holistic and integrated visions. In these situations, however, the vision will almost certainly be quite vague and the change will be an evolving, interactive process. The future state is not, and cannot, be known with certainty, and the management team must remain flexible, open to inputs and learning as they navigate through what will undoubtedly be turbulent waters.

Managing Change

Communicating the Vision

Senior managers must constantly and consistently communicate the vision that has been developed. There is always resistance to change, and communication is a valuable tool in overcoming both passive and active resistance. Of course, senior managers must also act consistently with the vision—"walk the talk" as Tom Peters once put it.[26] The CEO needs to develop a communication process, using a range of forums and media—talks, newsletters, possibly e-mail and TV and other multimedia approaches.

> Sir George Bull, when he was CEO of GrandMet (now Diageo), used a monthly taped message so that employees could listen to it in their cars. Reuben Mark, CEO of Colgate-Palmolive, a great believer in the importance of communication, used monthly videotapes until the Internet enabled the use of e-mail.

The great advantage of these approaches is that the CEO can control the way the message reaches employees, without the many filters that operate when a message is passed through the "chain of command." Senior management can thereby be assured that a simple, focused message is getting out and can constantly reinforce the vision for the future. Of course, they cannot be sure how their message is being perceived, and follow-up research with relevant audiences is an important source of feedback.

The Change Team

As we noted, CEOs cannot manage the whole change process. They need to establish a guiding coalition, a team to manage and oversee the change process. Such a team is generally made up of senior executives who can provide knowledge, commitment, and support. The team must be balanced in skills and expertise, but it also needs resources, power, credibility, and leadership skills.

Members of change teams are often seconded to a team on a part-time basis, keeping their normal responsibilities as well. Balancing these demands is difficult and also requires some astute assessment of the shifting sands of organizational politics. For most of us, the term *politics* carries negative overtones when applied to a firm, but Peter Block points out that all successful managers must understand the use of politics. Politics means the use of influence and, just like power, is in and of itself value-free—politics can be used to further good ends as well as bad.[27] Block believes, and we agree, that the effective use of politics (and, indeed, power) is a skill that must be mastered for a manager to be effective. Because organizations are political systems and change results in shifts of power within the firm, change leaders need the support of key power groups.

The members of the change team need to understand the concerns of the recipients of the change—what they are interested in and how they may respond to the change. In particular, there may be psychological issues for people to resolve. One approach to this understanding is to classify those parties (individuals and/or groups) that are key to the implementation of our change strategies along two dimensions. The first is the extent to which we believe we have their confidence: Do they trust us? The second is the extent to which we believe they will be in agreement with our proposed course of action (strategies and programs). The result is a trust/agreement matrix, as depicted in Figure 10.7.[28]

One might expect a fourfold classification to result from a 2 × 2 matrix, but Block also incorporated "fence-sitters," an intriguing and potentially troublesome constituency that he believes merits special attention. We now briefly examine the influence strategy for each of the identified groupings.

Allies, as the figure indicates, are those who are agreement with our ideas and trust us—a wholesome combination! For this group Block urges that we confirm their agreement and reaffirm the quality of the mutual relationship. He suggests being open with any problems or difficulties and seeking advice and input. Clearly, it would be mistake to take any group for granted, but that is also most likely to happen with this constituency.

Opponents trust us but disagree with our ideas. Here Block suggests that we reaffirm the quality of the relationship, then restate both our own position and, as we understand it, the position of the opponent. The objective should then be to engage in joint problem solving to attempt to resolve the differences.

Bedfellows represent a different challenge, for they are in a "marriage of convenience." The recommendation for them is to reaffirm their agreement with the strategy and to be open in acknowledging their caution and lack of trust. We should then clarify

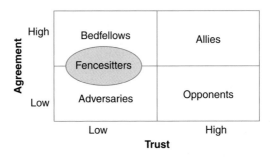

Figure 10.7   Trust/Agreement Matrix

what we are looking for, in terms of cooperation in implementation, and ask that the bedfellows do the same for us.

Adversaries are patently the most difficult to deal with. After stating our own position on strategy, we should state our best understanding of the adversary's position, doing so neutrally, without any evaluative comments. Block suggests that we then acknowledge our own contribution to any problems and end the meeting by stating our own plans to move ahead, but making no demands on the adversary.

Fence-sitters should first hear an explanation of the proposed strategy. We should then attempt to elicit their point of view and submit them to gentle pressure to accede to the proposed plan. They should then be encouraged to think it over and let us know what it would take for them to support the strategy.

Of course, we can give only a brief overview of Block's ideas in this chapter, but the basic idea that implementation will involve plotting out an influence strategy and distinguishing among the different parties whose cooperation we will need along such dimensions as trust and likely agreement is sound advice. Forgetting this admonition can lead to the debacle that resulted from Robert Ayling's clumsy strategy implementation at British Airways. His neglect of employees, and failure to achieve their trust and agreement, eventually cost him his job. As a CEO once said to one of the authors, "We have to recognize that ultimately, all power is granted from below."

Empowering Staff

Change will occur only if many people are involved and if innovation and risk taking are encouraged. The initial response to a change agenda on the part of many employees is at best guarded, with others apprehensive and some downright hostile. Empowerment is a key tool in building the leverage necessary to create the change. Participation reduces resistance to change as well as generating good ideas. The CEO can create enabling conditions by getting rid of obstacles and changing systems, structures, and people, but those who will accomplish the change have to build skills, growing and developing leadership abilities.

Short-Term Wins

Finally, important as it is to keep the ultimate vision in mind, it is vital to maintain enthusiasm in the interim. Short-term wins that are recognized, rewarded, and communicated throughout the firm provide positive feedback to those working on change efforts as well as other stakeholders. These wins provide tangible evidence of success, that the change process is under way and working, and constitute important symbolic communication.

Sustaining Change: The Organization of the Future

Creating and sustaining a different attitude toward change is essential to ensure that the firm does not slip back into fixed ways of thinking or doing things. Too often, managers and consultants construe the vision as an end-state, when it should be viewed as a continuing new beginning. Since we do not believe that the required pace of change will slow, it is essential that the vision be one of a firm that has the continuing capacity for self-renewal. Change becomes traumatic when a firm has not experienced it in many years. It becomes part of the landscape in a firm that has inculcated the capacity for self-renewal, and this philosophy should be a fundamental anchor of the new culture of the firm.

Indeed, a chapter on organizational change would be incomplete without some discussion of the organization of the future, for it is incumbent on us as authors to give you some insight into the changes you will be experiencing. Of course, there are a variety of opinions on how firms will have to evolve and change, but while reviewing the opinions of different authors, we will conclude the section by attempting to synthesize these opinions.

Kotter, for example, is convinced that successful firms of the future will have a high and persistent sense of the need to change, with teamwork at the top among people who can create and communicate a vision and create broad-based empowerment.[29] Others believe that *learning* will become increasingly important for organizational success and that the rate at which a firm can learn will in turn be a competitive advantage. In a changing world, organizations as well as individuals have to learn to do new things and to do old things differently, so that if a firm can speed up the learning process, it will achieve a competitive advantage.[30] At the same time, organizations need to forget, have to unlearn what no longer works due to a changing world. Yet, as Argyris points out, learning is an ongoing process with two activities: acquiring knowledge, insights, and associations and then taking action based on what has been learned: "Learning should be in the service of action, not simply discovery or insight."[31]

Individual learning can be distinguished from *organizational learning*, and Kim suggests that organizational learning is a fundamental requirement for sustained existence.[32] Organizations ultimately learn via their individual members, but organizational learning is not dependent on a single individual. Thus, for organizational learning to become a source of competitive advantage, knowledge must become structural or organizational, even though it may start as individual and tacit. Then if a specific individual leaves the firm, all the learning or knowledge possessed by that individual does not leave at the same time. In too many firms, high staff turnover produces high rate of knowledge loss. Organizational learning is typically captured in the *routines* and *processes* of the firm. These routines are an important part of a firm's memory, although ironically they may later inhibit change and introduce rigidity to the firm.[33]

There is a consensus across many different authors, academic and practitioner alike, that we can expect significant change in organizations in the 21st century. Many firms survived the 20th century using organizational concepts and practices derived from 19th-century thinking. They will not prosper in the years ahead, and to survive, their managers will have to manage far greater change more frequently. We return to this topic of the likely organization of the future in Chapter 14.

◎ 10.4 LEADERSHIP

The discussion of change management has underlined the importance of the leadership skills of managers, which we now examine.

Leadership involves the process of intentional influence by one person over other people. Influence may be based on rational processes or emotional ones. Further, the same person may be a leader in one situation and a follower in another.

Leader versus Manager

Following Kotter, we make a distinction between management and leadership.[34] They are distinctive but complementary systems of action. **Management** is about keeping the firm operating while coping with complexity. To manage, we develop systems and procedures to remove complexity, using devices such as standard operating procedures, planning, and budgeting systems.

In contrast, **leadership** is about change, developing visions and strategies, but also about aligning people with that vision and inspiring them to make it happen. Indeed, Kotter argues that many firms are overmanaged and underled. As we have seen, successful firms too often become arrogant and insular, isolated from their markets. With reduced efforts in innovation and creativity, they become bureaucratic, with rules for everything. Pressure for short-term performance by financial markets may result in too much concern with the present and not enough with the future, even though this may not serve shareholders' interests. Indeed, Rowe argues that strategic leadership is the ability to influence others to voluntarily make day-to-day decisions that enhance long-term viability while maintaining short-term financial stability.[35]

In increasingly turbulent environments, leadership matters as never before. The need to exhibit speed and flexibility, and to execute discontinuous change, requires effective leadership skills. Charismatic leaders are important: they provide vision, direction, and energy for their firms. Charisma alone, however, is not enough to build competitive, agile organizations. Charismatic leadership must be bolstered by institutional leadership through attention to details on roles, structures, and rewards. Moreover, since most organizations are too large and complex for any one executive or senior team to directly manage, the leadership of strategic organization change must be pushed throughout the company via education and empowerment. If managers at all levels own and are involved in executing the change efforts, they are much more likely to realize concrete benefits.[36]

Competences and Behaviors of Leaders

There has been considerable discussion of the extent to which leadership abilities can be easily taught or acquired. Certain personal traits of leaders—they should be visionary, able to handle ambiguity, interpersonally skilled, honest, capable negotiators, politically astute, and such attributes of good change managers have been reflected in much of our discussion in this book thus far. Other authors have focused on behaviors. It has been argued that leaders of the future will be involved in six activities:[37]

Determining the firm's purpose or vision

Exploiting and maintaining competencies

Developing human capital

Sustaining an effective organizational culture

Emphasizing ethical practices

Establishing balanced organizational controls

Another school of thought believes that successful managers understand and can practice a variety of leadership styles, selecting the one most appropriate to the situation and the person. Goleman, for example, identifies six different styles ranging from coercive to coaching, as shown below:[38]

Coercive—demands immediate compliance

Authoritative—mobilizes people toward a vision

Affiliative—creates harmony and builds bonds

Democratic—forges consensus through participation

Pace-setting—sets high performance standards

Coaching—develops people for the future

Effective leaders have mastered more than one style and are able to select the style which best suits the particular circumstances.[39]

10.5 SUMMARY

Increasing environmental turbulence and heightened levels of global competition necessitate that firms continually reinvent themselves. Organizations will have to change faster than ever and be prepared to change any, and all, of their characteristics. At any time, the firm is likely to be managing a number of change programs simultaneously, of varying levels of complexity, scale, and impact. For these reasons, we suggest that change management must become a core competence of any successful firm.

Any change program is risky, but so is the alternative of no change. While change can be managed, the process of change is adaptive and evolving, particularly for radical changes where the end-point is not always well understood. All change processes involve an element of disruption to established procedures, values, and political power within the firm, so an understanding of the recipients of the change—what their likely response will be, what resistance may be encountered—is fundamental to successful change.

Successful change management follows an interactive process, diagnosing the need for change, generating the vision of the future, managing the change, and finally ensuring that the change is sustained. Leadership plays a central role in the success of this process. The quintessential features of leadership are the ability to generate a vision and to have the industry knowledge and foresight to guide the firm through the turbulence and uncertainty. Leadership is about introducing change, aligning people with the vision, demonstrating enthusiasm and passion to inspire people to make it happen. Since the CEO is just one individual, any large change program requires a multidisciplinary team with sufficient financial and human resources.

REVIEW QUESTIONS

1. Discuss the factors that make organizational change a crucial task for strategic management.

2. How can managers improve their skills in anticipating and responding to change?

3. "It is more difficult for managers to detect the need for change than it is for them to develop the appropriate response." Discuss this statement.

4. What are the stages of the change process? Use examples of firms with which you are familiar to illustrate how the firms implemented each stage.

5. How does leadership influence the determination of a firm's strategy?

6. Do you believe that a given manager can develop a range of leadership styles? Discuss.

ENDNOTES

[1] S. L. Brown and K. M. Eisenhardt, *Competing on the Edge: Strategy as Structured Chaos* (Boston: Harvard Business School Press, 1998).

[2] J. Wind and J. Main, *Driving Change* (New York: Free Press, 1998).

[3] S. H. Haeckel, *Adaptive Enterprise: Creating and Leading Sense-and-Respond Organizations* (Boston: Harvard Business School Press, 1999).

[4] J. Bruce Harreld, "Building Smarter, Faster Organizations," in D. Tapscott, A. Lowy, and D. Ticoll, eds., *Blueprint to the New Economy* (New York: McGraw-Hill, 1998).

[5] Brown and Eisenhardt, *Competing on the Edge.*

[6] D. A. Ready, ed., *In Charge of Change* (Lexington, MA: International Consortium for Executive Development Research, 1995).

[7] D. K. Carr, K. J. Hard, and W. J. Trahant, *Managing the Change Process* (New York: McGraw-Hill, 1996).

[8] M. Y. Orgland, *Initiating, Managing, and Sustaining Strategic Change: Learning from the Best* (Houndmills, Basingstoke, Hampshire: Macmillan, 1997).

[9] N. Tichy and M. A. Devanna, *The Transformational Leader* (New York: Wiley, 1986).

[10] P. Killing, "Managing Change, the Urgency Factor," *Perspectives for Managers,* IMD, No. 1, February 1997, pp. 1–4.

[11] Ibid.

[12] John Whitney, personal remark to one of the authors.

[13] J. O. Whitney, *Taking Charge: Management Guide to Troubled Companies and Turnarounds* (Homewood, IL: Dow Jones–Irwin, 1987).

[14] E. Abrahamson, "Change without Pain," *Harvard Business Review,* July–August 2000, pp. 75–79.

[15] G. Hamel, "Revolution vs. Evolution: You Need Both," *Harvard Business Review,* May 2001, pp. 150–154.

[16] D. Nadler and M. B. Nadler, *Champions of Change: How CEOs and Their Companies Are Mastering the Skills of Radical Change* (San Francisco: Jossey-Bass, 1998).

[17] Ibid.

[18] M. Beer, "Why Change Programs Don't Produce Change," *Harvard Business Review* Nov.–Dec. (1990), pp. 158–166.

[19] S. C. Wheelwright and K. B. Clark, "Creating Project Plans to Focus Product Development," *Harvard Business Review,* March–April 1992, pp. 70–82.

[20] J. P. Kotter, "Leading Change: Why Transformation Efforts Fail," *Harvard Business Review,* 73, no. 2 (1995), pp. 59–67.

[21] J. P. Kotter, *Leading Change* (Boston: Harvard Business School Press, 1996).

[22] Nadler and Nadler, *Champions of Change.*

[23] Kotter, *Leading Change.*

[24] Tichy and Devanna, *The Transformational Leader.*

[25] Nadler and Nadler, *Champions of Change.*

[26] T. J. Peters and R. H. Waterman, *In Search of Excellence* (New York: Harper & Row, 1982).

[27] P. Block, *The Empowered Manager* (San Francisco: Jossey-Bass, 1987).

[28] Ibid.

[29] Kotter, *Leading Change.*

[30] B. Moingeon and A. C. Edmondson, eds., *Organizational Learning and Competitive Advantage* (London: Sage 1996).

[31] C. Argyris, "Education for Leading – Learning", *Organizational Dynamics,* 21, no. 3, (1993), pp. 5–17.

[32] D. H. Kim, "The Link between Individual and Organizational Learning," *Sloan Management Review* 35, no. 1 (1993), pp. 37–50.

[33] Ibid.

[34] Kotter, *Leading Change.*

[35] W. G. Rowe, "Creating Wealth in Organizations: The Role of Leadership," *Academy of Management Executive.* 15, no. 1 (2001), pp. 81–94.

[36] D. A. Nadler and M. L. Tushman, "Beyond the Charismatic Leader: Leadership and Organizational Change," *California Management Review* 32, no. 2 (1990), pp. 77–97.

[37] R. D. Ireland and M. A. Hitt, "Achieving and Maintaining Competitiveness in the 21st Century: The Role of Strategic Leadership," *Academy of Management Executive.* 13, no. 1 (1999), pp. 43–57.

[38] D. Goleman, "Leadership That Gets Results," *Harvard Business Review,* March–April 2000, pp. 78–90.

[39] D. Goleman, R. Boyatzis, and A. McKee, *The New Leaders: Transforming the Art of Leadership into the Science of Results* (London: Little, Brown, 2002).

CHAPTER 11

Designing Organizational Architecture

Learning Objectives

Upon completing this chapter, you should be able to:

- Recognize the decisions strategic managers have to make regarding firm architecture—structure, processes, and human resources
- Describe the major forms of organizational structure, together with their strengths and weaknesses
- Apply the principles of organizational structure at the business-unit and corporate level
- Appreciate the importance of process management and the nature of the possible conflict between process management and line management
- Articulate the role of information technology in process design and management
- Understand the importance of human resources in strategic management
- Be aware of the need for innovation in organizational architecture and why new forms have been developed.

In 1998, the U.S. firm EG&G appointed a new senior executive who swiftly became the CEO and chairman. The firm had been founded in 1947, mainly to provide a range of technical services for the U.S. government, such as incinerating the U.S. Army's chemical weapons stockpile. These businesses were generally low-growth and low-margin, a situation the new CEO was anxious to change. From the perspective of the CEO, the firm had some strengths such as a healthy balance sheet and limited activities in some growth markets, such as life sciences and digital imagining. At the same time, the firm was highly fragmented, with little synergy among its various businesses. Each of the 31 businesses seemed to possess a different culture. In addition, a substantial proportion of the senior managers of the firm had grown up with the firm through the government services businesses, which called for specific skills not always applicable to more competitive markets.

The firm developed a new strategy, designed to improve both its financial performance and its growth rate. One of the first steps was to consolidate the 31 businesses into 5 business units, necessitating a change in the structure of the firm. This consolidation was expected to achieve cost synergies, partly through the integration of the different sales forces. Some production was moved to China, Indonesia, and other lower-wage countries, necessitating more structural changes.

The operations of the firm were expanded in a limited number of new, attractive markets, reflecting a change in mission. The existing business portfolio of the firm was assessed on the basis of two characteristics: Could the business become one of the top three players in the industry, and could the business produce double-digit growth? As a result of this analysis, the government service business (the origin of the firm) was divested. Several other businesses were also divested, which provided some of the funds required for other changes, including acquisitions. These strategic decisions operationalized the dynamic portfolio approach adopted by corporate management. In 2002, the number of business units was reduced to three, partly from divestments, partly from consolidation.

The firm also developed more shared service organizations that operated across the entire firm, such as financial controls, information technology, and human resources. Their supply-chain management processes were updated with the establishment of a corporatewide material purchasing system. This resulted in the centralization of some processes. At the same time, there was a shift in power from the center to the business units. The number of staff in the center was reduced and staff in the business unit given more responsibility for their strategy.

Staff who could not or would not change were let go. New staff with the appropriate knowledge and skills were hired and given substantial responsibility. At the end of 2000, of the top 100 managers in the firm, 80% were new to their job and 50% were new to the firm. A new performance-based compensation scheme was also introduced. Training programs in Six Sigma were instituted for all staff. Leadership talent was developed by providing cross-functional and cross-business assignments. In 1999, the name of the firm was changed to PerkinElmer to symbolize the changes taking place.[1,2]

⊚ 11.1 INTRODUCTION

As the above example illustrates, strategic management is about more than simply developing a strategy; it is also about getting that strategy to work. To support the new strategy developed at PerkinElmer, senior managers made changes in structure, processes, and human resources, which we call **organizational architecture** and which is the topic of discussion for this chapter. A good strategy may be doomed by poor architecture. Without the support of an aligned and integrated structure, along with appropriate processes and the necessary human resources, failure is almost certain.

The design of architecture subsumes organizational structure, the design of certain processes within the firm, and critical human resource issues. Architecture determines the firm's formal role configuration, the processes it adopts to meet customers' needs, and the way in which it manages its own staff. The CEO needs to be involved, to some extent, in all these decision areas. In some areas, this involvement means establishing appropriate policies and procedures, for example, the incentive system to be used within the firm. In other areas, the CEO will take an active decision-making role, for example, in selecting a new organizational structure for the firm.

The traditional view is that the design of architecture is secondary to strategy development—that is, structure follows strategy[3]—and that architecture by itself does not generate superior economic performance. At the same time, as we noted earlier, strategy is not just about a good idea; it is about making that good idea happen. Architecture is certainly about making it happen, for it involves decisions about the type of people who comprise the firm, the culture of the firm, and the information systems and the structure adopted by the firm—all of which certainly affect performance. Another view, however, is that structure and strategy are so intertwined that there is really mutual causation. Said another way, the architecture has such a broad and multifaceted effect on the firm that it shapes its view of the world and its responses to it, that is, its strategy. So there is a strong interconnection between strategy and structure. We believe the distinction between strategy and architecture is useful but at the same time accept the concept of mutual causation.

So while we agree that generally architecture does not create competitive advantage, it can certainly contribute to inferior performance. In particular, a poor match between strategy and architecture will result in a lack of focus and integration, a lack of coordination among various organizational units resulting in wasted effort, indecision (or worse, conflict), slow decision making, and poor information for decision making—all of which can all produce inferior results.

What Is Organizational Architecture?

Designing organizational architecture requires decisions in three interrelated areas, as shown in Figure 11.1. A good architecture ensures consistency and alignment not only among these elements but also with the strategy being pursued by the firm. The three elements shown in Figure 11.1 are described below:[4]

> **Organizational structure** refers to the way in which tasks are differentiated and then coordinated. In addition, it indicates the way tasks have been defined and the hierarchy of the firm, indicating formal relationships and decision-making power.

> **Human resources** includes decisions on the selection, motivation, compensation, training, and succession planning for managers within the firm. In addition, the CEO must understand company culture and whether or not it is appropriate for current and anticipated strategic moves.

> **Processes** include decision making, planning and budgeting processes, workflows, and the increasingly important IT architecture of the firm. As noted in Chapter 3, information technology represents almost 50% of capital investment for U.S. firms, and top management must be intimately involved. Competitive advantage is more and more derived from information and knowledge, and ensuring that timely, accurate, and appropriate information is available to the workforce is crucial.

These three dimensions must be congruent with each other as well as with the strategy that has been developed.[5] As firms grow, they develop new structures, processes, and human resource systems to handle the increased complexity. At the same time, since these three dimensions are interlinked, they can make change more difficult due to the interdependencies, whereby change in one may require change in another. This has been referred to as structural inertia.[6]

Need for Innovation in All Characteristics

As we have highlighted throughout this book, organizations face a rapidly changing and unpredictable environment. Consequently, change must become an integral feature of the firm. Environmental change results not only in a changing strategy but also in ongo-

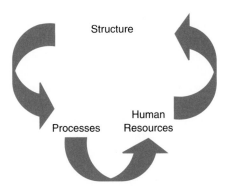

Figure 11.1 Organizational Architecture

ing and continuous change in the firm's architecture. Strategic management of the firm includes decisions about when and how to change this architecture.

Given the speed and unpredictability of external change, what organizational characteristics are likely to be critical in the future? We suggest that the following changes in organizational architecture are likely in the future:

Organizations will need to become increasingly flexible in order to cope with unanticipated changes. This includes increasing adaptability, the ability to sense and respond to external changes, and the ability of the firm and employees to experiment and learn.[7] A command-and-control approach will become less and less viable.

Creativity and knowledge will become more critical as the basis for competitive advantage. Organizations will need to create the conditions within which the creativity of their staff can be developed and allowed to flourish, and changes in rewards and structure will be needed to accomplish this. Architecture will need to contribute to reinventing the business.

With a higher rate of change in the environment, organizations will need to act faster, to make decisions faster, to launch new businesses faster. Greater adoption of information technology will provide one means of accomplishing this. These changes imply more empowerment, with decision making closer to where the action is and with less bureaucracy.

With increasing competition in product markets, firms will need to maintain high levels of efficiency, so they will focus on core activities at which they excel and outsource the rest. These trends mean that organizations may move to a quite different employment model, with a small core staff and contract staff around the core, as suggested by Handy.[8]

The automobile industry, in which all competitors are attempting to deliver precisely the car a customer wants, where and when he or she wants it, provides an excellent example of these changes. Car companies that are attempting to build to order, not to a forecast, are using the Internet to manage the supply chain with customers and suppliers. Toyota has operated such a system for some time in Japan, while the proportion of cars built to order in the United Kingdom increased from 10% in 1992 to 32% in 1999, with obvious organizational implications for manufacturers.[9]

In this chapter, we first examine the issue of organizational structure, looking beyond the organization chart per se to understand the underlying factors that drive the quest for better structures. We do this by first posing the classical dilemmas that managers must try to resolve via structure. We then examine the way in which structures have evolved to deal with the increased complexity of today's large global firms.

Next we examine processes. So many processes exist within a large firm that we cannot possible cover them all. However, we will underline the critical importance of a process-oriented perspective on the firm, examine the issues involved in reengineering such processes, and look in some detail at a few critical processes, such as the innovation process and the process involved in the design of an information architecture of the firm.

The final major section of the chapter will examine human resources. As we pointed out in Chapter 5, intangible assets increasingly account for the value of the firm, and our human resources are among the most vital of such assets. Accordingly, how we recruit, select, motivate, train, reward, promote, and deploy our people is more and more central to the success of the company. Whereas many firms pay lip service to this point, many are still far from strategically managing this valuable resource, and we hope to point you to some of the issues you should be considering if you are to become a good strategic manager.

⊚ 11.2 STRUCTURE

We have defined organizations as economic entities, voluntary collections of individuals (and assets as well) pursuing a common objective. Such entities have two fundamental characteristics—differentiation and integration. To obtain efficiency, organizations always have some degree of **differentiation,** whereby tasks are divided to allow for specialization and thus efficiency. But as soon as tasks are specialized, there is a need for **integration.** So tasks may be specialized between marketing and manufacturing, but then integration is required to ensure that manufacturing makes the products that marketing believes are demanded in the market place. This tension between integration and differentiation is at the heart of organizational design. Integration is holding the firm together, ensuring that the firm pursues a global or integrated direction. Differentiation derives from the employment of skilled specialists, increasingly necessary as the firm's environment becomes more competitive, and required competences evolve. As we will see, one way to achieve these dual goals of differentiation and integration is through structure, whereby tasks are subdivided and then integrated.

Structure often evolves historically; it is rarely the result of systematic analysis and planning. Structure evolves in response to strategic decisions, such as acquisitions or employment of staff with new skills, and in response to political pressure. Eventually, if not initially, such structures are likely to inhibit, rather than facilitate, strategy execution. Structural redesign is also difficult for many firms, not only because of inertia but also because it involves the redistribution of power, resulting in conflicts within the firm.[10] Further, after a firm has been in operation for some time, it develops a history and with this history comes a culture, a set of shared beliefs and assumptions about the world and how to succeed in that world. As with structure, such a culture can facilitate or inhibit strategy development and implementation. As we noted in Chapter 10, one of the most difficult strategic management tasks is to change the culture of a firm. This is made more challenging by the fact that culture is often very difficult to identify.

As noted earlier, firms should also strive to develop structures that encourage certain characteristics, yet these requirements may appear to be paradoxical. We want to encourage efficiency and creativity, flexibility and stability, centralization and decentralization, achieving integration and alignment while still retaining the ability of the firm to adapt to a changing environment. A classic organizational dilemma is how to balance the advantages of scale and specialization against the need for flexibility, adaptability, and creativity. A number of new organizational forms, such as the use of teams, alliances, and spinoffs, are designed to better achieve these twin goals.

Summarizing, modern firms are known by a number of characteristics:

- There is a division of labor, such as specialists in marketing, sales, accounting, finance operations, R&D, and human resources.
- There is some form of hierarchy, indicated by an organization chart, superior–subordinate relationships, tall or flat structures, and span of control (the number of subordinates reporting to a manager).
- Decisions are based on rules, policies, and standard operating procedures that seek to promote efficiency (and consistency). These may have both positive and negative characteristics but may inculcate a tendency to become inflexible and resist change—to become rule-based.

The Nature of Structure

Organizational structure shows how tasks in the firm are divided and then integrated to achieve coordination. Thus structure facilitates specialization within the firm, allowing members of the firm to develop and use specialized skills. In large firms, no one staff member is responsible for executing all tasks; instead, tasks are broken down into smaller, more specialized ones. Tasks within the firm are differentiated into roles such as finance, marketing, production, legal, and so on. Such specialization results in efficiency gains in the performance of individual tasks. Alternatively, such roles may be grouped into divisions or business units based on products or markets. As more skilled and specialized staff are added, differentiation within the business unit increases. This increased job specialization results in the need for increased coordination, whereby these disparate roles are integrated to ensure consistency. This coordination is achieved through control systems, culture, and so on. These principles of differentiation and integration are central to the design of organizational structure and result in the need to achieve an optimum trade-off between specialization and coordination.[11]

Structure will be influenced by the size, age, and diversity of the firm in terms of products, markets, and technology as well as the turbulence in the external environment. At the same time, consideration must be given to the cost of any structure. As the firm gets larger and more complex, the costs of operating the system will increase unless economies of scale can be demonstrated. So a firm may become unmanageable due to size and complexity.

The organizational structure also shows the *reporting* relationships and the *authority* and power relationships within the firm. Hierarchy is an essential ingredient in organizational life; it is present in all larger firms and organizations. Burns and Stalker[12] originated the idea of mechanistic and organic forms, where mechanistic forms are more rigid and the organic organizational forms are flexible. Where a firm or unit is positioned along this continuum depends on its environment, rate of change, and the degree of standardization of the product, service, or task. This relationship is an example of contingency theory, which suggests that there is no one best way to organize but that all ways to organize are not equally effective, since appropriate structure is contingent upon other factors.[13] In addition, since architecture must be considered in a total or integrative sense, structure may also be dependent of the human resources of the firm. One individual may be able to manage in a structure that may not suit others.

Nonetheless, while no single design will be best for all firms, there are some principles on which good design is based. We now discuss these principles.

Principles of Structural Design

Dynamic/Static Environments

Contingency theory suggests that there is no one best way to structure but that there are many possibilities, contingent on the situation being analyzed. So history matters, as does time orientation, task differentiation, external pressures, the technical system, size, and so on. One important variable of this type is the environment of the organization. In static environments, the mechanistic model of Burns and Stalker, to which many would apply the now almost-pejorative Weberian label of bureaucracy, was originally viewed as a great leap forward. By codifying rules to ensure that clients of organizations were treated in an equitable manner, Weber was contributing to human enlightenment by ensuring that individuals would not be subject to the whims of arbitrary or even despotic rulers and administrators. Over time, however, the connotations of the term have changed, and most of us today would equate it to ponderous, slow-moving, unthinking application of rules, more concerned with means than ends, preferring correct procedure to correct outcome.

These very connotations capture why the mechanistic and bureaucratic model is incapable of dealing with today's business environment. The speed of change means slow response cannot be tolerated, but it further means that change may outpace the organization's ability to cope. Let's be clear. Coordination cannot be achieved without some degree of predictability. March and Simon recognized this in their path-breaking work,[14] coining the phrase "standard operating procedure (sop)" to describe the rules that organizations develop to cope with recurring situations. Indeed, historically there have been guidelines for designing hierarchies—principles such as a clear line of command, reporting to only one person, clear accountability, responsibility coupled with authority, and span of control of seven.[15]

With the increased speed of change, however, the ability of the organization to develop rules is typically outpaced by change: we can't write and rewrite rules quickly enough! Further, with turbulence comes a different problem, which is the unpredictability of change. The consequence is that no matter how good a job we do in forecasting and planning, we will be unable to achieve 100% of our predictions. If this is the case, then we must build an organization that is flexible and can deal with the unanticipated changes that are a consequence of turbulence.

Tushman and O'Reilly adopted the phrase *ambidextrous organization* to capture the ability of organizing in different ways to deal with different situations.[16] The term *adhocracy* has been used to describe the innovative organization in contrast to *bureaucracy*, suggesting that we can put ad hoc teams and groups together to deal with situations as they arise, an approach that would be unnecessary in a predictable environment.[17] These ideas agree well with the Burns and Stalker concept of an *organic* organization,[18] but they are quite counter to the rigid hierarchies that characterized many 20th-century organizations. However, we see this type of change being implemented in many organizations today, as more and more firms recognize that change is needed. Devolution of responsibility, de-layering, the metamorphosing of functional organizations into business units, and the like—all provide illustrations of the general pattern of change toward more flexible and responsive structures. At the same time, we cannot leave this issue without pointing out the paradoxical nature of many of these changes, for at the same time that we urge organizations to be more flexible and responsive, we must simultaneously recognize that without some predictability of behavior, an organization ceases to be such and descends into chaos. Paradox is a fact of life in strategic management, and this will not be the only case we encounter as we examine organizational architecture.

Differentiation/Integration

The balance achieved between differentiation and integration is an important principle in the design of organizational structure.[19] Differentiation is the division of labor into specialized tasks, which allows employees to focus their abilities and be deployed for comparative advantage, thereby (in theory) developing efficiency gains. Thus activities may be grouped to achieve low cost via economies of scale. On the other hand, differentiation requires coordination to achieve integration. Firms only exist because activity coordinated by the firm is more efficient than activity coordinated by the market, so that resolving the coordination problem is vital to the efficiency and effectiveness of the business.[20] Business-unit managers must weigh the gains from specialization (and consequent differentiation) against the costs of integration.

Structure may also be influenced by decisions that have been made with respect to the role of the center, as discussed in Chapter 8. The style of the center affects not only the provision of corporate services but also the extent of differentiation and integration across business units. With a strategic planning style, there is extensive integration of strategy across the business units as the firm searches for competitive advantage. At the other extreme, financial control is characterized by few shared competences across businesses, coupled with tight financial controls. Associated with decisions about the style of the firm are decisions about the size and location of the head office. Firms with a financial style tend to have small head offices; firms with a strategic planning style tend to have larger head offices.

When discussing how businesses differentiate their activities, we can distinguish among vertical, horizontal, and spatial differentiation. **Vertical differentiation** is the number of management levels in the business, whether its structure is flat or not. The focus here is on the division of authority within the business—who has authority to make which decisions. **Horizontal differentiation** has a focus on the division and grouping of tasks. **Spatial differentiation** refers to whether distinct groups are developed within the firm for specific geographic areas. Differentiation involves combining the individual members of the firm into groups, with these groups typically demonstrating similarity by task (e.g., marketing or accounting), by product, or by geography. This differentiation in turn permits specialization and should lead to superior efficiency.

With horizontal differentiation, there is an increasing number of distinct positions at the same level within the firm. So we may have a number of accountants, all at the same level but with each undertaking specialized tasks. Horizontal differentiation may also occur with the formation of separate strategic business units discussed earlier—as when a new SBU is formed within the firm to permit a higher degree of specialization or focus on the needs of a particular market. Many firms now organize around so-called vertical markets, segmented on the basis of their customers' industries, and, as we will see later in the chapter, some are even organizing around customers themselves.

Vertical differentiation is reflected in an increased number of hierarchical levels within the firm. If the business unit is designed with many levels of management, then communication is difficult, information may be distorted, and there are limits on the ability of managers to make decisions. The business may also have too many middle managers, who add less value than their cost.

Global firms also generally need to differentiate themselves spatially in some way, such as when the firm designs an Asia–Pacific, Africa–Middle East, or European group to develop the specialized skills needed to understand specific geographic markets.

It should be clear from these examples that the more a firm is differentiated, the more difficult it is to integrate the various units. For example, a global firm may differentiate and set up a subsidiary in Argentina. This allows the firm to be more responsive to the local market. But now additional integration is needed to ensure coordination between the Argentina unit and, say, a German unit with the same product line. Developments in IT make this easier than in the past, but the integration issues remain. Too much differentiation can lead to disorder: integration and coordination become exceptionally difficult. However, too much emphasis on integration and coordination can lead to a stifling of creativity and innovation—everybody must agree, differences are not permitted!

There exist a variety of integrating mechanisms for achieving coordination, and they are not necessarily mutually exclusive. Integration can utilize lateral means, such as task forces, committees, conferences, and liaison functions as well as informal, direct, face-to-face contact. Vertical means include the formal hierarchical structure, wherein individuals higher up the organization have more authority to specify the nature of the cooperation. Additionally, rules and operating procedures can operate to facilitate cooperation.

Centralization/Decentralization

A related design consideration is the degree of authority and independence of each unit of the firm. Who has the authority to make which decisions determines the decision domain of a manager. **Centralization** is the degree to which decision-making authority is retained by senior management versus being devolved to the constituent units of the firm.

Centralization gives more control to the center but tends to increase the amount of information flowing into the center, which must then be processed so that a decision can be made and, subsequently, communicated. This has two consequences, neither of which is particularly desirable in contemporary environments. One is that it tends to produce slower decisions, and the other is that it increases the number of levels in the firm. Although both centralization and decentralization have advantages, in terms of the need for both lower cost (driven by intense competition) and speedy decision making (driven by the place of contextual change), the current trend in organizations is toward greater decentralization. This encourages empowerment and speeds response, since those closest to the action are making the decisions. We have witnessed many examples of firms downsizing, getting rid of a number of organizational levels to reduce costs in order to get decisions made at lower levels in the firm.

The classic organizational dilemma is to balance the advantages of scale against smallness. A structure of semiautonomous SBUs may produce flexibility and responsiveness but create problems of cost and control. In the worst case, information flows from business to corporate may be inaccurate, since the SBU manager wants to make his or her unit look good. SBU managers may also engage in political activity, forming alliances with other business-unit managers.

Such decisions on decentralization will usually be influenced by the strategy of the firm. For example, a strategy of cost leadership may require a structure with strong task specialization, centralized decision making, and formal work rules and procedures. By contrast, a strategy of differentiation and added value is more likely to require decentralization, more coordination and integration, and more use of teams. Likewise, a firm following a dominator strategy (as described in Chapter 7) will of necessity have to decentralize further, and it is no coincidence that Alfred Sloan was required to be an organizational innovator in order to implement the strategy he designed for General Motors. It is to Sloan that we owe the introduction of divisionalization and the reporting systems that permitted such a structure to flourish.

The environment in which the firm competes also influences centralization and decentralization decisions. Large, undifferentiated commodity-type markets are an environment much better suited to central management and control than is a heavily segmented and differentiated market, which will mandate a greater degree of decentralization.

Functional or Process Management

Another design issue is the consideration given to the importance of vertical *functions* as against different horizontal *processes*. We can think of these as two different perspectives on the firm. The traditional view has been to take a functional perspective, but firms have many important processes. For example, a process such as new product development draws on the skills of various functional groups, such as R&D, marketing, accounting, operations, and so on. Similarly, pricing decision processes may involve accounting, marketing, sales, finance, and general management. Is it more productive for shareholders to consider the firm as requiring managing a number of functions or a number of processes?

Ultimately, of course, we must manage both, but the adoption of total quality management (TQM) has undoubtedly encouraged many more firms to examine their processes more closely, as has the impact of information technology. Of course, business processes are not immutable, and the reduced cost and widespread availability of information technology has given many firms the opportunity to consider changing (reengineering[21]) their business processes. As we will see, however, there is often tension between function and process, and these tensions may defeat attempts at change.

Types of Organizational Structures

Organization structure has evolved over time along with the challenges faced by large corporations. Thus, although it is not our intent, as we review structural forms in this section, we also are recapitulating the historical evolution of the major corporation.

Functional Structures

The functional structure is likely to be used by firms with low levels of product and market diversity and in SBUs within a specific division of a multidivisional firm. Such a structure is illustrated in Figure 11.2, with a chief executive officer and managers for each of the major functions of the firm or business, such as marketing, accounting, human resources, and manufacturing. Such a structure permits development of specialization and consequent efficiency gains in these functional areas. A functional organization also permits economies of scale by bringing together in the one department activities that demonstrate substantial interdependencies—a cost accountant for product 1 may learn from the accountant for product 2 and vice versa.

With a functional structure, a major role for the CEO is ensuring integration among the departments. Thus manufacturing may want to reduce the product line to achieve higher product volumes of the remaining products, thereby improving economies of scale. Conversely, marketing may want to increase the line width to appeal to a broader market. Resolving this conflict, or integrating the two department views to get a common organizational view, is the CEO's responsibility.

This example also reveals one of the difficulties with such a functional structure: the tendency for the firm or business to develop functional "silos" between which there is very limited lateral communication at lower levels. Information flows are generally vertical—since the CEO needs to be kept informed—and are integrated only at the CEO level. This may result in slow decision making by the CEO, who has to resolve all disputes, while if the information has to pass through several vertical levels ("filters"), it may become distorted along the way.[22]

Many decisions will require coordination across functions to achieve integration and alignment. For example, the accounting department may suggest a price increase for a

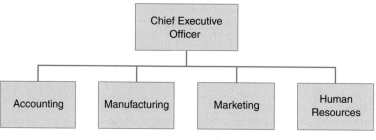

Figure 11.2 Functional Structure

product, but without understanding how this may affect demand and competitive position. Marketing inputs would then be required to make a good decision. Or marketing may want to improve product quality, but manufacturing is more concerned with minimizing costs. Making this type of decision so as to benefit shareholders requires obtaining inputs from all the relevant functional departments. Of course, not all integration is achieved via the CEO or general manager. Other means of achieving coordination and integration include task forces, made up of members from the different departments, or the use of liaison personnel operating at the interface between departments.

Functional structures work better when there is limited diversity of tasks within the function. When this is not the case, the functional department is itself generally organized by subfunction. A marketing department may be organized into sales, advertising, direct marketing, and market research subgroups. Again, there may be advantages of specialization and possible economies of scale, but the integration problems are further complicated. The emergence of these subfunctions is more likely as the company grows in size and the number of vertical levels within a functional department increases. The resulting structures can become very unwieldy and foster internal conflict. Marketing staff may, even unconsciously, regard manufacturing staff as the enemy, a group who are always opposing the wonderful ideas put forward by marketing, while accounting simply wants to postpone all "unnecessary" expenditure.

> As one CEO, troubled by such problems, commented, "The trouble with this company is that the functional elevators don't stop until they reach the 20th floor. I'm going to make sure that they stop much lower down!"

Apart from size, what really renders a functional structure dysfunctional is product, market, or technological diversity—and the resultant task diversity. If a firm is successful, it will grow, and as it grows, its mix of products, markets, and technologies inevitably becomes more complex. For this reason, most global firms are organized on a divisional basis, an innovation that permits them to handle diversity in products, markets, and technologies.

Divisional Structure

As firms became more diversified, it became apparent that the simple functional structure was retarding rather than facilitating strategy. Thus most large global firms now operate with some form of a divisional (or strategic business unit) structure, as shown in Figure 11.3. In such structures, responsibility for the performance of a unit is given to divisional managers, with the performance of the unit measured by the corporate center. Of course, which tasks are performed at the corporate level versus which are decentralized and which performance measures are used are all important topics in strategic management. Appropriate divisional control systems are neither so bureaucratic as to inhibit creativity by division personnel nor so loose as to endanger shareholder interests. However, encouraging divisions to draw on central resources and contribute to the total firm is often a challenging undertaking.

Responsibility for strategy development for each business unit (or possibly collections of business units) is delegated to the business-unit manager, who is also held accountable for the performance of the unit. In such a structure, corporate staff are responsible for corporate-level strategy, such as acquisitions and divestments, as well as the provision of certain corporate services.

Under such a structure, the *autonomy* of the business-unit manager will be influenced by the style adopted by the corporate center. The manager reports to the CEO in

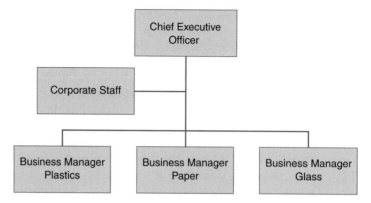

Figure 11.3 Multidivisional Structure

the corporate center and is therefore not truly independent. Corporate staff will decide on a set of controls to ensure that these business-unit managers meet their agreed-upon objectives, and with a strategic planning style, all strategy proposals must be approved by corporate staff. With a financial control style, the emphasis would fall primarily on the financial results to be achieved, with less concern from the center about the details of business-unit strategy. Such measures as EBITDA, cash flow, ROI, ROS, and, possibly, economic profit would be the prime corporate focus. Since each business is operated and evaluated as a relatively independent unit, a relatively standardized information system is required so that comparisons between the different units can be conducted.

Among the advantages of such a structure is the decentralization of decision making. Corporate management focus on strategic issues for the firm—capital allocation, overall direction, decisions to buy and sell businesses. Managers in the business are responsible for strategy and tactics at the business-unit level. This structure also improves accountability. Corporate staff have an advisory and audit function and hold division managers responsible for performance. Since units put up proposals to corporate for funds, competition for capital within the firm is a feature. This should improve allocation of capital, since cash flows go to corporate treasury and then back to divisions on a competitive basis.

One possible disadvantage when the firm becomes very diverse is that senior managers have a very limited understanding of the various business units. They can become very distant, preoccupied with financial markets, and have limited familiarity with the industry, competition, technology, and so on despite the fact that they have to make decisions on plans and strategies put forward by business-unit managers.

Within each division, the structure is normally organized on a functional basis, often resulting in duplication of many functions that exist in each division. Not all functions are decentralized. R&D, strategic planning, legal, and finance are often centralized corporate functions. However, the costs of any functional duplication are one of the disadvantages of divisionalization. The firm may miss possible opportunities for economies of scale that could be achieved by combining these functions. Ideally, however, the gains that come from detailed knowledge of the competitive situation of the business will outweigh the cost of duplication.

Such a structure will not remove all conflicts among lower-level managers. For example, there is often disagreement among the SBU managers over the allocation of corporate overheads. Depending on the style of the center, there may also be ambiguity as to who is responsible for SBU performance. Issues such as the definition of business units, reporting relationships, and transfer pricing may bedevil a divisionalized organization.[23]

An example of this divisional structure is provided by Ciba Specialty Chemicals.

Ciba Speciality Chemicals is a major producer of specialty chemicals with sales in 2003 of CHFB6.6, ($USB5.0).[24] The firm operates globally, with operations in some 120 countries. In 2001, senior management concluded that the company needed to increase customer focus, attain greater flexibility in operations, and respond faster to the marketplace. The firm reorganized as shown in Figure 11.4:

The company mission statement emphasizes the importance of innovation and superior products, and this is reflected by the high profile given to technology in the firm. The strategy is one of innovation and continuous operational improvement, and the firm has chosen to operate only in specialty chemicals, deliberately avoiding competing in the commodity chemical segment. To support this, the chief technology officer leads the effort to share core technical competences across the segments, as well as identifying new areas of opportunity. Environmental compliance is obviously a key issue for a chemical company, and this is reflected in the structure, with the legal and environmental reporting directly to the CEO

Ciba operates a number of groups, which it calls segments, each of which operates on a global basis, where these segments are differentiated on the basis of customer or market. Segment managers are responsible for marketing, R&D, production, and sales, while noncore support functions are provided by the centralized service units on a global basis, as shown in Figure 11.4. The Water and Paper Group supplies coagulants and retention products that improve the separation of solid/liquid mixtures. The Home and Personal Care Group supplies ingredients for skin and hair-care products and laundry products. In this way the firm believes that the different segments can develop integrated solutions tailored to the needs of that specific segment. The Ciba example provides an excellent illustration of a structure that is well aligned with the strategy of the company.

Group Structure
When firms are even larger, with a significant number of relatively independent businesses, these may first be assigned to broad product groups, with SBUs reporting to the

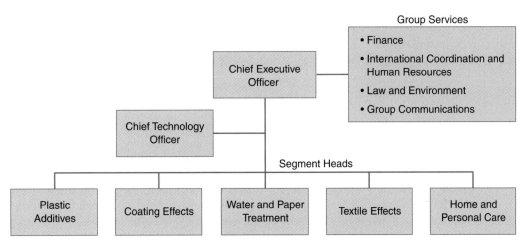

Figure 11.4 Organizational Structure for Ciba Specialty Chemicals
Source: 'Ciba Corporate Management," 2002: www.cibasc.com.
Reproduced by permission of Ciba Specialty Chemicals Inc.

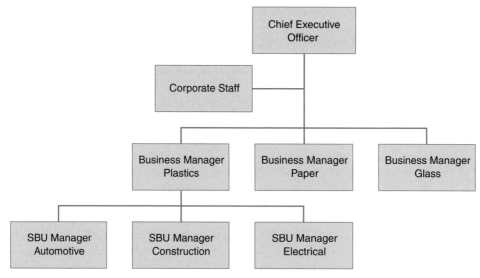

Figure 11.5 Group and Business Structure

different groups. The group structure of a hypothetical company is illustrated in Figure 11.5. The figure shows the detailed structure for only one group, the Plastics Group. This group has a group manager and possibly group-level staff. The group itself is made up of a number of SBUs, here automotive, construction, and electrical. Each of these SBUs is an independent business, competing in its own market against a defined set of competitors.

A group structure may be formed on the basis of products, markets, technologies, or geography:

Product: Commercial banks are often organized around product groups, such as lending, mortgages, current accounts, and so on.

Markets: This approach may keep more of a customer orientation and be more responsive to changing needs and meeting new customer requirements. Our Siemens example in Chapter 8 (Figure 8.1) featured groups for power, lighting, and so on.

Technologies: Such a structure is depicted in Figure 11.5, with groups for paper, plastic, and glass technologies.

Geography: Such groups might be regional within a continent or country but are probably most common in large global firms, many of which have groups for the U.S., European, Middle Eastern, African, Latin American, and Asian markets.

As with divisionalized structures, groups can result in lost economies of scale and higher costs. Groups may each employ specialist financial staff for reasons of accountability and focus. Staff within the business is naturally more focused on the needs of that business, whereas centralized staff will face more competing demands. Nonetheless, wasteful duplication must be avoided, and there is too often a tendency for group CEOs to empire-build. This is one of the critical organizational paradoxes to which we earlier referred.

Corporate management, which is responsible for the structure of the firm, needs to periodically consider whether to change the number and definition of SBUs to reflect changes in the environment and changes in firm strategy. The goal should be to combine structure and control systems so as to both motivate and control the business units' personnel. This does not imply complete uniformity, however, a growth business may need a quite different structure, incentive, and planning system from a more mature business unit.

Hybrid or Mixed Structure

Most global firms are hybrid structures, with some activities and functions undertaken in the corporate center and others at the group or business level. The choice is often among a product/technology structure, a market structure, and a geographic structure. In reality, however, most global firms will have some kind of hybrid structure, a combination of two of these dimensions. Further, the recent tendency has been to reduce the size of the corporate center, placing as much functional responsibility as is feasible into operating groups or divisions.

The size and nature of these corporate service staff will be influenced by the diversification strategy of the firm. When the firm has undertaken an unrelated diversification strategy, we are likely to see a structure with limited corporate staff—finance, legal, auditing, together with independent divisions or businesses. Such firms create value by efficient internal capital allocation or by buying and selling businesses. Firms that have undertaken a more related diversification may see greater advantage to a centralized staff for such functions as R&D.

Again, these firms require some integrating mechanism. To some extent this integration is accomplished by systems such as the planning system, since business-unit higher-level management must approve plans. We also see global firms using liaison staff, who try to straddle different groups or businesses, as well as temporary teams established on a project basis.

Global Structure

Global firms have a requirement for global efficiency. In many product fields there is a degree of customer convergence around the world, as is evident with consumer products such as DVDs, personal computers, jeans, and so on. Similarly, for industrial goods such as chemicals or steel, customers all require essentially the same product. So global competitors can take advantage of economies of scale to develop efficiencies, which may be unattainable by their local competitors. At the same time, global firms have to be sensitive to local needs and differences. Some of these local differences are related to culture, some are related to the fact that many products are part of a total use-system, some may result from government regulation, and so on. For example, different countries have specific legislation regarding the environmental impact of products, such that cars that can be sold in one country may not be able to be sold in another. Global firms need to balance off the desire to achieve cost advantages with the requirement to be flexible enough to respond to these local needs.

Bartlett and Ghoshal suggested four types of structures for global firms:[25]

International: The company has an international division, often regarded as an appendage by the firm.

Multinational: A corporate center manages a portfolio of multiple national entities, each of which may be regarded as a business unit.

Global: The company treats the world as an integrated whole and manages in a centralized manner, with little attention paid to local differences. Some large Japanese companies in automobiles and consumer electronics operate like this.

Transnational: These firms try to ensure that they do three things: use scale and cost leadership as one source of competitive advantage, adopt differentiation in product as a way to enhance performance, and, finally, use innovations, generally created at the corporate center, to gain new sources of revenue.

Transnational firms in the Bartlett and Ghoshal typology are attempting to get the best of both worlds: the advantages of scale with the flexibility of local operations. Thus operations around the world are not standardized. Some groups may be pursuing a differentiated strategy, while others pursue a low-cost strategy with standard products. Nonetheless, these companies encourage knowledge sharing (not all knowledge is assumed to be created at the corporate center), and they have procedures to share knowledge worldwide. Some activities, such as basic research, are centralized to protect core competences. On the other hand, applied research centers may be distributed around the world, with specialist R&D centers in different countries depending on the skills and markets within those countries. So innovation is both centrally and locally driven. Both Nestlé and Unilever follow such an approach.

Achieving a synthesis between global efficiency and local responsiveness represents a significant management challenge. Perhaps as a result, structures tend to be quite complicated.

> Unilever is now organized into two global divisions—Bestfoods and Home and Personal Care. Each of these in turn is organized into a number of regional groups:
>
> - Home and Personal Care Regions: Asia, Europe, Latin America, North America
> - Bestfoods Regions: Africa, Asia, Europe, Latin America, North America
>
> On the other hand, Ice Cream and Frozen Foods is a global business within Bestfoods, while DiverseyLever operates on a stand-alone worldwide basis.

Each region comprises a number of local operating companies, which are regarded as the core building blocks for Unilever, allowing rapid response to local needs.

There is certainly no single model of structure used by global companies; what is selected reflects their history and current concerns and the degree and nature of interaction among the units. Whatever basis is selected will need coordinating mechanisms.

Matrix Structure

A matrix structure is one in which there is a dual structure, combining both functional specialization and business product or project specialization. Such structures have always been common in firms that operate on the basis of projects, such as engineering construction firms like Bechtel or military contractors. Superimposed on a fairly standard differentiation of tasks into functions such as engineering, sales, and marketing is a further differentiation based on project or product. Each staff member works in a project team with specialists from other functions and has two bosses, a functional boss and a project boss. With this type of matrix structure, the appropriate skills and resources are assembled for each project. However, a significant proportion of large companies that are not project-oriented are now organized in a similar manner, generally on the basis of business group and geography, so it is important to understand the advantages and disadvantages of matrices.

Consider a structure formed around global product groups. Such a structure may allow the firm to achieve superior efficiency and quality but may also be weak in terms of customer responsiveness. If, for example, each group has a specialized sales force, there is not only a cost penalty but also the possibility of aggravating customers who prefer a single point of contact. In addition, the lateral flow of information among product groups is likely to be inhibited. Of course, if the company organized around markets instead, there would be commensurate difficulties in obtaining scale economics by product, for example. It was for this sort of reason that an exasperated IBM executive once exclaimed, "There is no best way to organize—there is only the least worst."

The problem is that managing a large diverse company with operations in multiple countries is a multidimensional problem, and the formal anatomy of the organization's structure cannot deal with more than two or three of these. A global matrix represents a way to deal with at least two dimensions. Instead of a vertical axis of functions, for example, it could be product groups, which provide specialist services such as R&D, marketing, and product design. The horizontal axis is the geographic groups—Europe, Asia and so on—so as to get a degree of local flexibility and better transfer of market information and experience.

Project-based matrices, while they may afford limited hierarchical control, permit project teams to grow, shrink, and change as required. It is therefore a very flexible structure—a classic example of adhocracy—but the costs are likely to be substantial, and it is often difficult to balance interests of function and project. In large companies operating across the globe, matrices exhibit similar problems. Members of the organization often have difficulty dealing with what are, in effect, dual reporting relationships, and priorities may well be ambiguous. Nonetheless, the debates spawned by differences over priorities can, if appropriately managed, significantly improve the resulting strategic decisions. Obviously, the culture of the company and its approaches to dealing with such conflicts will determine whether or not the process concludes productively or otherwise.

The resulting matrix structures of global firms can become very complex, as is shown by the Procter & Gamble example in Figure 11.6. P&G describes its structure as attempting to balance two divergent yet complementary perspectives: think globally and act locally. The company has five *global business units*, Fabric & Home Care, Beauty Care and so on as shown. These business units (probably what we would have called a group, since each involves a number of products) are encouraged to think globally, to create strong brands around the world, and to continually innovate in their chosen product areas. To attend to local needs, the firm also utilizes *market development organizations*. These are designed to think locally, to develop local knowledge and understanding, and to leverage corporate scale at the local level. The firm has seven of these, which span the world.

To achieve cost economies in back office transactional services, P&G has outsourced a number of these *global business services*, for example, human resources and payroll, to external suppliers such as HP and IBM, with P&G staff maintaining a planning and oversight role. P&G also has a number of centralized *corporate functions* which are charged with ensuring that functional capability is integrated across the firm, as well as certain functions that are really "corporate", such as finance and external relations.

This complex and therefore quite expensive structure is aimed at getting the best of all worlds: functional excellence, coordination and integration, cost efficiencies, innovation, and local responsiveness. Such is the challenge faced by the architects of today's global corporations.

Other Organizational Forms

As firms search for structures that assist strategy development and implementation, they often innovate with forms beyond the basic structures described above. A structure that supports strategy development and implementation, while simultaneously creating efficiency together with adaptability, speed, and flexibility, represents an ongoing challenge. Global firms face a particular problem, for employees in the various subsidiaries often feel that all decisions are made by remote figure at the head office who have no understanding of the competitive pressures in their marketplace.

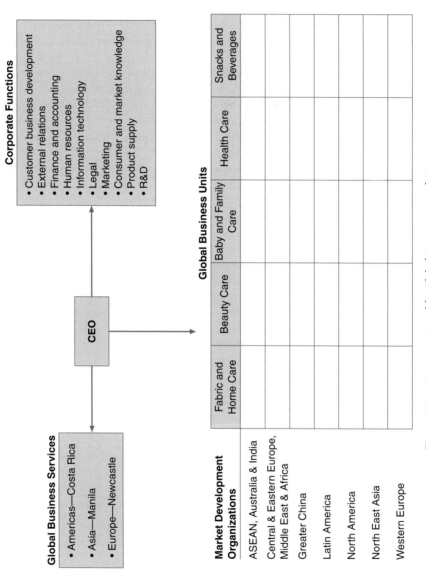

Figure 11.6 Procter & Gamble Global Organizational Structure

Source: P&G Annual Report, 2002: www.pg.com.

Reproduced by permission of The Procter & Gamble Company.

These new forms of organization share some common characteristics:

- The focus is on coordination rather than control. Cooperation is obtained through financial and professional incentives, with greater emphasis on social rather than managerial control.
- Individuals possess multiple organizational roles, which is seen as a way to reconcile complex patterns of coordination with high levels of flexibility and responsiveness.

Handy has noted that organizations of the future will have to deal with a number of *paradoxes,* combining bigness with smallness, creativity with efficiency, and prosperity with social acceptability, as well as having to reward the owners of ideas and the owners of the firm.[26] Knowledge staff will be increasingly unwilling to cede all property rights in their ideas to the firm.

These ideas suggest an incipient move away from bureaucratic structures and toward greater *flexibility:* organizations that can tap into the commitment and enthusiasm of people, encouraging them to develop their creativity. Customer pressure is also playing a part. Customers do not buy products from a function, but from a firm! Success in a competitive world will require much better integration across the various functions of a business, which has in turn increased the emphasis on a process view of managing.[27]

Current trends in organizational design that represent responses to these challenges include reduction in the number of layers; adoption of process teams; reengineering of processes; open communications; alliances with suppliers, customers, and possibly competitors; and adoption and use of information technology. These changes will require more training of and skill development by staff. Staff empowerment is likely to increase, although increases in autonomy will be coupled with better control systems. Control will continue to be based on both quantitative and cultural elements, but the latter are likely to become more important. We will also see continuing development of information systems that provide reliable and up-to-date information throughout the firm.

Networks and Alliances

As we noted in Chapter 3, competition increasingly occurs between whole networks and industry systems. Traditional joint ventures sometimes metamorphosed into other forms, sometimes contractually bound as a result of outsourcing decisions, but at other times consisting of quite informal, even ephemeral, relationships. The ideas that one company's strengths can offset another's weaknesses or that collaboration in a vertical value chain may be worthwhile are representative of the concepts that have fostered such alliances. Other firms, shy of merging or acquiring, see alliances as a form of courtship that may later lead to consummation in some form.

This organizational form may also be chosen when a firm wishes to enter a new business area but lacks the requisite assets—such as capital, skills, technology, and market access—or is unwilling to assume the risk and full entry costs itself, instead seeking an alliance with a partner firm. Although the immediate impact of such alliance announcements may appear threatening to competitors, problems often occur when the partners' alliance objectives and/or ability to provide needed resources diverge over time. Nonetheless, some succeed.

General Mills, a large U.S. producer of breakfast cereals, lacked export distribution. Swiss-based Nestlé, one of the world's largest food companies, had excellent European distribution but did not carry breakfast cereals. The two companies allied to form Cereal Partners, which has become a major competitor to Kellogg's.

Some of the more important alliances are vertical partnerships in which the company forms close linkages with its suppliers. In some cases these partnerships result from mutuality of interest and are positive-sum games (win–win situations), creating formidable supply-chain advantages. In other cases, "partnership" may be forced on the weaker firm by the relative market power of the other and be no more than a somewhat unpalatable way of forestalling potential supply-chain competition.

A major problem of alliances is how control is to be exercised. Who has control? How can firms operate both cooperatively and competitively at the same time? What will be the reaction of regulatory bodies to these networks—will they be seen as anticompetitive? These are all important questions that must be addressed by alliance partners.

11.3 PROCESSES AND PROCESS MANAGEMENT

As we have emphasized throughout this book, an increasingly competitive environment requires ever-higher levels of corporate performance. It is often claimed that the functional structure that underlies the superstructure of most firms inhibits this achievement. The traditional vertical division of work into functions, then into departments within these functions, and finally into tasks certainly permits a high degree of specialization as well as a decision hierarchy. Yet such functional specialization may or may not lead to high levels of customer satisfaction or financial performance. For example, if there is little coordination between marketing and manufacturing in new product development, and no research on customers needs is undertaken, it is unlikely that the company will achieve either customer satisfaction or profit from the new product.

When managers see their organizations in this vertical fashion, they tend to manage them in the same way: vertically. Such a perspective tends to ignore the customer and enamor managers with their own functional expertise. There is a distressing tendency, sometimes reinforced by reward systems, for managers to concentrate on functional optimization, with the firm generating functional silos across which there is little or no communication. Thus the key challenge of such functional structures is coordination across tasks, departments, and functions.[28] As we have seen, integrating mechanisms such as committees and task forces may assist in this coordination, but sometimes this is not sufficient and a more radical solution may be called for.

> No matter how a company chooses to organize, important issues will arise that cut across organizational lines. It was for this reasons that Jack Welch, when CEO of General Electric, endorsed the idea of the "boundaryless" organization.[29] While a devotee of process mapping and reengineering, he nonetheless exhorted his managers to cross organizational lines whenever they encountered a problem or opportunity that required it. His desire to create a more entrepreneurial GE was so strong that he said he would make so many people report to a manager that he would not be able to manage them. Empowerment by default meant that managers would have to lead rather than micromanage their subordinates.

From another perspective, the firm can be viewed as a set of **processes** that deliver products and services and receive funds for them and that, to perform well, it must excel in each of these processes. If we consider the firm from the customers' perspective, they have little interest in how the firm is structured and organized—they want products and services developed and delivered efficiently and effectively. If a product they have purchased requires service, they do not want to know where the service department is housed, how service is coordinated with spare parts, and so on.

Whereas some processes are generic, others are industry-specific. Industry-specific processes include loan processing in banking, claims processing in insurance, and car servicing in auto dealerships. Examples of generic processes include, but are not limited to:

Order generation and fulfillment

Product development

Customer service

Supply-chain management

In addition, there are a number of generic managerial processes, such as:

Planning

Budgeting

Cost analysis

Acquisition evaluation

Resource allocation

Competence transfer

In recognition of these concerns, many firms have realized that needed performance improvements remain out of reach when the business is organized in the traditional vertical fashion, which is hierarchically structured and functionally oriented. Today's competitive environment seems to require superb coordination between the functions as well as functional excellence.

There is real performance leverage in moving toward a flatter, more horizontal mode of organization in which cross-functional, end-to-end work flows link internal processes with the needs and capabilities of both suppliers and customers. This form of organizational design is horizontal in nature, with the business organized around processes not tasks. Owners are then assigned to these processes with responsibility for process performance and improvement. In this way, process teams, not individuals, are the principal building blocks for organizational design. This has been described as the horizontal organization,[30] and many businesses have undertaken reengineering to improve the costs and performance of their processes. Indeed, it can be said that a firm is only as effective as its processes.

A process-based organization may be thought of as a type of matrix organization, since the horizontal process-based structure is usually overlaid on the vertical functional structure. Of course, conflict between the vertical and the horizontal structures is possible, and disputes over power and authority may occur, as with a project-based matrix. Process managers should have end-to-end responsibility, since they are often asked to work to process measures, such as time to respond. Process managers attempt to improve performance on such measures to create a competitive advantage, but they often have to work through the functional structure to make improvements. Cooperative values are obviously a great help in avoiding destructive conflict in such matrices.

Key Process Management Activities

Strategic managers will be actively monitoring the development and/or effectiveness of a number of systems. In a multibusiness company, one of the most important challenges is to develop systems to encourage synergy between businesses. Best-practice sharing is one example of such a system. For example, manufacturing competence in quality may be transferred from one business to another, although without some kind of reciprocal benefit, the first business may not go out of its way to help! After all, it might be argued, other businesses benefit but do not contribute to the cost of developing the expertise. Clearly, appropriate culture can also facilitate transfer and must encourage learning. Businesses must be open to new ideas in areas where they are underperforming. Besides sharing best practice, other synergies may be possible. Thus a product innovation in one area helps another business develop and market a complementary product. Further, central services—such as R&D—provided by corporate may add value to a number of businesses, although the benefits may be hard to realize.

Decision-making processes and information flows must be specified for both the corporate and business-unit levels. The information system must include strategic control as well as monitoring activities to see what is being achieved and whether corrective action is needed. In this context, the balanced scorecard may be very useful.[31] Certainly, as will be discussed Chapter 12, performance management requires much more than a bottom-line focus!

Corporate staff also have to decide on the information technology platform to be used by the firm, and this is becoming ever more critical. It is the largest capital expense for many organizations, particularly service firms. For these it is often the infrastructure that enables new products, new organizational forms, and access to new markets. However, some firms are much more successful at generating value from their IT investments. We will discuss the IT infrastructure later in the chapter.

Business Process Reengineering

Business process reengineering (BPR) adopts processes as the building blocks of organizations. How a customer order is fulfilled, new products developed, or customer accounts processed should operate without regard to functional boundaries. If a phone system needs repair, customers don't care what department is responsible or who orders the parts—they just want the job done! Many of a firm's legacy systems and processes antedate the development of sophisticated information technology, and BPR capitalizes on these developments to transform, rather than merely automate, existing processes.[32]

The BPR philosophy is that each of the firm's processes should add value. These end-to-end processes cut across traditional function-based management structures. Reengineering requires improving these process and embraces the Japanese *kaizen* concept of continuous improvement. Of course, functions provide centers of expertise and knowledge in essential skills as well as constituting a means of collecting and disseminating information from outside the firm, which can then be internalized. However, the integration of functional activities is vital, for success can typically be achieved only through the efforts of more than one function.[33] Indeed, the late quality guru W. Edwards Deming pointed out that all important processes in the firm cut across multiple functions, and certainly such processes as product development or new market entry provide excellent examples of this transcension.

BPR was initially hailed as a magic cure-all for companies' problems. Certainly, the idea that a business should identify its core processes and then look at how they can be improved is extremely important. In practice, however, BPR usually runs into significant implementation problems. Because important processes cut horizontally across so many functions, their reengineering requires many persons and departments to change their work processes. The natural inertia present in so many large companies means that change is resisted, often very broadly, presenting significant obstacles to BPR proponents. Understanding the process and politics of organizational change is a necessary prerequisite for successful BPR. Further, processes require leadership, teamwork, and empowerment deep in the firm, and process management may well entail developing different reward systems, based at least partly on process measures.

Information Technology Infrastructure

As we saw in Chapter 3, the ratio of information technology (IT) investment to all other business investment is now about 85%. IT describes the firm's total investment in computing and communications technology, including hardware, software, telecommunications, devices for collecting and representing data (such as an ATM or PDA), and all electronically stored data. It is critical that these investments generate value for shareholders. Further, business units need to develop information systems within the parameters of the corporate information system, which involves an integrated set of technology choices regarding computers, operating systems, communications networks, data storage, and transmission.

The Internet has changed the cost of information, in terms of both availability and transmission, and thus the structure of markets and the terms of competition. Now businesses may have to compete in real time, share data in real time, and make deals in real time. For example, the Internet has revolutionized supply-chain management, and both suppliers and customers seek access to companies' information systems.[34]

> Starting in the 1980s, Federal Express offered its customers the ability to track packages by calling an 800 number. Nowadays, FedEx's Internet-based system enables customers to track packages, schedule pickups, and generate and print airbills, complete with bar codes, themselves. As a result, customer value has increased at the same time that FedEx's costs have been reduced.[35]

Aligning strategy and IT infrastructure is not easy, but it is becoming a key element in achieving success in the marketplace. Weill suggests four major areas for IT investment.[36]

- *Infrastructure:* This provides the basis for integration and subsequent flexibility. It is shared by many of the firm's businesses, coordinated centrally, and includes network services, provision of computing, database management, and intranet capability.

- *Transactional:* This supports the business by lowering costs and enabling greater throughput by automating basic repetitive transactions of the firm, such as accounts receivable and order processing.

- *Informational:* This permits better control of performance and quality and subsumes such activities as planning, communication, and accounting.

- *Strategic:* This enhances competitive advantage and encourages innovation, leading to improvements in sales and/or market position.

Infrastructure accounts for over half of the average firm's IT expenditure, and, whether IT is outsourced or not, strategic management must be actively involved in policy. Indeed, top management support is key to IT success, since, among other benefits, it reduces the associated political turbulence. Other factors that lead to successful IT implementation include a shared focus for the firm (in actionable terms) and an understanding of which activities must be centrally controlled and which decentralized. Key processes include continuous innovation, developing partnerships with customers, ongoing cost reductions, and increased operational effectiveness. If these conditions are fulfilled, IT can be the crucial element in achieving industry leadership:

> Dell's system requires no human intervention, from taking the customer order, to delivery of the components to Dell for assembly, to shipment to the customer. The system also has some intelligence, since it checks customer requirements and provides options.[37]

Major IT Initiatives

The last few years have seen large numbers of companies undertake major IT systems initiatives in a number of areas. We now review three of the most important.

Enterprise Resource Planning (ERP)

ERP systems are large computer applications allowing a business to manage all its operations, finance, human resources, requirements planning, and order fulfillment on the basis of a single, integrated set of corporate data. It promises improvements in efficiency, with shorter times between orders and payments, lower back-office staff levels, reduced inventory, and improved customer service.

Customer and sales data are entered into the ERP system, which produces a sales forecast, in turn generating orders for raw materials, production schedules, timetables for shifts, and financial projections; it also keeps track of inventory. The value of such a system lies in the use of common data: information has the same vocabulary and format.

While in the last decade businesses have invested some $USB300 in ERP,[38] the installation of many such systems has been traumatic, long, and expensive; it has also been hard to measure the benefits.

> In April 2003, the CEO of ICI, the U.K. chemicals company was forced to resign. His demise was due to the flawed implementation of ERP at ICI's Qwest subsidiary, which had resulted in alienation of customers and large-scale loss of business.[39]

Customer Relationship Management (CRM)

Another major systems application over the last few years is customer relationship management (CRM). CRM is typically viewed as a process of managing relationships with existing customers in order to maximize their loyalty and thus improve profitability. The firm's focus with CRM is to improve customer identification, conversion, acquisition, and retention. The objective is to improve levels of customer satisfaction, boost customer loyalty, and increase revenues from existing customers in the face of high competition, high customer turnover, and growing customer acquisition costs.

There is a focus on customer value as the business generates the ability to sell several products to one customer, to differentiate customers, and to maintain continuous customer interaction and participation. Customer value is viewed over a lifetime, not as a single transaction, and customers are assumed to require individualization.[40] Interestingly, many firms fail to comprehend that a relationship has to be two-way. They focus on the value *of* the customer rather than value *to* the customer, thereby failing to realize increases in shareholder value from the system investments they have made.

Supply-Chain Management

Many firms are focused on reducing the costs and improving the performance of the entire supply chain. The objective in supply-chain management is to remove inventory from the total system (including suppliers and customers) through better information and coordination, while maintaining levels of customer service. Costs are taken out of the entire industry value chain through this cooperative behavior. Wal-Mart, now the biggest company in the world as measured by revenue, has been a very successful exponent of these strategies.

Unfortunately, overhyped promises by sellers of IT systems have left many senior executives more uncertain than ever before about what can actually be achieved through IT use. Typical problems include lack of integration of systems, missed business opportunities, IT priorities not based on business needs, and an incoherent technology strategy resulting in the selection of incompatible options. Since new technologies come and go quite rapidly, it is perhaps not surprising that many firms are now outsourcing IT.

Knowledge Management Systems

As we have seen, strategy development and implementation are increasingly dependent on the acquisition and use of knowledge and information. For example, a retailer who has developed a knowledge management system with information on inventory, costs, customer preferences, and shopping patterns is likely to possess a competitive advantage.

Knowledge management systems consist of four interrelated activities:

Developing knowledge

Storing knowledge

Transferring knowledge

Using knowledge

We examine each of these activities in turn.

Developing Knowledge

Many companies believe that knowledge generation resides in functional groups such as R&D or marketing, but knowledge generation must exist for all processes and functional areas of the firm. Knowledge is no less important in finance (e.g., acquisition screening processes) or operations (e.g., better production scheduling). We need to develop and capture knowledge in both individuals and the firm. Achieving this goal demands understanding the conditions influencing creativity and innovation, such as attitudes toward risk and mistakes and high-performance teams. New knowledge frequently arises at the boundaries of the old, so that knowledge generation requires the creativity that accompanies conflict between different disciplines or perspectives.

The first step in knowledge management is to proactively manage how the firm consciously and intentionally develops new knowledge. At Nucor, success at knowledge creation has come from three elements: superior human capital, high-powered incentives, and a high degree of empowerment. These, together with a tolerance for failure, a high degree of accountability, and encouragement of creativity and experimentation, are seen as essential for knowledge development.[41]

Since much knowledge resides in the brains of the staff, there is a question of who benefits from this knowledge—the firm or the individual staff member. If individual staff members capture all the benefits of knowledge in the form of higher salaries, this may limit the extent to which the firm engages in knowledge-generating activities such as developing individuals via training and education.

Knowledge generation can also be accomplished by acquiring a firm or an individual. If we buy another firm, we generally acquire individuals as well as structured knowledge. Some firms, such as Cisco, seem to have been successful by buying young, high-potential firms and successfully integrating these in to the established culture. When this is done, we have to ensure that the high-potential staff remain with us. The firm may also use external sources of new knowledge such as universities, research institutes, the Internet, and alliances with competitors, customers, and/or suppliers. We can also rent knowledge by hiring a consultant, but then we should ensure that there is some transfer to the firm.

Storing Knowledge

Structured knowledge can be stored in a database or repository accessible via an intranet, which is a network of documents, reports, policies, and so on. Alternatively, information and knowledge may be stored in an external database, the largest of which is the Internet itself. Electronic storage is low-cost and has almost infinite capacity when material is stored in digital form, which also makes it easy to transmit and process. For example, the Internet search engine Google indexed 3.3 billion text documents as of September 2003.

When the firm develops an intranet, data security is paramount and firewalls must prevent unauthorized access or hacking. Nonetheless, not all knowledge is explicit and capable of being stored by these formal means. Substantial knowledge is stored in people's heads and is lost to the firm if they leave the firm.

Transferring Knowledge

To successfully manage knowledge transfer, managers need to nurture a culture that encourages sharing of insights. Knowledge transfer is not simply a technical issue, for although information technology and electronic connectivity can assist knowledge transfer, they must be embedded in a supportive culture. Data and information can be transferred electronically, but tacit knowledge is transferred most successfully through human networks. Knowledge is ultimately created in the human brain, and only the right organizational climate can persuade people to create, reveal, share, and use knowledge.

We can employ the concept of a **knowledge market** within a firm, the mechanism by which knowledge is shared. Generally this is not a very efficient market; in other words, we cannot assume that people in a firm will share knowledge freely. However, the concept of a knowledge market forces managers to consider the incentives for individuals to share their knowledge. Transfer will be influenced by such factors as whether reciprocity exists when information is shared, what incentives are offered, and whether the providers want to be known as knowledgeable persons or are altruistic.[42] To share knowledge, staff need to trust others and management. Employees are not likely to share their personal knowledge when they fear for their job. A supportive knowledge culture cannot survive without trust.

A lot of knowledge management techniques focus on codified knowledge, but most knowledge is tacit and is learned in doing. Such working knowledge is transferred in a different way—through stories, gossip, watching others, that is, by social interaction, not by technology.

From a competitive point of view, the most desirable state is when knowledge is widely shared within the firm and there is no leakage to competitors. In competitive markets, ease of imitation determines sustainability of a competitive advantage. Easy imitation rapidly dissipates the benefits of competitive advantage, speeding transition to a lower-margin commodity market. Knowledge that is context-specific, tacit, embedded in complex organizational routines, and developed from experience tends to be unique and difficult to imitate. To acquire this knowledge takes time, and the competitor cannot just speed this up by spending more.

Transferring Tacit Knowledge   By definition, tacit knowledge cannot be codified. Sharing such tacit knowledge requires both formal and informal systems. Managers may design formal systems for knowledge transfer through mentoring, training and other development activities, learning on the job, and discussion groups. But informal networks and discussion accomplish a substantial amount of tacit knowledge transfer. Tacit knowledge transfer generally needs extensive personal contact as well as an organizational culture that encourages transfer. Management can facilitate informal discussion at lunch or around the water cooler and can develop lists of "knowledgeable people", accessible to all employees of the firm. Such a system enables staff to identify the individuals who possess the knowledge they require.

Transferring Explicit Knowledge   Information technology enables firms to support the digital capture, storage, retrieval, and distribution of explicitly documented knowledge. The Internet itself is an example of a huge knowledge repository outside the company, and search engines such as Google provide fast and easy ways to search through a huge volume of material. Companies such as IBM, Lotus, Autonomy, and others are active developers of portals that provide a single point of entry to such databases, though the content must be carefully sourced and organized. The design and application of these portals has been facilitated by such developments as XML, a set of rules for defining data structures. Key elements of a document can be categorized according to meaning and searches undertaken via the attributes of a document. Such portals can be used to serve customers or to offer staff online tools.

An example of such a data warehouse would be a detailed description of projects set up by a consulting company so that consultants around the world can draw from the experiences of others.[43] Data warehousing captures and codifies explicit information, and this information can be mined, or analyzed and interpreted, to draw inferences that can then be applied to new situations. These data warehouses allow employees to share knowledge and insights. Instead of storing documents in personal files and sharing personal insights with a small circle of colleagues, individual staff can store documents in a common information base and use electronic networks to share insights with all members of the firm. We have already mentioned one such simple system, a list of individuals within the firm who can contribute knowledge on a specific task or problem—such a system is called a knowledge map.[44] This knowledge map is a quick guide to who knows what in the firm and is a useful method of transferring knowledge, provided an incentive is offered to staff to both list their expertise and share it.

> The consulting firm Accenture has developed Knowledge Xchange, while PricewaterhouseCoopers has developed Knowledge View, which provides staff members access to a directory of people organized according to expertise, questions, and issues so that they can obtain the best knowledge available within the consulting firm.

We also need to develop systems for transferring the structural knowledge of the firm; therefore processes need to be documented, and this document then becomes a knowledge map for that process.

With the growth in alliances and network forms of organization, there is an increasing need to transfer knowledge across the partners—and, again, information technology facilitates this. This can be accomplished by e-mail, intranets, or videoconferencing, which facilitate both tacit and explicit knowledge transfer. One example from the disc drive industry reveals the substantial cooperation between different firms. In numerous cases, some firms are responsible for design but others for manufacture. In this industry, much of the interfirm communication involves electronic transfer of data such as simulation results, with engineers being able to log on to a cooperating firm's computer system so that they can share information on design of components. Such a technology infrastructure—the network, software, and hardware—allows knowledge workers to work together on projects and is generally scalable and able to handle different formats such as Windows and Linux. E-mail is widely used to transfer documents, while video-conferencing allows us to "see" and communicate with people in remote locations.[45]

Using Knowledge

While companies talk about the importance of learning, intellectual capital, and knowledge management, they often fail at the vital step of transforming knowledge into action.[46] All too often there is a knowing–doing gap. The firm has to ensure that people are encouraged to use the knowledge systems that have been developed. People will only use these systems if they are convenient and the knowledge stored is seen as useful and relevant. Many knowledge management techniques focus on codified knowledge, but it has been suggested that much important knowledge is tacit knowledge, which, as we have seen, is more difficult to transfer and thus to use.

One other point is important to make. Using knowledge requires the correct culture—a culture in which people trust each other, in which people are allowed to make mistakes and to learn from those mistakes, and in which the right incentives for creation and transfer of knowledge are provided.

⊚ 11.4 HUMAN RESOURCES

We have defined strategic management as creating organizations that generate value. Building such an organization requires making many decisions that should ultimately be beneficial to shareholders. These include some important human resource decisions, such as selecting people for key positions, designing appropriate reward and incentive systems, building the competences required to compete successfully in the future, and organizing business processes and decision making to be successful.

As firms grow, so do their requirements in terms of capabilities—the skills embedded in the company's people, processes, and institutional knowledge. To build new competences often requires changes in the human resources of the firm. The CEO must encourage the emergence of a more strategic approach to managing human resources, something that has been lacking in too many companies, where the administrative or political considerations have too often outweighed the strategic.

> When Jack Welch embarked on his change program at GE, business managers were required to bring their human resource managers to planning meetings, or they could not attend themselves!

We first review the responsibilities of senior managers in building future competences. Then we focus on the critical issue of succession planning for senior management appointments, and we conclude by examining the critical human resource policies that senior management should be concerned with, since they can significantly shape the emergent values and culture of the organization.

Managing Resources and Competences

Growth requires building new capabilities, which means ensuring that the company's people have appropriate skills (whether via development or new hires), storing and sharing institutional knowledge, and putting in place the necessary processes for integrating and coordinating activities. Although less critical capabilities can be outsourced, management of the most important capabilities can determine whether or not shareholder value will be created.

> Sony is attempting to transform itself into a knowledge-led enterprise with a focus on open and broadband networks, where users will be able to freely send and receive high-resolution video images such as movies. This new communication paradigm means Sony must develop appropriate resources and competences in order to capitalize on the opportunity.[47]

A good corporate strategy is a carefully constructed system of interdependent parts. It directs executives' decisions about the businesses in which the firm will compete, the resources and capabilities the firm must develop, and the organizational architecture required for successful implementation. To align these elements in a multibusiness company is clearly a demanding task, one that requires senior management direction and involvement.[48]

Multibusiness firms also have advantages, however. They can provide a diverse range of experiences to more fully develop their managers. They can transfer skills and experience by moving managers or developing processes such as best-practice sharing, as discussed earlier in the chapter. In the modern firm, people—with their skills, motivation, and creativity—are critical to success. The CEO, together with the top-management team, must play an active role in senior appointments and management development, supported by human resources staff fully attuned to corporate and business strategies.

Succession Planning

The CEO must be personally involved in the selection, training, and development of the senior managers of the firm. For a global firm, this is likely to be the top 100 or 200 managers. This group must have the skills and competences required to develop and implement strategy. One of the most important of these activities is succession planning, which, since there is now a global market for senior management talent, must incorporate some redundancy.

The need for an active approach to human resource management is well illustrated by the data in Table 11.1. BHP is a large Australian resources company, now called BHP Billiton after a merger with a South African firm in 2001. The data show the characteristics of managers classified as "general managers" for two time periods, the 1980s and the 1990s. In the early 1980s, under the then newly appointed CEO Brian Loton, BHP made a significant change in its mission and strategy. The newly constituted senior management team concluded that the company then known as the "Big Australian" was approaching the limits of its growth within Australia and that it had to become a global resources firm, decreasing dependence on its local Australian base.

BHP's growth had already led to a critical shortage of general managers, but for the new strategy to be successful, the company had to make significant changes in the composition of its cadre of general managers. Such a change did not occur by chance. The issue was recognized and actively pursued by the firm's most senior managers, with the

TABLE 11.1   Profile of General Managers in BHP

	1980s	1990s
Age on appointment	47	44
Non-Australian nationality (%)	8	37
International experience (%)	4	46
Experience outside BHP (%)	8	44
Functional experience		
One function (%)	75	22
Two functions (%)	25	26
More than two functions (%)	–	63
Location experience		
One location (%)	49	8
Two locations (%)	42	20
More than two locations (%)	9	85

Reproduced by permission of BHP Billiton.

CEO playing a strong role. As a result, the composition of the general manager cadre had changed very significantly by the 1990s.

As can be seen, the nature of these general managers changed dramatically over the decade. The proportion of managers with experience outside BHP went from 8% to 44%, while the percentage of managers with international experience went from 4% to 46%. BHP deliberately changed selection criteria and recruitment practices, targeting managers from other resource firms around the world. Over a decade, the firm significantly altered the characteristics of its general manager population, a good example of aligning human resource practices with corporate strategy. In the next section, we examine these practices in more detail.

Managing Human Resource Policies

To ensure alignment with strategy, senior management must implement appropriate human resource (HR) policies. The "organizational inertia" to which we earlier referred is often embedded in obsolete HR practices, which reinforce the "old way" instead of supporting the emergence of the firm of the future. HR policies often play a critical role in shaping the firm's culture, and the CEO must therefore play an active role in influencing and approving the design of a number of HR policies, such as selection, compensation, and training for staff. Figure 11.7 illustrates some of these relationships, and we now examine each of the policy areas where we believe senior management should be actively involved.

Recruitment and Selection

As we noted earlier, without the right people and skills, the firm cannot succeed. As strategy changes, so will the types of individuals and skills needed. Strategic human resource planning can accommodate and facilitate these changes, but without strategic clarity and well-defined planning processes, such plans will not eventuate. As in our BHP example, senior management plays a critical role in ensuring strategic alignment of recruitment and hiring practices.

Recruiting new skills can also be helpful when the organization is attempting major change of the type discussed in Chapter 10. The assimilation problems may mirror those

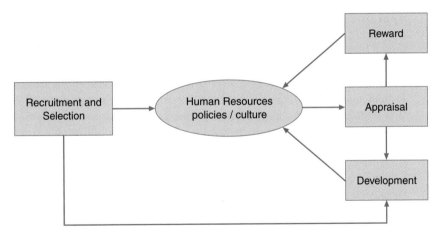

Figure 11.7   Human Resource Policies and Culture

of a merger or acquisition if wholesale hiring from "outside" occurs, and the lives of new members for the firm can be made quite difficult, even if they are hired into senior management positions.

Reward

Senior managers must guide the design of the firm's reward systems, for strategic management includes the need for supportive reward systems. There will often be three levels of rewards that need to be considered. One will be related to corporate performance, another to performance at the business-unit level, and the third to individual performance.

Incentive problems often arise from the principal/agent problem. Employees' personal objectives will usually differ from those of the business unit and shareholders. Appropriate incentives may influence or even induce the desired behavior from individuals, while inappropriate rewards ensure problems. Obviously, there are many other influences on behavior, including management style and firm culture, but the reward system is undoubtedly important.

Stern Stewart, the originator of economic value added (EVA), was originally a management compensation firm, and some firms have incorporated these concepts in their reward system to reflect corporate performance.

> Sony has indicated that it is progressively adopting EVA so as to improve return on invested capital. We assume that the compensation system will be revised to reflect EVA, thereby encouraging alignment.

Stock options, originally intended to align managers' and shareholders' interests, became widely used in the 1990s. Originally, eligibility for options was restricted to a very few senior managers, but in the last decade participation became much more widespread. Options have been particularly favored by fast-growing smaller firms, where cash is inevitably in short supply.

The board of the company is formally charged with responsibility for such schemes, but management has generally proposed them. Widespread concerns over the use of options have led such thought leaders as Warren Buffett to decry their use, while accountants have become increasingly preoccupied with how they are reported. Many believe that the use of options will decline in the future.

Appraisal

Appraising individual performance is usually complicated by the circumstances of different businesses. The origins of the PIMS project were in exactly such a dilemma. Because GE was one of the more diverse companies in the world at the time, Fred Borch and the senior management team recognized that appraising management performance was very difficult, given the very different characteristics of the businesses they managed. Borch charged a team of operations researchers, led by Sid Schoeffler, to solve the problem for him. By measuring a wide variety of business characteristics, the team developed a PAR model for ROI, showing what a manager with average luck should achieve when running a business with these particular characteristics.[49] If performance were ahead of par, either the manager had been exceptionally lucky or exceptionally capable.

The importance of the PAR model lies in the recognition that objectives and measures should be specific to the business and performance must be measured against these. In Chapter 12, we discuss the balanced scorecard as a general framework for assessing performance. In general, it is preferable if jobs specify outputs, not just duties, with performance targets clearly identified. However, it is equally important to recognize that the firm will need different management systems for different businesses. Growth businesses need builders and visionaries with appropriate styles and appropriate performance metrics. Mature businesses require a different approach and may be assigned very different objectives related to their role in the corporate portfolio. Corporate staff and business-level staff will generally work together in some cooperative arrangement to set standards for performance appraisal at the business-unit level.

A further refinement, adopted by a number of companies, recognizes that good performance is not just about achieving objectives but also about the way in which those objectives are achieved. As many are aware, large companies often distribute decision-making guidelines in an attempt to ensure ethical behavior in the marketplace. In a world where people are ever more the source of competitive advantage, however, it is vital to ensure that these critical human resources are managed appropriately.

To summarize, senior managers should design a reward system having both financial and nonfinancial elements, which will often involve both individual and group (business- and/or corporate-level) measures. Managers must also remember that rewards typically include a range of incentives such as salary increases, bonuses, recognition, promotion, choice of assignment, and so on.

Development

Corporate managers should play an important role in planning the development of the firm's managers. These activities should include further development for the most senior managers, who are often forgotten—or avoided for political reasons—when the HR department plans for development.

Promising managers need opportunities to broaden their skills and knowledge to prepare them for senior general management positions; leaving them in a single functional department for substantial parts of their career does both them and the firm a disservice. Clearly there are trade-offs that must be made between depth of expertise in a specialty and cross-functional breadth, but all senior positions will demand the latter, even if they carry functional titles.

Education, both inside and outside the company, plays an important role in the development process. In-company training and education can build *esprit de corps* and enable a focus on real company issues, whereas external experiences broaden perspectives across industries and geographies in ways than cannot be emulated inside a firm. A judicious combination of these two can support both corporate and individual goals in developing a well-rounded team of more senior managers.

Many firms have taken novel and exciting approaches to development, based on the concepts of *action learning*.[50] The aforementioned BHP, for example, has given junior teams of managers real assignments with project budgets as part of their development. The same company set up a junior "think tank" to advise on major investment decisions, arguing that because the firm's younger managers would inherit the consequences of these decisions, their input should be considered.

Other companies have taken the radical step of putting their own people to work for customers and vice versa. One of the authors has worked as a consultant with a company in which one of the supplier's salespersons went to work in the customer's receiving department, while a customer's buyer went to work in the supplier's customer service department. These are developmental experiences that can create insight and empathy on the part of both parties.

Human Resource Policies and Culture

A firm that has been in operation for several years and that has a history develops its own **culture**—widely shared basic assumptions, values, and beliefs that have a powerful influence on activities and operations. Culture includes assumptions about the nature of humans, about what is ethical and unethical behavior, about the importance of work for individuals. It also includes assumptions about innovation and creativity, who in the firm can manifest these, and the value of experimentation, as well as attitudes toward risk and failure. Many of these assumptions are implicit and are treated as axiomatic by members of an organization.

Human resource policies can have a very definite impact on the culture of a firm, and since organizational performance is influenced by culture and this impact can be positive or negative, strategic managers must, to the extent possible, manage the culture of the firm. A strong culture can be an inhibitor of change but can also replace supervisory activity and be a powerful form of control. Some firms are trying to replace formal control systems with cultural control, wherein employees share a common culture that aligns their interests with the firm's. Knowledge workers, in particular, are believed to be much more comfortable in such an environment.

Many corporate managements are currently talking about cultural values such as creativity/innovation, high ethical standards, transparency, and a focus on performance. In many cases, however, not only is the informal culture of the firm inimical to such values but the formal processes and, in particular, human resource policies act as inhibitors of the very values professed by senior management. To "walk the talk," as Tom Peters once put it,[51] strategic managers must align their processes and policies with the values they are advocating!

⑤ 11.5 SUMMARY

Designing the firm's architecture involves an important set of decisions for any strategic manager. As we discussed in earlier chapters, strategic management is about both generating strategy and ensuring that the strategy is implemented. These two stages of generation and implementation are mutually dependent; strategy shapes architecture and at the same time architecture shapes strategy. The CEO will be actively involved in these architecture decisions. Some decisions, such as the adoption of a new structure, are primarily the responsibility of the CEO. In other decision areas, the CEO must ensure that appropriate systems are in use. Systems such as the recruitment of senior managers, succession planning, promotion, and rewards, and the business planning systems in use need input from strategic managers. Since IT investment is now a major component of capital expenditure for any firm, decisions on IT processes cannot be left solely to technocrats; instead, such investments must contribute to business and firm strategy.

Architecture comprises three elements—structure, processes, and human resources. In a rapidly changing world, it is likely that the firm will need to innovate in all three. We suggest that in the future, firms will need to be increasingly flexible, to pay greater attention to creativity, to be concerned with recruiting and retaining high-caliber staff, to speed up decision processes, and to give more managerial attention to the knowledge assets of the firm.

Structure incorporates how the firm integrates two conflicting objectives—differentiation and integration. Differentiation reflects specialization, which is adopted to improve efficiency through the use of specialist staff. But such specialists often lose sight of the "big picture," and hence there is a need for integration, which can introduce considerable organizational tension. Structure includes decisions on the basis of differentiation—whether this will be by product or by geography—and this decision in turn determines the necessary integrative mechanisms. In their attempt to improve flexibility and responsiveness, many firms have reduced the level of vertical differentiation, eliminating layers of managers and resulting in considerable extra pressure on the remaining staff. Most global firms have adopted a matrix structure, organized on both a geographic and a business basis, where the corporate center provides a range of central services. Given the size and complexity of such firms, providing local autonomy while coordinating across the entire firm is a considerable managerial challenge.

Increasing competition also implies that firms have to look at process management. They need to identify those processes, which deliver value to customers, and manage these on an end-to-end basis. Such a structure can produce considerable tension in the firm, with conflict between the (vertical) business structure and the (horizontal) process structure and with issues of power and authority ensuing.

Finally, designing architecture involves decisions on the human resources of the firm. In any organization, people are a critical resource, and strategic managers need to ensure that the right people are hired and that the incentive systems in place align the interests of staff to that of the firm. With the increasing importance of intangible assets, particularly knowledge assets, there is likely to be heightened interest in knowledge management systems. Developing systems that facilitate the transfer of tacit knowledge across different units in the firm is a considerable challenge yet one that needs to be met, since this knowledge is often the basis of competitive advantage.

⟳ REVIEW QUESTIONS

1. Identify some of the central issues that managers need to consider in developing the appropriate organizational structure.

2. What are the benefits and disadvantages of organizing the multidivisional firm by product, by market, by technology, and by geography?

3. Why are so many global firms organized along matrix lines? What benefits does this structure provide and what problems does it generate?

4. With increasing developments in information technology and the changing workforce, do you believe firms will become more centralized or more decentralized in the future? Discuss.

5. Using the literature, review the success and failure of ERP and CRM applications.

6. "The CEO must play a central role in managing the human resources of the firm." Discuss this statement, with attention to what issues arise and what level of involvement is needed.

7. Why are firms adopting newer forms of architecture such as that represented by networks?

⊙ ENDNOTES

[1] H. Heimbouch, "Racing for Growth," *Harvard Business Review,* November–December 2000, pp. 148–154.

[2] PerkinElmer Annual Report, 2002: www.perkinelmer. com.

[3] A. D. Chandler, *Strategy and Structure: Chapters in the History of the American Industrial Enterprise* (Cambridge, MA: MIT Press, 1962).

[4] M. L. Tushman and C. A. O'Reilly, *Winning through Innovation* (Boston: Harvard Business School Press, 1997).

[5] Other models are the 7S's model and the congruence model. For the former, see R. H. J. Waterman, T. J. Peters, and J. R. Phillips, "Structure is Not Organization," *McKinsey Quarterly,* Summer 1980, pp. 2–20. For the latter, see D. A. Nadler and M. L. Tushman, *Competing by Design* (New York: Oxford University Press, 1997).

[6] Tushman and O'Reilly, *Winning through Innovation.*

[7] S. H. Haeckel, *Adaptive Enterprise: Creating and Leading Sense-and-Respond Organizations* (Cambridge, MA: Harvard Business School Press, 1999).

[8] C. Handy, *Beyond Certainty* (London: Hutchison, 1995).

[9] "A Long March," *The Economist,* July 14, 2001, pp. 63–65.

[10] M. Goold and A. Campbell, "Do You Have a Well-Designed Organization?" *Harvard Business Review,* March 2002, pp. 117–124.

[11] P. Lawrence and J. W. Lorsch, *Organizations and Environment* (Cambridge, MA: Harvard University Press, 1967).

[12] T. Burns and G. M. Stalker, *The Management of Innovation* (Oxford: Oxford University Press, 1994).

[13] J. R. Galbraith and D. A. Nathanson, *Strategy Implementation: The Role of Structure and Process* (St. Paul, MN: West, 1978).

[14] J. G. March and H. A. Simon, *Organizations* (New York: Wiley, 1958).

[15] J. W. Hunt, *Managing People at Work* (Maidenhead, UK: McGraw-Hill, 1992).

[16] M. L. Tushman and C. A. O'Reilly, "Ambidextrous Organizations: Managing Evolutionary and Revolutionary Change," *California Management Review* 38, no. 4 (1996), pp. 8–30.

[17] H. Mintzberg, *Structure in Fives: Designing Effective Organizations* (Englewood Cliffs, NJ: Prentice-Hall, 1993).

[18] Burns and Stalker, *The Management of Innovation.*

[19] Mintzberg, *Structure in Fives.*

[20] O. E. Williamson, *Markets and Hierarchies: Analysis and Antitrust Implications* (New York: Free Press, 1975).

[21] C. Coulson-Thomas, *Business Process Re-Engineering: Myth and Reality* (London: Kogan Page, 1996), pp. 254.

[22] March and Simon call this "uncertainty absorption." See March and Simon, *Organizations.*

[23] Hunt, *Managing People at Work.*

[24] Based on an exchange rate of 1.313 Swiss francs per US$; source—Federal Reserve Bank.

[25] C. A. Bartlett and S. Ghoshal, *Managing across Borders* (Boston: Harvard Business School Press, 1998).

[26] C. Handy, *The Elephant and the Flea* (London: Hutchinson, 2001).

[27] J. M. Hulbert, N. Capon, and N. F. Piercy, *Total Integrated Marketing: Breaking the Bounds of the Function* (New York: Free Press, 2003).

[28] F. Ostroff, *The Horizontal Organization* (New York: Oxford University Press, 1999).

[29] M. A. Devanna and N. M. Tichy, "Creating the Competitive Organization of the 21st Century: The Boundaryless Corporation," *Human Resource Management* 29, no. 4 (1990), pp. 455–471.

[30] Ostroff, *The Horizontal Organization.*

[31] R. S. Kaplan and D. P. Norton, "The Balanced Scorecard—Measures That Drive Performance," *Harvard Business Review,* January–February 1992, pp. 71–79.

[32] J. Ward and J. Peppard, *Strategic Planning for Information Systems* (Chichester, UK: Wiley, 2002).

[33] Lawrence and Lorsch, *Organizations and Environment.*

[34] J. Luftman and T. Brier, "Achieving and Sustaining Business—IT Alignment," *California Management Review* 42, no. 1 (1999), pp. 109–122.

[35] L. Downes and C. Mui, *Unleashing the Killer App: Digital Strategies for Market Dominance* (Boston, MA: Harvard Business School Press, 1998).

[36] P. Weill and M. Broadbent, *Leveraging the New Infrastructure* (Boston: Harvard Business School Press, 1998).

[37] Ward and Peppard, *Strategic Planning for Information Systems.*

[38] D. Jackson, *Becoming Dynamic* (Basingstoke, UK: Macmillan, 2000).

[39] Various contemporary news reports.

[40] A. Tiwana, *The Essential Guide to Knowledge Management* (Upper Saddle River, NJ: Prentice Hall, 2001).

[41] A. K. Gupta and V. Govindarajan, "Knowledge Management's Social Dimension: Lessons from Nucor Steel," *Sloan Management Review* 42, no. 1 (2000), pp. 71–80.

[42] T. H. Davenport and L. Prusak, *Working Knowledge: How Organizations Manage What They Know* (Boston: Harvard Business School Press, 2000).

[43] P. Gottschalk, "Strategic Knowledge Networks: The Case of IT Support for Eurojurislaw Firms in Norway," *International Review of Law, Computers & Technology* 14, no. 1 (2000), pp. 115–129.

[44] G. Probst, S. Raub, and K. Romhardt, *Managing Knowledge* (Chichester, UK: Wiley, 2000).

[45] J. E. Scott, "Facilitating Interorganizational Learning with Information Technology," *Journal of Management and Information Systems* 17, no. 2 (2000), pp. 81–113.

[46] J. Pfeffer and R. I. Sutton, *The Knowing–Doing Gap: How Smart Companies Turn Knowledge into Action* (Boston: Harvard Business School Press, 1999), pp. 314.

[47] Sony Annual Report, 2001: www.sony.co.jp.

[48] D. J. Collis and C. A. Montgomery, "Creating Corporate Advantage," *Harvard Business Review,* May–June 1998, pp. 70–83.

[49] R. D. Buzzell and B. T. Gale, *The PIMS Principles* (New York: Free Press, 1987).

[50] R. W. Revens, *The ABC of Action Learning* (London: Lemos and Crane, 1998).

[51] T. J. Peters and R. H. Waterman, *In Search of Excellence* (New York: Harper & Row, 1982).

CHAPTER 12

Measuring Organizational Performance

Learning Objectives

Upon completing this chapter, you will be able to:

- Direct the establishment of an appropriate system for managing corporate and business-unit performance

- Recognize the defects present in most companies' systems of performance measurement

- Analyze and implement measurement of the important non-financial parameters of organizational performance

- Explain the principles of leading indicators and anticipatory control to other managers in the organization

- Recognize the vital role of measurement systems in supporting the adaptation and evolution of strategy

---

Walt Disney is one of the oldest, and best-known, entertainment firms in the world. During the 1980s, the firm suffered some difficulties, and a new CEO was appointed to take over what was by then an ailing firm. After major expansion, by the late 1990s, its revenue had increased from $USB1.65 to $USB22 between 1984 and 1997, and operating income peaked at $USB4.3 in 1997. Market capitalization increased from $USB2 in 1984 to $USB86 in 2002, although this had fallen to $USB30 by March 2003. Over the last five years, Disney has experienced difficulties, which is reflected in its recent financial results. In the five years leading up to 2002, the total return to shareholders was –9.7%, while the S&P entertainment and leisure index increased by 44.6%.[1] In 2002, operating income was less than $USB3. and external financial analysts see little prospect for future increases. To add to Disney's woes, in 2002 Standard and Poors lowered its long-term credit rating from A– to BBB+.[2]

What are the reasons for Disney's poor recent performance, and what performance measurement system might have enabled senior management to prevent this decline? Some possible reasons for the deterioration are:

The loss of talented and creative staff
A shortage of talented senior executives
Too high a level of corporate complexity
Leadership style within the firm
Declining visitor numbers in several of its theme parks
Declining competitive advantage for ABC TV[3,4]

Generally, as these reasons indicate, the explanation for poor financial performance must be sought in non-financial measures. Possibly Disney was measuring its performance on non-financial variables but failing to identify those that drive financial performance? In early 2004, Disney was faced with a hostile takeover by Comcast, the U.S. cable giant.

⊚ 12.1 INTRODUCTION

Throughout this book, we have emphasized that the ultimate objective of a firm is to create value and that this is accomplished only when the revenue generated by the firm is greater than the costs incurred in generating that revenue. However, such value creation is the output of a complex process that we depicted in our strategic management model from Chapter 1, shown in Figure 1.5. As we have reiterated throughout this book, achieving high-level performance is an exceptionally difficult task, achieved by relatively few managers.

Managers need a good understanding of the context in which they operate—both the internal and external environment—to develop value-creating strategies. Such understanding, however, is a necessary but not sufficient condition for value creation. Innovation, creativity, and the collective organizational skills must be successfully applied to generating and implementing competitively superior strategies. Even when strategies are sound, however, management must also ensure that appropriate structures, systems, and processes are in place to facilitate implementation, for many brilliant strategies fail because of inappropriate organizational architecture. Only when these conditions are fulfilled does it make sense for us to start asking whether or not we are achieving our desired performance levels.

It follows from the above that any attempt to fully explain corporate performance would require a complete audit of the strategic management process that has served as the subject of this entire book. Such a broad ambit is beyond the scope of this chapter, but it is vitally important that we bear in mind that a good performance management system has to be much more comprehensive than the numbers that account for most of a company's annual report, which are inevitably backward-looking and often lacking in any diagnostic value. While we are strong advocates of the firm as a value-creating entity, we also know that it is naive and deceptive to treat a living organization merely as a set of accounting numbers.

We begin by giving an overall perspective on the issues of measurement and control. We elaborate on the importance of diagnosis, the role of non-financial and financial measures, focusing in particular on the increasing role of intangible assets in performance management, and the application of best-practice benchmarking. We also present an integrative model that will be used to organize the remainder of the chapter.

The next section covers the measurement of business-unit performance. We discuss the concept of a balanced scorecard, as well as introducing specific measures for some of the firm's intangible assets. We also explain the importance of presenting these measures in easily accessible formats, such that they can be widely shared and discussed within the organization.

Finally, we examine the issue of corporate performance measurement. We illustrate with corporate examples, showing how different companies have focused on the measures they see as critical to their success. Again, we show formats that facilitate communication to internal and external audiences. Abstruse indices that cannot be understood by large portions of the workforce are unlikely to serve our goal of performance improvement.

⊚ 12.2 PERFORMANCE MEASURES

The purpose of a measurement system is to help managers generate superior strategies and thus superior firm value. While most of this value generation takes place at the business-unit level, one of the means by which the corporate center can augment this business-level value creation is by ensuring that appropriate measurement and control systems are in place. Of course, value is not created by the measurement system, although it can be an essential diagnostic tool for management, supporting better decision making, or it can do exactly the reverse, contributing to a downward spiral. There is a saying that managers do what is inspected, not what is expected, and there is no doubt that poorly designed measurement systems produce a catalogue of deviant behaviors!

> Managers at Connex, then responsible for operating most of the southern railroad commuter lines into London, learning that their on-time performance was going to be measured by regulators on a particular day, instructed their drivers to go through stations without stopping if they were behind schedule. This way the company met on-time standards, but at the expense of stranding their passengers! In 2003, Connex was informed that it was losing the franchise to operate those lines.

Figure 12.1 depicts the interactive strategy and measurement process over time. We develop and implement strategy based on an understanding of context and supported by appropriate architecture. We then measure the results, ascertain where these depart from expectations (positively or negatively), identify the causes or drivers of these discrepancies, and then make appropriate revisions. It is vital to see the whole process as a dynamic and ongoing learning process rather than as a punitive or simply evaluative exercise.

Thus the strategy and architecture of the firm will change and evolve as the world moves forward. In an uncertain and turbulent world, strategy must have emergent features and must be contingent on unpredictable changes. Managers need a system to monitor the execution of the strategy and its underlying assumptions, to ensure that it remains successful, and to indicate how it may need to be revised and modified.

We now clarify a number of important concepts in performance measurement before introducing the model that will be used to structure the remainder of the chapter.

Shareholder Value and Firm Value

With more and more companies adopting the shareholder value approach, it is critically important to keep separate the concepts of *shareholder value* and *firm value*. From the perspective of the firm, it creates value when it earns a return greater than its cost of capital. The return that a shareholder receives, however, is a function of the dividends received and the level of share price appreciation. These two concepts are not identical. A company may be performing well and earning above its cost of capital, thereby creating firm value. However, shareholders may have paid too much for their shares or the overall stock market may be collapsing, in which case they cannot appropriate firm value in their returns. Over the long term, however, if the company is increasing value by creating economic profit, its shareholders should profit as a result.

Variables and Measures

In designing a measurement system, we need to be aware of the distinction between a *variable* and the *measurement* of that variable. We regard the concepts of "innovation" or "customer satisfaction" as variables. Identifying such variables requires a conceptual model of business, of which variables are relevant. We also need to distinguish between input and output variables. Typical output variables would be "profit" or "market share." Inputs are the variables that determine, or influence, the levels of these outputs. Normally these input variables can be considered as nested; thus "product quality" as a vari-

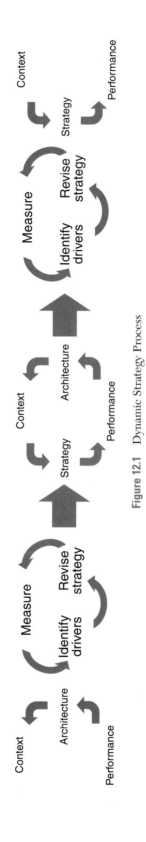

Figure 12.1 Dynamic Strategy Process

able may influence another variable, "customer satisfaction," which in turn may be related to the output financial variable "profit." In a complex system such as a business firm, there is seldom a simple connection between an input variable and an output variable; instead, there may be many inputs that influence a single output such as "profit."

Having identified a variable as being relevant to understanding the overall performance of the firm, we then need to construct a measure, an operational procedure that results in a specific measure, generally numeric, for each variable. So "customer satisfaction" may be defined as the score obtained from a customer survey. There can be considerable debate on how to measure a particular variable, such as "employee morale" or "synergy." The operational measure of the variable must be both valid and reliable.

Diagnostic Use

The underlying rationale for developing a performance measurement system is to facilitate strategy execution and to provide diagnostic information on how the strategy could be improved. This indicates that the measurement system must also incorporate an understanding of the *drivers* of firm value and clarify the relative importance of these drivers. Thus we need both outcome measures and performance drivers. We should be able to translate the business-unit or corporate strategy into a linked set of measures that define objectives and the mechanisms for achieving these. The specific measures adopted will depend on the strategy being executed and will, of necessity, require the development of *cause–effect* chains that link specific actions to corporate objectives.

Financial and Non-financial Measures

It should be clear that if we are to create value, we must have financial measures of performance. However, as was noted in Chapter 5, intangible assets now account for the majority of a firm's market capitalization. This reinforces the proposition that traditional financial measures must be complemented by non-financial measures. This increasing discrepancy has produced considerable concern in the business community and is leading to some changes in accounting practice.

> In the early 1990s, 11 leading British companies—including GrandMet, Cadbury Schweppes, Pearson, Reckitt and Colman, Guinness, and Reed—were sufficiently worried that they commissioned a special study of the topic by a leading accounting firm. They concluded that while the perception was that there existed no generally accepted framework of methods for valuing intangible assets, perception did not match reality and that, with due caution and consideration, reliable and consistent valuations for financial reporting purposes could be determined.[5]

All performance measurement systems must include measures of intangible assets such as product quality, brand equity, innovation, and knowledge, since these can all be drivers of financial success.[6] Otherwise management can be seriously misled, to the detriment of shareholders' interests.

While we give primary emphasis to the economic performance of a firm, reflecting the interests of shareholders, there are numerous other stakeholders, and managers need to know how well the firm is performing relative to these stakeholders; therefore customer, employee, and community measures will also be important. Yet our primary focus on shareholders is justified, since empirical studies indicate that increasing shareholder value does not conflict with the long-term interest of other stakeholders.[7]

Benchmarking

As pernicious as looking backward is looking inward. We have emphasized the increasing competitiveness of the business environment throughout the book, and unless the company is winning competitive battles, its prospects are poor. Thus, while telling ourselves we are doing better than we were previously may provide some solace, the real question must be: "Are we doing better than competitors?" Internal yardsticks against historical performance are not enough.[8] While historical analysis can improve existing performance, real best-practice exercises must encompass a wider realm.

"Best-of class" *benchmarking*[9] was a concept developed by Xerox, recognizing that many business processes are common across different industries. Thus most firms invoice clients in some form, electronic or otherwise, all have an accounts payable process, and so on. Earlier, we discussed organizational learning, and central to the best-of-class benchmarking concept is the idea that we can learn from others, not just in our own company or industry, but also outside it. Indeed, one can argue that if one learns only from one's own industry, one will never lead it. Thus we argue strongly for external comparison on any performance measure wherever this is even remotely feasible.

Need for a Set of Measures

Organizational performance is far too complex to be captured by a single, simple measure, particularly when the measurement system has a diagnostic focus. Further, reliance on any simple metric is likely to produce deviant behavior of the type exhibited by Connex. Thus evaluating performance requires an integrated set of measures that are supportive of the mission statement, foster proper implementation of the strategy, and capture the underlying complexity. Here we face a dilemma, for too simple an approach is likely to be deceiving and dysfunctional, but if the system becomes too complex, it will be too difficult for people to use prescriptively. Clearly, we must find an appropriate trade-off between simplicity and complexity. At the same time, since the firm is developing new strategies in response to a changing world, it will also need to revise and update its measurement system.

◉ 12.3 DEVELOPING A PERFORMANCE MEASUREMENT SYSTEM

We begin with the basic assumption that we are dealing with a multibusiness corporation. Consequently, we must develop a measurement system that is appropriate at both the business-unit and corporate levels. For each of these variables, we need to establish a measurement process that provides both a valid and a reliable measure of the variable under consideration. Further, building on our discussion in the previous section, we conclude that a good measurement system must include multiple variables, including leading indicators wherever possible, and that these will necessarily include non-financial as well as financial variables.

We should point out that performance measurement also has a cultural dimension. Successful firms have a performance culture, a culture where performance is measured and actions are taken on the basis of an analysis of this performance. Not only is performance taken seriously; so are the actions that flow from this analysis. Companies with substantial excess cash flow often make uneconomic investments in either mature businesses or in uneconomic diversification. Unless there is a strong performance culture in the firm, these strategies are likely to be adopted since they are in the interests of managers, despite the fact that they may well be destroying value. This illustrates that firms may suffer from the agency problem, where the goals of managers are not aligned with the goals of shareholders. Good performance measurement systems attempt to overcome this by utilizing a related management incentive system that aligns managers' remuneration with the performance measures.

Identifying and Designing Performance Measures

Figure 12.2 presents a process for identifying and developing performance measures.[10] We now review each step of the process.

Clarify Strategy and Agree on Objectives
A vital first step is to ensure that both strategy and objectives (including priorities among different objectives) are clearly defined, including a consideration of the interests of various stakeholders, in particular shareholders, customers, and employees. Once priorities are agreed upon, then specific improvement levels can be established for each objective. In doing so, it is important to remember our admonitions in Chapter 6. Big, hairy, audacious goals (BHAGs)[11] are all very well and good under certain circumstances, but objectives "stretched" to the point where people believe them to be unattainable are demotivating, not motivating!

Agree on and Implement Measures for Business Objectives
We must next develop a specific measure for each objective. The measure should clearly indicate how close we are to the intended target level, stimulate desired behavior, and,

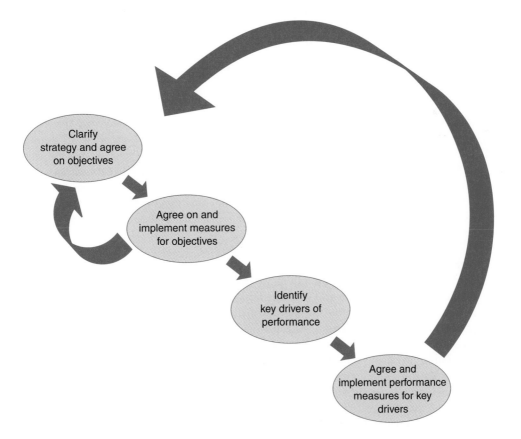

Figure 12.2 A Process for Identifying and Developing Performance Measures

wherever possible, avoid unintended dysfunctional consequences. We should also consider such issues as frequency of measurement, who will be responsible for measurement, and the source of the data to be used. We are great believers in redundancy, for no matter how carefully we try to anticipate the behaviors that measurement will produce, human ingenuity is such that we will undoubtedly fail to foresee all of them, as the following examples indicate.

> During Jack Welch's tenure as CEO, the much-admired General Electric Company achieved no fewer than 110 quarters of successive increase in earnings. Part of this achievement resulted from assuming that its pension fund would earn an annual return of 9.5% and taking a credit to profits of $USB1.74.[12]

Finally, implementation requires specifying who will be responsible for acting if performance fails to meet objectives and the general nature of managerial processes and remedial actions they will be expected to undertake should this be the case. Such specifications put teeth into the measurement process and are essential in supporting the kind of performance culture to which we previously referred.

It is important that the final set of measures be sufficiently comprehensive and that the management team "sign off" on the measures and the measurement and review process. In the case of corporate-level objectives, these should be agreed upon at the board level, whereas business-unit objectives should be established as a result of discussion and negotiation between business-unit and corporate management. The system itself should also be subject to review as strategy evolves over time.

Identify Key Drivers of Performance

A good performance measurement system is one that helps us to identity the drivers (causes) of performance, or a lack thereof, and therefore guides us in making decisions that will improve performance. These drivers include such concepts as customer service, R&D effectiveness, product quality, and employee development, among others. Identifying the key drivers of performance usually benefits from team-based contributions that, if properly managed, will increase the creativity and originality of thinking. Identifying such drivers is facilitated by the use of cause–effect chains, as is illustrated in Figure 12.3, which shows the determinants of customer satisfaction for an airline. This cause–effect analysis needs to be taken further to include the impact that customer satisfaction, among other variables, has on an outcome measure such as firm profitability. Clearly, some variables may have greater impact than others, and setting priorities again will be important.

Agree on and Implement Measures for Key Drivers

Once key drivers have been identified, we need to identify measures for each key driver. Again, we will seek measures that encourage appropriate behavior, identify persons responsible, and determine the nature of the actions that need to be undertaken to achieve improvements. These measures and targets should be agreed upon with the business team; again, involvement improves quality and commitment to the quality of the system. Involving the cross-functional business team is particularly helpful in identifying possible conflicts among measures in order to achieve integration and alignment. We can then set specific improvement targets in these identified areas.

Note that Figure 12.2 contained two feedback loops, for measures of objectives and drivers respectively. In addition, we should also schedule reviews of the complete system, for if measures are to be linked to strategy they must evolve with the strategy. In our experience, too many firms violate this basic principle, sticking rather rigidly with a

Figure 12.3 Cause–Effect Chain for Customer Satisfaction

Source: Adapted from A. Neely and M. A. Najjar, "Linking Financial Performance to Employee and Customer Satisfaction," in *Business Performance Measurement,* A. Neely, ed. (Cambridge, UK: Cambridge University Press, 2002).

given set of measures and puzzling perplexedly over why their strategies do not seem to get implemented. Finally, people must be compensated on the basis of these measures—and this may be one of the most important steps.

☺ 12.4 MEASURING BUSINESS-LEVEL PERFORMANCE

Both corporate and business-unit managers have an interest in measuring and assessing business-unit performance. Such assessment should determine whether or not the business unit has met its objectives, how its performance can be enhanced, and what its likely future performance will be.

As we have consistently stated, the purpose of the firm is to create value; therefore financial measures of a business's performance are clearly important. Yet we have already pointed out the limitations of traditional accounting data for managerial purposes. Kaplan and Norton recognized the same problem and developed the balanced scorecard, a widely adopted system illustrated in Figure 12.4.[13] The balanced scorecard supplements financial measures with a set of non-financial measures that provide better insight into the likely future performance of the business, thus providing a tool for *ex ante,* or anticipatory, control rather than *ex post* analysis. These non-financial measures include measures of both tangible and intangible variables.

The word *balance* is used to denote several ideas. Balance between financial and nonfinancial, balance between measures of past results and measures that will influence

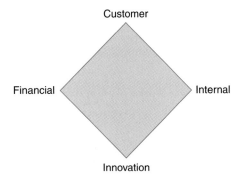

Figure 12.4 The Balanced Scorecard

future performance, and balance between more objective measures and more subjective measures. As we recommended earlier in the chapter, the approach eschews the use of a single measure. Instead, it adopts a set of measures providing insight into how the strategy of the unit may be adjusted to meet future goals and expectations.

The balanced scorecard measures business unit performance along four dimensions: *customer, internal, innovation* and *financial.* For each dimension there is a set of measures, with objectives established for each. We discuss each in turn.

Customer Measures

In a highly competitive world, any business unit must deliver value to customers and possess a strong customer orientation. Customers have many choices in where they purchase, and if the business does not understand these choices and how they are changing due to competition, then the future of the business may be at risk. As discussed in Chapter 7, an important element of business-unit strategy is choosing its horizontal positioning—which market segments the business will compete in. Within its chosen segments, the business must understand how customers define value in order to ensure customer loyalty and to attract customers from competitors. In addition, the business must measure how well it is performing with respect to such outcomes as customer satisfaction, customer retention, and acquisition of new customers. The scorecard also includes a number of more aggregate measures, such as market share in the total market or in selected segments and channels of distribution. Since details of the measurement system will depend on the specific business unit, we will discuss selected measurement examples, beginning with aggregate measures and then progressing to more detailed measures.

Customer measures of performance at the business-unit level include aggregate measures such as sales volumes and growth, both of which are critical measures for managers. These measures could be broken down by segment and benchmarked against figures for the economy or industry as a whole. Benchmarking against the total market permits analysis of market share by product, region, customer segment, channel, and so on, as illustrated below. Market share is an important output measure, since it controls for the effects of changes in market size and enables managers to assess competitive performance.

As an illustration, Table 12.1 shows the market share of Harley-Davidson, the motorcycle producer, in its target market, the 651+cc motorcycle market, in three geographic segments. While we have shown this information in tabular form, generally it would be displayed graphically for ease of viewing. From this we can see that Harley-Davidson has had little change in share in its two largest markets, North America and Europe, but is does appear to be increasing share in Asia, which possibly reflects its global strategy. This aggregate performance data would normally be supplemented with information on the total market size as well as on the market shares of competitors, such as BMW, Honda, and Yamaha.

Business-unit managers should also be asking themselves about the factors that contributed to sales volume and growth. Such a cause–effect analysis might lead them to

TABLE 12.1   Harley-Davidson Market Share by Segment

Segment	1999	2000	2001	2002
North America	47.7	44.6	43.9	46.4
Europe	5.8	6.8	6.7	6.6
Asia	18.5	19.5	20.4	21.3

Source: Harley-Davidson Annual Report, 2002: www.harley-davidson.com.

TABLE 12.2   Performance Measures, Segment 1

	2002	2003	2004
Relative value (index)			
Relative price (%)			
Relative quality (index)			
Customer retention (%)			
Sales from new customers (%)			
Customer satisfaction (index)			
Competitive advantage (index)			

look at more detailed measures for a specific market segment that drive volume, as illustrated in Table 12.2.

Each of the variables in Table 12.2, such as customer satisfaction, itself has drivers. Managers cannot improve customer satisfaction by dictate; there is no simple lever to turn. The drivers of customer satisfaction will depend on the nature of the business and the industry in which it competes, as was illustrated for an airline in Figure 12.3.

Such data, particularly if analyzed using competitive benchmarks, help assess how customers see the business. Business-unit managers must ensure that they are creating value for customers; a business whose competitive advantage is declining is likely to have problems in the future.

Brand Equity

As was discussed in Chapter 5, brand equity is an important component of the intangible assets of a business, and this must be measured and appropriate actions taken to maintain the value of any brands owned by the business. The magnitude of this brand equity can be very significant.

> In 1989 Ford paid $USB2.5 for the British car manufacturer Jaguar, whose book value was $USB0.4. The difference, $USB2.1, that was placed on Ford's balance sheet as "goodwill" is mainly accounted for by Ford's estimate of the value of Jaguar's brand equity.[14]

A number of approaches are used to measure brand equity, which are covered in more detail in Keller.[15] One method is the earnings approach, which compares the revenues earned by the brand in a product category with the revenues earned (or estimated) by a generic product in the same category.

> The Interbrand Group plc, a major brand consultancy, employs two factors in its earnings-based method. It uses annual after-tax profits less expected earnings for an equivalent unbranded product averaged over time, factored by a proprietary-developed multiplier purporting to measure "brand strength." Measures of brand strength are based on several factors, including leadership (the ability to influence the market), stability (survival ability based on degree of customer loyalty), market (invulnerability to changes of technology and fashion), geography (the ability to cross geographic and cultural borders), support (the consistency and effectiveness of brand support), and protection (legal title).[16]

Quite apart from the difficulties associated with any of the methods, just as with any item of value for which a liquid market does not exist, valuations may be wrong. This can lead to critical mistakes in making acquisitions.

In 1994, Quaker Oats purchased the Snapple brand of fruit and tea soft drinks for $USB1.7. Twenty-seven months later, it sold Snapple for $USM300, a loss of $USB1.4, which, together with $USM160 in operating losses in 1995–1996, amounted to roughly $USM2 per day during Quaker's ownership. (Quaker's 1996 sales were $USB5.2.)[17] Clearly, Snapple was not worth the $1.7 billion that Quaker paid.

Valuation, especially regarding the revenue function, always rests on assumptions about the behavior of customers, and these assumptions must be subject to scrutiny. How many customers in the target market will buy? How frequently? How responsive will they be to the various marketing programs we expect to be using, and how do we expect their tastes and preferences to evolve over time? Assumptions about these and other issues are present, at least implicitly, in every valuation exercise.

Internal Measures

With the high levels of competitive intensity in most markets, firms are under inexorable pressure to continually reduce costs and improve productivity of both labor and capital. The balanced scorecard system suggests that the business should have a set of key performance indicators (KPIs) to assess cost and productivity. Typical measures are shown Table 12.3, which includes measures of the business unit's internal processes, such as order entry, new product development, and supply-chain management. The business unit should identify those processes that have the greatest impact on customer satisfaction and develop performance measures for each. The specific measures will depend on the process involved but may include such generic measures as time, cost, quality, and innovation. The educational level of employees or the number of years of experience in the industry or the firm could be measures of staff skills. Note that a number of these will be intangible, since we are attempting to measure both human and structural capital within the business.

In the auto industry, J. D. Power Associates provides data on defects that are widely tracked within the industry. Auto manufacturers also track and benchmark their productivity statistics. A typical set of these data for European car factories is shown in Table 12.4.

Innovation and Learning Measures

In rapidly changing environments, firms must innovate on an ongoing basis. Innovation is a major contributor to business-unit growth, but innovation should not be construed

TABLE 12.3 Internal Performance Measures

Measure	2002	2003	2004
Unit cost ($US)			
Yield (%)			
Product defects (%)			
Process measures (index)			
Staff satisfaction (index)			
Staff skills (index)			
Competences (index)			
Productivity (output/employee)			
IT system use (index)			

TABLE 12.4 2002 Productivity of European Auto Factories (2001 in parentheses)

Rank	Manufacturer	Plant Location	Vehicles per Employee
1 (1)	Nissan	Sunderland, UK	99 (95)
2 (4)	Renault	Valladolid, Spain	89 (77)
3 (—)	Toyota	Valenciennes, France	88 (—)
4 (2)	Ford	Saarlouis, Germany	87 (87)
5 (6)	General Motors	Antwerp, Belgium	83 (76)
6 (12)	Renault	Novo Mesto, Slovenia	82 (69)
7 (13)	Honda	Swindon, UK	82 (67)
8 (3)	Toyota	Burnaston, UK	81 (87)
9 (5)	General Motors	Eisenach, Germany	80 (77)
10 (7)	General Motors	Zaragoza, Spain	80 (75)

Source: A. Jay, "Nissan Sunderland Retains Top Spot for Productivity," *The Daily Telegraph,* July 9, 2003, p. 27.

as consisting only of new products. As we have noted, innovation can subsume new business models, entry into new markets, new processes, distribution channels, organization structures, and the like. Since innovation is crucial to renewal, business-unit managers need measures of the success of their business with respect to innovation. At the same time as the firm is renewing itself, it must be learning. Too many firms repeat their mistakes because their memory resides only in the memories of individuals; it has not been transformed into structural knowledge.

Some of the variables that capture innovation and learning are illustrated in Table 12.5. Other indicators of innovation might include R&D expenditures as a percent of sales revenues or the number of researchers as a percent of the labor force. These are input numbers, and we would prefer output measures such as number of patents filed or the number of new products in a particular time period. One example of such a measure is used by 3M—the percent of sales from products new in the last five years. One of the reasons much research on innovation has focused on new product–related measures is that these are much easier to design than measures of other kinds of innovation. Channel and business model innovation is less frequent than new product launches in most businesses, while process innovation is even harder to measure.

Financial Measures

The firm is an economic entity whose purpose is to create value, so financial measures are critical. In Chapter 1 we defined value as economic profit—the residual after all costs, including the cost of the capital employed in the business, are deducted from sales revenues. However, economic profit is an outcome, and a good performance measurement system will also track the drivers of economic profit. We begin by looking at cur-

TABLE 12.5 Innovation and Learning Performance Measures

Measure	2002	2003	2004
Patents (number/year)			
Revenue from new products (%)			
New capabilities (index)			
Staff training ($US)			
R&D Expenditure ($US)			

TABLE 12.6   **Financial Measures of Performance**

Measure	2002	2003	2004
Economic profit ($US)			
Net income ($US)			
ROCE (%)			
ROS (%)			
Asset turnover (ratio)			
Current ratio (ratio)			

rent performance indicators, both outcomes and drivers. We then review measures that give insight into likely future performance.

Measuring Current Performance

Table 12.6 contains a typical set of financial measures that reflect recent performance of the business. A more detailed explanation of these terms is contained in Appendix B to this chapter.

We have given pride of place to a measure of *economic profit* since we argue that this should be the primary basis on which we should assess any business. Nonetheless, we should not expect all business units to make a positive economic profit all the time. We do expect that all businesses should *eventually* generate positive economic profit, but if the parent corporation is investing in the business to support its growth, short-term economic profit may be negative. In this instance, we can see the advantage of a business being part of a diversified firm, since the corporate center can provide capital for the business from internal or external sources.

We have also shown a *net income* figure in the table. This number is widely tracked and reported, and certainly managers do not like to see this decline. Several of the other measures in Table 12.6 are measures of efficiency. Return on capital employed (ROCE) is a measure of how productively the capital in the business is being utilized. For a positive economic profit, this must be above the business's cost of capital. The corporate level may use such a measure in allocating resources, although, as argued earlier, only future capital productivity is actually relevant. Return on sales (ROS), also known as net margin on sales, can be seen as another measure of the efficiency of the business: How much does the business keep of each dollar of sales? Margins are not a good performance measure of the business's overall profitability since they are strongly influenced by the level and nature of competition, being low in highly competitive markets. Margins are usually high for successful new products but decline as competitors follow the successful pioneer. Acceptable margins will also depend on the capital intensity of the business. As discussed in Appendix B to this chapter, capital-intensive firms need to earn a high margin on sales to be profitable. By contrast, a retailer may be quite profitable (defined in terms of ROCE) with net margins as low as 2% to 3%. Capital intensity is generally measured by the ratio of capital to sales, which is the inverse of the asset turnover ratio, and retailers generally have low levels of capital intensity.

> One of the major drivers of Wal-Mart's rise to become the world's largest corporation in sales revenues has been its competence in supply-chain management, which enables it to achieve phenomenal levels of stock turnover. One consultant described Wal-Mart as a cash-generating machine financed by its suppliers, so astute has the company become in financing its growth!

We have included asset turnover as one of the measures above since in our view most firms are actively engaged in reducing the level of capital tied up in the business, particularly working capital, through supply-chain initiatives.

Valuing Future Performance

The above measures of performance are focused on the present, on how well is the firm performing now. But strategy is about making decisions now whose consequences will be manifest some time in the future. So a technique is needed to estimate the current value of future results. The recommended method for accomplishing this is to calculate the net present value of the strategy over time.

The current value of a strategy is determined by the discounted value of the future free cash flow estimated to be generated by that strategy. We regard net present value (NPV) as the correct method for an economic evaluation of the future results of a strategy since it incorporates both net cash flows and the time value of money. In this formulation, net cash flow is the free cash generated by the strategy, including all investments in both fixed and working capital, and the discount rate is the firm's weighted average cost of capital.

The forecast of future cash flows is generally broken down into two time periods:

- A forecast period for which detailed cash flow projections are made (conventional practice seems to be to pick the arbitrary period of five years[18])

- A steady-state period to perpetuity, implicitly assuming no change in the firm's strategy

The calculation of net present value has some very real problems in application. First, at the practical level, it is difficult to develop estimates of the required numbers, since forecasts of sales, costs, and investments are needed over the forecast period of, say, five years. These numbers may have major errors, for it is unreasonable to expect perfect foresight with respect to future demand, competitor action, developments in technology, future market shares and prices, and so on, all of which will be fundamental to the development of cash flow numbers. Unfortunately, the "gimme a number" syndrome often means these numbers have an apparent accuracy, which can lead to a feeling of greater certainty. In addition, the realities of organizational life mean there may be an unconscious (or even conscious!) tendency for managers to bias their numbers to ensure that the NPV comes out at an acceptable level.

Second, NPV is of limited use when dealing with very innovative strategies. These are by their nature characterized by little in the way of historical data and information that can be utilized to predict the future.

Third, it is in the nature of NPV calculations that short time-horizon cash streams are weighted higher than cash streams that are in the distant future. With a discount rate of 15%, $1 in 10 years time is discounted to only 24¢ today. So most of the NPV is in the first few years, which may bias managers' choices toward those alternatives that promise to deliver short-term benefits. Indeed, given two alternatives of equal NPV, it is likely that most managers would choose the alternative that produces the earliest positive net cash flows.

Figure 12.5 depicts a typical cash flow profile of a strategy.

Despite the apparent high weighting to short-term results, when such a calculation is done, a large part of the NPV (perhaps as much as 80%) is in the residual value term. This is calculated using the simplifying but simplistic—if not heroic—assumption that the performance of the firm stays at its five-year level in perpetuity. Such an assumption is quite dangerous for strategies with heavy front-end investments and delayed payoffs, as many dot.com investors discovered!

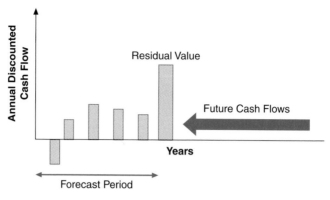

Figure 12.5   Future Cash Flows of a Strategy

NPV approaches can deal with risk by using a higher discount rate. As we have noted, the cost of capital will be different for different business units of a company. However, this does not address the different risk levels of individual projects. One way to deal with this is by subjectively adjusting the discount rate based on qualitative risk assessment. Kuczmarski, for example, argues that quite low discount rates should be used for strategies involving cost reduction or product extensions, with higher rates for more radical strategies.[19]

Other Methods: Simulation and Options

One way to handle some of the problems just discussed is to use simulation methods. If we are uncertain about an input variable to the financial model, a range of possibilities can be evaluated and a distribution of expected returns generated. In some applications, game theory may be useful, since it explicitly incorporates concepts of competitive reaction.

NPV also does not deal adequately with the benefits of flexibility. Faced with great uncertainty, more firms are making small investments in growing areas—through alliances, for example—to gain knowledge about whether to invest a substantial sum at a later date. This may permit greater flexibility, for the business may be able to shut down and restart, or refocus, an activity or expand partial to full ownership. The business could then be considered to have a call option—the right to buy.[20]

In summary, NPV is a good methodology to use for evaluating financial instruments, such as bonds, where the investor gets a guaranteed return for several years, but investment projects are typically more complicated. Management can intervene and change the direction of a strategy if it is not meeting expectations, while circumstances may change significantly from those initially envisaged, particularly in new areas. If NPV were foolproof, venture capital firms would not have to maintain such a large portfolio of projects! For this reason, there has been some interest expressed in the possibility of using option theory as a basis for evaluation.

Finally, we should point out that valuing future performance is not the same as influencing future performance. If business-unit managers are interested in leading indicators of future performance, they would be well advised to look at the various non-financial measures we have discussed, since they are likely to have predictive value.

🌀 12.5 CORPORATE PERFORMANCE MEASURES

The balanced scorecard is a performance measurement framework best suited to a business unit or single-business firm rather than a multibusiness corporation. Possibly as a

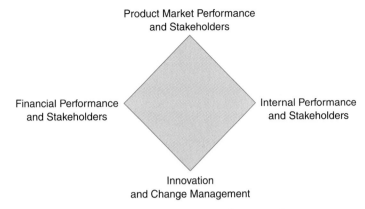

Figure 12.6   Corporate-Level Scorecard

result of this, and the fairly recent development of the balanced scorecard by Kaplan and Norton, there has been less effort devoted to the development of comparable non-financial measures at the corporate level.

In this section, we have adapted some of the basic principles of the balanced score-card to the corporate level of a multibusiness firm. Such adaptation is necessary since, for instance, the corporate level of a firm typically has no actual customers; customers purchase from its constituent businesses. For measures such as customer or employee satisfaction, or new product launches, it is possible to score each strategic business unit (SBU) and weight these scores to get an overall corporate measure that would enable a CEO to track corporate performance. However, there are also some quintessential cor-porate variables, such as scope and diversity that should also be of concern. Measures for these variables must be constructed for the firm as a whole; they cannot be created from weighted sums of scores for individual business units.

Our framework is shown in Figure 12.6, where performance of the firm is assessed in four areas: *external product/market, internally, financially,* and with respect to *innovation.* While innovation could be considered as an internal measure, we regard it as of sufficient importance to warrant special consideration. We now discuss each set of measures in turn.

Product/Market Performance and External Stakeholders

The firm has a number of external stakeholders, comprising customers of the business units as well as other entities such as suppliers, unions, pressure groups, and the com-munity. While the performance of the firm needs to be assessed from the perspective of each of these, we start with customers generally and then move on to other stakeholders.

For most corporate managers, growth itself is a vital performance measure; thus all firms monitor total sales revenue for the firm very closely and would prefer to see this measure increasing over time. Revenue may also be compared with some measure of economic growth, such as GDP, to see whether the firm is growing faster or slower than the overall economy.

As we discussed earlier, the ability to create a continuous stream of new businesses, representing new sources of profit, is a distinguishing characteristic of successful firms. For a firm to grow in terms of market capitalization, it generally requires a stream of new businesses. At the corporate level, this can be analyzed as shown in Figure 12.7.

Growth from existing businesses presents a different management challenge from growth of new businesses. Yet if the company is to survive, it must have a portfolio of growth alternatives, and senior management cannot afford to focus exclusively on cur-

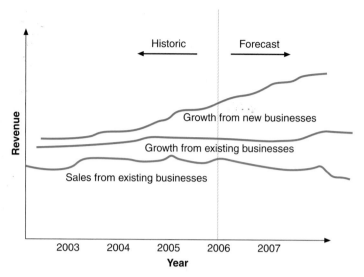

Figure 12.7 Sources of Corporate Growth

rent core business. Indeed, we should measure the performance of a diversified company in terms of its ability to spawn a stream of new business ventures, either from internal development or through acquisition.

As mentioned, the corporate level has no direct customers—they all exist at the business-unit level, so a measure of corporate-level customer satisfaction is hard to imagine. However, the corporate center should be monitoring performance on this critical dimension by determining the weighted-average customer satisfaction measure of its different business units, where the measure from a given business unit is weighted relative to the size of the business unit. The center will also be tracking business-unit market shares and may well be comparing the performance of each business in its chosen market, using dimensions such as market share, revenue, customer satisfaction, customer value, and competitive advantage.

Total revenue is a simple measure, but it is only one, and the firm needs to get more detail to properly analyze its position. At the corporate level, managers would also need to collect segment data—by business unit, by industry, by geographic market, or by type of business—to see how the business portfolio is evolving over time. The overall balance of a firm's portfolio is a critical leading indicator of both risk management and future value-generating potential. Such an analysis is shown in Figure 12.8, which shows the distribu-

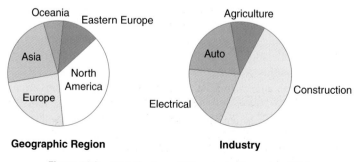

Figure 12.8 Distribution of Corporate Revenue, 2004

tion of corporate revenue both geographically and by industry. Such analyses would normally be done dynamically to reveal how the distribution of revenue is changing over time.

Brand equity may also be a major issue at the corporate level. If the firm makes heavy use of a corporate masterbrand, then a corporate health-check system is essential.[21] However, the center may well be interested in the stewardship of its business unit's major brands, in which case it will want to see the appropriate health-check tables. If the center is considering modifying its brand or business portfolio, it will also want to measure these brand equities, which may in any case be required to be reported on its balance sheet.

Finally, as we noted, the corporation may well be interested in tracking the perceptions of other important stakeholder groups. While the indices would be less elaborate, perceptual measures could equally well be used to track community perceptions of the firm, whether locally, regionally, nationally, or internationally.

Internal Measures and Internal Stakeholders

At the corporate level, the firm is structured as a set of business units, and hence internal measures are connected with the performance of these units as well as with several overall firm measures. In the preceding section, we examined several methods for analyzing the entire portfolio of businesses from a market perspective. Here we extend that discussion by indicating methods that can be used to assess the health of the business units.

Corporate Portfolio Performance Measures

To perform their agency role for the principals, corporate managers must delve more deeply into the performance of the business units comprising the firm's portfolio. Continuing with our key measure of economic profit, then, one form of analysis is the so-called value map,[22] a useful tool for resource allocation that demonstrates how businesses are contributing to the creation of value.

As shown in Figure 12.9, the **value map** plots the business units in the portfolio on two dimensions. The horizontal axis is the level of capital employed in the business (in dollars), giving an indication of the size of the business. The vertical axis is the spread generated by the business—its return on capital less its weighted average cost of capital. Consequently, the area for each business measures the total economic value it generates, which can be negative or positive. Negative economic profit is not necessarily bad; if the business has an objective of rapid revenue growth, we might expect negative

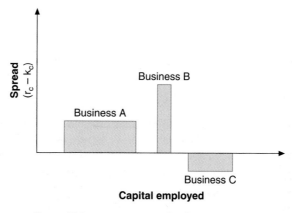

Figure 12.9   Economic Profit of Business Units

TABLE 12.7   Illustrative Corporate Overview of Business-Unit Performance

Measure	Business 1	Business 2	Business 3	Business 4
Percent sales revenue				
Percent assets				
ROCE (%)				
ROS (%)				
Sales growth (%)				
Percent profit				

economic profit since it will be investing in R&D, market development, staff development, physical capital, and so on in anticipation of future returns. The value map provides an interesting and insightful way to plot the portfolio of businesses in terms of the value created and the capital employed.

Such a chart helps corporate managers address several important questions: Should we continue to invest in high-value businesses, or are these now in saturated markets and not likely to return the cost of capital for any new investment? What about the businesses that are currently generating negative economic profit—what is their future, when can they be expected to shift to positive?

The corporate center might also construct an extensive set of performance measures for the firm's business units, comparing their growth, percent of total corporate sales, revenues, assets, economic or net profit, and so on. Similar analyses could also be constructed by geography or for established and new products. Table 12.7 illustrates such a performance table.

Aggregate Corporate Measures

As in the previous section, one class of measures could deal with the aggregation on a weighted basis of business-unit measures. GM, for example, could combine measures of defects per vehicle across its many nameplates to develop a measure for its vehicle-producing businesses as a whole. Corporate productivity numbers could be calculated by dividing the total number of vehicles produced by total GM employment. A similar but instructive measure would be sales per employee, while the ratio of these two ratios, benchmarked against the market, would tell corporate managers whether or not the corporation as a whole is trading up or down in the market. Similarly, the center could weight and combine employee satisfaction measures from business units or conduct central surveys of morale.

Other important measures, however, relate strictly to the corporation as a whole. We have already indicated that decisions on the degree and nature of diversification are critical corporate decisions. It is therefore important that senior management track and manage the level of diversification of the firm. Yet it turns out that there are few good measures of a corporation's extent of diversification. At first sight, it might seem that the simplest measure would be the number of different types of businesses that comprise the portfolio, so that we could use a measure like the number of four-digit SIC codes. However, this approach neglects any commonality across these different classifications, despite the fact that we know that the relatedness of a corporation's constituent businesses is important to its performance. One of the advantages of a diversified firm is its ability to share strategic resources and competences among its different businesses, so any measure neglecting this construct is bound to be defective. Unfortunately, few measures of relatedness have been developed and managers have routinely applied even fewer to monitor their firms' portfolios, although we do develop one possible such measure below.

Relatedness Measures

One measure used is the so-called entropy measure, based on the SIC codes.[23] These codes characterize business activity in terms of what the business does. It is a hierarchical system, in which a small number of major industry areas, such as mining and manufacturing, are in turn broken down into finer and finer subgroups. Thus, there are business areas defined by two-digit (broad) and four-digit (narrow) codes, as illustrated in Appendix A. Businesses belonging to different four-digit industries within the same two-digit group are treated as related, whereas businesses from different two-digit groups are treated as unrelated.

A measure of entropy for these groups may then be calculated, where entropy is a measure of the spread of businesses. If the total corporation comprises just one business, then entropy is zero. If the firm's portfolio is split equally among, say, N businesses, then entropy is defined as ln (N).

There are three different concepts—related, unrelated, and total entropy—to which the measure can be applied:

Total entropy is determined by the size distribution of revenue between the businesses at the four-digit level.

Unrelated entropy is determined by the size distribution of revenue at the two-digit level.

Related entropy is then obtained by subtraction of unrelated from total entropy.

This measure of related entropy could be used as a measure of relatedness among the businesses and plotted over time to monitor changes, identifying whether or not a firm is becoming less or more related in its businesses. Such a measure could also be used to evaluate the impact of any given acquisition on the relatedness of the firm's portfolio.

While this measure is one of the few available, it is not without its problems. It assumes that two businesses sharing the same two-digit SIC code have similar production and technology functions and are thereby related, but this may not be the case. Yet two businesses in different industries—say, a timber product and an adhesive—could nonetheless share a common or similar distribution system (e.g., both distributed through hardware stores) that could produce synergistic benefits. SIC codes would not provide a good measure of the type of relatedness. Nor does the entropy statistic measure the degree of relatedness between any two business units; it measures only the relatedness between the units of a total firm, so that relatedness operationalized in this way is, of necessity, a corporate statistic, not a statistic between two business units.[24]

Part of the difficulty with the measurement of relatedness is that the construct itself is poorly defined. Perhaps it should be viewed as multidimensional. Certainly, rather than defining it by relatedness among industries in which the firm competes, we could also construe relatedness with respect to the resources and competences of the various business units, the geographies in which they operate, and so on. It may be that it is the ability to transfer these competences, or geographic knowledge, between business units that is important.[25] Regardless, relatedness should be a factor in determining the benefits that may potentially be derived from the common ownership of a group of business units, the topic of our next section.

Synergy

In Chapter 9 we suggested that there are several different types of synergy that may be present in a firm and that may result in higher revenue or lower costs for the firm. These were:

> Cost savings from two businesses sharing common facilities
>
> Revenue enhancement from the ability to cross-sell across two businesses
>
> The transferring of best practices from one business to another
>
> Tax benefits gained by moving tax liabilities between businesses

All these are difficult to measure and evaluate, and the benefits in any case are likely to be firm-specific. It is, of course, the sharing of resources and competences that is the underlying rationale for the diversified firm. The answer to the question of what value a corporate center adds to its portfolio of business units is always synergy. Yet, despite the importance of the concept, there is no real theory of synergy, nor any specific measures of it. Thus, while we have some attempts to measure relatedness, as discussed above, there is no generally agreed-upon method for measuring synergy between any pair of businesses.

Competences

Innovation, growth, and change will all require new competences. There are several means open to the firm by which competences can be enhanced, such as buying in from outside, investing in training and development, and using temporary outside staff such as consultants. Corporate management should be asking what means should be adopted and what measures are in place to ensure that the required capabilities are being developed in a timely and cost-effective manner. The stock of competences is the structural capital that constitutes part of the firm's intangible asset base, and their management and protection is impossible without measurement. Senior managers also need to be questioning whether the current business model is still aligned with the market and whether the mental model of the firm needs to be revised and changed.

Employee Indices

Employees are critically important stakeholders, and their views and attitudes are vital to the firm's future success. The human capital represented by employees needs to be continually enhanced, since it is a critical component of the firm's intangible assets. Thus, internal analysis also requires measurement on a number of "soft" dimensions.

> Such major U.S. corporations as IBM and Texas Instruments began conducting employee morale surveys back in the 1960s, signifying early recognition of the importance of knowledge workers' morale to their corporate success.

Strategic management of the firm's human resources is ever more important, and the skills of staff, their levels of education and experience, their career development and job rotation, their leadership skills and motivation are all variables that we should consider monitoring. In addition, useful information can be gained by conducting interviews with those who elect to leave the firm and to determine their reasons for doing so.

Innovation and Change Management

Innovation and change management are, as we have pointed out, crucial for the long-term success of the enterprise. In Figure 12.7 we have already suggested one possible framework for assessing the success of innovations within the firm.

As we have pointed out innovation is more than just new products or new businesses. It includes new business models, new organizational forms, new leadership styles, and new capabilities. Some of these are relatively simple to assess. For example, most firms conduct R&D, and hence measures such as expenditures on R&D would be available. Related measures would be R&D output measures such as number of patents. But what about expenditures on innovation in other areas? For example, how much does the firm spend on understanding the changing needs of customers? What expenditures are undertaken to understand changing industry structure and relationships? What processes are in place to ensure that new business models are being generated? For many firms, information technology is becoming an important basis for competitive advantage. So another possible measure would be expenditures on IT systems.

Finally, the firm should be assessing how it performs at change management. Again, this may be a basis for competitive advantage. We may find that several firms in the same industry have come up with essentially the same strategy. Success, then, will go to the firm that is better at managing the change.

Financial Measures and Stakeholders

The final area for assessment covers such financial stakeholders as shareholders and capital markets. Most of the measures applicable to business units can be used at the corporate level, but in addition we can also track such corporate measures as market capitalization.

Corporate-level financial measures are much better developed than the non-financial measures we have just discussed. However, since there is a huge range of such measures, we will cover just some of the more important here. Some of the measures are also quite technical, and more detail on many of these measures is contained in Appendix B to the chapter.

Economic Profit

Because a firm is primarily an economic entity, financial measures are critical. However, the perspective of a senior manager on overall performance should not differ from that of an owner of the business. Indeed, if those managers are directors, they are legally obliged to take such a point of view, for they should be acting as agents of the owners. This is the underlying rationale for our continuous emphasis on the concept of economic profit: the firm that generates economic profit is meeting the interests of its owners. As we will see later in the section, senior managers will need additional information and analysis to fulfill their managerial roles, but measurement of economic profit is the most appropriate starting point for any discussion of financial measures.

As noted in Chapter 4, a widely adopted measure of economic profit is Stern Stewart's concept of economic value added (EVA). According to a 1996 survey of 1,300 U.S. firms conducted by the Institute of Management Accountants, 34% were already using EVA and another 45% anticipated using it in the future. However, the firms surveyed realized that financial measures were not everything, and some 90% indicated that greater use of non-financial measures would be desirable.[26]

EVA calculations for a number of US firms shown in the table in Table 12.8. As can be seen, firm performance alters substantially when we include an explicit capital charge. In 1997, General Motors made an accounting return, shown as ROCE, of 5.9%. To earn the net income which this implies ($USM5,561), the firm employed total capital of $USM94,268.[27] Given the industry in which it is located and its financial structure, GM is considered to have a weighted-average cost of capital of 9.7—which is the return that shareholders would expect given its risk. When this cost of

TABLE 12.8 EVA of Selected U.S. Firms

Firm	EVA ($USM)	Capital Invested ($USM)	Return on Capital Employed (%) (ROCE)	Cost of Capital (%) (WACC)
Coca-Cola	2,442	9,276	36	9.7
Ford Motor	1,719	55,995	12.1	9.1
General Motors	−3,527	94,268	5.9	9.7
IBM	−2,743	67,867	7.8	11.8
Merck	1,688	19,792	23.0	14.5
Microsoft	1,727	4,889	47.1	11.8
Walt Disney	−347	20,599	11.0	12.6

Source: R. A. Brealey and S. C. Myers, *Principles of Corporate Finance* (Boston: Irwin/McGraw-Hill, 2000). Reprinted by permission of McGraw-Hill.

capital is considered, the returns earned by GM were well below what shareholders expected, given the risk of their investment. Indeed, in 1997 GM destroyed $USM3,527 in shareholder value!

In the EVA calculations in Table 12.8, intangible assets have not been included—the figure used for capital invested is simply the net tangible assets of the firm. Firms such as Merck and Microsoft report low levels of invested capital, since most of their assets are intangible. Thus their capital charges are low and their EVAs look high. To further complicate matters, Microsoft did not expense options, thus inflating reported net income and economic profit.[28]

Investors, analysts, and senior managers will also be interested in other aggregate measures, such as market value added, market/book ratio, and earnings per share, which were reviewed in Chapter 4.

Other Financial Measures

At the corporate level, a number of ratios are utilized to assess how well the firm is performing financially. Return on capital employed (ROCE) measures how well the firm is using the capital under its control and is defined as net income/capital employed. ROE measures the return the equityholders are receiving and is defined as net income/shareholder's equity, where values for shareholders' equity, total assets, and capital employed come from the firm's balance sheet. Many companies also track the corporate margin on sales (ROS) and asset turnover (S/A) as financial productivity measures.

Figure 12.10 shows the ROE for Harley-Davidson over a 10-year period. As can be seen, the company suffered financially in the late 1990s and then underwent a turnaround in early 2002, with shareholders enjoying a return on their equity of 26% in that year.

A number of these ratios could be displayed in a convenient summary form, as shown in Table 12.9. These might well be attractively displayed showing trends in color, in what some have labeled a corporate "dashboard." In the next major section of the chapter, we will show examples of the dashboards used by several companies, which incorporate both non-financial and financial measures.

As Table 12.9 indicates, at the corporate level a measure of liquidity is generally essential, measured by the D/E ratio. This measure reflects the financial structure of the firm, whether it is financed by debt or equity, and is also a measure of financial risk, since high leverage means high financial risk. Fluctuating demand with high

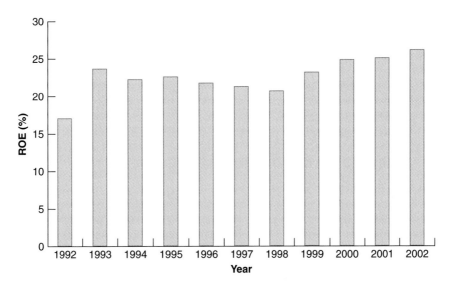

Figure 12.10 ROE for Harley-Davidson Inc.
Source: Harley-Davidson Annual Report, 2002: www.harley-davidson.com.

leverage will jeopardize the firm's ability to meet its periodic interest payments. Other liquidity measures are the amount of cash on hand and the current ratio (current assets/current liabilities). Another important liquidity measure is the interest cover, measured by net income/interest expense, which indicates the firm's ability to service its debt. Financially strong firms may have a ratio of 4 or more, and deterioration in this measure often leads to significant refinancing by the firm

Several of the measures in Table 12.9 are essentially measures of the operating performance of the firm. These are particularly important because they create a link between strategy decisions and financial performance. Consider, for example, return on equity, which, as shown in Appendix B to this chapter, can be expressed as:

$$\text{Return on equity} = \text{sales margin} \times \text{asset turnover} \times (1 + \text{financial leverage})$$
$$\text{where asset turnover} = 1.0/\text{capital intensity}$$

This simple model becomes a very useful diagnostic tool, since it can be used to identify the sources of variability in ROE and how it can be improved. To improve ROE the firm can do the following:

TABLE 12.9 Selected Financial Measures

Measure	2000	2001	2002	2003	2004	2005
Economic profit						
Market value added						
Net income						
Earnings per share						
Total revenue						
Annual sales growth						
Leverage						
Share price						

- Improve its net margins
- Improve its asset utilization
- Increase its financial leverage

Improving *net margin* means improving average realized prices or reducing costs. It is not always easy to improve margins, but we can see why firms are interested in cost reductions. A firm's ability to increase prices is influenced by its market power, which in turn is determined by its competitive advantages and the intensity of competition in the industries in which it competes. Margins usually decline over the life cycle of products, starting high and then declining as inflation-adjusted prices go down as a result of increased competition.

> IBM's profitability declined as the overall market shifted from high-margin mainframe computers, with relatively high barriers to entry and competitive advantage for the company, to low-margin personal computers. As the latter market became more competitive, IBM outsourced much of its production and began to focus on computer services.

Forecasts of future margins should generally be for them to decline. A changing product mix over time could also result in lower average margins as the firm markets a higher proportion of low-margin products. This emphasizes again the critical importance of innovation to value creation over the longer term.

Increasing *asset turnover* means reducing fixed or working capital, with the same level of net income. It is often easier to reduce working capital than fixed capital. Fixed capital is generally a characteristic of the industry we are in and is not easy to alter without a major technological breakthrough. In contrast, reducing working capital means reducing inventories or receivables (or allowing payables to expand). Such considerations drive companies' interest in supply-chain management, which has the potential to dramatically reduce working capital and thus improve asset turnover. Another way to think of this, and sometimes better, is in terms of investment intensity *(I/S)*—how many dollars of investment are needed to support a dollar of sales. If a firm is asset-intensive, as is true for aircraft manufacture or aluminum refining, it will need high margins to offset this factor in achieving a good return on shareholders' equity.

Another option is to increase *leverage* by replacing equity with debt or funding new opportunities with increased levels of debt. These are financial decisions that increase the financial risk of the firm. Some firms are already exposed to significant business risk. Business risk is derived from high fixed-cost intensity, which, if associated with variations in sales volume, can have devastating effects on net income when that volume falls. As we noted earlier, firms with high business risk due to their operating leverage would be well advised to keep lower levels of debt!

In summary, senior management should carefully monitor the components that contribute to shareholder return on equity. They must be cognizant of the relationship between the firm's business decisions and their financial consequences, and avoid the compartmentalization that is so often the result of a functional view of the firm.

Company Examples

Some companies have put considerable effort into developing a simple set of indicators that can quickly give senior managers an overview on how their firm is performing. We believe these simple systems, or "corporate dashboards" as they are sometimes called, provide an important tool for better management of the enterprise. However, they must be carefully constructed to incorporate the principles we discussed earlier. Senior managers, desirous of pleasing external stakeholders, are often very selective in the information they present. Such behavior often causes undesirable and unnecessary fluctuations in share prices, as expectations are raised and then dashed—scarcely serving shareholders! Such behavior can destroy the company when it becomes self-delusionary. Thus indicators should be carefully chosen, be linked to strategy, incorporate multiple measures, permit causal analysis, be meaningfully benchmarked, and encourage forward-looking behavior and decisions. In short, we must bear in mind all the cautions discussed in Section 12.2 of this chapter. Having said this, we will present some company examples even though they do not necessarily comply exactly with all the admonitions we have presented.

Our first example is from an anonymous health services company, whose dashboard is shown in Figure 12.11. The indicators in the figure compare the company's results for the current year with its plan. An upward-pointing arrow means that the firm has exceeded the planned value (desirable), a horizontal arrow means the company just about matched the plan, and a downward-pointing arrow means that the planned result was not attained.

The columns of Figure 12.11 bear some resemblance to the categories of corporate measurement we have been discussing. Column one deals mainly with financial results of interest to senior management and external stakeholders. Column two contains information that could be roughly grouped into an operating category, while column three deals with two measures of performance of financial markets. The final column contains a number of non-financial indicators of the type we have been discussing.

The overall pattern of Figure 12.11 suggests cause for concern. The company has achieved good operating results and has apparently pleased the stock market. However,

Figure 12.11　Health Services Company Corporate Dashboard

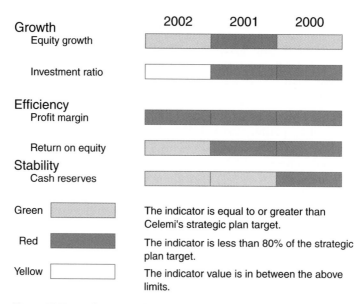

Figure 12.12   Celemi Tangible Asset Monitor—an Extraction
Source: Celemi Annual Report, 2002: www.celemi.com. © Dr. Karl-Erik Sveiby.

it appears that these financial results have come about primarily through raising prices, while relative quality has deteriorated. In general, the company has done a poor job of meeting its non-financial targets. Senior management should definitely be concerned that the firm may well have achieved good short-term results at the expense of its future. The combination of deteriorating relative quality, lower market share, and flat sales is likely to show up as poor future performance.

Another example, which does not have to be disguised, is provided by Celemi, a Swedish consulting firm specializing in providing corporations with advice on learning solutions for corporate change programs. In this industry, the value of the firm is determined primarily by its intangible assets. Thus Celemi, which has offices in Europe, the United States, and China, should, according to the principles we have discussed in this book, be paying considerable attention to measuring and managing these assets, and this is indeed the case. Of course, that does not mean that financial performance is neglected. Figure 12.12 shows how Celemi presents its financial results, while Figure 12.13 shows how it monitors its intangible assets. The structure of the Celemi tangible and intangible assets monitor has been developed by Dr. Karl-Erik Sveiby. Less conventional, and more interesting for our purposes, is the monitor for intangible assets, as shown in Figure 12.13.

Celemi's matrix for intangible assets has several noteworthy features. Notice the three themes of renewal, efficiency, and stability. The first is clearly related to our emphasis on innovation and growth, but with the three categories of clients/organization/people, they have also incorporated our internal classification of competence. The efficiency measures relate well to our productivity measures, but the stability measure is a fascinating addition, one that seems to have considerable merit when looking at intangible assets. We are a little uneasy with the division of "staff" and "expert" turnover into two different classifications, but turnover is nonetheless a measure important in any people-dependent business. Arguably, we should not seek zero turnover, for fresh blood and ideas may be invaluable, but too high a rate of turnover produces loss of learning and inefficiency.

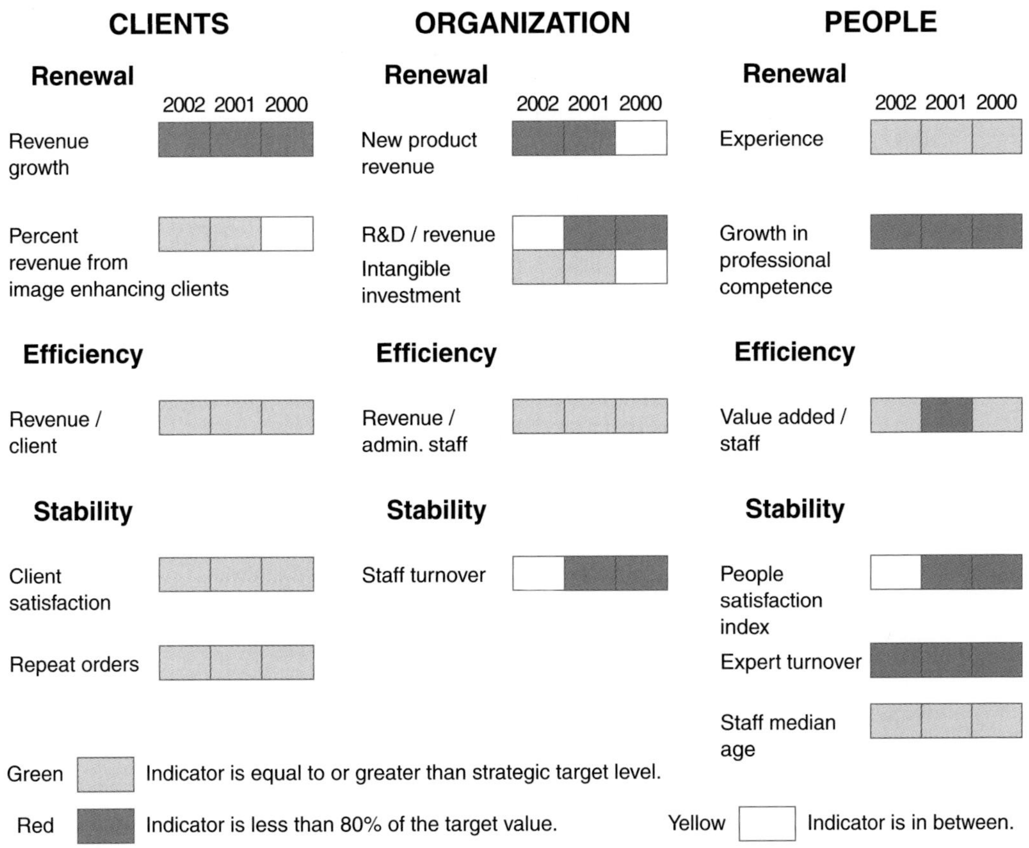

CLIENTS   ORGANIZATION   PEOPLE

Renewal   Renewal   Renewal

CLIENTS	2002	2001	2000
Revenue growth			

ORGANIZATION	2002	2001	2000
New product revenue			

PEOPLE	2002	2001	2000
Experience			

| Percent revenue from image enhancing clients | | | |

| R&D / revenue Intangible investment | | | |

| Growth in professional competence | | | |

Efficiency   Efficiency   Efficiency

| Revenue / client | | | |

| Revenue / admin. staff | | | |

| Value added / staff | | | |

Stability   Stability   Stability

| Client satisfaction | | | |

| Staff turnover | | | |

| People satisfaction index | | | |

| Repeat orders | | | |

| Expert turnover | | | |

| Staff median age | | | |

Green — Indicator is equal to or greater than strategic target level.

Red — Indicator is less than 80% of the target value.   Yellow — Indicator is in between.

Figure 12.13   Celemi Intangible Assets Monitor—An Extraction
Source: Celemi Annual Report, 2002: www.celemi.com. © Dr. Karl-Erik Sveiby.

12.6 SUMMARY

In this chapter we reviewed the importance of understanding that measurement should be embedded in a sophisticated understanding of the strategic management process, which is itself very dynamic. Too many companies take a static perspective on measurement, failing to link the process either to changes in the firm's environment or to its evolving strategy.

We then examined the considerations that enter into the design of a system. We examined the process as well as some of the pitfalls that can render the whole effort counterproductive. Among other factors, we emphasized the importance of multiple leading indicators, understanding cause–effect relationships, and the fact that performance measurement should subsume non-financial as well as financial measures.

We looked separately at the issues of measuring business-unit and corporate performance, reflecting the fact that most larger companies today operate in multiple businesses. This has been a recurring theme in the book, and we illustrated the different types of measures that pertain solely to the corporate level.

As we noted, measurement of performance has generally—and particularly at the corporate level—not kept up with changes in business. Thus not only are we lacking in good measures that might help senior executives make better diversification decisions (for so many have gone disastrously wrong!), but the measurement and management of the intangible assets that now constitute the majority of a company's value have lagged considerably. Fortunately, there are signs that the business community is waking up to these defects, and we hope and trust that we will see the much-needed development and changes in the practice of performance management.

◉ REVIEW QUESTIONS

1. Explain why measurement of financial performance alone is insufficient for the purposes of good management stewardship.

2. Contrast the measurement of business-unit and corporate performance.

3. Demonstrate how you would convince skeptical senior managers that their firm needed better measurement and management of its intangible assets. Be sure to make an economically justified argument for your point of view.

4. Choose a company with which you are familiar. Using published sources, analyze its performance management practices and recommend improvements.

5. Most companies measure themselves by comparing performance against the previous year. Explain why this may lead to problems, and illustrate your argument with examples from real companies wherever possible.

6. Select a firm that has suffered financial difficulties in the past three to five years. Using published sources, develop a set of variables, and measures of those variables, that could be leading indicators of the poor performance.

AU:
Reread
and
check
appendix

◉ APPENDIX A: MEASURES OF RELATEDNESS

Assume that the firm consists of N business units in total, where each is defined with respect to the four-digit SIC code.

Also assume that the firm consists of M (where $N > M$) groups of businesses, where a group is defined at the two-digit SIC code level.

Note that each of the N four-digit businesses is contained within one, and only one, of the M two-digit groups.

Also assume that p_i is the proportion of total firm sales represented by business i at the four-digit SIC level. So $\Sigma p_i = 1$.

Also assume that q_j is the proportion of total firm sales represented by business group j at the two-digit level. So $\Sigma q_j = 1$.

Then total entropy is defined as using the proportion of sales in each of the N businesses at the four-digit level:

$$DT = \Sigma p_i \ln (1/p_i) \text{ over the total on } N \text{ business units.}$$

The unrelated entropy is calculated, in a similar fashion, using the proportion of sales in each of the M two-digit SIC codes:

$$DU = \Sigma q_j \ln (1/q_j) \text{ over the total of } M \text{ business groups}$$

Related entropy is then defined as:

$$DR = DT - DU$$

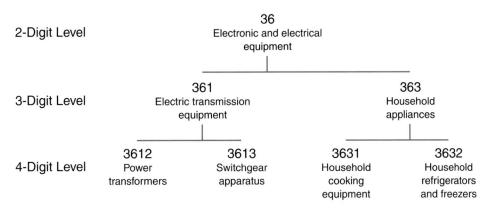

Figure 12.14 Illustrative SIC Codes

Source: J. A. Robins and M. F. Wiersema, "The Measurement of Corporate Portfolio Strategy: Analysis of the Context Validity of Related Diversification Indexes, *Strategic Management Journal* 24, no. 1 (2003), pp. 39–60.

This could be used to analyze the nature of the diversity of a firm over time. As the firm diversifies, is this diversification toward more related or toward more unrelated diversification?

An illustration of the hierarchical nature of SIC codes, indicating the relationship between two-digit and four-digit codes is given in Figure 12.14.

◉ APPENDIX B: FINANCIAL MEASURES OF PERFORMANCE

Economic Profit

Economic profit is a generic name for a range of approaches that have been developed to evaluate the ongoing performance of a firm, whether or not the current strategy is producing value for the equityholders. Economic profit is not always easy to calculate in practice, but the concept is clear—the firm as an ongoing entity should cover all its costs, including the cost of the capital employed by the firm, since this is not free.

Economic profit is defined by the relationship:

Economic profit = net operating profit after tax – capital charge for the capital employed by the firm

This can be written as

Economic profit = net operating profit after tax – capital employed in the firm × cost of that capital

If we denote economic profit by EP, then:

$$EP = NOPAT - (CE \times k_c)$$

where

NOPAT = net operating profit after tax

CE = capital employed

k_c = cost of capital, reflecting the firm's risk and financial structure

Defining ROCE (denoted as r_c) as NOPAT/CE, the above can be written as:

$$EP = CE \times (r_c - k_c)$$

where the term $(r_c - k_c)$ is referred to as the return spread, the difference between the return earned by the firm and its cost of capital.

Economic profit is not only a method of assessing the value of a firm; it can also be applied at the SBU level, forcing business managers to be cognizant of the capital employed in their business. As a result, economic profit can be used in an integrated financial management and incentive system. Economic profit is useful for evaluating the ongoing performance of a firm; it results in a net measure showing how much value has been created or destroyed by the firm during the period and is an intuitively appealing concept.[29] It is not the same concept as accounting profit, due to the adoption of a capital charge, but we regard it as a superior measure to use for management decision making.

Economic profit is comprised of three major terms, and we now discuss some of the difficulties in measuring each of these.

Net Operating Profit after Tax

Net operating profit after tax measures the results that the firm achieves on an ongoing and after-tax basis, with any nonoperating income from investments or restructuring costs excluded.[30] It is also calculated before interest, since the debt of the firm is counted as part of the capital and the cost of debt will be counted as part of the capital charge.

It is generally developed using the firm's financial system, often from an earnings-before-interest and tax value, and several adjustments are required to convert these numbers to the appropriate figures, including the following:[31]

R&D and advertising may be spread over several periods.

Depreciation is not added back; instead, it is treated as a true economic expense reflecting the operational use of equipment.

Adjustments may be made to eliminate the effects of gearing and other financial factors.

Capital Employed

Capital employed is calculated from the balance sheet as the sum of interest-bearing debt plus equity or from the asset side of the balance sheet as net fixed assets plus working capital. Again, several adjustments may be made. Since capital employed is a measure of operating assets, nonoperating assets such as excess cash and marketable securities are excluded. Any operating leases may be capitalized and added to fixed assets. There may also be adjustments to goodwill, the price premium paid for a prior acquisition of assets over the book value. There is a problem with intangible assets, since these are normally not on the balance sheet. But they should be included to ascertain the level of capital employed. If they are added to tangible assets, the capital employed in the firm increases substantially and the firm is less likely to earn an economic profit. These difficulties generate a degree of subjectivity in measuring economic profit, but if we look primarily at year-to-year changes, then the problem of measuring capital may disappear.[32]

Cost of Capital

The cost of capital is the weighted cost of debt and equity, reflecting the financial structure of the firm. The cost of debt is over all classes of debt on an after-tax basis. The cost of equity is generally determined by the capital asset pricing model, which reflects the risk of the firm.

Economic Value Added

The concept of economic value added (EVA) was developed by Stern Stewart, which has trademarked the acronym EVA. In recent years, EVA has garnered a following of prominent corporations that feel strongly about its ability to deliver improved company performance

As with economic profit, there is a question of how many and what adjustments have to be made to accounting numbers to be able to apply the EVA principle. For example, spending on intangible assets such as R&D, advertising, and systems development may be capitalized. Stern Stewart suggests that 8 to 11 adjustments to financial statements are typically required, which can introduce an element of subjectivity to the numbers.[33]

Financial Ratio Analysis

Most investors follow several other ratios derived from the financial statements of the firm. Here, we group these ratios into three groups—profitability, liquidity, and operational measures.

Profitability

A key figure for shareholders is return on equity, defined by:

$$\text{Return on equity (ROE)} = \text{net income/shareholder's equity}$$

Generally, net income is measured after all expenses, including interest, tax, and extraordinaries. ROE is a measure of how well the firm is delivering to the providers of the risk capital.

$$\text{Return on assets (ROA): net income/total assets}$$
$$\text{Return on capital employed (ROCE): net income/capital employed}$$

These are both measures of the efficiency of the firm—how well managers utilize the assets of the firm.

$$\text{Return on sales (ROS): net income/total operating revenue}$$

Margin measures how much the business keeps as profit from each dollar of sales, a ratio determined by prices and costs, which in turn are influenced by competitive intensity. We would expect margins to be low for intensely competitive mature markets.

Margin is not a good performance measure at the corporate level unless the businesses are very related, since it neglects the assets used to generate net income.

Liquidity

Liquidity measures are concerned with financial risk and the ability of the firm to service debt. Debt is cheaper than equity and is tax deductible. Leverage is normally measured by the ratio debt/equity (D/E). Leverage reflects the financial structure of the firm, whether it is financed by debt or equity. Is also a measure of financial risk, since high leverage means high financial risk, making it more difficult to meet the periodic interest payments.

Other liquidity measures are interest cover, measured by net income/interest expense, and the current ratio, measured by current assets/current liabilities.

Operating

The ratios developed above are interconnected and can be used to diagnose operating performance and how it can be improved.

As defined above,

$$ROE = NI/E$$

where NI = net income

E = shareholders equity

$$= NI/S \times S/E$$

where S = sales revenue
The second term, S/E, can be expanded to

$$S/E = S/CE \times CE/E$$

And since CE = D + E, this is can be written

$$CE/E = (1.0 + L)$$

where L = Leverage = D/E
Combining all these terms we can write:

$$ROE = NI/S \times S/CE \times (1 + L)$$

or a relationship that was utilized in the chapter, which is

$$\text{Return on equity} = \text{margin} \times \text{asset turnover} \times \text{leverage}$$

Another measure would be the dividend payout rate, defined as dividends/net income, while the earnings retention rate = 1 – dividend payout.

Value-Based Management

Value-based management is another term for estimating the future value of a strategy and is based on the concept of seven value drivers:[34]

- Revenue growth rate
- Operating margin
- Cash tax rate
- Working capital growth
- Capital expenditure
- The duration of competitive advantage
- The weighted average cost of capital of the firm

These are used these to forecast future cash flows using the formula

$$\text{Cash flow} = (\text{sales in year } t) \times (1.0 + \text{growth rate}) \times$$
$$(\text{operating profit margin}) \times (1.0 - \text{cash income tax rate}) -$$
$$(\text{incremental fixed and working capital investment})$$

Operating profit margin is the ratio of pre-interest, pre-tax operating profit to sales after depreciation. Incremental fixed capital investment is capital expenditure in excess of depreciation. Cash income tax rate does not include any deferred taxes relating to any deferred income or expenses.

Problems with Accounting Numbers

The Enron crisis of 2001 led to suspicion about the financial reports of U.S. firms. By 2002, investors, boards, and regulators were all concerned with the reliability of U.S. firms' financial reports. There is considerable pressure—and often strong personal incentives—for managers to report revenue and earnings growth that meets investor expectations. There is no doubt that managers can—and do—manipulate accounting earnings through different accounting methods for measuring revenue or valuing assets. There is sometimes a fine line between fraud and the understandable desire to give a positive interpretation to the numbers.

The source for all information on the financial performance of a firm is the accounting data prepared and disseminated by the firm. Given this, we regard it as important that managers have an awareness of some of the sources of subjectivity in accounting numbers so that they can try to restore investor confidence in the firm's public reports. The discussion below is centered on the two sets of information in the income statement and the balance sheet. More detail can be found in Sherman.[35]

Income Statement

The income statement shows the revenue and cost for the firm over a period—generally a year. It is based on an accrual system, whereby revenue and expenses are attributed to the specific time period even if they have not yet been incurred. These revenues and expenses are open to interpretation by management, although various accounting conventions are designed to minimize the impact of these differing interpretations.

The measure most closely followed by analysts, stockbrokers, and investors is net income or earnings, as reported in the firm's annual report. Net income is broadly measured as revenue minus certain expenses. Since both are reported on an accrual basis, net income is not a measure of cash flow. Net income is calculated after a combination of cash and noncash expenses, the most important noncash expense being depreciation. This presents some difficulties, since depreciation is a partly subjective number, based as it is on historical costs and assumptions about the economic life of an asset. Net income may also be reported as pre- or post-tax, and before- or after-interest expenses, further adding to the uncertainty.

Given the lack of uniformity, other common measures of income are earnings before interest and tax (EBIT) and earnings before tax, interest, depreciation, and amortization (EBITDA). While the latter is more closely related to cash flow, it is not a true measure, since changes in fixed and working capital are excluded.

Even though it may appear simple, there are difficulties associated with the measurement of revenue. Since the income statement is based on accruals, the revenue reported is that which is claimed to be relevant to the period. Revenue may be recognized when products are shipped, not when the actual payment is received. Similar complications with revenue occur when the customer makes payments over several years, as may be the case with large software installations. Do we count all the revenue in year 1? As an illustration, Enron counted all income in year 1 for projects that would take 12 years to complete, which many would argue is deceptive.[36]

There can also be uncertainty on how to measure costs. How are product returns handled, what is the basis of the estimates used, and have there been changes in the basis of estimation? What about restructuring costs? These should be seen as "one off" events and isolated from normal costs. But what if a restructure takes several years? Does the firm report these costs as "extraordinaries" for several years when they could be seen as normal costs of doing business? There can also be subjectivity in the measurement of depreciation. Depreciation is a noncash item, treated as a period expense. It reflects the decreasing value of a tangible asset over the period and is based on historical cost of the asset and the depreciation regime, which in turn is based on legal and tax considerations. Depreciation is also based on the useful life of the asset. If this useful life is extended, depreciation expenses are reduced and net income increased—with no change to the underlying economics of the firm. Further complicating depreciation is the fact that the historical cost of an asset may bear no resemblance to its current value or replacement cost.

As we discussed in Chapter 8, net income generally does not include any cost of stock options, and this may seriously distort the numbers. There does seem to be some evidence that more firms are now expensing options in order to provide a better picture of their financial performance. Net income can also be affected by company pension plans, as we saw earlier with GE.

The above illustrates some of the difficulties and subjectivity in measuring net income. Yet this one number is the basic element in calculating many performance measures—such as ROCE, ROS, ROE, and EPS—and any errors in measuring net income may make these measures quite erroneous.

Asset Valuation

The balance sheet is a statement of the firm's financial position at a point in time, showing the firm's liabilities and tangible assets. It is used for a number of measures, such as capital employed and leverage. Since fixed assets are valued at historical cost less accumulated depreciation, the values on the balance sheet may not bear any resemblance to the current value of the asset or its replacement cost. The balance sheet also ignores intangible assets such as patents, knowledge, satisfied customers, value of R&D, and the value of brand brand equity. These are all ignored in attempting to arrive at a "value" for the firm. This is despite the fact that expenditure on intangible assets such as R&D or advertising is often a key source of value creation—yet these expenditures are expensed, not capitalized. As a consequence, since the value of assets is reduced, measures such as ROI will be increased if intangible assets are excluded.

Other expenses such as lease expenses may be deducted, while another view is that the value of these leases should be capitalized and added to the capital base of the firm.

Accounting bodies are trying to get companies to record all financial assets and liabilities at their market value, but many banks and other large companies are resisting. Accounting bodies think that it is more useful to measure assets and liabilities at fair value (or market value) rather than historical cost. Since financial markets are now more volatile, the values of assets and liabilities are constantly changing. Banks in particular are concerned about this, as it will introduce more volatility into their earnings, which could increase the level of risk for the shares and thus their cost of capital. The value of loans would fluctuate with changes in interest rates, banks could be forced to write down loans if their credit quality was reduced, and these changes would have to be incorporated in the bank's income statement for the year.[37]

Funds flow shows the sources and application of funds over the period. It shows whether the entity is cash-positive or -negative over the period. The funds flow statement also shows many items not on the income statement, such as new equity and debt, cash from asset disposals, and divestments. It also shows investment in fixed and working capital, which are not on the income statement.

There has also been concern expressed at the accuracy of pro-forma financial reports. Many firms in the United States issue pro-forma earnings, an early report of the likely results of the firm over the next quarter or so. Some of these are very inaccurate, and the bias is toward extreme optimism. For example, in the first three quarters of 2001, the 100 largest NASDAQ firms reported pro-forma earnings of $USB20. When these same firms reported earnings under GAAP rules and conventions, these forecast profits had become a combined loss of $USB82.[38] The initial pro-forma statements had provided investors with extremely inaccurate data. The ethics of the firms involved must be questioned, since these reports of projected earnings would have had an impact of share prices.

Fortune magazine, not usually among the most critical observers of business practice, recently called on companies to "get rid of the absolutely funniest numbers ... things like adjusted earnings, operating earnings, cash earnings and Ebitda (earnings before interest, tax, depreciation and amortization)." *Fortune* continued, "If companies want to tout such random, unaudited, watch-me-pull-a-rabbit-out-of-my-hat figures in their press releases, well, fine. But investors should also immediately be able to compare these figures with full financial statements prepared in accordance with Generally Accepted Accounting Principles (GAAP) rather than having to wait 45 days or more for the company's SEC filing."[39]

International Accounting Standards

Accounting standards vary around the world, and this can have an impact on reported net income. The Dutch-based supermarket chain Royal Ahold disclosed that its earnings would have been 90% lower if prepared under GAAP rules in the United States as opposed to Dutch rules. For this firm, disputes arose from the treatment of goodwill, derivatives, and one-time gains on real estate costs, where the majority of the charges are noncash, affecting earnings but not cash flow.[40] Professional accounting bodies are attempting to develop common standards to make it easier to compare financial results across borders, which would increase transparency.

⊚ ENDNOTES

[1] M. Gunther, "Has Eisner Lost the Disney Magic?" *Fortune,* January 7, 2002, p. 64.

[2] M. Benz, "Recent Disney Performance Unacceptable: Eisner," *Amusement Business,* October 28, 2002, p. 9.

[3] M. Gunther, "As the Debate Heats Up on How Companies Should be Run, the Best Show in Town May Be at Disney," *Fortune,* October 14, 2002, p. 130.

[4] B. Orwall, "Eisner Contends Disney Is Primed for a Turnaround," *Wall Street Journal,* August 9, 2002, p. B1.

[5] *The Valuation of Intangible Assets* (London: The Economist Intelligence Unit, 1992).

[6] R. S. Kaplan and D. P. Norton, *The Balanced Scorecard* (Boston: Harvard Business School Press, 1996).

[7] T. E. Copeland, "Why Value Value?" *McKinsey Quarterly* 4 (1994), pp. 97–110.

[8] J. Holloway, J. Lewis, and G. Mallory, eds., *Performance Measurement and Evaluation* (London: Sage, 1995).

[9] For more details, see R. C. Camp, *Benchmarking: The Search for Industry Best Practices That Lead to Superior Performance* (Milwaukee, WI: Quality Press, 1989).

[10] Adapted from A. Neely, M. Bourne, J. Mills, K. Platt, and H. Richards, *Getting the Measure of Your Business* (Cambridge, UK: Cambridge University Press, 2002).

[11] J. C. Collins and J. I. Porras, *Built to Last* (New York: HarperBusiness, 1994).

[12] R. Waters, "Coming Clean," *The Financial Times,* February 2, 2002, p. 6.

[13] R. S. Kaplan and D. P. Norton, *The Balanced Scorecard*.

[14] J. M. Hulbert, N. Capon, and N. F. Piercy, *Total Integrated Marketing: Breaking the Bounds of the Function* (New York: Free Press, 2003).

[15] K. L. Keller, *Strategic Brand Management* (Upper Saddle River, NJ: Prentice Hall, 2002).

[16] N. Capon and J. M. Hulbert, *Marketing Management in the 21st Century* (Upper Saddle River, NJ: Prentice Hall, 2001).

[17] B. J. Feder, "Quaker to Sell Snapple for $300 Million," *New York Times,* March 28, 1997, p. D1.

[18] See, for example, A. Rappaport, *Creating Shareholder Value: A Guide for Managers and Investors* (New York: Free Press, 1998).

[19] T. D. Kuczmarski, *Managing New Products: Competing through Excellence* (Englewood Cliffs, NJ: Prentice Hall, 1988).

[20] T. E. Copeland and P. T. Keenan, "How Much Is Flexibility Worth?" *McKinsey Quarterly* 2 (1998), pp. 38–49.

[21] For an illustration of a brand health-check system, see Capon and Hulbert *Marketing Management in the 21st Century.*

[22] A. Black, P. Wright, and J. E. Backman, *In Search of Shareholder Value: Managing the Drivers of Performance* (London: Pearson Education, 1998).

[23] The United States Standard Industrial Classification (SIC) scheme is being replaced by a new system, the North American Industrial Classification Scheme (NAAICS), but we retain the more familiar SIC system.

[24] J. P. H. Fan and L. H. P. Lang, "The Measurement of Relatedness: An Application to Corporate Diversification," *Journal of Business* 73, no. 4 (2000), pp. 629–660.

[25] C. C. Markides and P. J. Williamson, "Related Diversification, Core Competencies and Corporate Performance," *Strategic Management Journal* 15 Summer (1994), pp. 149–166.

[26] M. W. Meyer, "Finding Performance: The New Discipline in Management," in *Business Performance Measurement,* A. Neely, ed. (Cambridge, UK: Cambridge University Press, 2002), pp. 51–62.

[27] Table 12.8 contains some rounding errors.

[28] In 2003, Microsoft announced that it would change this policy.

[29] J. L. Dodd, "EVA Reconsidered," *Business and Economic Review* 45, no. 3 (1999), pp. 13–18.

[30] A. Ehrbar, *EVA: The Real Key to Creating Wealth* (New York: Wiley, 1998).

[31] Ibid.

[32] G. B. Stewart, *The Quest for Value: The EVA Management Guide* (New York: HarperBusiness, 1991).

[33] R. Barker, *Determining Value* (Harlow, UK: Financial Times Prentice Hall, 2001).

[34] Black, Wright, and Backman, *In Search of Shareholder Value.*

[35] H. D. Sherman and D. S. Young, "Tread Lightly through These Accounting Minefields," *Harvard Business Review,* July–August 2001, pp. 129–135.

[36] A. Hill, J. Chaffin, and S. Fidler, "Enron: Virtual Company, Virtual Profits," *Financial Times,* February 4, 2002, p. 18.

[37] "Shining a Light on Company Accounts," *The Economist,* August 18, 2001, pp. 55–56.

[38] "Capitalism and Its troubles," Survey of International Finance, *The Economist,* May 18, 2002, p. 3

[39] "System Failure," *Fortune,* June 24, 2002, p. 39.

[40] S. Kapner, "Dutch Grocer to Expand Its Reports," *New York Times,* April 9, 2002, p. W1.

CHAPTER 13

Corporate Governance

Learning Objectives

Upon completing this chapter, you should be able to:

- Appreciate the importance of corporate governance
- Describe the roles of shareholders, managers, and boards in governance
- Understand the role of the board in strategy development
- Define the responsibilities of directors
- Understand the importance of board processes and structure
- Be aware of how corporate governance practices vary in different countries

In August 2000, Enron was one of the most admired firms in the United States, with published core values of respect, integrity, communication, and excellence. It reported revenue of $USB101, which made it the seventh-largest firm in the United States, while its stock reached a high of $US90. It was hailed by many as an exceptionally well-run firm whose success was due primarily to its high level of innovation. A year later, in November 2001, the share price had collapsed to US 26¢ a share and the firm filed for bankruptcy (under Chapter 11) on December 2, 2001.[1]

Enron began in 1985 with the merger of two natural gas pipeline firms, Houston Natural Gas and InterNorth, a Nebraska firm. The gas pipeline industry was then regulated, with producers selling gas at prices set by the government. In turn, pipeline firms sold gas to local utilities and large customers, also at regulated prices. With the coming of deregulation, Enron separated gas transmission from gas sales, deciding to move heavily into gas sales. It then quickly developed gas trading—buying and selling standard amounts of gas, both in the spot market and through long-term contracts of 2 to 10 years. It subsequently extended into gas futures, where a customer would be supplied with gas by Enron at a fixed price while Enron had to purchase the gas at a floating price. So Enron and the customer swapped floating prices for a fixed price, with Enron taking the risk on the contract.

Enron then expanded into trading a range of other products, including electricity, another U.S. market undergoing a degree of deregulation. It also expanded geographically, purchasing a water utility in the United Kingdom and power plants in Argentina, India, and the Philippines. Its business model was extended to other industries, offering futures in steel, paper, and water. In 1999, the firm launched Enron Online, an electronic commodities-trading business. With this business, Enron was a buyer or seller on all transactions, making Enron's credit standing critical, since other parties thought that they could trust Enron if any problems developed.

By 2000, Enron had become a complex, global firm, operating in industries far removed from its original, relatively simple gas transmission. In 2001, the board had five subcommittees, including a finance committee responsible for approving transactions over

$USM75 in value and an audit committee that was responsible for reviewing Enron's accounting procedures and approving the financial reports. There was also a compensation committee, which established compensation packages for directors and senior managers, and a nominating committee, which nominated new directors.

The audit committee was chaired by an emeritus professor of accounting and had five other members, only one of whom "appeared to have limited familiarity with complex accounting principles" (U.S. Senate hearings).[2] Several members had been on the board since 1985, although the nature of the business had changed substantially.

Following the collapse of Enron, the U.S. Senate conducted an investigation, which concluded that the board had failed to safeguard shareholders by allowing Enron to engage in high-risk accounting practices, inappropriate conflict-of-interest transactions, extensive undisclosed off-the-books transactions, and excessive executive compensation.

To illustrate, in 1999 the board permitted Enron's chief financial officer to establish private equity partnerships that did business with Enron. One of these produced $USB2 in funds flow for Enron in six months—yet was never questioned. Following an article in the *Wall Street Journal* which suggested that the CFO was being compensated by these private equity vehicles, the CFO admitted to the chairman of the compensation committee that he had received compensation from these private equity funds of $USM45, a far greater sum than he had received at Enron. At this time—October 24, 2001—the CFO was placed on leave.

The committee also found that the board had knowingly allowed Enron to conduct off-the-books activity designed to make its financial condition appear better than it was. In the end, the board knowingly allowed Enron to move at least $USB27, or almost 50% of its assets, off the balance sheet. The board was also criticized for the financial ties between the firm and some members of the board and for not ensuring the independence of the auditor.

The collapse of Enron had far-reaching implications, including the bankruptcy of its auditors, Arthur Andersen LLP, and major legislative changes designed to reduce the possibility of the same thing happening in the future.[3]

◉ 13.1 INTRODUCTION

What Is Corporate Governance?

The Enron example illustrates that investors and others are concerned with how well firms are being managed and whether they are delivering value to shareholders. Over the past few years, there have been numerous corporate frauds perpetrated by senior management, including:

- Misleading accounts
- Money being siphoned from employee pension funds
- Unjustified executive pay levels
- Collapse of firms with little or no prior warning of difficulties.

As a consequence, corporations and their boards are under intense scrutiny from governments, institutional investors, individual shareholders, regulators, and employees who share a desire to eliminate such problems. The U.S. pension fund TIAA-Cref, for example, has some $USB150 invested and wants to ensure returns for its members. *Business Week* regularly ranks firms in terms of their governance performance, while the huge compensations (particularly options) paid to senior managers, often unrelated to performance, have added to the concern. As a consequence, corporate governance—the nature, role, and activities of the board of directors, who are supposed to monitor and control the management of the firm—has become a hot topic.[4]

Corporate governance describes the relationship among shareholders, management, and the board in determining the direction and performance of the corporation.[5] It represents the processes through which ultimate corporate authority and responsibility are shared and exercised by shareholders, directors, and management to ensure that the firm delivers value to its stakeholders, particularly shareholders. As we will discuss, corporate governance is also concerned with broader issues such as other stakeholders, business ethics, crisis management, and guaranteeing legal compliance by the firm.

The essence of corporate governance is ensuring that the professional managers who actually manage the firm use assets efficiently in the pursuit of the firm's objectives. In fact, we could go further and suggest that the role of the board is to ensure that corporate management strives for and achieves above-average performance, taking due account of risk.[6] An ideal system of corporate governance would allow managers the freedom to manage coupled with accurate knowledge of shareholders to ensure that their expectations are known and satisfied. At the same time, shareholders would have sufficient information to know whether or not their expectations were being met together with market liquidity, so that they could easily sell their shares. Satisfying both of these requires a boardroom culture that facilitates open discussion, where directors are able to exercise objective judgment and hold managers accountable for the performance of the firm, in particular the efficient use of the assets of the firm.

Global Issues in Corporate Governance

Each country has its own distinct type of corporate governance reflecting its history as well as its legal, regulatory, and tax regimes. But all over the world, there are concerns with inadequate governance arrangements. Switzerland has had problems with Swissair and UBS, Sweden problems with ABB, Korea problems with Daewoo, Germany problems with Kirch, France problems with Vivendi, Italy with Parmalat, and, of course, the United States problems with Enron and WorldCom. As a result, countries are reexamining the way companies are managed. Germany has had a committee under the chairmanship of Gerhard Cromme, the head of ThyssenKrupp; France had the Verniot Report; and the United Kingdom has had several reports, the latest being the Hampel Committee in 1998.[7] The U.S. Congress passed the Sarbanes-Oxley Act, attempting to improve the governance of American corporations.

Flaws in the way in which companies are managed have focused attention on corporate governance and the role of boards of directors. At the same time, globalization—with the adoption of free-market systems and the removal of trade barriers, together with technological advances in communication and transportation—has led to higher levels of competitive intensity in both product and capital markets. As a consequence, investors, both institutional and individual, have recognized that the quality of corporate governance affects the firm's competitive performance and hence its ability to attract investment capital.[8] There is a growing recognition in all countries that the expectations of shareholders have to be met when the firm relies on the financial markets for debt and equity. At the same time, boards of directors need to give consideration to the needs of other stakeholders, such as customers, employees, suppliers, creditors, and the community.

This chapter discusses the role of the board and how it should exercise its role. It will also explore how this role varies according to the country in which the firm is located. We concentrate on corporate governance issues in large, publicly listed, and generally global companies.

✺ 13.2 THE MODERN CORPORATION

In all countries, **firms** are legal entities and as such can enter into contracts as well as sue and be sued by other legal entities, including individuals. In most countries, the modern publicly listed company has unlimited life and can have an unlimited number of shareholders. These shareholders can be individuals or other organizations, although in some countries there are some restrictions as to who can be a shareholder. For example, in the United States, banks cannot be shareholders of industrial firms, but this restriction generally does not hold in Europe.

The shareholders, who provide the equity capital for the firm, own the company. The liability of these shareholders is generally limited to the initial equity capital. Should a publicly listed company go bankrupt, with substantial debts, shareholders cannot be sued personally for these debts. This is not the case with other organizational forms such as a partnership, which normally has a limited number of partners. The partnership ceases on the death of a partner, and partners are jointly liable for the debts of the partnership. In return for their limited liability, however, shareholders of corporations give up the right to control the firm's assets to others—managers. Nonetheless, they should be able to expect that managers will act in the interests of the shareholders, not in the interests of the managers.

A distinguishing characteristic of such companies is the *separation* of ownership and control.[9] The shareholders own the company but have little or no control over the day-to-day running of the firm—or even the ability to obtain current information on the performance of the company. All managerial decisions are the responsibility of the professional managers, who are also accountable for regularly reporting on their performance. Of course, shareholders have the right to transfer their interests by selling their shares, but nevertheless, the firm's managers need to be held liable to some independent, competent, and motivated representative of the owners. This is the role of the board. Shareholders need to be able to hold the board, and through it the managers, accountable for the long-run firm performance, where this performance may include both financial and nonfinancial measures. Given the large number of shareholders of a modern firm, plus the fact that institutions will hold a significant proportion of shares, there may not be a strong sense of ownership among these shareholders. In most countries, the legal system imposes a fiduciary duty on the board to ensure that the firm is run in the long-term interests of shareholders. Since managers are given the power to make decisions and take reasonable risks, the challenge is how to grant them this power while holding them accountable for the use of that power.

Unfortunately, managers may act in their own interests, not in the interests of shareholders—what economists call an agency problem. A large number of shareholders and a weak board exacerbate this tendency. We return to the agency problem later in the chapter.

Global Institutional Arrangements

The legal system underlying the nature of firms and the style of corporate governance vary across countries, although there is some degree of overlap. While the legal system in each country reflects the culture, history, and development of that country, there does appear to be considerable convergence in the requirements for sound corporate governance processes.

United States/United Kingdom/Canada/Australia

The U.S./U.K. versions of governance put an emphasis on shareholder liquidity. If shareholders are unhappy with the performance of the firm, they can sell their shares on the stock market, and this is simple to do. Such a system requires full disclosure of financial data from firms, so that shareholders can make informed decisions, and insider trading is illegal. If firm does badly, a hostile takeover may ensue. In the United Kingdom there are two common legal forms for a company, PLC and Pty Ltd. A PLC (public limited corporation), such as ICI, can have an unlimited number of shareholders, while a Pty Ltd company has a limited number.

In the United States and the United Kingdom, the threat of takeover (the market for corporate control) is assumed to be a major check on managers and helps ensure that they satisfy shareholder expectations. In other countries, such as Germany, takeovers are relatively rare. There are also significant differences between countries in terms of the composition of shareholders; for example, in the United States and the United Kingdom, banks are restricted in their ability to hold equity—a restriction that does not apply in other countries, such as Japan.

In the United States, insider-trading laws discourage investors from taking large holdings. Indeed, both the New York Stock Exchange and the NASDAQ are considering changes to their listing rules that would make large investors (those owning more than 20% of stock) unable to be considered "independent," with implications for board committee membership.[10] The Sarbanes-Oxley Act is also expected to have considerable impact. For example, the act specifies that boards include a financial expert who must have knowledge in a number of areas, such as Generally Accepted Accounting Principles or preparing public company financial statements, among others, acquired either through education or work experience. As a result, firms may have to change the membership of their audit committees.[11]

Europe

In Europe there are two general legal forms for large companies. The first type is the **SA** (Societe Anonyme), the term used in France and elsewhere, or the **AG** (Aktiengesellschaft), the term used in Germany. These are public companies limited by shares, with an unlimited number of shares that are freely negotiable. Such firms in Germany must meet several legal requirements, such as conducting an annual meeting of shareholders, and adopting a two-board structure. The second type is **SARL** or **GmbH.** For example, in Germany BMW has the legal form of a GmbH. Large GmbH firms are also required to have a dual-board structure, with one having a significant proportion of employee representatives. Both types of companies have limited liability, but while the first has freely negotiable shares, the second does not.

Germany features an almost complete absence of open financial markets, in contrast to its product markets, which are generally open and competitive. Funding is often internal, and open markets play a minor role in any external funding. In the United States and the United Kingdom, financial institutions are restricted in their ability to hold equity, but this does not hold in Germany, where banks may own up to 12% of the company's shares.[12] Since banks play such a major role, this German system is sometimes considered to be an insider or a bank-based system, arising from the close contacts between firms and banks. In contrast, the U.S. and U.K. systems are often classified as market-based systems of capital supply: there are many opportunities for firms to raise debt or equity apart from banks.

Financial institutions in Germany are given more latitude to own shares in and exert control over large firms than is the case in the United States or the United Kingdom. In addition, bank financing is more common in Germany than in the United States. In Germany, share markets are considered to have less liquidity, and consequently shareholders (or their representative, such as a bank) carefully monitor the firms or have long-term links with the company. The firm provides limited data to shareholders, and there may be less protection against insider trading. As a result, hostile takeovers are less common in Germany.

As was discussed in Chapter 4, in several European countries (for example, Belgium) firms are given the right to offer *bearer* shares. With these, the holder does not need to register a name with the company; therefore the actual beneficial owner can remain anonymous, and such shares do not have to sold on the financial markets—they can be transferred privately. In Europe generally, many bearer shares are held by the banks, which can then vote on them. This adds to the power of the banks, since many shareholders do not tell their bank how to vote on the shares they have on deposit. So while banks in Europe do own shares in their own right, most of their power comes from these shares on deposit. For this reason, most large German firms have a bank representative on the supervisory board, generally from one of the three large banks—Deutsche, Dresdner, or Commerzbank banks.

The poor performance of some German companies is forcing them to look at restructuring, including divesting. Bayer AG has assumed the role of a holding company with Bayer Crop Sciences becoming a separate legal entity in October 2002. Deutsche Bank has also indicated that it intends to divest several of its industrial holdings. The bank has a number of interlocking directorships, so that it is creditor, shareholder, and board supervisor for several companies.

In many European countries there has been a history of state-owned companies, and there are still a number with varying degrees of autonomy from the state. At one extreme are the so-called government business enterprises or state-owned enterprises, still common in France. Air France and Credit Lyonnais, for example, have some degree of state control.[13] In the United Kingdom, the government holds "golden shares" in firms such as BA, although the EU authorities now frown on such arrangements. In Greece, the government still owns Olympic Airlines—but almost certainly wishes it didn't!

Despite the EU, there are still significant differences in the corporate governance mechanisms across countries, arising from the different legal, regulatory, and ownership frameworks. In 1995, private households in Germany owned only 14.6% of common stock of firms, compared with 47.9% in the United States. By contrast, in the United States other companies only owned 1.1% of company shares, compared with 58.0% in France.[14]

Asia

Corporate governance in Asia depends strongly on the country concerned and, again reflects its economic, social, and political development. In Southeast Asia, Chinese *family* business structures dominate, controlled by the family, with limited public shares. In these firms decisions are not delegated to nonfamily members, although long term personal relations are a central feature of Asian business.

Korea and Japan have a different system, with *chaebol* in Korea and *keiretsu* in Japan—these being groupings of large financial and industrial complexes such as Hyundai or Mitsubishi. Due to the existence of these groupings, Japanese firms rely on banks for a large proportion of their financing needs, although Japanese banks are limited to owning no more than 5% of the equity in any one firm. There is also less shareholder liquidity in these markets. In several countries, such as China, there are a substantial number of state-owned enterprises, and governance of these is deeply embedded in the country's political system.

As a result of recent corporate failures, there is considerable interest around the world in strengthening corporate governance procedures. In the United States and the United Kingdom it is directed at ensuring that the board is independent of management so that it can provide adequate guidance. In Germany and Japan, the pressure is to strengthen capital markets so that they can provide a discipline on management to improve its performance.

◉ 13.3 THE GOVERNANCE MODEL

Corporate governance is concerned with the relationship among shareholders, the board of directors, and management, as shown in Figure 13.1. However, other institutions and issues must also be considered. When one is reviewing firm performance, the role and values of stakeholders other than shareholders need to be understood. Determining the nature of these other stakeholders and their importance relative to shareholders is one of the tasks of the board. Furthermore, both boards and management need to develop relationships with financial markets to assist in the raising of new funds as well as to manage the firm's share price. We now discuss the three groups of Figure 13.1 in more detail.

◉ 13.4 SHAREHOLDERS AND BOARDS

As discussed in Chapter 4, shareholders of large global firms can be split into individual and institutional shareholders. The relative importance of these two groups varies by country, with the level of individual shareholders generally being low in Germany and Japan. In the United States and the United Kingdom, there has been a significant increase in the proportion of shares held by institutions, with implications for governance, since historically they have been passive investors. In addition, these institutions generally have only a small holding in the firm, say, less than 5%. By contrast, in Germany, an institutional investor may hold, say, 25% of the shares of the firm. Cross-shareholding—reciprocal share ownership by companies—is also very common in Europe, further reducing liquidity in the market for shares.

In all countries, shareholders are entitled to attend the annual general meeting, at which time the accounts are approved and the board elected. In Denmark, Belgium, the

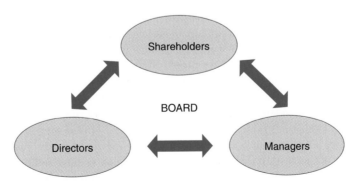

Figure 13.1 Corporate Governance Model

Netherlands, and Spain, among other countries, most shares are bearer shares, so notice of annual meetings must be published in both an official gazette as well as local and national newspapers. Holders of bearer shares have to deposit their shares with the company three to five days before the meeting in order to be able to attend. By contrast, in the United Kingdom, all shares are registered, and therefore the company has an address to which to mail announcements and agendas.[15]

Board members are usually elected at such an annual general meeting. The current board nominates members, and thus small shareholders often find it difficult to generate a major board shakeup. As noted, institutional shareholders have often been passive. If the firm is doing poorly, they simply sell their shares and find other investment opportunities. Furthermore, if these institutional investors are involved in detailed discussions with management on the future of the firm, any special knowledge could expose them to a risk of being accused of insider trading—taking advantage of information not available to other shareholders. In the United States, the Securities and Exchange Commission (SEC) has ruled that firms cannot reveal more information to institutional investors than they make available to private investors.

The board must also be aware of the mix of shareholders and their expectations. Different shareholders may want different things. Small shareholders (unless they are day traders) may be more patient, institutional investors more interested in the short term. The board may also be concerned with shareholder stability. If shares are held by a small number of shareholders, then the board may consider the share register to be unstable and the company could be a takeover target.

Research suggests that investors value corporate governance in both developed and emerging economies. Investors like companies that are well governed, have a majority of outside directors, and undertake formal evaluation of directors. They believe that directors should be shareholders and that their pay should be in the form of stock options. Then shareholders are willing to pay a premium. The value of this premium is higher in emerging economies—the role of the board is more important when accounting standards are lower. In a survey of institutional investors—such as money managers, mutual funds, and insurance companies—in several countries, it was found that investors were prepared to pay a premium of 18% for stock in a well-governed U.K. or U.S. company but that they were prepared to pay a premium of 27% for stock in a well-governed company in Indonesia.[16]

13.5 MANAGEMENT AND BOARDS

The **agency** problem arises when the objectives of managers differ from those of shareholders, in which case the agents (managers) may make decisions that are in their own interests and not in those of the principals (shareholders). In the modern corporation there is a separation of ownership (shareholders) from control (managers).[17] Due to this separation, managers may want to maximize firm size while shareholders want profits or earnings. Shareholders often want to reduce risk, which they can accomplish by investing in a number of firms. Managers may also say that they want to reduce risk, and this can become the rationale behind diversification. They often neglect the fact that shareholders can diversify more easily and cheaply than firms. Another manifestation of the agency problem is how free cash flow is handled. Jensen suggested that there would be conflict between managers and owners when there is a free cash flow—cash flow in excess of that required by all investments that have positive net present values when discounted at the relevant cost of capital. Managers often use this flow to fund acquisitions, which ultimately perform poorly, rather than returning it to shareholders.[18]

Shareholders are interested in financial returns, either short or long term. Managers may be interested in other things, such as the size, growth, and prestige of the company. Other areas of conflict between managers and owners would be the level and structure of executive salaries, the balance between dividends and retentions, and the priority given to growth or profit.

In the United Kingdom and United States, boards are elected to represent the interests of shareholders, and managers report to the board. It is often thought that managers enjoy a measure of discretion to pursue their own objectives without the need to seriously consider the interests of shareholders. The concern is that managers exercise power without responsibility and that boards are self-perpetuating oligarchies. Successful firms may become arrogant and insular, and a powerful CEO can take this to extremes. At one time, the same person held the following jobs at Sears Roebuck, the large U.S. retailer:[19]

- CEO
- Chairman of the board
- CEO of the largest operating division
- CEO of the worst-performing operating division
- Chairman of the nominating committee
- Trustee of the 25% of firm stock held on behalf of employees

If there is wide distribution of shares, any individual shareholder has little power to force a change in management. It is then vital that the board monitor senior management and ensure that the CEO works under its authority.

The agency literature suggests that outside directors provide important *monitoring* functions in an attempt to resolve, or at least mitigate, conflicts between management and shareholders. Management equity ownership may help to resolve this, but hostile takeovers may also provide a check on managers to deliver value. Indeed, the very existence of these phenomena is testimony to lack of accountability to shareholders.

The capital market was traditionally the market through which firms raised new capital, and that role still exists. But it is also a market where shares and other financial instruments are traded and in which control of a company can be acquired. This market is generally denoted as the market for corporate control, and this has been very active, although it seems to go in cycles. Shares can be seen as "trading chips," rather than ownership claims.

This market for corporate control implies that firms are subject to some discipline from the capital markets when they perform poorly. Poor performance will generally be reflected in low share prices. Other management teams may then decide to mount a takeover bid, suggesting that they are better able to manage the assets of the firm. Such a market includes leveraged buyouts as well as takeovers and may be facilitated by the ready availability of debt. In the United Kingdom about 25% of takeovers are **hostile,** initially rejected by the target management. Hostile takeovers are much less common in Europe and Japan, although they seem to be increasing, reflecting the increased activism of shareholders and their demand for performance. However, the market for corporate control acts as a spur to better management and results in the transfer of assets from poorly performing firms to successful firms.

The general threat of a takeover may act as an incentive for management to perform well. A question then may be how the board reacts to any such takeover offer: Does it respond in the interests of shareholders or not? Takeovers may represent a considerable threat to incumbent managers, since they are not likely to survive the takeover. Apart from the market for corporate control, there are other ways to minimize the gap between managers and shareholders—for example, tying the compensation of managers to shareholder return. Stock options for managers were supposed to align the interests of the two groups, but they have not always delivered as promised. Management options are offers to buy shares at a future date at a price that is close to or equal to the current price. Consequently, it is in the interests of managers to increase this share price, and thus the value of their options. By itself, this is not inimical to the interests of shareholders, who are interested in the same outcome, but managers may be encouraged to act fraudulently or not report news that could depress the share price.

🌀 13.6 THE ROLE OF DIRECTORS AND THE BOARD

The increasing complexity of the business environment, and of business itself, has resulted in changing roles of directors. There is more pressure for performance and for legal accountability. Outside directors differ from managers: they have no line responsibility and no staff. However, as directors they can request independent advice from external specialists, such as consultants or accountants, and the chairman cannot refuse reasonable requests for such advice. Executive directors should in theory be able to separate their role as executive from their role as director, but it is easy to see why they might find it difficult to do so.

Responsibilities of Directors

In most countries the role of directors is at least party defined by the legal system and generally includes the requirement to encompass a duty of loyalty, which means that directors should act in good faith to advance the firm's interests and not use information for personal gain. Directors are also required to exercise the care of a prudent person in the same or similar circumstances and to obtain adequate information to assist in fulfilling their responsibilities.[20] In summary, directors are required to do the following:

- To be honest; to act with integrity and good faith
- To exercise reasonable care, diligence, and skill
- To act in the interests of shareholders
- To present accurate and fair reports on finances to shareholders

In the United Kingdom and the United States, all directors bear equal responsibility for the performance of the company. Nonetheless, it may be difficult for directors who are not executives in the firm to gain the knowledge and skill required to monitor the firm's activities adequately. However, in the United States and the United Kingdom, some degree of independence from management is regarded as essential for outside directors. Outside directors should not have significant financial or personal ties to management or the firm. An outside director should not be a professional adviser or major supplier to the firm and should not have been employed as an executive by the firm in the recent past. However, it is not uncommon for these principles to be overlooked.

Directors are required to provide *overall direction,* rather than becoming involved in the day-to-day issues that are the responsibility of management. Directors' responsibility is to shareholders, meaning they should ensure that management is doing what it should be doing, since they have ultimate responsibility for the performance of the company. Directors cannot avoid this responsibility even if they want to. For example, given the turbulent environments we have discussed throughout the book, prudent directors would insist that management have a crisis management system in place, since shareholders' interests can be irrevocably harmed by ineptitude at such times. Associated with legal requirements and sanctions, directors can be sued by shareholders if the shareholders believe the director(s) are not fulfilling their legal responsibilities. They may be held personally liable for their own actions and those of the board. Penalties vary by country and can be severe. Directors are also liable for the decisions of any board subcommittee, such as finance or compensation.

In the United States, it is common for the same individual to be both the CEO and the chairman, although there is increasing pressure to change this practice.[21] The role of the CEO is to run the company, and the role of the chairman of the board is to run the board. These are not the same. As we will see, one important board role is to appoint the CEO. One might well ask how a board can remove an underperforming CEO when that individual is also chairman of the board making the decisions! A number of major U.S. corporations are now moving to cease this practice and follow the U.K. model of having a nonexecutive chairman. Indeed, about 90% of U.K. firms have different individuals handling the roles of chairman and CEO.

The role of the chairman is to ensure that the board operates effectively, to see that all members contribute effectively to the direction of the company, and to rigorously scrutinize proposals from the CEO. The chairman should ensure that there is interaction and discussion at board meetings. Board meetings should not therefore involve long and detailed presentations from management with no discussion.[22] Instead, the chairman must create a climate within the board that facilitates decision making and that does not inhibit open discussion and debate. Some decisions by the board may go against management: if management always gets what it wants, the board may be acting purely as a "rubber stamp."

> Following shareholder pressure because of poor performance, GM separated the roles of chairman and CEO in 1992. However, old practices die hard, and by 1996 they were again the same person: the CEO had become chairman.

Composition of the Board

An important characteristic of a board is the proportion of nonexecutive, or independent, directors. **Executive** directors are individuals who are currently employed by the firm in an executive capacity. For example, the CEO is an executive who is normally on the board, as are the chief financial officer and/or the chief technologist. Executive directors are expected to bring considerable expertise to the board; the question is their independence, particularly from the CEO.

Independent directors are outsiders who are supposed to be independent of management. We discuss in detail what it means for directors to be independent shortly, suffice it to say here that it means that they should not have had a relationship with the firm. There is still considerable discussion about the true degree of independence of these directors, since they may be CEOs of other firms and thus part of a network of CEOs.

Independent directors are expected to bring diversity and experience to the board, to provide new perspectives on the business and an independent assessment of both firm and management performance. Certainly in the United States, the trend over the past few years has been to increase the ratio of nonexecutive directors to executive directors. In 1990, 66% of directors on U.S. boards were independent; in 2001, the proportion was 78%.[23]

Qualified and truly independent external directors are not easy to find. For example, there may be a perceived conflict if a banker or lawyer is on the board. Many companies do not permit their senior managers to be on the boards of other companies, partly due to the increasing demands being placed on directors. To further align the interests of directors and shareholders, it has been suggested that directors must hold a minimum number of shares in the company.[24] Since the size of this recommended investment was $500,000, this is likely to further restrict the pool of potential external directors.

Independent directors are by definition individuals who are not currently executives of the company. Due to this, they are expected to bring an objective external perspective and a degree of independence to board discussions, since they are not employees under the authority of the CEO. In addition, the board may establish several subcommittees, such as an audit committee (to review the detailed financial performance of the firm), and some of these are required to be made up of nonexecutive directors. On the other hand, being outsiders, non-executive directors may not really understand the business. Independent directors cannot work from the command of detail that executives have. So they have to ensure that the board focuses on company performance and any changes that may imperil this. They should focus on what standards have been set for the firm and whether they are being met; whether management recommendations should be accepted and, if not, what further advice or information is needed; and whether policies are in place and being followed regarding, for example, ethics and compliance with the law.

In 2003, the New York Stock Exchange (NYSE) issued new rules on independence. Neither the individual nor a family member can have worked for the firm for the last five years. The individual must also have had no material relationship with the firm—which can include commercial, banking, consulting, legal, accounting, familial, or charitable relationships—for the last five years. The exchange is also suggesting that audit, nominating, governance, and compensation committees should be entirely independent and that independent directors must meet regularly without any executives present.[25]

An executive director is a director who is also a full-time executive of the company, an employee under some contract. A company executive who is also a company director appointed by shareholders is responsible under company law to act in the interests of shareholders. If a board has too many executive directors, this increases the separation between the board and the shareholders.

Chairman/CEO

A major debate in corporate governance is whether or not the chairman of the board and the CEO should be the same individual.

The role of the chairman is to ensure that the board operates effectively, to see that all members contribute effectively to the direction of the company, and to provide an objective review of proposals presented to the board by the CEO and senior management. Such a review requires interaction and discussion among board members, which may not be as vigorous if the CEO is also the chairman. Several researchers and commentators have suggested that this implies that the two roles of chairman and CEO should not be held by one individual.[26] How can the board monitor (and possibly terminate the employment of) the CEO if that individual is also chairman?

Despite this, in the United States it is common for the chairman and CEO to be the same person; in fact, it occurs in 80% of companies.[27] This makes if difficult to understand how the board can then effectively monitor the CEO. By contrast, in the overwhelming majority of U.K. firms, different individuals handle these two roles. Shareholders, with their concern about the agency problem, often want these two positions to be held by different individuals. In contrast, management often wants the positions to be combined so that the firm gets strong, unambiguous leadership. Little strong evidence exists on the link between board structure and performance, although there is some suggestion that when the roles are combined, there is a greater likelihood of bankruptcy. So board structure may be more salient in times of crisis.[28]

Competences of Directors

Because they act as a team, directors need a complementary mix of skills. Some skills need to be possessed by all; some will be more specialized. However, all directors are personally liable for board decisions; therefore one director cannot claim personal ignorance of say, derivatives, as an excuse for poor performance.

All directors need competences in finance, strategy, and global understanding, as well as such personal characteristics as intellect, integrity, courage, judgment, confidence, and so on. The composition of the board should match the needs of the firm and be characterized by diversity as well as cohesion. Board members need the ability to work with colleagues—remember that they can only be removed by shareholders at an annual meeting!

Board members must have the *will to act* when conditions require action and to "take on" management when this is required. Boards are sometimes constrained in this because directors meet infrequently and have no staff who could undertake independent analysis. Board members can request that independent advice be provided and this must then be made available to the entire board.

Thus board members need a thorough knowledge of the competitive position of the company's goods and services as well as a thorough understanding of industry structure, supplier relations, and customer needs. Board members must also be able to commit the time required to understand the issues facing the company. For this reason, some firms require that their board members limit the number of boards they join.[29]

Compensation of Directors

The most common board compensation is cash, except in the United States, where it is cash and stock. There is a global trend toward rewarding directors with a mixture of cash and stock, sometimes with options that cannot be exercised for several years in order to encourage board members to take a long-term perspective.[30] Director compensation may include other benefits, such as travel expenses and cars. Directors are generally provided with retirement benefits in the form of a pension. These benefits are being debated at present, both with respect to the level and linkage to either individual or firm performance.

◉ 13.7 BOARD OPERATIONS

As the criticism and scrutiny of boards have increased, so has the workload of directors. A global study of corporate governance in 188 firms found that the typical board of 12 members met 8 to 10 times per year for an average of 4.2 hours. It is not uncommon for global companies to have at least one meeting per year outside their home country.[31] Board chairmen spend 45 days per year, directors 21 days per year, on board matters. Membership on one or more board subcommittees can add considerably to the workload.

Board Processes

The culture of a board meeting is often not conducive to raising serious objections to a firm's strategic direction. Here the chairman plays a critical role, for outside directors must have the capability and independence to monitor the firm's performance and to change top management when performance does not meet expectations. This must be done while recognizing the boundary between directing and actually managing the company. Board culture and style are often such as to inhibit the free interchange of ideas. Meeting time is limited, agendas are too structured, and proceedings are dominated by presentations from the firm's executives. As a consequence, boards are often deferential to executive management, becoming reactive and focused on compliance. To be effective, boards must take the initiative, acting collaboratively to add more value. To improve effectiveness, some boards are providing counseling and advice to management, who may welcome the independent perspectives, judgment, and insight of external directors. Others are experimenting with different arrangements, such as meeting less frequently but for a much longer time period.[32]

The chairman and the CEO must perform a delicate balancing act. The chairman must ensure that the board is:

- Involved but does not micromanage the firm
- Challenging, but supportive of management
- Patient, but not complacent.

At the same time, the CEO must be able to:

- Share information without feeling vulnerable
- Seek advice without appearing weak
- Solicit input without appearing to relinquish control[33]

Board Tasks

We now discuss the tasks of the board, as summarized in Figure 13.2.

External

There is considerable debate on the degree and nature of the board's involvement in developing and implementing strategy. One school, with a legalistic approach, suggests that its role is to represent and protect shareholders' interests by ensuring effective management. Another view is more interventionist, arguing that the board should go beyond a strict control function and actively participate in strategy development. If this is the case, then directors must be carefully chosen to ensure that they have the necessary skills and are provided with adequate information.

It is generally accepted that the board does not develop strategy, that that is the responsibility of the executives. However, we believe that strategy development must be done in *cooperation* with the board, since it is ultimately responsible for the performance of the firm in creating value for shareholders. It is essential that the board be concerned with creating tomorrow, engaging in strategic thinking leading to a vision shared by directors and top management. This requires that board members have a well-devel-

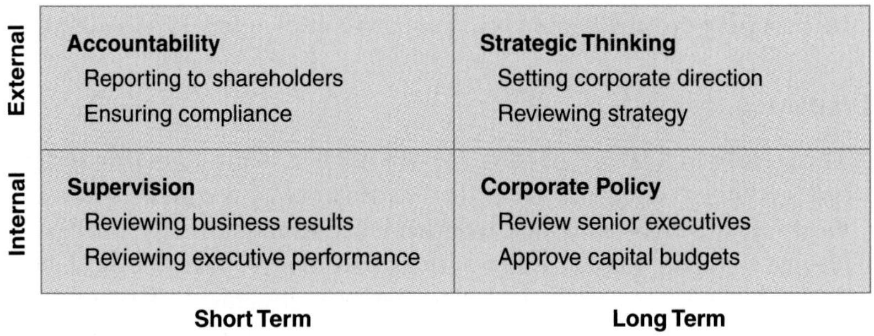

	Short Term	**Long Term**
External	**Accountability** Reporting to shareholders Ensuring compliance	**Strategic Thinking** Setting corporate direction Reviewing strategy
Internal	**Supervision** Reviewing business results Reviewing executive performance	**Corporate Policy** Review senior executives Approve capital budgets

Figure 13.2 Board Tasks

Source: Adapted from F. G. Hilmer, *Strictly Boardroom* (Melbourne: Information Australia, 1998).

oped sense of the firm's businesses, what is likely to work and what is not. In a global study of boards of directors, 54% of firms reported that the board is responsible for setting (as distinct from merely reviewing and approving) corporate strategy. Interestingly, this is less true in the United States, where only 21% reported that the board is active in setting strategy.[34] This finding, coupled with the fact that the CEO and chairman are generally the same individual in major U.S. firms, points to a general pattern there of executive dominance over the board.

In our view, top management has the critical responsibility for generating initiatives, doing the analysis, and interpreting results. The board must work out how to contribute to strategy without encroaching on this legitimate responsibility of management. This has several implications. First, the board must define what it means by performance— whether it is shareholder value, profit, cash, share price, short term or long term. Second, the board must make certain that a process for producing sound strategies is in place at the same time as it monitors current strategies to ensure that they are on schedule, on budget, and producing effective results.

Reviewing strategy requires that the board have considerable information on the firm and the industries in which it competes, including, but not limited to the following:

What environmental changes are expected? What discontinuities may occur? What are likely changes in markets, technologies, and currencies?

What are the good points and the weak points of the current strategy? Is it meeting our objectives? How should the domain of the firm change? Do we have the competences required to compete in the future?

What changes are expected in the competitive strategy of traditional and new competitors?

What is our current business model—how do we make money? What growth, risk, and returns are expected? Is our financing adequate?

What performance measures should the firm adopt? Total return to shareholders or cash flow? What time period and which firms should be used for comparisons?

Performing such a role puts considerable responsibility on the board. Its members must possess the time, the detailed knowledge, and the information support systems to allow them to perform this role satisfactorily. In this sense, the board needs expertise in *posing* questions to management and being able to interpret the responses. This highlights one possible problem with executive directors: their personal involvement may make them less objective when reviewing performance. In their board role, they must behave as director, not executive—a possible source of conflict.

In terms of their accountability responsibilities, directors are required to ensure that the firm has appropriate structures to reasonably assure compliance with all rules and regulations from stock exchanges and regulatory bodies. The board is responsible for reporting to shareholders and for preparing the annual report. This is a component of the board's role in shareholder communications—disseminating timely material to shareholders. The board must also be aware of shareholder expectations: What are these? Are they the same for all shareholders? Some shareholders may prefer a steady stream of dividends; others may prefer to see the firm minimize dividends to allow investment in growth. Microsoft, for example, paid its first dividend in 2003. Historically, large institutional investors were often treated differently with confidential briefings on the future of the firm, this being a disadvantage to small shareholders. The board must exercise care to ensure that shareholders are treated equally.

Contention can also arise over the handling of takeover offers. Does the board attempt to reject takeovers that seem to be in the interests of shareholders but not in their own personal interests or those of management? Managers are expected to turn strategic vision into operational reality, but directors represent shareholders and must evaluate strategy based on how the company's returns compare with those of other investment opportunities.

Internal

The most important internal role of the board is to ensure that the firm has the highest-caliber CEO and top-management team. The board therefore has a key role in planning *CEO succession.* Finding a new CEO is important: lack of such an individual can lead to a crisis in morale and investor panic. Responsibility for this rests with the board, which necessitates that it understand the firm's strategy and what this implies in terms of the skills of the new CEO.[35] Beyond the selection, evaluation, and, where necessary, *replacement* of the CEO, the board must also be actively involved in developing the compensation package for the CEO and senior executives. Possible measures for evaluating a CEO include business performance, accomplishment of long-term strategic objectives, and development of managers within the firm.

> In 2003 the shareholders of GlaxoSmithKline in the United Kingdom rejected a proposal to increase the salary of the CEO due to their concern at the continued poor performance of the firm.

The level of remuneration of senior executives and its relationship to firm performance has caused great concern to shareholders, institutions, governments, unions, and the public at large. The concern has been exacerbated by the fact that most firms have not reported management stock options as an expense when reporting to shareholders. If call options have been granted to the executive (at no cost), then the executive loses nothing should the share price fall. Many feel that such options are arguably an expense and should be reported to shareholders, as some firms (such as Coca-Cola) have announced they will do.[36] There is also a fear that senior executives may indulge in misleading behavior intended to increase share prices.

As part of the conformance role of the board, it must monitor the strategies adopted and report to shareholders on its stewardship. Thus the board is responsible for establishing a framework for the management of the economic entity, including a system of internal control, a business risk management process, and the setting of appropriate ethical standards.

Board members need to understand the relationship between risk and performance and the risk profile of the firm. They should ensure that processes are in place to manage risk at an acceptable level, where risk could involve financial loss, fraud, or some other crisis such as a currency collapse. Risk management subsumes the analysis of capital projects and the approval of capital budgets but should have a much wider purview. It means understanding where the firm is exposed and the magnitude of that exposure, as well considering whether the firm should take on a higher level of business risk. This is an area of governance that has become more important with the growth of a range of financial instruments such as derivatives and the turbulence in financial markets.

Board Committees

Most firms will have a number of subcommittees of the board. We now briefly review the role of some of the most important committees.

Audit Committee

This group oversees the financial systems and internal controls employed by the firm and is responsible for the *appointment* of the firm's auditors. These auditors are appointed by the board and report to the board, not to management. A major responsibility of this committee is to monitor the firm's auditors and to verify the accuracy and validity of financial information presented to the board and shareholders. The audit committee is generally made up of nonexecutive directors. In the United States, the NYSE requires all listed companies to have an audit committee comprised solely of independent directors. The performance of such committees has been a major concern in recent years, since many firms' financial statements have been inaccurate, if not fraudulent. To overcome this problem, it has been suggested that audit firms should not engage in consulting work with the firm and that the audit firm be rotated every few years.

Nominating Committee

This committee is responsible for nominating new directors of the firm and a new CEO. Concerns have been expressed that even with a nominating committee, CEOs may still suggest new board members, thus creating a board in their own image, not one that is truly independent. Shareholders at the annual meeting must approve all directors, but generally they find it difficult to elect individuals not approved by the current board. Directors are appointed for a limited term and cannot be removed by the board during their term of office. Individuals who are disruptive or who fail to contribute can only be removed by shareholders at the annual meeting. Shareholders vote on the appointment of directors, but they typically find it difficult to nominate new ones.

Remuneration Committee

This group makes recommendations on executive and CEO compensation arrangements and how this compensation relates to both individual and company performance. The committee is generally comprised of and chaired by independent directors. This is another major area of debate, since many CEOs seem to receive remuneration unrelated to the performance of the firm. Another issue has been salary paid to CEOs if their employment is terminated, since there have been examples of very large payouts. This group also has the challenging task of devising fees and remuneration for nonexecutive directors, including pension rights.

Governance Committee

Institutional and other investors are starting to demand that boards periodically evaluate themselves and review their effectiveness. As a result, it has become more common for global firms to have a governance committee. Its role is to review the board composition and committee structure and to assess board performance. The group should also assess board processes, such as information flows and agenda setting, to ensure open discussion at board meetings.

◉ 13.8 GLOBAL GOVERNANCE APPROACHES

Each country has its own distinct type of corporate governance, reflecting its unique history, legal system, and regulatory and tax regimes. But all over the world, managers are being forced to become more accountable to shareholders, and in all legal jurisdictions there are regulations on disclosure, insider trading, and takeovers. The discussion above was largely focused on governance arrangements under the Anglo-American system. We extend this to look at other regions of the world, looking at continental Europe and Asia.

Europe

The distinguishing feature of governance in Europe is the existence of a *two-tier* board structure in several countries. In the United Kingdom, Ireland, and some southern European countries such as Italy, Spain, Greece, and Portugal, a one-tier board system exists. In Germany, Switzerland, Austria, the Netherlands, and the Scandinavian countries there is a two-tier board system. To make it simpler, we will focus on the German system, although others are similar.

In Germany, the two boards are the *supervisory* board (Aufsichsrat) and the *management* board (Vorstand). The supervisory board has no direct management function and is responsible for major investment and long-term policy decisions. For larger firms, one-half of the members of this supervisory board are elected by employees and may include trade union representatives. The other half are elected by shareholders. This means that this board has no executives from the firm on it, not even the CEO. This supervisory board elects the management board, which is responsible for managing the firm on a day-to-day basis and normally has considerable autonomy.

This supervisory board has sometimes been seen by the management board as delaying decision making and as being a source of media leaks on firm strategy. More recently, given the difficulties in the United States, there is increasing interest in this two-tier model, particularly if the supervisory board is able to clarify the processes that govern its relationship with the management board.

This two-tier board structure reflects the German principle of co-determination—that firms are responsible to other stakeholders, such as employees, hence their presence on the supervisory board. However, concern has been expressed at the competence and independence of such employee directors. A person cannot legally be on more than 10 supervisory boards at the same time, but this number seems excessive. To encourage greater dialogue between its two boards, Siemens has changed its arrangements. The management board must now inform the supervisory board more systematically about its decisions, and all transactions worth more than 2% of the firm's equity must be approved by the supervisory board.[37]

There is a general legal maximum of 21 members for the supervisory board, although this can also depend on the size of the workforce. German boards are also characterized by few board committees; indeed, not all boards even have an audit committee.[38] Germany is also characterized by substantial equity cross-holding between firms, which means that it is extremely difficult to work out the true ownership of many firms. While there are liability rules against directors, these are not easy to implement, since shareholders need at least a 10% equity stake before they can sue directors for damages.

Asia

Asia is a diverse region, encompassing many different political and economic systems. We examine some of the more important differences.

Japan
Most large Japanese companies are stock companies, which are similar to U.S. public companies. At the same time, most large firms are associated with a financial *keiretsu*, characterized by extensive intragroup trade and a capital structure with elaborate cross-holdings of debt and equity, a strong domination by the group's main bank in corporate borrowings, and historically high levels of gearing financed by member banks. This cross-holding of debt and equity is a contingent governance mechanism that maintains

internal discipline, although it has been suggested that these banks have not excelled at monitoring firm performance.[39]

Governance in Japan is a one-tier system. Shareholders elect directors, and the Japanese Commercial Code requires that the board make important decisions, elect managers, and generally act with care and loyalty to the company. Boards are usually large and overwhelmingly male, generally comprised of current or former employees of the firm. It is uncommon for outsiders to be on the board, and given this board structure, it is not surprising that hostile takeovers are uncommon. Further, government officials may be members of the board.[40] This board structure reflects aspects of Japanese history and culture, and boards traditionally have seen their primary responsibility to employees, not shareholders, though this appears to be changing.

A typical Japanese board has 28 members, all executive, including the top management of the firm plus a president (who is the CEO) and a chairman (who is often the former CEO). There may be no independent directors and no board subcommittees to supervise management. For example, Canon in Japan has 26 board members: 1 president, 1 executive vice president, 3 senior managing directors, 6 managing directors, 12 directors, and 3 statutory auditors.

Southeast Asia

In Southeast Asia, Chinese family business structures dominate. These firms are controlled by the family and have limited public shares. There is little delegation of decision making to nonfamily members, although such firms do have a strong concept of trusted business partners.[41]

China

All large listed Chinese firms have active party secretaries who have their own agenda. In addition, nearly all listed Chinese companies, on the mainland as well as overseas, are still majority owned by the government or related entities. Intervention by party officials is out of sight of investors and unsupervised by regulators, so there is a potential conflict of interest between the board's responsibility to shareholders and to the party. The party provides a network outside of which promotion is impossible, bank credit inaccessible, and permission to list a company unattainable. In a Shanghai Stock Exchange survey of listed companies, 99% of the main business and staffing decisions, including those involving board appointments and salary, are made with the approval of internal party committees. The party, and links with the party, may be critical for getting access to credit and overseas markets, although smaller and newer private companies are much less likely to have a party committee.[42]

⊙ 13.9 SUMMARY

Arising from the scale and number of recent corporate crises, there is growing concern with improving corporate governance in many countries around the world. Shareholders are exerting pressure on boards to improve the governance of the firms that they direct and, since shareholders are the owners of the firm, their interests must be the board's primary concern. At the same time, the board must consider the interests of other stakeholders and ensure that the firm acts ethically and meets all legal requirements. Thus the board bears ultimate responsibility for organizational performance, while the managers are responsible for using the firm's assets, tangible and intangible, to ensure that the firm's objectives are met.

In the chapter, we examined the principles of corporate governance—the relationship among shareholders, management, and the board—in determining the direction and performance of the firm. Corporate governance is about how authority and responsibility are shared among shareholders, managers, and the board so that the firm generates value for all stakeholders, particularly shareholders.

Different countries with their own legal and financial systems have different systems of corporate governance, typified by the existence of dual boards in several countries. However, there is widespread concern with developing systems of governance that are more transparent for shareholders and result in superior performance. Directors are legally required to act in good faith, to act honestly and in the interests of shareholders. The challenge for them is how to do this when they are not involved on a day-to-day basis with the firm.

Of particular interest is the role of the board in the strategy of the firm. It is generally considered that strategy development is the responsibility of management—yet there is an inherent tension between this and the legal responsibility of the board for performance. In our view, the board should be closely involved in strategy but this involvement should be in the form of setting performance standards, questioning management on underlying assumptions, and asking the tough questions about the strategy.

While there is considerable interest in board structure, there should also be interest in board processes. Board structure is concerned with size, skills, number of meetings, subcommittees, and the role of independent directors. Processes need to be such that the board can work cooperatively with management to enhance performance. In too many firms, boards seem to be captured by management (particularly the CEO), resulting in the firm being run in the interests of managers, not shareholders. Boards must behave so that managers can act, both challenging and supporting management. At the same time, since it is ultimately responsible, the board must be prepared to change senior management, particularly the CEO, if performance is not satisfactory.

All of this is difficult when the board has limited information, meets infrequently, and has limited in-depth knowledge of the firm and its operations. This need to challenge and yet support management is part of the explanation for the importance of independent directors—they are supposed to have the independence to be able to challenge management, mainly the CEO, in ways that executive directors would find impossible. Hence board members must all be knowledgeable and skilled and must act as a team—boardroom fights and conflicts are not conducive to superior performance.

◉ REVIEW QUESTIONS

1. What is corporate governance and why is it important?

2. In your view, what role should the board play in the firm's strategy?

3. "The same individual should not be both chairman and CEO." Discuss this statement.

4. Select a recent example of poor corporate governance. How should the board have behaved?

5. Describe the differences between the German and the U.S. approach to corporate governance. What do you see as the advantages and disadvantages of each?

6. Do you think that all directors should have a substantial shareholding in the firm? What are the implications for both a small and a large shareholding?

7. What do you believe should be the role of the board in determining remuneration for top-level executives? Does current practice in your country conform to your ideas? Why or why not?

8. "The legal responsibilities of being a director of a publicly listed company are now so onerous that one would be foolish to accept such a position." Discuss this statement.

◎ ENDNOTES

[1] L. Fox, *Enron: The Rise and Fall* (Hoboken, NJ: Wiley, 2003).

[2] "The Role of the Board of Directors in Enron's Collapse," Permanent Subcommittee on Investigations, U.S. Senate, July 8, 2002.

[3] C. W. Thomas, "The Rise and Fall of Enron," *Journal of Accountancy* 193 (April 2002), pp. 41–48.

[4] J. A. Byrne, "How to Fix Corporate Governance," *Business Week*, May 6, 2002, pp. 69–76.

[5] R. A. G. Monks and N. Minow, *Corporate Governance* (Oxford: Blackwell, 2001), p. 1.

[6] F. G. Hilmer, *Strictly Boardroom* (Melbourne: Information Australia, 1998).

[7] R. Hampel, *Final Report/Committee on Corporate Governance* (London, The Committee and Gee Publishing, 1998), full text available at www.ecgi.org

[8] *Corporate Governance and the Role of the Board of Directors* (Chicago: Egon Zehnder, 2000), p. 39.

[9] A. J. Berle and G. Means, *The Modern Corporation and Private Property* (New York: Harcourt Brace, 1968).

[10] P. Plitch, "Governance Rules May Weed Out Directors with Large Holdings," *Wall Street Journal*, September 11, 2002, p. B5.

[11] B. Brown, "They Beat the Cheats but Scared the Brave," *The Australian*, May 23, 2003, special report, p. 4.

[12] M. Prevezer and M. Ricketts, "Corporate Governance: The UK Compared with Germany and Japan," in N. Dimsdale and M. Prevezer, eds., *Capital Markets and Corporate Governance*, (New York: Oxford University Press, 1994).

[13] For data on corporate holdings in the EU, see F. Barca and M. Becht, eds., *The Control of Corporate Europe* (Oxford: Oxford University Press, 2001).

[14] S. Prigge, "A Survey of German Corporate Governance," in *Comparative Corporate Governance—The State of the Art and Emerging Research*, K. J. Hopt, E. Wymeersch, and S. Prigge, eds. (Oxford: Clarendon Press, 1998).

[15] E. Wenger and C. Kaserer, "German Banks and Corporate Governance: A Critical View," in K. J. Hopt, E. Wymeersch, and S. Prigge, eds., *Comparative Corporate Governance—The State of the Art and Emerging Research*, (Oxford: Clarendon Press, 1998).

[16] P. Coombes and M. Watson, "Three Surveys on Corporate Governance," *McKinsey Quarterly* 4 (2000), pp. 74–77.

[17] Berle and Means, *The Modern Corporation and Private Property*.

[18] M. Jensen, "The Market for Corporate Control," in C. W. Smith, ed., *The Modern Theory of Corporate Finance*, (New York: McGraw-Hill, 1990).

[19] R. A. G. Monks and N. Minow, *Corporate Governance*, (Malden, Mass: Blackwell, 2003).

[20] W. T. Allen, "The Corporate Director's Fiduciary Duty of Care and the Business Management Rule under U.S. Corporate Law," in *Comparative Corporate Governance—The State of the Art and Emerging Research*, K. J. Hopt, E. Wymeersch, and S. Prigge, eds., (Oxford: Clarendon Press, 1998).

[21] J. A. Conger, E. E. Lawler, and D. Finegold, *Corporate Boards* (San Francisco: Jossey-Bass, 2001).

[22] A. Blake, *Dynamic Directors* (Basingstoke, UK: Macmillan, 1999).

[23] "The Fading Appeal of the Boardroom," *The Economist*, February 10, 2001, pp. 73–75.

[24] D. C. Hambrick and E. M. Jackson, "Outside Directors with a Stake: The Linchpin in Improving Governance," *California Management Review* 42, no. 4 (2000), pp. 108–127.

[26] P. Williams, "Corporate Conduct All Above Board," *Australian Financial Review,* August 20, 2002, pp. 60–61.

[26] Monks and Minow, *Corporate Governance.*

[27] Carlsson, *Ownership and Value Creation,* p. 47.

[28] Daily and Dalton, "CEO and Board Chair Roles Held Jointly or Separately."

[29] *Board of Directors Global Study* (Chicago: Egon Zehnder, 2000), p. 58.

[30] "The Fading Appeal of the Boardroom." *The Economist.*

[31] *Board of Directors Global Study.*

[32] D. Grady, "No More Board Games," *McKinsey Quarterly* 3 (1999), pp. 17–25.

[33] R. Charan, *Boards at Work: How Corporate Boards Create Competitive Advantage* (San Francisco: Jossey-Bass, 1998).

[34] *Board of Directors Global Study.*

[35] D. Carey and D. Ogden, *CEO Succession* (New York: Oxford University Press, 2000).

[36] "Clambering Back Up," *The Economist,* July 20, 2002, p. 51.

[37] B. Benoit, "Is Germany's Model Finding Its Level?" *Financial Times,* September 5, 2002, p. 7.

[38] K. J. Hopt, "The German Two-Tier Board: Experience, Theories, Reforms," in K. J. Hopt, E. Wymeersch and S. Prigge, eds., *Comparative Corporate Governance—The State of the Art and Emerging Research,* (Oxford: Clarendon Press, 1998).

[39] H. Kanda, "Notes on Corporate Governance in Japan," in K. J. Hopt, E. Wymeersch and S. Prigge, eds., *Comparative Corporate Governance—The State of the Art and Emerging Research,* (Oxford: Clarendon Press, 1998).

[40] T. Hoshi, "Japanese Corporate Governance as a System," in K. J. Hopt, E. Wymeersch and S. Prigge, eds., *Comparative Corporate Governance—The State of the Art and Emerging Research,* (Oxford: Clarendon Press, 1998).

[41] Blake, *Dynamic Directors.*

[42] R. McGregor, "The Little Red Book of Business in China," *Financial Times,* July 2, 2001, p. 9.

14

Strategic Management in Transition

Learning Objective

Upon completing this chapter, you should be able to:

● Recognize that strategic management is itself an evolving subject and that management of the firm of the future will bring new challenges.

14.1 INTRODUCTION

You may well be breathing a sigh of relief as you reach the end of this text, but relief is the last thing you should be looking for. Your journey is just beginning, and although we cannot claim anything near perfect foresight, we feel it is necessary to offer our views on what that journey is likely to involve. In doing so, we will inevitably reiterate some of the points we have emphasized elsewhere, but obviously we would not incorporate such redundancy if we did not feel that these ideas will be important to you in your future managerial career.

We have defined strategic management as the task of creating organizations that generate value in a turbulent world over an extended period of time. This task can be visualized as a process by which firms are transformed from one state to another, from one form to another, in response to a changing, turbulent, and uncontrollable world. Throughout this process, firms must be creating value in the present while investing in change programs to ensure continuing survival and value creation in the future. Figure 14.1 illustrates this process, emphasizing how the firm changes all its characteristics over time.

Citigroup in 2003 is not the same as what was Citibank in 1993, nor is Sony, nor Intel, nor any other firm. These firms have evolved, changing such characteristics as vision, structure, technology, products, markets, and people over the time period. As shown in Figure 14.1, the nature and form of the firm in, say, 2006 will be different from what it was in 2003.

This transition of the firm and its characteristics may occur through inaction, in which case the firm is not likely to survive. Or it can be managed, and we believe that the latter is preferable. Such change in the firm may be revolutionary and metamorphic, or it may be gradual and incremental. Driving these changes in a process of continual reinvention is the task of strategic management.

Figure 14.1 highlights that this change process within the firm occurs in an unpredictable, environment. The external context is continually changing over time. Some

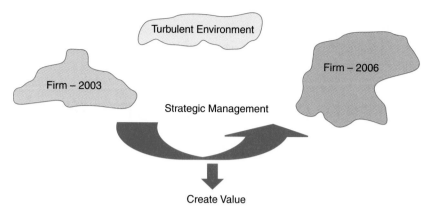

Figure 14.1   The Strategic Management Task

changes are due to actions of the firm, others due to the actions of other firms and such actors as governments or pressure groups. These events are both a threat and an opportunity. Strategic managers need both foresight and insight to work their way through the sometimes almost impenetrable fog created by change. Further, since some changes will be unpredictable in scale and scope, the strategy of the firm must be emergent and adaptable, as the world evolves in ways that were not initially well understood. Flexibility will be favored over rigidity.

Throughout this transition process, the firm needs to continually be creating value. If it does not, it is unlikely to survive. While this ongoing transition continues, there will be pressure from competitors, the end result of which may be to drive returns toward zero economic profit or below. Innovation is therefore essential to value creation, whether it be in technology, logistics, organization, business model, or some other aspect of the firm.

Managing ongoing change is an extremely difficult intellectual task. Organizations are not simple entities but complex collections of people (with all their foibles and good points), relationships, and processes. Intellect is certainly required to understand the world, yet management is not a purely intellectual exercise. It also requires action: making decisions, getting change accepted and implemented. Making decisions, monitoring the results, and modifying them as required constitute the flow of strategic management.

❂ 14.2 CONTEXT

Managers must perceive change, interpret it correctly, and then develop the appropriate strategy. All three steps are fraught with difficulty, as witnessed by the high rate of corporate demise. Sometimes managers fail to perceive change, possibly due to an obsolete mental model. Or such failure may reflect complacency among senior managers. Change often occurs on the periphery of the known, which makes it difficult to detect. For example, managers may place too much emphasis on current customers and not spend enough time identifying opportunities with new prospective customers.

Some generic, external changes that will become increasingly important in the future, are described below.

Globalization

You may feel we are beating a dead horse to emphasize globalization yet again, but intellectual recognition of the fact that business is increasingly global does not necessarily mean that the firm and its managers are capable of dealing with the consequent realities.

While the EU grows by adding countries to the union, many of its member country economies seem mired in low growth and increasingly stifled by regulation. Japan appears to be emerging from a period of stagnation. China is emerging as a manufacturing powerhouse, driven by indigenous change and the burgeoning of outsourcing by U.S. and European companies. Most other Asian countries are recovering from the travails of the mid to late 1990s, and the economic balance of the world's economy seems in an inexorable shift.

Despite recognizing that globalization means 24/7/365, however, few large companies seem capable of manning phones and offering services on the same timetable. Further, the ability to transcend cultural and geographic barriers, while increasingly important, is only slowly affecting the recruitment standards of large firms, which frequently lose the opportunity to hire multilingual employees with cross-cultural experience through outmoded employment practices.

No company today, regardless of size, is isolated from the impact of globalization. It will be your reality: prepare for it, relish it, and seize the opportunities it will present. For strategic managers of the future, the world is truly their oyster.

Competition

We have remarked throughout the book that you will be operating in an intensively competitive environment and have pointed out that that competition will be global. However, in Chapter 3 we pointed out a phenomenon that is likely to become even more pervasive as you pursue your careers—competition that crosses traditional industry boundaries. As we noted, the boundaries of an industry are increasingly blurred and indistinct. Over time, as a result of technological innovation, globalization, and deregulation, they have become permeable. You are well advised to carefully watch what you and your compatriots have traditionally thought were the boundaries of your industry or industries, for it is here that the innovations that may represent your most serious competitive threat are likely to occur.

Technology and Innovation

The rise of the information economy has already wrought profound change in almost every aspect of economic life. The digital revolution is far from over, and the networked economy will become all-pervasive. Not only will this and other technologies create opportunities for new products and markets; they will also demand new competences. In earlier eras, firms could achieve great success by responding to pre-existing wants and needs. In the 21st century, technological change will increasingly require that firms will have to create markets and market opportunities, a quite different challenge. The ability to innovate is, as we have seen, central to the longer-term challenge of creating firm value. Indeed, in a fast-changing world, the risks of inaction constantly rise. Finding and developing the individuals and talents required to cope with these challenges will preoccupy you as a manager.

⊚ 14.3 STRATEGY

Managing Paradoxes

As a strategic manager, you will be dealing with a more complex and faster-changing world than did any of your predecessors. You will need to bring intellect and passion to bear on your work. While you must strategize, you must also inspire; while you must implement, you must also be visionary; while you must be creative, you must also be ethical; while you must simplify, you must also cope with great complexity. These are the challenges that will test your mettle. While these requirements may seem hopelessly paradoxical, they constitute the gauntlet that has been cast in front of you. A fulfilling and exciting opportunity awaits those who can meet the challenge.

Changing Boundaries

As we noted, technology, globalization, and deregulation are changing industry boundaries everywhere. Yet these are not the only boundaries that will be affected. You will be faced with continually rethinking the mission and scope of the businesses and companies that you will manage. Outsourcing has changed the boundaries between the firm and its suppliers, while technology is changing the interface with customers. In the networked economy that many foresee expanding, the very notion of firm boundaries requires fundamental rethinking. Whereas your predecessors may have faced these decisions occasionally, you are likely to be thinking about them continuously. Making the appropriate trade-off between the internal assessment of existing competences and the external opportunities, while developing the competences required to exploit future opportunities, will be one of your major challenges.

Scale, Efficiency, and Flexibility

In the kind of world we have just described, the "rules" will themselves be changing. In the 20th century, we saw many firms rise to dominance of their industries by classic strategies. Size was undoubtedly important, sometimes bringing efficiency gains or market control, while vertical integration enabled behemoths to avoid the vagaries of the marketplace and achieve excellent returns for their shareholders. Yet, with size, there inevitably comes complexity. The vogue for downsizing that occurred in the 1990s was perhaps an indication that the challenges of managing large and diverse firms were becoming too great. Future advantages may flow from the ability to form networks, to become a virtual organization, driven in part by the increasing functionality and decreasing cost of communications. Barring great improvement in the concepts and tools of strategic management, we can expect other firms to reach the point where the market for corporate control tells them to voluntarily dismember themselves.

Furthermore, while not denying the advantages of scale in some instances, the battle between economies of scale and scope is likely to be ongoing. With increased affluence, the desire to be different seems to assert itself in an explosion of lifestyles and choices. The "one size fits all," "any color you like as long as its black" philosophy, so well suited to shortage economies, will not suffice in the affluent markets of the 21st century. While intense competition is likely to ensure that efficiency remains important, the ability of firms to be flexible and adapt to changing demands, and to deal with ever more complex and differentiated customer requirements, is likely to become even more important. The traditional business model of producing large quantities of standard products in the hope and expectation that someone will be willing to buy them rests on the critical assumption that we can adequately forecast the quantity, timing, and composition of demand. This assumption will become increasingly untenable, and where Dell has trod, others will almost certainly follow!

Ethics and Transparency

The standards of performance that will be expected of you will far outstrip those expected of your predecessors. The early part of the 21st century witnessed some particularly egregious examples of greed and dishonesty among senior executives. Societies around the world are making it clear that they are unwilling to tolerate such behavior. Even for those who believe the "invisible hand" is the ultimate criterion, however, the ethicists believe, and we agree, that the balance has shifted to the point where it is more profitable for large companies to behave ethically than to do otherwise. You should exhibit the highest standards of ethical behavior, avoid dual standards (e.g., tolerating behavior in one country that would not be tolerated in another), and clearly communicate expectations about how your personnel should behave—that is, clearly and consistently communicate your values. These actions are, of course, integral to being a good leader, and these leadership responsibilities are likely to become more rather than less important in the future.

Finally, given the ever-changing world, we can expect strategies to have shorter and shorter lives, so strategy renewal will come to the fore.

◎ 14.4 IMPLEMENTATION

Leadership in the Organization of the Future

Most people can understand the importance of the leader in a hierarchical organization. They recognize that in such a structure, all decisions recognized as important will rise to the top: hence the importance of the person at the top. Yet we have argued, we hope persuasively, that the knowledge-intensive organizations of the future will be much less hierarchical, with fewer levels of management, with more emphasis on fluidity and adaptability and less on rigidity and bureaucracy. Knowledge and expertise, rather than title or position, will comprise the main sources of influence on behavior. Multibusiness, complex firms will, of necessity, result in more decentralization and local autonomy, with leadership responsibilities diffused throughout the organization. Further, such firms will be networked with others in heterarchical relationships that will integrate best-of-class processes to achieve success in an intensively competitive world.

Paradoxically, we believe that the role of leadership will be even more important in such firm than it is in traditional hierarchies, although the leadership will, of necessity, be qualitatively different. In such firms, often networked as a result of outsourcing, leadership will be characterized by remote, rather than direct, control. Hence senior managers must lead in the crucial tasks of recruitment, selection, development, and reward. In performance management, there must be as much emphasis on how results are attained as there is on the results themselves, and reward systems must reflect this reality. As the firm's value becomes more and more dependent on intangible assets, the personal behavior of leaders and their performance in establishing standards for all will become correspondingly ever more important.

It is also important for strategic managers to act, to make decisions. Declining firms often decline over extended periods of time, as if managers are frozen in to immobility. They may perceive the need for change but seem unable to make decisions.

Intangible Assets

Throughout the book we have stressed the importance of intangible assets. The market capitalization of the firm is increasingly dependent on such assets, and this trend is unlikely to change. This has enormous implications for how we conceptualize and approach the tasks of strategic management.

Rather than being the harbingers of change, our business schools are today too often on its trailing edge. As the importance of intangible assets rises, most business schools seem to be increasing the emphasis on teaching the tools for managing tangible assets. As ethics becomes an issue of international importance, too many students become imbued with the idea that the "invisible hand" is the answer to all the challenges of decision making, abrogating any concept of personal responsibility.

Managing intangible assets means, at its core, mastering the management of human resources internally and customer and supplier relationships externally. If three-quarters of a company's value is based on such characteristics, and we preach value creation to generations of students, then why should not three-quarters of the curriculum be related to such issues? We know that is not the case, although without an understanding of accounting and finance, we would not be able to even have a discussion about what value management really means. Yet we repeat the argument we made earlier in the book. Our tools for managing intangible assets are nowhere near as highly developed as those for managing tangible assets, and you had better recognize that your success will increasingly depend on how well you manage the former, rather than the latter.

Finally, it is vital that the firm contain a diversity of views and voices, without becoming a Tower of Babel. It will be important to bring new staff into the firm, to get new ideas, new values, and new knowledge. The firm may even need to encourage and protect heretics, those individuals who challenge the existing orthodoxy.

Change

When the authors began their careers studying business, change was perceived as exceptional. Indeed, many of the characteristics that we today view as variable were then fixed. Industry structures, exchange rates, even interest rates were in many cases either fixed or subject to only occasional change.

Today, as we have seen, change is continuous. It is often unpredictable, seeming to outfox even the most prescient of forecasters. The world we are living in is not only fast-changing, it is also increasingly turbulent, and we see little likelihood that this will change in the future.

If change is continuous, the good news is that we should be learning how to handle it better. The bad news is that we must all learn to become better managers of change. If change is unpredictable, then we must learn how to make our organizations more resilient and flexible. We must seek people who either have or can acquire the ability to live with such change and who can tolerate the ambiguity that accompanies turbulence.

You must become ever more astute at managing such risks, lest you lose the firm that employs you to the savage swings of a fast-changing environment.

Competences and Opportunities

We have argued that the firm must not only nurture existing competences but also develop the competences required to create and exploit future opportunities. This is challenging enough in its own right, but in the world of today and tomorrow, building and keeping competences poses new problems. The social contract that used to exist between the firm and its workforce no longer exists. Companies battling turbulence by hiring then firing, expanding then refocusing, quickly find that the loyalty of their workforce is atrophying. Knowledgeable staff, usually in demand, will take responsibility for their own careers, behaving more like short-term contract employees than long-term servants. Marshaling, building, and retaining competences will continue to be important, but the difficulty of doing so will undoubtedly rise.

◉ 14.5 PERFORMANCE

Creating Value

Creating firm value has been a consistent and ongoing theme of this book. In a world where capital moves so freely from one application to another, there can be no alternative. Yet we were at pains to distinguish the idea of creating firm value from shareholders returns. Ensuring that the firm creates economic profit will, we believe, benefit all stakeholders, including shareholders, over the longer term. However, neither we nor anyone else can protect investors from the vagaries of the stock market as a whole, nor ensure that they buy low and sell high!

We have emphasized that the only way to create value is through innovation. This is not to say that continual improvement should be neglected. But the firm needs to explore the new, which requires creativity, different voices within the firm, and display a willingness to engage in experimentation.

Furthermore, strategic managers should resist the distressing tendency, too apparent in some firms, to assume that short-term profit maximization is the best route to creating firm value. Local optima do not guarantee a global optimum. Indeed, in competitive strategy, knowing that one's competitor is focused on short-term results can always be turned to advantage by a well-financed rival.

We do believe that aligning the interests of professional managers (agents) with those of shareholders (principals) is important to achieving better management of the firm. We also believe that a vigorous and independent board of directors is vital to ensure that managers avoid behavior that enriches themselves at the expense of the owners of the enterprise.

Non-financial Criteria

Finally, we have been at pains to point out that even good financial performance means measurement and management of a good many non-financial criteria. Interestingly, such criteria are more and more becoming important to some investors. Ethical considerations are now built into the investment strategies of a number of large pension funds, while new mutual funds have been created to target the many investors who wish to ensure that their monies are expended only on the shares of firms whose policies they endorse. Not only are such developments unlikely to disappear; we expect them to be manifest even more broadly in the future.

We wish you every good fortune in the journey that lies ahead of you. For a good strategic manager, learning will be a lifetime journey, and we can but hope that you have at least begun that journey well.

Glossary

Accounting profit   Reported on the income statement and is broadly measured as revenue minus certain expenses. Both revenue and expenses are reported on an accrual basis, and reported expenses include both cash and non-cash expenses. Accounting profit or net income can also be reported as before or after tax.

Acquisition   The firm expands its resources and competences by purchasing, or taking a controlling interest in, another firm.

Agency problem   An agency relationship exists when one or more persons (the principal) hire another person or persons (the agent) to perform a service or make decisions on their behalf. An agency problem arises when the agents make decisions that are in their own interests, not in the interests of the principals.

American depository receipts   Negotiable securities issued by a U.S. bank that are backed by the ordinary shares of a non-U.S. firm.

Balanced scorecard   A performance measurement system that combines qualitative and quantitative measures. Performance is measured along four dimensions: customer, internal, innovation, and financial.

Barriers to entry   Additional costs that need to be overcome if a firm is to enter an established industry and compete successfully.

Board of directors   The group elected by shareholders whose fiduciary duty is to run the firm in the long-term interests of shareholders. This is accomplished through their formal monitoring and control of senior executives.

Brand equity   The value the organization receives from its branded product or service compared with the value from an identical unbranded product or service. For many firms this value is a major intangible asset.

Breakout strategies   Revolutionary strategies that deliver a major improvement to customers. This improvement is large enough that it can be shared with customers to drive rapid growth, with some of the value retained to provide superior return to shareholders.

Business level strategy   How a unit of the firm competes successfully to create value in its chosen markets.

Business model   The method by which a business unit generates revenue and creates, and captures, value for itself.

Business portfolio   The collection of relatively independent strategic business units that collectively comprise the entire firm.

Capital structure   The proportion of debt and equity used to finance the operations of the firm, generally measured by the debt to equity ratio, which is also called the financial leverage of the firm.

Cash cow   A business unit with a dominant market share in a low-growth market.

Centralization   The degree to which decision-making authority is retained by senior management rather than being devolved to the constituent units of the firm.

Change agent   The individual or group that effects strategic change in an organization.

Competence   Combinations of resources, typically embedded in the firm's processes, which the firm is able to perform better than its competitors. A *core* competence is one which serves as a basis for its advantage over competitors.

Competitive advantage   The way in which the firm utilizes its resources and competences to generate a value-creating strategy that other firms find difficult to imitate.

Competitive business strategy   The basis on which a business unit elects to compete for customers while withstanding competitive endeavors.

Competitive environment   Other organizations and activities that compete, directly or indirectly with the firm, or phenomena that influence customer behavior.

Context   The world external to the firm and the internal resources and competences of the firm.

Corporate governance   The relationship between shareholders, management, and the board in determining the direction and performance of the corporation. It represents the processes through which ultimate corporate authority and responsibility are shared and exercised by shareholders, directors, and management to ensure that the firm delivers value to its stakeholders.

Corporate level strategy Deciding the overall purpose and mix of business, partners, geographic markets, technologies, and customers of the firm so that the total entity delivers value to stakeholders which is greater than the value delivered under any other organizational arrangement.

Cost leadership strategy An integrated set of actions designed to produce and deliver goods or services to customers at the lowest price, relative to competitors, with features that are acceptable to customers.

Cost of capital The return that the firm should earn to cover its capital base. This cost reflects the firm's capital structure, since debt and equity have different costs to the firm. This cost of capital is also used to discount expected future cash flows to calculate present value.

Cost of equity capital The return required by shareholders to compensate them for the level of risk involved in investing in the firm.

Culture The basic assumptions, beliefs, and values that are shared by members of an organization which operate unconsciously and which influence the way in which the firm conducts itself.

Customer analysis A detailed understanding of customers, their needs and values, and how these needs may vary within a given market.

Customer capital The value of the firm's relationship with its customers, including an understanding of customer's demands and preferences.

Customer value The benefits customers receive from a product, at a certain price, compared to the benefits they receive from a competitive product at a different price.

Deregulation The government policy of eliminating entry barriers and minimizing regulatory controls in selected industries to promote increased competition.

Derivatives A broad range of financial instruments whose returns are derived from the returns of other financial instruments. They are generally used to transfer financial risk, at a price, to other parties who are prepared to assume that risk.

Differentiation strategy Offering a product or service with features or characteristics that are valued by buyers, such that the offer is different from competitive offerings, and consequently a price premium can be charged.

Direct competitor Competitors producing essentially the same product or service.

Director Elected by shareholders to direct the firm. The director is required to act in good faith to advance the firm's interests and to exercise prudent care. *Executive directors* are managers currently employed by the firm. *Independent (or non-executive) directors* are individuals who do not have any significant professional or contractual relationship with the firm, except as a director.

Disintermediation The process whereby the function of an intermediary can be eliminated.

Disruptive technology A new technology which brings a new and different value proposition to the market.

Diversification A strategy in which the firm expands its current set of markets, products, technologies, or geographic regions. *Related diversification* is when the extension permits some sharing of current resources or competences. *Unrelated diversification* is when the extension involves little or no resource sharing.

Divestment The firm sells, or removes, one or more organizational units to another party.

Dog A business unit with a nondominant market share in a static or declining market.

Dominant logic A frame of thinking common to managers in the industry based on their education and experience which defines the firm and the industry and may limit creativity.

Downsizing Major reductions in the number of staff and functions within the firm to achieve significant improvements in productivity.

Due diligence Detailed analysis of a target firm, its financial strength, intellectual assets, its operations and the environment in which it operates which provides a basis for future forecasts.

Dynamic competences Mechanisms for building new resources and competences or reconfiguring existing ones.

Economic profit A generic name for a range of approaches that have been developed to determine whether a firm, on an on-going basis, is generating value. It is measured by revenue less all costs, where cost includes an explicit charge for the capital employed in the firm. Economic value added (EVA) is a trademarked name for one specific measure of economic profit.

Economies of scale Occur when the unit costs of a product, service, or activity decline as the size of firm, or plant, increases.

Economies of scope Occur when the cost of producing and selling two products together is less than the costs of producing and selling the two products separately.

Entry barrier   Characteristics that make it difficult for an organization to enter a specific industry.

Equity spinoff   The firm offers a minority position in a portion of the firm to new shareholders, through an initial public offering.

Experience curve   Occurs when the unit cost of a product or service declines with cumulative output—the total number of units that the firm has ever produced.

Financial markets   The markets where firms requiring investment funds come together with individuals and institutions with funds to invest.

First mover advantage   A competitive advantage possessed by the firm who pioneers a new product or feature.

Forward contract   A contract between two parties to buy or sell something at a later date at a price agreed to by both parties when the contract is written.

Functional structure   An organizational arrangement consisting of a chief executive officer and managers for the major functional areas such as production, accounting, marketing, R&D, and human resources.

Globalization   The process that enables the free movement of goods, services, people, skills, and ideas across political borders.

Hierarchically based exchange   A system in which goods are produced and exchanged between different units of the same firm, sharing common ownership.

Horizontal positioning   Deciding how many segments a business unit should compete in.

Human capital   The skills, knowledge, ability, experience, intelligence, creativity, and motivation of the individuals who comprise the firm's workforce.

Imputation credit   A tax system in which the firm pays tax (at the corporate tax rate) on dividends. This payment is a tax credit for the shareholder.

Increasing returns to scale   Occurs when the benefit of a product or service to an individual user increases as the total number of users of that product or service increases. Also called network effects and Metcalfe's Law.

Industry   A group of firms producing essentially the same product using essentially the same production technology. These firms would be seen as direct competitors to each other.

Industry foresight   The ability of managers to have superior understanding of the changes in the industry, customers, competitors, and technology and their likely future impact.

Industry structure   The major factors that impact, possibly differentially, on all firms in the industry. They are generally grouped into five categories: suppliers, buyers, entrants, substitutes, and rivalry.

Inflection points   Occurs when there is a substantial increase in the rate of change of a phenomena.

Initial public offering (IPO)   Occurs when a firm offers a tranche of equity to investors for the first time.

Innovation   Creating a new product, service, business model, process, or means of organizing.

Institutional investors   Financial institutions such as banks, mutual funds, and superannuation funds that hold an equity position in a firm.

Intangible resources   Resources and assets whose value is not included on the firm's balance sheet.

Intellectual capital   Knowledge, information, skills, and experience used by the firm to create value. It is generally partitioned in to three categories: human, structural, and customer.

Intellectual property   Structural capital that is owned by the firm and which can be legally protected.

Internal development   A strategy whereby new businesses are generated from within the firm. Generally it involves technological innovation.

Joint venture   Two or more firms combine parts of their operations and assets to form a jointly-owned and independent firm.

Junk bond   A bond issued by a firm that has a quality rating by one of the rating agencies of less than investment grade.

Knowledge   A combination of experience, values, and insight that reflects cognition and thinking by the individual when faced with a problem. *Explicit knowledge* can be codified and articulated in books, manuals, and reports. *Tacit knowledge* includes intuition, beliefs, and values and is difficult to articulate in a meaningful manner.

Knowledge intensity   The extent to which a product or activity is based on knowledge.

Latency   The time after introduction of a new technology before it is widely adopted.

Leadership   The process of intentional influence by one person over another.

Legacy assets   The historic assets, both tangible and intangible, owned by the firm.

Leveraged buyout   A restructuring strategy whereby a group, which often includes incumbent management, buys the firm's assets in order to take the firm private. Such a strategy is generally financed primarily with debt.

Leveraging resources   Aggressively using current resources to engender future growth.

Liquidity   The ability of the firm to meet its financial responsibilities such as paying staff, suppliers, and debt holders.

Low-priced strategy   A strategy whereby the firm offers products such that the price actually paid by customers is the lowest among the available alternatives.

Management incentive option   A form of compensation offered to senior managers in which they are given the right, but not the obligation, to buy at a given price a given number of shares in the firm up to a specified future date.

Market-based exchange   A system in which exchanges of goods and services occur between two separate and independent entities.

Market capitalization   A measure of the value of the firm, calculated as the number of shares outstanding multiplied by the current share price.

Market for corporate control   Different management groups vying for the right to manage the firm's assets.

Market segmentation   The process of grouping together actual and potential customers whose needs are similar so that target segments can be selected and the appropriate marketing program designed.

Market-to-book ratio   The market capitalization of the firm divided by the book value of capital employed by the firm.

Market value added   A measure of the value of the firm calculated as the current market capitalization of the firm minus the book value of capital employed by the firm.

Matrix structure   An organizational arrangement which involves two dimensions: generally geography and business.

Mental model   The set of assumptions held by managers and/or employees about the firm, its industry and environment, and the nature of competition.

Merger   A strategy under which two firms agree to integrate their operations on a friendly basis to strengthen competitive advantage.

Mission   A generalized statement specifying the domain of the firm, where and how it elects to compete, and its activities and operations.

Moore's Law   That the number of transistors on a computer chip will double every 18–24 months and consequently that the speed of microprocessors will double every 18–24 months.

Networks   An association of possibly competing firms established to develop a new industry that requires competences beyond those possessed by any individual firm.

Objectives   Quantitative targets to be achieved by the firm or one of its units.

Option   A contract in which the writer of the option grants the buyer of the option the right, but not the obligation, to purchase from or sell to the writer something at a specified price within a specified time. For this right the option writer charges the buyer a price called the option price. An option to sell is referred to as a put option, while the option to buy is referred to as a call option.

Organizational architecture   The organizational structure, process design, and human resource approach adopted by the firm.

Organizational processes   A coordinated and horizontal multifunctional set of activities that support the delivery of products and services to the customer.

Organizational structure   The firm's formal role configuration showing how tasks are divided and integrated, including the control mechanisms, authority, and decision-making processes of the firm.

Organizational values   A common set of beliefs that guide the behavior of organizational members.

Outsourcing   The transfer of a recurring, internal value creating activity to an external provider, where the arrangement is specified in a formal contract.

Path dependency   The concept that future developments of a product or technology are conditional on an earlier state.

Pecking order   The order in which firms generally use their three sources of funds: internal development, new debt, and new equity.

Privatization   The transfer or selling off of state owned firms and organizations to private ownership.

Problem child   A business unit in a high-growth market with a nondominant market share.

Punctuated equilibrium   A pattern of change characterized by periods of incremental change coupled with periods of revolutionary change.

Remote environment   The broad socio/technical/economic environment in which the firm competes. This environment is global in nature, exerts a powerful influence on strategy, and in many instances is slow acting. Due to the breadth of these changes it can be expected to affect a number of industries.

Resources   Stocks of important factors that the firm owns or controls. They are frequently grouped into tangible and intangible resources.

Resource-based view   A view of strategy that characterizes the firm as a unique collection of resources that can be combined to provide firm-specific advantages and thus are the basis for its success.

Risk   Uncertainty on how the future will develop. Total risk can be subdivided into two categories: business risk and financial risk. *Business risk* is the variability in operating cash flow. It is related to the nature of the firm and the uncertainty of future sales and costs. *Financial risk* reflects uncertainty of factors such as interest rates, exchange rates, and stock prices.

S-curve   A common pattern for technological change whereby improvements occur slowly at first, accelerate, and then slow down as the technology reaches its limit.

Stakeholders   Individuals or groups who can affect, and are in turn affected by, the strategic outcomes of the firm's activities.

Star   A business unit which has a dominant market share in a rapidly growing market.

Strategic alliance   A partnership in which two or more firms combine their resources and capabilities to pursue a mutual business opportunity. It may or may not result in the formation of a new business entity.

Strategic business unit   A unit of a firm that is relatively autonomous and responsible for developing its own strategy with its own products, markets, and competitors independent of other units within the same firm.

Strategic decisions   Decisions that affect the long-term well-being of the organization. Such decisions involve major resource commitments and are difficult to reverse, implying a long-term commitment.

Strategic drift   Occurs when the organization's strategy gradually moves away from relevance to the environment in which it competes.

Strategic management   Creating organizations that generate value in a turbulent world over a sustained period of time.

Strategy   The common theme underlying a set of strategic decisions.

Strategy-conduct-performance   A model of business that postulates that the dominant influence on firm performance are the structural characteristics of the industry in which the business competes.

Structural capital   Capital that is owned by the firm, not by a specific individual.

Substitute   A product or service that is capable of meeting the same customer needs as our own business but which does so in a very different manner. Also known as an indirect competitor.

Sustaining technology   Improves the performance of established products and services along the dimensions of performance that mainstream customers in major markets have historically valued.

Swap   A contract in which two parties agree to exchange the cash flows from an asset or liability. For example, the firm swaps a cash flow based on a floating interest rate for one based on a fixed interest rate.

Synergy   Occurs when two or more activities or processes complement each other so that the value created by the two units working together exceeds the value created when the two units operate independently.

Takeover   An unsolicited acquisition bid where the acquirer makes a direct appeal to the target's shareholders.

Total return to shareholders   The annualized return to shareholders from maintaining their investment in a stock over a period of time. It is calculated as the total of dividends received and share price appreciation over the time period.

Value chain   The activities within a firm that it has chosen to undertake in order to be able to compete. It is also used to describe the linked set of firms that together create a product or service.

Vertical integration   Occurs when a firm acquires or develops a business that is the current concern of either their customers (forward) or their suppliers (backward).

Vertical positioning   The decision by senior managers regarding which activities are best done under common ownership and which are best done under market-based transactions.

Vision   The ideal future state of the total entity. A mental image of a possible and desirable state of the firm.

Index